Directions for accessing your
Oxford University Press Digital Course Materials

W9-DFN-478

American Popular Music
From Minstrelsy to MP3

SIXTH EDITION

Larry Starr,
Christopher Waterman
with Brad Osborn

Carefully scratch off the silver
coating to see your personal
redemption code.

This code can be redeemed
only once.

Once the code has been revealed,
this access card cannot be returned
to the publisher.

Access can also be purchased online
during the registration process.

The code on this card is valid for
two years from the date of first
purchase. Complete terms and
conditions are available at
learninglink.oup.com

Access Length: 6 months from
redemption of the code.

OXFORD
UNIVERSITY PRESS

Your OUP digital course materials can be delivered several different ways,
depending on how your instructor has elected to incorporate them into his
or her course.

**BEFORE REGISTERING FOR ACCESS, be sure to check with your
instructor to ensure that you register using the proper method.**

VIA YOUR SCHOOL'S LEARNING MANAGEMENT SYSTEM

Use this method if your instructor
has integrated these resources into
your school's Learning Management
System (LMS)—Blackboard, Canvas,
Brightspace, Moodle, or other

Log in to your instructor's course
within your school's LMS.

When you click a link to a resource
that is access-protected, you will be
prompted to register for access.

Follow the on-screen instructions.

Enter your personal redemption
code (or purchase access) when
prompted.

VIA OXFORD learning link

Use this method if you are using
the resources for self-study only.
NOTE: *Scores for any quizzes you
take on the OUP site will not report
to your instructor's gradebook.*

**Visit
oup.com/he/starr-waterman6e**

Select the edition you are using,
then select student resources
for that edition.

Click the link to upgrade your
access to the student resources.

Follow the on-screen instructions.

Enter your personal redemption
code (or purchase access)
when prompted.

VIA OXFORD learning cloud

Use this method only if your
instructor has specifically instructed
you to enroll in an Oxford Learning
Cloud course. **NOTE:** *If your instructor
is using these resources within your
school's LMS, use the Learning
Management System instructions.*

Visit the course invitation URL
provided by your instructor.

If you already have an
oup.instructure.com account
you will be added to the course
automatically; if not, create
an account by providing your
name and email.

When you click a link to a
resource in the course that is
access-protected, you will be
prompted to register.

Follow the on-screen
instructions, entering your
personal redemption code
where prompted.

For assistance with code
redemption, Oxford Learning
Cloud registration, or if you
redeemed your code using
the wrong method for your
course, please contact our
customer support team at
**learninglinkdirect.support@
oup.com**
or 855-281-8749.

American Popular Music

American Popular Music

From Minstrelsy to MP3

SIXTH EDITION

Larry Starr
University of Washington

Christopher Waterman
University of California, Los Angeles

with Brad Osborn
The University of Kansas

New York   Oxford
OXFORD UNIVERSITY PRESS

Oxford University Press is a department of the University of Oxford.
It furthers the University's objective of excellence in research, scholarship,
and education by publishing worldwide. Oxford is a registered trademark of
Oxford University Press in the UK and certain other countries.

Published in the United States of America by Oxford University Press,
198 Madison Avenue, New York, NY 10016, United States of America.

Library of Congress Cataloging-in-Publication Data

Names: Starr, Larry, author. | Waterman, Christopher Alan, 1954- author. |
  Osborn, Brad, author.
Title: American popular music : from minstrelsy to MP3 / Larry Starr,
  Christopher Waterman, with Brad Osborn.
Description: Sixth edition. | New York : Oxford University Press, 2021. |
  Includes bibliographical references and index.
Identifiers: LCCN 2021020466 (print) | LCCN 2021020467 (ebook) | ISBN
  9780197543313 (paperback) | ISBN 9780197543351 (epub)
Subjects: LCSH: Popular music—United States—History and criticism.
Classification: LCC ML3477 .S73 2021 (print) | LCC ML3477 (ebook) | DDC
  781.640973—dc23
LC record available at https://lccn.loc.gov/2021020466
LC ebook record available at https://lccn.loc.gov/2021020467

Printing number: 9 8 7 6 5 4 3 2 1
Paperback printed by Quad/Mexico, Mexico

CONTENTS

4 "I Got Rhythm": The Golden Age of Tin Pan Alley Song, 1920s and 1930s 111

5 "St. Louis Blues": Race Records and Hillbilly Music, 1920s and 1930s 133

6 "In the Mood": The Swing Era, 1935–1945 166

7 "Choo Choo Ch' Boogie": The Postwar Era, 1954–1954   212

8 "Rock Around the Clock": Rock 'n' Roll, 1954–1959   260

9 "Good Vibrations": American Pop and the British Invasion, 1960s   304

10 "Blowin' in the Wind": Country, Soul, Urban Folk, and the Rise of Rock, 1960s 343

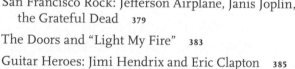

11 The 1970s: Rock Music, Disco, and the Popular Mainstream 391

12 Outsiders' Music: Progressive Country, Reggae, Salsa, Punk, Funk, and Rap, 1970s 433

Although we analyze many specific musical genres, performances, and pieces of music in this book, the following is a list of works to which we have lent particularly close attention, most often in the form of Listening Guides, but also as Boxes, or within the main text.

Preface

IT SEEMS SCARCELY POSSIBLE THAT WE ARE NOW AT THE POINT OF presenting the sixth edition of *American Popular Music: From Minstrelsy to MP3*, nearly twenty years after the book's initial publication. It is not possible to thank adequately the many students, colleagues, and other interested readers whose enthusiasm for the previous editions of the book has brought us to this point, and whose many helpful observations and suggestions have informed the creation of this new edition at every stage.

What distinguishes our book from others in this rapidly growing field is that it combines two perspectives not often found in the same place: the study of cultural and social history on the one hand, and the analytical study of musical style on the other. In presenting this introductory survey of the rich terrain of American popular music, we bring years of experience in teaching courses for a general student population and in lecturing on musical subjects to general audiences. This experience has taught us that it is neither necessary nor desirable to talk down, write down, or think down to such groups. People love music and can quickly grasp all kinds of intricacies and subtleties concerning music so long as what they read is free of jargon, clear, and unpretentious. We love American popular music ourselves—that is why we have written this book—and we have attempted to foreground this love for the subject in our writing, realizing that it is the most valuable common bond we share with all potential readers of our work.

Our Approach

We fully expect that students, teachers, and readers of all kinds will enter into a creative dialog with the material in this book. No general overview of a complex subject can begin to satisfy everyone. And since passions run high in the field of popular music, we anticipate that our particular perspectives, and particularly our choices of artists to emphasize and specific examples to study, may well provoke some controversy at times, whether in the classroom or simply in the mind of the reader. We have felt it better to identify clearly our own viewpoints and enthusiasms rather than try to hide behind a scrim of apparent objectivity. The opening chapter outlines particular *themes* and *streams* that serve as recurring reference points throughout the book, ensuring that our narrative focus and strategy are articulated at the outset.

Throughout the book, we strive to take as broad a view as possible of "popular music," but it is inevitable that some readers will find certain genres and styles either excessively prominent or underestimated, depending on their own tastes and viewpoints. We have tried in particular to avoid the trap of viewing the period from the 1960s to the present as exclusively the "age of rock." Those wishing a study of rock music per se are directed to our companion text, *Rock: Music, Culture, and Business* (Oxford University Press, 2012), written in collaboration with Joseph G. Schloss, which offers a different perspective on the American musical landscape from the period following World War II to the present day.

While we feel that this text provides a sound and reliable starting point for the study and appreciation of American popular music, we claim no more than that. We hope and expect that teachers who use this book will share supplementary and contrasting perspectives on the material with their students, and that individual readers will use the bibliography as an enriching source of such perspectives as well. We inevitably bring certain limitations of perspective, along with our passions, to our understanding of the broad trajectory of American pop, and it is certainly desirable for all readers to seek out other perspectives and modes of understanding as they pursue this subject further.

What's New?

The sixth edition of *American Popular Music* features exciting new digital teaching and learning tools that will prove essential to any popular music course:

- A new enhanced e-book includes links to stream every recording in the text with a free Spotify account, as well as in-text review questions, flashcards, historical performance videos, and more.
- New, regularly updated popular music activities that ask students to apply concepts discussed in the text to recent music. Popular music activities are updated every year, so they always feature music that will be familiar to students.

Even more flexible purchase and delivery options, allowing students to access material through their own learning management systems, via Oxford Learning Cloud, or in a stand-alone enhanced e-book. See the "Flexible Delivery Options" section of this preface for more details.

With the sixth edition, we've also made numerous updates to the text of *American Popular Music*:

- The text includes new, detailed discussions of significant female artists, such as Sister Rosetta Tharpe (Chapter 7), Bikini Kill (and the riot grrrl movement, Chapter 14), and Missy Elliott (Chapter 15).
- Chapter 15 has been completely reworked to accurately reflect the current landscape of American popular music, as the twenty-first century enters its third decade. This includes major new material: on technology and the music business; on contemporary rock stars, such as the Yeah Yeah Yeahs and TV on the Radio; on emo music; and on hip-hop (in addition to Missy Elliott, Drake, and updated material on Beyonce).
- Also in Chapter 15, a generous new section on "Popular Musicians Who Endured—and Endure!" allows readers an overview and review of major trends and styles covered in the book's preceding chapters, by virtue of a summary of the careers of artists such as Louis Armstrong, Aretha Franklin, Bob Dylan, and Tony Bennett.

Finally, with this new edition, we welcome Brad Osborn (University of Kansas) as a contributing author. Brad's expertise in popular music of the twenty-first century and music videos has been central to the revision of the book's last chapters.

Features

- **Listening Guides**. Rather than being separated out or introduced independently, the main musical discussions are integrated into the text at the points where they are relevant to the developing narrative; this approach seemed to us both logical and functional. Given the enormous diversity of the music covered, these Listening Guides follow various formats adapted to the nature of the material under consideration. For example, Tin Pan Alley songs lend themselves readily to discussions that separate out the song as a composition from any specific recording of the song; this approach seems counterproductive, however, for examples in which the recording itself *is* the song—that is, the primary document. Accompanying charts are used to represent and summarize, in outline form, the most important elements of many recordings that are discussed in some detail in the text. In some of the more general discussions in which the emphasis is on the impact of the recording as a whole rather than on its various parts, these charts are not as useful, so we have not provided them. The fact that we are dealing here to an overwhelming extent with *songs*—texted music—has enabled us to treat musical issues with some sophistication without having to employ musical notation, since lyrics may be used as points of specific orientation in the musical discussions. This keeps the focus on *listening* and opens the musical analyses to the widest possible audience without compromising depth of treatment.

- **Key Terms and Names**. We have sought to limit the use of specialized terms, to employ them only when clearly necessary, and to define them as they arise naturally in the course of study. Important and frequently employed terms appear in **boldface** and typically are defined in the text when first introduced, as well as given extensive definitions in the glossary at the end of the book. These terms will also be listed at the end of each chapter to aid in study. Important names are introduced in ***boldface italics*** and will also be found in lists at the ends of chapters, as well as in the index.

- **Boxes**. Boxes are used occasionally throughout this book to provide further insight and information on significant individuals, recordings, and topics in cases in which such material—although it may be useful—would interrupt the flow of narrative.

- **Timeline**. An illustrated timeline provided at points throughout the text surveys important landmarks in American popular music and places them in historical context.

- An appendix that illustrates basic musical concepts, including beat, tempo, rhythm, and form, is offered for students who do not have a background in musical analysis.

Digital Tools to Build and Enrich Your Course

All new print and electronic versions of *American Popular Music*, Sixth Edition, come with access to a full suite of engaging digital learning tools that work with the text to bring content to life and help students experience popular music actively.

Digital Access to *American Popular Music*, Sixth Edition, includes:

- An enhanced e-book that integrates the text's engaging narrative with a rich assortment of multimedia resources, including links to stream every recording in the text with a free Spotify account, as well as in-text review questions, flashcards, historical performance videos, documentaries on specific artists, and more.

- Assignable, regularly updated popular music activities that ask students to apply concepts discussed in the text to recent music. Popular music activities are updated every year, so they always feature music that will be familiar to students.

- Assignable chapter quizzes including written and audio questions.

Flexible Delivery Options

At Oxford University Press, we create high-quality, engaging, and affordable digital material in a variety of formats, and deliver it to you in the way that best suits your needs and those of your students. You can choose to have your students access the digital content for *American Popular Music* in one of the following ways:

- **In your local learning management system with Oxford Learning Link Direct.** Brings all of the high-quality digital teaching and learning tools for *American Popular Music* right to your local learning management system. Instructors and their LMS administrators simply download the Oxford Learning Link Direct cartridge from Oxford Learning Link, and with the turn of a digital key, incorporate engaging content from OUP directly into their LMS for assigning and grading. See the Additional Instructor Resources section for more information on Oxford Learning Link.
- **In Oxford Learning Cloud.** Ideal for instructors who prefer a user-friendly alternative to their school's designated LMS, Oxford Learning Cloud delivers engaging learning tools within an easy-to-use cloud-based platform. Pre-built courses can be adjusted to fit course needs. A built-in gradebook allows instructors to quickly see and easily monitor students' progress. Visit learningcloud.oup.com or contact your Oxford University Press representative to learn more.
- **In a stand-alone enhanced e-book.** Ideal for self-study, the *American Popular Music* enhanced e-book delivers the full suite of digital resources in a format that is independent from any courseware or learning management system platform. The enhanced e-book is available through leading higher education e-book vendors.

Additional Instructor Resources

Save time in course prep with valuable tools available for download on Oxford Learning Link:

- PowerPoint lecture outlines for each chapter
- A detailed Instructor's Manual
- Test banks in Word and LMS/VLE course import package formats
- Oxford Learning Link Direct cartridge for integrating the full suite of digital resources for *American Popular Music* into most learning management systems

Visit http://www.oup.com/he/starr-waterman6e or contact your Oxford University Press representative to request access.

Acknowledgments

We would like to thank our families, who put up with a great deal as our work under-went its extensive prenatal development: Leslie, Dan, Sonya, and Gregory Starr; and Glennis and Maxfield Waterman. We extend our gratitude to Maribeth Payne, our ini-tial, ever-patient editor at Oxford University Press, who convinced us to take this project on; to Jan Beatty, our second, ever-enthusiastic and helpful executive editor at OUP; to our current editor, Justin Hoffman, and to his gifted associate Olivia Clark.

We owe a substantial debt of gratitude to the many readers who offered extensive and helpful comments on our work in its various stages:

Norman Bergeron, *Temple College*
Richard Birkemeier, *California State University–Long Beach*
Charlie Dahan, *Middle Tennessee State University*
Joel Henderson, *Chattanooga State Community College*
Sanford E. Hinderlie, *Loyola University–New Orleans*
Catherine Hughes, *St. Joseph's University*
Steven Hymowech, *Fulton-Montgomery Community College*
Ian Ranzer, *Montclair State University*
Sanda Saltstrom, *Lone Star College–University Park*
Mary A. Wischusen, *Wayne State University*
Thomas Zlabinger, *York College, City University of New York*

At the University of Washington, our valued colleague Tom Collier has been a con-sistent and selfless source of assistance and encouragement. The course on American popular music out of which this book grew was shaped not only by faculty members but by several generations of graduate students as well—among whom we especially wish to cite Jon Kertzer, Peter Davenport, Stuart Goosman, Jun Akutsu, Cathy Ragland, Steve Nickerson, Miles White, Edgar Pope, James Cunningham, Sue Letsinger, and Andrew Killick. We would like to thank Richard Caceres, who designed the charts in the appen-dix on meter and form and created the associated audio tracks.

The many students who road-tested this book, both in its preliminary stages and in its first two editions, also merit our sustained thanks. Graduate assistants Elizabeth Knighton, Timothy Kinsella, Shelley Lawson, and Nathan Link at the University of Washington, and Sabrina Motley, Mark Eby, and Ann Mazzocca at UCLA gave invaluable and generous editorial assistance. A special shout-out is owed to University of Washington graduate Sarah Kolat, Ph.D., who dutifully read through the entire text of the fourth edi-tion, offered invaluable suggestions regarding updating it for a contemporary readership, and provided essential material on twenty-first-century divas. Scott Wardinsky helped us with the interpretation of Afro-Cuban song texts. Thanks also to Elisse La Barre of UC Santa Cruz for setting us straight on the origins of the band name the "Grateful Dead." We owe an additional debt of gratitude to the folks at Joel Whitburn's Record Research for their series of books containing *Billboard* chart data. There are plenty more folks to thank, but there's also a story waiting to be told, and we'd best get on with it.

Larry Starr, Professor Emeritus, University of Washington
Christopher Waterman, UCLA

American Popular Music

MAJOR EVENTS IN U.S. HISTORY	YEAR	IMPORTANT LANDMARKS IN AMERICAN POPULAR MUSIC
	1760s	First "pleasure gardens" open in American cities
American Revolution begins	1775	
Declaration of Independence adopted by delegates from the thirteen American colonies	1776	
American Revolution ends as Great Britain recognizes American independence	1783	
Constitution of the United States of America ratified	1788	
George Washington elected first president of the United States	1789	
Importation of slaves from Africa to the United States officially becomes illegal	1808	
Slave rebellion in Louisiana	1811	
War of 1812 between United States and Great Britain	1812–1814	
Fully steam-powered textile mills established in Waltham, Massachusetts	1814	Inspired by a battle during the War of 1812, Francis Scott Key publishes the lyrics for "The Star-Spangled Banner," which eventually becomes the U.S. national anthem

TIMELINE: 1760s–1899

MAJOR EVENTS IN U.S. HISTORY	YEAR	IMPORTANT LANDMARKS IN AMERICAN POPULAR MUSIC
Erie Canal constructed	1817–1825	
Andrew Jackson elected president	1828	New York debut of George Washington Dixon, first prominent white "blackface" entertainer
	1829	Thomas Dartmouth Rice introduces the song "Jim Crow," the first American pop song to become an international hit
Nat Turner leads slave rebellion in Virginia	1831	
	1843	First performances by the Virginia Minstrels lead to the standardized pattern for the minstrel show
War with Mexico	1846–1848	
	1847	First performance of "Oh! Susanna," Stephen Foster's first big hit (plantation song)
Uncle Tom's Cabin published	1852	
Henry David Thoreau publishes Walden, promoting a return to a more natural life	1854	Publication of Stephen Foster's sentimental "Jeanie with the Light Brown Hair"

MAJOR EVENTS IN U.S. HISTORY	YEAR	IMPORTANT LANDMARKS IN AMERICAN POPULAR MUSIC
 • Abraham Lincoln inaugurated as first Republican president • Civil War: Union victory secures end of slavery within the United States	1861–1865	
The Thirteenth Amendment to the Constitution officially outlaws slavery in the United States	1865	
The Fifteenth Amendment to the Constitution gives all citizens the right to vote, regardless of "race, color, or previous condition of servitude"	1869	
• Custer's last stand at Little Bighorn • National Baseball League founded, beginning "professional" baseball	1876	
	1877	 Thomas Edison invents his phonograph
	1878	African American composer James Bland, among the first black composers to publish a popular hit song, publishes "Carry Me Back to Old Virginny"
	1877	Emile Berliner introduces the first flat disc records, which soon become the industry standard
National strike held in support of an eight-hour work day	1886	
	c. 1890	• Birth of New York's Tin Pan Alley, which becomes the center of popular music publishing • The first "nickelodeons"—machines that play the latest hits for a nickel—are set up in public places. (These machines later become known as "jukeboxes.")

MAJOR EVENTS IN U.S. HISTORY	YEAR	IMPORTANT LANDMARKS IN AMERICAN POPULAR MUSIC
 Massacre of Native Americans at Wounded Knee, South Dakota	1890	
Strike by steelworkers in Homestead, Pennsylvania, against Andrew Carnegie leads to the crushing of the union	1892	Publication of Charles K. Harris's "After the Ball," the first "mega-hit" pop song
Pullman porters—mostly African Americans—strike for better wages and working conditions	1894	Producer B. F. Keith opens the New Theater in Boston, the first major vaudeville house
 Plessy v. Ferguson decision of U.S. Supreme Court affirms the legality of "separate but equal" (i.e., segregated) facilities for blacks and whites	1896	"All Coons Look Alike to Me," composed by the African American songwriter Ernest Hogan, launches the craze for "coon songs"
	1897	 Publication of John Philip Sousa's "The Stars and Stripes Forever," which becomes the official march of the United States
Spanish-American War	1898	
	1899	 Publication of Scott Joplin's "Maple Leaf Rag"; its popularity helps to kick the "ragtime craze" into high gear

Themes and Streams of American Popular Music

1

MANY PAGES OF THIS INTRODUCTORY CHAPTER COULD BE FILLED MERELY by listing the various terms and phrases that have been employed over time to categorize the many styles and forms of American popular music. Ragtime. Race music. Hillbilly. Swing. Country and western. Rock 'n' Roll. Alternative. Easy listening. Punk. Hip-hop. EDM. Indie. Americana. Emo. Crunk. Cowpunk. And so on, and on, and on . . .

But think for a moment. Why all these categories? Who listens to them? How do formats such as classic rock, urban contemporary, adult alternative, and Latin tropical take shape? What does this dividing up of musical genres and audiences tell us about American culture? And who's making money from all this?

We hope that this book will help you to think creatively and critically about such questions. Our goal is to get you to listen closely to popular music and learn something about its history and about the people and institutions that have produced it. We cover a wide range of music, starting in the nineteenth century and continuing up to the present. Listening to music is an important part of this study, and we hope that you will enjoy the recordings that we have chosen to highlight. But be forewarned—we cannot possibly do justice to all the music you like or all the musicians you admire (nor can we adequately denigrate the music you hate).

It is difficult to come up with a satisfactory definition of "popular music." In many cases popular music is defined by its difference from other types of music, especially "art music" or "classical music" on the one hand and "folk music" on the other. One problem with such categories is that they seem less reasonable when you begin to deal with particular examples. In some ways the "garage band" tradition of rock music—in which a bunch of people get together to play music for fun, sometimes copying songs from records and sometimes composing their own—is more like "folk music" than "popular music." In other cases—say, the ragtime piano pieces of Scott Joplin or the Beatles album *Sgt. Pepper's Lonely Hearts Club Band*—it is not easy to separate the "artistic" from the "popular." There have been times in American history when what we think of as classical music—say the operas of nineteenth-century Italian composers like Verdi and Bellini—were in effect popular music. Much of the music that people regard today as "folk music"—the recordings of the Weavers, the Kingston Trio, or Peter, Paul, and Mary—was performed by professional urban musicians and profoundly shaped by market forces.

In this book we use the term "popular music" broadly to indicate music that is mass-reproduced and disseminated via the mass media, that has at various times been listened to by large numbers of Americans, and that typically draws upon a variety of pre-existing musical traditions. It is our view that popular music must be seen in relation to a broader musical landscape in which various styles, audiences, and institutions interact in complex ways. This musical map is not static—it is always in motion, always evolving.

BOX 1.1 WHAT KIND OF STORY IS *HISTORY*?: "YOU ARE THERE" VERSUS WE ARE *HERE*

History is always a "story" of some kind, a story shaped in countless conscious and unconscious ways by the tellers. In writing a history like the present one, we have been consistently aware of the push and pull between what might be called "objective" factual data and what might be termed "subjective" contextualization and interpretation of that data. Of course an additional complication is that the apparent total opposition between "objective" and "subjective" viewpoints is deceptive and ultimately false. Objectivity is inevitably a relative, rather than an absolute, concept, and it is impossible to avoid subjectivity completely. (That doesn't mean, however, that there is no distinction between relatively objective and markedly subjective presentations of historical material.) Examples of relatively objective phenomena in our present field of study are: written records of recording dates, songs, and performers; the sound recordings themselves; data in the form of sheet music and record sales, airplay charts, and related indexes of popularity; and reliable contemporaneous accounts of popular music, performers, and culture at specific times (although such accounts are unavoidably colored by the subjectivity of their authors). Subjectivity manifests itself most obviously when evaluations of the aesthetic merit and long-term cultural impact of styles, trends, performers, and recordings are offered by the authors of histories.

A 1950s television program called *You Are There* attempted to place viewers at important historical events as they were occurring, as if time travel were literally possible—and with TV cameras in attendance! This exemplified an "objective" approach to the presentation of history. Many would argue, however, that what is most important is not the presumably "objective" data, but our assessment of historical *meaning* from the standpoint of the present—emphasizing in effect that "we are *here*," rather than trying to pretend that "you are there." And some would go further, asserting that our present-day assessment of meaning is not simply what is most important, but is also the only approach to the past we can realistically take! This dichotomy is encountered most powerfully in the study of popular music when we attempt to reconcile the data of past popularity with our present understanding of what music and which performers have proved most enduring and arguably significant over time. We will be referring to these issues at many points throughout this book.

Here is an illustration of the complexities involved: All indexes of popularity from the 1920s tell us that bandleader Paul Whiteman and singer Al Jolson were superstars—arguably *the* superstars of that decade—and that while trumpet player and bandleader Louis Armstrong and blues singer Bessie Smith certainly were contributors to the popular culture of that time, they ultimately were more marginal and less important figures. Yet in the twenty-first century, Armstrong and Smith are regarded as iconic central artists, essential immortals in the history of popular music, while Whiteman and Jolson have been relegated to the realm of nostalgia. Had you told a 1920s pop music fan that such an evaluation would come to pass in due time, that fan would probably have been surprised, if not incredulous—and if you were to tell a present-day jazz fan or cultural historian that you esteemed Whiteman or Jolson over Armstrong or Smith, you would probably be laughed out of the room. But our present perspective makes it far too easy to forget—or ignore—that Whiteman and Jolson were both very good at what they did, that there were significant cultural reasons for their popular acclaim, and that in fact they helped prepare the way for a broader public to fully appreciate the artistry of Armstrong and Smith. Belittling Whiteman and Jolson can lead us to significantly oversimplify and distort both history and aesthetics.

We find instances of this phenomenon of changing valuation throughout the history of popular music. In the later 1950s Pat Boone's records vastly outsold those of Chuck Berry, and for a time in the later 1960s albums by the TV-fabricated Monkees were outselling those of the Beatles!

You might stop to wonder how your present feelings about the value and importance of today's pop artists and recordings might seem to you sometime in the future—and how those feelings might come to be viewed by cultural historians in the future. Appreciating the extent to which such information is now unknowable, and understanding the complexity of the issues and perspectives that such uncertainty throws into relief will enhance your grasp of the richness and multidimensionality of our subject.

Theme One: Listening

Although this book covers a wide range of performers, styles, and historical periods, it is unified by several themes. First and foremost, we hope to encourage you to *listen critically* to popular music. The word "critical" doesn't imply that you must adopt a negative attitude. Rather, critical listening is listening that consciously seeks out meaning in music by drawing on knowledge of how music is put together, its cultural significance, and its historical development.

Even if you don't think of yourself as a musician and don't have much—or any—experience at reading musical notation, it is likely that you know much more about music than you think. You know when a chord sounds "wrong," a note "out of tune," or a singer "off-key," even if you can't come up with a technical explanation for your reaction. You have learned a lot about music just by growing up as a member of society, although much of that knowledge rests below the level of conscious awareness.

In everyday life, people often do not think carefully about the music they hear. Much popular music is in fact designed to not call critical attention to itself (a good example of this is the multimillion-dollar "background music" industry pioneered by the Muzak Corporation in 1934). Many types of popular music—big band swing, funk, punk rock, hard rap, thrash metal—seek to grab your attention but do not by and large encourage you to engage them analytically. The point of analyzing popular music is not to ruin your enjoyment of it. Rather, we want to encourage you to expand your tastes; to hear the roots of today's music in earlier styles; and, in the final analysis, to be a more critically aware "consumer" of popular music.

Formal analysis—listening for musical structure, its basic building blocks, and the ways in which these blocks are combined—can tell us a lot about popular music. We can, for example, discover that recordings as different as Glenn Miller's 1939 big band hit "In the Mood," Little Richard's rock 'n' roll anthem "Tutti Frutti," James Brown's "I Got You (I Feel Good)," the Doors' "Riders on the Storm," and the theme song of the 1960s TV show *Batman* all share the same basic musical structure, the twelve-bar blues form (to be discussed in Chapter 5). Similarly, tunes as diverse as George Gershwin's 1930 song "I Got Rhythm," the Penguins' 1955 doo-wop hit "Earth Angel," the Beatles' "Yesterday," and the theme of the 1960s cartoon show (and 1993 film) *The Flintstones* all have an AABA melodic structure. You don't have to worry about such technicalities yet; there will be ample opportunity to discuss them later on. The point here is simply to suggest that a lot of popular music draws on a limited number of basic formal structures.

Structure is not the only important dimension of music. In order to analyze the way popular music actually sounds—the grain of a singing voice, the flow of a dance groove, or the gritty sound of an electric guitar—we must complement formal analysis with the analysis of musical process. To draw an analogy to biology, there is an important difference between the *structure* of an organism—its constituent parts and how they are related—and the *processes* that bring these parts and relationships to life. Popular songs may be analyzed not only as composed "works" with their own internal characteristics but also as interpretations by particular performers; in other words, one must understand not only *song* but also *singing*.

Traditional methodologies, which focus on the analysis of written musical scores, are often of little use in helping us to understand popular music. In this book we frequently use concepts that are directly relevant to popular music itself: for example, the **riff**, a repeated pattern designed to generate rhythmic momentum; the **hook**, a memorable musical phrase or riff; and **groove**, a term that evokes the channeled flow of "swinging," "funky," or "phat" rhythms.

Another important aspect of musical process is **timbre**, the quality of a sound, sometimes called "tone color." Timbre plays an important role in establishing the "soundprint" of a performer. Play just five seconds of a recording by Louis Armstrong, Frank Sinatra, Johnny Cash, Aretha Franklin, Bruce Springsteen, Dr. Dre, Beyoncé, or Adele, and any knowledgeable listener will be able to identify the singer by the "grain" of his or her voice.

Instrumental performers may also have highly memorable soundprints. Some—such as Jimi Hendrix, Eric Clapton, and Eddie Van Halen—have become superstars. Others remain unknown to the general listening public, although their soundprints are very familiar: for example, James Jamerson, the master bassist of Motown; King Curtis, whose gritty tenor saxophone is featured on dozens of soul records from the 1960s; and Steve Gadd, studio drummer par excellence, who played on records by Aretha Franklin, Stevie Wonder, Barbra Streisand, Steely Dan, and Paul Simon during the 1970s.

Recording engineers, producers, arrangers, and record labels may also develop unique soundprints. We will encounter many examples of this, including the distinctive "slap-back" echo of Elvis Presley's early recordings on Sun Records; the quasi-symphonic teen pop recordings produced by Phil Spector; the stripped-down "back to basics" soul sound of Stax Records in Memphis; and the immense sampled bass drum explosions used by engineer Steve Ett of Chung House of Metal, one of the most influential studios in the history of hip-hop. You will learn more about the creative contributions of arrangers, engineers, and producers as we go along; for now, you should simply note that the production of a particular "sound" often involves many individuals performing different tasks.

Lyrics—the words of a song—are another important aspect of popular music. In many cases words are designed to be one of the most immediately accessible parts of a song. In other cases—the songs of Robert Johnson, Bob Dylan, John Lennon and Paul McCartney, David Byrne, Kurt Cobain, or Ice-T—the lyrics seem to *demand* interpretation, and fans take a great deal of pleasure in the process of figuring out their meaning.

Dialect has been a crucial factor in the history of American popular music. Some musical genres are strongly associated with particular dialects (e.g., country music with Southern white dialects, rap music with certain urban Black dialects, 1970s punk rock with working-class British dialects). The ability of African American artists such as Nat "King" Cole, Chuck Berry, and Diana Ross to "cross over" to a white middle-class audience was to some degree predicated upon their adoption of a "mainstream" (white American) dialect. In other cases the mutual incomprehensibility of varieties of English has been consciously emphasized, particularly in recordings aimed at consumption within ethnic communities. There are sometimes very good reasons to not be understood by the majority.

These are some of the dimensions of popular musical to keep in mind as you work your way through this book. Think about what attracts you to the music you like: the texture of a voice, the power of a guitar, the emotional insight of a lyric, the satisfying predictability of a familiar tune, the physical momentum of a rhythm. These are what make popular music important to people: its sound, the sense it makes, and the way it feels.

Throughout the book, we will be operating on the assumption that you are (or have been, or will be) listening to the music under discussion. When sustained attention is devoted to individual recordings, we offer separate Listening Guides to assist in your comprehension and appreciation of the musical elements of each selection.

Theme Two: Music and Identity (Individuality, Gender, and Race)

None of us is born knowing who we are—we all *learn* to be human in particular ways, and music is one important medium through which we formulate and express our identity. Think back to the very first pop song you remember hearing as a little kid, when you were, say, five years old. Odds are you heard it at home, or maybe in a car, or (depending on your age) over a transistor radio, a portable CD player at the beach, or on an audio streaming service such as Spotify or YouTube Music. The person playing that song may have been one of your parents, or an older brother or sister. Family members often influence our early musical values, and it is their values that we sometimes emphatically reject later in life. In elementary school other kids begin to influence our taste, a development closely connected with the ways in which we form social groups based on gender, age, and other factors. As we move into adolescence, popular music also enters our private lives, providing comfort and continuity during emotional crises and offering us the opportunity to fantasize about romance and rebellion.

As you grow older, a song or a singer's voice may suddenly transport you back to a specific moment and place in your life, sometimes many decades earlier. Like all human beings, we make stories out of our lives, and music plays an important role in bringing these narratives to life. Some popular songs—for example, Frank Sinatra's version of "It Was a Very Good Year," Dolly Parton's "Coat of Many Colors," Don McLean's "American Pie," and Missy Elliott's "Back in the Day"—are really *about* memory and the mixed feelings of warmth and loss that accompany a retrospective view of our own lives.

Popular music in America has from the very beginning been closely tied up with stereotypes, or convenient ways of organizing people into categories. It is easy to find examples of stereotyping in American popular music: the common portrayal of women as sexual objects; the association of men with violence; the image of African American men as playboys and gangsters; the characterization of Southern white musicians as illiterate, backwoods "rednecks"; the use of supposedly Jewish musical characteristics in songs about money; and the caricatures of Asian and Latin American people found in many novelty songs from the 1920s through the 1960s.

Stereotyping is often a double-edged sword. In certain cases popular performers have helped to undermine the "common-sense" association of certain styles with certain "types" of people: the Black country singer Charley Pride and the white blues musician Stevie Ray Vaughan are just two examples of performers whose styles challenge stereotyped conceptions of race and culture. The history of popular music in the United States is also replete with examples of minority groups who have reinterpreted derogatory stereotypes and made them the basis for distinctive forms of musical creativity and cultural pride—James Brown's "Say It Loud, I'm Black and I'm Proud," Merle Haggard's "Okie from Muskogee," Dolly Parton's "Dumb Blond," and the Village People's "Y.M.C.A." are only a few illustrations.

Pop music provides images of gender and sexual identity. In recent years, members of the LGBTQ communities have frequently employed popular music as a means of asserting, and expressing pride in, group and individual identities. For example, the lesbian sisters who perform as Tegan and Sara are a prominent Canadian pop/rock duo that has achieved significant commercial success well beyond the borders of their native country. While their music doesn't overtly discuss gay issues, their videos and their image explore sexual identity and the "love is love" theme, as in "Closer" from the 2013 album *Heartthrob*. The duo has also gained wide recognition with the song "Everything Is Awesome," from *The LEGO Movie*, and with a colorful Oreo commercial. In 2012, the album *Trespassing* by openly gay artist Adam Lambert (who appeared on *American Idol* in 2009) debuted at Number 1 on the *Billboard* 200. And an open letter published that same year by hip-hop/R&B artist Frank Ocean on his Tumblr blog, recounted his love for a young man when he was nineteen years old, and gained the public support of hip-hop figures such as Jay Z, Beyoncé, and Russell Simmons. This was a truly notable event in the field of hip-hop music, where homophobic slurs have long been an idiom of verbal aggression. And in 2019 Lil Nas X, whose hip-hop/country track "Old Town Road" became the longest-running hit in the history of the *Billboard* Hot 100 chart, became the first and only openly LGBTQ artist to win a Country Music Association award.

It is important to note that there is a distinction between openly LGBTQ artists and their "allies." Lady Gaga is a notable example of an LGBTQ ally. Her Born This Way Foundation, named after Gaga's 2011 hit single "Born This Way," is dedicated to empowering young people to create a "kinder and braver world." The LGBT Academy of Recording Arts and its OUTmusic Awards serve the community through political and social activism and artist recognition.

Ethnicity and race—including notions of "Black," "Latino," or "white" cultural authenticity—are also powerfully represented in popular music. Recent examples include Taylor Swift's "22" (2013), which is about being an upper-middle class white woman with very few things to worry about, and Kendrick Lamar's "Alright," from his album *To Pimp a Butterfly* (2015), a track that deals with race relations, police brutality, and growing up Black in Compton. Beyoncé's 2016 album *Lemonade* addresses issues of racism and sexism through both music and accompanying videos. And although the Black Lives Matter movement and associated protests against systemic racism (2020) did not have an unifying anthem such as "We Shall Overcome," participants sampled classic protest songs, including "Strange Fruit," composed by Abel Meerpol and recorded by Billie Holiday in 1939; Public Enemy's "Fight the Power" (1989); "Inner City Blues [Make Me Wanna Holler]" by Marvin Gaye (1974); and Kendrick Lamar's "Alright" (2015), and stimulated immediate musical responses such as Beyoncé's "Black Parade" and Lil Baby's "The Bigger Picture" (both released in June 2020). While the anti-racist protest movement of the 1950s and 1960s found its musical heart in a hymn composed by a Black Methodist preacher, Charles Albert Tindley, and published in 1901 under the title "I'll Overcome Some Day," the new generation of activists and allies sampled recordings from the past and composed songs specifically relevant to contemporary concerns.

People value music for many reasons: they use music to escape from the rigors of the work week; to celebrate important events in their lives; to help them make money, war, and love. In order to understand the cultural significance of popular music, we must examine both the music—its tones and textures, rhythms and forms—and the broader patterns of social identity that have shaped Americans' tastes and values.

Theme Three: Music and Technology

From the heyday of printed sheet music in the nineteenth century through the rise of the phonograph record, network radio, and sound film in the 1920s, and right up to the present era of digital recording, computerized sampling, and internet-based radio, technology has shaped popular music and helped disseminate it, more and more rapidly, to more and more people. Technology doesn't determine the decisions made by musicians or audiences, but it can make a particular range of choices more available to them.

It has often been argued that the mass media create a gap between musicians and their audiences, a distance that encourages us to forget that the music we hear is made by other human beings. To what degree has technology affected our relationship to music and, more importantly, to other people? This is by no means a simple issue. Some critics of today's musical technology would say that a much higher percentage of Americans were able to perform music for their own enjoyment a century ago, when the only way of experiencing music was to hear it performed live or to make it yourself. This long-term decline in personal music-making is generally attributed to the influence of mass media, which are said to encourage passive listening. However, nationwide sales figures for musical instruments—including electronic instruments such as digital

One of the earliest FM radio stations, Alpine, New Jersey, 1948.

keyboards and drum pads—suggest that millions of people in the United States today are busy making music. The onset of quarantining in response to the Covid-19 pandemic of 2020–2021 encouraged a marked increase in the purchase of music creation software such as Apple's GarageBand, as well as musical instrument sales by online vendors such as Sweetwater, Guitar Center, Reverb, and other retailers.[1] And more and more people are using portable and distributed technologies to create their own music.

In addition, although the mass media can encourage passivity, people aren't always passive when they listen to recorded music. Have you ever pretended to be a favorite musician while listening to music in private, perhaps even mimicking their voice or on-stage movements? Have you ever unconsciously sung along with your smartphone in a public setting? When you listen to music on headphones or earbuds, don't you enter into the music in your imagination and in an important sense help to "make" the music?

Although we tend to associate the word "technology" with novelty and change, older technologies often take on important value as tokens of an earlier—and, it is often claimed, better—time. Old forms of musical hardware and software—music boxes, player pianos, phonographs, sheet music, 78s, 45s, LPs, and CDs—become the basis for subcultures made up of avid collectors. In some cases older music technologies are regarded as qualitatively superior to new technologies. For example, some contemporary musicians make a point of using analog rather than digital recording technology. This decision is based on the aesthetic judgment that analog recordings, which directly mirror the energy fluctuations of sound waves, "sound better" than digital recordings, which break sound waves down into packets of information. Musicians who prefer analog recording say that this technology produces "warmer," "richer-sounding," and somehow "more human" music than digital recording.

Sometimes the rejection of electronic technology functions as an emblem of "authenticity," as, for example, in MTV's *Unplugged* series (1989–present), on which, for over thirty years, rockers such as Eric Clapton, R.E.M., Nirvana, and Miley Cyrus have demonstrated their "real" musical ability and sincerity by playing on acoustic instruments. (In 2020, during the COVID-19 pandemic, MTV launched *MTV Unplugged at Home*.) However, there are also many examples of contemporary technologies being used in ways that encourage active involvement, including **digital audio workstations** (DAWs), music creation software, karaoke machines, and technologies whose effectiveness depends upon the active participation of listeners. While revenues from musical instrument sales in the United States were relatively flat during the 2010s, the Covid-19 pandemic and the imperative to sequester at home has catalyzed a big increase in both profits and number of instruments sold. And even a cursory tour of the video-sharing website YouTube, launched in 2005, will confirm the existence of tens of thousands of musicians eager to share their work with a wider audience.

The latest method of music dissemination is online **streaming**, including services such as Spotify (by far the largest), Apple Music, and Tidal, an artist-owned company

---

1. Samantha Hissong, "Sales of Instruments and Music Gear Are Soaring. Will Quarantine Spark a Renaissance?" *Rolling* Stone.com (April 24, 2020).

whose investors include Shawn "Jay Z" Carter, Beyoncé, Jack White, Madonna, and Daft Punk. Subscription-based streaming services, projected to reach 1 billion paying customers by 2021, feature a wide range of artists and content, and offer high-definition audio quality. While a number of streaming services have pursued the strategy of offering restricted artist content—for example's Tidal's exclusive release of Kanye West's *The Life of Pablo* (2016) and Beyoncé's *Lemonade* (2016)—it seems clear that many buyers have not been willing to subscribe to multiple services in order to access the latest albums by superstars. While some of these services have been growing, even Spotify, founded in 2008, didn't turn an annual profit for a decade, and by the 2020s was facing robust competition from YouTube Music, rooted partly in the latter's appeal to younger consumers, indicating that the business model for music streaming is still evolving.

In the end, there is no easy way to summarize the evolving relationship between popular music, music-making, and technology. If it is true that technology has long been used in cynical ways to manipulate the public into buying certain kinds of music, it also remains the case that people frequently seek to exert creative control over the musical machines in their own lives.

Theme Four: The Music Business

In order to understand the history of American popular music, it is necessary for us to learn about the workings of the music business. The production of popular music typically involves the work of many individuals performing different roles. From the nineteenth century until the 1920s, sheet music was the principal means of disseminating popular songs to a mass audience. This process typically involved a complex network of people and institutions: the composer and lyricist who wrote a song; the publishing company that bought the rights to it; the song pluggers who promoted the song in stores and convinced big stars to incorporate it into their acts; the stars themselves, who often worked in shows that toured a circuit of theaters controlled by still other organizations; and so on, right down to the consumer, who bought the sheet music and performed it at home.

The rise of radio, recording, and movies as the primary means for popularizing music added many layers of complexity to this process. Up until the beginning of the twenty-first century, the process of making popular music was organized around a well-defined set of roles. In mainstream pop music, the **composer** and **lyricist** were important as the first creators of a work; the songs they wrote were then reworked to complement a particular performer's strengths by an **arranger**, who decided which instruments to use

The interior of the offices of the original Sun Studios as it has been restored as a museum.

as accompaniment, what key the song should be in, how many times it should be re-peated, and a host of other details. The advent of rock 'n' roll in the mid-1950s introduced a variation on this model, in which performers—think of Chuck Berry, Bob Dylan, and the Beatles—were also songwriters. The **A&R** (artists and repertoire) personnel of record companies sought out talent, often visiting nightclubs and rehearsals to hear new groups. The **producer** of a record played several roles: convincing the board of directors of a record company to back a particular project, shaping the development of new talent, and often intervening directly in the recording process. Engineers worked in the studio, making hundreds of important decisions about the balance between voice and instru-ments, the use of effects such as echo and reverb, and other factors that shaped the over-all sound of a record. The publicity department planned the advertising campaign to promote the record, and the public relations department handled interactions with the press. Business agents, video producers, graphic artists, copy editors, stagehands, truck drivers, the companies that designed and produced T-shirts and other forms of concert "swag," and the companies that produced musical hardware—often owned by the same corporations that produced the recordings—were also important links in the chain of popular music production and dissemination.

Of course, many of these roles are still important in popular music today, although the advent of digital distribution has in recent years profoundly challenged the music in-dustry's fundamental modes of operation. The traditional lines that once divided artist, publisher, record company, distributor, and consumer electronics manufacturer have become blurred. New modes of digital music distribution have forced both government and industry to re-examine the definitions of intellectual property and the rights of all the parties involved. It is in fact hard to know where to draw the boundaries of an industry that has splintered into a myriad of specialized styles, audiences, markets, and start-up companies while at the same time moving forcefully toward even greater levels of corporate consolidation.

Compared to other industries that make and disseminate consumer products, the music business has always been quite unpredictable. In the 1890s a new generation of twenty-something immigrants created novel techniques for promoting and disseminat-ing popular songs, generating a business that had barely existed before then. By the mid-1920s annual sales of recordings had surpassed sheet music sales, and radio had provided a new means of promoting them, but the business was still loaded with risk. By the 1980s and 1990s only about one out of eight records produced made a profit, and a handful of platinum albums—certified million-sellers like Michael Jackson's *Thriller* (1982), Madonna's *Like a Virgin* (1984), Nirvana's *Nevermind* (1991), and Dr. Dre's *The Chronic* (1992)—had to compensate for literally hundreds of unprofitable recordings made by less widely known musicians or faded stars.

During the first decade of the twenty-first century the music industry was profoundly impacted by the rise of internet-based digital technologies. Initially, downloadable audio was the dominant new format. As Apple's online iTunes Store (founded in 2001) rose to become the largest music retailer in the world, revenues from sales of recorded music in the United States dropped precipitously, from a high of $14.6 billion in 1999 to $6.3

billion in 2009. More recently, however, iTunes revenue fell dramatically from recorded music sales; growth dropped 14 percent in the first half of 2014 while streaming revenue rose 28 percent. Whether through downloads or streaming, the impact on the recording industry has been dramatic. The decline in physical sales caused large-scale layoffs within the industry, forced the closure of retailers such as Tower Records (2006), and impelled record companies, producers, studios, recording engineers, and musicians to seek new business models. As music technology and software increasingly made it possible for artists to create their own home studios, many recording studios in cities like New York and Los Angeles were driven out of business. Increasingly, live performance became the most profitable aspect of the industry. Today concerts bring in the majority of profits, and the sale of recorded music is an important but secondary source.

While the internet has encouraged the establishment of small artist-owned music labels and publishing companies, it is also important to realize that the music industry is at the same time becoming more consolidated on a global scale. As of 2016, three transnational corporations—Universal Music Group, Sony Music Entertainment, and Warner Music Group—controlled at least 80 percent of the world's legal trade in commercially recorded music. Each of these music corporations is part of a larger business conglomerate, and each has bought up smaller labels, using them as incubators for new talent. The market for recorded music has been predicted to decline from $57.3 billion in 2019 to $55.8 billion in 2020, due mainly to a massive economic slowdown across countries related to the Covid-19 outbreak and the measures to contain it.[2]

Even as it undergoes potentially revolutionary change, the music industry continues to permeate our daily lives. Any time you hear music in a restaurant or bar, at a mall, on an airplane, at a football or baseball game, or while waiting endlessly for a human voice on the telephone, the music industry is involved, and someone is reaping profits. We are almost continuously bathed in music, whether we are fully conscious of it or not, and modern technology places the entire history of recorded sound at our fingertips, twenty-four hours a day, seven days a week. To be sure, it is easier now than ever before to explore, expand your taste, and experience new sounds from all around the world. At the same time, the very ubiquity of music raises the risk that we will come to take it for granted, diminishing its deep and enduring significance as a means of individual and cultural expression, one of the hallmarks of being human.

Theme Five: Centers and Peripheries

The distinction between major and minor labels leads us to a final theme: the idea that much of the history of American popular music may be broadly conceptualized in terms of a center-periphery model. The "center"—actually several geographically distinct

---

2. https://www.marketwatch.com/press-release/insights-on-the-music-recording-global-market-to-2030—featuring-universal-music-group-sony-music-warner-music—researchandmarketscom-2020-08-28?mod=mw_more_headlines&tesla=y.

centers, including New York, Los Angeles, and Nashville—is where power, capital, and control over mass media are concentrated. The "periphery" is inhabited by smaller institutions and people who have historically been excluded from the political and economic mainstream. This distinction is by no means intended to suggest that the center is "normal" and the periphery "abnormal." Rather, it is a way of clarifying a process that has profoundly shaped the development of popular music in the United States—that is, the role of the musical "margins" in shaping mainstream popular taste and the workings of the music industry.

Until the mid-1950s the stylistic mainstream of American popular music was largely oriented toward the tastes of white, middle- or upper-class, Protestant, urban people. In economic terms, this orientation makes perfect sense, since it was these people who for many years made up the bulk of the expanding urban market for mass-reproduced music. From whom have the vital "peripheral" musical impulses come? The sources, as you shall see, are abundant: from African Americans, poor Southern whites, working-class people, Jewish and Latin American immigrants, adolescents, the LGBTQ communities, and various other folks whose "difference" vis-à-vis the mainstream has at times weighed upon them as a burden.

The history of popular music in the United States shows us how supposedly marginal music and musicians have repeatedly helped to invigorate the center of popular taste and the music industry. Regrettably, as we have recently been reminded, the people most responsible for creating the music that people in the United States and elsewhere consider quintessentially American have often not reaped an equitable share of the profits accumulated from the fruits of their labor.

Streams of Tradition: The Sources of Popular Music

Every aspect of popular music that is today regarded as American in character has sprung from imported traditions. These source traditions may be classified into broad "streams," and in this book we will focus on three very prominent ones: European American music, African American music, and Latin American music. Each of these three streams is made up of many styles of music, and each has profoundly influenced the others.

THE EUROPEAN AMERICAN STREAM

Until the middle of the nineteenth century, American popular music was almost entirely European in character. The cultural and linguistic dominance of the English meant that their music—including folk **ballads**, popular songs printed as sheet music, and various types of dance music—established early on a kind of "mainstream" around which other styles circulated.

At the time of the American Revolution, professional composers of popular songs in England drew heavily upon ballads, a type of song in which a series of **verses** telling a story, often about a historical event or personal tragedy, are sung to a repeating melody. This sort of musical form is called **strophic**. Originally an oral tradition passed

Castle Garden, New York City, in 1848, as depicted in a lithograph by Nathaniel Currier.

down in unwritten form, ballads were eventually circulated on large sheets of paper called **broadsides**, the ancestors of today's sheet music. While some broadside ballads were drawn from folk tradition, many were urban in origin and concerned with current events (much like today's tabloid newspapers). In most cases broadsides provided only the words to a song, along with an indication of a traditional melody—for example, "Greensleeves" or "Barbara Allen"—to which they were to be sung. Balladmongers hawking the broadsides sang the tunes on the streets, an early form of commercial song promotion. Composers of broadside ballads often added a catchy **chorus**, a repeated melody with fixed text inserted between verses.

The pleasure garden, a forerunner of today's theme parks, was the most important source of public entertainment in England between 1650 and 1850. Large urban parks filled with meandering tree-lined paths, the pleasure gardens provided an idyllic rural experience for an expanding urban audience. The pleasure gardens became the main venues for the dissemination of printed songs by professional composers, and many of the first widely popular song sheets were illustrated with sketches of these gardens and other romanticized rural scenes. In the 1760s the first American pleasure gardens opened in Charleston, New York, and other cities.

The English ballad opera tradition was also extremely popular in America during the early nineteenth century. These stage productions drew upon ballads, some of which had previously been circulated as broadsides. Perhaps the best known of the English ballad operas is John Gay's *The Beggar's Opera* (1728), designed to counter the domination of the British stage by Italian composers and musicians. In ballad operas the main characters were common people rather than the kings and queens of imported operas, the songs were familiar in form and content, and the lyrics were all in English rather than Italian.

The pleasure gardens and ballad operas both featured songs produced by professional composers for large and diverse audiences. Melodies were designed to be simple and easy to remember, and the lyrics focused on romantic themes.

The ballad tradition thrived in America, and songs were reworked to suit the life circumstances of new immigrants. In the early twentieth century folklorists interested in continuities with traditions of the British Isles (England, Scotland, Ireland, and Wales) were able to record dozens of versions of the old ballads in the United States. While today these songs are preserved mainly by folk music enthusiasts, the core of the tradition—including its musical forms and storytelling techniques—lives on in contemporary country and western music. In addition, vocal qualities derived from the Anglo-American tradition—notably the thin, nasalized tone known as the "high lonesome sound"—continue to be used in music today as markers of Southern white identity.

Published collections of Irish, Scottish, and Italian songs also influenced the development of early American popular song. Copies of Thomas Moore's multivolume *Irish Melodies* (a collection of Moore's poems set to Irish folk melodies, published in London and Dublin between 1808 and 1834) were widely circulated in the United States, and Scottish songs such as "Auld Lang Syne" (probably written in the late seventeenth century and still performed today on New Year's Eve) also enjoyed wide popularity. By the first decades of the nineteenth century, the Italian opera had also become very popular in the United States. Songs by Rossini, Bellini, Donizetti, and other Italian composers were published as sheet music, and the bel canto style of singing—light, clear, flexible, and intimate—had a major impact on the development of popular singing style.

Dance music was another important area of American popular music that was shaped by European influences. Until the late nineteenth century European American dance was closely modeled on styles imported from England and the Continent. Country dances—such as the contra dance, quadrille, reel, and square dance, in which dancers arranged themselves into circles, opposing rows, or squares—were popular. In the United States the country dance tradition developed into a plethora of variants, both urban and rural, elite and working class, Black and white. It continues today in country and western line dances and in the contra dances that form part of the modern folk music scene.

The nineteenth century saw a move toward couple dances, including the waltz, the galop, the schottische, and the ballroom polka, the last based on a Bohemian dance that had already become the rage in the ballrooms of Paris and London before coming to America. Later, in the 1880s, a fast dance called the one-step, based in part on marching band music, became popular. These couple dances are direct predecessors of the African American–influenced popular dance styles of the early twentieth century, including the two-step, the fox-trot, the bunny hug, and the Charleston (see Chapter 3).

In addition to the songs and dance music that were produced by professional composers for a largely urban audience, immigration brought a wide variety of European folk music to America. The mainstream of English-dominated popular song and dance music was from early on surrounded by a myriad of folk and popular styles brought by immigrants from other parts of Europe. The descendants of early French settlers in North America and the Caribbean maintained their own musical traditions. Millions of Irish and German immigrants came to the United States during the nineteenth century, seeking an escape from oppression, economic uncertainty, and—particularly during the potato famine of the 1840s—the threat of starvation. Between 1880 and 1910 an additional 17 million immigrants entered the United States, mostly from eastern and southern Europe. These successive waves of migration contributed to the diversity of musical life in the United States. European-derived musical styles such as Cajun (Acadian) fiddling, Jewish klezmer music (band music originally played for dances and weddings in central European Jewish communities), and the Polish polka—an energetic dance that was quite different from the "refined" style of polka discussed previously—each contributed to mainstream popular music while maintaining a solid base in their particular ethnic communities.

The Europeans who came to America also brought many traditions of religious music to our shores. The first distinctively American body of sacred music arose in the middle of the nineteenth century as part of a wave of Protestant religious activity and conversion that has been called the "Great Awakening." The type of music most closely associated with this period was a body of sacred songs called **spirituals**, which originated in breakaway movements such as that of the Separatist Baptists, who believed that their musical texts, like their religious expression, should be intensely personal, exuberant, and free from doctrinal restraints. The nineteenth century saw a series of widespread revivals led by evangelical ministers and characterized by the formation of new religious movements and denominations. "Camp meetings"—multiday, open-air religious services that attracted thousands of people from all denominations—spread in popularity during this period. Camp meeting hymns were designed to encourage religious fervor and commitment among participants and often featured **call-and-response** singing, with the preacher "lining out" or singing each line of a given song and the congregation repeating it in turn. (It should be noted that each of these developments also influenced the development of African American sacred music, discussed later in this chapter.)

Gospel music, a large body of sacred song with texts that reflect aspects of the personal religious experience of Protestant evangelical groups, first appeared in the 1850s in collections published for Sunday schools. (It is important to note that here we are discussing the white gospel music tradition. African Americans developed their own distinctive approach to gospel music, which we will discuss later.) The rise and expansion of gospel singing as a popular movement took place in the last three decades of the nineteenth century and was closely associated with both the intensification of Pentecostal revivalism after the Civil War and the work of the evangelist Dwight L. Moody and his musical associate Ira D. Sankey, who produced influential collections of gospel songs for use by congregations in cities such as Chicago. As compared with the Sacred Harp tradition, gospel music is more strongly influenced by popular songs, particularly in its use of repetition and memorable combinations of melody and text designed for mass consumption, and is usually accompanied with musical instruments, rather than sung **a cappella** (meaning without instrumental accompaniment). By the mid-twentieth century the boundary between gospel and secular popular music had become less pronounced, although country music stars often chose to make religious recordings under a pseudonym.

Of course, other religious traditions coexisted with Christianity, although their influence on American popular music was generally less explicit than that of gospel music. The style of Jewish folk songs and klezmer, as well as the sacred Jewish tradition of cantillation (chanting of scripture), influenced some of the melodic lines composed by the great Jewish songwriters of Tin Pan Alley and in so doing became part of the broader stylistic vocabulary of American popular music. (The plot of the very first sound film, *The Jazz Singer* [1927], is centered on a young Jewish cantor who becomes a pop music star, much to the consternation of his rabbi father; see Chapter 4.)

In fact, the line between sacred and secular song was rarely, if ever, absolutely fixed in American culture. This is readily illustrated by our long tradition of popular "Christmas music," which freely mixes songs of deeply religious import with songs of nonsectarian seasonal character. Popular musicians from the most wide-ranging ethnic, national, and religious backgrounds have regularly made contributions to Christmas music, often creating major hit records in the process. The seasonal tribute "White Christmas" (composed by Jewish songwriter Irving Berlin) is the most famous example of this crossover, but the tradition of Christmas hits can now be traced back over a century. Between 1905 and 1936 there were no fewer than six different hit recordings of "Silent Night" by six different artists; in more recent times, Barbra Streisand and the Temptations each brought forth their own successful versions of the song—which, we should recall, is an English translation of a German song of Christian devotion originally composed in 1818.

THE AFRICAN AMERICAN STREAM

Not all immigrants to the United States came willingly. Between 1 and 2 million people from Africa, or about 10 percent of the total transatlantic traffic in slaves, were forcibly brought to America between 1619 and the official abolition of the slave trade in 1808 (though an illegal trade continued for some years afterward). By 1860, on the eve of the American Civil War, there were almost 4 million slaves in the United States, out of a total population of around 31 million.

Any discussion of the genesis of African American music and its impact on American popular music as a whole must engage with the painful topic of slavery and the culture that the slaves forged. To begin with, the population of newly arrived slaves in the Americas was made up of Africans from many diverse societies, speaking mutually unintelligible languages. The cultural mix among slaves in the United States was made even more complex by the fact that many arrived after spending some years in English, French, and Spanish colonies in the Caribbean. These conditions encouraged the development of syncretic or "creolized" forms of cultural expression that drew upon various African and European (and sometimes Native American) precedents.

Listening Guide OLD-TIME MUSIC

"Barbary [Barbara] Allen" (Child Ballad #84), performed by Jean Ritchie; recorded 1960
"Soldier's Joy," performed by Gid Tanner and the Skillet Lickers; released 1929
"Soldier's Joy," fiddle solo performed by Tommy Jarrell; recorded early 1980s

Of the various strains of European music that fed into American popular music, the most widely distributed and lastingly influential came from the British Isles. The British music that played such a large role in the formation of country music, urban folk music, and other popular genres was itself made up of multiple traditions—English, Highland Scots, Scotch-Irish, Catholic Irish, and Welsh—but these musical sub-streams had much in common historically and stylistically and were often blended together by immigrant musicians in the New World. Musicians and fans of these early American styles often lump them together under the rubric of old-time music, a category that comprises string band music (ranging from fiddle and banjo duets to larger dance ensembles with guitar, mandolin, and autoharp); ballad songs, performed with or without instrumental accompaniment; sacred songs and church hymns; and a variety of functionally specialized music genres such as lullabies and work songs.

British settlers in America composed new songs and styles that reflected their own experiences and drew upon the music of other peoples with whom they came into contact, including German immigrants, the French-speaking Acadians of eastern Canada and Louisiana (where they are known as Cajuns), the Mexicans of Texas and the Southwest, and slaves from West Africa who were imported to fuel the growth of plantation agriculture in the Deep South. Certain aspects of the old British traditions—songs about Robin Hood or witchcraft, for example—fell by the wayside, but many other aspects, including certain melodies, song texts with references to "lords" and "fair-haired maidens," and specific musical scales and techniques, were preserved through a continual process of cultural adaptation that married the old with the new.

The rural "backcountry" of the American South—a huge area reaching from the coastal tidewaters of Virginia and isolated communities of the Appalachian Mountains to the "piney woods" of east Texas and the Ozarks region of Arkansas and Missouri—has been called "the fertile crescent of country music" (Peterson and Davis 1975). In the early twentieth century, when scholars began to seek evidence of the deep Anglo-Celtic roots of American music, they found many of the strongest links to the past in small communities located in relatively inaccessible areas such as the Appalachian and Ozark Mountains. This is not to say that these communities were completely cut off from contemporaneous developments in American popular music that were occurring in cities such as New York and Chicago. Just as it is impossible, despite the profound impact of racial segregation, to draw a strict boundary between "white" and "Black" traditions in the American South, so even the most isolated Southerners were exposed to the latest urban popular songs by way of traveling carnivals and "medicine shows"; gramophone recordings; and, beginning in the early 1920s, radio. One thing is certain: the people of the South shared a passionate commitment to music, and this commitment helped to preserve many aspects of the old traditions they and their forbears brought to America.

The British ballad tradition is one of the main roots of American music and is the predecessor of such diverse genres as urban folk music, country music, and rock 'n' roll. One of the most widely performed songs in this centuries-old tradition is "Barbara Allen," first definitively documented in London in 1666 and first published as a broadside ballad there around 1690 under the title "Barbara Allen's Cruelty: or, the Young-Man's Tragedy." Knowledgeable aficionados of folk music know the song as "Child Ballad #84," a reference to its inclusion in Francis J. Child's five-volume *English and Scottish Popular Ballads* (1882–1898), still the definitive anthology in its field.

It is impossible to know precisely when "Barbara Allen" was introduced to the English colonies in North America, but it is not unreasonable to speculate that the song was in wide circulation there by the eighteenth century. The ballad was included in some of the earliest recordings of rural American folk music and has been performed by popular artists as diverse as Bob Dylan, Dolly Parton, the Everly Brothers, Trini Lopez, big band singer Doris Day, the Grateful Dead, the Irish bagpiper Paddy Keenan, and film star John Travolta.

Ballads typically tell a story in a series of verses sung to a more-or-less set melody, and "Barbara Allen" is no exception. The outline of the story is relatively simple and varies little in its essentials from performance to performance. A young man (usually named William) is dying of unrequited love for the beautiful Barbara Allen, but when she is called to his deathbed, all she can say is, "Young man, I think you're dying." When he perishes of heartsickness, Barbara Allen is stricken with guilt and dies soon after. The song's final verses typically describe a thorny briar growing from her grave and a rose from his; eventually the two twine together, a symbol of the power of love to defy even death.

In order to stay alive, all traditions must change to some degree. Over the centuries, individual performers have embellished the melody of "Barbara Allen" and altered details of the story to accord with their own taste and the demands of their audiences. In some versions additional stanzas have been introduced to help listeners understand the young woman's cruelty, explaining that she had become jealous when she overheard William in a tavern making a toast to all of the young women in town, save her. Despite these minor variations, the essential narrative of love, rejection, death, remorse, and more death, concluding with an affirmation of the transcendental power of love, is what has defined "Barbara Allen" for generations of performers and listeners. It is, so to say, an enduring soap opera in song form.

To gain a more immediate understanding of the sound and sensibility of "Barbara Allen," we will explore a version of the ballad by the folk singer and song collector *Jean Ritchie* (1922–2015). Ritchie performs her version of the song—entitled "Barbary Allen"—in the style she learned growing up in an isolated, mountainous region of Kentucky. One of thirteen children born to a farming family, she began her performing career as a teenager at local country fairs and dances, and in the late 1940s became an inspiration for the first generation of urban folk musicians playing in the nightclubs and coffeehouses of Greenwich Village, a group that included both Woody Guthrie and Pete Seeger (see Chapters 5 and 7).

In the liner notes to the album *British Traditional Ballads (Child Ballads) in the Southern Mountains* (1961), Ritchie provides a first-person perspective on the ballad tradition:

> All of us, Mom, Dad, and all thirteen children could write, but these old songs and their music were in our heads, or hearts, or somewhere part of us, and

we never needed to write them down. They were there, like games and rhymes and riddles, like [butter] churning-chants and baby-bouncers and gingerbread stackcake recipes, to be employed and enjoyed when the time came for them. Nobody got scholarly about them and I have a feeling that's why they have been genuinely popular all these years.

Ritchie's solo rendition of "Barbary Allen," sung a cappella, is unaffected, beautiful, and haunting. She sings twelve four-line verses, and her vocal style includes subtle use of the melodic ornamentations typical of Appalachian hill country singing (and still in evidence in some contemporary country music). Her pronunciation of some words in the lyrics (including "slow-lie" for "slowly" and the name "Barbary") reflects the local dialect she grew up speaking in Kentucky.

Another important branch of old-time music is the string band tradition. Like the ballad song tradition, the repertoire of old-time string bands provides rich evidence of the impact of new environments on the traditions that English, Scots, Irish, and Welsh immigrants brought with them to the Americas. Some fiddle tunes—for example, "Soldier's Joy"—survived the transit across the Atlantic with their basic musical forms and titles intact. The names of other tunes, such as "Cumberland Gap" and "Cripple Creek," reflect the circumstances of the musicians who created them. In America, tunes from Britain also intermingled with Black fiddle styles, which

Jean Ritchie.

(continued)

Listening Guide OLD-TIME MUSIC (continued)

LISTENING GUIDE	"BARBARY ALLEN"		
TIME	**LYRICS**	**TIME**	**LYRICS**
0:00	*All in the merry month of May* *When the green buds they were swellin',* *Young William Green on his deathbed lay* *For the love of Barbary Allen.*	2:27	*"Oh yes, I remember in yonder's town* *In yonder's town a-drinkin'* *I gave my health to the ladies all around* *But my heart to Barbary Allen."*
0:23	*He sent his servant to the town* *To the place where she was dwellin'* *Sayin', "Master's sick and he sends for you* *If your name be Barbary Allen."*	2:52	*He turned his pale face to the wall* *For death was on him dwellin'* *"Adieu, adieu, you good neighbors all* *Adieu, sweet Barbary Allen."*
0:49	*So slow-lie [slowly], slow-lie she got up* *And slow-lie she came a-nigh [near] him* *And all she said when she got there* *"Young man, I believe you're dyin'."*	3:17	*As she was goin' across the fields* *She heard those death bells a-knellin' [ringing]* *And every stroke the deathbell give* *Hard hearted Barbary Allen.*
1:12	*"Oh yes, I'm low, I'm very low,* *And death is on me dwellin'* *No better, no better I'll never be* *If I can't get Barbary Allen."*	3:44	*"Oh Mother, oh Mother, go make my bed,* *Go make it both long and narrow* *Young William's died for me today* *And I'll die for him tomorrow."*
1:37	*"Oh yes, you're low and very low,* *And death is on you dwellin'* *No better, no better you'll never be* *For you can't get Barbary Allen.*	4:09	*Oh she was buried 'neath the old church tower* *And he was buried a-nigh [near] her* *And out of his bosom grew a red, red rose,* *Out of Barbary's grew a green briar.*
2:00	*For don't you remember in yonder's town* *In yonder's town a-drinkin'* *You passed your glass all around and* *around* *And you slighted Barbary Allen."*	4:35	*They grew and they grew up the old church* *tower,* *Until they could grow no higher* *They locked and tied in a true lover's knot,* *Red rose wrapped around the green briar.*

had roots in equally ancient and complex West African traditions. The banjo, a plucked stringed instrument with a piece of animal skin or plastic stretched over a circular frame, was an African American invention based upon African prototypes. Beginning in the eighteenth century, the banjo was adopted by white players, who developed their own approaches to playing the instrument. By the early twentieth century instruments such as the guitar, mandolin, autoharp, and double bass (and its country cousin the one-stringed bass, made with a broomstick and a metal washing tub) were being combined in various configurations as Southern farmers, mineworkers, ranchers, lumberjacks, railroad workers,

and sharecroppers used their musical skills to generate additional income. These semiprofessional practitioners played at dances, fiddling contests, political rallies, and "house parties."

"Soldier's Joy" (also known as "The King's Head") is one of the most venerable, popular, and widely distributed fiddle tunes in the old-time repertoire. The tune is believed to have originated in Scotland, first appearing in an English collection of dance music published in the 1770s, but was doubtless in wide circulation as part of oral tradition considerably before that date. The basic melody, consisting of two contrasting phrases repeated over and over with variations, is found in Scotland, Ireland, Wales, England, France, Denmark, Sweden, and Finland and is played by old-time fiddlers in the Americas from Canada to the Deep South. Though lyrics have been added to the song at various points in its development, the tune is often performed without them and remains closely associated with social dancing. "Soldier's Joy" is still included in the repertoires of many bluegrass string bands. In 1959, the height of the rock 'n' roll era, it reached Number 15 on the country music charts in a rendition by Hawkshaw Hawkins, and in 2010 the tune appeared as the theme of a Monster.com advertisement during Super Bowl XLIV, performed by a fiddling beaver.

We provide here two versions of "Soldier's Joy": first, one of the earliest commercially successful recordings of the song, performed by a string band made up of entertainers from Georgia; and second, a solo recording by a veteran performer from Kentucky who has preserved aspects of an older style of fiddle playing. Listening to two versions of the same tune will help give us an idea of both the stable, shared elements that define "Soldier's Joy" and the different approaches that individual performers have taken to the tune.

The **Skillet Lickers** were one of the very first Southern string bands to appear on commercial recordings. Their leader, **James Gideon (Gid) Tanner** (1885–1960), was a chicken farmer and part-time fiddler. In 1926, Tanner and three other musicians from northern Georgia—the blind guitarist and singer George Riley Puckett (1894–1946), fiddler Clayton McMichen (1900–1970), and banjo player Fate Norris (1878–1944)—came together to become Columbia Records' first successful "hillbilly" act (as Southern rural music was then marketed by the entertainment industry; see Chapter 5). Members of the

The Skillet Lickers.

Skillet Lickers had grown up steeped in the old Southern ballad and string band traditions and had gained experience performing at dances, house parties, and fiddle contests. Their stage act and recordings were distinguished by a high level of technical skill, a rough, hard-driving, dance-oriented sound, and the inclusion of raucous comedy skits that played upon stereotypes of the "country bumpkin" or "hayseed." In fact, the members of the Skillet Lickers were more musically sophisticated than many in their audience knew, and they were well aware of developments in urban popular music of the time, including early jazz.

The Skillet Lickers' recording of "Soldier's Joy," made in Atlanta in 1929, begins with a short comic recitation by fiddler Clayton McMichen that was intended to evoke the sensibility of the rural house parties enjoyed by so many of their Southern listeners:

> Well folks, here we are again, the Skillet Lickers, red hot and rarin' to go. Gonna play you another little tune this morning, want you to grab that gal and shake a foot and moan. Don't you let 'em dance on your new carpet. You make 'em roll it up!

The usual form of the fiddle tune is relatively simple, beginning with a musical phrase that is repeated almost exactly and is followed by a second, contrasting phrase, which is also repeated. This pattern, with its alternation of two basic musical phrases (which we call A and B), continues through the entire performance, with verses being sung only over the first (A) phrase each time through. The style is designed to accompany (and inspire) communal dancing, with the guitar playing a strong, steady bass pattern, the fiddle players attacking their strings vigorously with their horsehair bows, and the banjo playing rhythmic chords in the background.

After the instruments play through the entire form once, Riley Puckett sings the first verse, which is lifted from another popular old-time fiddle tune, "Chicken in the Bread Tray." The fact that this "borrowed" lyric fits into the musical form of "Soldier's Joy" so easily is a reflection of the fact that many old-time songs belonged to closely related tune families, the members of which could be interchanged in the flow of performance. The last two lines of this verse are traditional square dance calls, or lines shouted by a fiddler to give directions to the dancers.

After the sung verse, the fiddles take the lead on the second A phrase and play the two B phrases to finish the entire form of the tune. The melody is then picked up

(continued)

Listening Guide OLD-TIME MUSIC (*continued*)

again by Puckett, who sings another verse, derived from a venerable oral tradition of animal stories that reaches back to *Aesop's Fables* and finds its modern analog in Bugs Bunny cartoons. The final two sung verses, separated by instrumental sections, are more specifically associated with the tune "Soldier's Joy."

The precise origin and meaning of these verses has long been debated by aficionados of old-time music,

LISTENING GUIDE	"SOLDIER'S JOY"[3]	
TIME	**SECTION**	
0:00		Spoken introduction by Clayton McMichen
0:13	AA	Twin fiddle lead, with guitar and banjo accompaniment
0:29	BB	Twin fiddle lead, with guitar and banjo accompaniment
0:44	A	*Chicken in the bread tray scratchin' out dough,* *Granny, will your dog bite? No, child, no.* *Ladies to the center and the gents catch air* [dance instructions] *Hold her noose, don't let her rear* [hold on to your partner, don't let her go out of control]
0:52	A	Twin fiddle lead, with guitar and banjo accompaniment
1:00	BB	Twin fiddle lead, with guitar and banjo accompaniment
1:15	A	*Grasshopper sittin' on a sweet potato vine,* *Grasshopper sittin' on a sweet potato vine,* *Grasshopper sittin' on a sweet potato vine,* *'long come a chicken and says "you're mine."*
1:23	AA	Twin fiddle lead, with guitar and banjo accompaniment
1:38	B	Twin fiddle lead, with guitar and banjo accompaniment
1:46	A	*I'm a-gonna get a drink, don't you want to go?* *I'm a-gonna get a drink, don't you want to go?* *I'm a-gonna get a drink, don't you want to go?* *Oh Lord, soldier's joy.*
1:53	AA	Twin fiddle lead, with guitar and banjo accompaniment
2:08	BB	Twin fiddle lead, with guitar and banjo accompaniment
2:23		*25 cents for the morphine* *15 cents for the beer* *25 cents for the morphine* *That's gonna take me away from here.*
2:31	AA	Twin-fiddle rhythmic variant
2:45	B	Ends with "shave-and-a-haircut" lick often used at end of fiddle tunes

3. This listening guide follows the Skillet Lickers' recording.

but the reference to alcohol and the narcotic morphine as a means of escape (the "soldier's joy" of the title) probably stems from the period of the Civil War, when morphine was first used to treat battlefield wounds. The tune of "Soldier's Joy" is cheerful enough, but the lyric adds a tinge of dark, sardonic humor.

A second version of "Soldier's Joy" was performed by **Tommy Jarrell** (1901–1985), an influential old-time fiddler and banjo player from Mt. Airy, in the mountains of North Carolina. (The documentary film *Sprout Wings and Fly* [1983] is a touching portrait of the fiddler a few years before his death.) Jarrell precedes his performance with a brief verbal introduction:

> Well, here's a little tune called "Soldier's Joy." I do it just a little bit different from anybody else. I do it up on the [Army] bases part of the time, and it's in old-time D tuning, here's your tuning [plays the open strings of the fiddle to demonstrate].

Without getting too technical in musical terms, it is worth noting that the "old-time D tuning" to which Jarrell refers is different from the standard violin tuning used in classical music. Retuning the lowest pitched string of his fiddle allows him to play a drone (that is, a single repeated pitch that runs throughout the performance, rather in the manner of a Scottish bagpipe) at the same time that he plays a series of ornate melodic inventions around the basic musical form of "Soldier's Joy." The manner in which he plays the fiddle—with strong rhythmic momentum, a vigorous, saw-like, scratchy-sounding bowing technique, and an inspired sense of melodic embellishment—was said by Jarrell himself to represent an older style of playing common in his area of the Appalachian Mountains. That attribution is likely accurate; on the other hand, the relative freedom exhibited in Jarrell's performance, as compared with the more predictable repetition of the tune in the Skillet Lickers' recording, may also reflect the difference between a solo performance and an ensemble performance, in which musicians have to coordinate amongst themselves in order to create a group sound. (It also seems likely that the three-minute time limit imposed by the recording technology of the 1920s impelled the Skillet Lickers, like other musicians of the time, to organize their performances with an eye on the clock.)

Listening to these two examples—one a popular commercial recording made at the very dawn of what would later be called "country music," and the other an informal recording by an octogenarian Appalachian fiddler who learned his craft in the first decades of the twentieth century—will serve to give us some sense of the deep historical continuity and creative vitality of the Southern string band tradition.

The mix of other peoples with whom the slaves came into contact and the social and political structures that channeled their interactions also varied widely. In the South, home to the largest concentration of people of African descent until the northward migrations of the twentieth century, the mass production of crops such as cotton, tobacco, and sugar cane on plantations was made possible by the forced labor of thousands of slaves. People of African descent, who outnumbered whites in some parts of the Deep South, were usually confined to segregated quarters, forced to work long, grueling hours, and subjected to severe disciplinary action for violating the norms of a racially segregated society. In isolated areas like the Appalachian and Ozark Mountains, farms were much smaller, and slaves often lived in family units adjacent to their owners' homes, creating the possibility of more nuanced day-to-day interactions across racial lines. In the city of New Orleans, Louisiana, a creolized culture comprising French, English, Irish, African American, and Caribbean elements and influences developed.

If we think of the genres of African American music that have come to quintessentially represent the Deep South, Appalachia, and New Orleans—the Mississippi Delta–based electric blues of Muddy Waters and Howlin' Wolf, with its strong roots in West African aesthetics (see Chapter 7); the Black banjo music of Kentucky and the Carolinas, born out of a continual interchange between Black and white musicians (see the discussion of "Coo Coo" later in this chapter); and the uniquely hybrid style and sensibility of New Orleans jazz, captured in the early recordings of King Joe Oliver and Louis Armstrong (see Chapter 3)—we can glean a sense of how local geographical and social conditions helped to shape the development of African American music.

From the early eighteenth century on, observers cited the slaves' skill in music, dance, and verbal improvisation, attributions that have played a role in subsequent racial stereotyping. However, even if the association between "Blackness" and "musicality" has an ambiguous history, it cannot be denied that music, dance, and linguistic creativity were critical elements in the slaves' struggle for cultural survival, providing avenues for community building, social criticism, and the creation of identity. Stripped of their institutions, material possessions, family structures, and often their very names, the first generation of slaves in America began the process of constructing a coherent, resilient culture in a hostile environment. African American culture was built first and foremost out of what the slaves carried in their memories and were able to reconstruct in America, a process that often involved an emphasis on the nonmaterial, spiritual, and aesthetic aspects of culture, including music.

It is important to realize that the huge region of Africa from which slaves were drawn—the areas bordering more than eight thousand miles of Atlantic coastline stretching from current-day Senegal to Angola—is home to hundreds of different languages, cultures, and musical traditions. The music of West Africa is very diverse, ranging from impromptu performances of songs with hand-clapping to percussion music used to accompany social and ritual dance, virtuoso solo performances of historical epics by singers who accompany themselves on stringed instruments, and large ensembles of trumpets or flutes associated with political leaders such as kings and chiefs.

During the course of the nineteenth century the music of African American communities comprised an array of genres and styles, including work songs, lullabies and game songs, story songs (a Black parallel to the European American ballad tradition), and various instrumental types of music used to accompany dances and other important social events, ranging from fife-and-drum ensembles to brass bands and string band music that paralleled and influenced the old-time tradition discussed previously. However, it is widely agreed that the most impressive and extensive repertory created by the slaves was the Black spirituals.

During the "Great Awakening" of the early nineteenth century, increasing numbers of slaves converted to evangelical Christianity. The credo that all Christians are equal in the eyes of God was adapted by the slaves to fit their own situation and provided the basis for a widespread belief in the inevitability of a "Jubilee Day," on which all slaves would be freed. Though some white clergy complained about the enthusiasm with which the slaves performed the repertoire of spiritual songs that they learned in church, others encouraged enthusiastic call-and-response singing, improvisation, clapping, dancing, and even spirit possession (a phenomenon in which participants fall under the sway of the Holy Spirit, achieving a direct, personal communion with a higher power). All of these practices provided a bridge for the continuation of aspects of African worship within a framework of Christian belief.

The fear that slaves might use their own religious meetings to foment rebellion led many slave-owners to insist that they attend white-controlled churches. Whenever possible, however, the slaves organized their own informal spaces for worship (called "hush quarters"), where they forged alternative interpretations of the spirituals and the Bible itself that bore double meanings of religious salvation and freedom from slavery. When early white scholars of African American song wrote that the Black spirituals were mere imperfect copies of the texts and melodies of the white spirituals, they failed to perceive a deeper "invisible" layer of cultural invention in which the hymns were reinterpreted in accordance with the slaves' aspirations and beliefs, and performed in an energetic, improvisational, call-and-response style that invoked all the expressive power of African sacred traditions. In some cases the secret, encoded meanings of slave spirituals were quite specific, equating evil figures in biblical scriptures with slave masters and the notion of entering the Promised Land (Canaan) with fleeing to the North. It was in this context that Black preachers, in the absence of formal political power, became leaders of their communities, developing a style of semi-improvised, musically intoned sermonizing that was to shape the development of African American religious practice and the performance styles of popular musicians such as James Brown and Ray Charles (see Chapter 10).

Despite the richness and variety of African American musical traditions, it is possible to point to certain unifying traits, features that were to exert an enormous impact on popular music in the United States. Call-and-response forms are a hallmark of African and African American musical traditions. One very common form of call-and-response, found in genres such as gospel music, big band jazz, and rhythm & blues, is one in which a lead singer (or instrumentalist) and a group of singers (or players) alternate phrases, with the leader usually being allowed more freedom to elaborate his part. In much African music-making, repetition is regarded as an aesthetic strength, rather than a weakness, and many forms are constructed of relatively short phrases that recur in a regular cycle. These short phrases are combined in various ways to produce music of great power and complexity. In African American music such repeated patterns are often called riffs. The aesthetic focus of much African music lies in the interlocking of multiple repeating patterns to form dense **polyrhythmic** textures (i.e., textures produced by many rhythms going on at the same time). This technique is evident in African American musical styles such as funk, particularly the work of James Brown, and the digitally produced accompaniments ("beats") of contemporary hip-hop recordings.

The commonly expressed notion that African music is "all about rhythm" is an oversimplification, since melodic creativity, textural complexity, and linguistic expressiveness (including not only songs with words but also the use of "talking" instruments that can communicate verbal content) are also very important aspects of music-making

Listening Guide "LONG JOHN"

Performed by Lightning Washington and fellow convicts; recorded 1934

In African American work songs, musical performance was more than a mere accompaniment or diversion: it coordinated the work efforts of individuals, increasing efficiency and helping them avoid physical danger. The mechanization of agriculture during the twentieth century signaled, for better or for worse, the disappearance of much group cooperative labor and thus of the primary context for performing such songs. One of the

LISTENING GUIDE | "LONG JOHN"

TIME	LYRIC	TIME	LYRIC
0:00	Leader: *O the long John,* Response: *O the long John,* Leader: *He's a-long gone,* Response: *He's a-long gone,* Leader: *Like the turkey through the corn,* Response: *Like the turkey through the corn,* Leader: *He's a-long gone,* Response: *He's a-long gone.*	1:23	*"Well-a two, three minutes,* *Let me catch my win';* *In-a two, three minutes,* *I'm gone again."*
		1:35	*It's-a long John,* *He's long gone,* *He's-a long gone,* *He's-a long gone.*
0:14	*Well, my John said,* *In the ten chap' ten* [tenth chapter, tenth verse], *"If a man die,* *He will live again"*	1:47	*Well, my John said,* *Just before he ran,* *"Well, I'm goin' home,* *See Maryland."*
0:25	*Well, they crucified Jesus* *And they nailed him to the cross,* *Sister Mary cried,* *"My child is lost!"*	1:58	*It's-a long John,* *It's-a long John,* *With his long clothes on,* *Like a turkey through the corn.*
0:38	*O long John,* *He's long gone,* *He's long gone,* *In the corn, John.*	2:10	*Well, my John said,* *On the fourth day,* *Well, to "Tell my rider* [lover] *That I'm on my way."*
0:50	*O big eyed John,* *O John, John,* *It's-a long John.*	2:22	*It's-a long John,* *He's long gone,* *He's-a long gone,* *It's-a long gone.*
0:59	*Says-uh "Come on gal,* *And-uh shut that do'* [door]," *Says, "The dogs is comin'* *And I've got to go."*	2:33	*"Gonna call this summer,* *Ain't gon' call no mo',* *If I call next summer,* *Be in Baltimore."*
1:12	*It's-a long John,* *He's long gone* *It's-a long John,* *He's-a long gone.*	2:45	*He's-a long John,* *He's long gone,* *He's long gone,* *He's long gone,* *He's long gone,* [fades out]

few contexts in which work teams continued to be used to clear land, fix roads, and chop wood was the prison system, and it is in prison culture that the work song tradition continued to flourish. As one prisoner from Texas said in an interview, if a man couldn't sing and keep time when he entered prison, he'd better learn quickly or suffer the wrath of his cellmates, for such a man was a menace when working in a group with an axe or a pickaxe.

In this performance of "Long John," recorded at Darrington State Prison Farm in Sandy Point, Texas, a prison songleader named **Lightning Washington** sings about a legendary character who outran the police, the sheriff, and the bloodhounds and escaped to freedom. The leader-and-chorus, call-and-response song—accompanied by the percussive sound of the convicts chopping oak logs—offers a picture of the chase, full of excitement and focused energy. The performance

consists of a series of verses (with each line of text initiated by the leader and repeated by the group) that are alternated with a chorus sung by everyone ("It's-a Long John, he's-a long gone . . ."). In the first verse, Long John is described as running "like a turkey through the corn, through the long corn." In subsequent verses, his exodus from the Deep South to the Northern city of Baltimore, Maryland, is described in more detail. If "Long John" evokes the powerful image of a slave escaping to freedom, it also exemplifies the interaction between the sacred and secular realms of expression in its use of references to the Gospel of John 10:10 (the parable of the shepherd and the thief) and the crucifixion of Jesus.

In "Long John," as in the spirituals, biblical images of suffering function both as a metaphor for faith and redemption and as a medium for criticizing an oppressive system based on racial discrimination.

throughout the African diaspora. Having said this, it is nonetheless the case that rhythm—the musical organization of time—is an important focus for performers and listeners within this broad tradition.

One unifying feature of many African musical genres that sets them apart from most music-making traditions of Western Europe is the frequent occurrence of **syncopation**, or "off-beat" patterns, in which the sounds produced by musicians are played very precisely apart from or against the underlying steady pulse of the music (which is often reflected in the movements of dancers). This technique is grounded in the ability of competent musicians and listeners to maintain an internalized pulse that acts as a framework for organizing and interpreting musical time. This skill—which has been called the "metronome sense"—is a learned, unconsciously carried ability that is acquired over time within a particular cultural and musical milieu and is critical to both listening to and playing West African music. It is part of the nonmaterial culture—concepts, values, and schemes for interpreting the world—that West African slaves brought with them to America.

The notion that the underlying pulse of music can be strengthened by playing against it, rather than with it, is reflected in the common practice of accenting the **backbeat** (as, for example, when a gospel choir claps on the second and fourth beats of a steady four-beat pulse) and in the syncopation that runs through every African American musical genre from ragtime, the blues, and jazz to soul music, funk, and hip-hop. Playing against the pulse also helps to create the sense of "swing" or groove—a powerful but fluid sense of forward momentum—that is so often cited as a core aesthetic value in African American musical traditions. You will hear many examples of this rhythmic approach, which has deeply influenced American popular music, as we examine particular genres and songs.

Another important dimension of music is timbre, or "tone color," in which one's perception of the quality of a given sound is shaped by the relative strength of harmonics created by a fundamental frequency. (Without attempting to explain the physics involved in this phenomenon, we can say that timbre is what allows a blindfolded listener to tell the difference between a clarinet, a trumpet, a guitar, and a piano all playing the same pitch, say "middle C.") In contrast to the aesthetics of Western classical music, in which a "clear" or "pure" tone is the ideal, African singers and instrumentalists often make use of a wide palette of tone colors. Buzzing sounds are created by attaching a rattle or snare made of shells, beads, or metal rings to a drum or stringed instrument, and singers frequently use growling and humming effects, vocal techniques that can also frequently be heard in African American genres such as blues, gospel, and jazz.

Another key aspect of African musical practice that has carried over into African American music is an emphasis on improvisation. This is not to say that African music lacks fixed structures; however, as we have already suggested, these structures often take the form of repeated motifs (musical ideas) that form the basis for myriad subtle variations or provide accompaniment for melodic improvisation. The notion that the form of a musical piece functions as a platform for extemporization and the development of ideas in response to the context of music-making is a core aesthetic value of African American music that can easily be identified in genres ranging from the blues to jazz and hip-hop.

Improvisation is linked to another signal feature of this tradition: the dynamic interaction between performers and their audiences, who in many cases function as co-performers, adding to the texture and momentum of a musical event. In many traditions of the African diaspora, the social aspect of music is not easily separated from its acoustic properties. Rather, the two are intimately connected by a holistic conception of music as a mode of interaction among human beings and as a privileged technique for building and defending communities.

The issue of continuities in musical instruments—both their physical structures and the techniques for playing them—is a complex one. African drumming traditions did not persist as explicitly in the American South as they did in the Caribbean (e.g., Cuba, Jamaica) and South America (Brazil), in part because the making and playing of drums were suppressed by slave-owners—who were aware that drums were used to transmit coded messages—and condemned by religious authorities as being tied to "pagan" beliefs. Nonetheless, the method of organizing percussion into complexly layered multipart rhythms was carried forward in traditions such as Mississippi fife-and-drum music and the polyrhythmic hand-clapping that accompanies the songs of many African American genres, from children's game music to gospel music.

Other West African instruments were preserved in America and adapted to new circumstances. The diddley bow is an adaptation of the one-stringed zither, found in many parts of Africa. Typically homemade, the instrument consists usually of a wooden board and a single wire string stretched between two screws, and it is played by plucking while varying the pitch with a metal or glass slide held in the other hand. A glass bottle is usually inserted under the string as a bridge, which helps magnify the sound. The instrument is traditionally played by young, aspiring musicians, functioning as an entry-level introduction to the guitar. Many well-known blues musicians started out on the diddley bow, and some blues and rock musicians continue to feature it in performances. (The 1979 documentary film *The Land Where the Blues Began* shows the Mississippi musician Lonnie Pitchford making a diddley bow out of a wire nailed to a post on the front porch of his house. For a more contemporary view, see the 2009 rock documentary *It Might Get Loud*, which opens with White Stripes guitarist Jack White constructing a diddley bow from a piece of wood, three nails, and a Coke bottle.)

The instrument most commonly cited as evidence of continuity with West African traditions in the United States is the banjo. The earliest references to slaves playing a basic prototype of the banjo—a three- or four-stringed lute made from a dried gourd (calabash) covered with a stretched animal skin, with a wooden stick for a neck—come from the islands of the Caribbean in the late sixteenth century. The first accounts of the instrument (written variously as *banger, banjar,* and *banjo*) appeared in newspapers in the American colonies in the 1730s and 1740s.

Recent research has suggested that a likely African ancestor (or cousin) of the American banjo is the *akonting*, a three-stringed lute played by the Jola people of Senegal and the Gambia. Like the banjo, the *akonting* has a drone string that is played with the ball of the thumb, creating a single repeated tone during the course of a performance. Melodies are played on the other strings with downward strokes of the index fingernail in a manner strikingly similar to a technique documented in banjo instruction books from the mid-1800s, which banjo players today call "clawhammer," "frailing," or "thumping." While the physical makeup of the banjo changed with the advent of industrial production, there are strong continuities in the approach to playing the instrument in the performances of older African American musicians in the Appalachian region.

As late as the turn of the twentieth century there were still hundreds of Black banjo players playing what DeFord Bailey, an African American harmonica player on the popular country music radio show *Grand Ole Opry*, called "Black hillbilly music" (Wolfe 1990, 32). The fact that the banjo was broadly regarded as emblematic of Black culture is suggested by its adoption as a central instrument in the minstrel show (see Chapter 2), the dominant form of popular entertainment in the United States throughout most of the nineteenth century. The eventual rejection of the banjo by urban African American musicians in favor of the guitar may have had something to do with its association with minstrelsy, a genre that propagated unflattering stereotypes of Black people. Today the banjo is associated mainly with bluegrass, a branch of country music (see Chapter 7). The most prominent contemporary champions of the Black banjo tradition are performers like Rhiannon Giddens, who have dedicated themselves to preserving and celebrating overlooked African American musical genres.

African American variants of the ballad song tradition also flourished during the nineteenth and early twentieth centuries, with texts celebrating the courageous and often rebellious exploits of Black heroes and "bad men" such as John Henry and Stagger

Listening Guide "COO COO"

Performed by Dink Roberts; recorded 1974

This performance of "Coo Coo" reflects what the performer himself—an African American musician born and raised in the Piedmont area of North Carolina—regarded as an authentic, old style of banjo playing. **Dink Roberts** (1894–1984) began playing the banjo in the first decades of the twentieth century and built his repertoire of songs and playing techniques by "catching" them from older players. He developed his skills by playing for barn dances, house parties, and other "frolics," crossing the color line intended to separate Blacks and whites in rural North Carolina. Roberts was a type of musician known as a "songster," a tradition of African American secular music-making that predates the emergence of the blues (see Chapter 5). Songsters were known for their ability to play a wide range of musical genres, including folk songs, ballads, dance tunes, and popular songs of the day. They were also known for their mobility, traveling along the routes established by the extension of riverboats and the railroad.

Roberts, who was eighty years old when his version of "Coo Coo" was recorded, said that he learned the song when he traveled to the city of Greensboro, North Carolina, around 1910 (Conway and Odell 1995, 20). He begins by retuning his banjo to a specialized tuning system called "sawmill," similar to those used on the *akonting* and related African stringed instruments. Roberts's performance is a fluid call-and-response conversation between the singer and his instrument, and the song itself is a loose, semi-improvised series of lines and images, very different from the European American ballad tradition, which emphasizes narrative plots. Like many songs in the Piedmont banjo tradition, "Coo Coo" is less a story per se than an associative cluster of bits of reported conversation, brief melodies, and rhythms organized around an emotional core, in this case the singer's ambivalence about sexually independent women. (The coo coo or cuckoo bird, which has the habit of laying its eggs in other birds' nests, has

LISTENING GUIDE | "COO COO"

TIME	LYRIC	TIME	LYRIC
0:00	Brief banjo opening during which Roberts tunes the instrument		And, "Who's gonna kiss your red rosy cheeks?" And, "Mama's gonna kiss my red rosy cheeks." And, "I sure don't need no man."
0:04	Unaccompanied vocal; free rhythm: *"Where'd you get your brand new shoes, Clothes you wear so fine?"* *Said, "I got my shoes from a railroad man And a dress from a man in the mine."* [banjo starts to play toward end of this line]	1:13	Banjo instrumental response
		1:19	*Said, "My horses [are] hungry, And they sure won't eat your hay." Said, "They're knobbin' [nibbling] on the corn, tramplin' down your hay." And, "They sure won't eat your hay."*
0:20	Banjo instrumental response		
0:31	Verse sung with accompaniment in time: *Hey . . . "Where'd you get your brand new shoes, Clothes you wear so fine?"* *Said, "I got my shoes from a railroad man And a dress from a man in the mine." What you say?*	1:33	Banjo instrumental response
		1:39	*"Where'd you get your brand new shoes, Clothes you wear so fine?" Said, "I got my shoes from a railroad man And a dress from a man in the mine."*
		1:55	Banjo instrumental response
0:46	Banjo instrumental response	2:01	*Said, who's gonna do your lovin' when I'm gone* *Spoken: I don't know who's gonna do it.*
0:53	*Hey . . . "Who's gonna . . . glove your hand?" Says, "Daddy's gonna glove my hand."*		

been a traditional symbol of infidelity since well before the days of Shakespeare.) Roberts's banjo playing is structured around the repetition and variation of brief rhythmic phrases. Each of these phrases is made up of independent but interlocking parts produced by alternating thumb and finger movements, a technique commonly used by lute players in West Africa.

At the end of the piece, Roberts appears to start a new verse by singing, "Say, who's gonna do your lovin' when I'm gone?" He then abruptly changes course, providing the female character's spoken answer to this question: "I don't know who's gonna do it!" The notes accompanying this recording (Conway and Odell 1995) explain that another musician was standing across the room chatting with Roberts's wife, and that the younger man's quick laughter in response to the final line indicated that the old songster's wit had not been missed.

Dink Roberts's performance of "Coo Coo" has many of the elements of African American music that we have identified: call-and-response, syncopation, the use of short repeated phrases to build complex musical textures, improvisation, the use of song as a medium of social commentary, and a dynamic relationship between the performer and his audience.

Lee (a.k.a. Stagolee). In the late nineteenth century African American oral tradition began to feature tales and songs about merciless toughs who confronted and generally overcame their adversaries without hesitation or remorse. This was a departure from narratives of the pre–Civil War period, when tales of Black resistance were often personified in the image of the Trickster, a mythical character derived from African folklore who survived and often triumphed by outwitting his oppressors, rather than confronting them physically. It is worth taking a moment to reflect on why the image of the "bad man" entered African American tradition during the postbellum era.

After the Civil War, during the Reconstruction era (1865–1877), many former slaves, denied opportunities for advancement by the imposition of laws enforcing racial segregation, became sharecroppers. This meant that they farmed on land owned by former slave masters, and often on the very same plantations where they and their parents had been slaves. Sharecroppers were required to buy their farming supplies, food, and clothing on credit from a local merchant, or sometimes from a plantation store. When the harvest came, the cropper would pick the whole crop and sell it to the merchant who had extended credit. Purchases and the landowner's share were deducted and the sharecropper kept the difference—or added to his debt. This exploitative system, along with the rise of violence against African Americans, encouraged by white supremacist organizations like the Ku Klux Klan, impelled many African Americans to migrate to Northern cities such as New York City and Chicago in search of a better life.

In this context, the emergence of a compelling figure—amoral, tough, unafraid of authority, and willing to take matters into his own hands—makes perfect sense. While the cruel exploits of these characters were universally condemned by the narrators of the songs and tales that featured them, the overall impact was one of ambivalence. The bad men in Black folklore did provide emotional catharsis, an understandable reaction to racism, but they also offered hard lessons about the effects of violence within African American communities that echo today in debates about the social impact of gangsta rap music videos.

The quintessential prototype for the bad man character is Stagolee (also called Stackolee, Stackerlee, and Staggerlee). The earliest reports of this character date from the 1890s, and by the first decade of the twentieth century songs recounting his exploits had spread throughout the South. Half a century later Stagolee was still an active figure in African American oral traditions in Chicago, Detroit, Philadelphia, and New York City.

There are many versions of the Stagolee story, set in urban nightspots, gambling halls, and houses of ill repute, as well as in coal mines and on riverboats, but most of them share a few elements. The central event is a gun battle between Stagolee and another hard man, Billy Lyons, precipitated by Stagolee's anger at losing his Stetson hat while gambling. Billy is soon at Stagolee's mercy and begs for his life as a loving father and husband, to no avail. Stagolee himself ends up being executed, usually only after issuing a defiant statement that indicates his complete lack of regret. In some versions Stagolee proves very difficult to kill, his neck refusing to "crack" when he is dropped from the gallows. In others, he dies and goes to hell, where he begins his career anew, seizing control from Satan himself. A bad man indeed.

The influence of African musical aesthetics and techniques on American popular music has been profound. The history of this influence, which we shall examine in some detail, reveals both the creativity of Black musicians and the persistence of racism in the music business and American society as a whole. The origins of a distinctively American style of popular entertainment lie in the minstrel show of the mid-nineteenth century, in which white performers artificially darkened their skin and mimicked Black music, dance, and dialect. In the early twentieth century African American ragtime and blues profoundly shaped the mainstream of American popular song. The Jazz Age of the 1920s and the swing era of the 1930s and 1940s involved the reworking of African American dance music so it would appeal to a predominantly white, middle-class audience.

Although country music is typically identified as a "white" style, some of its biggest stars—for example, DeFord Bailey, Ray Charles, Charley Pride, Darius Rucker, and Lil Nas X (Montero Lamar Hill)—have been Black, and the styles of influential country musicians such as Jimmie Rodgers, Bob Wills, Hank Williams, and Willie Nelson have been strongly influenced by African American music. One could cite many more examples of the influence of Black music on the musical "mainstream" of America: 1950s rock 'n' roll was, in large part, rhythm & blues (R&B) music reworked for a predominantly white teen music market; the influence of 1960s soul music, rooted in gospel music and R&B, is heard in the vocal style of practically every pop singer today, regardless of ethnic identity; the tone and texture of guitar-based rock music owe a large debt to the electric urban blues of Muddy Waters and Howlin' Wolf; and rap music, based on African-derived musical and verbal traditions, continues to provide many white Americans with a vicarious experience of "listening in" on Black urban culture.

We could say, then, that with every passing year, American popular music has moved closer to the core aesthetic values and techniques of African music. Yet this way of phrasing the matter is somewhat misleading, for it directs attention away from the

Listening Guide "STAGOLEE"

Performed by Mississippi John Hurt (vocal and guitar); recorded 1965

Mississippi John Hurt in the 1960s.

We will listen to a version of the song "Stagolee" (also known as "Stack O'Lee"), performed by **Mississippi John Hurt** (1892–1966), a representative of the songster tradition mentioned previously in connection with Dink Roberts and "Coo Coo." Raised in Avalon, Mississippi, Hurt taught himself how to play the guitar at around age nine and began to play at local dances and parties while working as a sharecropper, often as part of a duo with a fiddle player. Hurt's first recordings for Okeh Records (1928) were commercial failures, and he continued his work as a farmer. He was "discovered" by a scholar in the early 1960s, and in 1964 appeared at the Newport Folk Festival and was recorded by the Library of Congress. Hurt's recordings helped to further the American folk music revival, and his songs have been performed by musicians such as Bob Dylan, the Grateful Dead, and Beck.

LISTENING GUIDE	"STAGOLEE"
TIME	**LYRIC**
0:00	GUITAR introduction
0:13	*Police officer, how can it be?* *You can arrest everybody but cruel Stagolee* *That bad man, ol' cruel Stagolee.*
0:26	GUITAR
0:38	*Billy Lyons tol' Stagolee, "Please don't take my life."* *Says, "I got two little babes and a darlin' lovin' wife."* *That bad man, ol' cruel Stagolee.*
0:50	GUITAR
1:03	*"What I care 'bout your two little babes, your darling lovin' wife?"* *Said, "You done stole my Stetson hat, and I'm bound to take your life."* *That bad man, ol' cruel Stagolee.*
1:16	GUITAR [hums melody twice]
1:41	*Boom-boom, boom-boom, with a forty-four [handgun]* *When I spied po' Billy Lyons, he's lyin' down in the floor.* *That bad man, ol' cruel Stagolee.*
1:53	GUITAR
2:05	*Gentlemens of the jury, what do you think of that?* *Stagolee killed Billy Lyons 'bout a five-dollar Stetson hat.* *That bad man, ol' cruel Stagolee.*
2:18	GUITAR
2:29	*Standin' on the gallows, with his head held way up high,* *At 12 o'clock they killed him, they was all glad to see him die.* *That bad man, ol' cruel Stagolee.*
2:42	GUITAR

(continued)

Listening Guide "STAGOLEE" (*continued*)

In this performance of "Stagolee," Hurt shows off his virtuoso fingerpicking guitar style, in which the thumb plays a steady bass pattern and the fingers play syncopated patterns that interlock with the bass. As with the banjo performance of "Coo Coo" by Dink Roberts, this use of the thumb and fingers to create a polyrhythmic musical texture is rooted in African stringed instrument techniques. Hurt also sets up a conversation between his voice and his guitar, which take turns on successive verses. "Stagolee" is a blend of European American and African American elements: on the one hand, the ballad form, designed to tell a story in a series of verses; on the other, the three-line verses and supporting harmonies of the blues. It is worth noting that Hurt himself cited a number of musicians, both Black and white, who influenced his performance style, not least among them Jimmie Rodgers, the first country music superstar (see Chapter 5).

fact that African Americans are Americans and that the ancestors of Black Americans arrived in the United States *before* the forebears of many white Americans. The complex history of interaction between European American and African American styles, musicians, and audiences demonstrates the absurdity of racism, just as it attests to the unfortunate tenacity of racial thinking in America.

THE LATIN AMERICAN STREAM

Latin America is a vast region that was colonized by southern European countries such as Spain, Portugal, and France. (The term "Latin America" derives from the fact that Romance languages, or languages descended from Latin, are predominant in these countries.) Musicians in the Caribbean, South America, and Mexico have developed a wide range of styles that blend African and European traditions and have in turn influenced popular music in the United States.

The first Latin American style to have a major international impact was the Cuban *contradanza*, an African-influenced variant of the French country dance tradition. (French colonists fleeing Haiti during the revolution of the 1790s had originally brought the dance to Cuba.) Beginning in the 1850s the contradanza became fashionable in Europe under the new name *habanera*, and its influence extended to the popular music of the United States in the last decades of the nineteenth century. The habanera's characteristic rhythm—an easily identified syncopated pattern, usually carried in the bass—was featured in compositions like Eduardo Sánchez de Fuentes's "Tú" (1892), widely considered the first Cuban hit song.

In the mid-nineteenth century the dissemination of such compositions and the arrival of sailors from Cuba brought the habanera to Montevideo, Uruguay, just across the Rio de la Plata from Buenos Aires, Argentina. By the 1870s local musicians were blending the habanera with rhythms from the African-derived *candombé*—a genre created by slaves from Angola and the Congo—to create a faster, more forcefully rhythmic dance style called the *milonga* (derived from a Congolese word for "argument" or "contest").

In the United States, the habanera influenced late nineteenth-century ragtime music and the popular blues compositions of W. C. Handy (see Chapter 5) and was an important part of what the great New Orleans pianist Ferdinand "Jelly Roll" Morton called the "Spanish tinge" in American jazz. Nor did classical music escape the influence of the habanera, with the most famous example being the oft-quoted aria from Georges Bizet's opera *Carmen*, which debuted in Paris in 1876. By the end of the nineteenth century the habanera, in one form or another, had become a well-established international phenomenon.

The next big wave of Latin American musical influence came just after the turn of the century from Argentina in the form of the tango. Initially played by musicians in the capital city of Buenos Aires, tango was influenced by the Cuban habanera rhythm, the African-influenced *milonga*, Italian and Spanish popular songs, and the songs of the guitar-playing Argentine *gauchos* (cowboys), who originally inhabited the vast, rolling grasslands, called the *pampas*, and were forced into poor neighborhoods in the city when ranchers fenced their lands. Associated with the *arrabales* (slums) and brothels of Buenos Aires, the tango was a couples dance featuring an insistent four-beat pulse, close physical contact, and subtle improvisational communication between the male and female partners. From its very beginnings the tango was associated in the popular imagination with sexuality, recklessness, and danger, as well as with the romantic image of the *gaucho*.

By the first decade of the twentieth century the tango had reached Paris, where its popularity was boosted by visiting bandleaders such as Francisco Canaro and international film and recording star Carlos Gardel. In the United States the tango was promoted starting around 1914 by dance stars Irene and Vernon Castle (a story we tell in more detail in Chapter 3). The tango was also popularized in America by the silent movie idol Rudolph Valentino, whose image as a "Latin lover" was promoted in films like *The Four Horsemen of the Apocalypse* (1921), which included a sizzling tango dance scene.

The next wave of Latin American musical influence was the rumba. The roots of the ballroom rumba style that became popular in the United States in the late 1930s (see Chapter 6) lie in Cuba. This type of music developed when the rural *son*—a Cuban parallel of country music—spread to the city of Havana, where it was played by professional dance bands. These musicians created a more exciting style by adding rhythms from the rumba, an urban street drumming style that was strongly rooted in African traditions.

A "refined" version of rumba, developed by musicians working at tourist hotels in Cuba, was introduced to the world by Don Azpiazú and his Havana Casino Orchestra. Azpiazú's 1930 recording of "El Manicero" ("The Peanut Vendor") became a huge international hit (see Chapter 3). Within a few months of its release, many dance orchestras in the United States had recorded their own versions of the song, a phenomenon later known as "covering" a hit song. The rumba reached its height of popularity in the United States during the 1930s and 1940s and was succeeded after World War II by a series of Cuban-based ballroom dance fads, including the mambo and the *cha-cha-chá*.

Listening Guide THE TANGO

"La Cumparsita," performed by Carlos Gardel, with guitar accompaniment by José Ricardo; recorded 1928
"La Cumparsita," performed by Francisco Canaro y Quinteto Pirincho; recorded 1951

"La Cumparsita" is the best-known composition from the tango tradition. Although tango music is most commonly associated with Argentina, "La Cumparsita" was composed in 1916 by the Uruguayan musician Gerardo Matos Rodriguez (1897–1948), the son of a Montevideo nightclub proprietor. The song was recorded by a dance orchestra in Buenos Aires that same year, and when Rodriguez visited Paris in 1924, he found that his composition had become a major hit in the capitals of Europe, with new lyrics by the Argentine poet Pascual Contursi (1888–1932). The "new" tango song was rechristened "Si Supieras" ("If You Knew"), and Rodriguez spent the subsequent twenty years in and out of court trying to regain his rights as its composer.

Carlos Gardel (1890–1935), the legendary French-born superstar of tango, died in a plane crash at the age of forty-four and is still celebrated as a national hero

in Argentina today. Suave and handsome, he grew up singing in bars, restaurants, and markets in the Buenos Aires neighborhood of Abasto, then dominated by Italian immigrants. From the time of his very first recording in 1917, Gardel's style was unique, inspired by the emotional expressiveness of the tango, operatic bel canto singing, and the songs of the Argentine *gauchos*. His 1928 version of "La Cumparsita" is typical of the very earliest tango performances, which featured only a solo singer accompanied with a guitar. This mode of performance naturally focuses the listener's attention on the song's lyrics (which can be found by searching online), which are tinged—we might say saturated—with the torment of love betrayed, a common theme in tango songs.

The voice of the narrator, abandoned first by his lover and then by their little dog, evokes the sensibility of the tango, expressed quintessentially by the *lunfardo* (urban slang) word *mufarse*—the ability to reflect upon one's destiny with a kind of bittersweet satisfaction (ideally in a Buenos Aires cafe, accompanied by a glass of good red wine). The idea that "life is an absurd wound"[4] flows through the poetry of tango.

The performance of Gardel's guitarist, *José ("El Negro") Ricardo* (1888–1937), demonstrates both the importance of Afro-Argentine musicians in the tango tradition and the role of the guitar as the original form of instrumental accompaniment for tango songs. While exercising care to never overpower Gardel's singing, Ricardo attacks the guitar's strings with gusto, supporting the emotional content of the lyrics with strong chords, melodies, and bass lines, keeping the tango rhythm moving, and demonstrating how his early experience performing unamplified in Buenos Aires dance halls and cafes equipped him to produce an assertive yet nuanced sound on the instrument.

An instrumental version of "La Cumparsita" by the Quinteto Pirincho, led by the Uruguay-born violinist and bandleader *Francisco Canaro* (1888–1964), is a good example of the other major context for tango performance, the traditional dance band (*orquesta típica*).

Carlos Gardel.

---

4. "La Última Curda" ("The Last Drink of the Day"), composed by Cátulo Castillo. Cited in Thompson 2005, p. 25.

Canaro, the son of poor Italian immigrants, learned the tango in Buenos Aires around 1908 and became a successful performer, composer, and bandleader who did much to promote the style through his performances at nightclubs in Paris. (He and his band were required to wear *gaucho* uniforms during their Paris performances, in accordance with prevailing stereotypes.) The Quinteto Pirincho exemplifies the tango *orquesta típica* of the early twentieth century, with two violins. piano, double bass, drum set, and the genre's most characteristic instrument, the *bandoneón*, a reedy-sounding cousin of the concertina and accordion. The *bandoneón* takes center stage in this performance, joining with the violins to play the song's melody and then breaking away to weave improvised melodies.

The music is organized around a strong four-beat pulse, combined with the syncopated stop-and-start of the habanera rhythm and short, sharply articulated sounds on the instruments. Expressive effects such as the *arrastre*, or "drag"—a sweeping gesture that tango musicians use to give the rhythm and the dancers a little push from time to time—add to the emotional intensity of the music. The musical arrangement dictates subtle changes in tempo and texture, and provides plenty of room for the *bandoneón* player to show off his virtuosity. Although this recording was not made until 1951, it was explicitly intended by Canaro as an homage to the sound of his earliest tango dance bands, which through their recordings and live performances helped to popularize the genre worldwide in the 1910s and 1920s.

In Cuba, the term rumba originally referred to a family of Afro-Cuban dances, the African-derived percussion-driven music that accompanies them, and the informal parties where such performances traditionally take place. Musicians who specialize in the genre are called *rumberos*, and the Cuban scholar María Teresa Linares has described the dynamic atmosphere of a traditional rumba, in which musicians and dancers compete fiercely—though usually good-naturedly—with one another as follows:

> Rumberos are selective. Everybody who participates has to be good, and everyone struggles to be the best. In fraternal combat they grab their turn at singing, or try to get a shot at playing the quinto [lead drum] to show off their licks, or they jump into the center to dance. There exists a gestural language for requesting permission to take over; courtesy and brotherhood require the yielding of the center to the next contender. (Sublette 2004, 257)

Competitive events that combine the values of individualism and community and help to articulate and manage tensions within an aesthetic framework are found throughout the African diaspora, from jazz "jam sessions" to the Brazilian martial art/dance/music genre *capoeira* and the "b-boying" dance and rapping competitions that enlivened early hip-hop culture. The Afro-Cuban rumba is part of this great Afro-Atlantic tradition.

Cuba did not abolish slavery until 1878, and the island was home to one of the largest concentrations of people of African descent in the Americas. Although there is evidence of African-style drumming and dancing during the period of slavery, when Cuba's slave population labored mainly on sugar cane and coffee plantations, the rumba itself does not appear in the historical record until the 1880s. The music that most Cubans today regard as the authentic rumba was in fact looked down upon by the middle and upper layers of society and was actively suppressed by Cuban authorities through the first half of the twentieth century, going undocumented in recordings until the late 1940s.

Although music drawing upon the traditions of Cuba's diverse African population can be found all over the island, the rumba's birthplace appears to have been the town of Matanzas, on the northern coast, east of the capital city of Havana. Matanzas was a center of African culture in Cuba, and the rumba's origins are associated with Afro-Cuban dockworkers and *Abakuá*, a male secret society that controlled much of the work on the docks and whose beliefs and ritual practices were largely derived from the cultures of southeastern Nigeria.

Variants of Cuban-inspired music in the United States have ranged from the exciting blend of modern jazz and rumba pioneered by Machito and Dizzy Gillespie in the 1940s to the tourist-oriented style performed by Desi Arnaz's orchestra on the *I Love Lucy* television show. The 1960s saw the emergence of salsa, a rumba-based style pioneered by Cuban and Puerto Rican migrants in New York City (see Chapter 12). The stars of salsa music include the great singer Celia Cruz and bandleader Tito Puente. In the 1980s Miami Sound Machine created a commercially successful blend of salsa and disco music, and "world beat" musicians such as Paul Simon and David Byrne began to experiment with traditional Afro-Cuban rhythms.

The Brazilian samba is another dance style strongly rooted in African music. The variant of samba that had the biggest influence in the United States was the *carioca*, a smooth style developed in Rio de Janeiro. The carioca was boosted in the 1940s by the meteoric career of Carmen Miranda, who appeared in a series of popular musical films. A cool, sophisticated style of Brazilian music called the bossa nova ("new trend") became popular in the United States during the early 1960s, eventually spawning hit songs such as "The Girl from Ipanema" (see Chapter 9).

Mexican music has long had a symbiotic relationship with styles north of the Rio Grande. At the end of the nineteenth century Mexican musicians visited the World's Columbian Exposition in Chicago (an early example of the World's Fair) and later toured throughout the United States, causing a sensation. Important styles of Mexican music today include *conjunto acordeon* ("accordion band"), a genre influenced by the European polka and played in northern Mexico and Texas; *rancheras*, romantic songs originally performed by a solo singer with a guitar that are today played by a wide range of ensembles; the *corrido*, a Mexican parallel to the ballad song tradition; *mariachi* ("marriage") music, a staple of the Mexican tourist trade, which is performed by ensembles of stringed instruments and trumpets; and *banda* ("band"), performed by groups made up of brass, woodwind, and percussion instruments that play a variety of genres of Mexican music and imported styles such as the Colombian *cumbia*. Country and western music has been influenced by Mexican styles since at least the 1930s. Mexican immigrants in California (*Chicanos*) have also played an important role in the development of rock music. Examples of this continuing influence are Ritchie Valens's 1959 hit "La Bamba," which was based on a folk tune from Veracruz; the mixture of salsa and guitar-based rock music developed in the late 1960s by guitarist Carlos Santana; recordings of traditional Mexican songs by Linda Ronstadt; and the hard-rocking style of the Los Angeles–based band Los Lobos. In cities like San Antonio and Los Angeles the presence of Mexican music is felt nearly everywhere, and *conjunto acordeon* and mariachi

Listening Guide AFRO-CUBAN RUMBA

"Enigue Nigue," performed by AfroCuba de Matanzas; released 1998

There are several distinctive styles of Afro-Cuban rumba; we will focus on the *guaguancó*, a couple dance in which a symbolic game of "rooster and hen"–style flirtation is enacted, featuring a symbolically sugges- tive move by the male dancer (the *vacunao*, or "vacci- nation"). Although rumba ensembles originally made use of box-like percussion instruments constructed from disassembled shipping crates—an innovation that partly stemmed from the need to avoid authorities on the lookout for "drums"—the typical rumba group today is centered on a group of three single-headed drums (of the type called "conga drums" in the United States) that are held between the knees of seated players and played with the bare hands. Two are low-pitched drums (*tumbadores*), which play interlocking rhythms with relatively limited room for improvisation, and the third is a high-pitched drum (*quinto*), which plays a lead role and is the showcase for musical virtuosity. The *quintero* plays intricate, constantly shifting improvisations that weave around the foundation supplied by the *tumba- dores*, while at the same time directing or responding to the movements of the dancers. In combination, these three drums are capable of creating music of staggering power and complexity.

Also central to rumba music are the *palitos*, two sticks used to play a precisely repeated pattern against the wooden side of one of the low-pitched drums, and the *claves*, two wooden dowels that are struck together in a different repeated pattern that interlocks with that of the *palitos*. The *palito*/clave combination is the heart of rumba music, in part because these steady patterns help drummers to orient themselves within the complex swirl of sound they create. Other instruments are occa- sionally added; on the recording we explore here, there is a *shekere*, a large rattle made of a dried gourd sur- rounded by a web of cords strung with beads or cowrie shells.

Rumba vocal parts alternate between solo singing and the sort of leader-and-chorus call-and-response patterns that are typical of much African and African American music. Our example of *rumba guaguancó*, entitled "Enigue Nigue," is typical in that it has three sections:

A. *La Diana*, an opening, improvised melodic passage sung in "nonsense syllables" by the lead singer.
B. *El Canto*, "the song," in which the lead singer sings verses that establish the identity of the piece and its central topic, and a group of singers answers with a repeated chorus.
C. *El Montuno*, a final climactic section organized around call-and-response patterns, in which the tempo accelerates, the energy of the performance increases, and both the drummers and the dancers reach peaks of virtuosity and self-expression.

"Enigue Nigue" is performed by Grupo AfroCuba, one of the leading contemporary proponents of traditional rumba, and is a characteristic example of the *guaguancó* style. Once the claves, *palitos*, and *tumbadores* estab- lish their repeating patterns, the *quinto* drum enters, trying out a few subtle rhythmic improvisations. The Diana section, in which the lead singer improvises solo melodies with no text, is brief in this performance. In the Canto section (which begins about forty-seven seconds into the track), the lead vocalist is joined in harmony by two other singers. They perform languid, stretched-out, Spanish-tinged melodies that lie across the framework of underlying rhythms like loose ropes, while the *quinto* drum continues to provide crisply articulated rhythmic interjections. The song announces the group's presence and shares their motivations.

The ***montuno*** section (which starts at around 3:04) is initiated with a vocal "call" by the lead singer ("Rumbero Enigue, Enigue, Nigue Caballero"), which is answered by the chorus ("Enigue Nigue, Nigue Caballero"), establishing the call-and-response struc- ture that will dominate the rest of the performance. The montuno section allows the *quintero* an opportu- nity to show off his technical prowess, playing dozens of complex polyrhythmic elaborations and inspiring the dancing couple's flirtatious interactions. In *rumba guaguancó*, the female dancer both entices and pro- tects herself from the man, who tries to catch her off-guard with a *vacunao*, tagging her with the flip of a handkerchief or throwing his arm, leg, or pelvis in her direction in an act of symbolic sexual contact.

(continued)

Listening Guide   AFRO-CUBAN RUMBA (*continued*)

To defend herself, she may cover her pelvis with her hand or use her skirt to protect the area in order to deflect the sexual energy away from her body. The virtuosity of the dancers' movements ideally matches that of the musicians. In an effective rumba performance, the drummer and the dancers continually exchange subtle cues. They compete for the approval of onlookers, but always within a cooperative framework, since the success of one depends upon the success of the other.

The montuno accounts for more than half of the total time of this performance, and it is typically the longest section of a *rumba guaguancó*, often continuing for a half hour or more in live performance. The basic idea of a distinction between a lyrical "song" (canto) and a rhythmically charged, dance-oriented section with call-and-response singing (montuno) has been carried forward in salsa music, which we will explore in Chapter 12.

LISTENING GUIDE	"ENIGUE NIGUE"	
TIME	**SECTION**	
0:00	*La Diana*	Opening section, beginning with percussion instruments followed by nonsense lyrics sung by the vocalist in call-and-response
0:47	*El Canto*	*Nosotros cultivamos el canto* (2X) *para divertirnos* *y para tener* *un rato de pasion con el amigo*
		por que *el a mi me dio otra idea* (2X) *para que el publico estimen* *a lo oir cantar este nueva agrupacion*
		Translation: We cultivate the song (2X) to enjoy ourselves and to have a slamming good time with friends because he gave me another idea (2X) so that the public would appreciate hearing this new group sing.[5]
3:03	*El Montuno*	Call-and-response section between vocalist and chorus, accompanied by percussion, with accelerating tempo

5. Translation by Scott Wardinsky, 2012.

musicians are able to augment their earnings by playing at community social events such as festivals, parties, and marriages.

The impact of the Latin American stream on American popular music is seen most obviously in the Latin dance and Spanish-language recordings that have become hits in the United States. Far more wide-reaching and arguably more important, however, is the way in which sounds and rhythms rooted in Latin American musical culture have found their place in a broad range of U.S. popular styles and genres—often without conscious

Listening Guide   MEXICAN MARIACHI MUSIC

"La Negra," performed by Mariachi Vargas de Tecalitlán; released 1959

The mariachi tradition originated in the western region of Mexico and is associated particularly closely with the state of Jalisco and the city of Guadalajara (known as "the capital of mariachi"). The term has various etymologies, including the French *mariage* (marriage), one of the social events at which mariachi groups commonly play. From the mid-nineteenth century through the 1930s, mariachi groups were small bands made up of violin, guitar, and other stringed instruments, just one of many types of music performed in villages and ranches around the Jalisco region. In the late 1930s, radio, the recording industry, and the fledgling Mexican film industry disseminated mariachi music more widely, and mariachi musicians began to move to Mexico City

and other big cities in order to pursue musical careers on a professional basis. In the process, mariachi groups expanded in size, adding trumpets and more stringed instruments, and their performance style became more polished. Today, successful mariachi ensembles may include up to four trumpets and eight violins.

Mariachi Vargas de Tecalitlán, the best-known mariachi group in Mexico, was founded in 1897 by Gaspar Vargas. The earliest iteration of the group was a quartet of two violins, a harp, and a five-stringed version of the guitar called a *guitarra de golpe*. By the time of their 1957 recording of "Son de la Negra" (popularly known as the "national anthem of mariachi"), the group had expanded to include a trumpet, four violins, two guitars, a

LISTENING GUIDE	"SON DE LA NEGRA"
TIME	**SECTION/LYRIC**
0:00	Instrumental introduction; singer calls out enthusiastically
0:22	Instruments play main melody
0:42	*Negrita de mis pesares, ojos de papel volando.* *Negrita de mis pesares, ojos de papel volando.* *A todos díles que sí, pero no les digas cuando* *Así me dijiste a mí, por éso vivo penando!* *Little dark-skinned woman of my regrets, eyes fluttering flirtatiously* ["like flying paper"] *Little dark-skinned woman of my regrets, eyes fluttering flirtatiously* *You tell everyone yes, but you never tell them when* *You said the same to me, and now I'm suffering!*
1:00	Instrumental; singer calls out enthusiastically
1:51	*Cuando me traes a mi negra, que la quiero ver aquí* *Con su rebozo de seda, que le traje de Tepíc.* *Cuando me traes a mi negra, que la quiero ver aquí* *Con su rebozo de seda, que le traje de Tepíc.* *When will you bring me to my sweetheart, whom I want to see here* *With her silk shawl, that she wears from Tepíc* [a town in the neighboring state of Nayarit]? *When will you bring me to my sweetheart, whom I want to see here* *With her silk shawl, that she wears from Tepíc?*
2:07	Instrumental; vocal calls
2:24	Syncopated figures
2:35	Return of regular rhythm; brief ending

(continued)

Listening Guide MEXICAN MARIACHI MUSIC (continued)

viheula (a small, five-stringed rhythm guitar), a *guitarrón* (a six-stringed acoustic bass guitar), and a harp. "Son de la Negra" has been traced back to the nineteenth century, but the song appeared in printed form only in 1940. The song's text is structured around the *copla* (couplet), a poetic form brought to the Americas from Spain that is made up of a series of four-line stanzas, with each line consisting of eight syllables.

"Son de la Negra" is in a driving triple (three-beat) rhythm and makes use of polyrhythms derived from Spanish music. (It's worth noting that the influence of Africa is by no means absent here, since Spanish music was strongly impacted by the 780-year occupation of much of what is now Spain by North Africans.) The violins and trumpet play in the modern urban style, with lots of vibrato—an expressive technique that involves varying the pitch of a held note—and the musical arrangement is carefully worked out, with well-rehearsed changes in tempo. The guitar and *viheula* players use a technique called *rasqueado*, in which they strum their instruments vigorously to create a scraping sound that propels the music forward. Members of the band call out *gritos* (yells) at various points during the performance. This traditional feature of mariachi music is used to build excitement among the audience, members of which often respond with their own *gritos*!

intent on the part of those involved. It may be said that Latin American sounds and rhythms have penetrated the collective unconscious of American popular music, just as aspects of European American song forms and African American performance styles have done.

> IN THIS CHAPTER we have discussed some unifying themes that run through the history of American popular music and have explored some of the diverse traditions that have contributed to this rich history. Now we will get more specific, beginning with an examination of the nineteenth century, when the music business and the first distinctively American styles of popular music began to take shape.

Key Terms

a cappella	dialect	polyrhythmic
A&R (artists and repertoire)	digital audio workstation (DAW)	producer
arranger		riff
backbeat	folk music	spirituals
ballad	gospel music	streaming
broadsides	groove	strophic
call-and-response	hook	syncopation
chorus	lyricist	timbre
composer	montuno	verses

Key People

Carlos Gardel	Jean Ritchie	The Skillet Lickers
Dink Roberts	José ("El Negro") Ricardo	Tommy Jarrell
Francisco Canaro	Lightning Washington	
James Gideon (Gid) Tanner	Mississippi John Hurt	

Review Questions

1. What are the main "themes" that will be studied in this book, and how do they relate to the history of American popular music?
2. Every aspect of popular music that is today regarded as American in character has sprung from three broad "streams." What are the three streams? Describe each of them.
3. What are some musical elements of European, African, and Latin music that have influenced American popular music?
4. What is a ballad? Typically, what musical form does a ballad follow?
5. What are some examples of the relationship between music and identity in American popular music?

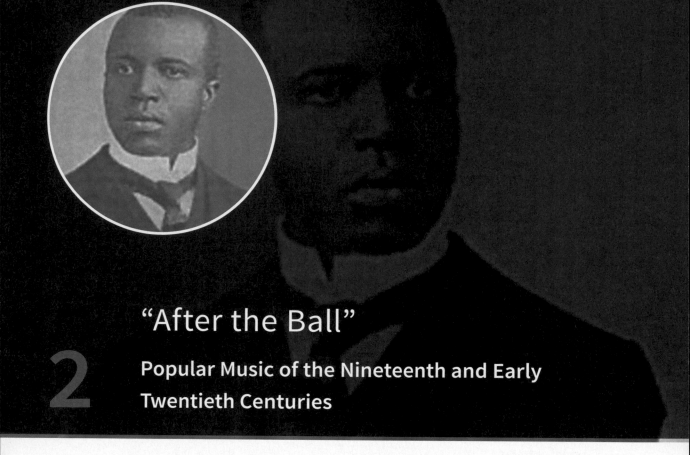

"After the Ball"

2 Popular Music of the Nineteenth and Early Twentieth Centuries

IN THIS CHAPTER WE TURN OUR ATTENTION TO POPULAR MUSIC OF THE nineteenth and early twentieth centuries. This period saw the birth of minstrelsy, the first distinctively American form of popular culture; the rise of the modern music industry; rapid expansion of the audience for popular music; changes in technology that supported the dissemination of music to a national audience; and the emergence of song and dance music styles that were to profoundly influence the subsequent development of popular music in the United States.

The Minstrel Show

The **minstrel show**, the first form of musical and theatrical entertainment to be regarded by European audiences as distinctively American in character, featured mainly white performers who artificially blackened their skin and enacted parodies of African American music, dance, dress, and dialect. Today blackface minstrelsy is quite appropriately regarded with embarrassment or anger. But an effective answer to the apparently reasonable question "Why not forget about it?" would be the famous statement by European-American philosopher George Santayana: "Those who cannot remember the past are condemned to repeat it." It would be difficult if not impossible to understand subsequent developments in the history of American popular culture without some knowledge of the minstrel show, and indeed the complexities and problems surrounding race relations in the United States continue to dominate contemporary news headlines and public and private discussions. Furthermore, there is good reason to believe that the common interpretation of minstrelsy as an unvarying expression of white racism oversimplifies the diverse and sometimes ambiguous meanings that this form of popular culture held at different times and for various audiences.

Recent scholarship on the evolution of blackface minstrelsy suggests that this seminal form of American popular culture emerged from rough-and-tumble, predominantly working-class commercial urban zones where interracial interaction was common, such as New York City's Seventh Ward. From this point of view, early blackface performers were the first expression of a distinctively American popular culture in which working-class white youth expressed their own sense of marginalization through identification with African American cultural forms. This does not mean that minstrelsy cannot also be read as a projection of white racism—in fact, this interpretation makes even more sense in the later years of minstrelsy (1840s–1880s), when, as we shall see, the portrayal of Black characters became more rigidly stereotypical. But, as is often the case with popular cultural forms, the meanings of blackface minstrelsy were neither fixed nor unambiguous.

Black characters were played by white actors in British comic operas of the eighteenth century, some of which became popular in America before the Revolutionary War. Most of the songs sung by these characters were European in character and written in a childishly simple style, often drawing upon Irish or Scottish melodies ("exotic" styles available to English composers). *George Washington Dixon* (180?–1861) was the first white performer to establish a wide reputation as a "blackface" entertainer. He made his New York City debut in 1829, and two of the earliest "Ethiopian" songs to enjoy widespread popularity—"Long Tail Blue" and "Coal Black Rose"—were featured in his act. Like their English predecessors, these songs were simple melodies in a European mold.

Thomas Durtmouth Rice (1808–1860), a white actor born into a poor family in New York's Seventh Ward, demonstrated the potential popularity (and profitability) of minstrelsy with his performance of the song "Jim Crow" (1829), which became the first international American song hit. Rice sang this song in blackface while imitating a dance step called the "cakewalk," an Africanized version of the European quadrille, which was a kind of square dance. (See the discussion of dance in the European American stream section of Chapter 1.) Ironically, the cakewalk was first developed by slaves as a parody of the "refined" dance movements of their white slave-owners. One ex-slave, interviewed in 1901, recalled the slave dances of the 1840s, the same period in which minstrelsy rose to mass popularity among whites:

> Us slaves watched the white folks' parties where the guests danced a minuet and then paraded in a grand march, with the ladies and gentlemen going different

ways and then meeting again, arm in arm, and marching down the center together. Then we'd do it, too, but we used to mock 'em, every step. Sometimes the
white folks noticed it, but they seemed to like it. I guess they thought we couldn't
dance any better! (Levine 2007, 17)

One could scarcely imagine a more striking example of the ironies of racial relations in mid-nineteenth-century America—the slaves performing a delicious parody
of European dance styles, while the whites watched with fascination, oblivious to the
fact that they themselves were being ridiculed! (Beginning in the 1850s, a version of
the cakewalk became popular among whites as a ballroom dance step. The rhythms
of the music used to accompany the cakewalk exemplify the principle of syncopation;
such "irregular" rhythms later became one important source of ragtime music, discussed later in this chapter.)

Soon after Rice introduced his Jim Crow character to New York in 1832, there was a
veritable explosion of blackface performance in venues ranging from formal theaters to
saloons, the latter often patronized by a racially mixed audience of urban workers and
craftsmen. Contrary to much of what has been written about early minstrelsy, which
suggests that the performers were exclusively white, recent research suggests that Black
and mixed-race performers participated in most of the minstrel shows that were held at
the local "dives" that featured such entertainment during this period. The musical and
linguistic heritage of early minstrelsy was just as mixed as its audience and practitioners. Scholars have suggested that the most likely inspiration for "Jim Crow" was not an
African American song but an Irish folk tune that had subsequently been transformed
into an English stage song. Although sheet music arrangements suggest that Rice's
song bore only an indirect relationship to African American folk music, we have no
direct evidence of the other musical aspects of his stage performances.

"Daddy" Rice's Jim Crow character spoke and sang in a dialect that was partly based
on pre-existing white rural characters (such as the Kentucky rifleman Davy Crockett)
and partly on the variety of Black and Creole dialects heard by Rice as a youngster growing up by the docks in New York's Seventh Ward.

> Come, listen all you gals and boys, I'se just from Tuckyhoe
> I'm goin' to sing a little song, My name's Jim Crow
> Weel about and turn about and do jis' so
> Eb'ry time I weel about I jump Jim Crow

The Jim Crow character used this hybrid dialect—neither Black nor white but something in between—to make fun of pretentious politicians and social elites, mangling
their "fancy" words and introducing a satirical subtext that Rice's high-class targets
found somewhat threatening:

> I make my infernal sensibilifications yieldify to de "Fox popular," as I tinks dey
> call de people's breath at de Walnut street Te-atre. . . . I am gwaing in short time
> to do like oder great hactors, publish my account ob men and manners in dese
> blessed States, and I trus I shall be unable to do dem as much justice as dey

desarve, on account ob my debility to use falsificationority as de foreignificated deatrical ladies do. (Lhamon 1998, 188–89)

This speech, from the introduction to Rice's 1835 autobiography *The Life of Jim Crow*, captures the subversive, Trickster-like quality of the Jim Crow character, a quality that has been forgotten in the subsequent concern over minstrelsy's role in promulgating racist stereotypes. Arbiters of public taste and morals, including newspaper and magazine publishers, politicians, and the clergy, ridiculed minstrelsy as an indicator of the depraved state of the lower classes and urged its rejection in favor of more refined (i.e., European-derived) forms of entertainment. For their part, the racially mixed, relatively impoverished audiences for early minstrelsy must have found Jim Crow's lampooning of the pretensions and "falsificationority" of the "foreignificated deatrical ladies" ("high-society" critics of minstrelsy) richly satisfying.

When Thomas Dartmouth Rice toured England in the 1830s, he became the first native-born American performer to export a type of music that was *perceived* abroad as quintessentially American in style and content. There is a terrible irony in the fact that the title of Rice's "Jim Crow"—arguably the point of origin of American popular music—was soon transformed into a derogatory epithet for African Americans and, from the 1870s until the 1950s, became the catchall term for the segregationist laws that excluded Blacks from white theaters, cemeteries, hospitals, restaurants, and schools.

The next big "Ethiopian" song hit was "Zip Coon," published in New York in 1834. The song was in the familiar verse-chorus ballad form, its verses sprinkled with images of banjo playing, wild dancing, and barnyard animals. The chorus consisted of the nonsense syllables "Zip a duden duden duden zip a duden day" (the direct ancestor of the song "Zip a Dee Doo Dah," featured in Walt Disney's 1947 cartoon *Song of the South*). Like "Jim Crow," the melody of "Zip Coon" is more closely related to Irish or Scottish than to African American song. The same melody was adopted by both Black and white country fiddlers, rearranged, and given the title "Turkey in the Straw." This song provides a good example of the continually evolving relationship between popular and folk music in the nineteenth century.

From the 1840s through the 1880s blackface minstrelsy rose to become the predominant genre of popular culture in the United States. As the genre was reworked for mass appeal by theatrical entrepreneurs and promoters and transformed into the more formally organized and predictable "minstrel show," much of its original subversive quality was lost. As the scholar W. T. Lhamon Jr. has phrased it, "The early Jim Crow was not the late Jim Crow. Jim Crow went from fond alliance to hateful segregation as the Civil War approached and then as the Nadir replaced Reconstruction" (Lhamon 1998, 191). As the fires of white racism were stoked, first by the escalating conflict between the states and then by postbellum fears of Black backlash and economic competition, minstrelsy both reflected and helped to promulgate the national obsession with symbols of racial difference. It was during this period that the most pernicious stereotypes of Black people—the old faithful slave (the "good negro") and the big-city, knife-toting dandy (the "bad negro")—became enduring images in mainstream American popular culture, disseminated by an emerging entertainment industry and absorbed by a predominantly white mass audience.

Beginning in 1843 with the first appearance of the Virginia Minstrels (led by the white banjo virtuoso Dan Emmett), more lengthy performances featuring a standardized group of performers became popular. This format became the classic minstrel show, organized around a sequence of more or less independent sketches and songs and featuring characters such as Mr. Interlocutor, a lead performer who sang and provided patter between acts, and Bones and Tambo, musicians who sat at either end of the line of performers.

By the mid-nineteenth century minstrel songs had become an important influence on the mainstream of American popular song. Many of these "plantation songs" were very successful as sheet music, and they were a dominant force in the development of nineteenth-century popular music. Some of these later minstrel tunes do show evidence

Cover of the published sheet music for "Zip Coon."

of African American influence, particularly in their irregular syncopated rhythms, but there is good reason to believe that few minstrel performers were able to capture the rhythmic and textural complexity of the Black musical traditions they purported to represent. The typical minstrel song of the early 1840s was sung by one member of the troupe, with accompaniment by a fiddle, one or more banjos, a tambourine (played by the character Tambo), and a pair of rib bones held in one hand and clacked together to create a syncopated rhythmic pattern (played by the character Bones).[1] Despite their incorporation of instruments used by some Black musicians, performances by white minstrels still had little to do with the African American musical traditions of the American South. Nonetheless, minstrel troupes competed with one another on the basis of their attention to supposedly "authentic" details of Southern Black culture.

Although the biggest celebrities of minstrelsy were white during the form's rise to national popularity, African American performers did appear in minstrel shows. In a practice that shows the arbitrariness of social distinctions based on race, light-skinned African American minstrels were required to apply blackface in order to prepare themselves for their stage roles as "authentic negroes." This practice adds yet another twist to the complex and often ironic interaction between African American and European American cultures. In this later stage of the evolution of minstrelsy, what was initially a parody of white culture created by African slaves and later popularized by the urban working class was in turn propagated by African American people whose physical appearance was not considered to match white stereotypes of "Blackness." We might cite this phenomenon as an example of the importance of popular culture as a key to understanding the development of racial identity in the United States, up to and including contemporary notions of whiteness and Blackness. Suffice it for now to say that in this regard, as in others, minstrelsy left a lasting imprint on American popular consciousness.

It should be stressed that in the formation and rise of the nineteenth-century minstrel show, we encounter many of the basic themes that will concern us throughout our survey of the history of American popular music. Minstrelsy arose during the 1830s as an expression of a predominantly white urban youth culture, which sought to express its independence through the appropriation of Black style. As minstrelsy became a mass phenomenon in the decades just before and after the American Civil War, its form became routinized and its portrayal of Black characters more rigidly stereotyped. This basic pattern, in which a new genre of music arises within a marginalized community and then moves into the mainstream of mass popular culture, in the process losing much of the rebellious energy that gave rise to it in the first place, will be encountered many times in this book.

Minstrel troupes toured the United States constantly from the 1840s until the 1870s, helping to create an embryonic national popular culture. Minstrels borrowed from the diverse traditions they encountered, adopting aspects of English, Irish, German, and

---

1. Examples of minstrel performance reenacted in the early 1980s can be heard on *Early Minstrel Show* (New World Records NW 338, 1985).

Advertising lithographs for minstrel (1896) and vaudeville (1899) shows.

African music, dialect, and dance and continually crossing the boundaries between folk and popular, rural and urban, Southern and Northern culture. The minstrel show is also the direct ancestor of vaudeville, a kind of variety show that became the dominant form of popular entertainment in late nineteenth- and early twentieth-century America (see Chapters 3 and 4). And while the mass success of the blackface minstrel show doubtless helped to reinforce racist attitudes among whites, minstrelsy also established a mobile performance tradition within which influential Black musicians such as W. C. Handy, Ma Rainey, and Bessie Smith could later flourish (see Chapter 5).

An Early Pop Songwriter: Stephen Foster

Stephen Collins Foster (1826–1864) is regarded as the first important composer of American popular song, producing around two hundred songs during the 1840s, 1850s, and early 1860s. He was probably the first person in the United States to make his living as a full-time professional songwriter, surviving on the fees and royalties generated by sales of sheet music for songs such as "Oh! Susanna," "Old Folks at Home," "My Old Kentucky Home, Good Night," "Jeanie with the Light Brown Hair," and "Beautiful Dreamer." His earliest musical experiences, growing up on the western frontier near Pittsburgh, were dominated by the sentimental song tradition that was derived from England and considered a mark of gentility by upwardly mobile Americans. Foster also knew and incorporated into his work the various song styles popular in midcentury

America: ballads, Italian light opera, Irish and German songs, and minstrel songs. In embracing both genteel traditions and less highly regarded but wildly popular traditions like minstrelsy, Foster demonstrated his versatility while establishing models for many later generations of American songwriters.

"Jeanie with the Light Brown Hair," a product of the nineteenth-century genteel song tradition, reemerged during World War II after several swing era dance bands performed it on the popular *Hit Parade* radio show. It was still sufficiently remembered in the 1960s to lend its name—or, to be more precise, a pun built on its first line—to the popular television series *I Dream of Jeannie*.

Although Foster was not the wealthiest popular songwriter of the nineteenth century, he was the most influential. He was a master at creating the simple but compelling combinations of melody and text that later popular composers would refer to as "hooks" (i.e., the basic musical or verbal idea that "hooks" the listener's ear). Foster's compositions were heard almost everywhere—in saloons, theater productions, variety shows, and band concerts. His biggest hit, a plantation song called "Old Folks at Home," sold over 100,000 copies of sheet music in 1851, the year it was published. On a per capita basis, this is equal to a million-seller in today's terms. Some of Foster's songs became part of American oral tradition, passed from generation to generation without the aid of musical notation. His songs have remained attractive vehicles for popular entertainers to the present day; the well-received compilation *Beautiful Dreamer: The Songs of Stephen Foster* (2004) is but one recent example of his enduring popularity.

Foster's success was supported by a number of social and technological factors. Minstrel troupes performed his songs on their tours, popularizing them across the country. In addition, the sheet music publishing business expanded during the mid-nineteenth century, fueled in part by the rapid growth of public music education, which allowed many more people to read and play the simple piano arrangements that accompanied popular songs. This trend was also encouraged by expanded domestic production of cheap pianos. The piano became a standard feature of the middle-class parlor—a cozy room outfitted with sofas, paintings, books, kerosene lamps and candles, and, if the family in question could afford it, a piano or reed organ. The parlor was a center of family life, a place for entertainment, conversation, and courting.

Foster's success as a "hit maker" occurred well before the rise of electronic mass media and was dependent on the ability of the public to read and perform the arrangements of his songs published on sheet music and in songbooks. During this period, people often

A portrait of Stephen Foster, looking wistful (and dreaming of "Jeanie," perhaps?).

Listening Guide "JEANIE WITH THE LIGHT BROWN HAIR"

Music and lyrics by Stephen Foster; published 1854; performed by Thomas Hampson; released 1992

"Jeanie with the Light Brown Hair" is an example of Foster's sentimental "Irish" style, which is strongly reminiscent of the songs of Thomas Moore (see Chapter 1). The most typical performance of this song would have featured a male singer with a high voice, who employed a slight Irish accent. "Jeanie" is also a prototypical example of a form that would become increasingly common in American popular music: the four-section song with an AABA melodic structure. The A sections begin identically, although their endings vary slightly (this is why we have chosen to call them A¹, A², and A³; see the following chart). The B section introduces a new melody and chords and acts as a musical "bridge" that leads us to the final A section. This basic structure, with its economical and easily comprehended balance between repetition and variation, was to become one of the most important popular song forms of the early twentieth century.

Forms such as AABA are not just technical features or blueprints for the composer. They also become the basis for listening habits. Once you have learned to hear a kind of song form, you expect things to happen in a certain order. The arrangement of a song—that is, the way in which the song is actually presented in a particular performance—may either delay elements or speed them up. A performer or arranger may even vary the order of the sections to create a certain effect. But these variations make sense only against the background of the listener's learned expectations.

The melody of "Jeanie" contains hints of its origin in Irish popular song. In melodic terms, there is plenty of conjunct (i.e., step-by-step) movement, which is contrasted with dramatic leaps up or down. See if you can identify the large melodic leaps as you listen: "I dream of Jeanie with the light [downward leap ↓] brown hair, / Borne like a [upward leap ↑] vapor on the summer air."

LISTENING GUIDE	"JEANIE WITH THE LIGHT BROWN HAIR"		
TIME	**FORM**	**LYRICS**	**DESCRIPTIVE COMMENTS**
0:00			Instrumental introduction
0:14	A¹	*I dream of Jeanie with the light brown hair . . .*	The main melody, meant to "hook" your ear
0:31	A²	*I see her tripping where the bright streams play . . .*	The melody repeats, with new words and a different ending
0:48	B	*Many were the wild notes her merry voice would pour . . .*	New melody, new chords, and new words
1:07	A³	*I dream of Jeanie with the light brown hair . . .*	This final A section has a new ending, which produces an effect of finality (called a cadence). The form then repeats itself for the following verses.

performed music in their homes. Amateur piano playing was widely considered a female specialization, an attractive feature in a prospective wife. The piano remained a center of domestic music-making in the United States until the 1920s, when commercial radio was introduced.

Foster's life—which ended in obscurity and poverty at the age of thirty-seven—illustrates the state of copyright enforcement in the mid-nineteenth century. His first success, the plantation song "Oh! Susanna" (1847), was sold outright to a music publisher for one hundred dollars. The publisher subsequently made thousands of dollars from the worldwide hit, but none of that money ever went to Foster. This was a typical situation for composers of the time, for the law covered the rights of music firms but not those of the composers of songs bought by the firms. A study of various arrangements of "Oh! Susanna" published between 1848 and 1851 indicates the ways in which numerous publishers profited from a single song. "Susanna" was published sometimes as a minstrel song but more often in wordless piano arrangements in the style of popular dance steps, including the quadrille, the quickstep, and the polka (the latest fashionable dance from Paris and London). All in all, twenty different arrangements appeared during the three-year period and were copyrighted by eleven different publishers.

Dance Music and Brass Bands

As we have already seen, American popular music has been closely bound up from its very inception with dance and the varied social functions of dancing, including courtship, entertainment, celebration of community, and the communication of ethnic and class identity. The earliest examples of published dance music in the United States were modeled strongly on styles popular in England, as was the case with popular song. Until the early twentieth century, social dancing among white Americans was dominated by offshoots of the contra dance, or country dance, tradition (in which teams of dancers formed geometric figures such as lines, circles, or squares) and by dances such as the waltz, mazurka, schottische, and polka, which were performed by couples. Many of these dances were originally modeled on the traditions of rural peasants, although the music and movements often bore little resemblance to the folk traditions from which they sprang. The adoption of country dances by the urban elite was an aspect of the romantic fascination with rural themes that we have already described in connection with the pleasure gardens of the eighteenth century (see Chapter 1).

The typical setting for dancing among the upper classes (and the upwardly mobile) was the ball, organized around a program of preselected music played by an orchestra and arranged to accompany a specific sequence of dances. A typical dance program of the late nineteenth century might include a waltz, a mazurka or polka, and a cotillion, itself a sequence of dances during which couples would continuously exchange partners. This succession of dances was overseen by a dance master, who called out the sequences of movements, sometimes referring to a book of instructions called a dance manual.

The grand ball, originally modeled on the aristocratic gatherings of European royalty, provided an important public venue for Americans who desired to demonstrate their refinement and knowledge of high culture. The following rules for male dress, published in a dance instruction book in 1867, give some sense of the close relationship between ballroom dancing and public demonstrations of gentility:

> The dress should be studiously neat, leaving no impression other than that of a well-dressed gentleman. Black dress coat, black or white vest, black trousers, white necktie, patent leather boots or pumps and black or white stockings, white kid gloves, hair well-dressed. Coats of fancy character and colors, velvet collars, and metal buttons are not proper for the opera or ball. (Stephenson and Iaccarino 1980, 31)

In general, ballroom dancing focused more on uniformity and restraint than on improvisation or the expression of emotion. Another nineteenth-century dance manual suggests that

> the upper part of the body should be slightly inclined forward, the hips backward—the forward inclination just enough to cause a tendency in the heels to rise from the floor; the head erect, legs straight, arms hanging by the sides, elbows very slightly turned outward so that the arms will present gently curved lines to the front. (Dodworth 1885, 24)

As the nineteenth century progressed, there was a shift away from the more formal dances based on the contra dance and toward an increased emphasis on couple dancing, a change that was regarded with alarm by some dance masters (perhaps because it threatened to put them out of a job!). Even the **waltz**, which first rose to popularity in the United States in the 1820s, was initially regarded as an "indecorous exhibition" of intimacy between men and women, and as a threat to public morality. By the end of the century, however, the waltz, with its lilting triple-meter accompaniment, circular movements, and smooth, graceful lines, had become the ultimate symbol of sophistication and romance.

As was the case with other adopted European customs, local variants of the grand ball tradition in America reflected the tastes and cultural values of particular communities. Uniquely American versions of the ball included the rough-and-ready miners' balls of the California Gold Rush—often accompanied by drinking and general rowdiness—and the slave balls held on Southern plantations, which satirized the elite dances of the white slave-owners (recall our discussion of minstrelsy earlier in this chapter). In addition, occupational and ethnic groups in big cities such as New York held their own imitations of the elite grand balls.

Throughout the nineteenth century there was a continual feedback between urban and rural, "high-class" and "low-class" dance styles. Urban professional musicians arranged folk dances and their associated music for mass consumption, and some of the popular songs published by big New York City music companies were incorporated into rural dance traditions such as the square dance. (Minstrel songs such as "Turkey in the Straw" and Stephen Foster's "Camptown Races" are good examples of the latter process.) The diversity of American popular dance was reinforced by waves of European immigrants, who brought distinctive dance music styles with them. Some of these styles were maintained solely in ethnic enclaves, while others circulated into the popular mainstream. At the same time, the mass influence of African American dance, which began to appear in the 1830s in the form of the cakewalk steps performed by white minstrels, intensified, rising to become the dominant force in American popular dance during the first few decades of the twentieth century (see Chapter 3).

From the Civil War through the 1910s brass band concerts were one of the most important musical aspects of American life. Although military bands made up of brass instruments (e.g., trumpets, cornets, trombones, and tubas) had been around since the birth of the United States, they spread rapidly during and after the Civil War (1861–1865). One conservative estimate suggests that at one point the Union Army had five hundred bands and nine thousand players, to which must be added the probably only marginally smaller number of musicians who served in the Confederate Army. While a number of these regimental bands continued to flourish after the war, many of the musicians who were decommissioned formed bands in their home communities. In addition, many colleges and high schools formed bands during this period. By 1889 a journalist was reporting that there were over ten thousand brass bands in the United States. Almost every town of note had a park with a band shell in it, and bands were formed in association with city governments, schools, churches, and business enterprises. As one contemporary observer wrote in 1878, "A town without its brass band is as much in need of sympathy as a church without a choir. The spirit of a place is recognized in its band" (Camus 1986, 133).

The brass band movement of the late nineteenth century drew energy from the interaction of patriotism and popular culture, as well as from the growing force of American nationalism. The lion's share of a band's repertoire generally consisted of patriotic marches, a type of music that in the wake of the Civil War became an important symbol of the unity of the nation. Marches stirred the emotions and were used to foster public support for the assertion of American military and economic power overseas (including U.S. involvement in the Panama Canal project and the Spanish-American War of 1898). Then, as today, brass bands were associated with national holidays such as the Fourth of July, and their music often held a special significance for those who had served in the armed forces during times of war. Many bands, however, also played arrangements of the popular sheet music hits of the day, including music for dance styles such as the cakewalk, polka, and waltz, and adaptations of classical music. This ability to move between patriotic music and the popular styles of the day reinforced the brass band's role as a community institution.

The most popular bandleader from the 1890s through World War I was *John Philip Sousa* (1854–1932), popularly known as America's "March King." The son of a trombonist in the U.S. Marine Band, Sousa eventually became its conductor and later formed a "commercial" concert band that toured widely in America and Europe. This band, arguably the first American pop "supergroup," made two dozen hit phonograph recordings between 1895 and 1918. (Sousa himself despised "canned music," and many of

John Philip Sousa holding a baton.

the recordings made under his name were actually directed by Arthur Pryor, who later became the most prolific conductor of brass band music in American history.) The Sousa band's repertoire included stirring patriotic marches by Sousa such as "El Capitan," "The Washington Post," and "The Stars and Stripes Forever" (the official march of the United States), as well as popular songs such as "In the Good Old Summer Time," complete with vocals. Sousa toured constantly, and the appearance of his band, which comprised more than fifty members, in cities and towns across the country created a sensation that could only be surpassed by a presidential "whistle-stop" tour. In addition to his activities as a bandleader, conductor, and composer, Sousa was one of the first musicians to negotiate royalty payments with publishers, insisting on a percentage of total sales of his compositions, and he was an important advocate of copyright reform.

"Business bands"—touring bands not connected to government institutions—were an important part of the American music business. Italian concert bands, led by charismatic conductors, were among the most popular groups of the 1890s. A newspaper headline that appeared in New York City in 1899 described the excitement and athletic appeal of an Italian brass band as follows: WOMEN ON TABLES IN HYPNOTIC FRENZY. BROADWAY PLEASED BY EXHIBITION OF ATHLETIC LEADERSHIP (Schwartz 1975, 216). Although we do not usually think of brass bands as purveyors of popular music, the American passion for bands was a truly national phenomenon and a powerful shaper of musical taste during the late nineteenth century. The brass band tradition also contributed to later developments in popular music, particularly the development of jazz, as we shall see in Chapter 3.

The Birth of Tin Pan Alley

By the end of the nineteenth century the American music publishing business, formerly distributed among a number of cities on the eastern seaboard and in the Midwest, had become centered in New York City. The established publishers, who had made their fortunes in classical music and genteel parlor songs, were, from around 1885 on, challenged by smaller companies specializing in the more exciting popular songs performed in dance halls, beer gardens, and theaters.

These new publishing firms—many of them founded by Jewish immigrants from Eastern Europe—set up their offices in a section of lower Manhattan, creating a dense hive of small rooms with pianos where composers and "song pluggers" produced and promoted popular songs. This stretch of 28th Street became known as **Tin Pan Alley**, a term that evoked the clanging sound of many pianos simultaneously playing songs in a variety of keys and tempos.

The 1890s saw the rise of the modern American music business, an industry aimed at providing "hits" for an expanding urban mass market. For the first time, a single song could sell more than a million copies. Sheet music sold for between twenty-five and sixty cents, and the wholesale value of printed music in the United States more than tripled between 1890 and 1909. Publishing firms such as T. B. Harms and Witmark and Sons hired teams of composers and lyricists to crank out new songs.

Popular songs, printed as sheet music, were promoted by song pluggers, whose job it was to promote a given company's product. Sheet music was sold by specialized music outlets, mail order houses such as Sears, Roebuck and Co., and large department stores such as Macy's and Montgomery Ward. A song plugger's typical workday might begin with a visit to a big department store, where he would deliver bundles of sheet music and sing the company's latest songs over and over to get customers' attention. It would typically end late at night in a saloon, where he might perform from his table, or backstage at a theater, where he might try to convince a popular singer to incorporate one of the company's songs into his act. The promotional strategies of the music publishers were evidently quite successful: by 1910 annual sales of sheet music in the United States had reached 30 million copies.

By the turn of the century **vaudeville**, a popular theatrical form descended from music hall shows and minstrelsy, had become the most important medium for popularizing Tin Pan Alley songs. Unlike minstrel shows, in which the entire cast remained onstage for the whole performance, vaudeville shows typically consisted of a series of performances—by singers, acrobats, comedians, jugglers, dancers, animal handlers, and so on—presented one after the other without any overarching narrative theme. There is a similarity here to the television "variety" shows that were popular from the 1950s through the 1970s. Every city in the country had at least one large vaudeville theater, and the music publishing firms sent representatives out along the theater circuit to make sure that performers lived up to the terms of their contracts and that local music stores had a sufficient stock of sheet music for the songs being promoted. By 1915 more than half a million dollars was being paid every year to vaudeville performers for song boosting.

Most performers had to provide their own transportation, lodging, costumes, songs, and arrangements, and they were dependent on the whims of powerful booking agents, to whom they paid substantial fees. Racial segregation meant that there was a separate chain of theaters for Black performers and audiences, as well as a separate booking agency, the Theatre Owners Booking Agency (TOBA, known informally as "Tough On Black Asses").

Tin Pan Alley songs—their forms, themes, and performance styles—dominated the mainstream American music industry for almost seventy years. The principles of popular songwriting established by Stephen Foster in the 1840s were further developed by Tin Pan Alley composers. The romantic parlor song remained popular, as did "Irish" and waltz songs. One of the most popular composers of the early Tin Pan Alley period was *Paul Dresser* (1857–1906), who wrote a series of sentimental and nostalgic

Listening Guide "AFTER THE BALL"

Music and lyrics by Charles K. Harris; published 1892; performed by Joan Morris (vocal) and William Bolcom (piano); released 1990

"After the Ball," published in 1892, was the first "mega-hit" pop song, eventually selling over 5 million copies in sheet music. The song's history reveals certain facets of the music business around the turn of the century. Its composer, **Charles K. Harris** (1867–1930), was a self-taught banjo player from Wisconsin who could not literally write music; instead, he dictated his songs to a professional musician. Aware that his new song needed boosting by a popular performer, Harris paid a well-known singer in a traveling theater production to incorporate "After the Ball" into his performance. It soon became the most popular part of the play, and audiences requested that it be repeated several times during each performance.

"After the Ball" became even more popular after it was performed by John Philip Sousa's band at the

LISTENING GUIDE	"AFTER THE BALL"		
TIME	**FORM**	**LYRICS**	**DESCRIPTIVE COMMENTS**
0:00	Introduction		Instrumental
0:06	A	Strophe 1: Verse *A little maiden climbed an old man's knee . . .*	This is the opening verse, designed to introduce the melody and chords and interest us in the story to follow.
0:18	A'	*Why are you single; why live alone? . . .*	
0:31	B	*I had a sweetheart, years, years ago . . .*	
0:44	A'	*List' to the story, I'll tell it all . . .*	
0:58	C	Chorus *After the ball is over, after the break of morn . . .*	Chorus (C), with new chords and melody, and new lyrics that begin and end with the title words of the song
1:35	A	Strophe 2: Verse *Bright lights were flashing in the grand ballroom . . .*	Back to the A melody, with new lyrics carrying the story forward
	A'	*There came my sweetheart, my love, my own . . .*	
	B	*When I returned, dear, there stood a man . . .*	
	A'	*Down fell the glass, pet . . .*	
2:28	C	Chorus *After the ball is over, after the break of morn . . .*	Another chorus; note that the lyrics and music are repeated exactly
3:09	A/A'/B/A'	Strophe 3 *Long years have passed, child, I've never wed . . .*	Back to the A music, with lyrics completing the story and revealing the narrative twist
4:05	C	Chorus *After the ball is over, after the break of morn . . .*	The final chorus (C)

1893 World's Columbian Exposition in Chicago. The M. Witmark Company, a powerful music publishing firm that had built its success publishing plantation songs, offered Harris $10,000 for all rights to the song. Harris declined the offer, published the song himself, and was soon clearing around $25,000 a month. His success demonstrated that popular music could be a lucrative business and encouraged young entrepreneurs to set up their own publishing firms during the 1890s. These small-scale enterprises, many of which were wiped out during later economic depressions, were the predecessors of the independent record labels that were to play so important a role in twentieth-century popular music.

"After the Ball" tells a tragic (if, from our viewpoint, rather unbelievable) story of mistaken identity, misplaced jealousy, and lost love. The song is clearly related to the ballad tradition (see Chapter 1) in its employment of a series of verses, sung over a fixed melody, to tell a story with a beginning, middle, and end. As is the case in some ballads, each verse of "After the Ball" is followed by a chorus,[2] a contrasting section consisting of a fixed melody and lyric that are repeated exactly each time around. Viewed as a whole, the large-scale structure of the piece thus consists of three main sections, or **strophes**, each made up of a verse and a chorus.

Although its basic verse-and-chorus structure is ultimately derived from the ballad tradition, the degree of emphasis placed on the chorus in "After the Ball" positions it as a predecessor of twentieth-century popular song forms. The chorus announces the title of the song not once, but twice, helping to embed it in the listener's memory; it both foreshadows and summarizes the sentimental message of the song; and it is, in melodic terms, the catchiest part of the song, cleverly designed to lodge itself in the audience's consciousness. "After the Ball" draws upon the centuries-old storytelling techniques of European American balladry, but it is also a perfect example of a pop song with a catchy hook, crafted to hold a mass audience's attention and generate millions of dollars in profit. In addition, "After the Ball" is a waltz, one of the most popular dance styles of the late nineteenth century. The song's mass appeal can only have been boosted by the fact that it was often included in the musical programs of ballroom dance orchestras.

2. The chorus is also often called a refrain. To avoid possible confusion, we reserve use of the term "refrain" in this book for Tin Pan Alley song forms in which the refrain constitutes a main, independent part of the piece. See the discussion of Tin Pan Alley songs in Chapter 4.

songs, including "The Letter That Never Came" (1885) and "On the Banks of the Wabash, Far Away" (1899; later adopted as the official state song of Indiana). *Harry von Tilzer* (1872–1946), sometimes referred to as the "Daddy of Popular Song," was another successful turn-of-the-century songwriter; his big hits included "A Bird in a Gilded Cage" (1900) and "I Want a Girl (Just Like the Girl That Married Dear Old Dad)" (1911). Von Tilzer was a calculating composer: one of his hints for aspiring songwriters was to keep their tunes to a limited range so that even a baby could hum them. The songs of Dresser and von Tilzer represent the commercial peak of the nineteenth-century parlor song.

"Plantation songs," descended from the minstrel song tradition, were also popular. One of the best-known and most successful composers of plantation songs was *James A. Bland* (1854–1911), the first successful Black songwriter. An ex–minstrel show performer from a middle-class background, Bland wrote some seven hundred songs, including "Carry Me Back to Old Virginny" (1878; for a long time the official state song of Virginia) and "Oh, Dem Golden Slippers" (1879). He became popular in Europe, where he performed concerts for large fees. It has been argued that Bland's plantation songs featured a somewhat more dignified portrayal of American Blacks than the crude "Ethiopian" songs, but it is not easy to distinguish his lyrics of "In the Evening by the Moonlight" (1880) from those written by other composers of plantation songs:

> *All dem happy times we used to hab' will ne'er return again,*
> *Eb'rything was den so merry, gay and bright,*
> *And I neber will forget it, when our daily toil was ober,*
> *How we sang in de ebening by de moonlight.*

In stylistic terms also, Bland's songs are similar to those of his white contemporaries. Although Bland has been criticized by some later observers for pandering to white misconceptions about Blacks and lionized by others for his supposed championing of "authentic" African American music, the reality is more complex. Bland, the product of a comfortable middle-class home, was determined to achieve the same level of economic success as his white contemporaries. Like many other Black musicians who have sought to gain access to mass markets, he had to work through the stereotypical images of Blackness that were already established in mainstream popular music.

The Ragtime Craze, 1896–1918

While songs derived from European musical traditions like "After the Ball" dominated the popular mainstream of late nineteenth-century America, this same period also saw the intensification of African American musical influence, a trend best represented by the growth of **ragtime**. Ragtime music emerged in the 1880s, with its popularity peaking in the decade after the turn of the century. In some regards ragtime was a descendant of minstrelsy, in which white musicians used simplified elements of African American musical styles to spice up their performances. However, the ragtime style also represented a more intimate engagement with African American musical techniques and values that was largely due to the increasing—if still unequal—involvement of Black songwriters and performers in the music industry (see Box 2.1).

Although it is impossible to pinpoint the precise origins of ragtime, it is generally agreed that the word itself derives from the African American term "to rag," meaning to enliven a piece of music by shifting melodic accents onto the offbeats (a technique known as syncopation). This technique of playing "against the beat," when done competently, actually has the effect of intensifying the beat and creating rhythmic momentum. It has been suggested that the basic patterns of ragtime music came from music for the banjo, a stringed instrument developed by slave musicians from African prototypes during the early colonial period. Ragtime was also influenced by Latin American rhythms such as the Cuban habanera (see Chapter 1) and by marching band music, which contributed the regular "oom-pah" bass so common in ragtime pieces. During

BOX 2.1 SCOTT JOPLIN AND "MAPLE LEAF RAG"

The best-known composer of ragtime music was an African American composer and pianist named **Scott Joplin**, born in Texas in 1868. He began to play piano around the town of Texarkana during his teens and received instruction in classical music theory from a German teacher. His first regular job as a pianist was in a cafe in St. Louis. Like other Black pianists of the time, Joplin developed a "ragging" piano style in which he improvised around the themes of popular songs and marches in a syncopated manner. In 1893 he attended the World's Columbian Exposition in Chicago, where he heard influential Black ragtime pianists such as Tom Turpin and "Plunk" Henry (and may also have heard John Philip Sousa's band performing "After the Ball"). While in Chicago he widened his knowledge of ragtime style and started a brass band. The following year, Joplin moved to Sedalia, Missouri, where he was to write most of his famous compositions. Between 1895 and 1915 Joplin composed many of the classics of the ragtime repertoire and helped to popularize the style through his piano arrangements, which were published as sheet music. Joplin's rags were also widely heard on player pianos. These elaborate mechanical devices were activated by piano rolls—spools of paper with punched holes that controlled the movement of the piano's keys.

Scott Joplin's first successful piece was "Maple Leaf Rag" (composed in 1898), named after the Maple Leaf social club in Sedalia, where he often played. The piece was published in 1899 and became a huge hit, spreading Joplin's fame to Europe and beyond. Other ragtime piano pieces had been published earlier—ironically, the first was "Mississippi Rag" (1897) by the white songwriter and bandleader William Krell. But it was "Maple Leaf Rag" that started a nationwide craze for syncopated music. A version of the piece, performed by Joplin himself, was recorded in 1911 on a piano roll.

The form and style of "Maple Leaf Rag" are typical of "classic" ragtime. The piece is carefully composed, and Joplin plays it as written. "Maple Leaf" consists of a succession of four distinct themes, presented in the order AABBACCDD. This type of form is common in marches and shows the interrelationship of the two genres. The right hand (treble) part plays syncopated ("offbeat" or "staggered") rhythms against the regular bass part, played by the left hand—a typical feature of piano ragtime style. The bass rhythm is derived from marching band music and a popular ballroom dance called the two-step. Most of the rhythmic interest comes from the interplay of the two hands. Although the writing down of these patterns tended to neaten things up, the traditional African principle of pitting rhythms against one another was preserved in piano ragtime. Many jazz pianists took Joplin's composition and brought it back into oral tradition, treating it as the basis for extended, rhythmically complex improvisations (listen, for example, to Ferdinand "Jelly Roll" Morton's version of "Maple Leaf Rag").

Scott Joplin, c. 1911.

the height of its popularity, from the late 1890s until the end of World War I, ragtime music was played by every imaginable type of ensemble: dance bands, brass bands, country string bands, symphony orchestras, banjo and mandolin ensembles, and—in the so-called classic ragtime style—by solo pianists.

The first piece of sheet music to bear the term "rag" was the unfortunately titled "All Coons Look Alike to Me," composed by the African American songwriter Ernest Hogan and published (complete with racist caricatures on the cover) in 1896. The so-called "coon song," popular among white audiences from the 1890s until World War I, was usually accompanied by a simplified version of the syncopated rhythms of ragtime piano music. Most of these songs continued the old tradition of using a dialect that purported to be "typical" of Black Americans' speech. Coon songs, regarded as comic by white audiences, helped to promulgate the stereotypes previously established in the minstrel show during one of the worst periods of racism in American history (see the conclusion to this chapter).

Other ragtime-influenced songs were less derogatory in content, although they also owed less to the style developed by Joplin and other Black pianists than they did to the popular craze for march songs by composers such as George M. Cohan (1878–1942), author of "You're a Grand Old Flag" (1907). A few of these tunes can still be heard

"The Maple Leaf Rag" by Scott Joplin.

today, including "A Hot Time in the Old Town Tonight" (Theodore Metz, 1896) and "Bill Bailey, Won't You Please Come Home?" (Hughie Cannon, 1902).

The growing market for ragtime songs at the turn of the century suggests a continuation of the white fascination with African American music first evinced in minstrelsy. In general, Tin Pan Alley composers at this time simply added syncopated rhythms and ersatz Black dialects to spice up otherwise bland popular tunes. The idea, then as now, was to create songs novel enough to stimulate the audience's interest but not so radical that they required a great deal of work on the listener's part. Just as the songs performed by blackface minstrels were largely European in style, most popular ragtime songs were vigorous march-style songs with a few "irregular" rhythms added for effect.

Racial imagery—the Black "other" evoked in music and dialect and visually portrayed on the covers of sheet music—became complexly intertwined with social class and generational identity. Morality plays about the degeneracy of poor whites—say, the descent of a young woman into drug addiction and prostitution—often used ragtime (and association with Blacks in general) as an indicator of depravity. Logically enough, some young whites appear to have embraced ragtime as a means of rebelling against the cultural conservatism of their parents and other authority figures, a pattern that became even more prominent during the so-called Jazz Age of the 1920s and the rock 'n' roll era of the 1950s. Ragtime is an interesting example of the complex crosscurrents of American musical history: rooted in talented Black musicians' mastery of European musical forms, the style circulated throughout society, spanning boundaries of race, class, region, and generation and being put to different uses by various communities.

The Rise of the Phonograph

The phonograph was invented in 1877 by Thomas Alva Edison and, at around the same time, by a French inventor named Charles Cros. These early machines transformed the energy of sound waves into physical impressions on a foil- or wax-coated cylinder, which could then be used to reproduce the original sounds. In 1887 Emile Berliner developed the flat gramophone disc, which was more durable, cheaper to produce, and easier to store than wax cylinders. In the 1890s the first "nickelodeons"—machines that played the latest hits for a nickel—were set up in public places. (These machines later became known as jukeboxes, and the term nickelodeon came to be used for movie theaters that charged five-cent admission.) By the turn of the century the American market in phonograph discs was firmly dominated by two companies, Columbia Records (formed in 1887) and the Victor Talking Machine Company (1901). In 1902 the twelve-inch shellac disc was introduced. Played at a standard speed of 78 rpm (revolutions per minute), these discs could hold up to four minutes of music. In 1904 the double-sided disc was introduced. This was the standard type of record issued for sale in the United States until 33⅓ rpm long-playing discs and 45 rpm singles were introduced in the late 1940s (see Chapter 7).

The first phonograph, invented by Thomas Alva Edison in 1877.

The first phonographs were largely regarded as toys and mnemonic devices, useful for preserving the voices of family members and presidents, but not as tools for the commercial distribution of music. The dramatic commercial possibilities of sound recording were first revealed by the famous singer Enrico Caruso (1873–1921), who recorded a series of opera arias in London in 1902. The American rights to these recordings were bought by the Victor Company, which released the discs in 1904 after Caruso's American debut. The discs sold very well, indicating the popular appeal of classical music in the United States. Immediately following Caruso's death in 1921, the Victor Company sold more than $2 million worth of his discs. (This established the notion of "death sales," a strategy that has been repeated in the music industry's postmortem promotion of records by Hank Williams, Janis Joplin, Jimi Hendrix, Jim Morrison, Johnny Cash, Kurt Cobain, Selena, Michael Jackson, and David Bowie.)

Hit records in the years preceding World War I fall into two broad thematic categories. The unsettling effects of change—immigration, social and geographical mobility, and technological innovation—encouraged the continuing popularity of sentimental songs, including both nineteenth-century compositions like "Old Folks at Home" (1851) and "After the Ball" (1892), and newly composed nostalgic songs such as "In the Good Old Summer Time" (1902) and "Down by the Old Mill Stream" (1910). At the same time there was a strong interest in syncopated ragtime songs such as "Bill Bailey, Won't You Please Come Home?" (1902) and "Alexander's Ragtime Band" (1911), which represented the progressive, stimulating side of change. These two cultural themes— reverence for home, family, and the "good old days" versus the celebration of novelty

The phonograph's appeal knew no limitations of region, age, race, or social class. It is seen here in a fashionable home setting (1908) and in a humble cabin (1939).

and excitement—continue to figure prominently in American popular music today. Interestingly, some of the bestselling early recordings were not musical performances at all, but comic monologues such as "The Preacher and the Bear" (1905) and "laughing records"—basically three minutes of contagious guffawing.

The purchase of a phonograph for the home parlor was a symbol of upward mobility. There is evidence, however, that not everyone was wholly pleased with this change in the soundscape of domestic life. In 1904 a New York immigrant newspaper called the *Daily Forward* published an article entitled "The Victrola Season Has Begun" (Victrola was a brand name that had become virtually synonymous with "phonograph"):

> God sent us the Victrola, and you can't get away from it, unless you run to the park. As if we didn't have enough problems with cockroaches and children practicing the piano next door. . . . It's everywhere, this Victrola: in the tenements, the restaurants, the ice-cream parlors, the candy stores. You lock your door at night and are safe from burglars, but not from the Victrola. (Howe 1976, 127)

Despite such misgivings, the popularity of phonographs increased steadily in the years before World War I. It has been estimated that by 1904 one out of every twenty-two households in the United States had a phonograph. By 1909 over 26 million discs and cylinders were being produced every year, and the upward climb of the modern record industry was well underway. (The discs were initially regarded as an inducement to buy the fancy furniture that enclosed the record player, and companies such as Victor and Columbia made both the "software" discs and the "hardware" to play them.)

The introduction of the phonograph in the late nineteenth century gave rise to a set of important philosophical and aesthetic issues that continue to inspire debate up to the present day. The process of mechanical recording introduced a phenomenon that has been termed *schizophonia*, meaning the splitting of sounds from their original sources (Schafer 1977, 90). From this perspective, sound recording introduces a gap between the original context and meanings of music—its connections to community life and individual identity—and its existence as sound, a purely acoustic phenomenon that can be reproduced and consumed by a huge audience. This development is decried by some contemporary critics as leading to the dehumanization of music. Others have argued that it was precisely this split between musical sound and live musical performance that enabled the phonograph to disseminate music to millions of people in America and around the world, spreading some styles far beyond their communities of origin. From this viewpoint, recorded music has become a medium by which people who will never meet face to face can communicate with one another over wide geographical and cultural distances, and thus an important basis for the creation (and constant reinvention) of a distinctively American culture. Whatever one's position on these matters, there can be no denying that the introduction of the phonograph during the late nineteenth century was an epochal step in the development of popular music.

THE PERIOD AROUND the turn of the twentieth century was one of deep and pervasive change in American society. In 1890 fewer than one out of four Americans lived in communities with a population over twenty-five hundred; by 1920 more than half lived in urban areas. During this era the transcontinental railroad system was nearly completed, the automobile began to replace the horse and buggy, and the first manned flight took place (1903). These new forms of transportation were favorite themes for songwriters, who penned such immortal tunes as "In My Merry Oldsmobile" (Bryan-Edwards, 1905). The Spanish-American War (1898) expanded America's imperial designs and created a general feeling of optimism. Industrialization and good economic conditions were the twin motors for a rapid expansion of the American middle class, which was mostly white, Northern, and urban. Apart from a brief economic downturn in 1907, the era of good feeling lasted until World War I.

This optimism did not extend to Black America, for the period around the turn of the century was one of the most difficult in history for American Blacks. The Supreme Court's *Plessy v. Ferguson* decision (1896) confirmed the legality of racial segregation, and harsh "Jim Crow" laws were imposed throughout the South, where most of the descendants of Africans still lived. In 1900 alone 107 lynchings of Blacks by white mobs were reported. "Coon songs" with offensive lyrics—written, ironically, by both white and Black composers—were frequently published, often set to ragtime music. By this time the pattern that began with minstrelsy had been reinforced: the commercial mainstreaming of African American music—often in the watered-down form of mildly syncopated dance music—was coupled with the disenfranchisement and denigration of Black people themselves.

By the 1910s many basic elements of the modern music business were firmly in place: a pattern of fierce competition between publishing companies; mass promotion of songs, spread across several different media (newspapers, the theater, department stores, mail-order catalogs); a highly asymmetrical ratio between hit songs and duds; and the dominance of a limited set of musical forms and lyrical themes. As we shall see in the next three chapters, the 1920s and 1930s gave rise to a number of important shifts in the production and consumption of popular music, including the supplanting of sheet music by phonograph discs, the rise of network radio and sound film, and the increasing influence of African American genres such as jazz and the blues. Yet all of these new developments played themselves out within institutional and musical frameworks that had already been established by the beginning of the twentieth century.

Key Terms

minstrel show	strophes	vaudeville
ragtime	Tin Pan Alley	waltz

Key People

Charles K. Harris	James A. Bland	Scott Joplin
George Washington Dixon	John Philip Sousa	Stephen Collins Foster
Harry von Tilzer	Paul Dresser	Thomas Dartmouth Rice

Review Questions

1. Describe the different musical forms discussed in this chapter: strophic form, verse-chorus, multisectional/march form, standard AABA song form.
2. How did a parlor song differ from a plantation song?
3. What are the musical elements found in ragtime piano music?
4. How does a waltz differ from a march? Give an example of each.
5. Describe vaudeville. How did vaudeville differ from the minstrel show?

TIMELINE: 1900–1945

MAJOR EVENTS IN U. S. HISTORY	YEAR	IMPORTANT LANDMARKS IN AMERICAN POPULAR MUSIC
	c. 1900	Jazz emerges in New Orleans
W. E. B. DuBois publishes *The Souls of Black Folk*	1903	
Theodore Roosevelt elected president	1904	Double-sided 78 rpm disc introduced
	1908	Composer W. C. Handy opens the first black- owned music publishing house
National Association for the Advancement of Colored People (NAACP) founded	1909	
	1911	Irving Berlin's "Alexander's Ragtime Band" published, becoming his first major hit
Henry Ford establishes first mass-production assembly line in Detroit, Michigan	1913	Irene and Vernon Castle hire black bandleader James Reese Europe and create a sensation performing the tango on Broadway
Panama Canal completed	1914	• ASCAP (American Society of Composers, Authors, and Publishers) founded to protect the rights of composers • "St. Louis Blues" published, a major hit for W. C. Handy
Ku Klux Klan (KKK) re-formed in Georgia to fight integration and modern social trends	1915	

MAJOR EVENTS IN U. S. HISTORY	YEAR	IMPORTANT LANDMARKS IN AMERICAN POPULAR MUSIC
• United States enters World War I • "Great Migration" of blacks from the rural South to Northern cities begins	1917	First recordings by the Original Dixieland Jazz Band spark national jazz craze
Armistice ends World War I	1918	Joe "King" Oliver leaves New Orleans to bring his Creole Band to Chicago
 Eighteenth Amendment (Prohibition) outlaws the sale and transportation of alcohol in the United States	1919–1933	
• Nineteenth Amendment gives American women the right to vote • For the first time, a majority of Americans live in urban areas rather than on farms • Beginning of the Harlem Renaissance, rebirth of African American culture	1920	 • First commercial radio stations established in the United States • "Whispering" becomes the first of a string of hit records for self-proclaimed "King of Jazz" Paul Whiteman • Mamie Smith's "Crazy Blues" inaugurates a craze for blues records
	1921	• Record industry sells over 100 million discs for the first time • *Shuffle Along* (Sissle/Blake) becomes the first successful all-black musical on Broadway • Al Jolson has a major hit with his recording of "April Showers"
	1923	 • Fiddlin' John Carson makes his first record, launching the country music industry • Duke Ellington brings his Washingtonians to New York's Kentucky Club
	1924	George Gershwin's "Rhapsody in Blue" is premiered by Paul Whiteman's Orchestra

TIMELINE: 1900–1945

MAJOR EVENTS IN U. S. HISTORY	YEAR	IMPORTANT LANDMARKS IN AMERICAN POPULAR MUSIC
	1925	• Electronic recording begins with the introduction of the microphone • Bessie Smith and Louis Armstrong record "St. Louis Blues"
	1926	• Blind Lemon Jefferson's "That Black Snake Moan" demonstrates the power and marketability of country blues styles • First nationwide commercial radio network (NBC) established
 Charles Lindbergh makes the first successful solo transatlantic flight	1927	• *The Jazz Singer*, starring Al Jolson, introduces sound film • Ralph Peer records Jimmie Rodgers and the Carter Family in Bristol, Tennessee, inaugurating the careers of the first major stars of hillbilly music • Gene Austin records "My Blue Heaven," which becomes the bestselling record of its era
	1928	Louis Armstrong records "West End Blues," launching the era of the great jazz soloists
Great Depression begins with the collapse of the New York Stock Market	1929	Delta blues guitarist/singer Charley Patton makes his first record
	1930	Don Azpiazú's "The Peanut Vendor" is released in the United States; its popularity reinforces the marketability of Latin American popular music and dance
 Franklin D. Roosevelt elected to his first term as president; New Deals era begins	1932	

MAJOR EVENTS IN U. S. HISTORY	YEAR	IMPORTANT LANDMARKS IN AMERICAN POPULAR MUSIC
Social Security Act gives guarantee of income to senior citizens	1935	• *Your Hit* Parade debuts on network radio • California appearance of the Benny Goodman Band inaugurates the Swing Era
Gone With the Wind published	1936	• Robert Johnson records his "Cross Road Blues," which becomes a standard for postwar Chicago blues musicians and later blues rockers like Eric Clapton • Producer/jazz fan John Hammond brings Count Basie's band to New York City
	1938	Roy Acuff, the first true modern country star, joins the *Grand Ole Opry*
	1940	• BMI (Broadcast Music, Incorporated) is founded to challenge the ASCAP monopoly over the licensing of music • Woody Guthrie composes "This Land Is Your Land" in response to the popularity of Kate Smith's recording of "God Bless America"
Pearl Harbor attacked by the Japanese; United States enters World War II	1941	
	1942–1944	AFM (American Federation of Musicians) recording ban helps precipitate the decline of the big bands and the rise of solo singers and other nonunion musicians
	1943	*Oklahoma!* by Rodgers and Hammerstein, the first modern "book" musical, opens on Broadway
	1944	Columbus Day Riot over Frank Sinatra's appearance at New York's Paramount Theater marks the first documented example of pop-star hysteria
World War II ends with the surrender of Japan	1945	

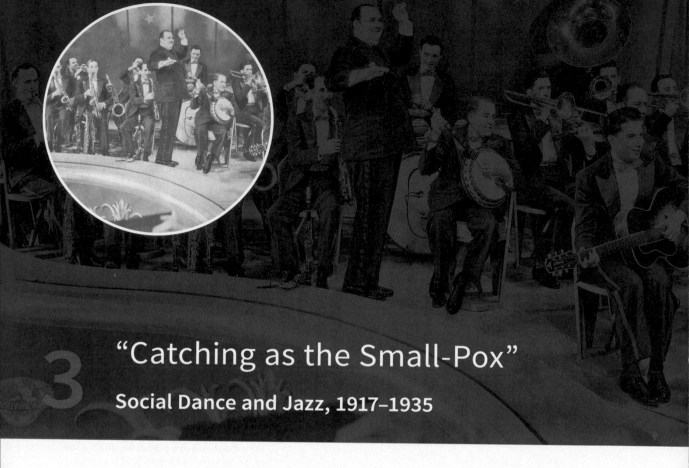

"Catching as the Small-Pox"

Social Dance and Jazz, 1917–1935

CHAPTERS 3 THROUGH 5 FOCUS ON THE 1920s AND EARLY 1930s, A PIVOTAL period in the history of American popular music. From World War I through the prosperity of the "Roaring Twenties" and into the depths of the Great Depression, mass media, the music business, and popular musical taste underwent a series of important changes. Although the popular songs and dance music of the so-called Jazz Age may sound old-fashioned to us now, these shifts in popular taste and the production and consumption of music established basic patterns that continue to affect us today.

World War I—regarded at the time as "the war to end all wars"—was a watershed event in the cultural history of the United States. The war reinforced American influence overseas, stimulated and reorganized the national economy, and demonstrated the horrifying as well as liberating possibilities of modern technology. The ready availability of jobs and development of the national transportation system during and after the war encouraged migration from the country to the city, as well as from the South to the North. Immigrants from central and eastern Europe continued to add to the cultural heterogeneity of the big cities, as they had during the first decade of the twentieth century.

The 1920s was a crucial period in the development of American popular culture. For the first time, millions of families owned a car, the quintessential symbol of independence and mobility. Telephones, which had previously been an exclusive luxury of the wealthy, now appeared in middle-class homes. Phonographs, **radio**, Hollywood films, and tabloid newspapers began to create a unified national popular culture, and a new generation of celebrity performers emerged, their faces and voices familiar to the inhabitants of cities, towns, and hamlets stretching from coast to coast. It was during this period that the modern American entertainment industry began to take shape.

The 1920s was also a period of mass law-breaking and social conflict. Modern organized crime rose to new heights during this time, partly in response to the possibilities for illegal profits offered by the Eighteenth Amendment to the Constitution of the United States (in effect 1919–1933), which prohibited the sale and transportation of alcohol. The Ku Klux Klan and other racist, anti-immigrant groups flourished during the 1920s and received a boost from the Great Depression, which threw millions of Americans out of work and exacerbated frictions between ethnic groups. Although African American traditions increasingly and directly influenced the popular culture of white America, the boundaries of racial segregation remained rigid.

During the 1920s unprecedented profit levels in the music business led to a bolstering of the centers of influence established at the end of the nineteenth century, especially the big music publishing firms and record companies in New York City. Organizations were set up to control the flow of profits from mass-reproduced music. The phonograph was introduced into millions of American homes, and advances in recording technology encouraged the development of new performance styles. Radio networks broadcast the latest songs and artists coast to coast, allowing people separated by thousands of miles to hear the same music simultaneously. The world of vaudeville entertainment went into a gradual decline, only to be supplanted in New York City's prestigious theater district, Broadway, by big musicals—extravaganzas featuring the songs of great Tin Pan Alley composers such as Irving Berlin, George Gershwin, Richard Rodgers, and Cole Porter. Hollywood films with synchronized sound—the "talkies"—became an important medium for promoting songs and "star" entertainers, and Los Angeles began to compete with New York City as a center of the national entertainment industry. Increasingly, the mass media shaped the daily experience of Americans, not only in the big cities, but also in towns and small rural communities throughout the country.

Technology and the Music Business

During the 1920s and 1930s the production and consumption of popular music was deeply influenced by new technologies, including radio and sound film, and by new institutions designed to protect the rights of composers and music publishers. While the Great Depression severely affected the phonograph and film industries, it helped to boost the popularity of radio, which provided consumers with a cheaper way to hear a variety of music, both recorded and live. The music industry became increasingly centralized during this period, and organizations were established to control profits accrued from the performance of popular music in Hollywood films and national radio broadcasts.

The record industry underwent a period of rapid expansion after World War I that was followed by a precipitous decline, caused in part by the introduction of radio and later exacerbated by the Great Depression. One important shift in the industry was its increasing reliance on phonograph records, rather than sheet music, as the main means of promoting songs and artists. The year 1919 saw the first hit song to be popularized in recorded form before it was released as sheet music. This song was "Mary," composed by George Stoddard and performed by Joseph C. Smith's Orchestra (one of the most popular dance bands of the time). The record, released by the Victor Company, sold a phenomenal 300,000 copies in three months and brought the composer $15,000 in royalties. Later that same year, Victor released the first phonograph record to sell a million copies—a fox-trot arrangement of the song "Dardanella," written by an African American composer named Johnny S. Black and performed by the Selvin Novelty Orchestra, a popular New York dance band. The term "novelty" was commonly used as a sales gimmick in those days. Selvin's version of the song "Dardanella" exemplifies the not uncommon genre of "Orientalism," in which "exotic" musical effects—in this case, banjos and a slithering saxophone—were employed, with the intention of sounding sufficiently unusual to be regarded as "Oriental." (There is a compound irony here, as a composer from one marginalized group wrote a song capitalizing on the stereotyping of another marginalized group in order to court success in the mainstream pop market. The song tells the story of an Arab sheik who professes his love for a woman and offers to add her to his harem.) The sales standard for hit records was raised again the following year, when a recording of the songs "Whispering" and "The Japanese Sandman" ("Oriental" exotica again!), performed by Paul Whiteman and His Ambassador Orchestra, sold 2 million copies worldwide.

By the early 1920s nearly 100 million records were being pressed each year in the United States. Records were no longer a byproduct of the manufacture of phonographs, and record companies no longer waited until sheet music sales of a given song had been exhausted before releasing a version of the song on record. In the mid-1920s an important threshold was crossed when total national sales of phonograph discs surpassed those of sheet music for the first time.

In 1925 electric recording, which used a new device called the **microphone**, replaced the older system of acoustic recording, in which performers had to project into a huge megaphone. While electric recording is regarded as a more "high-fidelity" technology than acoustic recording, its introduction also allowed recording engineers greater latitude in manipulating musical sounds to produce certain effects (e.g., inducing a feeling of intimacy between the singer and his or her listener). The development of the electric microphone allowed engineers to isolate and amplify particular sounds, including that of an individual human voice. As a result, a new manner of singing emerged, one that would have a significant impact on subsequent developments in American popular music. This intimate, gentle style, called **crooning**, was developed by a new generation of performers. Crooners such as Bing Crosby were the first modern superstars, with their public images carefully honed and promoted across various mass media.

The major competition for phonograph record companies came from a new medium, the radio network. Radio started out as a hobby for amateurs. In 1906 the first radio program in the United States—consisting of two musical selections and a poem—was broadcast from an experimental station in Massachusetts. After World War I the relaxation of military restrictions on broadcasting encouraged the growth of the industry. In 1920 the first three commercial radio stations in the United States were established: KDKA in Pittsburgh, WWJ in Detroit, and WJZ in Newark, New Jersey. Once it took root, commercial radio grew by leaps and bounds, with 564 stations licensed by 1922.

The idea of network radio was born in 1922 when telephone lines were used to transmit a running account of a football game from Chicago to New York. In 1926 the first nationwide commercial radio network—the National Broadcasting Company (NBC)—was established. Three other networks—the Columbia Broadcasting System (CBS), the Mutual Broadcasting System, and the American Broadcasting Company (ABC)—soon followed. By 1927 there were over one thousand radio stations in the United States.

Popular music was an important staple of commercial radio from its inception in the early 1920s. Stations carried live broadcasts of dance bands and singers, and the establishment of the national networks allowed a listener in Chicago or San Francisco to hear celebrities live from New York. The first music stars created by radio were the

Live radio broadcast at station WJZ, 1926.

Happiness Boys (Ernie Hare and Billy Jones), who began presenting their vaudeville-style act over WJZ in 1921. Increasingly, radio broadcasters went to the scene of musical performances rather than bringing the performers into the studio. The first such "remote" broadcast, recorded in 1921, featured a ballroom dance orchestra performing at the Hotel Pennsylvania in New York City.

The 1930s saw the further expansion of music broadcasting. Superstar crooners such as Rudy Vallee, Bing Crosby, and Russ Colombo competed for popularity on the air, sometimes engaging in well-publicized feuds. Sponsors—including cigarette, automobile, soap, and laxative companies—competed for access to the top shows and stars. The establishment of programs such as *Make Believe Ballroom* (1932) propelled **disc jockeys**—radio announcers who played records and provided entertaining patter, sometimes actually impersonating absent bandleaders—into an important position. Disc jockeys helped to demonstrate the commercial potential of radio by promoting the products of their shows' sponsors over the air.

Radio had a tremendous impact on the musical experience and social habits of Americans. During the Great Depression people who could not afford to buy a phonograph and discs were sometimes able to purchase a radio receiver and thereby enjoy a wide range of programming. Radio linked the smallest towns to the biggest cities and provided a source of excitement for working people. It became the most important medium for promoting songs and artists and for using music to sell other products.

Sound film, introduced in 1927, soon became an important means for the dissemination of popular music. The first film to exploit sound successfully was *The Jazz Singer* (1927), based on a successful Broadway play and starring Al Jolson, a vaudeville superstar of the 1910s and 1920s (see Box 4.2). The film, which tells the story of a Jewish cantor's son who becomes a success singing "jazz" songs in blackface, grossed the unprecedented sum of $3 million. Much of the film was silent, but sound was introduced at critical points, especially when Jolson sang several songs that had already been popularized on the vaudeville stage (such as "Toot Toot Tootsie" and "My Mammy"). The projectionist was provided with a set of single-sided 33⅓ rpm discs that contained the entire soundtrack of the film. He would mark certain points on the discs with colored crayon in order to allow precise synchronization of the film image with the music. (This technique is still employed today by old school hip-hop DJs, who use multiple turntables to create the "beats" that are key elements of rap performances.)

The first "all talking, all singing, all dancing" film musical, *The Broadway Melody*, was released by MGM in 1929. The film won an Oscar in 1930 for Best Picture of the Year, helping to establish musical cinema as a legitimate form. Within the period of a few years, the major Hollywood studios had produced over one hundred musical films.

Beginning in 1929 the Great Depression wiped out smaller studios and consolidated control in the hands of the major studios. In the period leading up to World War II, film became an increasingly important venue for popular music, challenging Broadway musical comedies and vaudeville shows. By the 1930s many of the biggest Tin Pan Alley music publishing firms had been bought up by Hollywood film companies.

Licensing and copyright agencies were set up to control the flow of profits from the sale and broadcast of popular music. ASCAP (the American Society of Composers, Authors, and Publishers) was founded in 1914 in an attempt to force all business establishments that featured live music to pay fees (royalties) for the public use of music. Until then copyright protection covered only the purchase and mechanical reproduction of published compositions; composers, lyricists, and publishers received no compensation from live performance of their music. After a series of legal battles that eventually reached the Supreme Court, ASCAP won its case in 1917, and all hotels, theaters, dance halls, cabarets, and restaurants were required to purchase a license from ASCAP before they could play music written or published by a member of the organization. Similar rulings were later handed down regarding radio stations and motion picture studios. By the 1920s almost all leading publishing houses and composers belonged to ASCAP, and by the mid-1930s some $10 million in licensing fees were being paid annually.

In the period between the two world wars the music industry exerted firm control over the production and promotion of popular music. The big recording and publishing companies couldn't really predict hit songs (any more than they can today), but they did limit the public's exposure to music outside the commercial mainstream. Apart from Tin Pan Alley songs (see Chapter 4) and the music of ballroom dance bands (see Chapter 6), the only other major forms of music available on phonograph discs were classical music, "race" and "hillbilly" records (see Chapter 5), and a variety of ethnic recordings, all of which were promoted to limited audiences. There was no serious competition for the big record companies, music publishers, and film studios, and the industry had an interest in making sure that things remained that way.

"Freak Dances": Turkey Trot and Tango

Around the beginning of the twentieth century, several fundamental changes took place in American social dancing that closely paralleled shifts in popular music. Most important was the intensified influence of African American dance, which had begun, quite indirectly, with the cakewalk dance of nineteenth-century minstrelsy. Starting around 1910 the craze for orchestrated versions of ragtime songs (see Chapter 2) gave rise to a succession of fads loosely based on Black styles, including the Texas Tommy, the turkey trot, the bunny hug, the grizzly bear, the Boston dip, the one-step, and—most popular of all—the foxtrot. Many of these ragtime dances appear to have developed initially in clubs and dance halls in cities such as San Francisco, Chicago, and Memphis, where they were observed by vaudeville entertainers who incorporated them into their acts. Professional dance teachers transmitted simplified versions of the steps to the public, and it was in this form that most ragtime dances made their way into the ballroom setting.[1]

---

1. A remarkable documentary tracing the development of African American social dance styles from the cakewalk era to the 1980s is *The Spirit Moves: A History of Black Social Dance on Film, 1900–1986* by Mura Dehn (issued on DVD in three parts, 2008, Dancetime Publications).

By World War I, a variety of ensembles were responding to public demand for the new styles of syncopated dance music. Although these groups varied in regard to both instrumentation and size, the typical cabaret dance band included a violin (the lead melodic instrument), two or more brass instruments, two or more reed instruments, and a "rhythm section" made up of piano, banjo or guitar, and drums, sometimes augmented by a string bass or tuba. At the grand balls of the nineteenth century, dance orchestras played music in strictly prearranged sequences, or "programs," but early twentieth-century dance bands began to make decisions on the spot, playing certain numbers in response to audience requests. A typical dance orchestra would have on hand arrangements in a variety of musical styles that were designed to accompany new dances such as the foxtrot and the tango, as well as the occasional nostalgic waltz. The popular songs of Tin Pan Alley, arranged either for a singer with dance band accompaniment or in a strictly instrumental setting, became a major portion of the dance music repertoire during this period. Responding to this emerging market, music publishers began to produce band arrangements of popular songs, complete with parts for individual instruments. This practice allowed dance bands across the country to perform the latest hit songs for local audiences.

The years around World War I saw the rise of hundreds of dance halls and cabarets in cities across America, set up to cash in on the succession of dance crazes that were sweeping the country. In big cities, restaurants and hotels built dance floors and hired live bands to entertain their customers. The cabaret—a term that by the mid-1910s had come to signify any establishment offering food, drinks, floor shows, and dancing—became both a laboratory for new dance steps and a major source of employment for musicians.

Dances such as the turkey trot represented a departure from the relatively restrained movements that had previously dominated social dancing among the white middle and upper classes. A newspaper article entitled "The Turkey Trot, Grizzly Bear and Other Naughty Diversions," published in 1912, included this description of the turkey trot:

> Starting as if in the good old-fashioned Two-Step, the dancers suddenly let go hands, the man slipping behind his fair companion, there is a little step and a hop, something like a turkey might be expected to do, then a fresh grip around the waist of the young lady, the man snuggles up ever so closely behind her and they hop, skip and jump and half run along. (Malnig 1992, 6)

While this may seem tame by today's standards, ragtime dances were regarded in some quarters as an outright threat to public morality. Mechanical devices called "bumpers" were sometimes inserted between the bodies of dancers to keep them separated by a respectable distance. The United Neighborhood Guild of Brooklyn went so far as to outlaw the turkey trot, the bunny hug, and other "shoulder-rocking, feet-dragging freak dances" within borough limits. As might be expected, the same moral authorities that disapproved of the new dance steps also took exception to the social contexts in which they were performed. Big-city cabarets were singled out for disapprobation, particularly after the prohibition of alcohol consumption in 1919, when they became associated with illicit activities such as drinking, gambling, and prostitution. Despite—or more likely because of—these associations, the "racy" cabaret atmosphere was increasingly emulated at dances held by fraternal organizations, social clubs, and ethnic associations in towns and cities across the country. Newspapers of the time reported the invasion of high-society balls by young people, who would secure a corner of the dance floor to perform the foxtrot.

Ragtime dancing and syncopated music went hand in hand. Popular African American bandleaders such as W. C. Handy, Wilbur Sweatman, Ford Dabney, and James Reese Europe (see the following section) composed ragtime arrangements specifically for the ballroom, and the most popular white orchestras of the day followed suit, including such numbers in their repertoire. Phonograph recordings of ragtime-influenced dance bands from the 1910s and early 1920s sound quite dated today, being typically rather rigid in rhythm and involving little or no improvisation. However, for most white Americans, who had little experience dancing to syncopated music, ragtime pieces apparently created a slightly disorienting or dizzying sensation. Descriptions of the time stress the titillating effect of offbeat rhythms, sometimes likening them to a pinch of pepper used to spice up an otherwise bland soup or stew. Of course, it is important to remember that the dancers' prior experience and cultural values conditioned these attributions of "spiciness." It seems likely that many African Americans would have found the mildly syncopated music performed by the most successful dance orchestras of the era neither stimulating nor scandalous.

Another stimulus for the general loosening up of American ballroom dancing was the tango, which developed during the late nineteenth century in Buenos Aires, Argentina (see Chapter 1). The tango—a blend of European ballroom dance music, Cuban habanera, Italian light opera, and the ballads of the Argentine *gauchos* (cowboys)—was introduced to New York City in 1910 by Maurice Mouvet, who performed the dance in a popular cabaret. The tango did not achieve mass popularity, however, until it appeared in a Broadway revue entitled *The Sunshine Girl* (1913), featuring the husband-and-wife dance team of Irene and Vernon Castle (see the next section). The Castles' performances of the tango and the turkey trot—actually rather staid versions of the original dances—created an immediate sensation and virtually eliminated the waltz from the musical comedy stage. The daring associations of the tango were reinforced by the rise of the so-called tango tea, an afternoon event at which society women took dance lessons (and sometimes formed romantic liaisons) with young male instructors. (Contemporary reports suggest that alcohol, not tea, was most commonly consumed at these events!) The tango craze soon encouraged the rise of other dance superstars, the most famous of whom was Rudolph Valentino, a dance teacher and gigolo who went on to become one of the great stars of silent film. Often cast in the stereotypical roles of the passionate Latin lover or fierce sheik, Valentino boosted the tango's popularity when he performed it in his first starring role, in the film *The Four Horsemen of the Apocalypse* (1921).

One of the main distinguishing features of the tango—and of the ragtime dances with which it was often alternated in an evening's dancing—was a bent-knee posture, quite different from the upright, straight-legged posture of earlier ballroom dances. This posture—common to many African-influenced dance traditions in the Americas—has the effect of freeing up the dancers' hips and upper body, and this mobility, when combined with the intimacy of contact between the male and female partner, was largely responsible for the morally daring aura that was attached to the tango. The Americanized tango popularized by Vernon and Irene Castle was a somewhat antiseptic version of the original, featuring a "promenade" in which the couple would embrace cheek to cheek and, with arms extended and knees bent, take long strides across the floor. As Irene Castle put it in her autobiography, "If Vernon had ever looked into my eyes with smoldering passion during the tango, we would have both burst out laughing" (Castle, Duncan, and Duncan 1980, 87).

The passionate associations of the tango were evoked musically by an insistent four-beat pulse, dramatic changes in volume, and sudden starts and stops. The typical instrumentation of a 1920s tango orchestra included a *bandoneón* (a kind of accordion), violin, bass, and piano. Performed onstage and in ballrooms and dance schools, and disseminated to a mass audience on phonograph records and silent films, the tango brought a new energy and intensity to American popular dance and the music that accompanied it.

James Reese Europe and the Castles

Vernon and Irene Castle—arguably the biggest media superstars of the years around World War I—seem unlikely candidates for the role of popular culture revolutionaries. Vernon Blyth was an Englishman who stumbled into American show business almost by accident, while Irene, born in New Rochelle, New York, had been rejected as a stage dancer for being too "awkward." Yet from 1912, when they debuted in New York City, until 1918, when Vernon was killed in a military airplane accident, the Castles did more than anyone to change the course of social dancing in America. They attracted millions of middle-class Americans into ballroom classes, expanded the stylistic range of popular dance, and established an image of mastery, charisma, and romance that later bore fruit in the work of dance teams such as Fred Astaire and Ginger Rogers (who played the Castles in a biographical film released in 1939). Patronized by the wealthy elites of New York City, the Castles democratized ballroom dance, bringing the elegance and excitement of the latest styles within the reach of millions of Americans.

Vernon was responsible for the couple's choreography and for breaking complex dance movements down into manageable sequences ("figures") that could be learned easily by nonprofessionals. Thus, while the tango was reputed to have 160 different figures, Vernon asserted that knowledge of six basic movements was sufficient for the "average ballroom Tango" (Castle and Castle 1914, 85). In a sense this process paralleled what publishers of sheet music had already done for decades in the realm of music—that is, producing simplified versions of songs for performance by people with little formal musical training. More importantly, Vernon Castle suggested that students "could do the Figures as they occur[red]" to them, in essence freeing dancers (especially the men) to create their own combinations of movements on the dance floor (Castle and Castle 1914, 108). This was a real departure from the practices of nineteenth-century ballroom dancing and an important source of the Castles' appeal—you could imitate their grace and virtuosity while (to a limited degree) doing your own thing on the dance floor.

The Castles' spectacular though brief reign as arbiters of popular taste relied in large part upon a savvy marketing campaign masterminded by a New York City socialite named Elizabeth Marbury. She wrote the laudatory introduction to the Castles' popular dance instruction manual, *Modern Dancing*, introduced them to the upper echelons of New York society, franchised their name and photographic image, and made sure that they took advantage of mass media such as newspapers and silent film. By the mid-1910s the Castles were being featured at such eponymous venues as Castle Park (at Coney Island), Castles-by-the-Sea (on Long Beach), and Castles-in-the-Air (on the roof of a theater in Manhattan), and their names appeared on clothing, phonograph records, books, and magazines. The promotional campaign for the Castles was a clear predecessor of the sort of cross-merchandising that is now commonplace in American show business and professional sports.

Vernon and Irene Castle in action.

Another key element in the Castles' success was their decision to hire a brilliant young African American musician as their musical director. *James Reese Europe* (1880–1919) was born into a middle-class family in Mobile, Alabama. In 1889 the family moved to Washington, DC, where young Jim Europe took violin and music theory lessons with the assistant director of the U.S. Marine Corps Band. Moving to New York City at the age of twenty-two, Europe found that there were few opportunities for even the most highly skilled Black musicians. He gradually developed a reputation as an accomplished pianist and conductor, playing ragtime piano in cabarets and acting as musical director for several all-Black vaudeville revues. In 1910 Europe founded the Clef Club, which functioned as a social club, booking agency, and trade union for African American musicians in New York City. (The main musicians' union, the American Federation of Musicians, did not admit Black performers.) He booked musicians into dance halls and ballrooms and staged concerts at Carnegie Hall with a 125-piece orchestra. These concerts attracted the attention of elite patrons and resulted in invitations to perform at private parties in New York, London, and Paris.

In 1913 Irene and Vernon Castle attended a private society party in New York City, where they danced to Europe's Clef Club Orchestra. Although they had already achieved some notoriety as dancers, the Castles were generally limited to dancing with whatever music the orchestra hired for a particular occasion could provide. These bands were often not able to provide the syncopated music required for the Castles' adaptations of ragtime dances, and Vernon realized immediately that Europe's band would be perfect for the job. From 1913 until 1918 Jim Europe composed music for all of the Castles' "new" dance steps and provided musicians for their live engagements. Although the instrumentation of Europe's Society Orchestra varied somewhat depending on context, a typical lineup included strings (violins, cello, and string bass), horns (cornet, clarinet, saxophone, trombone, and baritone horn), banjos, and drum set. Contemporary observers, both Black and white, emphasized the Europe band's superior ability to perform syncopated ragtime and tango arrangements and frequently remarked on the distinctiveness of their rhythmic approach and ensemble timbre. For many of Europe's high-society patrons, this music was an exciting and exotic, yet familiar brew.

While his career as a popular dance musician skyrocketed, Jim Europe continued to devote a great deal of energy to establishing a Black symphony orchestra that would specialize in performing the works of African American composers. These activities were interrupted in 1916, when Europe enlisted in the Fifteenth Infantry Regiment of the New York National Guard, an all-Black outfit. He was soon asked by his commander to form a military band. Since the best musicians in New York were reluctant to leave their regular jobs, Europe traveled to Puerto Rico to recruit players. Forbidden by U.S. Army regulations from fighting alongside white soldiers in World War I, Europe's outfit (now the 369th Infantry Regiment) was transferred to the French Army, which had already accepted African troops.

Europe's company—popularly known as the "Hell Fighters"—proved to be highly effective in combat and were the first Allied regiment to cross the Rhine River at the end of the war. The Hell Fighters Band played several concerts in Paris, creating a

Listening Guide "CASTLE HOUSE RAG"

Music by James Reese Europe; performed by James Reese Europe's Society Orchestra; recorded 1914[2]

In 1913 Europe's Society Orchestra became the first Black group to sign a contract with a record company. A series of recordings made by the Victor Company in 1914 includes the Society Orchestra's rendition of "Castle House Rag." While the sound quality of this recording is primitive by today's standards, it nonetheless gives us a sense of the style of Europe's band and some of its musical influences, including ragtime and marching band music. The recording was made by a relatively large version of the Society Orchestra, featuring violins, cellos, banjos, brass and wind instruments, and percussion (snare drum, cymbals, and orchestral bells). The musical form of "Castle House Rag" is typical of ragtime style (e.g., Scott Joplin's "Maple Leaf Rag"), with a series of themes arranged into a larger structure. In this case the structure is a bit more complicated: AABBACCDEEF. Each measure (basic rhythmic unit)[3] is two beats long.

LISTENING GUIDE	"CASTLE HOUSE RAG"		
TIME	**FORM**	**DESCRIPTIVE COMMENTS**	
0:00	Introduction (4 measures)	Violins foreshadow the syncopated melody of section A, while piano plays descending chords; section ends with cymbal crash	
0:04	A (16 measures)	Violins and piano play syncopated melody; snare drum plays march-like pattern that reinforces syncopations in the melody	
0:19	A (16 measures)	Repeat A	
0:35	B (16 measures)	New melody; section begins with dramatic effect, like a Sousa march; cymbal crashes and special (diminished) chords add to the dramatic effect. Second half of section is more ragtime-like.	
0:50	B (16 measures)	Repeat B	
1:06	A (16 measures)	Back to A	
1:21	Transition (4 measures)		
1:25	C (32 measures)	Section is relatively quiet, gentle: drums drop out and violins carry melody; stop time effect (where almost all the instruments drop out temporarily) featuring bells	
1:56	C (32 measures)	Repeat C	
2:26	D (16 measures)	Drums come back in, and the energy increases. The violins and trumpets introduce a new syncopated ragtime theme.	
2:41	E (16 measures)	Band plays collective improvisation on ragtime theme, led by cornet (Cricket Smith) and drums (Buddy Gilmore).	
2:56	E (16 measures)	Repeat E	
3:11	F (16 measures)	The intensity peaks! Drum solo, with other instruments playing stop time, ending with "shave and a haircut, two bits" figure	

---

2. The 1914 rendition of "Castle House Rag" by James Reese Europe's Society Orchestra is a low-fidelity acoustic recording made well before the advent of electronic microphones. A digitally recorded version of the piece is included on the album *Black Manhattan* by the Paragon Ragtime Orchestra (New World Records, 2003).

3. For a more complete discussion of the term "measure," see "Understanding Twelve-Bar Blues" in Chapter 5.

sensation and establishing the long-standing French enthusiasm for jazz. Returning to the United States in 1919, wearing the French government's Croix de Guerre, Europe took the Hell Fighters on a successful concert tour and began to lay plans for the next stage of his career. The Hell Fighters made a number of recordings for Pathé, a French company with a studio in New York. The future seemed bright for Jim Europe. But on May 9, 1919, he was stabbed by one of his band members after an argument and died that night. James Reese Europe, the most influential and popular African American musician of the early twentieth century, was buried with honors at Arlington Cemetery.

Jazz as Popular Music: The Original Dixieland Jazz Band, the Creole Jazz Band, and Louis Armstrong

Until World War I, the major influence on syncopated dance band music was ragtime. The next stage in the "African Americanization" of ballroom dance music was the so-called jazz craze, which began during World War I and continued through the 1920s.[4] Jazz—sometimes called "jass" or "hot music"—emerged in New Orleans, Louisiana, around 1900. New Orleans's position as a gateway between the United States and the Caribbean, its complexly stratified population—including culturally distinct white, Creole, and Black communities—and its strong residues of colonial French culture encouraged the formation of a hybrid musical culture unlike that of any other American city. The core impetus for jazz lay in the interaction between Black musicians, who tended to live "uptown" and had grown up surrounded by such African American musical genres as the spirituals and blues, and Creole musicians, who lived "downtown" and were more likely to have received formal European-style musical training.

There has been a good deal of argument about the origins of jazz. The term "jazz" itself carried multiple meanings in New Orleans, including strictly musical references ("speeding up" or "intensifying") and a variety of sexual associations. Jazz music emerged from the confluence of New Orleans's diverse musical traditions, which included ragtime, marching bands, the rhythms used in Mardi Gras and funerary processions, French and Italian opera, the Cuban habanera (referred to by early jazz musicians as "the Spanish tinge"), Tin Pan Alley songs, and both sacred (the spirituals) and secular (the blues) African American song traditions.

What were the earliest jazz bands like? The nineteenth-century dance music repertoire in New Orleans, as elsewhere, was dominated by the grand ball tradition, with its predetermined programs of polkas, mazurkas, schottisches, and quadrilles

---

4. In this chapter we are primarily concerned with jazz as a form of popular music, rather than with the internal evolution of jazz as an art form.

(see Chapter 2). Dance bands of the period typically included some combination of violin, guitar, mandolin, and string bass, and sometimes a wind instrument (clarinet or cornet, a close relative of the trumpet). A number of sources suggest that "hot" or "ratty" ragtime-based music was being performed in New Orleans by the 1890s, largely as an accompaniment for dancing. This sort of music was played at dance halls or honky-tonks such as the Pig Ankle and the Funky Butt, located in the city's tenderloin district. These often rowdy contexts for social dancing encouraged the addition of instruments such as the drum set, cornet or trumpet, trombone, and clarinet, which could project over the noise of a boisterous crowd. These wind and percussion instruments were also used in the large "official" bands connected with public institutions and the more informal neighborhood bands that performed in the streets during Mardi Gras.

Although jazz developed in New Orleans, the first recordings of the new music were made in New York City and Chicago. (This makes perfect sense when you consider that there were no recording studios in the South at that time.) The first recording to bear the designation "jass" was made in New York in 1917. It featured a white group from New Orleans called the Original Dixieland Jazz Band (ODJB). The leader of the group, cornet player *Nick LaRocca* (1889–1961), had started playing "hot music" with other white musicians as a teenager. The ODJB had already played for two years in Chicago before coming to New York to take up a steady engagement at Reisenweber's Restaurant in Manhattan. Within a few weeks the ODJB created a major sensation in New York City, attracting large crowds and quickly landing a recording contract with Victor Records. Their recording of "Livery Stable Blues" and "Dixieland Jass Band One-Step" was released in March 1917, and within a few weeks it had sparked a national fad for jazz music. The ODJB's biggest hit was their 1918 recording of "Tiger Rag," composed by LaRocca.

There is considerable controversy about the relationship of the music played by the ODJB, on the first phonograph recordings designated as jazz, to the style played by African American musicians in New Orleans. This controversy has been further fueled by the fact that the ODJB were white musicians who played and helped to commercialize a form of music pioneered by African American musicians. Nick LaRocca did not help matters with his patently false claim that white musicians in New Orleans had invented jazz. Those claims can be tested by juxtaposing the ODJB's 1918 recording of "Tiger Rag" with the 1923 recording of "Dipper Mouth Blues" by King Oliver's Creole Jazz Band, one of the first recordings of Black musicians from New Orleans. While the two ensembles are similar in structure, their approaches to the music are different in both style and sensibility.

While King Joe Oliver was an important figure in his own right, it may be that the most critical role he played was as a teacher and mentor of the brilliant young cornetist and singer *Louis Armstrong* (1901–1971). Armstrong, affectionately known as "Satchelmouth" or "Satchmo," built a six-decade musical career that challenges the

King Oliver's Creole Jazz Band in a pose that clearly references the "wilder," "novelty" aspects of African American jazz as it was perceived in the 1920s. (Compare to the more staid photographs of Paul Whiteman's band.)

distinction that is sometimes drawn between the artistic and commercial sides of jazz music. In addition to establishing certain core features of jazz—particularly its rhythmic drive, or swing, and its emphasis on solo instrumental virtuosity—Armstrong also profoundly influenced the development of mainstream popular singing during the 1920s and 1930s.

The outlines of Armstrong's early life are well known. He was born into poverty in the slums of New Orleans in August 1901, in what contemporaries called the "Black Black" (as opposed to Creole) community, and had his first encounter with the cornet at the age of twelve, in the band of the Colored Waifs Home. Armstrong emerged as an influential musician on the local scene in the years following World War I and subsequently migrated to Chicago to join the band of his mentor King (Joe) Oliver. In an interview years later, Armstrong recalled his arrival in Chicago with characteristically self-deprecating amusement:

> When I got to the Garden, King Oliver, Johnny Dodds, Honore Dutrey, Lil Hardin, Baby Dodds, Bill Johnson, were swinging some tune and it sounded so great until I was almost in doubt whether I should go in the place and report to Papa Joe or just go on back to N.O. on the next train. In fact, from the music that I was hearing I did not think I was good enough to ever sit in the band. Somebody must have told Joe Oliver about my dumbness— standing out there and refusing to come in—so Papa Joe came outside and

Listening Guide EARLY JAZZ RECORDINGS

"Tiger Rag," written by Nick LaRocca; performed by the Original Dixieland Jazz Band; recorded 1918

"Dipper Mouth Blues," written by King Joe Oliver; performed by the Creole Jazz Band; recorded 1923

Like many New Orleans jazz bands, the ODJB comprised a "frontline" of three wind instruments—cornet, clarinet, and trombone—and a rhythm section. In their recording of "Tiger Rag," made in New York in 1918, the rhythm section consists of piano and a "trap set," which includes snare drum, tom-tom, cymbals, and woodblock. (In live performance many bands also included a guitar or banjo and a string bass or tuba. Bass instruments were often left out of early recordings because of the tendency of low frequencies to make the needle of the acoustic recording machine jump.) Each instrument in this ensemble has a specific role. The cornet typically carries the main melody, with some embellishments; the clarinet weaves an active countermelody in and around the cornet part; and the trombone plays either a simple countermelody or the bass notes of the chords (sometimes using the "tailgate" technique of sliding or smearing from one note to the next). This style is sometimes referred to as "collective improvisation," since the players all simultaneously embellish their parts with personal touches. This music may also be called "polyphonic" ("many-sound") jazz, since in the earliest recordings all of the musicians tend to play together more or less continuously.

Another striking feature of this performance is the prevalence of syncopation. In our discussion of ragtime music, we noted that syncopation involves the accenting of offbeats and the creation of rhythms that pull against the main pulse of the music. In this piece the cornet player often plays a syncopated pattern, which places the rhythmic accents of his part between the regular pulses played by the rhythm section. The tension between the regular pulses and the syncopated patterns acts to intensify the forward propulsion of the dance rhythm.

How might this recording have struck the ear of an average white middle-class listener in 1918, someone accustomed to a diet of ballroom dance music and Tin Pan Alley songs? To begin with, the sheer energy of "Tiger Rag" must have been striking (and could have been exciting or repellant, depending on one's taste). The record starts abruptly, with all the players going full tilt, as though the needle has been dropped in the middle of an ongoing performance. The energy level remains high throughout, peaking at the end in a particularly intense

"shout chorus" (the classic "Hold That Tiger!" routine). This impression of unbridled intensity was an important part of the ODJB's appeal to an audience hungry for novelty and excitement (and perhaps had an effect parallel to that of early rock 'n' roll records on some listeners).

Like most rags, "Tiger Rag" consists of a series of musical phrases of regular length, presented one after the other and varied to hold the listener's interest. Unlike most popular music of the time, there is no strongly identifiable melody throughout much of the performance. This means that the listener's attention is focused on other aspects of the music, including the ensemble interaction, the variations played by individual instruments, and the rhythmic drive of the performance. The use of musical tricks such as stop time sequences (in which the band stops abruptly for a few beats and one instrument plays a brief solo) and unusual instrumental techniques (the glides and slides played by the trombone and clarinet) must only have increased the sense of novelty.

"Dipper Mouth Blues," recorded in April 1923, is one of the earliest recordings of African American jazz musicians from New Orleans, and it makes an instructive contrast with the recordings of the ODJB, released some five years earlier. Though the ODJB recordings were at the time much more successful in commercial terms, it is the Creole Band recordings that are now identified as the first authentic evidence of a mature jazz style. There can be little question about the superior musical artistry of the Creole Band, compared to which the ODJB sounds amateurish and even crass.

The Creole Jazz Band was led by the cornetist **King Joe Oliver** (1885–1938), who was born in rural Louisiana and moved to New Orleans as a youth, where he was inspired by the legendary cornetist Buddy Bolden. Beginning around 1907 Oliver played in brass bands, dance bands, and various small groups in New Orleans bars and cabarets, and the group he co-led with trombonist Kid Ory was considered the city's hottest in the 1910s. Oliver's popularity in New Orleans traversed economic and racial boundaries, and he was in demand for jobs ranging from rough working-class Black dance halls to white society debutante parties.

In 1918 Joe Oliver moved to Chicago to join the Creole Jazz Band, which had already established a reputation

(continued)

Listening Guide EARLY JAZZ RECORDINGS (*continued*)

LISTENING GUIDE | "TIGER RAG"

TIME	SECTION	DESCRIPTIVE COMMENTS
0:00	A	Entire band begins; cornet, clarinet, and trombone play countermelodies
0:15	B	Cornet and trombone alternate with clarinet
0:23	A	Repeat opening theme
0:31	C	Band playing countermelodies alternates with stop time sequences featuring clarinet
1:01	D	Drummer plays syncopated rhythms on woodblocks; countermelodies continue with brief clarinet stop times
1:32		Repeated band riff with clarinet freely improvising
2:03		"Hold that Tiger" riff with trombone slide
2:34		The "shout chorus"; whole group improvises, energy reaches a final peak

as the first New Orleans jazz band to tour outside of the South. In 1922 the group, led by Oliver, took up residence at Lincoln Gardens on Chicago's South Side, a balconied ballroom with a mirrored glass globe that threw beams of light around the dance floor. This iteration of the band was made up of leading jazz musicians, including Baby Dodds on drums, Honore Dutrey on trombone, Bill Johnson on bass and banjo, Johnny Dodds on clarinet, Memphis-born Lil Hardin on piano, and the twenty-two-year-old New Orleans cornetist Louis Armstrong playing second cornet.

A big part of the success of the Creole Band—and its excellent reputation in the eyes of contemporaneous musicians—can be attributed to Oliver's skill as a bandleader. He integrated his own cornet playing superbly with the playing of his ensemble and imposed strong, though not uncaring, discipline on his musicians. Like other early New Orleans cornetists, Oliver played in a style that emphasized short melodic phrases and a four-square rhythm, contrasting with the longer, more flowing, and more irregular phrases of the younger Armstrong (who will be discussed later in this section). He had a repertory of expressive musical gestures, some verging on theatrical novelty effects and others deriving from African American vocal styles. He was well known for his use of mutes, devices attached to the bell of the cornet that altered its volume and tone-color, including the plunger

mute "wah-wah" effects in his solo on "Dipper Mouth Blues." (This solo, which lasts three choruses, became part of the aural "textbook" of jazz and was memorized note-for-note by many trumpeters of the 1920s and 1930s.)

"Dipper Mouth Blues," although just as energetic as ODJB's "Tiger Rag," has a more relaxed and flowing rhythmic feeling, and its syncopations are played more smoothly. Improvisation plays a prominent role in the Creole Jazz Band's recording, while much of the musical material in ODJB recordings was prearranged and committed to memory. (Despite the fact that they played by ear, a comparison of different takes of the same pieces by the ODJB indicates that a great deal of their "spontaneity" was preplanned.) Although "Dipper Mouth Blues" has set melodies that establish its identity, the Creole Jazz Band's rendition of it is essentially an act of collective improvisation, grounded in African American musical aesthetics.

Only two minutes and eighteen seconds in length, "Dipper Mouth Blues," with its disciplined balance between composition (the melodies and harmonies that make the song recognizable) and improvisation (the solos and extemporized supporting parts), does not sound like any record made before it. To be fair, the differences between "Tiger Rag" and "Dipper Mouth Blues" may have as much to do with the five-year gap between them as with any absolute distinction between white and Black jazz styles. It has been suggested that the ODJB's recordings are rooted in the past—a tradition of semi-improvised ragtime ensemble playing common to white, Creole, and Black musicians in turn-of-the-century New Orleans—while the Creole Jazz Band recordings, featuring the brilliant young cornet player Louis Armstrong, point toward the future of jazz.

LISTENING GUIDE | "DIPPER MOUTH BLUES"

TIME	SECTION	DESCRIPTIVE COMMENTS
0:00	Introduction	Brief phrase played by cornets with stop time banjo chords
0:04	A (2x)	Blues form (see Chapter 5); the lead cornet plays the basic melody, while the second cornet, clarinet, and trombone improvise countermelodies around him
0:36	B (2x)	Clarinet solo by Johnny Dodds, accompanied by a stop time effect in the band
1:09	A	Return of opening strain; Armstrong takes over the lead cornet part
1:26	C (3x)	Cornet solo by Oliver using rubber plunger mute to create "wah-wah" effect, while band plays quietly in background; the end of Oliver's solo is marked by a musician shouting, "Oh, play that thing!"
2:14	A	The energetic "shout chorus," with the whole band improvising, and a brief "tag" to end

---

when he saw me, the first words that he said to me, "Come on in HEAH, you little dumb sombitch, we've been waiting for your Black ass all night. Ha ha." Then I was happy and at home just to hear his voice, and enjoyed every moment with him. (Giddins 2001)

Being required to play second cornet in support of King Joe Oliver developed Armstrong's musical sensitivity and knowledge of harmony and countermelody. In 1924, after playing with the Creole Jazz Band on what are regarded by many musicians and historians as the first real jazz records, Armstrong joined Fletcher Henderson's band in New York City, pushing the group in the direction of a hotter, more improvisatory style that helped to create the synthesis of jazz and ballroom dance music that would later be called swing (see Chapter 6). His sophisticated, flowing solos, with long syncopated phrases that seemed to depart from the structure of a song and then rejoin it, exerted a strong influence on New York jazz musicians. By the 1930s, as a result of his recordings and film and radio appearances, Armstrong was the best-known Black musician in the world. Between 1927 and 1939 he placed fifty-five singles in the Top 20, including his biggest hit, "All of Me," which was the bestselling record in America for two weeks in 1932.

Louis Armstrong's professional longevity was astounding. Although his popularity waned somewhat during the swing era and the 1950s, in 1964 he became the oldest musician ever to score a Number 1 hit with his version of "Hello Dolly!" (from the Broadway musical of the same name), the first single to push a Beatles record off the top of the charts.

Listening Guide   LOUIS ARMSTRONG: MASTER JAZZ TRUMPETER AND VOCALIST

"West End Blues," written by Joe Oliver; performed by Louis Armstrong and His Hot Five; recorded 1928

"Ain't Misbehavin'," written by Thomas Waller and Andy Razaf; performed by Louis Armstrong and His Orchestra; recorded 1929

Armstrong as Master Trumpeter

The most important and influential of Armstrong's recordings of the late 1920s is the instrumental "West End Blues" (1928), a piece that he had mastered while playing with King Joe Oliver, who composed it in honor of a popular picnic and entertainment area in New Orleans. Louis Armstrong and his Hot Five's recording of "West End Blues" had some commercial success, but its real importance lies in its impact on the development of jazz as an art form. As the jazz critic and musician Gunther Schuller once put it, "'West End Blues' served notice that jazz had the potential capacity to compete with the highest order of previously known musical expression. Like any profoundly creative innovation, 'West End Blues' summarized the past and predicted the future" (1968, 89).

The final moments of the recording sound carefully arranged, but Earl Hines later said, "How the ending was going to be we didn't know. We got to the end of it and Louis looked at me and I thought of the first thing I could think of, a little bit of classic thing that I did a long time ago and I did it five times and after I finished that, I held the chord and Louis gave the downbeat with his head and everybody hit the chord at the end" (Hines 1977).

"When it first came out," Hines said, "Louis and I stayed by that recording practically an hour and a half or two hours and we just knocked each other out because we had no idea it was gonna turn out as good as it did." The Hot Five's "West End Blues" is many things: a popular blues song, performed with grace and soul; a three-minute, seventeen-second intervention in jazz

LISTENING GUIDE | "WEST END BLUES"		
TIME	SECTION	DESCRIPTIVE COMMENTS
0:00	Opening cadenza	The piece opens with a startling fifteen-second trumpet cadenza—one of the most influential and hard-to-imitate solos in jazz history—Armstrong's virtuosity and expressive power on the trumpet were placed on full display for the first time. It falls into two sections, the first a serpentine melodic phrase that lands on a stirring high note, and the second a longer and equally complex descent to the lower register of the trumpet, full of surprises and changes of direction.
0:15	1st Chorus	The band establishes a slow, stately tempo; Armstrong plays the melody, with clarinetist Jimmy Strong first playing in harmony and then joining trombonist Fred Robinson to fill in between phrases.
0:50	2nd Chorus	The trombone takes the lead, with drummer Zutty Singleton switching to hand cymbals and pianist Earl Hines playing a steady tremolo (rapidly repeated notes) in the background.
1:24	3rd Chorus	Features a lugubrious call-and-response duet between the clarinet (playing in a low register) and Armstrong singing, introducing the wordless "scatting" technique that was to so profoundly impact jazz vocalists.

TIME	SECTION	DESCRIPTIVE COMMENTS
1:59	4th Chorus	Earl "Fatha" Hines, the great jazz pianist, takes over for the next chorus, playing an innovative and varied solo supported by a solid, steady "stride" in his left hand, while everyone else in the band listens.
2:33	5th Chorus	The final chorus of "West End Blues" is carefully arranged, with the clarinet holding a long note, the trombone playing squarely on the first beat of each phrase, and the banjo and piano holding the steady pulse together. Armstrong's elaboration on the melody takes off with him landing again on a sustained high note (held with a carefully modulated vibrato), and then a four-note, bluesy melodic pattern that pulls against the pulse, repeated five times in rapid sequence.
2:58	Tag	Introduced by piano riffs followed by concluding trumpet phrase.

history; and a performance that balances precomposed material and improvisation with extraordinary grace and skill.

Armstrong as Vocalist

Armstrong's **scat singing**—employing nonsense syllables—on "West End Blues" set the stage for the prominent featuring of his vocals on his following recordings. It was Armstrong's singing that helped establish him as a mainstream figure in popular music. His approach was radical for its time, in terms of both his vocal timbre and the extent of his departure from strict adherence to a song's original melody and lyrics. In its timbre, Armstrong's voice was anything but "pretty" in the conventional sense, but his intensity and enthusiasm dominated his singing to the extent that its rough-hewn quality came to be seen as an asset rather than as a liability. He opened the door to generations of singers who lacked "beautiful" voices but offered instead something more gripping and perhaps more "authentic" to their audiences: Muddy Waters, Big Mama Thornton, James Brown, Bob Dylan, and the list could go on and on. As an interpreter of song, Armstrong treated a song's melody and lyrics with the same freedom he brought to his work as an innovative jazz instrumentalist, utilizing his limitless imagination, his peerless musicianship, and his sense of humor to bring songs old and new to seemingly spontaneous life.

Armstrong was adding vocals to his recordings by the mid-1920s, and in 1929 scored a significant hit with "Ain't Misbehavin'," a song composed by *Thomas*

"Fats" Waller (1904–1943), with lyrics by Andy Razaf. "Ain't Misbehavin'" was featured in the Broadway show *Hot Chocolates* (1929), one of several successful Black musicals that followed in the wake of *Shuffle Along* (which will be discussed shortly in the section on "Dance Music in the 'Jazz Age'"). It is worth noting here that Fats Waller was himself a very popular Black entertainer who combined his prowess on an instrument (jazz piano) with singing, much in the mold of Armstrong.

Armstrong's recording of "Ain't Misbehavin'" features a complete sung refrain that is heard between two instrumental statements of the same music (both of these spotlighting Armstrong on solo trumpet). In singing "Ain't Misbehavin'," Armstrong freely omits some words from the original source to make some of his phrases more concise rhythmically. He also adds or repeats words to lengthen other phrases, and even inserts some brief scatsinging—at the end of the bridge ("B") section. He continually employs syncopation in inventive and unexpected ways. In other words, his singing employs jazz improvisation techniques to both lyrics and music; there is no separation between Armstrong's approach to playing his instrument and his approach to vocal performance. Nevertheless, the basic melody of "Ain't Misbehavin'" is always apparent, as is the import of the lyrics. Armstrong's fine sense of humor is on display during his final instrumental rendition of the refrain; in the first stop-time passage of that section, he quotes from George Gershwin's already-famous *Rhapsody in Blue*, and he later offers several "false endings"

(continued)

Listening Guide LOUIS ARMSTRONG: MASTER JAZZ TRUMPETER AND VOCALIST (*continued*)

Louis Armstrong in 1934.

before the ultimate breathtaking ascent to a concluding high note.

Although none of the leading jazz-influenced crooners of the 1930s—including the reigning pop superstar Bing Crosby—were able to directly appropriate Armstrong's rough, gravelly tone color, rhythmic drive, or gift for vocal improvisation, all were profoundly influenced by Armstrong's treatment of popular songs. His approach was shaped by the aesthetics of early New Orleans jazz, in which the cornet or trumpet player usually held the responsibility of stating the melody of the song being played. Throughout his career Armstrong often spoke of the importance of maintaining a balance between improvisation (or "routining," as he sometimes called it) and straightforward treatment of the melody. "Ain't no sense in playing a hundred notes if one will do," Armstrong is reported to have said on his seventieth birthday. In addition, Armstrong infused all of his vocal performances with his own warm and ebullient personality, making his approach a precursor to the highly personalized treatments of songs typical of later genres such as rhythm & blues and rock 'n' roll. Armstrong himself claimed that if it hadn't been for jazz, there would never have been rock 'n' roll.

LISTENING GUIDE	"AIN'T MISBEHAVIN'"	
TIME	**SECTION**	**DESCRIPTIVE COMMENTS**
0:00	A	Instrumental opening featuring Armstrong playing a muted trumpet
0:15	A'	Slight variation of the melody, continuing in trumpet
0:29	B	Contrasting ("bridge") section, featuring a violin
0:43	A'	Saxophones play the final section of the melody
0:58	A	*"No one to talk with ..."* Armstrong on vocal; note syncopation of the melody; scatting at the end
1:13	A'	*"I know a certain one ..."*
1:28	B	*"Jackie Horner, in the corner ..."*
1:43	A'	*"I don't stay out late ..."*

TIME	SECTION	DESCRIPTIVE COMMENTS
1:59	A	Trumpet resumes the lead, this time without mute (for contrast)
2:14	A'	
2:30	B	Dramatic ascending trumpet notes, building to the final section
2:46	A"	Note "false" endings, preceding the ultimate high note in the trumpet

And in 1988, some sixty-five years after his first groundbreaking recordings with King Joe Oliver, Louis Armstrong once again broke into the Top 40 with a rendition of "What a Wonderful World." (Originally released in 1967, the song's reappearance on the charts was catalyzed by its inclusion in the soundtrack for the film *Good Morning, Vietnam*, starring Robin Williams. When this, his last hit record, appeared, Armstrong had been dead for nearly seventeen years!)

In 1974 the Hot Five's 1928 recording of "West End Blues" was inducted into the Grammy Hall of Fame, and in 1990 Louis Armstrong was posthumously inducted into the Rock 'n' Roll Hall of Fame, a fitting tribute to the continuing influence of the man whom Bing Crosby asserted was "the beginning and the end of American music." In 2002, his Hot Five and Hot Seven recordings were inducted into the Library of Congress's National Recording Registry, the first year for this program that honors recordings of historic importance to American culture.

Dance Music in the "Jazz Age"

The recordings of the ODJB helped to spark an era in American popular culture that is commonly referred to as the Jazz Age. Although jazz music was initially regarded by the music industry as a passing fad or novelty, its impact on the popular music mainstream represented an important cultural shift. A new subculture emerged from the white upper and middle classes, symbolized by the "jazz babies" or "flappers" (emancipated young women with short skirts and bobbed hair) and "jazzbos" or "sheiks" (young men whose cool yet sensual comportment was modeled on that of the film star Rudolph Valentino). This movement involved a blend of elements from "high culture"—the novels of F. Scott Fitzgerald, the paintings of Pablo Picasso, the plays of Eugene O'Neill—and popular culture, particularly styles of music, dance, and speech that were modeled on Black American prototypes. The idea of the Jazz Age was promoted by the mass media, especially the burgeoning Hollywood film industry.

Following on the heels of the ragtime fad, the jazz craze represented the intensification of African American influence on the musical tastes and buying habits of white Americans. This process did provide expanded opportunities for some Black musicians, including the songwriting team of *Noble Sissle* (1899–1975) and *Eubie Blake* (1887–1983), who had begun their career with James Reese Europe's orchestra in 1916. In 1921 Sissle and Blake launched the first successful all-Black Broadway musical, *Shuffle Along*. This show, which included jazz-influenced songs such as "I'm Just Wild about Harry," was innovative in a number of regards. It was one of the first shows to portray romantic relationships between Black characters without resorting to degrading stereotypes, and it even included a "serious" love duet entitled "Love Will Find a Way." (It is reported that the promoters of *Shuffle Along* sat near the stage door the first night, fearing that violence would break out when the song was premiered!)

The continued viability of this show, and the continuing historical interest surrounding it, was made evident in 2016 by the Broadway production of *Shuffle Along, or the Making of the Musical Sensation of 1921 and All That Followed*, which revived the music and the book of the 1921 hit while telling the backstage stories of its original production.

The seating arrangements for the 1921 *Shuffle Along* were also innovative—for the first time, Blacks, usually restricted to the balconies of theaters, could sit in sections previously reserved for whites. The Jazz Age was also an era of racial inequality, however, in which the first successful sound film, *The Jazz Singer*, featured a white vaudevillian performer singing in blackface. African American musicians still had to adapt to white stereotypes. For example, the orchestra of *Shuffle Along*—comprising sophisticated and fully literate musicians—had to memorize their parts so they could appear to be playing by ear. "White people didn't believe that Black people could read music," Blake later explained. "They wanted to think that our ability was just natural talent" (Morgan and Barlow 1992, 113).

While the jazz craze did increase opportunities for some Black musicians, the world of dance orchestras remained strictly segregated. The most successful Black dance bands of the 1920s—McKinney's Cotton Pickers and the Luis Russell, Bennie Moten, Duke Ellington, and Fletcher Henderson orchestras—were able to extend their appeal across racial boundaries. Although the record companies began in the mid-1920s to establish special segregated catalogs for "race music" (see Chapter 5), the most popular Black dance bands were listed in the mainstream popular catalogs as well. African American musicians appeared with increasing frequency in fancy downtown cabarets and hotel ballrooms (although they could enter these places only as employees, not as customers). During the late 1920s white jazz fans began to frequent nightclubs in African American neighborhoods. In New York's Harlem and the South Side of Chicago, these "Black and tan" cabarets offered their predominantly white clientele an exotic array of jazz music, floor shows with scantily clad dancers, fancy drinks, and images of Africa and the Orient. Performing at Harlem's famous Cotton Club, the great jazz pianist and

Noble Sissle (standing) and Eubie Blake (at piano), c. 1920s.

composer Duke Ellington developed a style that he called "jungle music," which featured dense textures and dark, growling timbres. (In later, more politically correct times, Ellington bemusedly referred to his early style as "rainforest music"!) As in earlier periods, African American musicians had to work through the stereotypes of Blackness that were prevalent in white society. Nonetheless, there is no denying that the 1920s saw an expansion of opportunities for Black musicians in the cosmopolitan centers of the North.

It will come as no surprise that the most economically successful dance bands of the 1920s and 1930s were led and staffed by white musicians. Many bands maintained a "book" of written arrangements representing various styles of music—jazz numbers, Tin Pan Alley songs, and even the occasional waltz. As dozens of bands sprang up to feed the social dance craze, increasing competition encouraged bandleaders to focus on attracting particular segments of the audience. (This tendency was reinforced after 1929, when the Great Depression cut into the market for live and recorded music.) Many bands tended to specialize in one of three main categories: "hot," "sweet," or "Latin." The hot bands, including the Coon-Sanders Nighthawks, the Jean Goldkette Orchestra, and the Casa Loma Orchestra, specialized in syncopated jazz arrangements.

These bands were particularly popular at college dances. Sweet bands, like Guy Lombardo and His Royal Canadians, played romantic and nostalgic music. Although Lombardo's band was ridiculed by jazz fans for its "cornball" or "Mickey Mouse" style, the Canadians went on to sell over 100 million records. (The great jazz trumpeter Louis Armstrong praised the band for its warm sound and high standards of musicianship. For his part, Lombardo claimed that Black audiences loved his music, as long as he didn't try to play *their* music!) "Charmaine!" was released by Columbia Records in 1927 and was the first of Lombardo's twenty-six Number 1 hits, dominating the charts for seven weeks. This recording is a good example of the sweet dance band style, with a light beat that seems almost to float above the ground. The fact that "Charmaine!" is a waltz song with a sentimental lyric must only have added to its nostalgic effect.

PAUL WHITEMAN

By far the most successful dance band of the 1920s was the Ambassador Orchestra, led by *Paul Whiteman* (1890–1967). Even now it is hard to comprehend the scale of Whiteman's commercial success, which in some regards has not been equaled by any musician since. Like James Reese Europe before him, Whiteman was both a fine musician and an astute businessman. However, his role in the history of jazz is ambiguous. On the one hand, his assumption of the title "King of Jazz" was clearly a public relations ploy, part of an attempt to promote a watered-down, "safe" version of jazz to the public. Whiteman's claim that he had "made an honest woman out of jazz" only threw fuel on the fire, as it seemed to some to imply that African American music needed uplifting by white musicians. On the other hand, Whiteman did make some important contributions to jazz, widening the market for jazz-based dance music (and paving the way for the swing era), hiring brilliant young jazz players and arrangers, and establishing a level of professionalism that was widely imitated by dance bands on both sides of the color line. He also defended jazz against its moral critics (whom he called "jazz-klanners") and carried on aspects of Jim Europe's vision of a symphonic version of jazz. In fact, the 1924 debut of George Gershwin's *Rhapsody in Blue* featured Whiteman's band.

Born in Denver, Colorado, Paul Whiteman began studying music at the age of seven. He initially heard syncopated dance music while he was living in San Francisco before World War I. Soon thereafter he formed a seven-piece dance band, which played around the area until 1916, when he enlisted in the U.S. Navy. During the war he directed a forty-piece concert band. After the war, his band played at a hotel in Los Angeles, becoming a favorite of Hollywood film stars, and in 1919 moved to Atlantic City, New Jersey. That same year, Whiteman made his first recordings, including instrumental versions of "Whispering" and "The Japanese Sandman," which, as we have already noted, set a new sales record.

"Whispering" contained the musical seeds of Whiteman's future successes. The arrangement is played at a medium tempo, with a straightforward, bouncy foxtrot rhythm that was appropriate for ballroom dancing in the style popularized by Irene and Vernon Castle. After a brief introduction, the main melody is introduced on the cornet and violin. The second time through, the melody is picked up by the Swanee (slide)

Paul Whiteman and his Orchestra, in the film *The King of Jazz*, 1928.

whistle, a novelty that apparently played an important part in selling the record. (After Whiteman's hit recording, it became almost unthinkable to perform "Whispering" without at least one chorus of whistling.) In the last chorus, the lead instruments take a somewhat looser, more syncopated approach to the melody, although the spontaneity is kept within careful limits. Hints of jazz influence in "Whispering" include a strummed banjo that stresses the offbeats; a bit of syncopation in the cornet and trombone parts, and especially in the last chorus; and some mildly energetic woodblock playing by the drummer, vaguely reminiscent of the ODJB.

This mixture of syncopation and careful arrangement, rhythmic pep and gentility, was to become the core of Whiteman's symphonic jazz. As the record quickly sold out of stores nationwide, the Victor Company realized that it had a gold mine on its hands. Whiteman's first record not only challenged the sales of reigning recording stars such as John Philip Sousa and Enrico Caruso but also surpassed the success of the ODJB recordings. There is even evidence that the Victor Company urged the ODJB to adopt Whiteman's "sweeter" approach to syncopated dance music on its last recordings.

"Whispering" was the first of an amazing string of hit records. Between 1920 and 1934 the Whiteman band had twenty-eight Number 1 records and 150 records that ranked among the Top 10, a feat unmatched by any other recording artist in the entire history of American popular music. His orchestra, which comprised only ten players in 1920, had expanded to more than twenty by the end of the decade. In 1927 Whiteman began to hire some of the leading white jazz musicians of the time, including the brilliant cornetist Bix Beiderbecke and the Dorsey brothers, Jimmy and Tommy, who would later achieve success as bandleaders in the swing era (see Chapter 6). At concerts and dances he used a small "band-within-a-band," made up of the best jazz musicians in his orchestra, to play "hot" music. Whiteman hired pioneering dance band arrangers—Ferde Grofé and Bill Challis—to craft his band's book (library of music), and he helped to promote jazz-influenced crooners such as Bing Crosby. Like the Castles, Whiteman franchised his music and his image. (A good-humored, portly man with a pencil-thin moustache, Whiteman embodied the good times and cheer of the years before the Great Depression.) By 1930 there were eleven official Paul Whiteman bands playing official Paul Whiteman arrangements in New York City, seventeen Paul Whiteman bands on the road, and forty others established in hotels and dance halls around the country. The "King of Jazz" had become an industry.

Whiteman's autobiography, entitled simply *Jazz*, gives us some insight into the attitudes and experiences that shaped his career. Early on in the book he describes an epochal event in his life, which occurred when a fellow classical musician took him to a dance hall in San Francisco:

> We ambled at length into a mad house. Men and women were whirling and twirling feverishly there. Sometimes they snapped their fingers and yelled loud enough to drown the music—if music it was. My whole body began to sit up and take notice. It was like coming out of the Blackness into bright light. My blues faded when treated to the Georgia blues that some trombonist was wailing about. My head was dizzy, but my feet seemed to understand that tune. They began to pat wildly. I wanted to whoop. I wanted to dance. I wanted to sing. I did them all. Raucous? Yes. Crude—undoubtedly. Unmusical—sure as you live. But rhythmic, catching as the small-pox and spirit-lifting. That was jazz then. I liked it, though it puzzled me. Even then it seemed to me to have vitality, sincerity and truth in it. In spite of its uncouthness, it was trying to say something peculiarly American, just as an uneducated man struggles ungrammatically to express a true and original idea. (Whiteman and McBride 1974, 33)

Although Whiteman meant this description as a defense of the inherent value of jazz—he considered himself a "jazz missionary"—this excerpt also illustrates a less laudable set of attitudes common among white Americans in the 1920s and 1930s. Jazz music, and African American culture more generally, were defined either negatively ("raucous," "crude") or by the absence of certain criteria of civilization (couthness, musicality, grammaticality). The references to "fever" and "small-pox" suggest that the point of contact between Black and white culture—described earlier as a "smoke-hazed, beer-fumed room"—was regarded as a zone of potential contagion. Whiteman's description of his jazz epiphany was couched in terms of a set of values common to millions of white Americans during the 1920s (and shared to some degree by many members of the African American middle class).

Whiteman begins his book by identifying African music and the slave trade as origin points of jazz: "Jazz came to America three hundred years ago in chains." But African Americans are as absent from the rest of his story as they were from his orchestra. Whiteman demonstrates the hybrid nature of his music by referring to the cultural diversity of his musicians: Italians, Irishmen, Scots, Norwegians, and Germans! This whitewashed image of what Whiteman called "America's melting pot" is even more strikingly presented in the 1930 sound film *The King of Jazz*, in which Whiteman appears as a magician stirring a bubbling cauldron into which all of the ingredients of jazz are thrown, one after the other. We are shown English ballads, Scottish bagpipes, an Irish jig, an Austrian waltz, Italian opera, Spanish flamenco, and even Russian balalaikas, but there is no evidence at all of the ethnic groups most responsible for the creation of jazz (African Americans) and its inclusion in popular song, theater, and film (Jewish immigrants). These striking absences give us a glimpse of the limits of white middle-class perceptions of American culture during the 1920s.

Caricature of Paul Whiteman by Miguel Covarrubias, c. 1924. Whiteman is shown holding sheet music, and a viola (Whiteman's first instrument) is encompassed within the image.

While it is easy to regard the music labeled as jazz by the recording industry as a watered-down version of the improvised "hot" music pioneered by musicians in New Orleans, some religious and political authorities fiercely criticized the influence of jazz music on white youth. Jazz was widely associated with feeble-mindedness, crime, and immorality and explicitly linked with immigration and interracial sex as primary causes of national degeneration. A survey of articles published in the *New York Times*—generally regarded as a paragon of responsible journalism—reveals a pattern of association among jazz, social dancing, and various forms of "deviance," including alcohol consumption, indiscriminate sex, effeminacy, suicide, bestiality, insanity, and indigestion (Merriam 1964, 241–44). A religious authority quoted in the *Times* in 1934 asserted that "jazz was borrowed from Central Africa by a gang of wealthy international Bolshevists from America, their aim being to strike at Christian civilization throughout the world" (Merriam 1964, 243). The frequency of references to Africa, "savagery," "cannibalism," and "cave men" in these moralistic criticisms of jazz suggests that their primary motivation was really to prevent musical mixing between Blacks and whites out of fear that this intermingling might encourage interracial miscegenation and thus compromise the social privileges enjoyed by whites.

What factors contributed to the tremendous impact of jazz on mainstream popular music? First, the new music from New Orleans arrived at just the right moment to feed into the craze for syncopated dance music that had already swept the nation. It is clear that the white audience for such music initially regarded jazz basically as an updated form of ragtime, and many of the most popular early jazz band recordings feature music that is basically indistinguishable from ragtime. There is abundant evidence that jazz was from the beginning positioned in the music business as a kind of novelty music, or, as Duke Ellington once put it, a form of musical "stunt." Early recordings of jazz-influenced popular music often included raucous effects such as barnyard animal noises, and advertisements for popular jazz bands featured wacky poses, silly hats, and carnival-like attractions. (The African American bandleader Wilbur Sweatman was advertised for his

Listening Guide   "EAST ST. LOUIS TOODLE-OO"

Written by Duke Ellington and Bubber Miley; performed by Duke Ellington and His Washingtonians; recorded 1927

Among the African American dance bands of the late 1920s and early 1930s, none was more interesting in musical terms than the Washingtonians, led by **Edward Kennedy "Duke" Ellington** (1899–1974). Ellington is widely regarded as one of the most important American musicians of the twentieth century. Born in Washington, DC, the son of a Navy blueprint maker and a teacher, both of whom were amateur pianists, Ellington came from a middle-class background and received formal musical training at a young age. While his parents preferred genteel parlor songs and operatic airs, at the age of fourteen Ellington began to hang around the bars and pool halls where ragtime pianists played, and he formed his first dance band while still in high school. From 1917 through 1919 Ellington launched his musical career, painting commercial signs by day and playing piano with his band—The Duke's Serenaders—by night. His entrepreneurial side and personal charm were in evidence from early on: when customers would ask him to make a sign for a dance or a party, he would ask them if they had musical entertainment; if not, Ellington would ask if he could play for them. Ellington's sophisticated, refined manner was reinforced by his regal nickname, which he credited to a childhood friend: "I think he felt that in order for me to be eligible for his constant companionship, I should have a title. So he called me Duke" (Ellington 1976, 20).

In the early 1920s Ellington's band, rechristened the Washingtonians, began playing syncopated dance music in New Jersey and New York City. In 1923 an expanded and improved version of the band, including musicians from New York, Washington, DC, Boston, and, eventually, New Orleans, debuted at a Broadway nightspot called the Kentucky Club. This four-year engagement provided a steady income for Ellington and the band as well as a venue for developing his music. They made their first recording in 1924, and three years later, the Washingtonians were heard by a song publisher and promoter named Irving Mills, who arranged a recording contract for them with Columbia Records. Mills also secured them a regular engagement at the renowned Cotton Club in Harlem—an offer that King Joe Oliver had unwisely turned down—where the band played for dancers and accompanied exotic revues. There they developed Ellington's "jungle music" style, characterized by dense textures, complex harmonies, and muted, growling sounds in the brass. While this style reinforced the stereotypes of Black culture that many of the white patrons of the Cotton Club came to see and hear, it also provided Ellington with the basis for a unique approach to big band arrangement. Radio broadcasts from the club made Ellington famous across America and also gave him the financial security to assemble a top-notch band.

While he had the same basic musical resources at hand as other big band arrangers, Ellington was an experimenter. Although he was a fine jazz pianist, it has with some justification been said that the orchestra was Ellington's real instrument. He devised unusual musical forms, combined instruments in unusual ways, and created complex, distinctive tone colors, sometimes by putting instruments in extreme registers (e.g., the clarinet playing the lowest note and the trombone the highest note in a chord). Ellington was also a painter, and he described his approach to big band arranging as akin to creating visual textures. Ellington's experiments were aided by the remarkable stability of his band, some of whose members worked with him for almost fifty years. (The baritone saxophonist on "East St. Louis Toodle-Oo," Harry Carney, worked with Ellington from 1927 to 1974, dying just four months after Duke.) Ellington grew to know the individual players' strengths and weaknesses and often wrote parts specifically for particular musicians. Though no one could doubt that Duke was the leader, his band was always a collaborative enterprise.

"East St. Louis Toodle-Oo," recorded in 1927, was the Washingtonians' theme song and is a good illustration of Ellington's early style that was on show at the Cotton Club. The song was originally titled "East St. Louis Toad Low" and was intended to evoke the slow gait of an old man bent over with arthritis, walking low as a toad. The recording features trumpeter **James "Bubber" Miley** (1903–1932), a South Carolina–born musician who had heard King Joe

Duke Ellington and His Orchestra, c. 1930.

Oliver as a young man and was strongly influenced by Oliver's use of mutes. Miley created his signature sound—much in evidence on "East St. Louis Toodle-Oo," a piece he cowrote with Ellington—by combining two types of mutes and creating a deep growl in his throat, which made it sound as though his trumpet were talking. Though Miley left the Washingtonians in 1929 and died three years later of the effects of alcoholism, he exerted an important impact on the sound and style of Ellington's band. (It is a reminder of the times to note that after leaving Ellington Miley spent some time playing with an otherwise all-white society band that required him to either stand behind a screen or dress as an usher and stand off to the side of the stage when he played.)

The Washingtonians were a ten-piece band with six horns (three brass and three reeds) and a rhythm section of piano, bass, drums, and banjo. This recording reflects the ragtime- and jazz-influenced style of syncopated dance music in the late 1920s. The band's bouncy, "two-beat" rhythm, with the banjo playing sharply on the offbeats, is reflective of the dance styles of the time.

This tongue-in-cheek musical portrait of an old man approaching the end of his days, performed by a group of twentysomething musicians, gives us a glimpse of the skill and talent that would in later years position Duke Ellington as one of the towering figures of twentieth-century American music. Ellington's music arguably reached its pinnacle during the swing era, and his contributions during that period will receive attention in Chapter 6.

LISTENING GUIDE	"EAST ST. LOUIS TOODLE-OO"	
TIME	SECTION	DESCRIPTIVE COMMENTS
0:00	Introduction	The reeds play a sinuous melodic line, which rises and then falls gradually.
0:11	A (repeated once)	Bubber Miley enters and plays a solo over the reed line, using his mutes and vocal cords to create a dark, buzzing timbre, an important dimension of the band's "jungle music" sound.
0:35	B	In the middle of Miley's solo, a new melody and set of harmonies is introduced, shifting briefly from a dark, brooding minor key to a more upbeat major key.

(continued)

Listening Guide "EAST ST. LOUIS TOODLE-OO" (*continued*)

TIME	SECTION	DESCRIPTIVE COMMENTS
0:49	A	Miley returns to the minor opening theme.
1:01	C	Trombone solo by "Tricky Sam" Nanton in a major key (accompanied only by the rhythm section and baritone sax)
1:27	A	Clarinet solo by Rudy Jackson (playing over a restatement of the opening melody in the reeds). During the second statement of the melody, listen for drummer Sonny Greer's syncopated "splashes" on the cymbals, which he uses to punctuate and add excitement to the clarinet solo.
1:50	C	Ellington's arranging skills come to the fore, as the brass and reed instruments play a melody together in harmony.
2:20	C	This time only the reeds playing the melody in harmony.
2:33	C	Brass and reeds play together again.
2:47	A	Abbreviated return of opening theme on muted trumpet.

ability to play three clarinets at the same time!) From the point of view of many in its white audience, jazz was heady, daring, humorous, and slightly dangerous, a way to experience Black culture without having to come into close proximity with Black people.

In addition, the potential audience for jazz was expanded as a result of the great South–North migration that started during World War I. Seeking employment in the factories built during the war and in other businesses that sprang up in the economic boom years before the Great Depression, millions of Southerners pulled up roots and moved to Chicago, Detroit, and New York. This population provided a ready-made support system for jazz musicians, particularly in neighborhoods dominated by African Americans, such as the South Side of Chicago and New York's Harlem. As we have already noted, more and more whites began to visit night spots in Black neighborhoods, creating a web of interactions that, though always unequal, did support jazz musicians.

The Rise of Latin Dance Music: "El Manicero"

Beginning in the early 1930s, bands staffed with Latin American musicians, such as Don Azpiazú and His Havana Casino Orchestra and Xavier Cugat's Waldorf Astoria Orchestra (see Chapter 6), began playing refined arrangements of South American and Caribbean dances in the ballrooms of New York City. While influences came to the United States from many parts of Latin America, including Mexico and Argentina (recall our discussion of the tango earlier in this chapter), the strongest Latin impact on popular dance music from 1930 on was exerted by Cuba, a former Spanish colony some ninety miles off the coast of Florida, home to one of the largest per capita populations of African descent in the New World.

The origins of the Cuban dance styles that rose to popularity in the United States and Europe between the world wars lie in two genres of music: the *son*, a late nineteenth-century rural song tradition that migrated to the city, where it was performed by groups called *conjuntos*; and the *danzón*, a mildly Africanized style of ballroom dance music performed in urban ballrooms by larger, more formal ensembles called *orquestas*. There are many fascinating parallels between the development of music in Cuba and the development of music in the United States, including the emergence of the country blues and its subsequent movement to and transformation in the city (see Chapter 7). In addition, the class distinction drawn between *conjuntos* and *orquestas* broadly parallels that between dance "bands" and "orchestras" in the United States.

The term *son*, derived from the Spanish verb *sonar*, "to sound," is used in many parts of Latin America (notably Mexico, where it is freely applied to local musical traditions; see our discussion of "La Bamba" in Chapter 8). The Cuban *son* developed in the island's countryside around 1880 and was initially performed by farmers and workers who toiled in the island's sugar plantation economy. The rural *son* was a strophic song form that alternated verses with a vocal refrain (the *estribillo*). When available, a variety of instruments were used to provide a polyrhythmic accompaniment. The combination of African and Iberian elements—complex polyrhythms and call-and-response singing on the one hand, and a singing style and poetic form derived from Spanish folk traditions on the other—formed the basis of later developments in Cuban music and eventually exerted a lasting impact on popular music in the United States.

At around the same time a ballroom dance tradition, typically performed by ensembles with brass, reeds, violins, piano, string bass, and percussion instruments, emerged in Cuba's towns. In addition to the standard ballroom repertoire of waltzes and one-steps, these *orquestas* accompanied Cuban dances, particularly the *danzón*. In the capital city and port of Havana, the *danzón* met and mingled with the *son*, which had reached Havana around the time of the First World War. In responding to the demands of urban audiences for a more up-to-date, cosmopolitan sound, musicians formed the *son conjunto*, typically a six- or seven-piece ensemble featuring a trumpet playing lyrical, jazz-like improvisations.

Until 1930, "Latin" or "Spanish" music in New York and other American cities basically meant tango. That year saw the first visit to New York of a major Cuban dance band, Don Azpiazú's Havana Casino Orchestra. *Justo "Don" Azpiazú* (1893–1943) and his group gave American audiences their first taste of authentic Cuban music. They were a huge hit, attracting an audience that included Cuban and Puerto Rican immigrants but also reached across ethnic lines.

The centerpiece of Azpiazú's stage show was a song titled "El Manisero" ("The Peanut Vendor"), composed by the Cuban pianist Moises Simon (1889–1945) and sung by Antonio Machin (1904–1977), who was billed in his New York appearances as "the Cuban Rudy Vallee." Machin's performance of "El Manisero" was a variant of the Cuban *son* called a *pregón*, a vocal improvisation modeled on the calls of street vendors in Havana.

For "El Manisero," Machin came onstage at the Palace in costume, pushing a vendor's cart, throwing peanuts into the audience, singing "*Maníííí, Maníííí ...*" ("Peanuts ..."), and exiting again dramatically at the end, with a line of his own invention: "*Me voyyyyy, Me voyyyyy ...*" ("I'm going away ..."). (Sublette 2004, 395)

In 1930 the Havana Casino Orchestra recorded "El Manisero" (released into the market as "El Manicero") at RCA-Victor's studios, and the recording catalyzed a transnational craze for Cuban music. The label affixed to the phonograph disc categorized the song as a "Rumba Fox Trot," but any knowledgeable Cuban listener would have recognized "El Manicero" as a *son pregón*. Although the term "rumba" was soon being used by the music industry as a catch-all rubric for a variety of Latin music styles, in Cuba itself the term rumba was—and still is—applied first and foremost to a complex set of percussion-driven dances that are closely bound up with Afro-Cuban religion and hew much closer to their African origins than the *son*. (See the discussion of Machito and his Afro-Cubans in Chapter 6.)

The first thing to listen for in this recording of "El Manicero" is a repeated rhythmic pattern called the *clave* (literally, "key"), which is often referred to as the "heartbeat" of Cuban music. The clave is a syncopated pattern consisting of five strokes over a regular eight-beat pulse:

CLAVE	X		X		X		X	X	
PULSE	X	X	X	X	X	X	X	X	

Clave and Pulse

This pattern is ultimately derived from West African music, and cognate forms of it are found in a number of traditions in the Americas, including the Brazilian bossa nova and the syncopated "shave and a haircut, two bits" rhythm immortalized by 1950s rock 'n' roller Bo Diddley. In Cuban music the pattern is played by knocking together two resonant wooden dowels, which are themselves called claves (recall our discussion of *rumba guaguanco* in Chapter 1).

No written record exists of the instrumentation used in the recording session, but a short film of the band made in 1930 shows a thirteen-piece ensemble with three percussionists (claves, maracas, and *bongó*—a small, high-pitched pair of drums), five winds (three reeds and two trumpets), string bass, piano, *tres* (a small guitar), and two violins. The claves and maracas play repeated parts, the bongó player fills in with improvised patterns, and the muted trumpet plays improvisations over the groove in the style of the great Havana *son conjuntos*.

It is interesting to consider the enthusiastic reception of this song by its huge non-Spanish-speaking audience in the United States, who would not have understood Moises Simon's poetic evocation of a peanut hawker pushing his cart through the streets of Havana. Clearly, what moved these listeners initially was the sensibility and novelty of the music, rather than the poetry of the lyrics. In what appears retrospectively as a stroke of genius, the song had already been copyrighted in 1929 by the music publisher E. B. Marks, who profited immensely from its worldwide success in an era when sheet music revenues were still a larger source of profit than the sales of records.

The success of "El Manicero," one of the bestselling records of 1931, spawned dozens of imitations and kicked off a "Peanut Vendor" craze across the United States, a flash of brightness amid the deepening gloom of the Great Depression. Among the many versions of the song that appeared soon after the success of the Havana Casino Orchestra's record was a rendition by Louis Armstrong that made it onto the charts. Azpiazú later wrote that "within a week there existed a Havana Royal Orchestra, a Havana Novelty Orchestra, and a Havana God-Knows-What" (Roberts 1998, 78). In 1931 he scored similar successes in Europe and spent a number of years commuting between New York and Paris. However, by 1940 the craze for his style of Latin dance music had subsided, and he returned to Cuba, where he died of a heart attack in 1943, largely forgotten.

JAZZ MUSIC, AN African American tradition that originated in New Orleans and flowered in Chicago and New York City, was the anthem for the first well-defined youth culture to emerge from white America. Rebelling against the horrors of mechanized warfare and the straight-laced morality of the nineteenth century, millions of college-age Americans adopted jazz as a way to mark their difference from their parents' generation. Admittedly, the ability of youth to indulge in the sort of up-to-date pastimes portrayed in Hollywood films and novels such as Fitzgerald's *The Great Gatsby* was strongly affected by their position in society—after all, not everyone could afford luxury automobiles, champagne, and top-flight dance orchestras. However, jazz's attraction as a symbol of sensuality, freedom, and fun does appear to have transcended the boundaries of region, ethnicity, and class, creating a precedent for phenomena such as the swing era (see Chapter 6), rhythm & blues (see Chapter 7), and rock 'n' roll (see Chapter 8). In the next chapter, we turn to the rise of the Tin Pan Alley tradition of popular song, which was to dominate the mainstream of popular taste for over half a century.

Key Terms

conjuntos	microphone	scat singing
crooning	*pregón*	
DJs (disc jockeys)	radio	

Key People

Edward Kennedy "Duke" Ellington	Justo "Don" Azpiazú	Paul Whiteman
Eubie Blake	King Joe Oliver	Thomas "Fats" Waller
James "Bubber" Miley	Louis Armstrong	Vernon and Irene Castle
James Reese Europe	Nick LaRocca	
	Noble Sissle	

Review Questions

1. What were the new technologies that changed the sound of popular music during the 1920s?
2. What were the stylistic features found in early jazz?
3. Around the beginning of the twentieth century, several fundamental changes took place in American social dancing, closely paralleling shifts in popular music. Describe these changes.
4. What factors contributed to the tremendous impact of jazz on mainstream popular music?
5. Who billed himself as the "King of Jazz"? Why is this term deserved or not deserved?

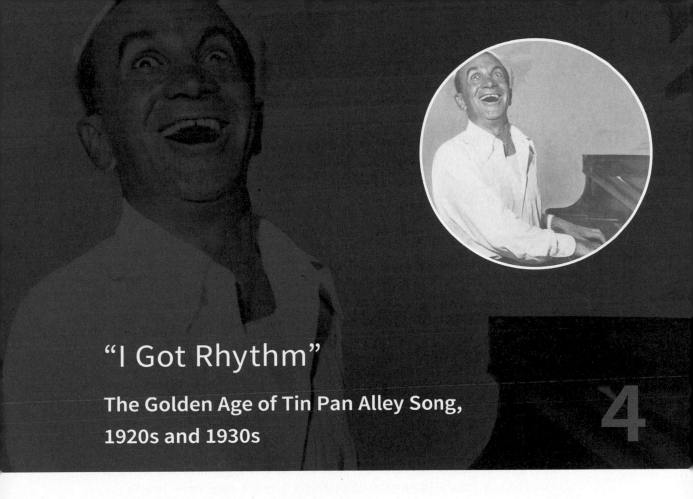

"I Got Rhythm"

The Golden Age of Tin Pan Alley Song, 1920s and 1930s

4

DURING THE 1920s AND 1930s CERTAIN CHARACTERISTIC MUSICAL structures and styles of performance dominated popular song. Professional songwriters, working within a set of forms inherited from nineteenth-century popular music and influenced by the craze for ragtime and jazz music, wrote some of the most influential and commercially successful songs of the period. The lure of fame and financial success on a previously unknown scale attracted composers and lyricists with diverse skills and backgrounds. *Irving Berlin* (1888–1989) grew up poor in the Jewish ghetto of New York City, began his career as a singing waiter, and achieved his first success writing ragtime-influenced popular songs (see Box 4.1). Richard Rodgers (1902–1979), who produced many of the finest songs of the period in collaboration with lyricists Lorenz Hart and Oscar Hammerstein II, was the college-educated son of a doctor and a pianist. *Cole Porter* (1891–1964) was born into a wealthy family in Indiana and studied classical music at elite institutions such as Yale, Harvard, and the Scola Cantorum in Paris. And *George Gershwin* (1898–1937) became the songwriter who perhaps did the most to bridge the gulf between art music and popular music; the son of an immigrant leatherworker, he studied European classical music but also spent a great deal of time listening to jazz musicians in New York City (see Box 4.3). The songs written by these men and a few others

Portrait of Cole Porter, c. 1956.

represent an achievement in terms of both quality and quantity that appears extraordinary to this day. The Tin Pan Alley composers produced many **standards**, songs that remain an essential part of the repertoire of today's jazz musicians and pop singers. When musicians and critics now speak of the "Great American Songbook," they are referring to a body of work dominated by the golden age of Tin Pan Alley.

Jewish immigrants, particularly those from central and eastern Europe, played a key role in the music business during the early twentieth century as composers, lyricists, performers, publishers, and promoters. The rise of anti-Semitism in eastern Europe during the 1880s had encouraged the emigration of millions of Jews. Few of the first waves of immigrants wrote or spoke English upon arrival, and many of them had little experience of big-city life, but by and large these people felt a strong impetus to become— and especially to have their children become—"real Americans." By 1910 Jews made up more than a quarter of the population of New York City. Young entrepreneurs from the burgeoning neighborhoods of the East Side had secured a foothold in a variety of businesses, including the entertainment industry. Some of the hundreds of Jewish performers who worked the vaudeville circuit went on to become major celebrities on Broadway and in Hollywood, including *Al Jolson* (1886–1950), Sophie Tucker, George Jessel, Jack Benny, George Burns, and Milton Berle.

The life stories of these performers suggest several reasons for the high proportion of Jewish involvement in the entertainment industry. Lower-class immigrants, denied the possibility of upward mobility for centuries, poured their ambition into music, dance, and comedy, perfecting their skills on the streets of New York before gaining a foothold in vaudeville. By the turn of the century many of the biggest theatrical booking agencies were managed by Jews, and young performers did not face the degree of anti-Semitism present in other established businesses. And for aspiring songwriters—such as Irving Berlin, Jerome Kern, George Gershwin, and others—the music business offered a kind of rough-and-tumble justice: if you could write songs that made money for the music publishers, you were a success.

Tin Pan Alley Song Form

During the 1920s and 1930s this new generation of composers and lyricists explored the possibilities of song forms inherited from the nineteenth century, including the AABA structure exemplified by "Jeanie with the Light Brown Hair" and the verse-and-chorus form exemplified by "After the Ball" (see Chapter 2). Let's take a quick look at the most common form of Tin Pan Alley songs, which, in effect, fused these two to produce a

BOX 4.1 IRVING BERLIN (1888–1989)

Irving Berlin (born Israel, or Isadore, Baline) is often cited as the most productive, varied, and creative of the Tin Pan Alley songwriters. His professional songwriting career started before World War I and continued into the 1960s. It has been said that Berlin often composed from three to seven songs a week; as of 2012, the Irving Berlin Music Company held the rights to over 1,200 of the composer's songs, a good number of which have remained favorites into the twenty-first century, such as "White Christmas," "God Bless America," "There's No Business Like Show Business," "Cheek to Cheek," and "Blue Skies."

Like many Tin Pan Alley composers, Berlin was a European immigrant; he was born in Temun, Russia, in 1888. His family fled that violently anti-Semitic environment in 1892, and settled in New York City's Lower East Side, a haven for displaced Jews. The Balines began their life in America in desperate poverty. Young Israel was on the streets by the age of eight, selling newspapers, and at fourteen he left home for good. He worked as a guide for a blind street musician, as a saloon pianist, and as a singing waiter. Like many other Tin Pan Alley tunesmiths, Berlin began his career as a song plugger: as a teenager he was paid five dollars a week by the songwriter Harry von Tilzer to join in "spontaneously" from the audience when von Tilzer's songs were performed at music halls.

The song that first brought Berlin mass acclaim was "Alexander's Ragtime Band," published in 1911. The song actually had little to do with ragtime as performed by the great Black ragtime pianists of the day, but it sold 1.5 million copies almost immediately. After World War I Berlin set up his own publishing company and founded a theater for the production of his own shows.

Like other Tin Pan Alley composers, Berlin wrote songs for the Broadway stage as well as for the new medium of sound film (he wrote music for eighteen films). An Irving Berlin song, "Blue Skies," was

Irving Berlin at the piano, c. 1903.

performed by Al Jolson in the first talkie, *The Jazz Singer*. The first motion picture featuring an entire score written by Berlin was the Marx Brothers' debut movie, *The Cocoanuts*, produced in 1929. The 1942 film *Holiday Inn* introduced one of Berlin's most successful songs, "White Christmas," which was also the title song for another popular movie in 1954. Music for the 1946 Broadway musical *Annie Get Your Gun*, composed by Berlin, probably included more hit songs than any other show ("They Say It's Wonderful," "The Girl That I Marry," "Doin' What Comes Naturally," and "There's No Business Like Show Business," among others). Berlin was the most prolific and consistent of the Tin Pan Alley composers, with an active songwriting career spanning almost sixty years.

---

verse-refrain form, with an AABA refrain. This schematic structure, in the hands of the more inventive composers, allowed for all sorts of interesting variations.

- First, the **verse**. The verse usually sets up a dramatic context or emotional tone. Although verses were the most important part of nineteenth-century popular songs, they were regarded as mere introductions by the 1920s, and today the verses of Tin Pan Alley songs are infrequently performed. Verses functioned in theatrical contexts during the heyday of Tin Pan Alley by offering a transition from spoken lines to singing in the Broadway musicals of the period.

- Then, the **refrain**, the part that is usually considered "the song" today. It is usually made up of four sections of equal length, in the pattern AABA. The A section presents the main melody, the basic pattern of the lyrics, and a set of chord changes to support them.
- The music of the A section is then repeated with new lyrics; often some slight melodic changes will be introduced, making this A'—that is, a variation of A.
- The B section, or **bridge**, is then introduced. The bridge presents new material—a new melody, chord changes, and lyrics.
- Finally, the A melody and chord changes are repeated with new lyrics (and sometimes with further melodic alterations or an addition called a "tag," producing an A", a second variation of A), bringing us back to the "top" of the song.

Such song forms became the basis of listening habits; in those days, just as today, audiences were conditioned to hearing particular musical forms. A listener familiar with the AABA form would probably approach a new song (or a new recording of an old song) with the expectation that the A section would at some point be followed by a contrasting section with different chords, words, and melody (the bridge), and that the performance was likely to end with the repetition of the A section.

The relationship between typical Tin Pan Alley songs and the old strophic verse-and-chorus form may be heard with particular clarity on one of the big hit records of 1927, *Ruth Etting*'s "'Deed I Do" (See the Listening Guide). The songwriters provided the singer with sheet music consisting of a verse, with two different sets of lyrics, and an AABA refrain; this was not uncommon. What was relatively uncommon was that, on her recording, Etting sang through the entire verse-and-refrain structure *twice*, in order, so that we hear the following on the record: verse 1—then AABA refrain; then verse 2 (same verse music, new words)—then AABA refrain (same refrain music, same refrain words). In this instance, the recording is a literal presentation of the sheet music as a large strophic structure with two-part (verse-refrain) strophes, clearly revealing the song's roots in nineteenth-century traditions.

Composers, singers, and arrangers—the individuals who bore responsibility for creating a musical environment (through the choice of key, tempo, instrumental accompaniment, and so on) that would match a given singer's vocal strengths to a particular song—became adept at fulfilling listeners' expectations while introducing just enough unexpected variation to keep the listener's attention. The attractiveness of a popular song or its rendering on a particular recording had much to do with achieving a balance between predictability and novelty. Although a lot of mediocre music was produced by Tin Pan Alley composers, the best songwriters were able to work creatively within the structural limitations of standard popular song forms.

Listening Guide   "'DEED I DO"

Music by Fred Rose, lyrics by Walter Hirsch; performed by Ruth Etting; recorded 1926

"'Deed I Do" is a clearly structured song that employs the form most typical of Tin Pan Alley: an introductory verse is followed by an AABA refrain. The verse, typically, is shorter than the refrain. The refrain has a wider-ranging, more memorable melody than the verse, and it also presents the title lyrics of the song—three times. The published music offers two sets of lyrics for the verse, whereas the refrain, functioning like the "chorus" in old verse-and-chorus songs, has just one unvarying set of lyrics. On Ruth Etting's recording of the song, she sings both sets of verse lyrics, resulting in a performance with two large verse-and-chorus strophes. (Compare this listening chart to those for "Jeanie with the Light Brown Hair" and "After the Ball" in Chapter 2 to see the similarities and differences between the form of this characteristic Tin Pan Alley song and the forms of its sources in earlier American popular music.) While the verse is sung first, the record actually begins with the accompanying band playing the "A" music of the catchy refrain. This functions as a hook, and enables listeners who have heard the song before to recognize immediately that this is indeed "'Deed I Do." Ruth Etting's performance of this unpretentious song is appropriately straightforward and sincere. It is not an entirely artless performance, however; during the second occurrence of the refrain, notice how she varies the melody of the "A" sections with little vocal ornaments, turning what could have been a mere repetition into a gentle intensification.

Ruth Etting (1907–1978) was one of the most popular singers of the late 1920s and early 1930s. "'Deed I Do," recorded late in 1926, became her biggest hit to date in

Ruth Etting singing on the radio, c. 1930s.

1927. The song with which Etting came most to be associated was "Love Me or Leave Me," which she performed onstage in the show *Whoopee!* (1928). That song, in turn, became the title of a 1955 movie based on Etting's life and career in which Doris Day, a major female singer of the next generation, sympathetically portrayed the older star.

LISTENING GUIDE | "'DEED I DO"

TIME	FORM	LYRIC	DESCRIPTIVE COMMENTS
0:00	Instrumental Introduction		Band plays the main melody of the refrain as a "hook"
0:12	Verse 1	*I was oh, so blue . . .*	Voice enters with the first verse
0:38	Refrain: A	*Do I want you? . . .*	
0:50	A	*Do I need you? . . .*	
1:03	B (Bridge)	*I'm glad . . .*	B section is the bridge

(continued)

Listening Guide "'DEED I DO" (*continued*)

TIME	FORM	LYRIC	DESCRIPTIVE COMMENTS
1:15	A	*Do I love you?...*	
1:28	Verse 2	*There are lots of others...*	Same music as Verse 1, with new lyrics
1:53	Refrain: A	*Do I want you?... (etc.)*	Main tune again, with same lyrics as before; voice adds melodic ornaments for variety
2:06	A		
2:19	B		
2:31	A		

What Were Tin Pan Alley Songs About?

Tin Pan Alley songs did not, by and large, deal directly with the troubling issues of the 1920s and 1930s: racism, massive unemployment, and the rise of fascism in central and eastern Europe. Only a few songs written by Tin Pan Alley composers even mention the Great Depression, during which some historians estimate that 60 percent of Americans were unemployed. The Tin Pan Alley song "Brother Can You Spare a Dime?" (1932) stands almost alone in its serious treatment of poverty. In general, popular songs and the musical plays and films in which they appeared were designed to help people escape the pressures of daily life.

Both the lyrical content of Tin Pan Alley songs and their typical mode of performance were linked to the prominence of privacy and romance as cultural ideals. For many centuries the notion of a right to privacy was largely restricted to economic, intellectual, and religious elites. The development of middle-class culture in America during the late nineteenth and early twentieth centuries depended in large part on the adoption of elite manners and tastes, within the limits imposed by one's income. Middle-class aspirations were focused on the ownership of a home, and the cozy parlor, with its piano and mass-reproduced artworks, as a center for family activities, and courtship became a primary symbol of the homeowner's control over domestic space. This move toward privatization—which has culminated in the development of aural cloisters such as the portable digital music player and the hermetically sealed automobile—is reflected in embryonic form in the content and style of the popular songs of the 1920s and 1930s.

The ideal of romantic love, a theme inherited from European song and poetic traditions, is also reflected in the lyrical content and performance style of Tin Pan Alley songs. Unlike the old European ballads—in which the action of characters is often narrated from a vantage point outside the singer's own experience—the first-person lyrics that are characteristic of Tin Pan Alley songs (suggested in such song titles as "What'll I Do?" "Why Do I Love You?" "I Get a Kick Out of You," and "Somebody Loves Me") allow the listener to identify his or her personal experience more directly with that of the singer. This first-person mode of address is reminiscent of elite poetic forms such as the sonnet, but Tin Pan Alley songwriters by and large avoided the flowery language of the Shakespearean ode, opting instead for a more down-to-earth manner of speech. (Songs like "Jeepers Creepers, Where'd You Get Those Peepers?" took a vernacular approach to describing the loved one's physical charms, while the floweriness of Elizabethan love poems was expressly satirized in the 1927 song "Thou Swell," written by Rodgers and Hart for their Broadway musical *A Connecticut Yankee*.) The idea that any working stiff could experience the bliss of romantic love—and, after a period of courtship, settle down and buy a home (his metaphoric "castle")—was widely disseminated by the mass media. Similarly, "torch songs"—songs that described the heartbreak of separation or of a romance gone sour—provided a ready-made outlet for the fear and uncertainty that many people experienced during the Great Depression.

The development of a singing style called crooning reinforced these links between popular music and personal experience. Listening to the early recordings of vaudeville performers such as Al Jolson or Sophie Tucker, whose exaggerated styles were developed for performances in large theaters, one feels that one is being "sung at" (or sometimes even "shouted at"). A Ruth Etting, **Gene Austin**, or Bing Crosby recording, made after the introduction of the electric microphone in the mid-1920s, is an altogether different sort of musical experience—a *private* experience. The singer's silky, gentle, nuanced voice invites you to share the most intimate of confidences; it speaks to you alone. Sometimes, the listener imaginatively enters the voice of the singer, and a kind of psychological fusion occurs between two individuals who will never actually meet face to face.

The lyrical content and performance style of Tin Pan Alley songs thus reflected the efforts of professional composers to tap into the aspirations of an expanding and ethnically mixed but predominantly white middle class. These songs were also popular among other audiences, however, including the large numbers of Southern whites and African Americans who migrated to urban centers during the 1920s and 1930s. This wide-reaching popularity suggests that the images of romantic love and domestic bliss evoked by these songs, as well as the urbane sophistication of the superstar crooners who sang them on phonograph records and radio and in Hollywood films, exerted an appeal that crossed boundaries of race, region, and class. As we shall see in Chapter 5, many early blues and "hillbilly" musicians were influenced by the forms of Tin Pan Alley songs and by the manner in which they were performed.

Conversely, because Tin Pan Alley songs were closely linked to white middle-class identity, it is easy to overlook the influence that Black music and musicians exerted on the composition of such songs. The turn of the century saw the increasing influence of African American traditions, especially ragtime, on the style and sensibility of mainstream popular music. This trend continued into the 1920s and 1930s with the popularity of songs and dance music influenced by blues and jazz. Although the mildly syncopated music that white audiences called jazz often bore little resemblance to the

Listening Guide "MY BLUE HEAVEN"

Music by Walter Donaldson, lyrics by George Whiting; published 1924; performed by Gene Austin; recorded 1927

Gene Austin's interpretation of the George Whiting–Walter Donaldson song "My Blue Heaven," released by the Victor Company in 1927, was the bestselling record of its era. (Not until Bing Crosby recorded "White Christmas" in 1942 did any record sell more copies.) It also exemplifies a great many typical characteristics of this era of American popular music. Consequently, we will examine this song and this recording in considerable detail.

Gene Austin was one of the first crooners, singers who mastered the electric microphone after its introduction in 1925. He was a tremendously popular performer in the late 1920s: it is estimated that his recordings for Victor sold 86 million copies, an incredible number at the time. Although crooning is perhaps most associated with male vocalists of this era, like Austin and Bing Crosby, the approach was successfully adopted by female singers as well. Ruth Etting was an enormously successful practitioner of the style.

A careful listening to "My Blue Heaven" will reveal many features found in other Tin Pan Alley music of its period. We will also point out some features that might account for the unique success of this recording.

Basic Description

The record begins with a brief instrumental introduction, which serves to identify the tune of the refrain so that anybody who has heard a previous performance of "My Blue Heaven" can immediately recognize the song from the outset. This instrumental introduction functions as a kind of hook. (Ruth Etting's recording of "'Deed I Do" employs the same strategy.)

Next, the voice enters and sings its own introduction. The lyrics and music here serve to set the scene for the main part of the song. This portion is the verse. Images of evening and homecoming in the lyrics establish the peaceful physical setting and the gentle emotional tone of the song. Once the verse is finished, neither its words nor its music are heard again; we are fully prepared for the important business at hand.

The remainder of the record presents the refrain of "My Blue Heaven." This is where the most memorable tune and the most important words are found. As may be seen in the following chart, the refrain is heard a total of three times in succession. This repetition ensures that

it will be quite familiar to the listener after only a single playing of the record.

Form

The two-part verse-refrain form is of course typical of Tin Pan Alley songs. "My Blue Heaven" is also typical insofar as its verse is shorter than its refrain. Although the verse-refrain form evolved out of the verse-chorus structure of strophic songs like "After the Ball," verses by this time usually assumed merely an introductory character and tended to have less verbal and musical interest than refrains. The lesser importance of Tin Pan Alley verses is reflected by the fact that they were often omitted altogether in recordings and other performances or were occasionally played by the instruments alone as introductions to or interludes in the vocal part. There is no one typical form for a verse. In "My Blue Heaven," the verse has two clear sections, both of equal length and with nearly identical music.

The refrain of "My Blue Heaven" falls into four sections, which follow the typical AABA design. (This formal design was already present in nineteenth-century songs; see the earlier discussion of "Jeanie with the Light Brown Hair" in Chapter 2.) The first, second, and fourth sections have identical music and similar lyric construction, and all end with the crucial words of the title, "my blue heaven." The third section provides needed variety by presenting different music and a different rhythmic and rhyme arrangement in the lyrics; this is the bridge (sometimes called the release). There is a satisfying balance of repetition and contrast in this design, which helps explain why AABA forms were favored by the composers of Tin Pan Alley songs.

Why was "My Blue Heaven" so phenomenally successful? There is no single right answer, of course, but we can conjecture that its success was due both to the nature of the song itself, as written by Whiting and Donaldson, and to the sound of Gene Austin's particular recording of it.

The Song

The lyrics of "My Blue Heaven" were written to appeal to the deepest aspirations of the Tin Pan Alley listening public. With just a few well-chosen images of benign nature ("when whippoorwills call") and domestic serenity ("a smiling face, a fireplace"), the lyrics present a familiar and comfortable version of the "American dream": one's own home and family, offering a peaceful refuge from the pressures of the world outside. The picture is deliberately both sketchy enough and suggestive enough to appeal to a multitude of persons.

A nice poetic touch in the lyrics appears in the bridge section of the refrain, which links the earlier bird imagery to human domesticity through the metaphor of the "nest." Note also the gentle pun as the "nest" is "nestled." Such poetic touches added to the sense of "classiness" exuded by many Tin Pan Alley songs, a sophistication that doubtless appealed to many in their intended audience.

However, it is probably the music of the refrain that accounts, more than anything else, for the appeal of "My Blue Heaven." It is that mysterious and distinctive phenomenon: a great tune that, once heard, is remembered, and remembered with affection. Particularly in the A sections, which begin with gentle upward curves of melody and fall to a satisfying sense of rest with the long notes on "my blue heaven," there is a feeling of inevitability both in the shape of the tune itself and in its perfect matching with the sense and the sound of the lyrics.

The Recording

Everything on Gene Austin's record of "My Blue Heaven" reinforces the feeling of quiet intimacy and tranquility that characterizes the song's melody and lyrics. It may be this impressive mating of song and performance that contributed to the record's popularity.

The choice of a solo cello (discreetly accompanied by a piano) to play the instrumental introduction was an inspired one. It immediately set the record apart from others of its time; much more typical would have been the choice of a dance band or an orchestra. The solo instrument instantly establishes the desired tone of special intimacy. Also, the association of the cello with "high-class" symphonic and chamber music conveys an implied sophistication that obviously struck a chord with the record's intended audience. Like the poetic effects in the lyrics discussed previously, the choice of instrument may be seen as gently flattering the record buyer's taste and cultural aspirations (or pretensions). Cello and piano remain the chief instruments heard throughout this uninterruptedly soft and gentle record.

Keeping the accompaniment unobtrusive is essential, for Austin's vocals scarcely rise above a tuneful whisper. This vocal style is the perfect example of crooning. Austin's performance would not have filled any but a small room, but the electric microphone picks up every detail of his delivery for the record without his ever having to exaggerate or stress anything. Crooning was still quite new in 1927, so apart from being intimate and therefore highly appropriate for this song, it was also felt at the time to be excitingly novel—and probably sexy in an understated way.

In the first half of the third presentation of the refrain, the melody is whistled in a warbling style reminiscent of the song of the whippoorwill. (The whistler is Robert MacGimsey, famed for his ability to whistle two or three notes at the same time.) Austin weaves his voice in and around the whistled melody, singing soft nonsense syllables. At certain points he speaks some of the words, creating the sense that he is talking directly to the listener. These techniques offer variety and also underline the atmosphere of intimacy and informality. At the very end, Austin effects a sense of conclusion by having his voice rise, instead of fall, on the concluding notes of the refrain.

LISTENING GUIDE	"MY BLUE HEAVEN"		
TIME	**FORM**	**LYRIC**	**DESCRIPTIVE COMMENTS**
	Instrumental introduction		Solo cello introduces the main melody of the refrain as a "hook"
0:17	Verse	*Day is ending . . .*	Voice enters
0:29		*Night shades falling . . .*	Melody of the second half of the verse slightly varies from that of the first half (their endings differ)
0:42	Refrain: A	*When whippoorwill calls . . .*	Main tune of the song
0:57	A	*I turn to the right . . .*	

(continued)

Listening Guide "MY BLUE HEAVEN" (*continued*)

TIME	FORM	LYRIC	DESCRIPTIVE COMMENTS
1:12	B	*A smiling face...*	B section is the bridge
1:25	A	*Just Molly and me...*	
1:40	Refrain: A		Cello takes over the melody; voice in background
	A		
2:09	B	*A smiling face...*	Voice dominates again
	A	*Just Molly...*	
2:36	Refrain: A		Whistled "bird sounds" represent the whippoorwills
	A		
3:05	B	*A smiling face...*	Voice dominates again
	A	*Just Molly...*	Voice goes up, instead of down, at the end to mark the conclusion

music that had developed in New Orleans, the so-called Jazz Age was nonetheless an important stage in the "Africanization" of American popular music and dance.

What Makes a Song a "Standard"?

If popular songs endure at all, they endure most commonly as occasions for nostalgia. Precisely because they capture the flavor of their time so tellingly, most popular songs sound unavoidably representative of their particular era. For the most part, it is difficult to imagine modern-day performances of old pop songs in anything but a nostalgic context.

Some popular songs, however, possess a continuing appeal that surpasses nostalgia. Since the nineteenth century, certain of Stephen Foster's songs have been performed so frequently that they may be said to belong to a stable core repertoire of American popular song. For a song to achieve such a status was relatively uncommon before the Tin Pan Alley era. But the period of the 1920s and 1930s yielded a sizable body of standards, songs that have remained in active circulation for more than seven decades. "My Blue

Listening Guide   "APRIL SHOWERS"

Music by Louis Silvers, lyrics by Buddy DeSylva; published 1921; performed by Al Jolson; recorded 1921

A brief discussion of another popular song from this era will afford us a broader overview of Tin Pan Alley song-writing and performance styles. Al Jolson's hit record of the Buddy DeSylva–Louis Silvers song "April Showers," recorded in 1921, reveals the sound and style of the pre-microphone period as exemplified by one of the most compelling and popular singers of the entire Tin Pan Alley era. "April Showers" was so successful and became so identified with Jolson that he recorded it several times during his career; listening to his recording from 1932 illuminates further aspects of his distinctive approach to performance.

Basic Description

Like "My Blue Heaven," this song is a slow, sentimental ballad with a verse-refrain structure. And, as shown in the following chart, Jolson's recordings of "April Showers" are patterned almost exactly like the Gene Austin recording of "My Blue Heaven": instrumental introduction, sung verse, sung refrain, repetition of the refrain. (In "April Showers" the refrain is heard twice, rather than three times.)

But the effect of "April Showers" on the listener is totally different from that of "My Blue Heaven" because of the special impact of Al Jolson's style. Where with Austin everything is quiet and intimate, Jolson's dominating, larger-than-life approach turns this pastoral song into a grand statement. The opposite approaches were the result, to some extent, of differences in the two singers' personalities and vocal abilities, but they were also decisively influenced by technology—or, in Jolson's case, by the lack of it.

Jolson first made his reputation as a stage entertainer in the period before electronic amplification was possible (see Box 4.2). Consequently, his voice and gestures were cultivated to fill a large space without assistance. This ability made him an ideal recording artist for the pre-1925 period, before the electric microphone came into use as an aid to small voices and intimate interpretations. His 1921 "April Showers" demonstrates the dominating character of his voice and interpretive style; despite the primitive technology, all of the song's lyrics and all of Jolson's musical gestures come across clearly and strongly. By 1932, of course, modern electric technology

was available. Nevertheless, Jolson not only stood by the style that first brought him success but also—if anything—emphasized and enlarged it. His 1932 "April Showers" is even more dramatic and "theatrical" than his version of 1921, as if Jolson consciously set out to reaffirm his roots and distance himself from the crooning style being cultivated by the younger generation of recording artists.

Form

As in "My Blue Heaven," the primary interest of "April Showers" lies in its refrain. This refrain can also be divided into four sections, showing a pattern of repetition and contrast. Here, however, the pattern is ABAC, rather than the more common AABA. (The ABAC pattern is probably the second most common form for a refrain in a Tin Pan Alley song.)

The first and third sections of the refrain in "April Showers" begin in a musically identical fashion, but the third section continues with a slight alteration of the earlier melody and a change in the accompanying chords. The B and C sections are of equal length but are musically different; the C section brings the melody and chord structures to a satisfying sense of conclusion.

The Song

"April Showers" is similar to "My Blue Heaven" and many other Tin Pan Alley songs in its employment of genteel nature imagery. Here the imagery is not put in the service of a love song but illustrates some homespun philosophy with which all listeners were doubtless familiar: "Every cloud has a silver lining." The words of the verse clearly establish that the ensuing nature descriptions of the refrain are to be interpreted metaphorically, as representative of the sequence of life's moods, with the assurance that unhappiness will eventually give way to better times.

Musically, "April Showers" possesses a memorable refrain in which the melody leaps repeatedly upward. This movement illustrates, in a sense, the sky-borne images of the words: rain showers, clouds, a bluebird. It also gives the tune a consistently uplifting feeling, which complements the underlying optimistic attitude the words seek to convey. Such a melody makes a perfect vehicle for a charismatic, big-voiced entertainer like Al Jolson; it is not surprising that his first (1921) recording of "April

(continued)

Listening Guide "APRIL SHOWERS" (continued)

Al Jolson accompanying himself on the piano, 1932.
Photo by Harold Stein.

Showers" put his indelible stamp on the song, which remained associated with him for the rest of his career.

The Recordings

Jolson totally dominates "April Showers" from the moment of his entrance.[1] His exaggerated diction, his tendency to slow down and elongate the notes at the ends of phrases, his frequent swellings in loudness—all these characteristics make for a highly theatrical performance. (One can readily picture the gestures that probably accompanied his live performances of the song.) Nothing could be more "stagy" than Jolson's spoken portion of the 1932 recording, which makes for an amusing comparison with Gene Austin's occasional understated speaking in "My Blue Heaven."

In the 1921 recording Jolson is accompanied by an orchestra that plays an elaborate and decorative accompaniment suitable to the flowery sentiments of the song. The orchestral introduction of this version presents a melodic phrase from the song's refrain, providing an identifying hook (similar to that which opens "My Blue Heaven"). The same hook is repeated to conclude the song, resulting in an agreeable sense of overall symmetry. By 1932 the song was so well known that such a hook was unnecessary. Thus the brief introduction played by the dance band accompanying Jolson in the 1932 "April Showers" does not present any music from the verse or the refrain. Its function is purely anticipatory, providing some ascending, billowy "cloud" music that settles down gently to prepare listeners for the singer's entrance. There is also no concluding instrumental passage in this later recording.

In his 1921 recording (see the Listening Guide) Jolson simply sings through the refrain twice. Some attempt to make the repetition a varied and intensified experience is evidenced by such touches as the singer's more exaggerated treatment of the word "violets" at the end of the B section and his extended lingering on the word "song" within the concluding C section. In the later 1932 version, Jolson breaks into rhythmic speech during the repetition of the refrain, considerably heightening the impact of the performance as a whole and giving the record an overall feeling of steadily building intensification. Paradoxically, by returning to his old theater techniques, Jolson created a new version of "April Showers," reinvigorating his own standard tune—and giving his fans, many of whom doubtless already owned his 1921 recording, a reason to buy this later version. (A contemporary analogy is the creation of remixes of popular tunes, in which a new version of a hit song is created by re-engineering the recorded material.) One might well wonder whether the particular intensity of the 1932 "April Showers," with its firm admonition to see life's brighter side, wasn't also deliberately tailored to suit the anxious national mood of this Depression-era year, a mood considerably different from that of the prosperous 1920s.

It would be understandable if a modern listener's initial reaction to Jolson's recordings was to find them excessively mannered and impossibly old-fashioned. But Jolson's influence on the style of American popular entertainment should not be underestimated. An

---

1. Jolson's 1932 version of "April Showers" is obviously patterned after his original 1921 recording, which was a big hit. You can compare it with the original on the Spotify playlist in Dashboard.

emphasis on theatricality, on the performer and the performance as well as on the song—or even more than on the song—clearly has endured in the work of such disparate later entertainers as Elvis Presley, Tina Turner, Michael Jackson, Madonna, Metallica, Beyoncé, and Lady Gaga.

LISTENING GUIDE | "APRIL SHOWERS"

TIME	FORM	LYRIC	DESCRIPTIVE COMMENTS
0:00	Instrumental introduction		Orchestra plays a "hook" phrase from the end of the refrain melody
0:09	Verse	*Life is not a highway . . .*	Voice enters
0:32	Refrain: A	*Though April showers . . .*	Main tune begins with a series of leaping gestures
0:47	B	*And if it's raining . . .*	
1:02	A'	*And where you see clouds . . .*	Begins just like the first A section but changes at the end
1:16	C	*So keep on looking . . .*	New music brings the refrain to a conclusion
1:38	Refrain: A		Voice repeats the refrain, with slight variations added for the sake of interest and intensification
1:53	B		
2:09	A'		
2:24	C		
2:50	Instrumental conclusion		Orchestra repeats the "hook" from the introduction

---

Heaven," "April Showers," and "How Deep Is the Ocean?" are all examples of Tin Pan Alley ballads that have become standards.

Let us now examine another standard from this era in an attempt to illustrate another type of Tin Pan Alley song and to understand some of the factors that might account for its enduring appeal. The George and **Ira Gershwin** standard "I Got Rhythm" illustrates the impact of African American musical styles on Tin Pan Alley composition. George Gershwin's intense interest in jazz—he knew many of the prominent Black bandleaders of the time and often heard them perform—left its mark on "I Got Rhythm," a song that combines structural elegance with rhythmic vitality.

"I Got Rhythm" was first introduced in the stage show *Girl Crazy* by twenty-one-year-old **Ethel Merman** in 1930 and became an instant sensation. The song was quickly recorded by many artists. Its enduring appeal is already suggested by the fact that Merman sensed a market for it as late as 1947, when she made the recording we will

BOX 4.2 AL JOLSON: A VAUDEVILLIAN POP STAR

Al Jolson (1886–1950) billed himself as "The World's Greatest Entertainer." He was the most popular performer of his generation, and his career overlapped the era of vaudeville stage performance and the rise of new media in the 1920s.

Born in Russia in 1886, Jolson migrated to the United States at the age of seven and grew up in a Jewish immigrant enclave in New York City. He began touring with a circus and a minstrel troupe at age thirteen, rose to success as a singer of "coon" songs in blackface, and made his Broadway debut in 1911. An advertisement that appeared in the music trade journal *Billboard* in 1907 touted Jolson as the "Blackfaced Comedian with the Operatic Voice. Never Idle." Jolson's energetic stage performances were in fact a major source of his popularity—it is said that he had trouble making his first studio recording because he couldn't force himself to stand still in front of the megaphone (the cone-shaped acoustic amplifier that preceded the electric microphone). Jolson was one of the first performers to use a "runway" that extended from the stage out into the audience, a technique that is now common in large pop, rock, and country music concerts.

In 1927 Jolson starred in *The Jazz Singer*. The following year he appeared in *The Singing Fool*, one of the most successful early Hollywood sound films. His career went into a slump during the late 1930s but was revived after World War II by the film *The Al Jolson Story* (1946), in which a younger actor played the lead role and Jolson supplied the vocals.

Many aspects of Jolson's style were derived from the nineteenth-century traditions of minstrelsy and vaudeville—he often performed in blackface, spoke and sang (often a mixture of the two) in a loud "stage voice," and used exaggerated gestures appropriate for the large theaters in which he had learned his craft. A parallel career was that of his near-contemporary **Sophie Tucker** (1884–1966), another Jewish American vaudeville star, who was known as "the last of the red-hot mamas" and who made a specialty of "Negro songs." (Tucker's signature hit, "Some of These Days," was written by the African American composer Shelton Brooks; recorded initially in 1911, it became an even bigger hit in 1927 when Tucker, taking a page from Al Jolson's book, re-recorded it for the electric microphone era.)

Jolson was probably the first superstar to fully use the possibilities of all the new media available to him. (Sophie Tucker, by comparison, never achieved parallel success in the movie medium, although she did appear in films.) The influence of his style is still clearly heard in the work of Ethel Merman, whom we shall meet shortly, and of too many others to list. Al Jolson is the ancestor of contemporary pop stars.

examine. This performance essentially recaptures the style and arrangement of 1930. That such a treatment produced a record that did not sound significantly dated in 1947— and that still has an immediate appeal more than fifty years later, for that matter—is indicative of the popularity and stature of this song.

Tin Pan Alley and Broadway

The close proximity of the music publishers on Tin Pan Alley to the stages of Broadway made the center of American popular music publishing and the center of American musical theater performance near neighbors. But this was not merely a happy accident of Manhattan geography; rather, there has been a long-standing and mutually beneficial relationship between popular songs and Broadway shows, and this relationship was

Listening Guide "HOW DEEP IS THE OCEAN?"

Lyrics and music by Irving Berlin; performed by Bing Crosby; recorded 1932

This recording of "How Deep Is the Ocean?," another Tin Pan Alley standard, offers a fine example of Bing Crosby's style. Like Gene Austin, **Bing Crosby** (1904–1977) was a crooner and became by far the most popular representative of the style. (Sales of his records have been estimated at more than 300 million.) However, a comparison of Crosby's performance here with that of Gene Austin in "My Blue Heaven" will immediately reveal Crosby's greater range and expressivity. Without ever losing the sense of intimacy essential to crooning—and to the interpretation of this deeply personal song—Crosby, unlike Austin, constantly varies his dynamics (relative softness and loudness) within individual phrases, becoming gradually louder to gently press certain questions ("How far would I travel . . .?") and softening to color the pathos of "And if I ever lost you." Crosby doesn't hesitate to make the ending of this performance a relatively emphatic high point, turning the final questions in effect into a strong declaration of love; the singer projects certainty that his queries have no real, measurable answers. Other distinctive characteristics of Crosby's style are his use of delicate vocal ornaments to emphasize certain words (listen to the expressive trembles, for example, in "How many *times*

a day do I think of *you*?") and the general rhythmic freedom of his performance in terms of his willingness to place words just ahead of or behind the beat, an approach that is especially noticeable in the repetition of the refrain, for which the accompanying orchestra provides a steady rhythmic pulse throughout.

Irving Berlin's song, written for the film *Face the Music*, has a clear verse-refrain structure. The verse is short, consisting simply of four phrases, each one a question. The emphasis on questions continues into the refrain, of course, which falls musically into the ABAC type of pattern that we have seen before in "April Showers." One interesting technical feature is the way that the refrain moves from a beginning in a **minor** key to an ending in a different **major** key—also a feature of another famous Berlin song, "Blue Skies"—while the verse presents this pattern in reverse. The constant use of questions (every single line in the song except for "I'll tell you no lie" is a question), which alternate from the personal ("How much do I love you?") to the metaphoric ("How deep is the ocean?") and back, makes this song intimate, intense, and ultimately unique. Its lasting appeal to performers and audiences is no surprise.

never more fruitful than in the 1920s and 1930s—the so-called golden age of the Tin Pan Alley song. Tin Pan Alley at this time offered a seemingly endless supply of fine new songs, written by a new generation of exceptionally talented composers and lyricists for contemporary audiences, while Broadway's musical shows presented songs to new crowds receptive to contemporary entertainment on a daily basis. In strictly economic terms, then, Tin Pan Alley supplied a product for which Broadway had a demand, and Broadway in turn offered an outstanding showcase for that product: an abundance of exposure necessary if the product was to maximize its appeal to consumers. The relationship could also function in reverse. If a new song first introduced in a Broadway show began to captivate audiences on a nightly basis, a savvy Tin Pan Alley publisher would want to publish the tune as sheet music and interest many performers in presenting and recording it in order to achieve widespread distribution of the marketable product and maximize profit from it.

Listening Guide "I GOT RHYTHM"

Music by George Gershwin, lyrics by Ira Gershwin; published 1930; performed by Ethel Merman; recorded 1947

Basic Description

"I Got Rhythm" introduces us to an up-tempo Tin Pan Alley song. Such songs, of which there are many, often do not differ essentially from the slow ballads in form. As may be seen in the accompanying chart, "I Got Rhythm" follows the verse-refrain structure, and its refrain is in a typical AABA form. The musical style of up-tempo Tin Pan Alley songs is often very different from that of the ballads, however, because it is in the up-tempo numbers that African American influences are most obvious. In particular, the refrain of "I Got Rhythm," with its consistent syncopation, conveys a jazz-influenced flavor that is unlike anything we have heard in the previous Tin Pan Alley examples.

In terms of performance style, an up-tempo Tin Pan Alley song might naturally lend itself to a larger-scaled, more intensely rhythmic style than that exemplified, say, by Gene Austin's crooning in "My Blue Heaven." Ethel Merman's model is clearly more along the lines of Al Jolson and other pre–microphone era performers. (This is not surprising, since the song was introduced in the setting of a stage musical, where the practice of miking performers became common only in the second half of the twentieth century.) Merman was, in fact, a famous "belter" of songs, whose ability to fill an entire theater with her vocal presence became legendary, and she represents the continuing importance of this performance tradition through the 1930s, 1940s, and beyond.

What were the up-tempo Tin Pan Alley songs about? There were up-tempo love songs, of course. The faster pacing also lent itself to novelty songs, such as "Yes, We Have No Bananas" from the late 1920s or "The Music Goes 'Round and Around" from the 1930s. One of the immediately distinguishing characteristics of "I Got Rhythm" is its resistance to such categorization. It is sort of a love song ("I got my man"), but this aspect seems almost an afterthought, and its rhythmic drive is certainly novel, but the song is in no sense a jest. Most essentially, perhaps, the song seems to be about the pleasures of music itself: "I got rhythm, I got music" are among the most famous words ever to come out of Tin Pan Alley.

Form

In seeking to understand the distinction of a song like "I Got Rhythm," an examination of form certainly helps. Surprisingly, what is most formally distinctive about the song is not its refrain but the length and complexity of its verse—and the rich relationship that this verse establishes with the ensuing refrain. Unlike many Tin Pan Alley standards, in which the verse carries little weight, a great deal is lost when the verse to "I Got Rhythm" is omitted in a performance.

Gershwin's verse is nearly as long as his refrain, and it possesses its own intricate internal form (see the following chart). In contrast to many Tin Pan Alley verses, it is notably tuneful itself and could almost serve as a refrain; in fact, it seems to be proceeding like an AABA refrain form, but it never completes itself. Instead of presenting a final A, Gershwin leaves the verse hanging open and proceeds right into the song's refrain—which then presents its own completed AABA form, in effect providing closure on two different levels. Structural sophistication of this order is the mark of an unusually gifted composer and an unusually fine song.

All listeners will notice the striking difference in musical character between the verse and the refrain, accentuated in Ethel Merman's recording by the slower, flexible tempo of the verse and its more delicate orchestral accompaniment. The verse is rhythmically straightforward, offering scarcely a hint of the syncopation that will become a constant feature of the refrain. As a technical note, we may also observe that the verse and the refrain differ both in key and in mode, with the verse being in a minor key that moves at the start of the refrain to a major key that is higher than the original minor key.

Obviously, everything in both Gershwin's composition and this performance of it is calculated to ensure that the verse of "I Got Rhythm" will set up and complement the refrain. This fundamental contrast between the two main sections of the song also perfectly reflects the meaning and structure of the lyrics: the verse essentially poses a question (in effect, "Why am I so happy?"), which is answered by the refrain. In tandem, they produce a whole of remarkable variety and richness.

The Song

Ira Gershwin's many fine song lyrics run a gamut from the highly sophisticated to the disarmingly straightforward. The play of rhythm and rhyme in the words to a song like "Embraceable You," to mention just one example, is breathtaking. On the other hand, the lyrics of "I

Got Rhythm" flow so naturally and effortlessly that one is unconscious of any artistry at all—and yet this effect is precisely the result of great creativity. One clever feature of the lyrics is the presence of questions in the words of both the verse and the refrain that are included for clearly different purposes. The questions in the verse are real questions, while the refrain's repeated question ("Who could ask for anything more?") is obviously rhetorical, a reflection of the singer's feeling that all important questions have actually been answered.

Many aspects of the music in "I Got Rhythm" have already been mentioned. The celebrated refrain, like its lyrics, has the effect of simplicity itself. It is certainly and obsessively *about* rhythm, as the four-note rhythmic pattern first introduced—appropriately enough—on the words "I got rhythm" is applied over and over to changing words and changing note patterns. In much African American music a pattern that is repeated to create rhythmic momentum is called a riff, and it is likely that Gershwin derived the main musical motive, or compositional idea, of his song from jazz-influenced dance band music, in which riffs are a common stylistic device. In "I Got Rhythm" every four-syllable phrase of text is set to this same rhythmic pattern ("I got rhythm," "I got music," "I got my man," "Old Man Trouble," "I don't mind him," and so forth). The pattern loses one note on the three-syllable line that ends the bridge, "'Round my door," but the only really significant break from this rhythmic obsession comes on the closing lines of the A sections, "Who could ask for anything more?"

How is it that these repeated rhythms engender excitement rather than monotony? There are several reasons. Like the riffs used in Black dance band music of the time, the syncopated "I Got Rhythm" pattern is inherently exciting, since it begins off the beat and only the third of its four notes actually falls with the beat. This technique of "playing off the beat," commonly used in

African American music, actually serves to intensify the listener's experience of the regular pulses that underlie the music. Furthermore, Gershwin ensures that the melodic shapes paired with this rhythm sometimes ascend, sometimes descend, and sometimes, as in the bridge, emphasize repeated pitches. The sense of rhythmic release on the "Who could ask for anything more?" lines is especially marked, since the new rhythmic pattern here is much more aligned with the beat than is the prevailing four-note one.

The refrain of "I Got Rhythm" is also associated with a characteristic pattern of chord changes. We mention this connection only because the chord sequence has become so widely used in jazz improvisation that it is referred to as "rhythm changes," after the title of this song. This label is a further reflection of the song's enormous popularity and influence.

The Recording

This exuberant song is ideally suited to Ethel Merman's full-throttle approach, and she holds nothing back. The slowing of tempo just before the refrain begins, and again just before the end of the record, is a theatrical device of obvious and proven effectiveness. In the repetition of the refrain, Merman's long-held high notes create a sense of climax rather than of rehashing—and also avoid the risk of rhythmic monotony that might arise from too many additional literal repetitions of the four-note rhythmic pattern. (An attentive listener will notice that even in the first presentation of the refrain, Merman introduces some spontaneous small variations in this prevailing rhythmic pattern. This is a performer's privilege, of course, and in this case a natural result of having performed the song for over fifteen years.) Merman's move to a high note at the very end in place of the expected conclusion of the melody also allows the performance to end literally at a high point.

LISTENING GUIDE	"I GOT RHYTHM"		
TIME	FORM	LYRIC	DESCRIPTIVE COMMENTS
	Instrumental introduction		Assertive rhythms and sound of full orchestra anticipate the refrain
0:09	Verse: a	*Days can be sunny . . .*	Voice enters; slower, flexible tempo; soft accompaniment
0:21	a'	*Birds in the tree . . .*	Begins just like the preceding a section but changes at the end

(continued)

Listening Guide "I GOT RHYTHM" (*continued*)

TIME	FORM	LYRIC	DESCRIPTIVE COMMENTS
0:35	b¹	*I'm chipper all the day . . .*	b section is the same length as either a section but subdivides readily into two parallel parts that begin the same and end differently, mimicking the two preceding a sections. The formal effect of b is similar to that of a bridge.
0:45	b²	*How do I get that way? . . .*	

Orchestra picks up tempo and volume, leading into:

TIME	FORM	LYRIC	DESCRIPTIVE COMMENTS
0:57	Refrain: A	*I got rhythm . . .*	Refrain enters with completely new music, introducing the four-note rhythmic motive
1:05	A	*I got daisies . . .*	
1:13	B	*Old Man Trouble . . .*	Melody changes for the bridge, but the rhythmic motive persists
1:21	A'	*I got starlight . . .*	Melody is extended and altered at the end to effect a conclusion and accommodate repetition of the line "Who could ask for anything more?"
1:31	Refrain: A		Voice holds high note, returning to words and tune only for "Who could ask . . ."; orchestra plays the melody in a big, "jazzy" style
1:39	A		High note again
1:47	B	*Old Man Trouble . . .*	Voice sings the bridge, adding spontaneous variants in words and melody
1:55	A'		High note again; voice goes up instead of down at the end to produce a big conclusion, set off by the slowing of tempo prior to the final high note

Many songs became successful without being heard in shows, of course. But the nature of Broadway's musical shows in the period just following World War I was such that it was a relatively simple matter to incorporate Tin Pan Alley songs of many kinds into them. Revues, which featured sequences of diverse skits, songs, dances, and performers and bore such titles as "Follies" and "Scandals," were the obvious successor to vaudeville and remained popular with audiences of the time. Many different writers

BOX 4.3 GEORGE GERSHWIN (1898–1937)

The career and achievements of George Gershwin are unique. At the time of his tragically early death at the age of thirty-eight (from a brain tumor), he was already world famous, and to this day he remains probably the most widely known of American composers. Alone among his many distinguished Tin Pan Alley contemporaries, Gershwin sought and achieved success in both the world of concert music (*Rhapsody in Blue*, *An American in Paris*) and the world of popular music.

Ironically, it was Gershwin's acquaintance with the popular bandleader Paul Whiteman (see Chapter 3) that brought about his successful entry into the "classical" sphere. Whiteman commissioned *Rhapsody in Blue* from Gershwin for a 1924 concert, ambitiously titled "An Experiment in Modern Music," in which Whiteman and his orchestra set out to demonstrate the evolution of American popular music from "primitive" to more "sophisticated" forms. While virtually all the other music performed by the Whiteman ensemble on this occasion has been forgotten, *Rhapsody in Blue* quickly achieved national and international success as an engaging example of new and distinctively American music.

Both Gershwin's popular songs and his "classical" works demonstrate a sophisticated incorporation of stylistic devices derived from African American sources—such as syncopated rhythms and blue notes (see Chapter 5)—that far surpasses the rather superficial use of such devices in most other white American music of the time. Gershwin's greatest composition, *Porgy and Bess* (1935), which he called an "American folk opera," represents his most thorough synthesis of European classical, mainstream popular, and African American stylistic influences—a synthesis that remains his own but also celebrates the wide diversity of American culture.

George and Ira Gershwin, c. 1920s.

could contribute songs to a single show of this type, and new songs could be introduced (or substituted for others that had worn out their welcome) to freshen things up if the show had a long run. And although musical shows with integrated story lines and scores composed by a single person (or a composer/lyricist team) also attracted audiences, the emphasis that the vast majority of these productions placed on plot and characterization was decidedly secondary to the emphasis they placed on good songs and dancing. This meant, in effect, that the shows generally revolved around the musical numbers, rather than vice versa. In these types of shows, consequently, it was also not a complicated matter to interpolate new songs or to make substitutions. It is indicative that Berlin,

Porter, the Gershwin brothers, Rodgers and Hart, and other prominent songwriters of this period all wrote songs for many Broadway shows during the 1920s and 1930s. But with very few exceptions, it is their *songs* that are remembered and that continue to live today, not the shows from which they came.

The synergetic relationship between Tin Pan Alley and Broadway is well illustrated by the early career of George Gershwin. (For an overview of Gershwin's achievements, see Box 4.3.) Starting in his late teens, Gershwin was employed in Tin Pan Alley, demonstrating at the piano the songs of others to performers while he composed his own songs, looking for a smash hit and hoping eventually to write for the Broadway stage. In 1919 Gershwin worked with lyricist Irving Caesar to create a song called "Swanee," an upbeat representative of a long-established genre—sentimental songs about the American South. ("Swanee" even quotes Stephen Foster's "Old Folks at Home"!) The song seemed destined for oblivion, however, until Al Jolson heard Gershwin play the song at a party and decided that he liked it enough to interpolate it into his current long-running hit show *Sinbad* in order to add some new life to the production. As performed by Jolson, "Swanee" was a sensation. He quickly recorded it, and it became one of his biggest hits, as well as the greatest commercial success Gershwin had with any song during his lifetime. "Swanee" established Gershwin as a newly marketable composer, and he was soon in demand by producers of musicals to write for Broadway. The rest, as they say, is history. Although Gershwin wrote many songs that were independent of Broadway shows, most of the Gershwin standards have their origins in his Broadway musicals.

With the tremendous success of the musical *Show Boat* (produced in 1927, with music by Jerome Kern and lyrics by Oscar Hammerstein II), a new chapter opened in the history of the Broadway theater. *Show Boat* was, for its time, a musical show of unprecedented seriousness and depth; it addressed racial issues and presented a complex plot in which characters were allowed to experience genuine sorrow as well as joy. There was an attempt in *Show Boat* to tie the songs more obviously to specific characters and situations. Songs from the musical became popular, but they were known as songs from *Show Boat*. The trend toward musicals in which plot, character, and musical numbers are conceived as a highly integrated whole followed a winding path but was clearly in the ascendancy by the 1940s; the partnership of Oscar Hammerstein II and Richard Rodgers, which began in 1943 with *Oklahoma!*, marks the triumph of this conception. With that triumph, the intimate ties between Tin Pan Alley and Broadway clearly began to fray, although songs from Broadway musicals could still become chart hits. When rock 'n' roll took over the pop charts in the later 1950s, any close relationship between Broadway music and mainstream pop hits essentially dissolved. Not until *Hair* opened in 1968 did Broadway have a musical that seriously employed elements of rock style, and even though songs from *Hair* did become pop hits, such a phenomenon remains to this day the exception rather than the rule. We will return occasionally to the fascinating relationship between Broadway and the American pop charts in later chapters of this book.

POPULAR SONG BOTH reflected and helped to shape the profound changes in American society during the 1920s and 1930s: the intermixing of high and low cultures, the adoption of new technologies and expansion of corporate capitalism, the increasingly intimate interaction of white and Black cultures during a period of virulent racism, and the emergence of a truly national popular culture. These songs no longer dominate popular taste as they used to. Nonetheless, they continue to be rediscovered by new generations of musicians and listeners. Tin Pan Alley and the singing style known as crooning were important (if often unrecognized) influences on rhythm & blues and rock 'n' roll during the 1950s and 1960s. Many Tin Pan Alley songs are still used by contemporary jazz musicians as a basis for improvising. Current pop stars still perform them—for example, Elvis Costello's recording of "My Funny Valentine" (composed by Richard Rodgers and Lorenz Hart), Willie Nelson's version of "Blue Skies" (Irving Berlin), Bono's duet with Frank Sinatra on "I've Got You Under My Skin" (Cole Porter), and the Smashing Pumpkins' revival of "My Blue Heaven" in 1996. In the early 1990s the veteran crooner Tony Bennett appeared on MTV's Unplugged series, finding a new audience among fans of "alternative" music who valued the combination of emotional intensity and sophistication in Bennett's style and in many of the old standard songs themselves.

In Chapters 3 and 4 we have examined two key developments in the history of popular music of the 1920s and 1930s—the influence of jazz on popular taste and the rise of the Tin Pan Alley song tradition. Now we turn our attention to music that at the time existed only on the margins of the popular music marketplace. Genres such as the blues and so-called hillbilly music (later known as country music) grew out of Southern folk music traditions, were shaped by the migration of millions of Southerners from the country to the city, and eventually came to exert a profound influence on the development of American popular music.

Key Terms

bridge	minor	standards
major	refrain	verse

Key People

Al Jolson	Gene Austin	Ruth Etting
Bing Crosby	George Gershwin	Sophie Tucker
Cole Porter	Ira Gershwin	
Ethel Merman	Irving Berlin	

Review Questions

1. What is the form of most Tin Pan Alley songs?
2. What role(s) did Jewish immigrants from central and eastern Europe play in the music business in the early twentieth century?
3. What is a standard?
4. Name three Tin Pan Alley composers and describe their contributions to American popular music.
5. In what ways did popular song both reflect and help shape the profound changes in American society during the 1920s and 1930s?

"St. Louis Blues"

Race Records and Hillbilly Music, 1920s and 1930s

5

AS WE HAVE SEEN, MANY OF THE BESTSELLING SONGS OF THE 1920s AND 1930s were produced by professional tunesmiths who worked for a small number of music publishing firms, all of which were situated within an area of Manhattan less than one square mile in extent (the musical equivalent of Wall Street). Although some composers and lyricists were able to work creatively within the constraints of a narrow range of song forms (including the AABA and ABAC forms analyzed in the last chapter), powerful institutions at the center of the music industry—including the recording and publishing companies, Hollywood, Broadway, and ASCAP—were more interested in guaranteeing profits than in encouraging musical diversity or experimentation.

Despite the essential conservatism of the music industry, it was during the years between World War I and World War II (1918–1940) that companies targeted some specific new audiences and, in the process, recorded and disseminated types of music—particularly genres derived from the folk traditions of the American South—that had previously been ignored. This process of musical diversification was encouraged by the migration of millions of people from rural communities to cities such as New York, Chicago, Detroit, Atlanta, and Nashville in the years following World War I. These migrants constituted an audience both for music that reflected their rural origins and for new, distinctively urban styles of music that were derived from the older oral traditions. The prevailing economic conditions also encouraged companies to seek out secondary markets. In 1921 the American record industry sold over 100 million discs for the first time. This peak was followed by a decline in the demand for phonographs and discs, a shift that was due in part to the expansion of commercial radio, which provided people with a cheaper means of access to a variety of programming. However, throughout the 1920s the market for performers working in idioms related to Southern folk traditions continued to grow, countering the overall trend.

The terms *race* and *hillbilly* were used by the American music industry from the early 1920s until the late 1940s to classify and advertise Southern music. "Race records" were recordings of performances by African American musicians produced mainly for sale to African American listeners. "Hillbilly" or "old-time" music, on the other hand, was performed by and mainly intended for sale to Southern whites. The record companies that released this material—including small independent labels and the large record companies of the time—usually advertised it in racially segregated catalogs and brochures. Although there were some exceptions, the music industry in general reflected the broader patterns of segregation that were more widespread in American society. Paradoxically, as we shall see, these records were also one of the main means by which music flowed across the boundaries of race.

Although a clear distinction was drawn between race music and hillbilly music—each of which comprised dozens of specific styles—the two had a number of important features in common. Both bodies of music originated mainly in the American South and were rooted in long-standing folk music traditions. As they entered the mass marketplace, both blended these older rural musical styles with aspects of national popular culture, including the minstrel show, vaudeville, and the musical forms, poetic themes, and performance styles of Tin Pan Alley pop. Race music and hillbilly music both grew out of the music industry's efforts to develop alternative markets during a national decline in record sales and were disseminated across the country by new media—including electric recording, radio, and sound film—and by the process of urban migration, which affected the lives of millions of rural Americans during the 1920s and 1930s. Additionally, both bodies of music provided the basis for forms of popular music that emerged after World War II (rhythm & blues, country and western, and rock 'n' roll), extending their appeal across regional and ultimately international boundaries.

Race Records

Although the Victor Company had released records by the Dinwiddie Colored Quartet as early as 1903 (advertising them as "genuine Jubilee and Camp Meeting Shouts sung as only negroes can sing them"), recorded performances by African American artists in the first two decades of the twentieth century were basically in the Tin Pan Alley mold, including ragtime- and jazz-tinged dance music and "coon songs" in a minstrel-show mold aimed mainly at the white market. It was not until the 1920s that the idea of recording material closer to African American folk traditions—and the associated idea of selling such material to an African American audience—took hold in the record business.

The music industry's discovery of Black music (and Southern music in general) can be traced to a set of recordings made in 1920 that featured the Black vaudeville performer *Mamie Smith* (1883–1946). Perry Bradford, a successful Black songwriter and music store owner, brought Smith to the attention of the Okeh Record Company and suggested that she replace Sophie Tucker in a recording session. A record that featured Smith performing two of Bradford's songs was released in July 1920, and although Okeh made no special effort to promote it, sales were unexpectedly high. Smith reentered the studio two months later and recorded "Crazy Blues," backed with the song "It's Right Here for You (If You Don't Get It . . . 'Tain't No Fault of Mine)." Okeh advertised "Crazy Blues" in Black communities and sold an astounding seventy-five thousand copies within one month (at that time, five thousand sales of a given recording allowed a record company to recoup its production costs, meaning that any further record sales were almost all profit). Mamie Smith's records were soon available at music stores, drugstores, furniture stores, and other outlets in Northern and Midwestern cities and throughout the Deep South.

The promotional catchphrase "**race music**" was first applied by *Ralph Peer* (1892–1960), a Missouri-born talent scout for Okeh Records who had worked as an assistant on Mamie Smith's first recording sessions. Although it might sound derogatory today, the term "race" was used in a positive sense in urban African American communities during the 1920s and was an early example of Black nationalism; an individual who wanted to express pride in his heritage might refer to himself as "a race man." The term was soon picked up by other companies and was also widely used by the Black press. The performances released on race records included a variety of musical styles—blues, jazz, gospel choirs, vocal quartets, string bands, and jug-and-washboard bands—as well as verbal performances such as sermons, stories, and comic routines. Not all recordings featuring African American artists were automatically classified as race records. For example, recordings by Black dance orchestras or jazz bands with a substantial white audience—such as James Reese Europe's Clef Club Orchestra—were listed in the mainstream pop record catalogs (see Chapter 3). A few records by African American artists even found their way into the hillbilly catalogs.

The emergence of race records set a pattern that has been repeated many times in the history of American popular music, in which talented entrepreneurs, often connected with small, independent record labels, take the lead in exploring and promoting music outside the commercial mainstream. Okeh Records, under the direction of Ralph Peer, was the first label to send mobile recording units into the South, seeking out and recording local talent. Traveling in a car with recording equipment and a team of two engineers, Peer recorded in Atlanta, Memphis, New Orleans, Dallas, and other cities and towns in the South. Paramount Records, the second company to enter the race music market, began in 1922 as a subsidiary of the Wisconsin Chair Company. Although recorded music may seem like a strange sideline for a furniture company, the combination in fact made perfect sense: the company made phonographs and the wooden cabinetry that enclosed them, and the software side of the business (the production and sale of discs) reinforced the hardware side (the production and sale of phonographs). Helped by the business acumen and community connections of J. Mayo Williams, one of a handful of influential African American men involved in the management side of the record business, Paramount became one of the most important race record labels. Its records were sold by traveling salesmen and shop owners throughout the country, and a thriving mail-order service allowed the company to cultivate a substantial rural audience.

The large record companies took several years to catch on to the new trend. Columbia Records started its successful race series in 1923, and Vocalion/Brunswick Records entered the field in 1926, while the relatively conservative Victor Company—which had heard and rejected Mamie Smith in 1920—waited until 1927 to jump in. We will see this same process—in which small independent record labels develop new musical trends and markets, while the big record companies wait several years before moving in to capitalize on them—repeated in the 1950s with rock 'n' roll, in the 1970s with reggae and punk, in the 1980s with rap music, and in the 1990s with alternative rock.

The 1920s also saw the emergence of African American–owned record companies. The first of these was Black Swan, founded in 1921 in New York by Harry Pace, a former partner of the bandleader and songwriter W. C. Handy (see Box 5.1). In announcing the new company, Pace stated that it intended to meet "a legitimate and growing demand" among the 12 million people of African descent in the United States. Bandleader Fletcher Henderson—later the inspiration for the big band swing style of the 1930s and 1940s (see Chapter 6)—was the label's musical director. Black Swan managed to buy its own pressing plant and eventually expanded its catalog to include hillbilly and operatic, as well as race, records. The range of businesses that sold race records is indicated by this announcement, placed by Black Swan in Black newspapers in 1923:

> We Want Live Agents Everywhere! Music stores, drug stores, furniture dealers, newsstands, cigar stores, manicuring and hairdressing parlors, delicatessen shops and all other places of business catering to retail trade.

By 1927 a total of some five hundred race records were being issued every year. Throughout the 1920s African Americans bought as many as 10 million blues and gospel recordings a year, almost one per person, an astonishingly high figure when compared with the mainstream record market, especially considering that many Black people lived in poverty. Although detailed information on the consumption of recorded music by African Americans during this period is sketchy, it seems clear that even in the most isolated communities, the phonograph was an important part of everyday life. A survey of rural communities in Alabama in 1930

W. C. Handy, "Father of the Blues," c. 1900, when he was working as a trumpeter/bandleader.

> ## BOX 5.1 THE "FATHER OF THE BLUES": W. C. HANDY
>
> The most influential of the classic blues composers was **William Christopher Handy**, born in Alabama in 1873. The son of a conservative pastor who forbade him from playing guitar (an instrument often associated with the devil, as well as with the lower classes), Handy instead channeled his musical talents into playing the cornet. He went on to receive a college degree and became a schoolteacher. To augment his income, Handy also worked as a freelance musician, taking the job of bandmaster for a minstrel troupe and eventually forming his own dance band. In 1908 Handy cofounded the first African American–owned music publishing house in partnership with Harry Pace, who would later go on to found Black Swan Records.
>
> For a period of some twenty-five years Handy toured the South, where he became acquainted with forms of music that had not been allowed into his house during his boyhood. As we shall see,
>
> Handy's blues actually owed much to Tin Pan Alley song forms but also drew substantially on African American folk traditions. W. C. Handy's first sheet music hit was "Memphis Blues" (1912), composed as a campaign song for Boss Crump, the famously crooked mayor of Memphis, Tennessee. His biggest hit was the song "St. Louis Blues" (1914), which went on to become one of the most frequently recorded American songs of all time. To capitalize on his success, Handy moved to New York City, where his dance band made a number of recordings and attracted a large, racially mixed audience. Regarded by many white Americans as the originator of the blues, Handy christened himself "Father of the Blues" and wrote a fascinating autobiography about his career. W. C. Handy died in 1958, the same year that Nat "King" Cole played him in a film adaptation of his autobiography.

found that 13% of Negro families—most of them living in grinding poverty—owned phonographs, bought on installment plans from local merchants. Many young people in these communities thus grew up with the sound of a phonograph as part of their everyday experience. Migrants from rural communities who had relocated to urban centers returned periodically, bringing with them the latest hit records and creating a continual flow of musical styles and tastes between city and country.

It is clear that the music business did not create race music or its intended audience out of thin air. It would be more accurate to say that the basis for an African American audience already existed and the companies, hungry for new markets, moved to exploit (and in some cases shape) this sense of a distinctive Black identity. This process in turn helped to create a truly national African American musical culture—for the first time, people living in New York City, Gary, Indiana, Jackson, Mississippi, and Los Angeles could hear the same phonograph records at around the same time. It was during this period that the first generation of national Black music stars emerged, including Bessie Smith, Blind Lemon Jefferson, and Robert Johnson.

Classic Blues

One of the most influential kinds of music disseminated on race records was the **blues**, a musical genre that emerged in Black communities of the Deep South—and especially the region from the Mississippi Delta to East Texas—sometime around the end of the nineteenth century. In the beginning, the influence of this tradition on the American pop mainstream was quite indirect, taking the form of professionally composed "blues songs" that were filtered through the sensibilities of Tin Pan Alley and vaudeville and shaped by the commercial needs of the music industry. In 1914 Prince's Orchestra, the studio ensemble that provided backing for many of Al Jolson's early recordings, released the first in a series of "blues" dance arrangements, numbers in a fox-trot style that bore little if any resemblance to the music played in Southern Black communities but were nonetheless an important aspect of African American influence on mainstream popular dance (see Chapter 3).

In this context, it is perhaps understandable that the first blues records by African American singers—such as Mamie Smith's "Crazy Blues"—were not the **country blues** performed by sharecroppers and laborers in the Mississippi Delta and East Texas, but blues songs (sometimes called **classic blues**) written by professional songwriters eager to cash in on the national fascination with "authentic Negro music." Some of the most prominent composers of these Tin Pan Alley–style blues songs were middle-class African American men who also led popular dance orchestras and composed ragtime songs (a genre that overlapped with blues songs). In many cases these songwriters viewed the folk traditions of the Deep South from a distance and thus came to the blues as partial outsiders.

Classic blues songs were performed by nightclub singers such as *Alberta Hunter* (1895–1984), billed as the "Marian Anderson of the Blues"; *Ethel Waters* (1896–1977), who entertained the growing African American middle class in New York, Chicago, and other Northern cities; and singers who performed in a somewhat rougher style, such as *Gertrude "Ma" Rainey* (1886–1939), popularly known as the "Mother of the Blues," and *Bessie Smith* (1894–1937), the "Empress of the Blues." Unlike their more refined middle-class counterparts, Rainey and Smith had developed their singing styles in the rough-and-tumble Black vaudeville and tent shows that crisscrossed the country in the early decades of the century. Their early recordings, released during the height of the so-called blues craze (1920–1926), sold well among both whites and Blacks and signaled the emergence of a style of performance that was more directly and deeply informed by African American musical traditions than either nineteenth-century minstrelsy or the ragtime-tinged pop songs of the early twentieth century.

The recordings of Bessie Smith and other classic blues singers were an important part of the process by which African American musical styles and musicians shaped the taste of the predominantly white mass audience during the 1920s and 1930s. But it would be a mistake to think that the mainstream popularity of these records means that they were not equally popular in Black communities. In her autobiography, the great gospel singer Mahalia Jackson wrote about the classic blues recordings she heard as a child in New Orleans during the 1920s:

> Everybody was buying phonographs—the kind you wound up on the side by hand—just the way people have television sets today—and everybody had records of all the Negro blues singers—Bessie Smith . . . Ma Rainey . . . Mamie Smith . . . all the rest. The famous white singers like [Enrico] Caruso—you might hear them when you went by a white folks' house, but in a colored house you

heard blues. You couldn't help but hear blues—all through the thin partitions of the houses—through the open windows—up and down the street in the colored neighborhoods—everybody played it real loud. (Jackson and Wylie 1966, 29)

Although American cities, towns, and villages were still segregated along racial lines, recordings like Bessie Smith's version of "St. Louis Blues" created a kind of bridge or middle zone between Black and white communities of taste. This middle zone proved to be fertile ground for the growth of distinctively American styles of popular music. The popularity of Bessie Smith's "St. Louis Blues" may well be attributed in part to the fact that a wide audience was already familiar with the song. Prince's Orchestra had the first hit recording of it in 1916, having already achieved popular success two years earlier with their version of W. C. Handy's "Memphis Blues." The Original Dixieland Jazz Band recorded its performance of "St. Louis Blues" in 1921, which may in turn have finally prepared the way for a popular recording of the piece by Handy himself, leading his own orchestra, in 1923. Meanwhile, the first vocal version of the song to achieve wide sales was a 1920 hit by white singer **Marion Harris** (1896–1944), one of the major recording stars of the late 1910s and early 1920s. Comparing Harris's performance with that of Bessie Smith can easily make the former seem self-conscious and excessively genteel, but the comparison is inherently unfair. In terms of her own style, Harris treated Handy's song with respect and sensitivity. The vocal ornaments and slides that she incorporated into her singing (echoed in the instrumental accompaniment, which is provided by Prince's Orchestra) may strike us today as the musical equivalent of minstrel-era blackface, but they almost certainly reflected a sincere attempt on Harris's part to evoke "authenticity" in her presentation. Just as Paul Whiteman's dance-band music, with its aspects of jazz influence, helped pave the way for the mainstream acceptance of what we now call "real" jazz (e.g., the music of King Oliver's Creole Jazz Band), a recording like Marion Harris's "St. Louis Blues" helped prepare the wide public appeal that greeted Bessie Smith's version of the song five years later—a version that many would now call definitive.

Bessie Smith's 1925 "St. Louis Blues" was the kind of recording that introduced much of white America—and a large section of Black America—to African American classic blues. It was typical insofar as it represented a hybrid approach to both blues composition and blues performance. W. C. Handy's "St. Louis Blues" and Bessie Smith's interpretation of it are both some distance removed from what might today be regarded as the most "authentic," or at least the most roots-conscious, type of blues, namely, the "down-home" rural or country blues represented by composer/performers such as Charley Patton, Blind Lemon

Bessie Smith in a studio portrait by Carl Van Vechten, 1936.

Listening Guide "ST. LOUIS BLUES"

Music and lyrics by W. C. Handy; published 1914; performed by Bessie Smith, accompanied by Louis Armstrong, cornet, and Fred Longshaw, reed organ; recorded 1925

"St. Louis Blues" is more regular and predictable in its use of blues materials than typical rural examples of the form. In this song, W. C. Handy, a middle-class African American composer (see Box 5.1), combined elements borrowed from the country blues (discussed later in this chapter) with structural elements borrowed from Tin Pan Alley. The formal clarity of Handy's composition is respected by Bessie Smith and her accompanists, even as they use the song's structure as a springboard for subtle improvisations.

Basic Description

"St. Louis Blues" is a longer and more complex song than we have encountered heretofore, a result of composer Handy's fusion of blues with Tin Pan Alley elements. Hence, Bessie Smith's performance presents the song just one time through, without any repetitions; this is all she has time for in a record that nevertheless runs over three minutes in duration. The song's lyrics depict a representative blues subject and mood in their lament over love gone wrong and their projection of a desire to escape the scene of unhappiness. The slow tempo of this performance helps to accentuate the feeling of despair—notice especially the moaning quality of Smith's drawn-out vowel sounds.

Smith is accompanied on this record by reed organ and cornet. The organ is somewhat unusual; a more common choice would have been piano, but the less rhythmically emphatic organ certainly reinforces the singer's projection of hopeless lassitude. The cornet player is jazz great Louis Armstrong (see Chapter 3). Notice how Armstrong's cornet replies to each sung phrase, engaging in call and response with Smith in a manner that is typical of much African American music. Call and response is a common feature of blues and jazz performances of all types and periods.

Form

As may be seen in the accompanying chart, the form of "St. Louis Blues" is based on the AABA model commonly seen in Tin Pan Alley songs. In this instance, the final section is really a C, as it has a new melody, but is related to the earlier A sections by virtue of its identical length and

its use of the same basic progression of chords. These A and C sections are representative of **twelve-bar blues**, a formal concept so important in the history of American popular music that it demands our attention here. In the next section of the chapter we explain some of the musical elements that make up twelve-bar blues.

The Song

"St. Louis Blues" begins as if it might be a kind of strophic folk blues, with two opening presentations of a typical blues format in both lyrics and musical structure. As we shall see, Southern rural blues songs often adhere to this format throughout. A major factor in the impact and complexity of Handy's song is that it sets us up for a repetitive structure and then deviates brilliantly and expressively from our expectations. The A music never returns, and instead we hear a succession of two new sections, B and C, after which the song concludes. (Handy might well have derived the inspiration for the form of "St. Louis Blues" from ragtime music, which often minimized large-scale elements of return or dispensed with them entirely.)

When the lyrics turn from a tone of general lament to the specifics of place and situation with the mention of the "St. Louis woman," the typical blues music of the A sections gives way to a B section of contrasting form and character, as well as striking length. In one sense, B functions like a bridge, insofar as it separates the opening and closing sections based on the traditional blues. But unlike almost all standard bridges of Tin Pan Alley songs, this B music presents an independent and memorable tune with its own distinctive structure (a-b-a-b; see the accompanying chart), and it is in fact longer than any other individual section of the song. This B tune—arguably the one that people most remember and identify with "St. Louis Blues"—is the central core of the song, virtually a song-within-a-song, rather than a transition in any sense. This emphasis is only fitting in music that accompanies lyrics that identify the villain of the piece and describe her allure.

The music of the B section, with its more graceful, insinuating rhythm (along with its change to a minor key from the prevailing major one) hints strongly at

Latin American dance music, suggesting aspects of both the habanera and the tango. This tone evokes at once the exotic and cosmopolitan nature of the "St. Louis woman," with music obviously far removed from the unpretentious, more down-home flavor of the blues sections that portray the jilted singer and her feelings. Precisely at the time Handy published "St. Louis Blues," ballroom dance stars like Vernon and Irene Castle were making the tango the new definition of urban sophistication and sexiness in dance (see Chapter 3).

As already noted, the C section once again presents a blues chord structure, providing return on one level while offering even further variety with its new melody line and lyrics. Handy himself said of "St. Louis Blues," "Here, as in most of my other blues, three distinct musical strains are carried as a means of avoiding the monotony that always resulted in the three-line folk blues." While we may well disagree with the statement that strophic folk blues are inevitably monotonous, and while we may appreciate that Handy may well have made such a statement primarily to distance himself—as a middle-class, educated, urban Black man—from poor, uneducated, rural members of his race, the remarkable richness of "St. Louis Blues" is indisputable. This piece, which synthesizes aspects of European American music (Tin Pan Alley song form), African American music (twelve-bar blues), and Latin American

music (habanera and tango dance rhythms), is as representative as any we could name of the achievements of twentieth-century American popular song.

The Recording

W. C. Handy's published sheet music for "St. Louis Blues" presents a composition that uses "blue" melodic inflections and rhythmic syncopations to a degree unusual for its time. In notating his song, Handy still needed to balance his interest in evoking effects of pitch and rhythm that originated in African American folk tradition against the inherent limitations of a European-based system of musical notation. Bessie Smith's performance of "St. Louis Blues" adds yet another layer of complexity to Handy's already rich synthesis. Although Smith was by no means a rural blues singer herself, she approached the song as one intimately familiar and comfortable with many of the varied oral traditions of African American music, and consequently her performance treated Handy's composition with considerable—but never inappropriate—freedom.

Handy's published composition contains many written **blue notes**—"bent" or "flattened" tones that lie outside traditional European-based scale structures and reflect particular African American melodic characteristics. Blue notes probably reflect the long-range influence of African scales (and have to

LISTENING GUIDE	"ST. LOUIS BLUES"		
TIME	FORM	LYRICS	DESCRIPTIVE COMMENTS
0:00	Introduction		Single held note on organ and trumpet
0:04	A	*I hate to see . . .*	Twelve-bar blues, with call and response between voice and cornet
0:49	A	*Feelin' tomorrow . . .*	
1:33	B: a	*St. Louis woman . . .*	B section has its own distinctive melody and internal form; call and response continues
1:47	b	*Pulls my man around . . .*	
2:02	a	*Wasn't for powder . . .*	
2:16	b	*The man I love . . .*	
2:28	C	*I got them St. Louis blues . . .*	C section returns to the twelve-bar blues format, but with a new melody; call and response continues to the end

(continued)

Listening Guide "ST. LOUIS BLUES" (*continued*)

be notated as "altered" flat notes in European-based musical notation). In addition to Handy's written blue notes, Bessie Smith adds *additional* blue notes of her own to her performance, intensifying the African American flavor even further. The effect of blue notes is profoundly expressive and easy to hear, as blue notes in the melody generally clash poignantly with notes in the underlying chord. To help you locate and appreciate their effect, we will notate the first A section of the recording as an example. Below are the lyrics for this section. The particular words and syllables on which Smith sings the most prominent blue notes have asterisks above them—single asterisks for those blue notes she takes from Handy's own notation and double asterisks for those she has added on her own to enhance the performance:

```
            **          *
I hate to see the eve-nin' sun go down.
    **      **     **        *
I hate to see the eve-nin' sun go down.
    **         **      *    *   *
It makes me think I'm on my last go-round.
```

Handy's written composition also calls for a great deal of rhythmic syncopation, or rhythms that play "off" or "against" or "between" the main beats that define the meter of the piece. In fact, Smith's performance goes even further in playing around the main pulse established by the accompaniment. Louis Armstrong's improvised cornet responses to Smith's vocal phrases are perfectly aligned with the singer's own stylistic approach; like Smith, Armstrong continually incorporates blue notes and syncopation into his melody lines. Without ever upstaging the singer, he maintains and underlines the pervading feeling of intense melancholy. But notice also how no two of his responses are ever precisely the same.

A further analysis of this performance would necessitate detailed comparisons between Handy's sheet music and the auditory data of the recording; such an examination would become quite academic and is obviously beyond the scope of this book. The miraculous thing is that all the intertwined and overlapping complexities that went into the making of this recording resulted in nothing remotely academic in effect: the performance comes across as immediate, direct, sincere, and emotionally devastating.

Jefferson, and Robert Johnson (all of whom we shall meet shortly). But as we have already seen, it was often the very process of musical hybridization that enabled marginal music to begin crossing over into the mainstream of American popular music.

Bessie Smith, along with other Black singers who toured and performed in Northern urban centers, adapted her repertoire and performing to suit the tastes of her audiences and came to represent the style called, perhaps paradoxically, classic blues. It was the unprecedented success of the classic blues singers and records that eventually prompted interest in the roots of the blues and led to the later recordings of rural Southern practitioners of the form. Bessie Smith's 1925 recording of "St. Louis Blues" was an early crossover hit, selling well among whites as well as Blacks. Although there were no official industry charts for hit records at the time, it has been estimated that Smith's "St. Louis Blues" must have reached the equivalent of Number 3 on the mainstream pop charts. (Even more remarkable is the fact that Bessie Smith's first Columbia recording, "Down Hearted Blues," was the bestselling record in America for four weeks in 1923.) Smith's ability to attract an audience that crossed the color line during the 1920s has been credited with single-handedly saving Columbia Records from bankruptcy during that period. "St. Louis Blues" will now serve as our introduction to the blues.

Understanding Twelve-Bar Blues

A **bar**, or **measure**, is simply a rhythmic unit of music, consisting of one accented beat followed by one or more unaccented beats. Beats are equal measures of musical time; when you tap your foot or your finger to a tune, you are sensing and measuring its beats. Most popular music with which Americans are familiar is organized in bars of two, three, or four beats, following one right after another in regular patterns. For example (accented beats are indicated in bold):

March: **One**, two; **One**, two; **One**, two; etc.
In the march, each rhythmic unit of **One**, two is a bar.

Waltz: **One**, two, three; **One**, two, three; **One**, two, three; etc.
In the waltz, each rhythmic unit of **One**, two, three is a bar.

Blues: **One**, two, three, four; **One**, two, three, four; **One**, two, three, four; etc.
In the blues, each rhythmic unit of **One**, two, three, four is a bar.

It is the pattern of accented and unaccented beats that creates the characteristic rhythmic organization that we associate with specific types of music. Marches are typically "in two," to accord with the regular motion of two feet; waltzes are invariably written with three-beat bars; most blues and jazz—and much Tin Pan Alley music of either ballad or up-tempo type—have four-beat bars.

Twelve-bar blues refers to a particular arrangement of four-beat bars. The bars are themselves grouped in fours, and each group of four bars corresponds to a unit—a line or a phrase—in the lyrics and is also associated with characteristic chord changes. (In an instrumental blues, it is the recurring pattern of chord changes by itself that creates the form.) This is easy to hear in the initial A section of "St. Louis Blues." Let us consider the lyrics first. In following the chart below, rely on the organ for rhythmic orientation, as it clearly articulates each beat:

Beats: 1 2 3 4   1 2 3 4   1 2 3 4   1 2 3 4
Bars: 1   2   3   4
Lyrics: I hate to see   the evenin' sun go down. [Cornet response . . .]

Beats: 1 2 3 4   1 2 3 4   1 2 3 4   1 2 3 4
Bars: 5   6   7   8
Lyrics: I hate to see the evenin' sun go down. [Cornet response . . .]

Beats: 1 2 3 4   1 2 3 4   1 2 3 4   1 2 3 4
Bars: 9   10   11   12
Lyrics: It makes me think I'm on my last go-round. [Cornet response . . .]

The three-line poetic stanza, in which the second line is a repetition of the first, is extremely common in twelve-bar blues and is an obvious clue to the presence of that form. The same pattern is present in the lyrics of the second stanza, the second A section of "St. Louis Blues":

> *Feelin' tomorrow like I feel today,*
> *Feelin' tomorrow like I feel today,*
> *I'll pack my grip and make my getaway.*

The issue of harmony in the twelve-bar blues is obviously a complex one, since the progression of chords, even in examples of classic blues, is by no means absolutely systematic or consistent. Still, the twelve-bar blues does tend to be marked by specific chord changes at particular points in the pattern. The thing to remember is that the chord changes need not be limited only to these typical ones; a given performance may add further changes at other points. If we call our starting chord the "home" chord (musicians would call it the **tonic**), the following chart shows the most important, typical points of change in the twelve-bar blues pattern:

Bars	1	2	3	4	5	6	7	8	9	10	11	12
Chords	"Home" [tonic chord]				Change 1 [subdominant chord]		"Home" [tonic chord]		Change 2 [dominant chord]		"Home" [tonic chord]	

Twelve-bar Blues

Note that the chords at changes 1 and 2 are different from one another; thus there are three essential chords that define the skeleton of the musical structure. (Musicians call the chord at bar 5 the subdominant and the chord at bar 9 the dominant.) Although there are additional chord changes, this basic skeleton is clearly in evidence in the two A sections of "St. Louis Blues," and it is good listening practice to try to pick it out. This same chord skeleton is present in the twelve-bar C section that concludes the song, even though the vocal melody paired with it is different. This is why C is also a twelve-bar blues, even though its pattern of lyrics is also different, presenting three different lines in the stanza instead of having a repeated line.

The Country Blues

What was the initial inspiration for the twelve-bar sections and blue notes of popular songs like "Crazy Blues" and "St. Louis Blues"? In his autobiography, W. C. Handy described an encounter with what he called "the weirdest music I had ever heard" at a train station in the Mississippi Delta in the year 1903:

> A lean, loose-jointed Negro had commenced plunking a guitar beside me while
> I slept. His clothes were rags; his feet peeped out of his shoes. His face had on it
> some of the sadness of the ages. As he played, he pressed a knife on the strings of

the guitar in a manner popularized by Hawaiian guitarists who used steel bars. The effect was unforgettable. His song, too, struck me instantly.

"Goin' where the Southern cross' the Dog"

The singer repeated the line three times, accompanying himself on the guitar with the weirdest music I had ever heard. The tune stayed in my mind. When the singer paused, I leaned over and asked him what the words meant. He rolled his eyes, showing a trace of mild amusement. Perhaps I should have known, but he didn't mind explaining. At Moorhead the eastbound and the westbound met and crossed the north and southbound trains four times a day. This fellow was going where the Southern cross' the Dog, and he didn't care who knew it. He was simply singing about Moorhead as he waited. (Handy 1941, 78)

The music Handy heard that day was the country blues (also referred to as "rural," "down-home," or "folk" blues). Although country blues had existed for decades before the first vaudevillian blues songs appeared on record, rural musicians who played in a style closer to the roots of the tradition were not recorded by phonograph record companies until the mid-1920s. Most scholars agree that the folk blues first emerged in the Mississippi Delta, a region of fertile land that stretches some two hundred miles along the river from Memphis, Tennessee, in the north to Vicksburg, Mississippi, in the south. In the nineteenth century the Delta had been the site of some of the most intensive cotton farming in the Deep South and was home to one of the largest populations of slaves in North America. After the Civil War many former slaves were relegated to the position of tenant farmers, or sharecroppers, still tied to the land owned by white farmers and living in conditions of extreme poverty. Some men were compelled to work on the levees, a huge system of earthworks designed to protect the fertile Delta farmlands from flooding. To escape this exploitative system and gain some measure of freedom, others took to the road, working on the railways and riverboats.

The blues was the music of this impoverished Black workforce, and it provided a dynamic, flexible framework for publicly recounting aspects of individuals' experiences. The earliest blues appear to have been influenced by various types of African American folk music that already existed in the late nineteenth century. These included "jump-ups," songs based on short repeated phrases that were often used as accompaniment for dancing; African American story songs such as "John Henry" and "Frankie and Johnny," which show influences from the English ballad tradition; work songs, rhythmic songs used to accompany and coordinate agricultural labor; and field hollers or "arhoolies," stylized cries sometimes used to communicate across the fields.

As we saw in the analysis of "St. Louis Blues," the basic features of classic blues form are (1) a twelve-bar structure made up of three phrases of four bars each with (2) a basic three-chord pattern and (3) a three-line AAB text. In fact, the rural blues that provided the inspiration for classic blues songs displayed a much wider range of forms. There are eight-bar and sixteen-bar country blues; a rural blues singer may drop or add a couple of beats in order to better express himself, resulting in 11½- or 12½-bar forms; and some blues use more than three chords, while others are based on a repeated rhythmic-melodic pattern (a riff) and do not really use chords at all. In addition, distinctive regional styles of blues developed that were based in the Mississippi Delta, the Piedmont region of the Carolinas and Virginia, East Texas, and other parts of the South.

In order to understand the evolution of musical forms such as the blues, it is important to consider how songs are produced and how they are disseminated from one person or group to another. In the early twentieth century the country blues was an entirely oral tradition, in which versions of a song were passed down from generation to generation, learned by ear and carried in memory. Because the blues was essentially a personal form of music-making, individual musicians could construct their own versions of existing songs or assemble new songs from parts of others. The Tin Pan Alley way of making music, in contrast, depended on writing songs down in a standardized form. In addition, the music industry's reliance on sheet music as a means of distributing music to the public meant that songs often had to be simplified in order to allow customers without specialized musical training to perform them at home. Thus the neat and tidy form of classic blues songs is in part a byproduct of the process of musical notation, which tends to create a standardized and authoritative version of any particular popular song.

The process of recording, which began to affect the blues tradition in the 1920s, was another means of transmission that shaped the evolution of the blues. To take one example, Bessie Smith's 1925 recording of "St. Louis Blues," with its slow tempo and personal expressive touches, became a kind of model on which other performers based their versions. During the early 1920s many blues musicians in the South, having heard the classic blues recordings of Bessie Smith, Ma Rainey, and other vaudeville-influenced singers, added the songs to their repertoires. Later in the 1920s, when rural blues artists began to be recorded, certain melodies, lines of text, and styles of performance were spread on phonograph records, helping not only to create a nationwide audience for the blues but also to establish shared ideals of an authentic "deep blues" sound. These cases show how sound recording—a process rooted in urbanization and industrialization—can become part of the process of oral tradition.

CHARLEY PATTON

One of the earliest known pioneers of the Mississippi Delta blues style was *Charley Patton* (ca. 1891–1934). Patton, the son of sharecroppers, was a charismatic figure whose performance techniques included rapping on the body of his guitar and throwing it into the air. His powerful rasping voice, strong, danceable rhythms, and broad range of styles made him ideal for Saturday night dances and all-day picnics.

Patton's reputation and ability to secure work were boosted by his work as a recording artist. Between 1929, when he was "discovered" by Henry Speir (a white record store owner from Jackson, Mississippi, who served as a talent scout for Paramount and other companies) and 1934, the year he died, Patton recorded nearly seventy songs. His recorded repertoire included not only blues but also African American ballads, ragtime, Tin Pan Alley hits, and even church songs (which he recorded under a pseudonym, Elder J. J. Hadley). Charley Patton's recordings are the best evidence we have of a first-generation bluesman apart from the Texan Blind Lemon Jefferson, whose work is discussed later in this chapter.

The popularity of blues performers and blues recordings in rural Black communities throughout the South stemmed from the genre's ability to explore the shared concerns

Listening Guide "TOM RUSHEN BLUES"

Written and performed by Charley Patton; recorded 1929

Charley Patton's "Tom Rushen Blues," recorded by Paramount Records, has a twelve-bar form, three chords, and an AAB text (with a few minor variations, typical of rural blues performances). Patton sings in the rough, heavy voice typical of Delta blues, and his emphatic approach to guitar playing is also representative of the style. The lyrics of the song focus on Charley Patton's overnight incarceration in the Bolivar County, Mississippi, jailhouse after being arrested for drinking moonshine (homemade liquor, common in the South during the era of Prohibition). The real-life characters include Holloway, a friend of Patton who was also arrested for drinking moonshine; marshal Tom Day; and deputy sheriff Tom Rushing (whose name appears to have been mistranscribed by the staff at Paramount Records). The blues scholar David Evans interviewed Tom Rushing more than fifty years later, and Rushing still remembered Patton fondly. The blues singer had apparently brought Rushing a copy of the record when it was released!

The story itself is impressionistically presented, with general observations about life interspersed into the progression of events. The basic outlines of this story are not hard to follow: a drunk Charley Patton is unceremoniously carted off to jail, where he spends the night. But a closer examination reveals additional layers to this text, encoded meanings that any listener in the know—that is, anyone familiar with the conditions of everyday life in small-town Mississippi during the 1920s—would be able to extract.

The use of encoded, or hidden, meanings in the blues has its roots in many earlier genres of African American music. The songs of slaves could embody secret messages that were impossible to state directly in the presence of masters or overseers; a famous example is the folk song "Follow the Drinking Gourd," which described

symbolically certain landmarks on the Underground Railroad, a path runaway slaves could follow to the North and freedom. (The "drinking gourd" was code for the Big Dipper, which could be used in the night sky to locate the North Star and thus lead the runaway in the right direction.) Work songs or prison songs might contain encoded messages about bosses or wardens that would lead to punishment if stated outright. The presence of encoded meanings was a great source of the blues' power and influence; we will encounter this phenomenon at many other points in our survey of American popular music.

In "Tom Rushen Blues" Patton does not attack the institutionalized racism of the times in explicit terms. The critique of white privilege in "Tom Rushen," as in many other rural blues, is conveyed within an ironic framework. In the next-to-last stanza, the incarcerated bluesman slyly reveals that marshal Tom Day is concerned with losing an upcoming election and thus is being forced to wander "from town to town," much in the manner of an itinerant blues musician. This humorous way of dealing with serious issues—despair (the blues), alcoholism, and, at a deeper level, racism and small-town politics—is typical of many blues lyrics. Patton manages to poke fun at everyone, including himself; in the last line, he simultaneously protests his arrest and admits his culpability ("I'm gonna tell you folkses just how he treated me; Aw he dogged me here an' I was drunk as I could be").

This combination of dysphoria and humor, earthiness and philosophy, typifies the best country blues. As in the romantic songs of Tin Pan Alley, we view the world through the window of another person's experience. Unlike the romantic pop song tradition, however, the blues provides a gritty, realistic engagement with everyday life, offering metaphoric revenge and a mordant sense of humor as the best available antidotes to oppression.

of African Americans through the details of personal experience, often presented in striking poetic images. Unlike European-derived ballads, in which a story is usually presented in narrative fashion—that is, in a linear sequence recounting the actual order of events—blues songs more frequently resemble a series of evocative snapshots, assembled around a theme or set of themes: lost love, sexual desire, work, violence, loneliness.

Blind Lemon Jefferson: The First Country Blues Star

Although the genre appears to have originated in the Mississippi Delta, the first recording star of the country blues was the Texan *Blind Lemon Jefferson* (1893–1929). Born without sight, Jefferson adopted the typical life of a traveling street musician at a very young age, wandering from place to place, performing for whoever would listen, and living on handouts and the hospitality of friends while hoping for steadier engagements that could bring in more income. His first records were released in 1926, after an enthusiastic market for blues had been established by more modern artists, and Jefferson's songs were advertised even then as "real old-fashioned blues by a real old-fashioned blues singer." Like Charley Patton, Jefferson recorded popular ragtime numbers as well as blues and recorded church songs under a pseudonym, the Reverend L. J. Bates. However, Jefferson's East Texas style differs from Patton's Mississippi Delta blues in a number of ways: the vocal quality is generally more nasal and clearer, and the guitar accompaniments are sparser in texture and less rhythmically steady, generally subordinated to the vocal performance. Jefferson often used his guitar as an extension of his voice rather than as an accompaniment to it; he frequently played single-string passages on his guitar to answer a vocal line (another example of call-and-response technique).

Blind Lemon Jefferson, like many other race record artists, was denied any share of the profits generated by his hit records, and in the end he died destitute. Jefferson was buried in an unmarked grave in Texas, where a grave marker was finally dedicated by his fans in 1967. A sermon by the Chicago preacher Reverend Emmett Dickinson entitled "Death of Blind Lemon," released by Paramount Records in 1930, gives some indication of his importance in the African American community:

> Let us pause for a moment
> And look at the life of our beloved Blind Lemon Jefferson who was born blind.
> It is in many respects like that of our Lord, Jesus Christ.
> Like Him, unto the age of thirty he was unknown,
> And also like Him in a short space of a little over three years
> His name and his works were known in every house.

Robert Johnson: Standing at the Crossroad

If the recordings of Charley Patton and Blind Lemon Jefferson put us in touch with the roots of the blues, those of *Robert Johnson* (1911–1938) seem to point almost eerily toward the future. Indeed, no country blues artist had a greater influence on later generations of blues and rock musicians than Johnson. His work was especially revered by the British guitarist Keith Richards of the Rolling Stones and by Eric Clapton, whose band Cream released a celebrated cover of Johnson's "Cross Road Blues" in 1968. Eventually,

Blind Lemon
Jefferson, c. 1928.

Johnson's posthumous reputation was such that when his complete output was reissued on two CDs in 1990, the set quickly became a surprise million-seller.

Robert Johnson's brief life is shrouded in mystery and legend, much like the history of the blues itself; it is the stuff of which myths are made. Little is known of his early years. His guitar playing was so remarkable and idiosyncratic that stories circulated claiming Johnson had sold his soul to the devil in order to play that way: when performing for an audience, he apparently turned in such a position as to conceal his hands so that nobody could see what he was doing to produce his sounds. Only eleven records containing twenty-two songs by Johnson were released during his lifetime. Yet by late 1938 his fame had spread sufficiently that the American music talent scout and promoter John Hammond sought him out to appear with major African American folk and jazz artists in a "Spirituals to Swing" concert in New York City's celebrated Carnegie Hall—only to discover that Johnson had very recently died, apparently a victim of poisoning by a jealous husband.

Listening Guide "THAT BLACK SNAKE MOAN"

Written and performed by Blind Lemon Jefferson; recorded 1926

Listening to Jefferson's version of "That Black Snake Moan," recorded by Paramount Records, it is easy to grasp why music like this would have struck a middle-class Black musician like W. C. Handy—not to mention the white advertising copywriter for Paramount Records!—as "weird." Jefferson's voice has a moaning quality, sliding among pitches and sometimes sounding closer to speaking than singing. The moaning quality is accentuated by the textless vocalizations, such as "aay" or "mmm," with which Jefferson punctuates the beginnings of many phrases in the song. The melodic character of the vocal part is restricted essentially to brief, repeated ideas; each of the six three-line stanzas is set to essentially the same music, and all the repeated lines of text are set to the same repeated music. These features are probably what led W. C. Handy to refer to the country blues as "monotonous."

Furthermore, there is little feeling of chord progression in "That Black Snake Moan," as the guitar part is characterized more by single-note playing than by the strumming of chords. Additionally, the rhythmic feeling of the piece is unpredictable throughout, with individual phrases lasting shorter or longer than expected, according to the performer's pleasure. (The suspicion that Jefferson never played this song exactly the same way twice is validated by the existence of another, quite different recording of "Black Snake Moan" made by the singer.) Indeed, as Jefferson is the only performer here, he is not even obligated to keep a steady beat going, since he does not have to keep time with anybody else. While some parts of the song seem to have a clearly marked pulse, others do not, and it is frustrating to try to tap your foot regularly to this record. What establishes this song as blues is the form of the text and the presence of blue notes in the melody—not the more formalized chordal and rhythmic patterns found in classic blues performances.

If we listen closely to what Jefferson actually *does* with his seemingly restricted materials, we may come to appreciate an expressive intensity in his work that could leave Tin Pan Alley records sounding impoverished by comparison. The variety in vocal timbre and rhythmic approach that Jefferson brings to each successive stanza of his song is remarkable. The repetitive

textual and melodic structures are nothing more than a skeleton on which Jefferson builds a largely improvised performance of risky, and striking, immediacy. One can actually feel the pain of the bedbug bite in the third stanza and the weariness in the singer's heart as he asks his lover in the fifth stanza, "What's the matter now?"

Of course, lyrics like these demand a completely different approach than do those of a Tin Pan Alley song. It is instructive to compare the lovers' relationship in "That Black Snake Moan" with the idealized middle-class one articulated in the lyrics to "My Blue Heaven," recorded in New York City the next year (see Chapter 4). There is a blunt realism in Jefferson's words, with their descriptions of poverty and erotic desire. Whereas the "I" who hurries to "my blue heaven" is a kind of generic figure—is it the singer, the listener, the listener's spouse, or an imaginary lover?—there is no question that the person whose life is described in "That Black Snake Moan" is literally the singer himself; when he asks his "baby" for fifty cents, she addresses him by name: "Lemon, ain't a dime in the yard."

The sexual image around which the song is organized—the snake as phallic symbol—is typical of blues lyrics. Sexual puns and the theme of erotic love were an important part of the appeal of blues and other race records—Jefferson's "Black Snake Moan" recordings were his bestselling records, and blues musicians like Bo Carter made a living from double-entendre songs such as "Let Me Roll Your Lemon," "Pin in Your Cushion," and "My Pencil Won't Write No More." The sexual content of blues songs was, of course, also a source of middle-class outrage. The frankness of sexual discourse in rural African American culture, not atypical of farming communities where the facts of life are observed daily, ran counter to the social mores of "respectable" society and the religious establishment, both white and Black.

The lyrics of "That Black Snake Moan" are even further from the tradition of narrative storytelling in Anglo-American ballads than are the lyrics of Charley Patton's "Tom Rushen Blues." There is no precise chronological ordering of events here, and certain stanzas could be placed in a different position without affecting our overall understanding of what transpires. Obviously a sexual encounter is being described, but apart from that, it is not clear where or when certain exchanges of dialogue are actually taking place, nor is it important to know. The singer is obviously addressing his significant other at times, but other lines seem to be addressed to an outside listener, or quite possibly to the singer himself. This nonlinear approach to storytelling actually relates these lyrics to certain long-standing and sophisticated oral traditions in West Africa, wherein the roots of this approach certainly lie. By learning about varied aspects of an occurrence, the people involved in it, and their surroundings, we gain an overall feeling for what happened. Using relatively few carefully chosen words overall, Blind Lemon Jefferson manages to convey to us a distinct sense of himself, his environment, his sexual partner, the nature of their interaction, and the way they both feel about that interaction. As we have already suggested, this is a very different way of communicating human experience than that typically deployed in mainstream Tin Pan Alley songs of the 1920s and 1930s.

LISTENING GUIDE	"THAT BLACK SNAKE MOAN"
TIME	LYRICS
0:00	Guitar introduction
0:10	*Aay, ain't got no mama now.* *Aay, ain't got no mama now.* *She told me late last night, "You don't need no mama no how."*
0:37	*Mmm, black snake crawlin' in my room.* *Mmm, black snake crawlin' in my room.* *And some pretty mama had better come an' get this black snake soon*
1:03	*Oow, that must be the bedbug—you know, a chinch* [another small insect] *can't bite that hard.* *Oow, that must be the bedbug—you know, a chinch can't bite that hard.* *Ask my baby for fifty cents, she say, "Lemon, ain't a dime in the yard."*
1:33	*Mama, that's all right, mama, that's all right for you.* *Mama, that's all right, mama, that's all right for you.* *Say baby, that's all right, most any ol' way you do.*
1:59	*Mmm, what's the matter now?* *Mmm, honey, what's the matter now?* *Tell me what's the matter, baby. "I don't like no black snake no how."*
2:23	*Well, wonder where is the black snake gone?* *Well, wonder where is the black snake gone?* *Lord, that black snake, mama, done run my darlin' home.*

Early Country Music: Hillbilly Records

Hillbilly music, later rechristened "country and western music" or simply "country music," developed mainly out of the folk songs, ballads, and dance music of immigrants from the British Isles. It would be a mistake, however, to regard early country music recordings as examples of a pure and untouched rural culture. By the end of World War I even the most isolated rural communities had felt the influence of urban institutions, tastes, and technologies. The first Southern musicians to be commercially recorded grew up under the influence of minstrelsy, vaudeville, circuses, and the medicine show—a traveling spectacle complete with glib-talking "doctors" hawking dubious bottled potions

Listening Guide "CROSS ROAD BLUES"

Written and performed by Robert Johnson; recorded 1936

Johnson's music, like Charley Patton's, is representative of Mississippi Delta blues, a much heavier, more emphatic style than the Texas blues of Blind Lemon Jefferson. "Cross Road Blues" serves as a fine example of Johnson's artistry. Johnson's guitar here is forcefully rhythmic, and while the song as a whole exhibits the freedom of phrasing also seen in "That Black Snake Moan," there is a much stronger feeling of regular pulse throughout "Cross Road Blues." Unlike Jefferson, Johnson uses the guitar principally as a chordal instrument, and his aggressive, rapid strumming of chords gives his work a flavor that anticipates the electric guitar styles of rock music. This modern feeling is abetted by the wide range of timbres Johnson obtains from his acoustic guitar; note his effective alternations of high-pitched, strained chordal sounds with low-pitched, fuller chordal sounds. He also makes use of the "bottleneck" technique common among Mississippi Delta blues guitarists. To achieve this effect, the guitarist slips the sawed-off neck of a glass bottle over a finger on his left hand, which allows him to produce smooth glides between individual pitches. In the hands of a great guitarist like Johnson, the bottleneck technique can even be used to imitate the sound of a human voice. Johnson's creative use of guitar timbres is mirrored in his singing, which also veers eerily from high to low and from strained to gruff colors, as if depicting through sound itself the desperation expressed in the words of the song. The expressive intensity of the performance is given shape by the form of the blues, which is heard in the basic chord sequences as well as the poetic structure of the piece.

Although the lyrics of "Cross Road Blues" are not encoded in a typical way, they are certainly personal. Just where the "crossroad" is, what its special significance might be for the singer, and whether it even refers to a specific place at all or just functions as a metaphor, are all unknowable mysteries. (The image probably represents a continuity with West African mythologies, in which the crossroad figures as a place of uncertainty, danger, and opportunity, as well as a symbol of destiny.) Even in 1936 the name Willie Brown in the last stanza would have been recognized only by those who really knew their country blues (he was a mentor of Johnson's). In terms of narrative technique, "Cross Road Blues" hardly tells a story at all. Like some of the greatest lyric poetry, it uses words to evoke an emotional and spiritual condition—in this instance, a condition of harrowing darkness and despair.

and musicians ranging from Swiss yodelers and Hawaiian guitar bands to country fiddlers. The first generation of hillbilly recording artists was also familiar with the sentimental songs of Tin Pan Alley, and this material became an important part of the country music repertoire, alongside the older Anglo American ballads and square dance tunes.

Interestingly, it was the race record market, established in the early 1920s, that led to the first country music recordings. The first commercially successful hillbilly record, featuring a North Georgia musician named Fiddlin' John Carson, was made by Okeh Records in 1923 during a recording expedition to Atlanta. This field trip, led by Ralph Peer and a local record store owner named Polk Brockman, was actually aimed at locating new material for the race record market. As Ralph Peer later recalled:

> Brockman began scouting around but to my amazement he didn't know of any Negro talent. . . . Finally there was this deal where he wanted me to record a singer from a local church. This fellow had quite a good reputation and occasionally

worked on the radio. So we set a date with this fellow but his father was ill in some other town and he just couldn't make the date. So to take up my time, my distributor brought in Fiddlin' John Carson. He said Fiddlin' John had been on the radio station and he's got quite a following. He's really not a good singer, but let's see what he's got. So the beginning of the hillbilly [recording industry] was just this effort to take up some time. . . . I can't claim that there was any genius connected with it—not on my part, not on his part. (Porterfield 1979, 93)

Peer apparently had no inkling of the commercial potential of Carson's fiddle playing and singing on songs such as "The Little Old Log Cabin in the Lane" and "The Old Hen Cackled and the Rooster's Going to Crow," which Peer later described as "pluperfect awful." Polk Brockman, having a better sense of the local music scene, ordered five hundred copies of the disc for circulation in the Atlanta area. These sold out within a month, without any attempt to promote or advertise them, and Peer realized that the sales indicated an audience for country music among rural Southerners and recent migrants to the city. Although this realization may have been a bolt from the blue for Peer and his Northern recording company colleagues, the way had in fact been well prepared: Carson had already spent some forty years touring the South and building a reputation as a championship fiddler, and his fame had recently been reinforced by a series of appearances on radio station WSB in Atlanta.

The new medium of radio was crucial to the rapid growth of the hillbilly music market. In 1920 the first commercial radio station in the United States, KDKA in Pittsburgh, began broadcasting, and by 1922 there were more than five hundred stations nationwide, including eighty-nine in the South. Many farmers and working-class people who could not afford to buy new phonograph records were able to purchase a radio on a monthly installment plan and thereby gain access to a wide range of programming. That early radio played a large role in popularizing hillbilly music and a practically nonexistent role in promoting race music is not difficult to explain. Most radios, and all radio stations, were owned by whites. There simply were no Black disc jockeys until the late 1930s, when Jack Cooper started his race music show in Chicago. This white domination of the industry meant that radio played almost no role in popularizing race music, which was much more dependent on the phonograph (and correspondingly suffered more when radio began to eat away at record sales in the later 1920s and 1930s).

The first station to feature country artists on a regular basis was WSB in Atlanta, which began broadcasting in 1922. In 1923 WBAP in Fort Worth, Texas, aired the first hour-long radio show featuring country music, an innovation soon copied by WLS in Chicago (*National Barn Dance*) and WSM in Nashville (the famous *Grand Ole Opry*). The "barn dance" format, the predecessor of televised country music shows (exemplified by the relatively late but famous *Hee-Haw*) typically featured a variety of musical performers as well as comedians specializing in cornball humor that relied on stereotypes of rural "hicks," "rubes," and "rednecks." The musical performers on barn dance shows included string bands (featuring some combination of fiddle, guitar, banjo, and mandolin), solo and duet singers (performing in a wide range of vocal styles and often accompanying themselves on stringed instruments or piano), white gospel singers,

Hawaiian guitar bands, harmonica players, saw players, whistlers, and yodelers. (One country music radio veteran remarked that the first country music radio shows exploited "anybody who could sing, whistle, play a musical instrument, or even breathe heavy"!) (Wiggins 1986, 69) Radio did more than any other medium to popularize hillbilly music among both Southerners and a wider audience.

Most hillbilly musicians of the 1920s and 1930s did not start out as full-time professional musicians. The country music historian Bill C. Malone has noted that the majority were employed as textile mill workers, coal miners, farmers, railroad men, cowboys, carpenters, wagoners, painters, common laborers, barbers, and even occasionally as lawyers, doctors, or preachers. One important exception to this rule was **Vernon Dalhart** (1883–1948), a Texas-born former light-opera singer who recorded the first big country music hit. Dalhart's recording career, which had begun in 1916, had started to wane by the early 1920s, and he talked the Victor Company into letting him record a hillbilly number in an effort to cash in on the genre's growing popularity. In 1924 Dalhart recorded two songs: "Wreck of the Old 97," a ballad about a train crash in Virginia; and "The Prisoner's Song," a sentimental amalgam of pre-existing song fragments best known for the line "If I had the wings of an angel, over these prison walls I would fly." Although Dalhart's tenor voice bore unmistakable traces of his experience as a singer of sentimental songs and light classics, he adopted a Southern dialect and performed in a plaintive manner that country music fans found appealing. This two-song recording was the first big hillbilly hit, a million-seller that contributed to the success of the fledgling country music industry, made Vernon Dalhart a major star, and helped to ease the Victor Company's financial woes. From 1924 on, Vernon Dalhart recorded only hillbilly songs, and he did more to popularize early country music than any performer except the "Singing Brakeman," Jimmie Rodgers, whom we shall meet shortly.

It is instructive to compare Dalhart's early success in the hillbilly field to the classic blues recordings of Mamie Smith and Bessie Smith. Each represents a process of hybridization between Southern folk music and Tin Pan Alley pop. These singers all stand at some distance from the rural origins evoked by their songs, yet all are able to perform in a style respectful of those origins. Recordings such as "St. Louis Blues" and "The Prisoner's Song" are early examples of a phenomenon that will become more important as we move on through the history of American popular music: the crossover hit, that is, a record that moves from its origins in a local culture or marginal market to garner a larger and more diverse audience via the mass media.

Pioneers of Country Music: The Carter Family and Jimmie Rodgers

Country music has always really been about the relationship between the country and the city, home and migration, the past and the present. This thematic core is not surprising if we consider the main audience for this music during the 1920s: rural people whose way of life was being radically transformed by the mechanization of agriculture and changes in the American economy, and migrants who left home behind to find jobs and establish new lives in the city. Early country music records provide us with a stereoscopic image of tradition in a period of rapid change: on the one hand, ballads and love songs celebrating the good old days, family, hearth, and home; on the other, tales of broken love, distance from loved ones, and restless movement from town to town. These two images are perhaps best personified by two of the most popular acts of early country music: the Carter Family and Jimmie Rodgers. The Carters and Rodgers were both "discovered" by Ralph Peer at a recording session in Bristol, Tennessee, in August 1927. Boosted by hit records and radio appearances, both acts exerted a profound influence on successive generations of country and western musicians.

The *Carter Family*, born in the isolated foothills of the Clinch Mountains of Virginia, is regarded as one of the most important groups in the history of country music. The leader of the trio was A. P. "Doc" Carter (1891–1960), who collected and arranged the folk songs that formed the inspiration for much of the group's repertoire; he also sang bass. His wife Sara (1899–1979) sang most of the lead vocal parts and played autoharp or guitar. Sister-in-law Maybelle (1909–1978) sang harmony, played guitar and autoharp, and developed an influential guitar style that involved playing the melody on the bass strings while brushing the upper strings on the offbeats for rhythm. This technique was so identified with Maybelle Carter that it has become known as the "Carter Family lick." The Carter Family's repertoire included adaptations of old songs from the Anglo American folk music tradition, old hymns, and sentimental songs reminiscent of turn-of-the-century Tin Pan Alley hits. As Bill Malone puts it, "Theirs was a music that might

The Carter Family: Maybelle, Sara, and A.P. (from left to right), pictured on the cover of their first song-book, c. 1928.

borrow from other forms, but would move away from its roots only reluctantly" (Malone 1985, 65). Between 1927 and 1941 the Carters made over three hundred recordings for a half-dozen companies. Their most popular songs include "Wildwood Flower," "Wabash Cannon Ball," "Keep on the Sunny Side," and "Can the Circle Be Unbroken," all of which are still performed by country musicians today. Rehearsing at home, they crafted traditional materials into three-minute gems designed for the 78 rpm phonograph discs of the time.

The Carter Family were not professional musicians when their recording career started in 1927—as Sara put it when she was asked what they did after the Bristol session, "Why, we went home and planted the corn." The Carters' image, borne out in radio appearances and interviews, was one of quiet conservatism: their stage shows were simple and straightforward, and they generally avoided the vaudeville circuit and promotional tours. Despite their image of being firmly rooted in the rural past, however, the Carters' approach to working with folk music sources set a pattern that would shape the country music business for years to come. Doc Carter went on periodic song-collecting trips,

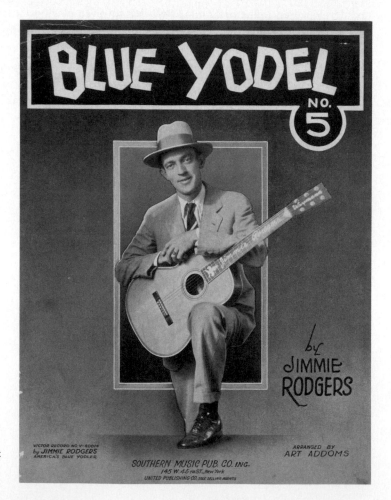

Sheet music for Jimmie Rodgers.

Listening Guide THE RECORDINGS OF JIMMIE RODGERS

"Blue Yodel No. 2," written and performed by Jimmie Rodgers; recorded 1929
"Waiting for a Train," written and performed by Jimmie Rodgers; recorded 1928
"Dreaming with Tears in My Eyes," written by Jimmie Rodgers and Waldo L. O'Neal; performed by Jimmie Rodgers; recorded 1933

One major reason for Jimmie Rodgers's success was his receptivity to African American influences, complemented by his ability to reflect those influences in original compositions and performances that proved appealing to a substantial white audience. In a highly successful series of recordings called "blue yodels," he adapted the poetic and musical forms of the blues, as well as certain aspects of blues performance styles, to his own purposes. The first such record, called simply "Blue Yodel" (also known by its opening words, "T for Texas"), was a million-seller; its appearance high on the pop charts in 1928 indicated that its appeal was not limited to a rural audience but had "crossed over" to the mainstream urban audience as well. Some of the later records in this series bore specific names (such as "Blue Yodel No. 8 [Muleskinner Blues]" or "Anniversary Blue Yodel," the seventh in the series and another pop hit), while others went by homely numerical titles (such as "Blue Yodel No. 2"); all, however, were informed by Rodgers's distinctive approach to what can only be called "white man's blues."

Rodgers's blue yodeling was a "high, lonesome sound" (to use a phrase that has come to be generally associated with white rural music) that was somewhat analogous to the textless moans and howls heard in blues recordings by rural Black artists and that served much the same purpose: to underline the intensity and depth of the singer's feelings. Rodgers used this vocal effect on a large number of his recordings, not just those with "blue yodel" in their titles. As for the actual "Blue Yodel" recordings, taken as a group, they demonstrate a significant diversity in formal approach, lyrical content, and instrumentation. Some of the lyrics conceal encoded sexual messages.

"Blue Yodel No. 2" is particularly close to rural Black models. Here Rodgers sings a loosely connected series of stanzas that suggest the familiar poetic and musical patternings of twelve-bar blues. The song has a highly personal tone—a not uncommon characteristic in Rodgers's blue yodels. Rodgers's performance of this song conveys a sense of freedom through unpredictable phrasing and of course through the yodels that occur between stanzas. These characteristics parallel the techniques of the Black bluesmen we have studied. But there are obvious stylistic differences as well. Rodgers uses the guitar strictly as accompaniment, making no attempt to set up any kind of melodic response (as with Blind Lemon Jefferson) or rhythmic contrast (as with Robert Johnson) to his vocal. With its simple and repetitive figures, the guitar part also creates a greater sense of chordal and rhythmic regularity than tends to be present in performances by rural Black artists. (Even on those infrequent occasions when Rodgers offers a substantial guitar solo, as he does in "Blue Yodel No. 8 [Muleskinner Blues]," it is clear that he is in no sense a guitar virtuoso like Jefferson or Johnson—nor did he aspire to be.) Furthermore, notwithstanding his occasional evocation of blue notes and the sliding effects in his yodels, Rodgers's vocal melodies stay much closer overall to European American scale structures than do the blues melodies of African American performers. This, of course, is unsurprising; what is remarkable is the extent to which Rodgers *did* manage to assimilate elements from Black music successfully into his style.

If "Blue Yodel No. 2" has as its subject a typical lover's complaint, "Blue Yodel No. 8 [Muleskinner Blues]" may be regarded as Rodgers's adaptation of the African American field holler, a work song meant to ease the pain and tedium of physical labor. "Muleskinner Blues" uses the typical chord progressions of twelve-bar blues to accompany three-phrase stanzas in which the third phrase is an extensive yodel rather than a textual statement.

Perhaps Rodgers's most enduringly popular record was "Waiting for a Train," released in 1928. It is a hobo song with a dark feeling that is reinforced by Rodgers's lonesome yodel. Certainly no record demonstrates his forward-looking versatility more thoroughly. Instead of the typical solo guitar accompaniment, an

(continued)

Listening Guide   THE RECORDINGS OF JIMMIE RODGERS (*continued*)

ensemble consisting of steel guitar, cornet, clarinet, and string bass joins the standard guitar in backing up Rodgers's vocal. The steel guitar is a particularly progressive touch here, and it makes the record sound remarkably modern in comparison to many others of its time; actually it was not until the mid-1930s that the sound of a steel guitar became commonplace in country bands and was indelibly identified with the country sound (see Chapter 6). On the other hand, the cornet and clarinet clearly evoke the small jazz ensembles of the late 1920s and link "Waiting for a Train" to the wider spheres of mainstream dance and pop music. The unusual instrumentation gives the record an almost jaunty character at times, effectively counterbalancing the downbeat aspects of Rodgers's lyrics and underlining the resilience of the hobo, who at least possesses the will to survive and the wisdom to appreciate "the moon and stars up above."

Although "Waiting for a Train" was recorded over a year before the stock market crash of October 1929, its lyrics seem to anticipate the Great Depression, when countless rural Americans lost their homes and farms and had to live by luck and their wits alone, like the protagonist in Rodgers's song. The mythic figure of the outcast—the resourceful, lone wanderer—presented so effectively in "Waiting for a Train" has proven to be a potent force in country music up to the present time; the songs and public personas of Merle Haggard, Willie Nelson, and many others, would be unthinkable without it. Yet, for all his progressive qualities, Rodgers remained grounded in tradition. He based "Waiting for a Train" on an old folk song. Reflecting meaningfully on the past while pointing toward the future, "Waiting for a Train" encompasses a duality that is characteristic of much of the finest Southern music, both white and Black.

"Waiting for a Train" is based on a strophic form, but Rodgers employs a number of strategies to avoid monotony. He freely varies the basic melody as he goes along—a technique common in music based on oral traditions, as we have already observed in our examples of rural African American blues. (A particularly expressive example of this flexibility is the way he bends the melody upward to portray "the moon and *stars* up above.") In addition, Rodgers achieves a large-scale structural shaping by varying the close of every third strophe to produce a firm cadence while allowing the other strophes to end inconclusively. The cadences are reinforced with a blue yodel, which adds yet another element to the already rich stylistic amalgam. The two groups of three strophes are separated by an instrumental interlude, thus giving the record a firm and convincing overall form.

Additional facets of Rodgers's extensive contribution to Southern music may be illustrated by a quick look at the tender love song "Dreaming with Tears in My Eyes," recorded in 1933. Although this was a newly composed song (by Rodgers and Waldo L. O'Neal), it also looks to the past: its prominent triple meter clearly recalls the waltz songs of the late nineteenth century. However, if its rhythm reminds us of a song like "After the Ball" (see Chapter 2), its homespun and delicate lyrics have little in common with the melodrama and wild coincidences of that earlier pop hit. These lyrics provide a wonderful example of humble, virtually invisible artistry. With their abundant open vowel sounds, they "sing" beautifully, and the triple meter of the music is already explicit in the natural rhythms of the words. Rodgers's melodic line gently rises and falls with the inflections one would use in speaking these words. Although the components that make up "Dreaming with Tears in My Eyes"—words, rhythm, melody, and chords—might seem simple to the point of cliché if considered separately, their synthesis produces an elusive kind of art that achieves an effect of remarkable directness, intimacy, and poignant honesty.

Waltz songs remained popular in country music throughout the twentieth century and into the twenty-first. These waltzes are frequently songs of sentiment, like "Dreaming with Tears in My Eyes," that use straightforward materials and aspire to the kind of natural yet artful expression achieved so memorably in Rodgers's song. But this effect is not easy to achieve. Rodgers left country music a rich and enduring, but challenging, legacy when he died of tuberculosis eight days after recording "Dreaming with Tears in My Eyes."

Listening Guide "SOUTHERN GOSPEL MUSIC, BLACK AND WHITE"

"Gospel Ship," written by A. P. Carter; performed by the Carter Family; recorded 1935
"The Sun Didn't Shine," written by Roosevelt Fennoy; performed by the Golden Gate Quartet; recorded 1941

"Gospel Ship" and "The Sun Didn't Shine" exemplify the general importance of sacred music in Southern culture and the popularity of commercial recordings of this music. They also introduce us to some of the significant differences between white and Black styles of **gospel music**.

As we have seen, the Carter Family was the first prominent "group" act in country music. Much rural music was heard and nurtured in informal family settings, of course; the unprecedented popularity of the Carter Family as recording and performing artists opened the gates for a succession of family-based acts that continues to this day. Well-known examples from country music include the Blue Sky Boys, the Everly Brothers, the Louvin Brothers, Alabama, the Judds, and the Dixie Chicks (two of whom are sisters). In the musical culture of a family like the Carters, there was no firm separation between secular and religious music, and they recorded both types extensively. Their gospel recordings typically present their own unpretentious arrangements of old folk hymns, with two of the most enduringly famous examples being "Can the Circle Be Unbroken" and "Gospel Ship." The Carters' performance style on such records is an utterly straightforward, unadorned one, whose plainness was seen by the performers and sympathetic listeners as indicative of the humility and devotion that marked authentic religious faith. This aesthetic of plainness was a long-standing feature of the culture of Protestant immigrants from Britain and Ireland.

In African American communities, religious music has tended to be centered more exclusively in the church. Rural Black churches made extensive use of music, and this encouraged the development of a distinctive style for African American gospel music and led to the emergence of talented performers in that style. The great Black gospel groups like the Golden Gate Quartet were not family acts but typically comprised unrelated individuals who came together through a common interest in and talent for singing religious music, often in a local church or school choir. Black gospel music thus developed an independent identity that was separate not

only from white religious traditions, but also to a certain extent from other musical traditions in the Black community itself. Black gospel artists were expected to perform sacred music only, not to indulge in "dirty" music like the blues. This explicit division between religious and secular music remained an important characteristic of African American culture for a considerable period of time. Still, this division was not absolute. Country blues artists such as Skip James, Blind Willie McTell, and Bukka White recorded sacred material along with characteristic blues. In the late 1930s, a figure emerged out of Black gospel music who would aggressively challenge this division, along with many other unwritten "rules": *Sister Rosetta Tharpe*. We will take up her story in Chapter 7, as an artist who in the 1940s achieved the unprecedented feat of placing uniquely styled gospel recordings high on the "race records" charts. By the 1960s, "soul music" had emerged as a new genre of secular music that consciously incorporated stylistic elements from Black gospel.

In contrast to the restrained white gospel music exemplified by the Carter Family, Black gospel music tended to favor extroversion and an intense expressivity; this music can be highly ornate, and it emphasizes the personal and ecstatic aspects of religious experience. These characteristics are clearly evident in the Golden Gate Quartet's performance of "The Sun Didn't Shine," with its remarkable displays of vocal virtuosity and rhythmic intricacy. Of particular interest in this performance is the extended, seemingly improvised, virtually textless buildup to the final chorus. Here the background voices assume the sound and role of insistent percussion instruments (portraying "the hammer ...heard in Jerusalem's streets"), while the lead vocalist, Henry Owens, hums and moans in a sacred transformation of blues techniques, immersed in his contemplation of the crucifixion.

Especially when it is juxtaposed with the brilliance of "The Sun Didn't Shine," the homely simplicity of the Carter Family's "Gospel Ship" might strain the appreciative faculties of today's sophisticated, largely urban

(continued)

Listening Guide "SOUTHERN GOSPEL MUSIC, BLACK AND WHITE"
(continued)

audience for popular music. We could call attention to the unique dark vocal timbre of lead singer Sara Carter; her voice and the way she uses it call immediate attention to the significance of the words she is singing. And we could cite the firm, clean guitar style of Maybelle Carter, whose "Carter Family lick" became one of the most widely imitated guitar sounds in country music.

Finally, we might point to how the final verse of "Gospel Ship" as sung by Sara Carter expresses the feelings of many "hillbillies" of abiding religious faith who had to endure the scorn of "sophisticated," "higher-class" people. While the upper classes might be "ashamed" of their poorer neighbors, "Gospel Ship" argues, the faithful will ultimately have the last laugh in heaven.

BOX 5.2 SOLO WOMEN'S VOICES IN COUNTRY MUSIC

The first major country hit by a solo female artist was "I Want to Be a Cowboy's Sweetheart," a tribute to life on the open range, recorded in 1935, that was written and sung by *Patsy Montana* (1908–1996). Montana's birth name was Ruby Blevins, and actually she came from Arkansas! "I Want to Be a Cowboy's Sweetheart" is a straightforward strophic song; what distinguished Montana's performance was clearly her virtuosic yodeling, heard at the beginning and ending of the recording and between the strophes of the song. Perhaps the yodeling was intended to serve as a tribute to the recently deceased "blue yodeler" Jimmie Rodgers, or perhaps this was a case of gender-based one-upmanship by Ms. Montana (or perhaps neither). Regardless, the yodeling remains impressive even today, as does Patsy Montana's effortless and engaging singing.

The darkly colored voice of Lily May Ledford is the only one heard on the 1938 recording of "Pretty Polly" by the *Coon Creek Girls*, the first all-female country string band. Ledford's voice occupies a point in the spectrum quite far from Patsy Montana's bright soprano. The singer's own banjo establishes a breathless pace from the outset, and she proceeds to sing this tale of cold-blooded murder with relentless, unsettling intensity. "Pretty Polly" has its source in British broadside balladry (see Chapter 1), but the Coon Creeks Girls' version of the song is an exceptionally compressed one, leaving much of the story open to the listeners' conjectures and interpretations. The sole, very brief, instrumental break on the record is

Lily Mae Ledford of the Coon Creek Girls.

strategically placed between the start of Willie and Polly's journey into the countryside and Polly's expression of fear (her first words heard in this version)—what happens during this interlude? (Does Willie seduce her—or even rape her—after luring her with the promise of marriage?) We then learn that Willie has been planning to murder her from the beginning, since her grave has already been dug. Arguably, this story is the more disconcerting because of the many mysteries surrounding it.

"Pretty Polly" is a traditional ballad musically insofar as it is a strophic song with many strophes, but one significant feature of the Coon Creek Girls' version is its three-line lyric stanzas, with the first line repeated each time (*a-a-b*). This format is not found in British sources (compare it with the four-line stanzas of "Barbary Allen," discussed in Chapter 1), but it is of course widespread in American twelve-bar blues songs. Does "Pretty Polly" then show the influence of African American song structures on European American-based country traditions? It seems at least plausible that this is the case. At any rate, the very short three-line stanzas contribute strongly to the distinctive, headlong pace of this recording.

The Coon Creek Girls' "Pretty Polly" can open up a provocative consideration of country-music aesthetics. Some relatively early country music, like this recording and many by the Carter Family, might give the impression of lacking emotion to some listeners unfamiliar with the roots from which this music springs. And it is true that "Pretty Polly" can seem rather monochromatic on the surface, especially considering the highly dramatic, even gruesome story that is conveyed by the lyrics. On the other hand, the steely, unyielding qualities of the tempo, of the banjo accompaniment, and especially of Lily May Ledford's vocal performance, can produce a nearly frightening impact on the attuned listener; the record arguably is that much more chilling for its unrelenting "coldness." The singer, after all, assumes the voice of the remorseless murderer for much of the song, and the final lyrics tell us that only the birds (not the singer!) are left to mourn Polly's death. Particularly affecting, then, is the one striking expressive deviation in the vocal performance: the singer's lingering on the long "Oooh" that initiates Polly's plea to have her life spared.

Probably the most popular female performer in country music during the 1930s was **Lulu Belle** (born Myrtle Eleanor Cooper, 1913–1999), a star of radio's *National Barn Dance*. She performed as half of the duet team Lulu Belle and Scotty, with Scott Wiseman (who became her husband), but she possessed a captivating solo voice as well. That voice may be heard on the record "Remember Me (When the Candle Lights Are Gleaming)" from 1940, a song written by Wiseman. Lulu Belle opens the final (third) strophe of this song as a solo, after demonstrating the lovely blend she and her husband could achieve during their performance of the first two strophes. Lulu Belle and Scotty may be seen and heard in the 1944 film *National Barn Dance*.

gathering material from both Black and white musicians and reworking it to suit the Carters' vocal and instrumental format. At the urging of Ralph Peer, Doc copyrighted all of the songs that the Carters recorded, whether or not he had actually composed them himself. Of course, the line between original compositions and folk songs is a blurry one, since most composition is consciously or unconsciously based on pre-existing material, and any folk song is bound to exist in multiple variants, shaped by the tastes and values of particular performers. Ralph Peer published all of the songs through his own Southern Music Company and split the profits fifty-fifty with Doc.

If the Carter Family's public image and musical repertoire evoked the country church and the family fireside, *Jimmie Rodgers* (1897–1933) was the quintessential rambler, a footloose man who carried home in his heart but drank deeply of the changing world around him. He was the most versatile, progressive, and widely influential of all the early country recording artists. The ex–railroad brakeman from Meridian, Mississippi, celebrated the allure of the open road and chronicled the lives of men who forsook the benefits of a settled existence: ramblers, hobos, gamblers, convicts, cowboys, railway men, and feckless lovers. Rodgers's devil-may-care personality and his early death from tuberculosis contributed to his charismatic mystique, a sort of white parallel to the Black bluesman Robert Johnson. He was early country music's biggest recording star, and his influence can be seen in the public images of Hank Williams, Waylon Jennings, Willie Nelson, and almost every contemporary male country music star.

Popular Music and the Great Depression

The Great Depression (1929–ca. 1939), which threw millions of Americans out of work, had a major impact on the music industry. In 1927, 106 million phonograph discs were sold nationwide; by 1932 annual sales had plummeted to only 6 million. Many small record companies—including those that had pioneered in the fields of race and hillbilly music—were wiped out overnight. Large companies such as Columbia and Victor were forced to reorganize and consolidate. Most people simply did not have the spare income to spend on records, despite the introduction of discs that cost as little as ten cents apiece, and network radio became even more influential as a result.

The race record market was crushed by the economic downturn, which hit African American consumers particularly hard. The first Black-owned music publishing and film production companies were also wiped out in the early 1930s. Increasingly, record companies relied on established artists and cut back on the field expeditions that had characterized the early years of the race record business. The most successful African American musicians of the Depression era were those whose records were featured in the mainstream record catalogs, particularly jazz-oriented dance orchestras, discussed in some detail in the next chapter.

Hillbilly record sales were also affected by the Depression, although not as severely as race records. However, although sales declined in absolute numbers, hillbilly music actually increased its share of the overall market during the economic downturn. In 1930, as the Depression consolidated its stranglehold on millions of families, both rural and urban, hillbilly records accounted for fully 25 percent of the total American market. Paradoxically, despite the general downturn in sales, it was during the Depression that the country music business was really established, with the biggest stars signing lucrative advertising contracts and appearing on radio and in Hollywood movies. In 1933 Billy Hill's recording of "The Last Roundup"—a romantic cowboy song—was a huge hit, selling 100,000 copies, crossing over to the pop charts, and helping to establish the "western" music market. Hill's success also set the scene for popular cowboy singers such as Gene Autry and Roy Rogers, discussed in the next chapter.

Given that popular music of the early twentieth century tended to scrupulously avoid any mention of social problems, how, if at all, was the terrible impact of the Great Depression on the lives of Americans expressed in popular music? During the 1930s, while Tin Pan Alley and Hollywood provided vivid fantasies of life among the elite, some hillbilly and blues singers injected a note of social realism into popular music. They chronicled the suffering of the homeless and unemployed: the Dust Bowl farmers whose

Woody Guthrie (reading the *HoBo* News) relaxes in New York's Central Park with fellow folksinger Burl Ives before a radio appearance, 1940.

way of life was threatened by ecological, as well as economic, disaster; and the textile and mine workers of the South, whose attempts to unionize were resisted—sometimes violently—by big business. Examples of songs that dealt with the Depression include the rare down-to-earth Tin Pan Alley song "Brother, Can You Spare a Dime?" (a Number 1 hit for crooners Bing Crosby and Rudy Vallee in 1932); hillbilly star Uncle Dave Macon's "All In Down and Out Blues," which argued that "Wall Street's propositions were not all roses"; and Casey Bill Weldon's "WPA Blues," which described a government demolition crew destroying dilapidated housing still occupied by African American families.

One of the musicians most closely associated with the plight of American workers during the Great Depression was ***Woodrow Wilson "Woody" Guthrie***. Born in Oklahoma in 1912, Guthrie began his career as a hillbilly singer, performing the songs of the Carter Family and Jimmie Rodgers. With his father dead and his mother committed to an asylum, Guthrie quit school at sixteen and spent years wandering throughout the Southwest. In the late 1930s he migrated to California as part of the stream of impoverished "Okies" described in John Steinbeck's novel *The Grapes of Wrath*. These experiences turned Guthrie toward composing songs that were more overtly political in nature, including "This Land Is Your Land," "Talking Dust Bowl Blues," and "Ludlow Massacre." After 1940 he was known primarily as a protest singer—his political orientation was summarized by a sign on his guitar that read "This Machine Kills

Fascists"—and was a direct influence on later urban folk musicians such as the Weavers (see Chapter 7) and Bob Dylan (see Chapter 10).

A prime example of Guthrie's writing and performing style is "Do Re Mi," a song he recorded several times during the 1940s. The lyrics offer a warning to people who might want to follow the path of Guthrie himself, by fleeing the Dust Bowl for the supposedly green pastures of California: unless they have some of their own *do* re mi (that is, *dough*), they should not expect hospitality at the state border. The song is in a straightforward verse-chorus form, and Guthrie sings it in an unpretentious fashion, accompanying himself on the guitar. The homespun ambience of his performance, and his employment of the "Carter Family lick" during the guitar solo, reveal clearly Woody Guthrie's country roots.

WHILE THE GREAT Depression marked the end of an important period in the development of American popular music, it was also a significant time of transition. From around 1935 through World War II, as the national economy began to recover, the music business expanded and underwent certain major transformations. Musical styles and cultural themes that had first emerged in clear form after World War I were updated by a new generation of performers. These musicians, in adapting to new social and historical circumstances, elaborated the long-standing conversation between Northern and Southern, urban and rural, and white and Black musical traditions, ultimately creating a style of dance music (and a cultural movement) called swing.

Key Terms

bar (measure)	country blues	tonic
blue notes	gospel music	twelve-bar blues
blues	hillbilly music	
classic blues	race music	

Key People

Alberta Hunter	Gertrude "Ma" Rainey	Robert Johnson
Bessie Smith	Jimmie Rodgers	Sister Rosetta Tharpe
Blind Lemon Jefferson	Lulu Belle	Vernon Dalhart
Carter Family	Mamie Smith	William Christopher Handy
Charley Patton	Marion Harris	Woodrow Wilson "Woody"
Coon Creek Girls	Patsy Montana	Guthrie
Ethel Waters	Ralph Peer	

Review Questions

1. What is a "race" record? How were these records marketed?
2. How did classic blues differ from country blues?
3. What are the common musical features of the twelve-bar blues?
4. How did the East Texas style of bluesman Blind Lemon Jefferson differ from the Mississippi Delta style of bluesman Charley Patton?
5. Why was radio more influential in the development of hillbilly music than in the development of race music?
6. What role did women play in country music during this period?
7. Compare the styles of Jimmie Rodgers and the Carter Family. What similarities and differences did they have?

"In the Mood"

6 The Swing Era, 1935–1945

DESPITE THE COMMERCIAL HOOPLA ASSOCIATED WITH THE JAZZ AGE, WE have seen that the influence of jazz on mainstream popular music was really rather indirect during the 1920s and early 1930s (recall our discussion of Paul Whiteman, the "King of Jazz," in Chapter 3). Some historians of popular music argue that the early years of the Great Depression (1929–1935) were in fact marked by a shift in mainstream popular taste away from "hot" syncopated dance music and toward a "sweeter" style of ballroom music more in keeping with the subdued mood of the times. Beginning in 1935, however, a new style of jazz-inspired music called **swing**—initially developed in the late 1920s by Black dance bands in New York, Chicago, and Kansas City—transformed American popular music. (The music of the swing era experienced a revival in the late twentieth- and early twenty-first centuries, and swing dancing continues to be popular among dancers to this day.)

The word "swing" (like "jazz," "blues," and "rock 'n' roll") is derived from African American English. First used as a verb for the fluid, "rocking" rhythmic momentum created by well-played music, the term was used by extension to refer to an emotional state characterized by a sense of freedom, vitality, and enjoyment. References to "swing" and "swinging" are common in the titles and lyrics of jazz records made during the

1920s and early 1930s.[1] However, it was the music industry that, around 1935, began to use "swing" as a proper noun, the name of a defined musical genre. (When the music business gets involved in promoting a style of music, it typically adopts colloquial terms that are verbs or adjectives and turns them into nouns—that is, into *things*, marketable objects that can be promoted, sold, and bought by a mass audience. More recent examples would be "grunge" and "techno.")

Between 1935 and 1945 hundreds of large dance orchestras—the best known of which were directed by celebrity bandleaders such as **Benny Goodman**, Tommy Dorsey, Duke Ellington, Count Basie, and Glenn Miller—dominated the national hit parade. These **big bands** appeared nightly on the radio, their performances transmitted coast to coast from hotels and ballrooms in the big cities, and featured on **jukeboxes**, coin-operated record players installed in nightclubs and restaurants. Many of the bands criss-crossed the country in buses, playing for dances and concerts at local dance halls, theaters, and colleges. The big bands were essentially a big-city phenomenon, a symbol of sophistication and up-to-dateness, and their occasional tour appearances in small towns generated a great deal of excitement. (In this sense the big bands played a role similar to traveling minstrel and vaudeville shows, which had largely died out by the late 1930s.)

Swing music was part of a broader cultural and aesthetic movement that included dance styles, modes of dress, and even architecture. Gradually supplanting the intimate cabarets of the 1920s, huge ballrooms, designed to cater to a larger and more diverse audience, sprang up during the 1930s. These new dance halls were constructed in keeping with the taste of the times, complete with streamlined modern designs of chrome, steel, and glass, evoking the power and forward momentum of airplanes and diesel trains. Photographs of dance bands taken during the heyday of the big bands also indicate a shift in visual presentation from the publicity shots of 1920s "syncopated orchestras," in which musicians mugged and struck unusual poses, to the sleek, sophisticated, and erudite image of swing bands and bandleaders adorned in fine suits and scholarly eyeglasses.

Swing music also played an important economic role. Record sales in the United States had plummeted from the 1921 high of $106 million in retail sales to only $6 million in 1933 (a decline of over 90 percent). By the late 1930s, largely as a result of the popularity of swing, the record industry had begun to recover: between 1935 and 1945 well over half of the records that sold more than a million copies were made by big dance bands. It is no exaggeration to state that swing music pulled the American music industry out of the Great Depression.

Swing Music and American Culture

Swing music provides us with a window onto the cultural values and social changes of the New Deal era.[2] The basic ethos of swing music was one of unfettered enjoyment—"swinging," "having a ball." (This "let's party" attitude was doubtless encouraged by the

---

1. For example, Duke Ellington's well-known composition "It Don't Mean a Thing If It Ain't Got That Swing" was first recorded in 1932.
2. The New Deal was an ambitious set of public programs put into place by the administration of Franklin D. Roosevelt that was designed to pull the country out of the economic depression of the early 1930s.

repeal of Prohibition in 1933.) Like the voting bloc that elected Franklin D. Roosevelt to four terms in office, the audience for swing spanned the social boundaries that separated ethnic groups, natives and immigrants, Southerners and Northerners, city dwellers and country folk, and the working class, the expanding middle class, and progressive members of the educated elite. Democratic in spirit, swing music was actually quite regimented in performance—planned and written down in advance by professional arrangers and often read note-by-note by musicians, with relatively little room for individual improvisation. This highly structured way of making music—a shift from the ideal of collective improvisation that had characterized early New Orleans jazz—has been shown by some scholars to correlate with the increasing bureaucratization of American life during the New Deal era, which saw the growth of government institutions, labor unions, and big business.

If this connection between music and society seems a bit far-fetched—after all, many dance bands of the 1920s also played from written arrangements and improvised little—it certainly cannot be denied that the swing era saw the growth of bureaucracy in the music industry. The swing craze was controlled and, at least in part, manufactured by large New York–based booking agencies, corporations formed to represent professional musicians and promote their music. The largest of these was MCA (Music Corporation of America), which, after barely surviving the Depression, rose to become the dominant booking agency for big dance bands. MCA and other agencies served as liaisons among the bands, the radio networks, and commercial advertisers. (Most successful bands had commercial sponsors such as tobacco, beer, and automobile companies.) The agencies also managed the bafflingly complex logistics of nationwide tours. In 1937, when total profits from the swing music industry reached $80 million, $15 million went to the booking agencies. It is perhaps no wonder that MCA—a cold, efficient, and businesslike enterprise—was viewed with a mixture of appreciation and distrust by musicians, who called the corporation the "Star-Spangled Octopus." (These large booking agencies continue to play an important—some would say oppressive—role in the music business today.)

During the swing era network radio was the most important means of promoting popular music. A big band simply could not hope to achieve any significant level of popularity without constant radio exposure. Swing bands appeared live on remote broadcasts from dance halls and hotels, as well as on regularly scheduled studio-based programs. Interestingly, some of the most desirable places for a swing band to perform were hotels and ballrooms where they might actually expect to lose money. These venues were important because they had a "wire"—a connection to a local radio station—that allowed them to be used for live broadcasting. (The most famous of these "remote" venues was the Pennsylvania Hotel in New York City, which played a key role in launching the careers of Benny Goodman, Tommy Dorsey, Glenn Miller, and other top bandleaders of the era.)

The 1930s also saw the appearance of radio shows featuring phonograph records rather than live performances. The most famous of these were the *Make Believe Ballroom* shows, broadcast from New York and Los Angeles. These shows featured disc jockeys, radio personalities who spun records and attempted to create the ambience of a live broadcast from a hotel. The first Top 10 radio show was *Your Hit Parade*, sponsored by Lucky Strike cigarettes. Introduced in 1935, the show began with the following announcement:

> Your Hit Parade! We don't pick 'em, we just play 'em. From North, South, East, and West, we check the songs you dance to . . . the sales of the records that you buy . . . and the sheet music you play. And then, knowing your preferences, we bring you the top hits of the week!

The announcement of top hit songs began with a dramatic drumroll and ended with the performance of "the top song in the country, Number One on Your Lucky Strike Hit Parade." This show, one of the most popular of the radio era, is the ancestor of the Top 40 shows of the rock 'n' roll era and MTV's music video countdown.

As is often the case with popular music, swing was put to all sorts of political uses. Some left-wing activists saw swing music as a utopian embodiment of racial democracy and the common interests of working people. Other leftists regarded it with suspicion, seeing its mass popularity and the fervor of its fans as possible precursors of totalitarianism. Conservative commentators decried swing as an outgrowth and intensification of the moral decline marked by the ragtime and jazz crazes of the 1910s and 1920s. One prominent psychiatrist blamed a wave of sex crimes on the music, while another played Tommy Dorsey records for monkeys and gorillas, reporting that the former enjoyed swing, while the latter—being largely terrestrial, not arboreal primates—did not. Religious authorities were generally not thrilled with the new music or the often acrobatic styles of dance, called "jitterbugging," that it accompanied (a topic that we will discuss shortly). In an October 1938 article in the *New York Times* Archbishop Beckman of New York went so far as to argue that "we permit, if not endorse, by our criminal indifference, 'jam sessions,' 'jitter-bugs,' and cannibalistic rhythm orgies to occupy a place in our social scheme of things, wooing our youth along the primrose path to hell!"

These criticisms of swing—with their references to sexual deviance, animals, and cannibalism—echo the racist tone of attacks on syncopated dance music during the 1920s, which we discussed in Chapter 3. American society remained segregated along racial lines, even as the country spent hundreds of thousands of lives and billions of dollars fighting World War II. (It is ironic that while the war was ostensibly an attempt to save the free world from the racism of the Nazis, the U.S. Army itself remained largely segregated.) Nevertheless, personal relationships and the exchange of stylistic influences between Black and white musicians on the whole became more direct and intimate. Although ballrooms remained segregated in certain parts of the country, photographs of big band concerts and dances during the late 1930s and the war years provide evidence that big-city swing audiences were also decidedly mixed in racial terms. Some of the most popular white swing bands met with success at venues in predominantly African American neighborhoods such as Harlem's Apollo Theater, while the most successful Black dance bands always counted substantial numbers of white fans among their audiences.

The influence of Black English on the speech of white youth also became more direct during this period. Terms such as "cool," "hip," "with it," and "in the groove" evoked a particular attitude or stance toward life—aware, sensually attuned, and in control of the situation—that has its roots in a distinctive African American aesthetic of personal comportment. (Linguists have traced the etymology of the term "hepcat" to "hipikat," a word used by the Wolof people of Senegal to describe a person who is particularly finely attuned to his surroundings, literally a person with his "eyes wide open." Many words in American English—including "jazz"—appear to have roots in African languages.)

The dance styles that paralleled swing music provide further evidence of the increasing centrality of Black styles and sensibilities in American popular culture. Beginning in the late 1920s, dancers at the Savoy Ballroom in New York City—located on Harlem's "main stem," Lenox Avenue—began to develop a style called the lindy hop, named in honor of Charles Lindbergh's solo transatlantic flight in 1927. The lindy differed from the popular jazz dance styles of the early 1920s—the bunny hug, turkey trot, and fox-trot—in several important ways. While the older dances emphasized bouncy, up-and-down movements, the lindy was smoother, with more fluid horizontal movements. In addition, the lindy provided greater scope for improvisation, including the "breakaway," a moment when dancers would part company and dance solo, exhibiting their skill. (The Savoy Ballroom had a special section of the dance floor, called the "Cat's Corner," that was set aside for these displays.) Gradually, this virtuosic element of the lindy became more prominent and began to incorporate judolike "airsteps," in which the man would spin his partner, slide her between his arched legs, flip her over his back, and so on. Naturally the bands sought to play music that would appeal to and encourage the dancers, and consequently swing dancing and swing music exhibited a mutual back-and-forth influence upon one another. The clothing worn by lindy dancers matched the streamlined and somewhat formal aesthetic of the new ballrooms: expensive (or at least expensive-looking) jackets, ties, and loose trousers for the men, billowing skirts and silk blouses for the women. Loose clothes were not only "hip" in appearance but also perfectly suited for the acrobatic moves of the lindy hop.

It is impossible to discuss the development of swing music, the lindy hop, or the clothing and speech styles with which they were associated without some reference to New York's Harlem and its famous nightclubs and dance halls, which included the Savoy Ballroom, the Cotton Club, and the Apollo Theater. Originally populated by European immigrant groups, Harlem was by the late 1920s home to a substantial, well-educated, and relatively prosperous Black middle class. Much of the attention of scholars has focused on the "high art" aspects of the "New Negro" movement, later called the Harlem Renaissance, exemplified by the poetry of Langston Hughes and the paintings of Aaron Douglas. However, the cultural energy and creativity of Black New York was also expressed through popular cultural forms, both in live performance and over the mass media. It could be argued that Harlem was the portal through which Black styles and sensibilities entered American mass culture from the 1920s through the 1940s.

Although the creative impulses of the Harlem Renaissance came mainly from the Black middle class, "Black and tan" nightclubs like the Cotton Club were generally owned and operated by Italian and Jewish mobsters. The Cotton Club's audiences were predominantly white, encompassing people with a genuine interest in jazz music and other aspects of cosmopolitan Black culture as well as those who came to Harlem in search of something akin to an exotic tourist experience (a practice called "slumming"). The most successful dance orchestras at the Cotton Club—led by Duke Ellington and Cab Calloway—provided musical accompaniment for stage acts featuring scantily clad "brown beauties," men in ape costumes, and jungle scenery. This scene—in which Black performers presented caricatures of themselves to white consumers—is in some ways reminiscent of nineteenth-century minstrelsy. However, the steady income provided by the well-known Harlem nightclubs and dance halls gave many Black musicians an opportunity to develop successful careers in music.

It can be argued that the swing era—a period during which Black people often attended concerts by white dance bands and whites began to study and imitate Black culture with greater passion and in greater numbers than ever before—did represent a step forward in cultural communication across racial boundaries. At the same time, we must recognize that this was not a relationship of full equality. Only a handful of dance bands were racially integrated (Benny Goodman was a pioneer in this regard), and even the most popular of Black dance bands faced serious economic and social disadvantages vis-à-vis their white competitors. Between 1935 and 1945 the four most popular big bands led by white musicians—the Tommy Dorsey, Benny Goodman, Glenn Miller, and Jimmy Dorsey Orchestras—racked up a total of 292 Top 10 records, of which sixty-five were Number 1 hits. In contrast, the four most popular Black swing orchestras—led by Duke Ellington, Count Basie, Jimmy Lunceford, and Chick Webb—scored only thirty-two Top 10 hits, three of which made it to Number 1 on the charts. While these figures may reflect broad differences in the economic status of Black and white Americans, they were also shaped by the Black musicians' difficulty in getting equal airtime on the radio and in having their records included among the selections on the coin-operated jukeboxes that sprang up in thousands of restaurants and nightclubs across the country during this period. (Very few radio stations featured African American disc jockeys during the swing era. The first well-known Black DJ was Jack Cooper, who began broadcasting in Chicago in the late 1930s. There were few others until after World War II.)

Finally, although swing is regarded today as nostalgic music, it is important to remember that its core audience initially consisted of college-age adults and teenagers. Avid young dancers called "jitterbugs" studied the recordings of their favorite bands, spent hours perfecting dance steps, formed fan clubs, bought fan magazines, and sometimes trailed their favorite bands from town to town. (As you might expect, the swing craze was regarded with suspicion by many parents, who continued to patronize the older-style "sweet" bands led by musicians like Guy Lombardo.) In general, the big bands brought a youthful energy back to

Jitterbug dancers, Washington, DC, 1943. Photo by Esther Bubley.

Listening Guide "WRAPPIN' IT UP (THE LINDY GLIDE)"

Composed and arranged by Fletcher Henderson; performed by Fletcher Henderson and His Orchestra; recorded 1934

There are a number of differences between swing and the jazz-tinged syncopated dance music that preceded it in the 1910s and 1920s (see Chapter 3). These differences can best be illustrated by listening to the band widely credited with inspiring the rise of swing, **Fletcher Henderson** (1898–1952) and His Orchestra. The Henderson band that recorded "Wrappin' It Up" in 1934 is considerably larger than most syncopated dance bands of the 1920s, which typically included only eight or nine musicians. By contrast, Henderson's big band comprises five brass instruments (three trumpets and two trombones); four reed instruments (saxophones and clarinets); and a rhythm section consisting of piano, bass, drums, and guitar, for a total of thirteen musicians. This expansion of the dance band was correlated with the development of an ensemble sound that was smoother, fuller sounding, and, in structural terms, simpler than the polyphonic, collectively improvised style of New Orleans jazz. To be sure, the influence of the rich orchestral textures developed by James Reese Europe and Paul Whiteman is evident in many big band recordings of the swing era. However, big band arrangers used the expanded instrumental resources of their ensembles in a manner different from that employed by most syncopated orchestras of the 1920s.

One of the signal features of swing music is a thorough application of the call-and-response technique central to African American musical traditions such as gospel music and the blues. Beginning in the late 1920s, Black dance band arrangers began to apply this principle to ensemble writing, treating the brass and reed instruments as separate sections and setting them off against one another. This basic approach—in which "conversations" were set up between parts of a band—was later adopted by white bands.

In addition, there was a change in the rhythmic organization or "feel" of the music. Rather than the "boom-chick," two-beat rhythms of much syncopated dance band music of the 1920s—correlated with the erect postures and largely up-and-down movements of the fox-trot and other popular dances of the time—the

rhythmic feeling of swing music is more continuous and flowing. This effect is created by having the bass player play on all four beats in a measure, rather than just the first and third beats, a technique referred to by jazz musicians as "walking" the bass. The drummer adds to this effect by playing all four beats with his bass drum pedal (a technique called "four on the floor") and playing a regular tapping pattern on his largest cymbal (a "ride" cymbal). In some bands, the guitarist would also play chords on every beat. In addition to this steady pulse, a good swinging groove depended on accents on the offbeats, that is, the second and fourth beats of each four-beat measure. These offbeat accents might be supplied by the rhythm section or the horn arrangements. This combination of a steady, fluid pulse with an accent, or "push," on every other beat creates the basic conditions for swinging.

Of course, there are many subtleties to creating a swing feeling in music, including seemingly tiny adjustments in the relationships among instruments in the rhythm section, and between the rhythm section as a whole and the reed and brass sections. If this all seems a bit abstract, simply play the Original Dixieland Jazz Band's 1918 recording of "Tiger Rag" back to back with Fletcher Henderson's 1934 recording of "Wrappin' It Up," and you'll get a more direct sense of the musical qualities we are attempting to describe here. "Tiger Rag" does have intensity; a bouncy, rhythmic feeling; and lots of syncopation—but it doesn't swing. "Wrappin' It Up," on the other hand, has all of the characteristics we have described: a big, full, smooth ensemble texture; lots of call-and-response patterns between the brass and reeds; and a steady, flowing groove, with the bass, drums, and guitar playing on all four beats, while giving a slight push to beats 2 and 4.

Big band arrangements commonly drew upon musical structures that should by now be familiar to us: the twelve-bar blues form and the thirty-two-bar Tin Pan Alley song form. Fletcher Henderson's "Wrappin' It Up" falls into the latter category: its basic structure is ABAC, with each section being eight measures in length (and each measure, as is typical of swing music, being four beats in length). It should be fairly easy to hear the basic structure of the arrangement, since the beats are emphasized by the rhythm section.

"Wrappin' It Up" begins with an eight-measure introduction, in which the call-and-response relationship between the reeds and the brass is established from the first moment. In the first measure the brass play a syncopated figure, which is answered in the second measure by the reeds. Measures 3 and 4 repeat this exchange. In the next two measures (5 and 6) the brass and reeds exchange even shorter figures (two beats in length), and everyone joins together in the last two bars (measures 7 and 8), launching us

into the main body of the arrangement. The rest of the following chart presents the thirty-two-bar ABAC form, which is repeated four times with all sorts of interesting variations, including the addition of an extra measure on the first and third times through the form.

Working with a few basic musical ideas and techniques, Henderson holds the listener's interest, alternating call-and-response patterns between the brass and reeds with **soli** scoring—musical passages in which a group of instruments play a melody together, often in harmony. (In swing arrangements, these passages often sound like improvised solos that have

LISTENING GUIDE	"WRAPPIN' IT UP"		
TIME	**FORM**	**DESCRIPTIVE COMMENTS**
0:00	Introduction (8 measures)	Bars 1–4: Brass and reeds play call-and-response figures (each one measure in length)
0:05		Bars 5–8: Brass and reeds play shorter call-and-response figures, then join forces to launch us into the main body of the arrangement
0:09	A (8 measures)	Reeds play main theme, punctuated by brief brass responses
0:18	B (8 measures)	Reeds and brass play call-and-response patterns
0:28	A (8 measures)	Soli section, with brass and reeds playing melody together in harmony
0:37	C (10 measures)	Soli section concludes (with extra measure added)
0:48	A (8 measures)	Saxophone solo, supported by soft brass chords
0:57	B (8 measures)	Saxophone solo, supported by soft brass chords
1:06	A (8 measures)	Saxophone solo, supported by soft brass chords
1:15	C (8 measures)	Saxophone solo, supported by soft brass chords
1:24	A (8 measures)	Trumpet solo with reed soli backgrounds
1:33	B (8 measures)	Rapid call and response between brass and reeds
1:42	A (8 measures)	Trumpet solo with reed soli backgrounds
1:51	C (10 measures)	Trumpet solo with reed soli backgrounds (with extra measure added)
2:01	A (8 measures)	Call and response between brass and reeds
2:11	B (8 measures)	Clarinet solo, supported by soft brass chords in background
2:20	A (8 measures)	Reed soli (harmonized melody)
2:29	C (8 measures)	Whole band soli—soft sustained piano note at end

(*continued*)

Listening Guide "WRAPPIN' IT UP (THE LINDY GLIDE)" (continued)

been written down for multiple instruments.) There are also three improvised solos that are performed over various types of backgrounds played by the other instruments. Fletcher Henderson's "Wrappin' It Up" is a great example not only of the rhythmic flow and texture of swing music but also of the balance between simplicity and complexity that characterizes the best big band arrangements.

The Listening Guide outlines the basic structure of the arrangement. Don't worry if you can't follow all the details in the arrangement right away. You might begin by listening all the way through a few times to see if you can keep track of the beats, measures, and larger ABAC form. Then go back and listen for the individual sections, solos, use of call and response, soli sections, and so on.

American popular music. At its best, swing was an exciting, brash, vital music, inspired by Black aesthetics and consonant with the growing optimism of a nation emerging from a devastating economic depression. Although most of the big bands vanished from the scene after World War II, the musical and cultural influence of swing continued to be strongly felt in postwar rhythm & blues and country and western music (see Chapter 7), as well as, eventually, in rock 'n' roll (see Chapter 8).

Benny Goodman: "The King of Swing"

Many genres of popular music are accompanied by stories describing a "founding moment," that is, an attention-grabbing performance or recording that establishes a musical era and brings a new audience into being. For the swing era that mythic event occurred in the summer of 1935, when a dance band led by a young jazz clarinetist named Benny Goodman (1909–1986) embarked upon a tour of California. Goodman was born in Chicago, the son of working-class eastern European Jewish immigrants. He made his first records under his own name in 1927 and worked as a freelance musician during the Depression years. Benny Goodman's career was boosted by *John Hammond* (1910–1987), an influential jazz enthusiast and promoter who also helped Bessie Smith, Billie Holiday, Count Basie, and (much later) Aretha Franklin, Bob Dylan, and Bruce Springsteen receive recording contracts with Columbia Records, where he worked as an A&R man. Hammond arranged Goodman's first recording dates with Columbia and pushed the band in the direction of the more strongly jazz-influenced music played by most Black dance bands.

In 1934 the Goodman band got its first big break. The National Biscuit Company was promoting its new Ritz cracker and decided to sponsor a national radio program called *Let's Dance*. This show featured three bands that represented the three main dance music styles of the time: a sweet band, a Latin band, and Goodman's band, playing "hot," syncopated music. Under constant prodding from John Hammond, Goodman soon hired more jazz musicians. He also purchased a group of Fletcher Henderson's arrangements, which became the center of the Goodman band's collection of charts. Goodman was not only a skillful jazz improviser but also an astute businessman and a strict disciplinarian, insisting that his musicians play their parts with perfect precision. (His laser-beam stare and readiness to fire miscreants were legendary among jazz musicians.) Benny Goodman brought to Henderson's arrangements a kind of neatness, smoothness, and control—a sound that appealed to the predominantly white, middle-class audience who was the main target of record companies and radio sponsors—without losing the swing feeling of the music.

Although initial audience reaction was not enthusiastic, the band went on a grueling cross-country tour of one-nighters, ending up in California. The tour had not been a great success: audiences did not warm to the "hot" arrangements that the band wanted to play, instead insisting that they play only sweet numbers. (The tour bottomed out in Denver, where dancers actually asked the band to give them their money back.) When they finally arrived at the famous Palomar Ballroom in Hollywood, relieved that the tour was almost over, the Goodman band was astounded to find lines of fans extending all the way around the block. Apparently their popularity had been built up by network radio appearances, though not in the way you might expect. The Goodman band had always played last on the New York–based show *Let's Dance*, not appearing until after midnight, when many in the audience had already gone to bed. But on the West Coast, where they were heard earlier in the evening, they had begun to build a long-distance following among teenagers and young adults, who loved the swinging approach that Goodman had borrowed from Fletcher Henderson.

This, then, was the birth of swing, a national cultural phenomenon of unprecedented proportions, created on the one hand by the intensified impact of Black musical styles and aesthetic values on popular dance music, and on the other by the intervention of the mass media. Other white dance band musicians—including Jimmy and Tommy Dorsey, Glenn Miller, and Artie Shaw—saw a golden opportunity, and dozens of swing bands sprang up overnight. (By the late 1930s *Metronome* magazine listed three hundred bands nationwide, and this number only scratched the surface!) As we have seen, swing became an industry, with the bands, radio networks, Hollywood studios, and corporate advertisers continually promoting one another, generating tens of millions of dollars in annual profits and pulling the recording industry out of its Depression era slump.

In a seeming echo of the hype surrounding Paul Whiteman's public image, the press crowned Benny Goodman the "King of Swing." However, there are several major differences between the so-called kings of jazz and swing. While Whiteman remained a classical musician all his life, Goodman was in fact a fine (if often underrated) improviser who studied jazz closely. While Whiteman's band played syncopated ballroom dance music in a style that borrowed its name from jazz, Goodman's group really was a jazz band, performing music closely modeled on the innovations of African American musicians, composers, and arrangers. And while Paul Whiteman's dance orchestras of the 1920s never included musicians of color, Goodman was the first prominent white

Benny Goodman performing at the
400 Restaurant, New York City, c. 1946.

bandleader to hire Black players, beginning with the pianist Teddy Wilson in 1936 and then attracting the brilliant young electric guitarist Charlie Christian, vibraphonist Lionel Hampton, and trumpeter Cootie Williams.

It is clear that Benny Goodman owed a key element of his success to the adoption of a style innovated by Fletcher Henderson and other African American musicians. It is also evident that Goodman's success was determined not solely by his musicianship and business savvy but also by the relatively privileged access to radio airplay, recording contracts, and corporate backing that he and other white musicians enjoyed. However, it is not fair—as has sometimes been done—to imply that Goodman was himself a racist, simply because he was a successful white musician in a cultural environment that was inherently unfair to musicians of color. His decision to hire Black musicians led to the integration of other prominent big bands, including those led by Artie Shaw

Listening Guide   "TAKING A CHANCE ON LOVE"

Composed by Vernon Duke, lyrics by John Latouche and Ted Fetter; arranged by Fletcher Henderson; performed by Benny Goodman and His Orchestra; recorded 1940

The Goodman band's 1940 recording of "Taking a Chance on Love," which reached Number 1 on the Hit Parade chart published in the influential trade journal *Billboard* in 1943, provides us with a good example of the group's popular approach. The arrangement is by Fletcher Henderson, who had by this time become a regular member of the Goodman band. Henderson makes use of the basic techniques of swing arranging, including call and response between reeds and brass and soli sections with a melody played in harmony. "Taking a Chance on Love" also illustrates a common aspect of the repertoire of big bands: orchestrated versions of popular Tin Pan Alley songs. Composed by the Tin Pan Alley songwriter Vernon Duke (with lyrics by John Latouche and Ted Fetter), the song was popularized in a Broadway musical (and subsequent Hollywood film) called *Cabin in the Sky*.

This recording illustrates a dimension of big band swing performances that we have not yet mentioned: the inclusion of a male or female crooner who was featured on selected arrangements that were interspersed among the purely instrumental numbers. Today we are used to the idea that singers, rather than nonsinging instrumentalists, are generally the biggest stars in pop music. During the heyday of the big bands, however, it was the bandleader's name and not the singer's that appeared on the record label. On this recording the singer is Helen Forrest (1918–1999), who, although her name is little known today, was in her time regarded as one of the greatest of the big band crooners. Her warm, fluid voice and clarity of phrasing were much admired

by musicians, and she eventually worked with three of the most prominent bands of the swing era (those of Goodman, Artie Shaw, and Harry James).

The form of the song "Taking a Chance on Love" is the familiar thirty-two-bar AABA song structure. Henderson's arrangement includes an interesting instrumental introduction that is twenty-four measures in length. The introduction opens with a five-bar section in which the brass play a melodic line and the reeds respond. Then the band plays two iterations of the A section of the song, with the brass carrying the melody in the first four measures (interrupted by responses from the reed section) and then handing it off to Benny Goodman's solo clarinet in the second four measures. The second of these A sections is short-changed by one measure, shifting instead into a four-measure phrase played by the reeds, which moves us into the vocal section of the arrangement. The form of the introduction is thus 5+8+7+4=24 measures, a somewhat unusual structure that—reflecting Henderson's mastery of the art of big band arrangement—sounds completely natural.

Once we get into the vocal section, it is easier to follow the form. (It no doubt helps to have someone singing the melody and lyrics!) The vocal follows the AABA structure of the song, with Helen Forrest's voice supported by various combinations of reeds and brass. Forrest sings the song through once (AABA), and then the band takes over with another rendition of the song, with a saxophone solo in the B section (the bridge) and a brief tag to conclude the recording.

LISTENING GUIDE	"TAKING A CHANCE ON LOVE"		
TIME	**FORM**	**LYRICS**	**DESCRIPTIVE COMMENTS**
0:00	Introduction (24 measures)		
0:06	Opening section (5 measures)		Bars 1–3: Brass and reeds play call and response
0:11			Bars 4–5: Reeds play soli phrase
0:19	A (8 measures)		Bars 1–4: Muted brass play melody of the song, reeds respond

(continued)

Listening Guide "TAKING A CHANCE ON LOVE" (continued)

TIME	FORM	LYRICS	DESCRIPTIVE COMMENTS
0:27			Bars 5–8: Solo clarinet plays melody, reeds respond
0:40	A (7 measures)		Bars 1–6: Muted brass play melody, reeds respond
0:42			Bar 7: Brass and reeds play melody together
0:50	Linking section (4 measures)		Reeds play soli phrase, answered by brass, and lead us into the vocal section
Vocal (32 measures)			
1:08	A (8 measures)	*Here I go . . .*	Vocal with saxophone backgrounds
1:23	A (8 measures)	*Here I slide . . .*	Vocal with saxophone backgrounds
1:42	B (8 measures)	*I thought . . .*	Vocal with brass backgrounds
1:42	A (8 measures)	*Things are mending . . .*	Vocal with saxophone backgrounds
Instrumental (32 measures)			
1:58	A (8 measures)		Brass begin melody, solo clarinet takes over (saxophone backgrounds throughout)
2:15	A (8 measures)		Brass begin melody, solo clarinet takes over (saxophone backgrounds throughout)
2:32	B (8 measures)		Saxophone solo, punctuated by brass
2:49	A (8 measures)		Brass begin melody, solo clarinet takes over (saxophone backgrounds throughout)
3:06	Tag		Brass play melody, reeds play final chord

(whose band included the singer Billie Holiday) and the drummer *Gene Krupa*. On the one hand, the integration of formerly all-white big bands meant better pay and wider exposure for some African American musicians. On the other hand, integration made things even more difficult for all-Black dance bands, who—as the Negro Leagues experienced during the desegregation of baseball in the late 1940s—saw some of their most promising talent, and a portion of their audience, drain away.

Duke Ellington in the Swing Era

During the Swing era, *Duke Ellington*—whose 1927 recording of "East St. Louis Toodle-Oo" we explored in Chapter 3—continued to develop his unique approach to jazz composition and arrangement. Like most jazz-based dance ensembles, his band grew in size, from ten musicians in 1927 to fifteen in 1941, when the band's new theme song, "Take the 'A' Train," was recorded. Despite Top 10 hits like "Caravan" (1937), "I Let a Song Go Out of My Heart" (1938), "Don't Get Around Much Anymore" (1941), and "Do Nothin' Till You Hear from Me" (1944), Ellington's idiosyncratic approach generally meant that his band enjoyed less commercial success than more mainstream-sounding dance orchestras during the height of the big band craze. As Ellington once said, "Jazz is music, swing is business," and despite remaining a savvy businessman throughout his six-decade career, he never abandoned his artistic aspirations.

By the time the swing era opened in 1935, Duke Ellington had already been leading a band for almost twenty years and making records for over ten. After leaving the Cotton Club in 1931, the Ellington band toured widely, making successful appearances in cities as far away as Paris and London, and the band's reputation was augmented by its recordings, network radio broadcasts, and the public relations efforts of Ellington's manager, Irving Mills. However, there is some evidence that the new generation of swing bands that rose to popularity in the wake of Benny Goodman's breakthrough threatened to displace Ellington and other long-standing bands in the hearts of younger listeners. (In 1936 a writer for *Variety* reported that students at Dartmouth University

Duke Ellington and his band at the Hurricane Club in New York City, 1943, photographed by Gordon Parks.

Listening Guide "CARAVAN"

Composed by Juan Tizol and Duke Ellington; arranged by Duke Ellington; performed by Duke Ellington and His Orchestra; recorded 1937

In 1937 the Duke Ellington Orchestra played a return engagement at the Cotton Club, now relocated to midtown Manhattan, during which they featured a new piece entitled "Caravan." The song was adapted by Ellington from an improvised melody played at a rehearsal by the Puerto Rican–born valve trombonist Juan Tizol (1900–1984), who had been with the band since 1929. "Caravan" had first been recorded the year before by a seven-piece group drawn from the Ellington band—part of an effort by Duke to create a more intimate "chamber music" context for his music—and had sold moderately well in that version. Ellington was to rework his arrangement of "Caravan" many times over the years, but the 1937 recording, the first by the full fifteen-piece band, is unique in its subtlety and freshness.

"Caravan" is in the familiar thirty-two-bar AABA form. It begins with the drummer Sonny Greer (1895–1982), who met Ellington in 1919 and had played with him ever since. One of the major differences between

LISTENING GUIDE	"CARAVAN"	
TIME	**SECTION**	**DESCRIPTIVE COMMENTS**
0:00	Introduction	Opens with the sound of a suspended metal gong being struck with a soft mallet, a sound evoking exotic stereotypes of the "Orient." Greer establishes a gentle but insistently pulsating groove on his drums using mallets, which create a softer, darker-sounding effect than drumsticks.The bass players—Ellington employed two during this period to deepen the bottom end of the band's sound, another notable difference in the context of swing music—support Greer's drumming with a steady pulse, while Duke sprinkles piano chords into the mix.
0:10	A (repeated once)	Haunting minor key melody played on valve trombone by Juan Tizol, complemented by a countermelody on the baritone saxophone and the growling wah-wah sound of trumpeter Cootie Williams. Tizol plays the melody in a straightforward, almost "classical" fashion in the first two A sections.
0:45	B	Tizol improvises on the major-key B section, with the support of sustained chords played by three clarinets.
1:02	A	Clarinetist Barney Bigard's fluid elaboration on the melody is backed by muted brass and a rhythmic pattern played by Greer on temple blocks (hollow wooden percussion instruments derived from East Asian musical traditions).
1:19	A	Muted trumpet solo by Cootie Williams, whose first, long note seems to come out of nowhere, sneaking up on us. Like Tizol and Bigard, Williams bases his solo in the two A sections on the main melody, though he plays with a stronger swing feeling, and uses blue notes and the plunger mute "wahwah" technique effectively. (If you listen closely you can hear the band as a whole begin to gel rhythmically in response to his playing, which is backed by a syncopated figure in the saxophones and temple blocks.)
1:55	B	Harmonized melody by the saxophone and the clarinet accompanied by temple blocks.
2:12	A	Tizol returns with the A theme to lead to the end—an unusual unresolved chord and a final splash from the gong.

the Ellington band and its competitors was the role of the drummer. In most swing bands, the drummer kept time and drove the band forward with a strong, dance-oriented pulse. In the Ellington band, Greer's contribution was more broadly musical—he added to the overall texture of the sound with his use of wire brushes, mallets, and "exotic" percussion instruments. (Interestingly, Ellington never wrote drum parts out for Greer, relying instead on his innate sense of discretion. Greer, for his part, did not specialize in the sorts of flashy drum solos that were featured by most swing bands, focusing instead on supporting the work of his fellow musicians.)

The main theme is played by the piece's coauthor, Juan Tizol, on the valve trombone (a version of the instrument with depressible keys, like a trumpet, rather than a slide). Tizol, whose father was a well-known bandmaster in Puerto Rico, was trained in the Italian style of concert band playing, which emphasizes a relatively light tone and fast vibrato, both of which can be heard here. Although the rhythmic feeling cannot be identified as a specific Latin American rhythm (say, a rumba), it does evoke the generalized, habanera-inspired "Spanish tinge" identified by Jelly Roll Morton as a key feature of early jazz (see Chapter 1).

The fittingly mysterious denouement for "Caravan" is a carefully arranged experiment in instrumental textures and timbres. Inspired by a brief improvised phrase—a thing of the moment that most bandleaders would have discarded—Ellington's arrangement supports Tizol's serpentine melody with subtle, carefully modulated instrumental accompaniments. The rhythmic feeling shifts back and forth between Latin American and swing phrasing, and the arrangement is enlivened with "exotic" percussion and bluesy jazz improvisations. The title of the tune (like its lyrics, composed later by Ellington's manager, Irving Mills) evokes the image of a lonely caravan snaking through a moonlit Middle Eastern desert, a reprisal of the conflation of Latin romance with the image of the proud Arab sheik first presented in the films of Rudolph Valentino (see Chapters 1 and 3).

Even if "Caravan" is essentially a less humid variation of the "jungle music" exotica of Ellington's earlier career, there can be no denying that the 1937 recording stands apart from the bulk of unimaginative writing that characterized the swing era. Over the years "Caravan" has been recorded by a wide variety of musicians, including Nat King Cole, Chet Atkins, the Carpenters, the Ventures, Les Paul, Bobby Darin, Phish, and Latin artists such as Tito Puente and Perez Prado. It has also appeared in the movies *Chocolat*, *Ocean's Eleven* (2001), and *Sweet and Lowdown*, as well as the television programs *The O.C.* and *The Simpsons*. For people of a certain age who grew up hearing "Caravan" mainly as an accompaniment for corny circus acts and an excuse for flamboyant drum solos, Ellington's original conception of the piece provides both a refreshing earwash and a reminder of his uniqueness.

felt that "Ellington's weird chords have grown stale" [Hasse 1993, 196].) Unlike contemporaries such as Goodman, Count Basie, the Dorsey Brothers, and Glenn Miller, Ellington was not only a skilled instrumentalist and bandleader but also an innovative composer and arranger, intent upon exploring sonic textures, colors, and moods and absorbing and extending the creative gifts of his talented musicians. This creative approach may have limited his appeal to the mainstream audience. Additionally, it is important to remember that racial prejudice still played a major role during the swing era in limiting the economic mobility of African American musicians, no matter how brilliant.

Kansas City Swing: Count Basie

Although big bands relied heavily on arrangements of popular Tin Pan Alley songs, the blues—with its twelve-bar structure, three-chord pattern, blue notes, and call-and-response patterns—also remained a mainstay of swing music. Of all the big bands, the one most closely associated with the blues tradition was led by the jazz pianist *William "Count" Basie* (1904–1984). Born in New Jersey, Basie gained much of his early experience as a player and bandleader in Kansas City, Missouri. In the 1920s Kansas City was in many ways still a frontier town, with a famously crooked mayor named "Boss" Pendergast whose administration tacitly encouraged the development of a lively—and, during Prohibition, largely illegal—nightclub scene. Many of the greatest jazz musicians honed their improvisational skills in "K. C." at competitive all-night jam sessions or cutting sessions. These Olympian contests provided a chance for budding virtuosos to test their musical skills and endurance against one another.

During the 1920s and early 1930s Black dance bands in Kansas City developed their own distinctive approach to playing hot dance music. **Territory bands** such as the Bennie Moten Orchestra and Andy Kirk's Blue Devils toured the southwestern United States, developing a hard-swinging, powerful style with lots of room for improvised solos. The Kansas City style was more closely linked to the country blues tradition than the style

Count Basie.

of the New York bands, and it relied more heavily upon riffs. Few of the jazz musicians in Kansas City had the formal music education of East Coast musicians like Fletcher Henderson. As a consequence, they often played with a looser, less precise feeling and relied heavily on "head charts," arrangements that evolved during jam sessions and were written down only later, almost as an afterthought. In rhythmic terms, the Kansas City bands tended to swing more intensely and with greater abandon than the East Coast dance bands.

One important influence on the rhythmic conception of the K. C. bands was the **boogie-woogie** blues piano tradition, which sprang up during the early twentieth century in the "southwest territory" states of Texas, Arkansas, Missouri, and Oklahoma and became a popular fad during the swing era. The style developed in the environment of the barrelhouses, rowdy nightspots patronized by the men who worked in the lumber and turpentine camps of the area. Solo pianists, a cheap and readily available form of entertainment, responded to the rowdy environment of the barrelhouses by developing a powerful style that could be heard over the crowd noise. In boogie-woogie performances the pianist typically plays a repeated pattern with his left hand, down in the low range of the piano, while improvising polyrhythmic patterns with his right hand. The greatest boogie-woogie piano players—men like Pete Johnson, Albert Ammons, Meade Lux Lewis, and Pine Top Smith—were said to have "a left hand like God," an admiring reference to the volume, steadiness, and authority of their bass patterns. Big band musicians from Kansas City were strongly influenced by the boogie-woogie style, especially its rhythmic drive and heavy reliance on riffs. (During the war boogie-woogie became a national fad, spawning a series of hit records with names like "Boogie Woogie," "Boogie Woogie Bugle Boy," and even "The Booglie Wooglie Piggy." The genre was later to exert a strong influence on rock 'n' roll through the influence of "southwestern" musicians such as Big Joe Turner and Jerry Lee Lewis.)

In 1936 John Hammond, who had recently helped start Benny Goodman's career, heard Count Basie's band on a late-night shortwave radio show in Chicago. "I just happened to tune in to an experimental radio station at the very top of the dial, just beyond the last station on the regular AM wavelength," he later recalled. Excited by the band's loose but energetic sound, Hammond worked to sign Basie on with MCA and to secure engagements for the band in Chicago and New York City. Although the band's roughhewn style did not catch on immediately, Hammond was able to get Basie a recording contract with Decca, a new record company interested in capitalizing on the swing craze. Basie's recollection of the contract he signed with Decca is a good example of the disadvantageous position of Black musicians at that time vis-à-vis the music industry:

> Without realizing what I was doing, I had agreed to record twelve records a year for $750 a year outright, no royalties! I didn't know anything about royalties. John [Hammond] couldn't believe it. He couldn't get us out of that contract, but he was able to get Decca to raise the musicians' pay. . . . I guess I just had to learn some things the hard way. (Basie and Murray 1995, 167)

Listening Guide "ONE O'CLOCK JUMP"

Composed by William Count Basie; arranged by Eddie Durham and Buster Smith; performed by Count Basie and His Orchestra; recorded 1937

"One o'Clock Jump," recorded by Decca in 1937, was the Count Basie Orchestra's theme song. It is an excellent example of the Kansas City bands' relaxed but energetic rhythmic approach, their emphasis on jazz improvisation, and their reliance on informal and flexible head arrangements. In structural terms, this recording of "One o'Clock Jump" consists of ten choruses of twelve-bar blues. The basic arranging technique involves the heavy use of riffs and call-and-response patterns—divided between the brass and the reeds—and a succession of improvised jazz solos. The closest thing to a melody, in the sense that the term would be used in the Tin Pan Alley songwriting tradition, does not appear until the next-to-last chorus. Listening to this recording, one has the feeling that the band could probably go on all night, as long as there were still soloists waiting in line to play.

The recording begins with an eight-bar piano boogie-woogie introduction and two improvised twelve-bar blues choruses by Basie, his piano supported gently but energetically by the rest of the rhythm section (Jo Jones on drums, Walter Page on bass, and Freddie Green on guitar). Then there is a key change, the band enters, and we hear a series of solos on saxophone, trombone, saxophone again, and finally trumpet, each supported by background riffs. (Although this section seems largely improvised, it is worth noting that the order of the solos alternates between reeds and brass, and that each reed instrument is supported by brass and vice versa.)

After these solos, Basie plays another chorus in his famously elegant "two-fingered" style, and then the entire band comes in. The final three choruses of riffs are what identify "One o'Clock Jump" for swing fans and musicians alike. This is an important point, for while riffs were one of several key techniques for East Coast arrangers such as Fletcher Henderson, here the basic identity of the piece lies in its riffs, which are continually tossed back and forth between the brass and the reeds. In a piece like this, the horns seem almost to become part of the rhythm section—their function is less to play a melody than to help propel the music along with greater and greater intensity.

Superstar of Swing: Glenn Miller

From 1939 until 1942 the *Glenn Miller* (1904–1944) Orchestra was the most popular dance band in the world, breaking records for both record sales and concert attendance. Miller had worked as a trombonist on numerous recordings before launching his own band in 1937. Like other bandleaders, his popularity was boosted by live radio broadcasts from hotels and dance halls. Miller developed a peppy, clean-sounding style that appealed to small-town Midwesterners as well as the big-city East and West Coast constituency that had previously sustained swing music. In terms of sheer popular success, the Miller band marked the apex of the swing era, racking up twenty-three Number 1 recordings in a little under four years.

Listening Guide "IN THE MOOD"

Composed by Joe Garland and Andy Razaf; arranged by Glenn Miller; performed by Glenn Miller and His Orchestra; recorded 1939

The Glenn Miller Orchestra's 1939 recording of "In the Mood," which held the Number 1 position on the charts for twelve weeks, was the biggest hit record of the swing era. "In the Mood" is probably the best-known swing recording, and its structure is easy to follow. Like the classic blues of W. C. Handy, "In the Mood" alternates the twelve-bar blues form with an eight-bar bridge phrase reminiscent of Tin Pan Alley songs. The main riff—that is, the featured saxophone part by which most people remember the recording—had been around for quite a while before Miller got hold of it. (Fletcher Henderson, for example, had used it in

LISTENING GUIDE	"IN THE MOOD"		
TIME	**FORM**	**DESCRIPTIVE COMMENTS**
0:00	Introduction (8 measures)	Bars 1–4: Saxophones play syncopated "fanfare" figure
0:05		Bars 5–8: Brass take over main melody
0:12	A (12-bar blues)	Saxophones play the main riff, with brass responses (two-measure phrases)
0:29	A (12 measures)	Repeat
0:47	B (8-bar phrase)	Saxophones play a different riff, brass answer (two-bar phrases); last two bars everyone together, with crescendo to push us into the next phrase
0:58	B (8 measures)	Repeat
1:10	B (8 measures)	Two saxophones take turns soloing (two-bar phrases); brass play last two bars
1:22	B (8 measures)	Repeat
1:34	Connecting phrase (4 measures)	Brass for two bars, then brass and reeds together (rhythm section stops for first two bars, comes back in for second two)
1:40	B (8 measures)	Trumpet solo, with saxophone and trombone riff accompaniment
1:52	B (8 measures)	Repeat
2:03	Connecting phrase (2 measures)	Whole band
2:06	A (14 measures)	Main riff returns in the saxophones, with trombones playing a sustained low note in response; extra two-bar phrase is added for suspense
2:27	A (14 measures)	Same music, but quieter
2:48	A (12 measures)	Same music, even quieter (listen for cowbell in background, very softly)
3:06	A (19 measures)	Same music comes back two measures before you expect it—*loudly*!!! At the end of this section there is another musical trick—the chorus is extended by an additional six bars, delaying and intensifying the final resolution to the tonic chord.

(continued)

Listening Guide "IN THE MOOD" (*continued*)

an arrangement as early as 1930.) Miller's contribution was to position this venerable riff as the centerpiece of an uncluttered arrangement constructed from simple building blocks and varied in ingenious ways to hold the listener's interest. A particularly famous aspect of "In the Mood" is its "trick" ending, in which the band gets quieter and quieter (and the arranger adds and subtracts a few measures here and there, so you're not quite sure when they will move to the next section) and then explodes into a big finish.

Although it lacks the energetic momentum and bravado of Count Basie's "One o'Clock Jump," "In the Mood" was one of the most commercially successful applications of the blues form in the history of American popular music. Jazz critics have tended to make fun of Miller's music, considering it shallow and unadventurous, both a reminder of the sweet music of Paul Whiteman's band and a harbinger of the schmaltzy mainstream pop music of the 1950s. Nonetheless, there is no denying his tremendous success as a popular musician, and it is worth taking a moment to consider the basis of his music's attraction for millions of Americans.

One of the most obvious qualities of "In the Mood"—and other Miller hits such as "Chattanooga Choo-Choo," "Tuxedo Junction," and "A String of Pearls"—is

its predictability. After the first time you have heard "In the Mood," its trick ending can never again come as a surprise. Rather, the pleasure comes from anticipating and then re-experiencing something one already knows by heart. The pleasures of "In the Mood" are those neither of passion nor of inventiveness; rather, they are the pleasures of the familiar, the comfortable, the expected. And if we take a moment to imagine ourselves living in a country about to enter a global war, a conflagration that was to bring tragedy to every community in the United States, it is perhaps easier to understand the appeal of such qualities.

Today we view World War II from afar, through black-and-white photographs or old movies about the heroism of soldiers. This sense of distance makes it hard for us to imagine what it was actually like for people on the "home front," living with the knowledge that an officer might show up at their door at any moment to report the death of a loved one. To be sure, "In the Mood," like most big hits of the swing era, was escapist in both content and outlook. But people sometimes need a means of escape, however temporary, from the anxieties of life. This has all along been one of the most important functions of popular music: in times of great stress or tragedy, it simply helps people to carry on.

Jazz Singers: The Boswell Sisters, Billie Holiday, and Ella Fitzgerald

During the swing era, several female jazz singers emerged as important artists on their own. Jazz singers tend to fall between the cracks, so to speak; they are rarely given detailed coverage in most accounts of popular music because they are "jazz" singers, but most jazz histories treat jazz as music overwhelmingly dominated by instrumental performers. Because jazz singers worked typically with prominent instrumentalists, in big bands or in small groups, their vocal contributions tended to get short shrift. During the swing era, band singers were often not even acknowledged on the record labels by name. The main attractions, whether live or on records, were the bands and their leaders. (We have seen how the recording of "Taking a Chance on Love" was credited to "Benny Goodman and His Orchestra"—poor Helen Forrest! But her situation was typical for band singers.) While most swing bands had one or more regular vocalists performing with them, a group that included both male and female singers, only rarely did those singers emerge from their band experience with enough of a popular following to have records issued under their own names. Two of them who managed to do so in the late 1930s were Billie Holiday and Ella Fitzgerald, both of whom must be counted among the great singers of any generation.

An important link between the early vocals of Louis Armstrong, which essentially defined jazz singing (see the discussion of "Ain't Misbehavin'" in Chapter 3), and those of Billie Holiday and Ella Fitzgerald is found in the recordings of the *Boswell Sisters* from the early 1930s. This sibling trio (Connie—later Connee, Martha, and Helvetia [Vet] Boswell) had a relatively brief recording career, but their records set a remarkably high benchmark for jazz vocal performance—and for future sister acts and "girl groups." Many of the greatest solo jazz singers, Ella Fitzgerald in particular, cited Connie Boswell as a fundamental influence.

The Boswells regularly recorded with some of the finest jazz musicians of the time, including the Dorsey brothers. An excellent example of their artistry is their 1932 version of Duke Ellington's "It Don't Mean a Thing (If It Ain't Got That Swing)" (with words credited to Irving Mills). The sisters' breathtakingly rapid group scat singing reveals their thorough absorption of Armstrong's vocal innovations, while the opening solo vocal demonstrates a comfortable familiarity with blues-derived styles. The intricate tempo-shifting arrangement on the recording as a whole anticipates the sophistication that characterizes the best big band records of the swing era.

The Boswell Sisters' "It Don't Mean a Thing (If It Ain't Got That Swing)" incorporates three distinctly different treatments of Ellington's AABA song. A brief instrumental introduction immediately prepares the listener for striking contrasts to come; the band starts things up in a moderate, steady tempo and then leaves the next phrase to a solo violin, which slows down as it draws out its melody. Returning to the opening tempo, a solo voice enters and presents the first AABA in call-and-response with the band; note the bluesy slides in Connie Boswell's performance. The next AABA suddenly doubles the speed, with the three sisters singing in rhythmic unison as they create an original scat "language" based on the key words of the song. Within each of the "A" sections here, the dizzying scat alternates with a smooth wordless "baa . . .," creating, in effect, call-and-response between two styles of vocalizing. The tempo slows down as this part of the recording concludes, and then a mournful, nearly dirge-paced instrumental interlude presents two "A" sections. Finally, the performance returns to the fast tempo for a last vocal trio AABA. This final presentation offers the "straightest" (but still swinging!) approach of all to Ellington's original song, paradoxically reversing the expected order—in which the performance would begin with a "straight" reading of the melody, and only following that would the musicians take liberties with it. A brief coda allows the Boswell Sisters a summarizing rapid-fire statement: "Doesn't mean a thing without the swing!"

Billie Holiday (1915–1959) possessed a voice with one of the most distinctive timbres ever recorded, somewhat akin to a reed instrument in its quiet but penetrating

Billie Holiday singing at the Downbeat Club in New York, c. February 1947.

intensity. She achieved chart success under her own name, while performing with great jazz instrumentalists, such as pianist Teddy Wilson and tenor saxophone player Lester Young.

Among Billie Holiday's most famous and enduring records is that of her own song "God Bless the Child" (co-written with Arthur Herzog Jr.) from 1941. Its somber music, and the lyrics' philosophical acceptance of aloneness and the need for self-sufficiency, have rendered the song timeless in its beauty and relevance, while Holiday's performance is a model of poignant understatement. On this recording, as on so many of her others, the singer's uncanny ability to phrase with the utmost naturalness and ease—as if speaking the lyrics—is evident, while she never loses the underlying rhythm of the music. To offer just one of many possible examples, in the "A" sections of this AABA song, notice particularly the ending lines: "God bless the child that's got his own, that's got his own." The first time Holiday sings "that's got his own," she deliberately accelerates ahead of the beat, to emphasize this essential and positive message. Then she slows down the repetition of these lyrics, relaxing back into the basic tempo of the music, while enjoying the long "o" vowel in "own"; this provides another form of emphasis that also conveys the necessary sense of conclusion.

Ella Fitzgerald (1917–1996) had such a long and distinguished performing and recording career that it resists any easy summary. By the age of twenty-one, she had a major hit, the novelty "A-Tisket, A-Tasket," recorded with Chick Webb's orchestra, and from that point on she brought her distinctive jazz sensibility to an exceptionally wide range of material. She made records with Louis Armstrong, Count Basie, and the rhythm & blues star Louis Jordan (see Chapter 7), among many others.

During the 1950s, Fitzgerald recorded an acclaimed series of "songbook" albums, each devoted to the songs of a major figure from the golden age of Tin Pan Alley (Irving Berlin, Cole Porter, George Gershwin, etc.). Attesting to the "classic" status that this repertoire had attained by this time, Fitzgerald's "songbook" albums proceeded to become classics themselves. As exemplars of jazz vocal performance at its best, her performances respect the songs as compositions, while employing rhythmic flexibility and elements of improvisation that render the songs newly fresh and meaningful. A fine example of her approach is the recording of "Too Darn Hot" from *Ella Fitzgerald Sings the Cole Porter Songbook* (1956). Remaining close to Porter's written melody at first, Fitzgerald allows herself greater and greater improvisatory freedom as the performance progresses. By the time we reach the end, both a firm impression of Porter's song and a completely individual, distinctive performance of it have been provided.

Vocal Harmony Groups

Although dance bands dominated the charts between 1935 and 1945, the bestselling record of the swing era—leaving aside Bing Crosby's 1942 recording of "White Christmas," a perennial holiday bestseller—featured a performance by an African American vocal harmony group, the Mills Brothers, accompanied only by guitar.

The American vocal harmony group tradition includes many streams, both white and Black, sacred and secular, rural and urban. Some of the earliest commercial recordings, made in the 1890s and 1900s, feature performances by professional vocal quartets singing Stephen Foster songs, Tin Pan Alley hits, and ragtime numbers. During the early twentieth century "jubilee" groups, usually in the form of male vocal quartets, became popular in Black churches, and many of these appeared on race records. (The Golden Gate Quartet, discussed in Chapter 5, was part of this tradition.) The 1920s and 1930s also saw the rise of a new generation of popular vocal trios and quartets who included hot syncopated songs in their repertoires. (Many of the biggest pop singers of the Jazz Age in fact began their careers singing with such groups; for example, Bing Crosby's first appearances with the Paul Whiteman Orchestra were as a member of a vocal trio called the Rhythm Boys.)

During the swing era vocal harmony groups such as the Boswell Sisters (whom we've already studied), the Andrews Sisters, the Ink Spots, and the Mills Brothers remained popular. The *Andrews Sisters* are still widely remembered today—thanks in part to their irresistible upbeat wartime recording of "Boogie Woogie Bugle Boy" (1941), revived by the pop singer Bette Midler in the 1970s. Like the Mills Brothers, the Andrews Sisters incorporated elements of jazz style into their pop recordings, such as scat singing and melodic improvisation (both of which are clearly present in "Boogie Woogie Bugle Boy," adding to its broad appeal).

The *Mills Brothers*, however, were the most successful and longest-lived of these swing era vocal groups. Unlike many "brother" and "sister" groups, the original Mills Brothers really were siblings. Born in Ohio, Herbert (1912–1989), Harry (1913–1982), Donald (1915–1999), and John Mills Jr. (1911–1935) perfected a secular version of the African American jubilee quartet tradition in the late 1920s. Their smooth, jazz-influenced style appealed to a broad audience, and they were one of the first Black musical groups to be broadcast on network radio and to score commercial success in the mainstream pop music market. (One key to their success was the brothers' ability to mimic the sound of various musical instruments. Their 1931 recording of the Original Dixieland Jazz Band's "Tiger Rag," one of the bestselling records of that year, featured an imitation of a New Orleans–style jazz band.) In 1935 John, the group's bass singer and guitarist, died and was replaced by his father, John Sr. With seventy hit records spread over almost four decades, the Mills Brothers were the most popular vocal harmony group of the twentieth century. Their recordings had a huge impact on vocal harmony ("doo-wop") groups of the rock 'n' roll era and exerted an influence as far afield as South Africa, where a 1950s vocal group actually called itself the African Mills Brothers.

Listening Guide "PAPER DOLL"

Music and lyrics by Johnny S. Black; published 1915; performed by the Mills Brothers; recorded 1942

"Paper Doll," the Mills Brothers' biggest hit, was recorded in 1942 and became a chart success in 1943. The record sold 6 million copies—an unprecedented figure—and stayed on the pop charts for thirty-six weeks, twelve of them at Number 1. The phenomenal success of "Paper Doll" is partly attributable to a recording ban, which barred instrumental musicians from making records for a period during the war and thereby cleared the field for vocal groups. But this cannot account for the record's singular appeal, which was due mainly to the Mills Brothers' polished performance, a sophisticated vocal arrangement of an old Tin Pan Alley love song composed in 1915 by the African American songwriter Johnny S. Black, which in other hands might have seemed hopelessly old-fashioned to swing era listeners.

"Paper Doll" expresses the anxieties of a young man who has decided to fashion an inanimate lover—a paper cutout of a woman—in order to protect himself from the treachery of "real live girls." The mildly misogynist tone of the lyrics—which place blame for the narrator's problems on the putative fickle-mindedness of young women—makes an interesting contrast with the Victorian high-mindedness of "After the Ball" (1892; see Chapter 2), in which the male narrator's suspicions of his female partner's infidelity are proved unfounded. From our viewpoint the song may seem almost a parody of itself—just another day in the life of a nerd—but ragtime era listeners apparently interpreted it as a straightforward expression of heartache.

Let's fast-forward to 1942 and the Decca Record Company's studios in New York City, where the Mills

TIME	FORM	LYRIC	DESCRIPTIVE COMMENTS
	LISTENING GUIDE | "PAPER DOLL"		
0:00	Guitar introduction		
	"Slow" section (refrain)		
0:05	A (8 measures)	*I'm gonna buy...*	Slow, sentimental style, with the guitar marking each beat
0:32	B (8 measures)	*When I come home...*	There is a brief reminiscence of the opening A music toward the end of B (*I'd rather have...*), which gives a general sense of rounding to the form.
	"Fast" section (double-time feel)		
	Verse		
0:59	First part (8 measures)	*I guess I had a million dolls...*	Note "walking bass" effect, typical of swing music
1:23	Second part (8 measures)	*I'll tell you boys...*	Second part of verse begins with same music as the first but ends differently
	Refrain		
1:46	A (8 measures)	*I'm gonna buy...*	
2:10	B (8 measures)	*When I come home...*	

Brothers reharmonized, rearranged, and breathed new life into the thirty-year-old song. (They apparently spent only fifteen minutes in the studio to record the song, which was not expected to be a huge hit.) The only instrumental accompaniment in this arrangement is a guitar, which plays a brief introduction. The brothers sing through the refrain as the guitar articulates each beat, with the bass notes landing on beats 1 and 3 and the lead voice supported by rich, dreamy vocal harmonies. Then they abruptly switch gears, introducing the verse and singing the refrain in a more active rhythm typical of swing music. (Although the music seems to have speeded up, if you count along you will discover that the tempo has remained the same. For example, although the second refrain feels as though it's moving twice as fast as the first, the words are really moving at the same speed. This technique, in which the speed of the bass part is doubled, is called "double-time feel.") This rethinking of the presentation of the song's form offers a good example of what we might call the "arranger's art." The brothers alternate vocal techniques, sometimes singing in close harmony—rather like a saxophone soli section in a big band arrangement—sometimes in unison, and occasionally allowing the lead voice to go it alone. The cheerful, lively approach of the latter part of the arrangement puts the lyrics into an entirely new context and suggests that the Mills Brothers knew that the swing era audience would have had a hard time taking the song seriously if it were presented only in a sentimental fashion.

Country Music in the Swing Era: Roy Acuff, Singing Cowboys, and Western Swing

Although the big bands dominated the pop charts, the appeal of so-called hillbilly performers and their music, based in Anglo-American folk traditions, continued to grow between 1935 and 1945. Uprooted by the Great Depression, the mechanization of agriculture, and ecological catastrophes such as the Dust Bowl drought of the late 1930s, millions of white Southerners migrated in search of industrial employment, forming enclaves in urban centers such as Nashville, Atlanta, Detroit, Chicago, Cincinnati, St. Louis, and Los Angeles. This mass population movement created a new urban audience for hillbilly music, a genre referred to by its increasingly cosmopolitan listeners, and eventually by the music industry, as country and western music, or simply country music.

At the same time, the appeal of country music also appears to have spread among many people who were not born in the South. During the late 1930s listeners throughout the country were exposed to country music on the radio, including the far-reaching fifty-thousand-watt stations located just across the border in Mexico and in North American cities such as Fort Worth, Texas (WBAP); Chicago (WLS); and Nashville, Tennessee (WSM). By the end of World War II there were over six hundred hillbilly radio programs on the air nationwide. Many people who looked down their noses at country music, making fun of the singers' nasal voices, "hick" dialects, and conservative cultural values, still listened to shows such as WSM's *Grand Ole Opry*, and many found their musical tastes shaped by the experience.

A number of other factors contributed to the expansion of country music during the war. The formation of BMI provided opportunities for country songwriters to publish their compositions and receive royalties. The American Federation of Musicians' recording ban, which kept members out of the studios, created more recording opportunities for hillbilly musicians, most of whom were not allowed to join the union. New record companies such as Capitol Records, based in Los Angeles, achieved success in part because of their large rosters of country recording artists. A number of small **independent record labels ("indies")** specializing in hillbilly music also sprang up during the war, particularly in towns such as Nashville, Cincinnati, and Los Angeles, with their large populations of Southern migrants. After the recording ban ended, major companies began to pay more attention to country music, and popular mainstream artists such as Bing Crosby and the Andrews Sisters released bestselling versions of country songs. By the close of the war, the American music industry had awakened to the commercial potential of country music, which by some estimates provided nearly a third of its total revenues.

The war helped to expand the audience for country music, not only by stimulating rural-urban migration on the home front, but also by bringing millions of servicemen from the North and Midwest into more intimate contact with their Southern-born counterparts. While co-residence did not automatically confer musical brotherhood, many Americans who had previously paid little or no attention to hillbilly music began to develop a taste for it. As heard over the Armed Forces radio network, on "V-discs" ("Victory discs") produced by the U.S. government for servicemen, and at USO concerts designed to boost the morale of the troops, music rooted in the old traditions of the American South played an important role in the daily lives of servicemen and had a profound and lasting impact on their musical sensibilities.

Themes of sentimentality, morality, and patriotism, already prominent in hillbilly recordings of the 1920s, played a key role in country music's popularity during the war. Prominent country music stars composed and recorded songs such as "Smoke on the Water," "Gold Star in the Window," "Cowards over Pearl Harbor," and "Hitler's Last Letter to Hirohito," which were targeted at servicemen and the families they had left behind. One survey of American soldiers in Europe actually found that the GIs preferred hillbilly musician Roy Acuff to the big band crooner Frank Sinatra by a substantial margin. Attacking a Marine position on Okinawa, a Japanese *banzai* charge reportedly used a battle cry designed as the ultimate insult to Americans: "To hell with Roosevelt, to hell with Babe Ruth, to hell with Roy Acuff!"

The object of this epithet was **Roy Claxton Acuff** (1903–1992), the most popular hillbilly singer of the swing era. Like many other country music performers, Acuff began his career with a traveling medicine show and in 1935 formed his own band, the Crazy Tennesseans. In 1938 he joined the regular cast of WSM's *Grand Ole Opry* and soon became its biggest star. Acuff performed in a style that was self-consciously rooted in Southern folk music. He sang old-timey songs in a sincere, unaffected style with a pronounced Southern twang, and his band used instruments derived from the Southern string band tradition, including the fiddle, banjo, and guitar. In general, Acuff was a traditionalist, accepting only those innovations that fit within the framework of musical traditions he had learned growing up in Tennessee.

Listening Guide "GREAT SPECKLED BIRD"

Written by Reverend Guy Smith; performed by Roy Acuff and His Crazy Tennesseans; recorded 1936

Roy Acuff's initial rise to fame was in large part due to the popularity of two songs that are still closely associated with him, "Wabash Cannonball" and "Great Speckled Bird." The latter song—widely regarded as the national anthem of country and western music—was Acuff's first hit record. Recorded in Chicago in 1936, Acuff's rendition of "Great Speckled Bird" crossed over to the mainstream pop charts, reaching Number 13 on the *Billboard* Hit Parade in 1938. (Acuff's recording is actually titled "Great Speckle Bird," but we are using here the name by which the song has become generally known.) Following in the tradition of gospel-derived performance established by the Carter Family and other early country music performers (see Chapter 5), the lyrics—composed by a Southern preacher—portray the church as an embattled group of individuals. The speckled bird is a metaphor for the church, a sign of God's word (as inscribed in the Bible) and a vehicle for the salvation of the faithful. This image is drawn from Jeremiah 12:9, "Mine heritage is unto me as a speckled bird, the birds round about are against her." The huge commercial success of Acuff's recording of "Great Speckled Bird"—and the song's subsequent incorporation into the services of many Pentecostal Holiness churches—was in large part due to the song's religious theme. During a time of profound change, in which millions of families were uprooted from a rural way of life, the church became a touchstone of moral and cultural continuity.

The traditional ethos of "Great Speckled Bird"—one source of its great appeal to Southern-born listeners—is reinforced by Acuff's straightforward, unadorned vocal performance, and by the form of the song, derived from the strophic pattern of Anglo-American ballad singing. (In this case the sixteen-bar strophe is performed a total of five times.) The melody of "Great Speckled Bird" is also quite similar to that of "I'm Thinking Tonight of My Blue Eyes," a song popularized by the Carter Family, and its familiarity to many of Acuff's listeners may also account in part for its success.

Although his reputation rested upon a folksy, down-home approach, Acuff was not averse to using technological innovations that fit within the framework of the Southern string band tradition. His recording of "Great Speckled Bird" features a new version of the standard six-string guitar called the Dobro, which uses a round metal plate (a resonator) to amplify the sound of the strings. On this recording the blunt edge of a steel knife is used to play melodic patterns on the Dobro, allowing the player to glide between pitches, interweaving with the singer's voice. (This technique, pioneered by Hawaiian and African American guitarists in the early twentieth century, is called "bottleneck" playing.) Acuff was a shrewd businessman—in 1942 he responded to wartime changes in the music industry by cofounding a music publishing company, Acuff-Rose, which went on to make millions of dollars from the expanding postwar market for country songs.

SINGING COWBOYS

Another important development of the late 1930s and 1940s was the rise of the singing cowboy. The heroic image of the old cowhand, popularized after World War I in cheap dime novels, published collections of cowboy songs, and the movies of silent film stars such as Tom Mix, was adopted by many country musicians during the Depression years as a substitute for the often-denigrated image of the hillbilly. Like the South, the Wild West has long been a place in the American imagination, a repository of images and stories that Americans tell themselves about their history, their traditions, and their character. However, images of the South in American popular culture, whether positive or negative in tone, typically evoke tradition, religious morality, and the past, while the West is popularly associated with movement, independence, and the future. From the 1930s through the 1950s, as country musicians sought to reach a wider audience, the term "western" became a substitute for "hillbilly." Many country singers, whatever their place of birth, wore cowboy hats and shirts and adopted nicknames such as "Tex," "Slim," "Hank," or "the Lone Cowboy." (The cowboy image remains a potent factor in country music, as may be seen in the careers of country singers such as Garth Brooks, Kenny Chesney, and Blake Shelton.)

The first successful singing cowboy was *Gene Autry* (1907–1998), a musician born in Texas. In the early 1930s Autry's musical career received a boost from regular appearances on the *National Barn Dance*, broadcast nationwide from the Chicago radio station WLS. Autry's early performances actually included few cowboy songs: he was a hillbilly singer, known for his imitations of Jimmie Rodgers. His big break came in 1934, when Autry moved to Hollywood and got a bit part in a cowboy movie. In a series of over ninety movies for various film companies—including a number of popular serials, the cinematic ancestors of today's weekly television series—Autry institutionalized the image of the singing cowboy, a heroic figure as adept with his voice and six strings as with a six-shooter.

In his filmed performances and popular recordings, Autry developed a style designed to reach out to a broader audience, with a less pronounced regional accent, a deep baritone voice, and a touch of the crooner's smoothness. Like Roy Acuff, but to an even greater degree, Autry was able to score crossover hits in the pop as well as the hillbilly market, and he paved the way for other western recording artists, including Roy Rogers, Patsy Montana, Tex Ritter, and the Sons of the Pioneers. In spreading his own fame, Gene Autry helped to bring country music to a much wider and more diverse audience—including the millions of fans of cowboy movies—and to establish the "western" component of country and western music. (By the 1940s some prominent Black popular musicians were making cowboy films, though none of these referred to the very real tradition of nineteenth-century African American cowboys.)

The increasing professionalism of country music and the close links between western themes in popular music and Hollywood films are particularly evident in the recordings of the vocal group Sons of the Pioneers. This group originated as a vocal trio in 1933 at the instigation of Len Slye (1911–1998), who later left the group and became a film and television star under the name Roy Rogers. The Sons of the Pioneers sang in many cowboy movies and represented the cosmopolitan side of western music. They specialized in sophisticated vocal harmonies, influenced to some degree by the Mills Brothers, and were known for writing their own songs, including "Tumbling Tumbleweeds," "At the Rainbow's End," and "Cool Water," all composed by group member Bob Nolan.

WESTERN SWING

Another important part of the "western" element in country music during the swing era was **western swing**, a concatenation of country fiddle music, blues, boogie-woogie, and swing music. The genre developed in Texas and accordingly reflected that state's

Listening Guide "COOL WATER"

Written by Bob Nolan; performed by Sons of the Pioneers; recorded 1941

"Cool Water," recorded in 1941, was a bestseller in the country music market and reached Number 25 on the pop charts. It features the vocal trio's smooth, carefully rehearsed harmonies and the lead singing of Bob Nolan, backed by guitar, fiddle, and bass. The recording opens with the guitar and fiddle playing the basic "hook" of the song ("Cool, clear water"). The song's structure is strophic, with a series of verses, each consisting of solo lines sung by Nolan and responses from the trio, and a repeated chorus, sung in unison by the three men.

The implied scenario of this recording would have been familiar to most listeners, a cliché straight from the Hollywood cinema: two cursed souls (a man and his horse?) crawling through the desert's "barren waste" and praying for water to quench their terrible thirst. The impact of the song's lyric lies in its use of the first-person voice and its verbal imagery, which impressionistically conveys the singer's experience: dehydrated to the point of madness, he hears the voices of swaying shadows and sees the night stars as pools of water. In each

verse the singer seems to rest and take stock of his situation. In the chorus—sung by all three men in unison, with an insistent, almost march-like rhythm—he strives to keep moving forward through the "burning sand," only to collapse into a hallucinatory fantasy, the mirage of a big green tree. Throughout the recording the voices and the fiddle drift lazily from pitch to pitch, fluctuating precariously in energy, and the dreamlike quality of the recording is underpinned by the obsessive repetition, in falsetto, of the single word, "water." It is this distant, tantalizing, almost ghostly voice that gives us a sense of the desert's unforgiving vastness, the man's helplessness, and his stubborn hope for salvation. More than half a century after its release, "Cool Water" remains a remarkable example of musical craftsmanship, in which the skills of songwriting, arrangement, and studio recording are brought together with imagery derived from Hollywood films to create something that is more than just a song. In less than three minutes, the Sons of the Pioneers manage not only to tell us a story but also to show us a movie.

diverse musical traditions, including cowboy songs; German and Czech polkas; and Texas-Mexican (Tejano) genres such as *corridos* (narrative ballads in Spanish), *conjunto acordeon* ("accordion band" music), and **mariachi** ("marriage" music played by ensembles consisting of violins, guitars, and two or more trumpets). (A market for Mexican and Tejano recordings had sprung up in the late 1920s as record companies sought to create Latin American parallels to the race and hillbilly record business.)

The seminal figure in the national popularization of western swing was *Bob Wills* (1905–1975), a fiddler from East Texas whose musical career ran from the 1920s through the 1960s. Raised in a family of fiddle players, Wills played with several dance bands in the Southwest before forming his own group, the Texas Playboys, in 1934. During the late 1930s the band established itself in Tulsa, Oklahoma, making daily radio appearances, playing nightly in a local ballroom, and going on tours of the "southwest territories." (This geographical area—encompassing Oklahoma, Arkansas, Kansas, and Texas—was also home to the boogie-woogie piano blues and the big band tradition of Count Basie and other Black "territory bands," both of which exerted an influence on western swing.) In 1943, after being discharged from the army, Bob Wills relocated to California. There he opened his own nightclub and attracted huge audiences,

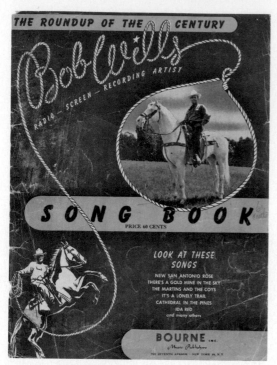

Cover of a Bob Wills songbook, 1940.

composed in part of migrants from the southwest territories who were already familiar with his music. The Texas Playboys' style became so popular in California that even mainstream swing bands were asked by dancers to add western swing–style numbers to their repertoires.

The heart of the Texas Playboys' style was Southern string band music, and many of Wills's most popular arrangements were based on old fiddle tunes and other types of dance songs that he had learned as a young man. To this traditional core he added elements from big band swing, including call-and-response riffs and instruments such as trumpets, saxophones, and the drum set. This balance between traditionalism and innovation was the key to Wills's ability to build a large and diverse audience that bridged the long-standing division between mainstream pop and country music.

Bob Wills's success was also based on his ability to hire and retain first-rate musicians, many of whom were versed in blues and jazz as well as hillbilly and cowboy music. Among the best remembered of these were the guitarist Leon McAuliffe, responsible for making the electronically amplified steel guitar a permanent part of country and western music, and vocalist Tommy Duncan, whose stylistic flexibility and warm baritone voice were an important part of the band's sound. During the Texas Playboys' performances Bob Wills acted as impresario, cracking jokes, calling out musicians' nicknames, and emitting enthusiastic cries and whoops of encouragement.

Although western swing bands did not dominate the country charts after World War II, the style exerted a permanent influence on country music, particularly in the introduction of amplified steel guitar and drum set, the incorporation of African American and Latin American musical influences, and the emphasis placed in live performances on improvised instrumental solos (called "takeoffs"). Western swing has been revived from time to time—the most notable example being the group Asleep at the Wheel, which had a number of hit records during the 1970s and 1980s—and Bob Wills is today widely regarded as one of the pioneers of modern country and western music.

Latin Music in the Swing Era

The swing era was a crucial period for the development of Latin music in the United States. During the 1930s and 1940s an ever-greater number of Latin American musicians immigrated to New York City, Los Angeles, and other American cities, bringing with them more nuanced and diverse versions of music from their home countries. Some of

Listening Guide "NEW SAN ANTONIO ROSE"

Written by Bob Wills; performed by Bob Wills and His Texas Playboys; recorded 1940

The Texas Playboys' biggest hit was their recording of "New San Antonio Rose," which was a country bestseller and reached Number 11 on the pop charts in 1940. (Bing Crosby recorded his own version of the song in 1941, which reached Number 7 on the pop charts, suggesting once again the crossover potential of country music, if not always of the original performers themselves.) The structure of the song is the thirty-two-bar AABA form, familiar to us from the Tin Pan Alley song, and the performance exemplifies the unique blend of stylistic elements achieved by Wills. The sixteen-piece ensemble combines a string band (fiddle, banjo, and three guitars, including McAuliffe's electrified steel guitar) with a big band (piano, string bass, drums, two trumpets, and six saxophones).

LISTENING GUIDE	"NEW SAN ANTONIO ROSE"	
TIME	**FORM**	**LYRIC/DESCRIPTIVE COMMENTS**
0:00	Introduction	Brief big band swing style introduction
0:04	AABA (32 bars)	The trumpets and saxophones play the main melody, while the rhythm section maintains a bouncy dance rhythm. Wills is heard yodeling the song's title. The section concludes with a brief harmonized brass fanfare.
0:44	Verse AA	Tommy Duncan begins the song: (*Deep within my heart . . .*). His singing is supported with soft harmonies in the brass and reeds and occasionally interrupted by Wills's trademark vocal interjections.
1:21	B	Vocal supported by trumpet duet, played in the style of a Mexican mariachi band
1:40	A	Vocal supported by harmonized saxophones
1:59	B	Trumpet duet in style of a Mexican mariachi band
2:16	A	Harmonized saxophones play the main melody. Ends with a short harmonized riff for the band.

these musicians formed their own outfits, while others joined existing American dance bands. That Black bandleaders such as Chick Webb and Cab Calloway were among the first to hire Latin American musicians reflects in part the continuing segregation of the dance band scene along racial lines.

Although most American dance bands still kept a few tango arrangements in their repertoire, the Argentine style, associated in the popular imagination with Rudolph Valentino and the silent film era, had become dated by the late 1930s. Following the enormous success of Don Azpiazú's Havana Casino Orchestra (see Chapter 3), Cuban musical genres such as the *son*, the *danzón*, and the bolero (a languorous, medium-tempo romantic genre influenced by the music of Haiti and Mexico) continued to infiltrate ballroom dance music. During the swing era a new generation of Cuban musicians migrated from Havana to the ballrooms and dance clubs of New York City and were heard both in "downtown" hotels and nightclubs patronized by the city's elites and in an emerging "uptown" scene in East Harlem patronized by Cuban and Puerto Rican immigrants. This generation of musicians had grown up with African-derived musical traditions and created novel fusions of Afro-Cuban music with big band jazz, a development that led to the rise of the mambo, Latin jazz, and, decades later, salsa music.

Although the Cuban stream was dominant, other Latin and Caribbean traditions also influenced the pop mainstream during the swing era. A ballroom dance called the beguine, introduced to the United States in the mid-1930s, was loosely based upon the *biguine*, a dance from the French Caribbean island of Martinique. The calypso, a topical song genre from the island of Trinidad, made its appearance toward the end of the swing era, spawning Number 1 hits such as the Andrews Sisters' "Shoo-Shoo Baby" (1944) and "Rum and Coca Cola" (1945). Mexican genres such as mariachi music and *corrido* ballads influenced country and western music, particularly in the American Southwest, as we have seen. Finally, our last major stream of Latin American influence, the Brazilian, reached the United States in the mid-1930s via popular Hollywood films such as *Flying Down to Rio* and *Down Argentine Way*, which featured Americanized versions of the samba—an African-derived dance-and-percussion genre associated with spectacular pre-Lent street celebrations called *Carnaval*—and the carioca, a ballroom version of the samba.

To be sure, most of what passed for "Latin" or "Spanish" music in the United States prior to World War II was quite generic, including hit records such as "She's a Latin from Manhattan," recorded by Victor Young's dance band in 1935; and the Cole Porter song "Begin the Beguine," which was recorded by Xavier Cugat and the Waldorf-Astoria Orchestra in 1935 and became a Number 1 hit for clarinetist Artie Shaw and his orchestra in 1938. Novelty songs such as "Rhumboogie" (1940), "Jitterhumba" (1941), and "You Don't Play a Drum (You Just Beat It)!" (1941), which debuted in Hollywood films with titles like *Argentine Nights* and *Blondie Goes Latin*, were basically swing numbers larded with a few south-of-the-border musical stereotypes. Although none of these songs reflected a detailed knowledge of Latin American musical traditions, they played an important role in filtering Latin influences into mainstream popular music in the United States, often at a subliminal level.

The bandleader who did the most to popularize Latin music during the swing era was the Spanish-born violinist, bandleader, and film star **Xavier Cugat** (1900–1990), known as the "Rhumba King." Cugat moved with his family from Catalan to Cuba at the age of five and was playing in a professional theater orchestra in Havana by age twelve. In 1915, during the height of the tango craze, he migrated to New York and began working as a musician. Around 1920 Cugat moved to Los Angeles, where he found employment as a cartoonist, appeared in several movies (including Valentino's

Xavier Cugat leading his band, c. 1940s.

Four Horsemen of the Apocalypse), and led a dance band called the Gigolos at the famed Coconut Grove.

In 1932 Cugat returned to New York and began a three-decade stint at the Waldorf-Astoria Hotel, home to the most prestigious of Manhattan's ballrooms. His basic strategy was to play standard American ballroom dances such as the fox-trot and then insinuate Latin rhythms, song texts, and instruments (such as the maracas and claves) into them. In addition to Afro-Cuban percussion instruments, he incorporated the accordion, associated most strongly with Argentine tango, and the marimba, a tuned percussion instrument popular in Mexico and Central America but absent from Cuban music. His band was a training ground for Latin music stars, including Desi Arnaz of *I Love Lucy* fame, and Cugat himself was an unabashed showman who made full use of theatrical effects to woo his audiences, including holding a chihuahua in one arm as he conducted with the other. He once said:

> Americans know nothing about Latin music. They neither understand nor feel it. So they have to be given music more for the eyes than the ears. Eighty percent visual, the rest aural. . . . To succeed in America I gave the Americans a Latin music that had nothing authentic about it. Then I began to change the music and play more legitimately. (Roberts 1998, 87)

Listening Guide "BRAZIL"

Written by Ary Barroso; performed by Xavier Cugat and His Waldorf-Astoria Orchestra; recorded 1943

Although many of his early hits were Cuban-influenced, Xavier Cugat's bestselling record was a lushly orchestrated samba titled "Brazil (Aquarela Do Brazil)" ["Watercolor of Brazil"], which reached Number 2 on the charts in 1943. Composed in 1939 by the great Brazilian composer Ary Barroso (1903–1964), "Brazil" introduced a new genre to Brazilian popular music—the *samba-exaltação*, a samba exulting in the beauties of the land. The song was introduced to American audiences in the 1942 Walt Disney animated feature *Saludos Amigos* (in which it was nominated for an Oscar for Best Song) and in the Hollywood musical *The Gang's All Here* (1943), in which it was memorably performed by the Portuguese-born singer and dancer Carmen Miranda (1909–1955) with a giant pile of tropical fruit on her head.

One of the most-recorded songs of all time, "Brazil" has perhaps become overly familiar through repetition—as a staple of the tourist trade, performed in hotel bars and ballrooms worldwide; as a duet between Donald Duck and the Brazilian parrot Jose Carioca; as a slick Top 20 disco hit by the Ritchie Family (1975); and as the iconic musical theme of Terry Gilliam's satirical film *Brazil* (1986). Given all these layers of imitation and reinterpretation, it is worth going back to one of the earliest versions heard by listeners in the United States to understand the song's initial appeal.

To understand the differences between Brazilian and American interpretations of "Brazil," it is interesting to consider the meanings conveyed by the Portuguese and English versions of the lyrics as published and distributed in the form of sheet music. Ary Barroso's original lyrics describe Brazilians "swinging" and "swaying" to the groove of the samba, dark-skinned Bahian women trailing their skirts through the parlors of white upper-class Brazilians, and the powerful African deities who are invoked in ceremonies of the Afro-Brazilian religion called *Candomblé*. The American sheet music version, by contrast, empties the song of its culturally specific content, substituting romantic verses such as "Where hearts were entertaining June, we stood beneath an amber moon, and softly murmured, 'Someday soon.'" This is another indication that Latin American music in the United States was filtered through existing stereotypes of tropical romance and passion that were bolstered by Hollywood films and the tourist trade.

The Waldorf-Astoria Orchestra's arrangement of "Brazil" (recorded in New York in 1941) opens with a rhythmically free treatment of the song's opening phrase by the Mexican American vaudevillian and singer La Chata (Beatriz Escalona, born in San Antonio, Texas, in 1903). In the very first measure after the vocals, the rhythm section establishes a flowing samba rhythm, played on *pandeiro* (large tambourine), *tamborim* (small tambourine), and Cuban maracas, substituting for the traditional Brazilian *rêco-rêco* (small basketry rattles). Other instruments used in the arrangement include the *cavaquinho*, a small Brazilian guitar with four strings, and the accordion, evoking the *bandoneón* used in Argentine tango music.

The musical logic of "Brazil" is centered on two elements: first, a one-measure syncopated pattern, repeated over and over to create momentum (and to "hook" the listener's ear), and second, a sweeping, almost cinematic melody with an ABCD form that is constructed out of a limited set of melodic elements yet never quite comes back around to repeat itself in the manner of a typical Tin Pan Alley song.

Throughout the arrangement the rhythmic pattern and the melody are tossed from instrument to instrument, and extra measures are introduced at important transition points. While the samba pattern generates a feeling of groove through repetition (like an engine moving the song down its track), the melody—played by various combinations of strings and winds, and at one point on the accordion—soars above its rhythmic base, rising and falling, never quite repeating itself, and in the end settling back to earth and folding itself into the embrace of the samba groove. This effect is emphasized by the accompanying wordless phrases sung by the chorus at various points, which also rise and fall in pitch.

It could be argued that the formal structure and musical texture of "Brazil," a song that to this day functions as an emotionally saturated symbol of Brazilian national identity, juxtaposes the logic of European song composition and the vitality of Afro-Brazilian music, quintessentially embodied by the polyrhythmic samba. We could even go so far as to suggest that Ary Barroso's song evokes the meeting of Europe and Africa, modernity and roots, in an elegant package perfectly suited as a symbolic vehicle for a rising, diverse Latin American nation like Brazil.

Throughout the swing era, Cuba continued to exert its influence on popular dance music, culminating in the emergence in New York City of two genres that would shape the future of Latin music in the United States: mambo (see Chapter 7) and Latin jazz. The musician who did most to introduce authentic Afro-Cuban music into big band jazz was the Havana-born composer, arranger, clarinetist, and trumpeter *Mario Bauza* (1911–1993), often called the "Father of Latin Jazz." A talented musician whose early experiences included playing classical music in the Havana Symphony and studying American jazz via recordings and radio, Bauza came up through the ranks of dance bands in Havana. In 1930, traveling on the same ship as Don Azpiazú's Havana Casino Orchestra, Bauza moved to New York City, where he played with a succession of top Black dance bands.

While working with bandleaders Chick Webb and Cab Calloway, Bauza met the young jazz trumpeter *John Birks ("Dizzy") Gillespie* (1917–1993), who had a strong interest in, but little knowledge of, Afro-Cuban music. As Bauza recalled later, "I'd stay up with Dizzy [and other musicians] . . . teaching them how to feel some of the simpler Cuban rhythms. Dizzy would sing the drum patterns using nonsense syllables, like 'Oop-bop, sh'bam'" (Palmer 1988). These onomatopoeic sounds, apparently derived from Afro-Cuban polyrhythms, eventually lent their name to the dominant postwar genre of jazz, bebop. Gillespie went on to champion the blending of Afro-Cuban music and modern jazz, hiring a number of prominent Latin musicians. In the late 1940s his band premiered such classics of the genre as "Manteca" and "Cubano Be, Cubano Bop." (The latter featured the drumming and singing of the Cuban musician Chano Pozo, whom we will discuss in greater detail shortly.)

In 1937 Bauza arranged for his brother-in-law, the Havana-born bandleader and singer Frank Grillo, who worked under the name *Machito* (1909–1984), to join him in New York. In 1940 Machito launched his own band, the Afro-Cubans, and Bauza soon joined him as musical director. This was a new sort of dance band, staffed by musicians who were familiar with the phrasing and rhythmic feel of jazz and were also able to understand and perform the complex interlocking rhythms of Afro-Cuban music. The Afro-Cubans were the first band in New York to use the full battery of percussion instruments that formed the core of Cuban dance music: maracas, bongó, conga (a single-headed African-derived drum held between the player's legs and beaten with bare hands), and timbales (a pair of parade-style drums mounted on a stand along with a metal cowbell). Bauza brought in the arranger John Bartee from Cab Calloway's band, and together they pioneered a fiery hybrid of Afro-Cuban music, big band jazz arrangement techniques, and modern jazz improvisation.

Machito (holding maracas) and his band, c. 1947.

Listening Guide "NAGÜE"

Written by Luciano (Chano) Pozo; arranged by Mario Bauza and John Bartee; performed by Machito and His Afro-Cubans; recorded 1941

Although it did not dent the pop charts, the Afro-Cubans' 1941 recording of "Nagüe," composed by the great Cuban drummer and singer Luciano (Chano) Pozo (1915–1948), arranged by Mario Bauza and John Bartee, and sung by Machito, gives a good sense of the intensity and drive of the rumba-based percussion music that would eventually become the mainstream of the family of Latin music styles known as salsa. The instrumentation of the Afro-Cubans on this session comprised three saxophones, two trumpets, string bass, piano, and three percussionists—Antonino "El Cojito" Escollies on timbales, Lorenzo "Chiquitico" Gallan on *tumba* (large conga drum), and Bilingüe Ayala on bongó.

The African-derived term "Nagüe" is Cuban slang for "bud(dy)" or "bro(ther)," and the song's brief lyrics recount in dialogue form a verbal exchange between two tough-guy characters on a street in one of Havana's *barrios*, the challenging urban milieu in which the composer Chano Pozo grew up.

Nagüe, nagüe, nagüe, nagüe	Brother, brother, brother, brother
Nagüe, nagüe, nagüe, nagüe	Brother, brother, brother, brother
¿Qué tú hace' por aquí?	What you doin' around here?
¿Qué tú hace' por aquí?	What you doin' around here?
Ando en busca de [u]na chamaca	I'm looking for a girl
Que yo tengo por aquí	That I have around here
Ando en busca de [u]na chamaca	I'm looking for a girl
Que yo tengo por aquí	That I have around here
Nagüe, nagüe, nagüe, nagüe	Brother, brother, brother, brother
Nagüe, nagüe, nagüe, nagüe	Brother, brother, brother, brother

"Nagüe" was the Afro-Cubans' theme song during the band's earliest performances at New York dance clubs such as La Conga, and it instantly signaled to knowledgeable listeners—including Latinos in the expanding *barrio* of East Harlem—a deeper, grittier, more authentic engagement with Caribbean culture than was afforded by the polite "rumbas" performed by ballroom orchestras. The form of the arrangement would also have been familiar to listeners knowledgeable about Cuban music, since it is an elaborated version of a two-part structure long in use by Havana dance bands: an initial, formally arranged statement of the song (what American musicians would call the "head" of the arrangement), followed by an improvisational section anchored in African-derived call-and-response patterns and a repeating melodic-rhythmic loop called the "montuno" (see Chapter 1). This basic form, designed to build excitement, became an essential aspect of postwar Latin styles such as the mambo and, decades later, salsa music.

"Nagüe" opens with an instrumental introduction six measures in length, orchestrated with complex harmonies of the sort increasingly favored by the more progressive swing arrangers. Tony Escollies immediately establishes the groove on the timbales, driving the band forward. After the introduction, Machito sings the entire song, beginning with the four-measure *coro* (the chorus)—"*Nagüe, nagüe, nagüe, nagüe*"—followed by the verse, twelve measures in length ("*¿Qué tú hace' por aquí?* . . ."), and a restatement of the four-measure *coro*. The singing is accompanied by sinuous melodic lines in the saxophones that are punctuated by brass "punches." This compact structure, twenty measures in length overall, is the kernel for what follows.

After an instrumental interlude of five measures, the trumpets and saxophones come together to play the entire *coro*-verse-*coro* structure of the song. This is followed by a third statement of the song, again sung by Machito and supported by the reeds and brass. The reeds and brass repeat the *coro* one additional time and then hand it over to the vocal chorus, and we launch into the second major section of the arrangement, the montuno.

And here is where the real difference becomes apparent between what Bauza and Machito and their compatriots were up to and the more restrained, generic approach taken by their ballroom-based counterparts such as Azpiazú and Cugat. The montuno section opens with a soaring vocal improvisation over the repeated *coro*, setting up a call-and-response texture. Then the percussion takes over for twelve increasingly intense measures, with Bilingüe Ayala playing a rhythmically complex bongó solo over the interlocking patterns of the cowbell, timbales, and conga, with all of the other musical layers stripped away to reveal the pulsing heart of the groove. This momentum is extended as the vocal solo-and-*coro*, call-and-response formula is reintroduced, and the arrangement closes with a final chord, or, more accurately, a single note played in octaves by the whole band.

The sense of a direct connection to African-derived tradition in the montuno section of "Nagüe" is intensified by the vocalist's inside references to aspects of life in Cuba unknown to most Americans, including *Abakwá*, an Afro-Cuban men's secret society that originated from fraternal associations in Nigeria and Cameroon. Chano Pozo, the song's composer, was himself an *Abakwá* initiate, and this is one of the first instances in a recording made in the United States of a direct reference to the African-based religious movements that grew out of slavery and served as a deep reservoir for Cuban culture.

While "Nagüe" never reached the pop charts, we have included it as an instructive example of a musical collaboration that connects deep traditions with modern sensibilities and in so doing establishes a space for subsequent developments in popular style. Mario Bauza played a pivotal role in negotiating the meeting of American jazz and Afro-Cuban music. Machito was the first bandleader to move the percussionists out from behind the horns and put them in the frontline of the band. It is difficult to know what additional impact Chano Pozo might have exerted on Latin music in New York City had he not been murdered at the age of thirty-three.

These musicians' collective knowledge of the wellspring of African values and techniques that energizes Cuban music introduced something truly powerful into American popular music. They developed an aesthetic that would continue to bear fruit years later in recordings such as Perez Prado's 1949 "Mambo No. 5" (see Chapter 7) and Santana's 1971 hit "Oye Como Va" (see Chapter 11), the latter composed by another member of Machito's Afro-Cubans, the renowned timbalist and bandleader Tito Puente.

ASCAP, the AFM, and the Decline of the Big Bands

The swing era lasted almost exactly a decade, ending almost as suddenly as it had begun. By the close of 1946 many of the top dance bands in the country—including the band that started the swing craze, the Benny Goodman Orchestra—had either broken up or formed smaller, more economical units. There is evidence that mainstream popular taste had already begun to shift during the war, away from the brassy exuberance of the big bands and toward lushly orchestrated, sentimental recordings by popular crooners. However, the sudden decline of the big bands involved changes in the music business as well as shifts in popular musical taste.

Some swing bandleaders had joined the armed forces, leading dance bands made up of enlisted men. These bands toured Europe and the Pacific, playing for the Allied troops. A number of well-known musicians were killed in the war, including Glenn Miller, whose plane went down over the English Channel in 1944. On the home front, the music business was affected by shortages in gas and vehicles, which made it difficult for the bands to travel to engagements; by the limits on the supply of shellac for pressing phonograph records; by restrictions on ownership of radio receiving and broadcasting equipment; and by the imposition of a 20 percent entertainment tax and a midnight curfew (called a "brownout"), both of which discouraged people from going out to hear live music.

The situation of the big bands was also adversely affected by a series of struggles among powerful institutions in the music business, including the record companies, the radio networks, the music licensing agencies, and the musicians' union. To begin with, the four big radio networks—NBC, CBS, ABC, and Mutual—were engaged in a bitter feud with ASCAP, which had grown tremendously since its founding in 1914. By 1939 ASCAP had licensed around 90 percent of Tin Pan Alley songs. The organization had already been working for a number of years to ensure that its members—the composers and music publishing companies—received royalties from the radio industry for the broadcast of their songs. As profits from network radio broadcasts rose—partly stimulated by the big band craze—ASCAP turned up the legal pressure on the networks to turn over a larger portion of their revenues.

In 1940 the radio networks counterattacked and formed a rival licensing agency called Broadcast Music, Incorporated (BMI), which was specifically designed to challenge ASCAP's monopoly. Although BMI was not initially expected to survive for long, its "open door" policy allowed songwriters working outside Tin Pan Alley to claim royalties from the use of their songs by the broadcast media. This gave a boost to musicians working in the idioms of country and western and rhythm & blues, genres that had largely been ignored by ASCAP, and which rose in economic importance during and after the war.

In 1941 the struggle between ASCAP and the radio networks came to a head, and ASCAP called a strike, withdrawing the rights to broadcast any material composed by their members. This move wiped out overnight a lion's share of the big band repertoire, which, as we have seen, relied heavily on arrangements of popular Tin Pan Alley songs. The quality of songs produced by BMI-licensed composers was at first not equal to that of the top ASCAP songwriters, who included among their ranks Irving Berlin, the Gershwins, Cole Porter, Rodgers and Hart, and others. The bands, unable to play either their most popular arrangements or their theme songs on the air, had to quickly assemble a replacement repertoire free of ASCAP songs. Big band arrangers were sometimes forced to turn to older materials, such as classical music themes and nineteenth-century popular songs like "Jeanie with the Light Brown Hair," "London Bridge Is Falling Down," and "My Old Kentucky Home." The battle between ASCAP and radio reached ridiculous extremes. For example, jazz musicians have traditionally often quoted bits of popular song melodies when playing improvised solos. During 1941 ASCAP began to take note of the appearance of melodic phrases from licensed songs in the solos of swing musicians and to charge for their use. This meant that all "improvised" solos had to be written out and approved by the radio networks before they could be played on the air.

To further complicate matters, on August 2, 1942, the musicians' union AFM (the American Federation of Musicians) called a strike against the recording companies. James Caesar Petrillo, president of the AFM, claimed that the union's members—including the musicians in all of the top dance bands—were not being properly compensated for their performances. In particular, he wanted the recording companies to make sure that musicians received a share of royalties when their records were played on radio broadcasts and coin-operated jukeboxes, which now numbered some 400,000 nationwide. While many musicians disagreed with Petrillo's decision—they recognized better than he the importance of recording and broadcast media to the future of their profession—he stuck to his guns, and for more than a year no major record company made any records with instrumentalists. Recording had already been curtailed by the wartime shellac shortage, and record companies chose to focus on vocal performances, particularly those of star crooners backed by choirs. (At that time the union did not consider singers to be "musicians" and thus did not allow them to join.) In 1943 Decca and Capitol Records—both new companies—signed a new contract with the union and were able to resume recording instrumental music. The biggest companies, Columbia and Victor, however, did not agree to the AFM's demands until 1944. By that time the swing bands had been dealt a severe blow, and within a year or two many of the professional dance band musicians whom Petrillo had claimed he was protecting were thrown out of work. This, along with other developments, created the conditions for the postwar success of other styles of music, including country and western and rhythm & blues (see Chapter 7).

THE SWING ERA represented the peak of jazz's influence on popular music. After World War II many jazz musicians moved in other directions, less concerned with record sales than with artistic achievement and instrumental virtuosity. Basic to this change was the emergence of a new jazz idiom called bebop, pioneered principally by the great alto saxophonist **Charlie Parker** (1920–1955) and trumpeter Dizzy Gillespie. Bebop flourished in small ensembles (often quartets) rather than in big bands, and was music made for attentive listening rather than for dancing. In the small group format, highly individual expression—focused on the players' originality and improvisational skill—became the center of interest and was prized above all other attributes. Bebop was not music intended to be played by the average big band musician, nor was it music intended for the typical pop music enthusiast. It is easy to understand why bebop musicians did not produce big hit records, but it was not their goal to do so; in response to charges that their approach was "elitist," creating music in which melody, chord changes, rhythm, and form could all be quite difficult to follow, they might have cited the purpose of advancing jazz as a modern art form rather than pandering to mass-market expectations.

Of course bebop did not by itself account for the decline of the big swing bands following the war. An economic downturn, along with the altered cultural landscape that we will examine in the next chapter, made it increasingly difficult for many of the bands to function profitably, and many accordingly called it quits. Meanwhile the singers who had appeared with big bands became even bigger celebrities in their own right, overshadowing bandleaders, who had formerly enjoyed the spotlight. Another branch of swing music, performed by small

(continued)

groups and christened "rhythm & blues" by the record industry, maintained its function as social dance music and came to dominate musical taste in African American communities during the postwar era. At the same time, so-called hillbilly music continued its move to the city and accounted for an increasing share of the market. In the next chapter we will examine these postwar developments, precursors of the rise of rock 'n' roll.

Key Terms

big bands	jukeboxes	territory bands
boogie-woogie	mariachi	western swing
independent record labels ("indies")	soli	
	swing	

Key People

Andrews Sisters	Ella Fitzgerald	John Hammond
Benny Goodman	Fletcher Henderson	Machito
Billie Holiday	Gene Autry	Mario Bauza
Bob Wills	Gene Krupa	Mills Brothers
Boswell Sisters	Glenn Miller	Roy Claxton Acuff
Charlie Parker	John Birks ("Dizzy")	William "Count" Basie
Duke Ellington	Gillespie	Xavier Cugat

Review Questions

1. What musical elements can be heard in 1930s big band swing music?
2. Describe the various ways in which radio affected swing music.
3. What made Harlem important to the development of swing music during the 1930s?
4. Describe ASCAP, BMI, and the AFM recording ban. What effect did these groups have on big band swing during World War II? How did the strike help create conditions that led to the success of rhythm & blues and country and western music after World War I?
5. Briefly outline the various styles of country music in the swing era, including the styles of Roy Acuff, singing cowboys, and western swing.

MAJOR EVENTS IN U. S. HISTORY	YEAR	IMPORTANT LANDMARKS IN AMERICAN POPULAR MUSIC
While visiting the U.S., Winston Churchill warns of an "Iron Curtain" descending over Eastern Europe	1946	Louis Jordan's "Choo Choo Ch'Boogie" tops the R&B charts for eighteen weeks, popularizing his jump band style
	1947	Les Paul pioneers the use of overdubbing, releasing his own recordings with up to eight different guitar parts
• Marshall Plan begun by U.S. to rebuild Europe • Berlin Wall divides East and West Berlin • First McDonald's fast food restaurant opened	1948	• Ampex tape recorder is introduced and quickly becomes a fixture of the recording industry • Columbia Records introduces the LP (long-playing) record • Nat "King" Cole is the first black musician to host a weekly radio series
NATO (North Atlantic Treaty Association) formed for the mutual protection of Europe	1949	• RCA Victor Corporation introduces the 7-inch, 45 rpm single disc • Perez Prado's "Mambo No. 5" ignites the mambo craze among non-Latin listeners
• Rise of Joe McCarthy and his anticommunist crusade • Beginning of the Korean War	1950	• Patti Page scores a massive hit with "The Tennessee Waltz," demonstrating the pop potential of country music • The Weavers' smash "Goodnight, Irene" demonstrates the pop potential of folk music
Dwight D. Eisenhower elected president	1952	
Execution of Julius and Ethel Rosenberg for supposed passing of secrets to the Soviets	1953	• Ruth Brown's "Mama, He Treats Your Daughter Mean" tops the R&B charts for five weeks • Honky-tonk star Hank Williams dies on New Year's Day while being driven to perform a concert

MAJOR EVENTS IN U. S. HISTORY	YEAR	IMPORTANT LANDMARKS IN AMERICAN POPULAR MUSIC
Brown v. Board of Education decision of U.S. Supreme Court outlaws racial segregation in public schools	1954	Muddy Waters has his biggest hit with "Hoochie Coochie Man," which reaches number three on the R&B charts, spreading the Chicago blues style
Beginning of Montgomery, Alabama, bus boycott marks the start of the civil rights movement	1955	• "Rock Around the Clock" (recorded by Bill Haley and the Comets) becomes the first number one rock 'n' roll pop hit • Chuck Berry records "Maybellene," launching his career as a great and highly influential rock songwriter and guitarist
	1956	• Elvis Presley begins his recording career for RCA Victor and his reign as the "King of Rock 'n' Roll" • Dick Clark begins his long tenure as host of the popular *American Bandstand* TV program
• Little Rock, Arkansas, public schools are desegregated, leading to protests • Soviet Union launches *Sputnik*, the first successful satellite • Jack Kerouac's *On the Road* published, popularizing the Beat Generation	1957	
Peak of postwar "baby boom" birth rate; 19 million teenagers have $9 billion of disposable income	1958	Ritchie Valens brings a Latino tinge to rock 'n' roll with his hit "La Bamba"
Alaska and Hawaii admitted as states	1959	• Berry Gordy Jr. starts Motown Records in Detroit • "The Day the Music Died": a tragic airplane crash takes the lives of Buddy Holly, the Big Bopper, and Ritchie Valens

MAJOR EVENTS IN U. S. HISTORY	YEAR	IMPORTANT LANDMARKS IN AMERICAN POPULAR MUSIC
 • John F. Kennedy elected president, the youngest man and first Catholic to hold this office • Students sit-in at lunch counters—beginning in Greensboro, North Carolina, and spreading through the South—to protest segregation	1960	 Chubby Checker's recording of "The Twist" sets off a spate of dance records and crazes
	1961	Phil Spector founds his Philles label, beginning to make his famous "Wall of Sound" recordings
• John Glenn becomes the first American to orbit the Earth • Cuban Missile Crisis	1962	• James Brown records *Live at the Apollo,* and the album's huge success establishes the market for concert recordings • Ray Charles's album *Modern Sounds in Country and Western Music* breaks new ground in the mingling of styles in American popular music • The Rolling Stones play their first gigs at small London blues clubs • Bob Dylan signs with Columbia Records
 • March on Washington in support of racial equality brings 200,000 to the nation's capital • Betty Friedan publishes *The Feminine Mystique*	1963	• The Beach Boys' first hits popularize the "California sound"  • First cassette tape manufactured by Philips Electronics of the Netherlands

THE POSTWAR ERA, 1946–1979

MAJOR EVENTS IN U. S. HISTORY	YEAR	IMPORTANT LANDMARKS IN AMERICAN POPULAR MUSIC
• Beginning of major hostilities between the United States and North Vietnam • Passage of the Civil Rights Act • President Lyndon Johnson launches the "War on Poverty" • Ford Mustang introduced, launching the "pony car" craze	1964	• "Beatlemania" breaks out in the United States, marking the beginning of the British Invasion • "The Girl from Ipanema" is a major pop hit, launching the bossa nova craze • Sam Cooke's "A Change Is Gonna Come" weds social protest with R&B
• Unrest over racial issues and Vietnam hostilities begins to take the form of major public demonstrations, continuing for many years • Voting Rights Act passed	1965	• Bob Dylan "plugs in" at the Newport Folk Festival, certifying the arrival of folk rock • First eight-track tape players offered as an option on the popular Ford Mustang
• National Organization for Women (N.O.W.) founded	1966	
• Six-Day War between Egypt and Israel • Supreme Court declares interracial marriage constitutional	1967	• Aretha Franklin's "Respect" becomes an anthem of racial and female empowerment • The Beatles' *Sgt. Pepper's Lonely Hearts Club Band* sets the standard for the rock "concept album"
• Assassinations of Martin Luther King Jr. and Robert Kennedy • Richard Nixon elected president	1968	*Hair,* the first rock musical, opens on Broadway
• Stonewall Riot in New York City marks the beginning of the gay rights movement • Chicago Seven trial follows rioting at the Democratic National Convention • Apollo 11 lands on the moon	1969	First Woodstock Festival attracts hundreds of thousands to concert site in New York State
	1970	• Janis Joplin and Jimi Hendrix die of drug overdoses • Miles Davis releases the jazz rock masterpiece *Bitches Brew*

MAJOR EVENTS IN U. S. HISTORY	YEAR	IMPORTANT LANDMARKS IN AMERICAN POPULAR MUSIC
• Watergate break-in marks the beginning of the downfall of Richard Nixon • Nixon visits China and Russia, beginning a new opening with both nations	1972	The film *The Harder They Come* establishes the popularity of reggae in the United States
	1973	Pink Floyd releases *The Dark Side of the Moon,* one of the bestselling rock albums of all time
Richard Nixon resigns the presidency in the wake of the Watergate scandals	1974	
U.S. military involvement in Vietnam comes to an end	1975	• Cassette and eight-track tape sales account for one-third of the market in recorded music • Donna Summer's "Love to Love You Baby" launches the Disco Era
• Jimmy Carter elected president • Apple Computer, Inc., is founded and introduces its first product, the Apple 1	1976	• First popular digital sampling keyboard is introduced • The compilation *Eagles/Their Greatest Hits* is released, eventually becoming the bestselling album of all time in the United States • *Wanted: The Outlaws,* the first alternative country album, reaches the pop Top 10 • The Ramones' first album certifies the arrival of punk rock
	1977	 • The film *Saturday Night Fever* helps push the popularity of disco to its height • Dolly Parton's "Here You Come Again" reaches number one on the pop charts, representing the crossover of country music into mainstream pop
• Nuclear accident at Three Mile Island • Iran takes Americans hostage, beginning a long ordeal	1979	• "Rapper's Delight" (recorded by the Sugar Hill Gang) establishes the commercial potential of hip-hop • Sony introduces the Walkman, a portable cassette player with headphones, in Japan, revolutionizing how people listen to music

"Choo Choo Ch' Boogie"

7 The Postwar Era, 1946–1954

THE DECADE LEADING UP TO THE EMERGENCE OF ROCK 'N' ROLL IS OFTEN portrayed as a period of musical stagnation or, at best, gestation. In fact, it could be argued that the postwar decade was one of the most interesting, complex, and dynamic eras in the history of American popular music. The entertainment industry grew rapidly after the war, and in 1947 record companies achieved retail sales of over $214 million, finally surpassing the previous peak, established more than a quarter of a century earlier in 1921. This growth was supported by the booming postwar economy, as well as by a corresponding increase in the disposable income of many American families.

In particular, record companies began for the first time to target young people, many of whom had more pocket money to spend on records than ever before. During World War II the demand for workers in military-related industries meant that many teenagers took on adult responsibilities, working for wages while continuing to attend high school. The idea that teenagers had the right to earn a salary of their own led after the war to the widespread practice of a weekly allowance in return for doing household chores. Many young adults spent a considerable portion of their income on films, jukeboxes, and records. A survey of record retailers conducted in 1949 estimated that people under twenty-one constituted fully one-third of the total record-buying population of the United States, a great increase from previous eras. Although the music produced by the largest record companies was still mainly aimed at an older audience, the increasing importance of a new marketing category—the teenager—was a harbinger of the rock 'n' roll era (see Chapter 8).

Many of the hit records of the late 1940s and early 1950s were romantic songs, performed by crooners—sweet-voiced singers who used the microphone to create a sense of intimacy—with orchestral string backing. The sentimentality of these songs can be gleaned from their titles: "Prisoner of Love" and "(I Love You) For Sentimental Reasons" (1946), "My Darling, My Darling" and "You're Breaking My Heart" (1949), "Cold, Cold Heart" and "Cry" (1951), "No Other Love" and "You You You" (1953), all Number 1 pop hits. Big band swing—the dominant jazz-based popular music style of the World War II era—was also supplanted by the romantic "light music" of Jackie Gleason, Percy Faith, and Mantovani and His Orchestra. These recordings typically featured string orchestras or choruses, with an occasional light touch of the exotic—maracas, castanets, a harpsichord, or a vaguely Latin rhythm. (These "easy listening" records soon became a mainstay of Muzak, a corporation that since the late 1930s had supplied businesses with recorded music that was designed to subliminally encourage worker productivity.) Romantic vocal and orchestral recordings were interspersed on the hit charts with catchy, light-hearted novelty songs, including Number 1 hits such as "Woody Woodpecker" (Kay Kyser, 1948), "The Thing" (Phil Harris, 1950), "I Saw Mommy Kissing Santa Claus" (Jimmy Boyd, 1952), and "The Doggie in the Window" (Patti Page, 1953).

The roots of this musical conservatism are not difficult to pinpoint. Although there was a brief depression just after the war (see the later discussion of "Choo Choo Ch' Boogie"), the national economy expanded rapidly during the postwar decade, fueled by the lifting of wartime restrictions on the production of consumer goods, the increased availability of jobs in the industrial and service sectors of the economy, and the G.I. Bill, which provided educational and job opportunities for returning servicemen. After the uncertainty and personal sacrifice of the war years, many people simply wanted to settle down, raise a family, and focus on building their own futures. For millions of Americans who had served in the armed forces or come to the city in search of work during the war, or whose immigrant parents and grandparents had fled poverty earlier in the century, the years following the war represented the first opportunity to buy a home. If we also take into account the underlying uncertainties and tensions of the postwar era—including the threat of nuclear war and Cold War conflicts in Europe and Asia—it makes perfect sense that many new members of the American middle class preferred popular music that focused on romantic sentiments and helped to create a comforting sound environment in the home.

The economics of the music industry also played a role in this conservative trend, as well as in the uneven quality of much mainstream pop music produced at this time. During the postwar decade we see clearly for the first time a phenomenon that has helped to shape the development of popular music in the United States ever since: a constant tug-of-war between, on the one hand, the efforts of the music business to predict (and therefore control) the public's consumption of music; and, on the other hand, the periodic eruption of new musical fads, usually based in youth culture. In general, the center of the music business—like many other sectors of corporate America—became increasingly routinized after the war. Music was now a product, sold in units, and listeners were consumers.

The idea of **Top 40 radio programming**—another attempt to control the uncertainty of the marketplace—was developed in the early 1950s by Todd Storz, a disc jockey in Omaha, Nebraska. Storz observed teenagers dropping coins in jukeboxes and noticed that they tended to play certain songs repeatedly. He applied this idea to radio programming, selecting a list of forty top hits, which he played over and over. The idea spread quickly, and within a few years many radio stations were playing the same set of songs. The ability of radio stations to control the public's exposure to new recordings led to a practice called **payola**, in which record companies paid DJs to put their records into "heavy rotation." By the mid-1950s this profitable practice had come under legal scrutiny, ending the careers of some prominent record executives and disc jockeys.

If the late 1940s and early 1950s were generally profitable for the music business—publishing firms, licensing agencies, record corporations, and radio networks—it was also a period of uncertainty. The executives who ran these powerful institutions, and who were therefore in charge of deciding how much and what sorts of music would be recorded and broadcast, were mainly veterans of an earlier era. Many of these men looked down their noses at the idea of producing music for a teenage audience, and this attitude limited their ability to spot and exploit new trends.

At the same time, the increasingly rapid turnover of hit songs on the radio and jukebox meant that record companies started producing many more records than the public was willing to buy. In general, the big record companies competed by saturating the market with records, sometimes sending as many as 100,000 copies of a new record out to stores, with a guarantee that they could return all of the discs they didn't sell. This is clearly not a sound business strategy, and it adversely affected the overall quality of pop music during the early 1950s—one record company executive referred to the technique of market saturation as "throwing a lot of shit at the wall to see if anything sticks" (Clarke 1995, 311).

In general, the major record companies of the period—RCA Victor, Columbia, Decca, and a new Los Angeles–based company, Capitol Records—experienced considerable growth. However, it was during the postwar era that musical genres regarded as marginal by the industry came to influence even more strongly the musical tastes of middle-class white Americans. As we saw in the last chapter, country and western music expanded its audience during the war, and this trend continued through the early 1950s. The market for Black popular music, rechristened rhythm & blues, also expanded as a result of postwar prosperity—the income of the average Black family tripled during the war—and a growing (though still small) white audience, whose musical conversion had been prepared by the swing era. The market was supported by a new generation of independent record labels, such as Chess (Chicago), Aladdin (Los Angeles), Atlantic (New York), King (Cincinnati), Sun (Memphis), and Duke/Peacock (Houston). In addition, a new licensing agency (BMI) and new publishing houses were eager to work with songwriters outside the Tin Pan Alley mainstream. As a result, with the increased access to the airwaves and the introduction of the new medium of television, country music and rhythm & blues experienced a golden age.

In retrospect, the music business of the late 1940s and early 1950s could be envisioned as a Jurassic scenario, in which huge, slow, powerful carnivores ruled the roost but were kept in continual competition with lighter, smaller, faster beasts. These little omnivores—"indie" record labels, renegade radio DJs, talented musicians who had for various reasons been excluded from the wellsprings of profit, and entrepreneurs and hustlers of all stripes—shared a double advantage over the big boys. First, they were musically omnivorous, feeding on styles outside the mainstream of popular music; and second, they were more keenly attuned to changes in the environment, particularly the increasing importance of the teenage market for popular music. Although many of the little guys did get eaten, in the long run it was precisely these adaptive qualities that allowed them to play an indispensable role in the development of American popular music.

Popular Music and Technology in the Postwar Era

During the decade following World War II the music industry was affected by the introduction of new technologies for the reproduction and transmission of musical sound and visual images. **Magnetic tape recording**, developed by the Germans and the Japanese during the 1930s, offered a number of advantages over the established methods of recording music. In the recording studio, tape was better able to capture the full range of musical sounds than the older process of recording directly onto "master" phonograph discs. In addition, tape recording allowed musicians to re-record over the unsatisfactory parts of previous performances and to add layers of sound to a recording (a process called "overdubbing"). The greatest innovator in this field was the guitarist and inventor Les Paul (1915–2009), who beginning in 1947 released a series of tracks featuring up to eight guitar parts that were recorded in his garage studio. The amazing thing about Paul's early experiments with "overdubbing" is that they were made on wax discs rather than magnetic tape. He would record a track onto a disc and then use another disc to re-record the first track plus a second track, and then use another disc to re-record a third track with the first and second parts plus a new part, and so on. (To add to the technical complexity of the process, Paul recorded some tracks at half the normal speed, so that they were higher in pitch and sounded twice as fast when played back!) It is said that Paul discarded some five hundred test discs in perfecting this early overdubbing technique.

The arrival of audio tape made the process of overdubbing far easier; by the late 1940s recording studios were using audio tape, rather than master discs, to produce most recordings, and some artists (notably Bing Crosby) had begun to use tape to pre-record their appearances on radio. In 1948 the Ampex Corporation, backed by Crosby, introduced its first tape recorder, a machine that soon became a mainstay of the recording industry. That year Crosby gave Les Paul the second reel-to-reel tape recorder ever produced for sale by Ampex, and Paul immediately began tinkering with the off-the-shelf model, creating the first multitrack recordings ever on tape by adding a second recording head and additional circuitry. The year 1949 saw the introduction of a two-track recorder, which could record simultaneous inputs from two microphones and thus produce stereo effects. While tape recorders were not initially successful as a home consumer item, the advantages of magnetic recording were felt immediately in the music industry.

The postwar era also saw fierce competition over new disc technologies, known as the "Battle of the Speeds." In 1948 Columbia Records introduced the twelve-inch long-playing disc (LP). Spinning at a speed of 33⅓ rotations per minute (rpm), the LP could accommodate more than twenty minutes of music on each side, a great improvement over the three- to four-minute limitation of 78 rpm discs. In addition, the LP was made of vinyl, a material at once more durable and less noisy than the shellac used to make

Les Paul at the controls in his Oakland, New Jersey, home, 1953.

78s. In introducing the new discs at a Columbia Records board meeting, an executive put a fifteen-inch stack of LPs next to an eight-*foot* stack of 78s containing the same amount of music in order to convince shareholders and the press to back the new technology. Interestingly, although the LP opened up the possibility of longer uninterrupted recordings—a great advantage for fans of classical music and Broadway musicals—most pop music LPs were "albums" of three-minute performances. This suggests that what had seemed to be a technological restriction from the engineering point of view—the three-minute limit of 78 rpm phonograph records—had long since become a musical habit. To this day, many pop music recordings are no longer than four minutes in length.

In 1949, responding to Columbia's innovation, the RCA Victor Corporation introduced yet another new disc format, the seven-inch 45 rpm single. The 45, which was actually closer to the old 78 rpm discs in overall recording time, required a special mechanical record changer that fit the large hole at the center of the disc. However, 45s had at least one decided advantage from the consumer's viewpoint. Using a record changer, the listener could load a stack of singles, thus preprogramming a series of favorite recordings, each of which would begin less than fifteen seconds after the end of the previous record. This ability meant that consumers could focus their spending power on their favorite recordings, rather than buying a prepackaged series of songs by a single artist on an LP. (And of course, a single 45 cost much less than a single LP—another appeal for teenagers living on an allowance from their parents.) Building on the basic principles of the jukebox, the marketing of 45s pointed the way forward to today's digital technologies, which allow consumers to program specific tracks in any order they choose.

In the end, the Battle of the Speeds was resolved by a technological compromise, in which turntables were set up to accommodate all three existing formats (78, 45, and $33\frac{1}{3}$ rpm). LPs continued to serve as a medium for albums of pop songs and longer musical works such as Broadway cast recordings, while the 45 became the favored medium for distributing hit singles.

Radio broadcasting was also affected by technological changes in the postwar period. In addition to the older AM (amplitude modulation) broadcasting technology that had dominated the field since the early 1920s, the postwar period saw the rapid growth of FM (frequency modulation) broadcasting. FM radio, which used higher frequencies than AM, had better sound quality and was not as easily subject to electrical disturbances such as lightning. (By the late 1950s FM was also being used for stereo broadcasting.) The first commercial FM broadcast took place in 1939, and by 1949 around seven hundred FM stations were operating in the United States, along with well over one thousand AM stations.

Of all of the new electronic technologies of the postwar era, television exerted the most profound influence on American culture. The development of television broadcasting, foreseen by science fiction writers of the nineteenth century, started in earnest in the 1920s. At the 1939 New York World's Fair RCA introduced its first fully electronic television system to the public. (At that time a television set cost $660, more than half the price of a new automobile!) During the war production of television was interrupted, but in the postwar years, with the economy booming and cheaper sets available, the new medium took off. In 1946 it was estimated that Americans owned six thousand television sets; this figure shot up to 3 million in 1948 and 12 million in 1951. For better or for worse, by the early 1950s television had become the central focus of leisure time in millions of American households.

Television's massive success rested on its ability to fuse the forms and functions of previous media, including radio, the record player, and cinema. Like Hollywood film, television was a multiple medium, combining sound and moving images. Like radios and record players, the TV set could be brought into the family parlor (now called a "living room") and incorporated into the daily round of domestic life. TV quickly became the main outlet for corporate advertising, and by 1952 the four big networks—NBC, CBS, ABC, and Dumont—had begun to turn significant profits. TV broadcasters used a great deal of recorded and live music, and the postwar era saw the eruption of complex legal disputes over fees to be paid for the use of songs on the air (a recapitulation of the battles between radio and the music business during the 1930s and 1940s). To be sure, there can be no doubt that the new medium was perceived by the record industry as a threat. (In 1949 retail sales of records fell drastically, while sales of television sets increased by some 400 percent!) However, by the mid-1950s, television had become the most important medium for launching new performers and recordings, and established stars such as Perry Como, Nat "King" Cole, Tommy Dorsey, and Jackie Gleason were hosting their own weekly variety shows. These shows, with their mixtures of widely varying acts (singers, comedians, dancers) resembled in many ways the old live vaudeville shows.

The Rise of the Star Singers

By 1946 the main focus of popular attention had shifted away from celebrity instrumentalist/bandleaders such as Benny Goodman, Count Basie, and Glenn Miller and toward a new generation of crooners. Many of the top singers of the late 1940s and early 1950s—such as Frank Sinatra, Perry Como, Nat "King" Cole, Doris Day, Jo Stafford, and Peggy Lee—had started their careers during the swing era. In the early 1950s these pop stars were joined by a younger generation of vocalists who specialized in sentimental ballads, novelty numbers—cheerful, disposable songs that often resembled advertising jingles—and crooner-style cover versions of country and western and rhythm & blues hits. These vocalists were promoted to the expanding teenage audience.

The musicians' union recording ban of 1942–1944—which had banned instrumentalists from recording but did not apply to even the most musically gifted vocalists—encouraged a number of big band singers to begin recording under their own names, sometimes with choral accompaniment. Those singers with the most entrepreneurial savvy, or the best business agents, were able to parlay this opportunity into long-lasting success. In addition, the music industry's mastery of cross-media promotion—on radio, films, and television—reached new heights. Following in the footsteps of Bing Crosby, many of the biggest singing stars of the postwar era also became film stars (e.g., Frank Sinatra and Doris Day) or hosted their own television shows (e.g., Perry Como and Nat "King" Cole).

Frank Sinatra at the microphone, 1947.

Frank (Francis Albert) Sinatra (1915–1998) was one of the first big band singers to take advantage of changes in the music business. Born into a working-class Italian family in Hoboken, New Jersey, Sinatra attracted public attention in 1935 when he appeared as a member of a vocal quartet on a popular radio show called *Major Bowes' Amateur Hour*. From 1937 to 1939 he worked as a singing waiter at the Rustic Cabin, a nightclub in New Jersey. (Although the job paid little, Sinatra wisely kept it because the place was wired for radio broadcasts.) In 1939 the bandleader Harry James hired him, and later that same year he joined the Tommy Dorsey Orchestra.

In 1942, against Tommy Dorsey's wishes, Sinatra convinced the Victor Company to let him make a solo recording and soon thereafter bought out his contract with the Dorsey band. A series of appearances on the national radio show *Your Hit Parade* helped him build a national following, particularly among younger listeners. During the AFM strike Sinatra continued to work in the studio, performing with choral accompaniment on several hit records. The magnitude of Sinatra's celebrity became clear for the first time in December 1942, when he appeared at the Paramount Theater in New York

City with the Benny Goodman Orchestra. Goodman, introducing Sinatra, suddenly found himself confronted with thousands of screaming young women. (The startled bandleader—himself no stranger to celebrity—is reported to have blurted out, "What the f— is *that?*")

Promoted on radio, at the movies, and in the press (even in biographical comic books aimed at high school–age females), Sinatra's popularity soared, culminating in the first documented example of modern pop hysteria, the so-called Columbus Day Riot of 1944. The occasion was a return engagement at the Paramount Theater by Sinatra and the Goodman band, and thirty thousand fans—including thousands of teenage girls, called "bobby soxers" after the style of the socks they tended to wear—showed up to claim tickets. The Paramount could seat only thirty-six hundred people, and many fans refused to leave after the first show, triggering a riot among fans lined up outside the theater. In a sense, Sinatra was the direct predecessor of the teen idols of the rock 'n' roll era and the Beatles after them. Falling into a "Sinatrance," young women cried, screamed, and tore their hair. They followed the singer everywhere, fighting for pieces of his clothing and treating his used cigarette butts like sacred objects. The press and public bestowed various nicknames on Sinatra: he was "Swoonatra," "The Sultan of Swoon," or simply "The Voice."

Oddly handsome, with a triangular head, golf-ball Adam's apple, and jug-handle ears, Sinatra projected a combination of confidence and vulnerability. Asked to explain his early popularity, Sinatra later conjectured that he represented to those at home all the local boys that were gone, drafted into the war. It is also undeniable that Frank Sinatra's early success lay partly in his keen business sense, his access to media exposure, and his sheer stamina. (In 1946 he did as many as forty-five shows a week, singing eighty to one hundred songs a day!) Furthermore, he was a highly skilled singer and a talented interpreter of popular songs, respected by the musicians with whom he worked.

Sinatra's approach to singing took shape in response to his early hero, Bing Crosby. In a 1965 article Sinatra wrote:

When I started singing in the mid-1930s everybody was trying to copy the Crosby style—the casual kind of raspy sound in the throat. Bing was on top, and a bunch of us . . . were trying to break in. It occurred to me that maybe the world didn't need another Crosby. I decided to experiment a little and come up with something different. What I finally hit on was more the bel canto Italian school of singing.[1] . . . That meant I had to stay in better shape because I had to sing more. It was more difficult than Crosby's style, much more difficult. (quoted in Pleasants 1974, 189)

Sinatra's combination of Crosby's crooning style with the bel canto technique of Italian opera was further enriched by other influences. In addition to female jazz and cabaret

1. Bel canto, a technique used by opera singers, emphasizes breath control, a fluid and relaxed voice, and the use of subtle variations in pitch and rhythmic phrasing for dramatic effect.

singers such as Billie Holiday and Mabel Mercer, Sinatra talked about the influence of instrumental soloists on his vocal approach:

> The thing that influenced me the most was the way that Tommy [Dorsey] played his trombone. He would take a musical phrase and play it all the way through without breathing, for eight, ten, maybe sixteen bars. How in the hell did he do it? Why couldn't a singer do that, too? Fascinated, I began to listen to other soloists. I bought every Jascha Heifetz record I could find, and listened to him play the violin hour after hour. His constant bowing, where you never heard a break, carried the melody line straight on through, just like Dorsey's trombone. It was my idea to make my voice work in the same way as a trombone or violin—not sounding like them, but "playing" the voice like those instruments. (Pleasants 1974, 192)

In performance, these various stylistic influences combined with Sinatra's mastery of the microphone, which he regarded as an extension of his vocal instrument. While Bing and other early crooners seemed to be *overheard* by the microphone, Sinatra and others of his generation *played* it, subtly shifting it to achieve certain tone qualities, accentuate melodic passages or lyric phrases, and avoid the "popping" of consonants. Perhaps it was this approach to his craft—that of an instrumental musician—that helped him avoid the lachrymose sentimentality of many crooners of the postwar era. Although Sinatra's popularity took a nosedive in the early 1950s—largely as a result of well-publicized difficulties in his personal life—his success in later years (see Chapter 8) was in no small part due to the connection his audience perceived between his voice and his personality, each of which suggested a delicate balance between emotionalism and rationality, deep feeling and technical control.

While few postwar crooners were able to match Frank Sinatra's artistry or longevity, this does not mean that he faced no serious competition. Despite the very small number of African American artists on the pop music charts of the early 1950s, it could be argued that the greatest postwar crooner—in both musical and commercial terms—was a Black musician, *Nat "King" Cole* (1917–1965). Nathaniel Coles was born in Montgomery, Alabama, and his family moved to the South Side of Chicago when he was only four years old. His father was pastor of a Baptist church, and young Nat was playing organ and singing in the choir by the age of twelve. He made his first recording in 1936 as a member of the Solid Swingers, a jazz band led by his brother Eddie Cole. Nat Cole, a brilliant piano improviser, exerted a strong influence on later jazz pianists such as Oscar Peterson and Bill Evans. He moved from Chicago to Los Angeles in 1937 and formed his own group, the King Cole Trio.

Nat "King" Cole was by far the most successful Black recording artist of the postwar era, placing a total of fourteen recordings on the Top 10 pop charts between 1946 and 1954. Along with the Mills Brothers and Louis Jordan, Cole was one of the first African American musicians to cross over regularly to the predominantly white pop charts. Although he continued to record a range of material—including jazz performances with the King Cole Trio—Cole's biggest commercial successes were sentimental ballads accompanied by elaborate orchestral arrangements: "(I Love You) For Sentimental

Oscar Moore, Nat "King" Cole, and Wesley Prince, New York, NY, ca. July 1946.

Reasons" (1946); "Nature Boy" (1948); "Unforgettable" (1950); his biggest hit, "Mona Lisa" (1950), which sold over 5 million copies; and "Too Young" (1951), perhaps the first teenage love ballad.

Given the racial prejudice prevalent in the American music industry and society as a whole, Nat "King" Cole's professional success was truly remarkable, comparable to the baseball career of Jackie Robinson, who became the first Black player to enter the major leagues in 1947. Promoted by Capitol Records as a "sepia Sinatra," Cole was the first Black musician to host his own weekly radio series (1948–1949) and the first to have a network television show (1956–1957). He recorded hundreds of songs for Capitol Records, helping to keep the new Los Angeles–based company afloat during its early years. Cole entered a field dominated exclusively by white artists and bested all but the most popular of them in both artistic and commercial terms. Unlike many pop crooners of the time, Cole thought of himself first and foremost as a musician, an artist who sang because his public wanted him to sing. In response to jazz critics who lambasted him for his success as a pop crooner, Cole noted that critics weren't the ones who bought records: "They get 'em free."

Urban Folk Music: The Weavers

During the early 1950s a new genre of popular music called "urban folk" showed up on the pop charts. This genre combined a number of seemingly contradictory tendencies. It was inspired by rural folk music yet performed by urban intellectuals. It drew inspiration from the populist protest songs of Woody Guthrie (see Chapter 5) yet was used by the record industry to generate millions of dollars in profits. Many urban folk recordings were seemingly harmless sing-alongs, designed to invite audience participation. Yet only a few years after the initial burst of public interest in this music, some of its best-known practitioners were being persecuted for their political beliefs. And the record industry really didn't know what to do with urban folk music. Was it "folk music"? Or "country and western"? Or perhaps "novelty music"?

The first urban folk group to achieve commercial success was the Weavers, a quartet led by singer, banjo player, and political activist **Pete Seeger** (1919–2014). The Weavers, formed in 1948, grew out of an earlier group called the Almanac Singers, which had included Seeger and Guthrie. With a repertoire based on American and international folk songs, the Weavers performed at union rallies, college concerts, and urban coffeehouses. The group was "discovered" at a New York City nightclub by Gordon Jenkins, managing director of Decca Records, and between 1950 and 1954 they

Listening Guide "NANCY (WITH THE LAUGHING FACE)"

Music and lyrics by Jimmy Van Heusen and Phil Silvers; performed by Frank Sinatra with the Axel Stordahl Orchestra; recorded 1945

Frank Sinatra's 1945 recording of "Nancy (With the Laughing Face)," which peaked at Number 10 on the *Billboard* charts, provides us with an example of the singer's style at the dawn of the postwar era. One big change from his recordings of the swing era is immediately apparent: string instruments dominate the instrumental accompaniment to Sinatra's singing. The song, which has a conventional thirty-two-bar AABA form, was cowritten by the Tin Pan Alley veteran Jimmy Van Heusen and television and film comedian Phil Silvers in honor of the birth of Sinatra's daughter, Nancy. (Part of the song's appeal for audiences lay in the fact that its lyric could be interpreted on more than one level.)

The brief orchestral introduction begins with four bars of waltz rhythm (three beats per bar) and then shifts into the four-beat meter of the song. As Sinatra's voice enters ("If I don't . . ."), the orchestra slows down, creating a sense of anticipation. (This stretching of the tempo for expressive purposes is called tempo rubato, an Italian phrase that literally means "stolen time.") Sinatra sings straight through the song's AABA form,

backed by an orchestra that includes strings, brass, and a harp. (The tempo is quite slow, so you will have to count carefully to follow the form.) He stretches the time slightly in several places to create drama—another example of tempo rubato. The orchestra then takes over again for five measures, and Sinatra sings a final A section, followed by an orchestral coda (a concluding section).

Sinatra's voice is relaxed and unforced, with warmth and a slight vibrato, and his hard-earned ability to sing long, uninterrupted passages allows him to connect the phrases of the song into one smooth contour. In this performance, as in all of his best recordings, Sinatra conveys the central emotion of the song to his listeners while at the same time maintaining a certain distance, an ability to keep the feeling of the moment in perspective. The arrangement complements Sinatra's voice beautifully, and the subtle tempo changes, the prominence of the harp (associated in the popular imagination with angels), and the brief references to waltz time at the beginning and end all contribute to the romantic atmosphere of the recording.

LISTENING GUIDE | "NANCY (WITH THE LAUGHING FACE)"

TIME	FORM	LYRIC	DESCRIPTIVE COMMENTS
	Orchestral introduction (8 measures)		4 measures of triple (waltz) time plus 4 measures of four-beat time; strings playing in tempo rubato
0:13	A (8 measures)	*If I don't . . .*	Strings and harp
0:43	A (8 measures)	*She takes . . .*	Muted trumpets (hint of big band sound)
1:12	B (8 measures)	*Have you ever . . .*	Tempo slows down for dramatic effect
1:40	A (8 measures)	*I swear . . .*	
2:11	Orchestral interlude (5 measures)		Tempo rubato
2:24	A (8 measures)	*Keep Betty . . .*	
2:54	Orchestral tag (coda) (8 measures)		Tempo rubato; music closely related to the introduction

Listening Guide "NATURE BOY"

Written by Eden Ahbez; performed by Nat "King" Cole, accompanied by Frank De Vol's Orchestra; recorded 1948

"Nature Boy" was the first record to present Nat "King" Cole's voice with full orchestral accompaniment, and it is also one of his most interesting pop recordings. Released in 1948, Cole's record held the Number 1 position on the *Billboard* pop charts for eight weeks. "Nature Boy" was composed by Eden Ahbez (1908–1995), a songwriter whose creative frame of reference was about as far from the professional songwriting business as can be imagined. Ahbez can best be described as a proto-hippie: a long-haired, bearded vegetarian who lived in the hills and deserts around Los Angeles with only a sleeping bag, a bicycle, and a juice squeezer. "Nature Boy," which Ahbez claimed was inspired by his studies of yoga and Eastern religions, was originally part of a suite of songs called the *Gospel of Nature*. Although the mystical message of "Nature Boy" may in fact be related to Ahbez's studies of Asian philosophy, musicologists have noted that the melody of the song is similar to that of a Yiddish folk song called "Shvayg mayn harts" ("Be Still, My Heart"), and a lawsuit resulting from this similarity was settled out of court. (Popular Jewish music had long provided inspiration for the melodic "orientalisms" in Tin Pan Alley songs.)

"Nature Boy" is a good example of the importance of the arranger in developing certain kinds of popular music. As we have learned, the arranger is a musician who takes a song—typically a melody with words and a few basic harmonies—and fashions it into a finished musical product. The multitude of choices made by an arranger—what key, what tempo, which instruments to use, and so on—are crucial elements both in the overall sound of a recording and in the success of the artists and record companies who pay for his services. We have already discussed the importance of arrangements in big band music; in many cases the arrangers hired by a bandleader were the most important factor in shaping the band's distinctive sound. After the war, as studio recording became more elaborate and technologically refined, the role of the arranger became even more important.

Frank De Vol's arrangement of "Nature Boy" is an example of the difference an arranger can make. The song itself is quite brief, and its ABAB structure, made up of eight-bar sections, appears rather mundane at first glance. "Nature Boy" does have a few distinguishing musical features. Its opening melodic phrase begins with an ear-catching upward leap, followed by a descent

("There *was* a boy . . ."), a pattern that reappears several times in the course of the song. The song is in a minor key, which occurs infrequently in mainstream popular music but is common in Jewish music and is associated in the popular imagination with sadness, longing, and exotic images of the "Orient." It is the orchestral arrangement, however, that makes this record work, along with Cole's honeyed baritone voice. In providing a dramatic musical context for Ahbez's vision of a mysterious boy who arrives one day with a utopian message for humankind, De Vol reached deeply into his professional bag of tricks.

The first moments before Cole's voice enters are complex and carefully crafted. We first hear a lonely French horn, playing a melodic phrase that foreshadows that of the song itself ("There was a boy . . ."). The strings enter soon afterward, and for a moment it is hard to find the basic pulse of the music. (This is an extreme example of tempo rubato, a technique discussed previously in connection with Sinatra.) In this swirl of sound a flute and an oboe play tag, tossing melodic phrases back and forth. None of these choices are arbitrary: the French horn and flute have long been used in orchestral music to evoke the countryside, and the oboe is a stereotyped signifier of "Eastern" music. Suddenly the orchestra begins to play in a steadier tempo, and we move into the vocal part of the arrangement.

Unlike Frank Sinatra, who sought to connect the notes of a melody in a continuous stream of breath, Cole treats each note as a somewhat distinct entity, often leaving just a bit of space in between them. (It has been suggested that this approach may have been influenced by Cole's long experience with the piano, an instrument that, unlike the violin or trombone, cannot glide between pitches.) This singing technique seems particularly appropriate in the case of "Nature Boy," in which Cole has to make the most out of a very small number of words. Notice also how he explores and savors the tone color of certain vowels, particularly evident here on words such as "boy" and "love." The intimacy of Cole's baritone voice and his unique ability to caress the lyric of a song allow him to draw the maximum effect from each word of the text.

As we begin the song the orchestra seems almost to breathe along with Cole, pausing slightly after each of the first two lines—"There was a boy . . ." (the flute plays birdsong-like phrases), "A very strange enchanted boy . . ."

(more birdsong)—and then speeding up slightly ("They say he wandered very far, very far . . .") and slowing toward the end of the phrase ("Over land and sea . . ."). Here we pause, building anticipation slightly, and then begin to breathe again: "A little shy . . ." (the oboe takes over, adding its exotic flavor), "And sad of eye . . ." (more oboe), "But very wise . . ." (strings cascade upward, then downward, like water), "Was he . . ." (flute and oboe together). This structure then repeats itself with new lyrics, but with many of the same arranging techniques applied. However, just before we reach the last two lines of the lyric—the punchline of the song, if you will—the orchestra grabs our attention with a more emotional swirl of sound, like leaves blowing into a whirlpool and then settling. As the fateful lines are delivered, the orchestra gets out of the way almost entirely, leaving Cole's voice and piano fully exposed.

At this point—two-thirds of the way through the recording—De Vol hands the melody to Cole's piano, which receives only light support from the orchestra. Things move along somewhat predictably until, suddenly, a violinist seems to stride in from the wings, playing an ardent passage reminiscent of Hollywood interpretations of gypsy music. As the tempo slows down and the orchestra once again moves out of the way, Cole drives the last two lines home again, just to make sure we get the point: "The greatest thing you'll ever learn is just to love and be loved in return." The end of the recording brings back the flute birdsong and the exotic oboe, and we "fade to black." (The studio fadeout, still a novelty in the late 1940s, was an effect made much easier to produce with the advent of magnetic tape recording.) Whatever one feels about the ultimate value of Eden Ahbez's message, there can be no doubting the formidable technique at work here, both in Cole's vocal performance and in De Vol's evocative orchestral setting.

BOX 7.1 THE BROADWAY MUSICAL AFTER WORLD WAR II

Rodgers and Hammerstein's musical *Oklahoma!*, which opened in 1943, was still going strong on Broadway at the end of World War II and continued to run for a record-breaking 2,212 performances. This show inaugurated a period in which the work of Rodgers and Hammerstein, and their ideal of a musical show in which all the songs and dances were specifically conceived for the characters performing them and their positions in the plot of the show, dominated Broadway. The reign of Rodgers and Hammerstein, marked by such still-beloved works as *South Pacific* (1949), *The King and I* (1951), *The Sound of Music* (1959), and the previously mentioned *Oklahoma!*, ended only with Hammerstein's death in 1960. When the goal of writing songs for Broadway shows became that of producing the most appropriate songs for a very specific show and consequently rendered obsolete the goal of simply writing an effective hit song that *could* be fit into a show (or into a number of different shows), the appearance of Broadway songs on the pop charts naturally became a less common occurrence. It would be an error, however, to assume that such occurrences ceased completely; love songs or catchy up-tempo numbers that were originally fashioned for specific plots and characters could occasionally transcend the specificity of their origins and become major hits, even for several singers. An outstanding example of this is the beautiful "Some Enchanted Evening" from *South Pacific*, which in 1949 yielded six Top 10 hit records for six different artists—one of whom was the opera singer who introduced it in the show, Ezio Pinza. (Among the others were Perry Como, Bing Crosby, Jo Stafford, and Frank Sinatra.) Examples of other big hit songs taken from Broadway shows during this period are the novelty number "A Bushel and a Peck" from Frank Loesser's *Guys and Dolls* (1950) and the tender,

(continued)

BOX 7.1 **THE BROADWAY MUSICAL AFTER WORLD WAR II** (*continued*)

self-mocking "Hey There" from Adler and Ross's *The Pajama Game* (1954), the latter a Number 1 hit for pop star Rosemary Clooney.

The new LP proved a perfect medium for Broadway show original cast albums, and it is the bestselling album charts that help us to gauge the full impact of Broadway during this period of American popular music. In addition, all of the musicals mentioned previously were made into very successful movies during the 1950s (or, in the case of *The Sound of Music*, during the 1960s), and movie soundtrack albums often were even more popular than their Broadway cast counterparts, serving to further disseminate the songs from the original musicals. The movie soundtrack albums from Rodgers and Hammerstein's *Oklahoma!*, *South Pacific*, *The King and I*, and *The Sound of Music* were all Number 1 bestsellers (*South Pacific* held the top slot for thirty-one weeks in 1958–1959!) and all of them stayed on the top album charts for years.

placed eleven records in the Top 40. It is difficult to gauge what impact the Weavers might have had on pop music had they been allowed to sustain their early success. Three members of the group, including Seeger, were accused of being Communists during the early 1950s.[2] (Their main accuser later admitted that he had fabricated the charges and went to prison for perjury.) Decca Records, unwilling to withstand the heat, dropped their contract, and the Weavers never again appeared on the pop music charts. Seeger, however, continued to play a leading role as a champion of folk music and a populist activist.

The Weavers' sing-along version of "Goodnight, Irene," composed by the Louisiana-born musician Huddie Ledbetter (better known as Leadbelly or Lead Belly, 1885–1949), was the most successful of their recordings, reaching the Number 1 position on the pop charts in 1950. The strophic form of the song is clearly related to the folk ballad tradition, with a series of verses and a recurring chorus ("Irene goodnight, Irene goodnight . . ."). Of course, this is not folk music in any strict sense. On "Goodnight, Irene," as on their other hit records of the early 1950s—"Tzena, Tzena, Tzena," "So Long (It's Been Good to Know Ya)," "On Top of Old Smoky," and "Wimoweh"—the Weavers are accompanied by the orchestral arrangements of Gordon Jenkins, who also worked with Frank Sinatra, Nat "King" Cole, and other pop stars. Despite the folksy informality of much of their later work, the Weavers' "Goodnight, Irene" and other hits on the Decca label are *pop* records, through and through. They helped to define a niche in the popular market for folk-based popular music, a genre that came to include the later work of the Kingston Trio (see Chapter 8); the songs of Peter, Paul, and Mary; and the music of Bob Dylan (see Chapter 10). In addition, the Weavers' use of international materials—including Israeli,

---

2. In the environment of the Cold War there was an upsurge of anticommunist sentiment in the United States. This led to hearings in the House of Representatives by the so-called Un-American Activities Committee, in which many people were targeted for alleged subversive activities and intentions. In the entertainment business, many careers were temporarily derailed or totally destroyed by this process.

Lead Belly, the composer of "Goodnight, Irene," and the Weavers (Pete Seeger, Lee Hays, Fred Hellerman, Ronnie Gilbert).

Cuban, and South African songs—makes them among the first world beat artists, a category of popular music that would not emerge in defined form for another thirty years (see Chapter 14).

The Mambo Craze (1949–1955)

The mambo, the most popular form of Latin dance music in the United States in the years just before the rise of rock 'n' roll, was a branch of the Cuban tradition that reaches back to Don Azpiazú (see Chapter 3), Xavier Cugat, and Machito (see Chapter 6), and beyond them to the headwaters of the rumba, the *son*, and the *danzón* (see Chapter 1). The term "mambo" was originally derived from the word for "song" or "story" used in the language of the BaKongo people of central Africa, who exerted a profound influence on the formation of Afro-Cuban culture beginning in the sixteenth century. In musical terms the mambo is difficult to define precisely, and its history is disputed by musicians. It seems clear that at some point in the 1930s Cuban musicians began to use the term to refer to a discrete section of certain compositions. In this usage, the mambo was an extension or intensification of the montuno, the second half of the two-part form common to much Cuban dance music (recall our discussion of Machito's "Nague" in Chapter 6). The mambo section was designed to ramp up the energy on the dance floor, and, like the montuno, it relies upon a repeated melodic-rhythmic figure in the horns, juxtaposed with call-and-response singing and either a vocal or an instrumental solo.

The variant of mambo that created an international craze during the 1950s drew upon these principles to create an up-tempo, highly energized, polyrhythmic variant of big band music. In creating this style, pioneering arrangers such as René Hernandez and Perez Prado (see the Listening Guide in this chapter) separated the saxophone section from the other wind instruments and gave it responsibility for playing the montuno's repeated patterns that interlocked rhythmically with the percussion, string bass, and piano. In many mambo arrangements, the trumpets enter after the saxophones and rhythm section, playing loud, bright, and sometimes dissonant figures against the montuno pattern. The groove is sometimes punctuated suddenly by an instrumental break—which may itself be interrupted by a vocal interjection (such as "Unh!")—creating momentary uncertainty in the listener, ratcheting up the tension, and propelling the music forward when the band re-enters in high gear.

The musician who did the most to popularize the mambo, throughout both Latin America and in the United States, was the pianist, organist, and bandleader *Damaso Perez Prado* (1916–1989). Born in the town of Matanzas in eastern Cuba, Prado moved to Havana around 1940, where he worked his way up through the ranks of local dance bands. In 1948 he settled in Mexico City, a popular destination not only for American tourists but also for expatriate Cubans. Influenced by American big band recordings—particularly those of the Stan Kenton Orchestra, one of the first bands to experiment seriously with Cuban music—Prado formed his own group. He began recording a series of mambo singles for the Mexican branch of RCA Victor. Some of these recordings were released into the Latin market in the United States, and a few—notably his first record, "Mambo No. 5" (1949)—crossed over to a non-Latin audience, helped in part by a second recording ban imposed upon its members by the American Federation of Musicians. "Mambo No. 5" is a quintessential example of the style that captivated American listeners at the beginning of the 1950s.

The temporal limitations of the recorded medium—the three-minute 78 rpm disc, which was still in wide use in Latin America—do not give us a good sense of how this piece was performed at concerts and dances. In live performance, Prado's band had the ability to whip audiences into a state of ecstasy, using the principle of repetition enlivened by dramatic and unpredictable breaks that toyed with the listener's expectations. Prado himself contributed not only on piano, but also by dancing, leaping, and shouting onstage, exhorting his band to ever greater heights of "mambo madness." This is quintessential music for the dance, with its focus on rhythmic flow, melodic motifs that are mixed and matched in various patterns, and the element of musical surprise—the breaks requiring that dancers keep moving in time without the band, which inevitably comes back just in the nick of time to rescue them.

On the strength of hits like "Mambo No. 5," which sold well throughout Latin America, Prado was soon the toast of the elites of Mexico City. His popular appeal among the less wealthy was boosted by a series of mambo recordings in honor of working-class occupations such as telephone operators, firemen, and gas station attendants. He even reached out to college students and their professors, recording the "Normal School Mambo," the "Mexico University Mambo," and the "Polytechnical Institute Mambo."

The B-side of "Mambo No. 5," an arrangement entitled "Que Rico el Mambo," was released in the United States by RCA in 1950 under the title "Mambo Jambo." A cover

Listening Guide "MAMBO NO. 5"

Written by Perez Prado; performed by Perez Prado and His Orchestra; recorded 1949

Like many of Prado's most commercially successful recordings, "Mambo No. 5" has a modular form and is constructed out of a small number of melodic-rhythmic building blocks, which are combined and recombined throughout the piece. Although grounded in earlier Cuban dance music styles, "Mambo No. 5" abolishes the traditional two-part head-montuno structure; in a sense, the montuno section has been folded back into the form as a whole, so that repeated interlocking patterns in the horns dominate the entire composition. The mambo was associated in the popular imagination with romance, excitement, and excess. However, it is in fact a tightly regimented musical form, a simplification of the formal and rhythmic complexity of Afro-Cuban music for audiences new to the style. This audience's attention was often focused on mastering new dance steps, which were in turn often simplified versions of the original forms from which they were derived.

LISTENING GUIDE	"MAMBO NO. 5"	
TIME	**DESCRIPTIVE COMMENTS**
0:00	Opening figure by trumpets, punctuated at the end by Prado's signature "Unh"
0:06	Main melodic motif stated by saxophones and percussion
0:18	Motif continues now accompanied by trumpets performing a series of complementary two-measure patterns
0:29	Trumpets change to a harmonized ascending two-measure pattern, ending with a fanfare and Prado's "Unh"
0:46	Saxophones pick up the melodic riff, joined by harmonized trumpets, followed by a percussive break and Prado's "Unh"
1:06	Saxophones play the main melodic motif; trumpets join with trilling riffs and then harmonized chords leading to another break
1:23	Vocalists begin the repeated chant "*Si, si, si, yo quiero mambo*" ("Yes, yes, yes, I love to mambo") accompanied by percussion; ending with harmonized horns and "Unh!"
1:44	Saxophones play main motif; on third repeat, trumpets again join with counter-harmonized figure; leading to break
2:10	Saxophones begin a descending riff in a new rhythmic pattern; after several statements, trumpets play counter figure in harmony
2:38	Trumpets play two separated chords followed by a single full-band chord to end the piece.

version that same year by the American bandleader Dave Barbour reached Number 27 on the pop charts, inspiring RCA to move more of Prado's recordings out of their "Spanish" (Latin) listings and into the mainstream pop catalog. By 1951, when Prado's band played in the United States for the first time, his fame had already spread. He achieved the peak of his success with the hugely successful "Cherry Pink and Apple Blossom White," the Number 1 pop single in the United States for ten weeks in 1955, and the second most popular single of the entire early rock 'n' roll era, bested only by Elvis Presley's "Don't Be Cruel"/"Hound Dog." His other Number 1 single (which topped both the pop and R&B charts) was "Patricia" (1958), a slinky instrumental track spotlighting Prado's organ playing that is nowadays a favorite of retro lounge music fans. Despite its relative tameness by rock era standards, "Patricia" has a long association with sensuality, strengthened by the song's appearance in a controversial strip-tease sequence in director Federico Fellini's classic *La Dolce Vita* (1960), as background music in the 1969 film *The Graduate*, and more recently as the theme for HBO's series *Real Sex*.

As has been the case with much of the music introduced to the United States from Latin America, the mambo craze started by Perez Prado gave rise to hundreds of imitations, ranging from the ridiculous (usually) to the sublime (rarely). In 1954 veteran Jewish American vaudeville performer Sophie Tucker recorded "Middle Age Mambo," and Atlantic Records star Ruth Brown scored a Number 1 R&B hit with the single "Mambo Baby"—a performance with little if any discernible relationship to the mambo as played by Perez Prado. The year 1954 also saw the release of the most successful mainstream pop song to hitch its wagon to the runaway mambo engine, Perry Como's "Papa Loves Mambo" (Number 4 pop), a song that explicitly linked dancing the mambo with middle-aged sexual rejuvenation: "Papa loves mambo, Mama loves mambo, Havin' their fling again, younger than spring again, feelin' that zing again, wow—UNH!!"

Rosemary Clooney, c. 1950s.

We have spent a great deal of attention in this book discussing the deleterious, if important, effect of racial and ethnic stereotypes on the development of American popular music. But understanding the impact of ethnicity and ethnic perceptions on music requires that we appreciate the good-humored and creative adaptations of these stereotypes that have from time to time also been part of this history. Clooney's record was a big hit among Italian Americans and has become part of the repertoire of nostalgic pop music in that community, thanks in part to the song's inclusion in films such as *It Started in Naples* (1960) and *Married to the Mob* (1988). It is important to note in this connection that the core audience for Latin music during the 1950s included Blacks and Jews, along with Italians, all of whom helped to support the dance club scenes in cities like New York and Los Angeles and to push records of genres like the mambo and its simplified successor, the

Listening Guide "MAMBO ITALIANO"

Written by Bob Merrill; arranged by Mitch Miller; performed by Rosemary Clooney; recorded 1954

In many ways the most interesting of the mambo-inspired pop hits was "Mambo Italiano" (Number 9 pop, 1954) by the former big band singer **Rosemary Clooney** (1928–2002), aunt of the film star George Clooney. "Mambo Italiano" is a sassy, funny, and very catchy tune that conflates Latino and Italian American stereotypes (as performed by an Irish American singer). The recording opens with Clooney's emotional, vibrato-saturated performance of the first four lines of text, sung in tempo rubato over a harpsichord background that conjures the sound of mandolins, richly evocative of Italian music and the homeland. The lyrics are replete with Italian-American references, with language straight out of a Mafia movie (including references to "Napoli," "mozzarella," "goombah," and "paisano").

As the groove kicks in for four measures, the young female protagonist is yanked rudely back to New York (or perhaps New Jersey), and Clooney belts out her mambo in a dialect that will be instantly familiar to fans of classic gangster films and the television show *The Sopranos*: "Hey, mambo! Mambo Italiano . . ."

In musical terms, the AABA structure of "Mambo Italiano" is straight out of Tin Pan Alley, and its rhythm is more akin to a Latin dance style called the bolero than to a mambo in the Perez Prado fashion. At the same time, the arrangement does incorporate features intrinsic to the latter genre, including frequent rhythmic pauses and group-chanting of a refrain. The song text employs Italian American slang (*goombah*) and culinary metaphors to evoke cultural identity—we are, for example, urged to reject mozzarella and instead to savor both enchiladas (a Mexican and Central American dish) and *bacalà*, the Italian name for a dish made of dried salt cod that is also widely popular in Latin America. "Mambo Italiano," written by Bob Merrill (composer of the 1950s hit "The Doggie in the Window"), is an anthem to hipness that plays on common ethnic stereotypes while at the same time urging traditionalist "squares" to get with the latest dance craze.

cha-cha-chá, to the top of the pop and R&B charts during the 1950s. It could be argued that part of Latin music's success in the years just before the emergence of rock 'n' roll lay in its ability to transcend taste differences between communities in a society still divided on the basis of race and ethnicity.

Southern Music in the Postwar Era

After World War II the market for forms of popular music rooted in the traditions of the American South re-emerged with new vigor. The old categories of "race music" and "hillbilly music" underwent a series of name changes, reflecting shifts in social attitudes and the music industry's perception of the economic potential of Southern music. In 1942 *Billboard* began for the first time to list these records, subsuming them under the single category "western and race," a hybrid designation that was soon changed to "American folk records." In 1949 *Billboard* began using the terms **rhythm & blues** and **country and western** as more dignified and up-to-date replacements for "race" and "hillbilly," respectively.

During the late 1930s and 1940s millions of people migrated from the rural South in search of employment in defense-related industries. Cities such as Chicago, Detroit, Pittsburgh, New York, Washington, DC, Nashville, Atlanta, and Los Angeles all became home to large populations of transplanted Southerners, whose musical tastes were doubly shaped not only by their experience of rural traditions but also by the desire to forge new, urbanized identities (and thereby distance themselves from the stereotyped image of the "hick" or "rube"). This migrant population greatly expanded the target audience for Southern-derived music, providing a steady source of support for the urban honky-tonks, juke joints, and lounges where country and western and rhythm & blues groups played.

Radio also played a crucial role in the popularization of these types of music. There was a substantial increase in the number of radio stations catering specially to transplanted Southerners, some capable of saturating the entire country's airwaves, and others low-wattage affairs with a broadcasting radius of only a few miles. The country music radio business was positively booming in the late 1940s and early 1950s, with new shows modeled on Nashville's *Grand Ole Opry* coming on the air in all of America's major cities and out of hundreds of small stations that sprouted up in rural areas. During the war a number of white disc jockeys began to mix Black popular music in with their usual diet of pop records, and 1949 saw the inauguration of the first radio station dedicated exclusively to playing music for a Black audience—WDIA in Memphis, Tennessee, featuring the popular blues musician and disc jockey B. B. King. (Although this station catered to a predominantly Black audience in the Mississippi Delta area, it was in fact owned by white businessmen.) In 1953 a nationwide survey in *Billboard* reported that pop music accounted for an average of thirty-one hours per week of radio programming, with country music occupying eleven and a half hours, and R&B two and a half. (The rest of the time was taken up with news, sports, comedy, and drama.) While these figures may not seem impressive at first glance, the fact that country music was being heard more than an hour a day on average and that R&B recordings were getting any airplay at all on mainstream pop radio stations is an indication of the expanding audiences for these styles.

The jukebox business—which had expanded greatly during and just after the war—also played an important role in promoting country and western and rhythm & blues records. In addition, the movieola—a type of jukebox that played short musical films or "soundies" on demand and was thus an ancestor of today's music videos—also played a part in popularizing Southern-based musicians. The AFM recording ban of 1942–1944 and the rise of BMI (described at the end of Chapter 6) provided many Southern-born musicians with new opportunities for recording. Because many of these performers did not belong to the musicians' union, the ban on studio recording did not apply to them, and they were free to continue making records. Similarly, the success of BMI at licensing Southern-born songwriters was based on ASCAP's long-standing refusal to admit these musicians as members. In the end, the combined prejudice of these mainstream music institutions against rural, Southern, and Black musicians backfired.

Finally, the success of country and western and rhythm & blues music (and other non-mainstream styles such as the polka and Mexican American music) was indebted to the re-emergence of dozens of small independent record labels during and just after the war. As in the 1920s, this new generation of "indies" was made possible by a strong national economy and by the activity of small-scale entrepreneurs eager to create new market niches, develop specialized audiences, and exploit areas of America's musical map that the major companies did not perceive as significant. These small record companies played an important role in country music and, as we shall see, almost completely dominated the R&B field.

Rhythm & Blues

Although *Billboard* adopted a new designation in 1949 for what had formerly been called "race records," in some ways the commercial logic underlying the category hadn't really changed much since the 1920s and 1930s. Like the older term, "rhythm & blues" described music performed almost exclusively by Black artists and produced mainly (at least at first) for sale to African American audiences.

R&B, as the genre came to be known, was a loose cluster of styles rooted in Southern folk traditions and shaped by the experience of returning military personnel and hundreds of thousands of Black Americans who had migrated to urban centers such as New York, Chicago, Detroit, and Los Angeles during and just after the war. The top R&B recordings of the late 1940s and early 1950s included swing-influenced "jump bands," Tin Pan Alley–style love songs performed by crooners, various styles of urban blues, and gospel-influenced vocal harmony groups.

The reappearance of small independent record labels during and just after the war provided an outlet for performers who were ignored by major record companies such as Columbia, RCA Victor, and Capitol. The development of portable tape recorders made record producers and studio owners out of entrepreneurs who could not previously have afforded the equipment necessary to produce master recordings. Each company was centered on one or two individuals who located talent, oversaw the recording process, and handled publicity, distribution, and a variety of other tasks. These label owners worked the system in as many ways as time, energy, and ingenuity allowed. They paid radio DJs payola to promote their records on the handful of stations that played Black music. They visited nightclubs to find new talent, hustled copies of their records to local record store owners, and occasionally attempted to interest a major label in a particular recording or artist with crossover potential.

Most "indie" label owners worked a particular piece of musical and geographical territory. However, they also had dreams of the huge financial success that would accrue to the label that found a way to cross R&B records over to the pop music charts. The middle-class white audience for this music, and the big record companies' and radio networks' interest in it, were growing—but the competition was fiercer than ever. By 1951 there were over one hundred independent labels slugging it out for a piece of the R&B market, and few of them lasted more than a few months.

Indie owners often put their names down for composer credits on songs they recorded and thereby often earned more royalties from a given song than the actual composer. (This was a long-standing practice in the music business—for example, Ralph Peer was listed as co-composer of a number of hillbilly songs, and Irving Mills, Duke Ellington's manager, was listed as co-composer of some of Ellington's most popular songs.) In the postwar era artists and record companies often tried to cash in on the potential popularity of a recording by creating their own (sometimes almost indistinguishable) versions of it and listing themselves as co-composers. Although the most famous examples of this practice involve white musicians (and major record companies) exploiting songs first recorded by Black artists (and independent record companies), the profit motive led to a variety of interactions, including pop versions of hillbilly songs and Black versions of Tin Pan Alley songs. In general, this practice—called covering a song or making a **cover version**—was crucial to the increasing crossover success of Black music (and, to a lesser degree, Black musicians) during the 1950s. (We shall examine this process more closely in Chapter 8.)

JUMP BLUES

Jump blues, the first commercially successful category of rhythm & blues, flourished during and just after World War II. During the war, as shortages made it more difficult to maintain a lucrative touring schedule, the leaders of some big bands were forced to downsize. They formed smaller combos, generally made up of a rhythm section (bass, piano, drums, and sometimes guitar) and one or more horn players. These jump bands specialized in hard-swinging, boogie woogie–based party music, spiced with humorous lyrics and wild stage performances.

The most successful and influential jump band was the Tympany Five, led by *Louis Jordan* (1908–1975), an Arkansas-born saxophone player and singer who began making recordings for Decca Records in 1939. Jordan was tremendously popular with Black listeners and, like Nat "King" Cole, was able to build an extensive white audience during and after the war. But Jordan himself regarded Cole as being in "another field"—the pop field. Although Cole enjoyed greater financial success, in the end Jordan had a bigger impact on the future of popular music, inspiring a number of the first rock 'n' roll artists (see Chapter 8). As the rock 'n' roll pioneer Chuck Berry put it, "I identify myself with Louis Jordan more than any other artist" (Shaw 1986, 64). James Brown, the godfather of soul music, was once asked if Louis Jordan had been an influence on him. "He was *everything*," Brown replied (Chilton 1994, 126).

Jordan's first big hit, "G.I. Jive," reached Number 1 on *Billboard*'s "Harlem Hit Parade," as the R&B chart was labeled in the early 1940s; it held the top spot on the pop music charts for two weeks and sold over a million copies. From 1945 through 1948 Jordan, working with a white record producer named **Milt Gabler** (1911–2001), recorded a string of crossover hits, including "Caldonia" (Number 1 R&B, Number 11 pop, 1945), "Stone Cold Dead in the Market" (an adaptation of a calypso from Trinidad, which reached Number 1 on the R&B chart and Number 7 on the pop chart in 1946), and "Ain't Nobody Here but Us Chickens" (Number 1 R&B, Number 6 pop, 1946). The popularity of the Tympany Five was reinforced by a series of films featuring the band. These short musical features were rented to individual movie theaters and shown as a promotional device a few days before the band was due to hit town. (Louis Jordan was a gifted comedian, as well as a musician, and many of the films had a decidedly wacky tone. One was a musical parody of Western movies, with Jordan in full cowboy gear, astride a horse, with his sax slung across his back.) Jordan's films were like his records, insofar as they were popular in white as well as Black movie theaters, even in the Deep South. However, the fact that his music appealed to an interracial audience should not lead us to assume that Jordan's career was unaffected by racism. An article published in 1944 described what was to become a standard practice for booking popular Black musicians:

Louis Jordan and his Tympany Five, c. 1946.

Listening Guide "CHOO CHOO CH' BOOGIE"

Music and lyrics by Milt Gabler, Denver Darling, and Vaughan Horton; performed by Louis Jordan's Tympany Five; recorded 1946

"Choo Choo Ch' Boogie," Louis Jordan's biggest hit, exemplifies key elements of the jump blues style of R&B. Released in 1946 by Decca Records, the song topped the R&B charts for an amazing eighteen weeks, reached Number 7 on *Billboard*'s pop hit list, and sold over 2 million copies. "Choo Choo Ch' Boogie" was cowritten by Milt Gabler, Jordan's producer, and two country and western musicians who worked at a radio station in New York City. The title of the song draws a parallel between the motion of a railroad train—a metaphor of mobility and change long established in both country music and the blues—and the rocking rhythm of boogie-woogie music. Boogie-woogie, which had experienced a craze during the swing era, provided an important link between rhythm & blues and country music during the postwar period, a connection that was to prove important in the formation of rock 'n' roll.

"Choo Choo Ch' Boogie" consists of a series of verses in twelve-bar blues form, alternated with an eight-bar chorus, a structure that combines elements of African American music and Tin Pan Alley song. (We have encountered this compositional strategy before, in W. C. Handy's song "St. Louis Blues"; see Chapter 5.) The song's lyric describes a situation that would have been familiar to many Americans, particularly to ex-GIs returning to the United States during the postwar economic downturn of 1946, when jobs were temporarily scarce and the future seemed uncertain. The song brings back a character from the Great Depression era: the poor but honest hobo, hopping freight trains and traveling from city to city in search of work. The protagonist arrives home, weary of riding in the back of an army truck, and heads for

the railroad station. His initial optimism is tempered as he searches the employment notices in the newspaper and realizes that he does not have the technical skills for the few positions that are open. (The history of encoded lyrics in African American popular music—discussed in Chapter 5 in connection with the country blues—suggests that African American listeners may have interpreted the line "the only job that's open needs a man with a knack" as a comment on the employment practices of the many businesses that favored white over Black veterans.) Despite his misfortune, however, our hero remains cheerful, and the lyric ends with an idyllic description of life in a shack by the railroad track.

The arrangement—devised by Gabler and Jordan—opens with a twelve-bar instrumental introduction in which the horns (a trumpet and two saxophones) imitate the sound of a train whistle, while the rhythm section (piano, bass, and drums) establishes a medium-tempo boogie-woogie rhythm. (This infectious four-beat dance rhythm, common in Jordan's recordings, is sometimes called a "shuffle.") The rest of the arrangement follows a clear blueprint, alternating the song's two basic building blocks, twelve-bar verse and eight-bar chorus. After the introduction the form should be easy to follow: first a verse, sung by Jordan and backed by riffs in the horn section; then a chorus, also sung by Jordan; followed by a twelve-bar boogie-woogie piano solo. The whole structure is then repeated (with a twenty-bar saxophone solo instead of a piano solo). The record concludes with a ten-bar instrumental tag, comprising an eight-bar chorus and an extra two bars at the very end.

LISTENING GUIDE	"CHOO CHOO CH' BOOGIE"		
TIME	**FORM**	**LYRIC**	**DESCRIPTIVE COMMENTS**
	Instrumental introduction		Twelve-bar blues; during the first four bars, the horns imitate the sound of a train whistle
0:17	Verse 1	*Headin' for the station . . .*	Twelve-bar blues
0:34	Chorus (8 measures)	*Choo choo, choo choo, ch' boogie . . .*	

TIME	FORM	LYRIC	DESCRIPTIVE COMMENTS
0:45	Piano solo		Twelve-bar blues
1:02	Verse 2	*You reach your destination . . .*	Twelve-bar blues
1:19	Chorus (8 measures)		Same chorus as before
1:30	Saxophone solo (20 measures)		Twelve-bar blues followed by an eight-bar chorus
1:58	Verse 3	*Gonna settle down . . .*	Twelve-bar blues
2:14	Chorus (8 measures)		
2:26	Instrumental tag (10 measures)		Tag includes a brief vocal interjection

> Due to the Louis Jordan band's popularity with both white and colored audiences, promoters in larger cities are booking the quintet for two evenings, one to play a white dance and the other a colored dance. (Chilton 1994, 107)

As R&B artists like Jordan began to attract a more diverse audience, the separation between white and Black fans was maintained in various ways. Sometimes white R&B fans sat in the balcony of a segregated theater or dance hall, watching the Black dancers below in order to pick up the latest steps. At other times a rope was stretched across the middle of the dance floor to "maintain order." Then, as at other times, the circulation of popular music across racial boundaries did not necessarily signify an amelioration of racism in everyday life.

BLUES CROONERS

If jump bands represented the hot end of the R&B spectrum, the cool end was dominated by a blend of blues and pop singing that was sometimes called the blues crooner style. The roots of this urbane approach to the blues reached back to a series of race recordings made in the late 1920s and 1930s by pianist **Leroy Carr** (1905–1935) and guitarist **Scrapper Blackwell** (1903–1962). Carr, born in Indianapolis, Indiana, developed a smooth, laid-back approach to blues singing that contrasted sharply with the rough-edged rural blues recordings of Charley Patton and Blind Lemon Jefferson, and he attracted a national Black audience. The late 1930s jazz recordings of the King Cole Trio, with its instrumentation of piano, bass, and guitar, were a more immediate influence on postwar blues crooners, although Cole's later recordings took him well into the pop mainstream.

In 1944 a Black GI from Nashville, Tennessee, named *Cecil Gant* (1913–1951) walked up to the stage at a war bond rally in Los Angeles and asked if he could play a few songs on the piano. The crowd loved him, and Private Gant, the "G.I. Sing-sation," was soon signed by a new independent record label called Gilt-Edge. Later that year Gant recorded a love song called "I Wonder," sung in a gentle, slightly nasal, bluesy style and accompanied only by his own piano playing. "I Wonder" reached the Number 1 position on *Billboard*'s "Harlem Hit Parade" and also attracted attention from some white listeners. Unfortunately, Gant was never able to repeat the success of his first hit, although he made dozens of recordings for various independent record labels.

The most successful blues crooner of the late 1940s and early 1950s was a soft-spoken, Texas-born pianist and singer named *Charles Brown* (1922–1999). Brown, who had studied classical piano as a child, graduated from college in 1942 at the age of twenty. He moved to Los Angeles in 1943 and joined Johnny Moore's Three Blazers, a small combo that played pop songs for all-white parties in Hollywood and a more blues-oriented repertoire in the Black nightclubs along LA's Central Avenue. His smooth, sensitive, somewhat forlorn vocal style (sometimes called "cocktail blues") attracted attention, and he began to develop a national reputation with the release of "Drifting Blues," one of the top-selling R&B records of 1945 and 1946. In 1948 Brown left to form his own quartet and had a Number 1 R&B hit the following year with "Trouble Blues."

Over the next three years he recorded ten Top 10 hits for Aladdin Records—one of the dozens of independent labels popping up in Los Angeles at the time—and became one of the most popular R&B singers nationwide. A handsome, dapper, gracious man, Brown projected an image of ease and sophistication. His repertoire—which included blues, pop songs, and semiclassical numbers such as the *Warsaw Concerto*—suggested a man in touch with his roots but not constrained by them. Brown was never able to break through to the pop charts—Columbia Records offered him a solo contract in 1947, but he turned it down out of loyalty to his bandmates. But he was rediscovered by a new generation of R&B fans in the 1980s and went on to develop a successful international touring career, culminating in a Grammy nomination.

ELECTRIC BLUES

A very different urban blues tradition of the postwar era, **Chicago electric blues** was derived more directly from the Mississippi Delta tradition of Charley Patton and Robert Johnson. Chicago was the terminus of the Illinois Central railroad line, which ran up through the Midwest from the Mississippi Delta. Although Chicago's Black neighborhoods were well established before World War II, they grew particularly rapidly during the 1940s as millions of rural migrants came north in search of employment in the city's industrial plants, railroad shops, and slaughterhouses. The South Side's nightclubs were the center of a lively Black music scene that rivaled New York's

Listening Guide "BLACK NIGHT"

Written by Jessie Robinson; performed by Charles Brown and His Band; released 1951

"Black Night," one of Charles Brown's most successful recordings, held the Number 1 position on the R&B charts for fourteen weeks in 1951. The fact that "Black Night" did not show up on the pop charts can in part be attributed to the record's dark mood, slow tempo, and somber lyrics.

In formal terms, "Black Night" is a twelve-bar blues, although the very slow tempo can make it hard to hear the overall structure of the song at first. It also exemplifies the continuing importance of the blues in Black popular music, not only as a musical form, but also an emotional state and a perspective on the world. This is a truly haunting recording, with Brown's subdued voice accompanied only by the sparse textures, blue notes, and dirge-like tempo of the rhythm section and the mournful tenor saxophone of Maxwell Davis. The lyric conveys a deep anxiety about the future and a fear of loneliness evoked by the coming of night. Advertisements for the record in Black newspapers and magazines typically suggested that the record would make listeners forget their own troubles, but this song also spoke volumes to a people weary of deferred promises. After 1952 Brown's blues ballad style became less popular as the urban Black audience's taste shifted toward more hard-edged singers, perhaps reflecting the growth of active resistance to racial segregation.

Harlem and LA's Central Avenue. The musical taste of Black Chicagoans, many of whom were recent migrants from the Deep South, tended toward rougher, grittier styles that were closely linked to African American folk traditions but also reflective of their new urban orientation.

Chicago electric blues was a response to these demands. It could be argued that the rural blues tradition had almost completely died out as a commercial phenomenon by the time of World War II as the urbanizing Black audience sought out more cosmopolitan forms of entertainment. From this point of view, the mid-1930s recordings of Robert Johnson (see Chapter 5) represent the final flowering of the Delta blues. (Unlike white Southerners, who tended to regard older forms of music with nostalgia, Blacks had every reason to want to forget their rural past.)

However, the old Delta blues style didn't really die out; rather, it emerged in a reinvigorated, electronically amplified form. The career of **Muddy Waters (McKinley Morganfield)** (1915–1983) exemplifies these developments. Waters was "discovered" in the Mississippi Delta by the folk music scholars John Work and Alan Lomax, who recorded him in 1941 for the Library of Congress. (Waters apparently had some difficulty in getting copies of these recordings, but when he did they were played on jukeboxes in the Delta and became regional hits.) In 1943 he moved to Chicago and found work in a paper mill, while continuing to perform as a musician at nightclubs and parties. In response to the noisy crowds and the demand for dance music, Waters switched from the acoustic to the electric guitar in 1944 and eventually

Listening Guide "HOOCHIE COOCHIE MAN"

Written by Willie Dixon; performed by Muddy Waters; released 1954

"Hoochie Coochie Man," composed by *Willie Dixon* (1915–1992), Chess Records' house songwriter, bass player, producer, and arranger, is perhaps the best example of the latter theme. The song was Waters's biggest hit for Chess Records, reaching Number 3 on the R&B charts in 1954. (Although none of Waters's recordings crossed over to the pop charts, his music later played an important role in inspiring rock musicians such as the Rolling Stones—who adopted their name from one of his songs—and Eric Clapton.)

This recording typifies Chicago urban blues, with its loud volume and dense textures; buzzing, growling tone colors; and insistent beat. "Hoochie Coochie Man" is also an example of a common variation on the blues form, a sixteen-bar blues. The first eight bars of the song feature the stop-time technique, in which the beat is suspended in order to focus attention on the singer's voice. (In essence, this is equivalent to the first four bars of a twelve-bar blues, made twice as long by the application of the stop-time technique.) Then the regular pulse is re-established, and the last eight bars are played. Because the lyric of the stop time section changes each time (like a verse) and the words in the second eight-bar section are repeated (like a chorus),

the song combines the blues form with a strophic verse-chorus structure.

The lyric of "Hoochie Coochie Man" is essentially an extended boast, related to the African American tradition of "toasts," fantastic narratives that emphasize the performer's personal power, sexual prowess, and ability to outwit authority. The song draws a direct link between the personal power of the singer (quintessentially expressed through sex) and the Southern folk tradition of mojo, a system of magical charms and medicines such as the Black cat bone and John the Conquerer root. This image of supernatural power applied in the service of personal goals was ultimately derived from the cultures of West Africa, and it tapped a common reservoir of experience among Waters's listeners, many of whom were not many years removed from the folk culture of the rural South. In essence, the lyric of "Hoochie Coochie Man" is an argument for the continuing relevance of deep traditional knowledge in the new urban setting, and it is easy to see why this would have been an attractive message for recent urban migrants. "Hoochie Coochie Man" can also be heard as a direct ancestor of contemporary "gangsta rap" recordings, which project a similar outlaw image in response to the challenging conditions of urban life.

LISTENING GUIDE | "HOOCHIE COOCHIE MAN"

TIME	LYRIC	DESCRIPTIVE COMMENTS
0:00	Brief introduction	Stop-time figure played by instrumentals
0:08	Verse	*"The gypsy woman told my mother . . ."* Vocal accompanied by same stop-time figure
0:35	Chorus	*"But you know I'm here . . ."* Accompaniment takes regular rhythm
1:01	Verse	*"I got a black cat bone . . ."*
1:27	Chorus	
1:54	Verse	*"On the seven hours . . ."*
2:22	Chorus	Piano becomes more prominent, playing a rhythmic chord figure, to accompany final chorus

expanded his group to include a second electric guitar, piano, bass, amplified harmonica ("blues harp"), and drum set. During the late 1940s and early 1950s he was the most popular blues musician in Chicago, with a sizeable following among Black listeners nationwide.

Waters's approach to the blues is different from that of blues crooners like Charles Brown and represents direct continuities with the tradition of Charley Patton and Robert Johnson. Like many of the great Mississippi guitarists, Waters was a master of bottleneck slide guitar technique. He used his guitar to create a rock-steady, churning rhythm, interspersed with blues licks, which were counterpoised with his voice in a musical conversation. The electric guitar, which could be used to create dense, buzzing tone colors (by using **distortion**) and long sustained notes that sounded like screaming or crying (by employing **feedback**), was the perfect tool for extending the Mississippi blues guitar tradition. Waters's singing style—rough, growling, moaning, and intensely emotional—was also rooted in the Delta blues. Furthermore, the songs he sang were based on themes long central to that tradition: on the one hand, loneliness, frustration, and misfortune ("I Feel Like Going Home" and "Still a Fool"); on the other, independence and sexual braggadocio ("Just Make Love to Me" and "Mannish Boy").

Vocal Harmony Groups

Another important thread in the tapestry of postwar rhythm & blues was **vocal harmony groups**. (Although this tradition is today sometimes called "doo-wop," the earliest performers did not use this term.) In previous chapters we have come across variants of the African American vocal harmony tradition, both sacred (the Golden Gate Quartet) and secular (the Mills Brothers). During the postwar era this tradition moved into the R&B market as young singers trained in the Black church began to record secular material. Many of these vocal groups were made up of high school kids from the Black neighborhoods of cities such as New York and Washington, DC, and interviews with the singers indicate that these groups served a number of functions: a means of musical expression, an alternative or adjunct to urban gangs, and a route to popularity. Few members of these groups initially saw singing as a way to make a living; this perception changed rapidly after the first vocal R&B groups achieved commercial success.

The vocal harmony group most responsible for moving away from the pop-oriented sound of the Mills Brothers and creating a new, harder-edged sound that was more closely linked to Black gospel music was the Dominoes, led by vocal coach Billy Ward, a strict disciplinarian and savvy entrepreneur. In 1950 Ward started rehearsing with a number of his most promising students and a seventeen-year-old tenor singer named *Clyde McPhatter* (1932–1972), whom he hired away from a gospel group. The Dominoes' first big hit was "Sixty Minute Man," recorded in New York City and released by the independent label Federal Records in 1951. A large part of the song's popularity was due to its lyric, which catalogued the singer's lovemaking technique in some detail, from "kissin'" to "teasin'" to "pleasin'" and finally to "blowin' my top." The combination of a naughty lyric, rocking dance rhythm, and bass lead vocal caught the attention of the R&B audience, and "Sixty Minute Man" monopolized the Number 1 spot on the R&B charts for fourteen weeks during the summer of 1951. It was also one of the first vocal group R&B records to cross over to the pop charts, where it reached the Number 17 position—doubtless without the assistance of AM pop radio.

But it was the Dominoes' next big hit, "Have Mercy Baby," that pushed vocal group R&B firmly in the direction of a harder-edged, more explicitly emotional sound. Recorded in Cincinnati, Ohio, and released by Federal Records in 1952, "Have Mercy Baby" was the first record to combine the twelve-bar blues form and the driving beat of dance-oriented rhythm & blues with the intensely emotional flavor of Black gospel singing. The song's commercial success (Number 1 R&B for ten weeks in 1952) was in large part due to the passionate performance of the Dominoes' lead tenor, Clyde McPhatter, the former gospel singer from North Carolina. McPhatter, the son of a Baptist preacher and a church organist, was like many other R&B musicians insofar as the Black church played a major role in shaping his musical sensibility. While in formal terms "Have Mercy Baby" is a twelve-bar blues, it is essentially a gospel performance dressed up in R&B clothing. With a few changes in the lyrics—perhaps substituting the word "Lord" for "baby"—McPhatter's performance would have been perfectly at home in a Black Baptist church anywhere in America. The sheer intensity of McPhatter's plea for redemption—you can actually hear him weeping during the fadeout ending—spoke directly to the core audience for R&B, many of whom had grown up within the African American gospel music tradition.

To be sure, this mixing of church music with popular music was controversial in some quarters, and McPhatter and later gospel-based R&B singers faced occasional opposition from some church leaders. But in retrospect the postwar confluence of the sacred and secular aspects of Black music, as well as its commercial exploitation by the music business, seem almost inevitable. Although it did not appear on the pop music charts, "Have Mercy Baby" attracted an audience among many white teenagers, who were drawn by its rocking beat and emotional directness. In addition, the Dominoes were featured on some of the earliest rock 'n' roll tours, which typically attracted a racially mixed audience. Although McPhatter soon left the Dominoes to form a new group called the Drifters, the impact of his rendition of "Have Mercy Baby" was profound and lasting—the record is a direct predecessor of the soul music movement of the 1960s and the recordings of Ray Charles, James Brown, and Aretha Franklin.

BOX 7.2 **SISTER ROSETTA THARPE, 1915–1973**

Sister Rosetta Tharpe merits a prominent place in any discussion of African American music during the mid-twentieth century. Exactly *where* that place should be located is an altogether more complicated matter. Raised in the church, and starting her performing and recording career as a gospel artist in the late 1930s, Tharpe quickly gained recognition as a songwriter and as a powerful performer of her own, as well as traditional, sacred songs. Gifted with an exuberant, extroverted vocal style that set her apart as a female gospel performer, she also was a remarkable virtuoso on the guitar (acoustic and also, eventually, electric), with which she accompanied her singing. Not merely an unconventional artist within the gospel field, she quickly proved herself unclassifiable—equally at ease fronting a big band in a number like "I Want a Tall Skinny Papa" as she was singing and playing solo her own soon-to-be classic religious songs like "This Train." Boundary-crossing and defying easy categorization, Tharpe was unsurprisingly a controversial figure during her lifetime. But the many recordings she left are indisputably those of an innovative and major artist.

A representative example of Tharpe's stylistic versatility and diversity is her 1945 recording of "Strange Things Happening Every Day," which became an anomalous Number 2 hit on the "race records" charts of that year. The idea of a traditional song with obviously religious import sharing chart space with the aggressively secular records that dominated the rhythm & blues market of that time might seem a "strange thing" indeed!—that is, until one actually listens to Tharpe's arrangement on this recording. "Strange Things Happening Every Day" would have been as welcome on a dance floor as any contemporary jump blues by Louis Jordan. All of its stylistic hallmarks—Tharpe's powerful belting, shouting vocal; her call-and-response with the band

members on the song's chorus; the fast-moving, boogie-woogie flavored beat of the accompanying Sam Price Trio (piano, bass, and drums)—fit in comfortably with the most popular Black music of the period. From the instrumental introduction on throughout the record, Tharpe's outstanding guitar performance is at center stage right along with her.

Her playing, which alternates strong, rapid melodic plucking with forceful chording, has obvious antecedents in the style of country blues artists from the 1920s and 1930s, but it just as clearly anticipates the rock 'n' roll style of a performer like Chuck Berry. (In fact, Tharpe was a major influence on early rockers, Black and white, and she made a big impact later on the "British Invasion" musicians of the early 1960s.) The unusual and potent mixture of influences heard on "Strange Things Happening Every Day" also informs the other side of this record, "Two Little Fishes and Five Loaves of Bread," in which a Biblical story is recounted via a minor-key version of the twelve-bar blues. The close kinship between Tharpe's sacred material and the secular music of her time was demonstrated by the ease with which "This Train," a song closely associated with her, was adapted by songwriter Willie Dixon and performer Little Walter to become the huge rhythm & blues hit "My Babe."

Perhaps it was the unclassifiable nature of Sister Rosetta Tharpe's achievement that led to her eclipse from popular consciousness for a long period following her death. Significant reissues of her recordings in recent decades have, however, rekindled enthusiasm. A new musical about Tharpe's life and work, *Shout, Sister, Shout!*, has played to acclaim at regional theaters. Taking its name from another song closely linked to Tharpe, the show has served to revive further interest in this important and pioneering figure.

R&B Women: Ruth Brown and Big Mama Thornton

Like many other genres of popular music, rhythm & blues played an important role as a stylized medium for enacting sexual politics. This form of expression was particularly important during the postwar period as Black families came under the disintegrating pressures of social change and individuals sought to cope with the sometimes alienating

"Miss Rhythm," Ruth Brown, c. mid-1950s.

experience of urban life. We have already seen several portrayals of male identity in R&B, including Charles Brown's dejected lover and Muddy Waters's magically charged mojo man. Here we want to briefly examine images of male-female relationships in the work of two influential female R&B singers, Ruth Brown and Willie Mae "Big Mama" Thornton.

Ruth Brown (1928–2006), also known as "Miss Rhythm," was born in Virginia. As a child she participated in two streams of the Black church tradition: the AME (African Methodist Episcopal) denomination and the Baptist denomination. In musical terms, the Methodist services she attended were relatively restrained, relying on the accompaniment of a piano and a big church organ, whereas the Baptist ceremonies, held in a rough-hewn country church, were often ecstatically emotional and featured only hand-clapping and tambourine as accompaniment. Both of these streams can be detected in Brown's later work, which ranged from crooner-style ballads to jump band blues songs.

Although her parents initially resisted the idea of her singing outside the church, Brown began her professional career at the age of sixteen and in 1949 signed with the new independent label Atlantic Records. Chart figures suggest that Ruth Brown was the most popular Black female vocalist in America between 1951 and 1954. It is said that she almost single-handedly kept Atlantic Records alive during its precarious early years, so much so that the label was nicknamed "The House that Ruth Built."

The song with which Ruth Brown was most closely associated was "Mama, He Treats Your Daughter Mean," which held the Number 1 position on the R&B charts for five weeks in 1953 and reached as high as Number 23 on the pop charts. Brown, the daughter of a respectable, churchgoing family, did not feel comfortable with the song at first:

> That tune, I didn't want to do. I thought, when I first heard it, "That's the silliest mess I have ever heard." At that time, I wasn't having too much of a problem [with men], so I felt like, "What is she talking about, Mama he treats your daughter mean. . . . Mama, the man is lazy, almost drives me crazy." I wasn't dealing with that kind of a lifestyle, so it didn't make sense to me. (Deffaa 1996, 35)

According to Brown, the song was recorded quickly, without much rehearsal, and its crossover success on the R&B and pop charts was a surprise. The form of "Mama, He Treats Your Daughter Mean" is another example of the blending of blues and Tin Pan Alley–derived forms. The song's A section is a sixteen-bar blues. (Unlike Willie Dixon's "Hoochie Coochie Man," the twelve-bar form here is expanded by adding four extra bars in the middle of the song; rather than the a-a-b text form typical of twelve-bar blues, the lyric follows an a-a-a-b pattern.) The B section is also sixteen bars in length. The band plays the song at a medium tempo, with the horns (saxophones and trumpets) riffing behind the singer.

Listening Guide "MAMA, HE TREATS YOUR DAUGHTER MEAN"

Written by Johnny Wallace, Herbert J. Lance, and Charles Singleton; performed by Ruth Brown; released 1953

LISTENING GUIDE | "MAMA, HE TREATS YOUR DAUGHTER MEAN"

TIME	FORM	LYRIC	DESCRIPTIVE COMMENTS
0:00	Introduction		Unaccompanied tambourine, followed by riffing harmonized saxes and strummed electric guitar.
0:12	A	*Mama, he treats your daughter mean...*	This section (A) is a 16-bar blues consisting of 4 phrases: the first phrase (*Mama...*) is sung three times, and the last phrase (*He's the meanest...*) is a response, with contrasting melody and lyrics.
0:41	B	*Mama, he treats me badly...*	
1:14	A	*Mama, he treats...*	Trumpets and saxophones begin playing harmonized responses to each vocal line.
1:45	B	*Mama, this man is lazy...*	
2:16	A	*Mama, he treats...*	
2:45	End riff		

Key characteristics of Brown's vocal style are evident on this record, including a warm, somewhat husky tone; a strong rhythmic feeling; and the little upward squeals she places at the end of words such as "mama," "man," and "understand." This style fits the somewhat complaining tone of the song, in which a young woman turns to her mother for help in dealing with a good-for-nothing lover. (It is worth noting here that Brown's next hit record, "Wild, Wild Young Men," presents a much more energetic and empowered female protagonist.) One of the most memorable features of the recording—one that can be seen as a link to the church music of Brown's youth—is the solo tambourine, which starts the record and continues throughout.

Brown was paid less than seventy dollars for recording her biggest hit, in addition to a promised royalty of 5 percent of sales. As was often the case in the R&B business, she received few of her royalties, since the cost of studio time, hiring musicians, and songwriters' royalties were charged to her account. One of the biggest stars of the postwar era, Brown ended up leaving the music business entirely for a decade and working as a domestic servant in order to raise her children. She was rediscovered in the 1970s and worked to publicize the plight of older rhythm & blues artists who had been denied their share of profits by record companies. This led to the founding of the Rhythm & Blues Foundation, which was established to provide support for older artists who are in need. In the 1980s she appeared in the Broadway show *Black and Blue* and won a Tony Award in 1989.

"Big Mama" Thornton (1926–1984), born in Montgomery, Alabama, was the daughter of a Baptist minister. She began her professional career as a singer, drummer, harmonica player, and comic on the Black vaudeville circuit and later settled in Houston, Texas, working as a singer in Black nightclubs. Her imposing physique and occasionally malevolent personality helped to ensure her survival in the rough-and-tumble world of con artists and gangsters. One producer and songwriter who worked with Big Mama described her in vivid terms (in the liner notes to the 1992 MCA release *Big Mama Thornton: Hound Dog/The Peacock Recordings*):

> In rehearsal she'd fool around, pick up one of those old microphones with a heavy, steel base with one hand and turn it upside down with the base in the air and sing like that. She was a powerful, powerful woman. She had a few scars, looked like knife scars on her face, and she had a very beautiful smile. But most of the time she looked pretty salty.

In the early 1950s Thornton arrived in Los Angeles and began working with Johnny Otis (Veliotes), a Greek American drummer, promoter, bandleader, and nightclub owner who lived in the Black community and was a major force in the R&B scene. Looking for material for Big Mama to record, Otis decided to consult two white college kids who had been pestering him to use some of the songs they had written. After hearing Thornton's powerful singing, Jerry Leiber and Mike Stoller ran home and composed a song that they felt suited her style: "Hound Dog." The combination of Leiber and Stoller's humorous, country-tinged lyric, Johnny Otis's drumming, and Thornton's powerful, raspy singing produced one of the top-selling R&B records of 1953, which stayed at Number 1 for seven weeks. ("Hound Dog" was the first hit written and produced by the team of Leiber and Stoller, who were to become a major force in early rock 'n' roll music; see Chapter 8.)

Of course, most people today know "Hound Dog" through Elvis Presley's version of the song, recorded by RCA Victor in 1956. If you are familiar only with Presley's version, then the original recording may come as something of a revelation. From the very first phrase ("You . . . ain't . . . *nothin'* . . . but a houn' dog . . ."), sung initially unaccompanied, Thornton lays claim to both the song and our attention. Her deep, raspy, commanding voice, reprimanding a ne'er-do-well lover, projects a stark image of female power rarely—if ever—expressed in popular music of the 1950s. The bluntness of the lyric is reinforced by the musical accompaniment, which includes a bluesy Delta-style electric guitar, a simple drum part played mainly on the tom-toms, and hand-clapping on beats 2 and 4. The tempo is relaxed, and the performance is energetic but loose. The basic form of the song is a twelve-bar blues, but the band adds a few extra beats here and there in response to Thornton's phrasing, another feature that links this urban recording to the country blues. The guitar solo in the middle of the record combines blues licks with figures that anticipate the budding rock style; Mama playfully urges on the guitarist with shouted asides. The final touch, in which the all-male band howls and barks in response to Big Mama's commands, reinforces not only the humor of the record but also its feeling of informality, giving you the sense that these are not distant pop stars but people you could get to know and maybe even party with.

Although both records are intended to create a humorous effect, the defiant attitude of "Hound Dog" makes an interesting comparison with the complaining tone of "Mama, He Treats Your Daughter Mean," a quality that Ruth Brown herself apparently did not find particularly appealing. Both songs were composed by men and sung by women, and both implicitly rely on the "offstage" presence of a male persona, a lazy, deceitful jerk. But the similarities between the two songs and performances end there. "Hound Dog" was designed specifically to fit Thornton's strong, rough-hewn persona. "Mama," written by professional tunesmiths with no particular singer in mind, presents the image of a female narrator unable to deal with the male problem in her life. One woman expresses her frustration with cute little squeals; the other growls her anger. One gossips; the other threatens to inflict physical harm. One—we might imagine—is a somewhat spoiled middle-class teenager; the other is an older woman from a working-class background. Of course, these are stylized images, exaggerated for dramatic effect, but it is their very exaggeration that allows them to convey popular conceptions of sexuality and gender identity in a particular place and time.

BOX 7.3 THE PRINCE OF WAILS: JOHNNIE RAY

In the early 1950s the former big band crooners were joined by a younger generation of pop singers. As the record industry began to explicitly target the newly affluent teenage audience, these young singers were cultivated by the record companies, who created their public images and promoted their recordings on radio and television. Of all the new singers who rose to popularity during this period, the most memorable (and in some ways the most interesting) was *Johnnie Ray* (1927–1990). Partially deaf since childhood—the result of an accident suffered during a Boy Scout expedition—Ray nevertheless became one of the biggest international pop stars of the early 1950s. Crowned the "Prince of Wails" and parodied as the "Guy with the Rubber Face and the Squirt Gun Eyes," Ray created an idiosyncratic style based partly on African American modes of performance and in so doing paved the way for the rock 'n' roll stars of the later 1950s.

During the late 1940s Johnnie Ray spent several years performing in nightclubs in Detroit, where he worked alongside Black rhythm & blues performers, and was eventually discovered by and signed to Okeh Records (the former race and hillbilly label, revived after the war by Columbia Records). During this period he developed a highly emotional performance style that involved sighing, sobbing, and stretching each syllable of a song out over as

Johnnie Ray, "The Prince of Wails," in full flight, c. 1955.

(continued)

BOX 7.3 **THE PRINCE OF WAILS: JOHNNIE RAY** (*continued*)

many melodic notes as possible (a practice called **melisma**, common in African American singing traditions). He was the first white pop performer to remove his microphone from the stand and go down into the audience, seeking direct contact. His stage act was dynamic: Ray writhed, wept, and fell to his knees. In 1952 *Billboard* described one of Ray's concerts as "a masterful display of showmanship that evoked a mass hysteria resembling a Holy Roller meeting. It was hard to say who screamed more—Ray or the customers."

Many older musicians and fans detested "Cry" (1951), Johnnie Ray's biggest hit, with a passion. (Television comedians of the early 1950s loved to lampoon Ray's tendency to burst into tears while performing, and Frank Sinatra apparently used his name as an expletive.) But Johnnie Ray's melodramatic, over-the-top approach appealed to the expanding white teenage audience for popular music. Interestingly, his records apparently also sold well in Black communities. "Cry" reached Number 1 on both the pop and the rhythm & blues hit parades, meaning that Ray was the only white performer to reach the top of the Black charts between 1946 and 1956, when Elvis Presley's "Hound Dog" performed the same feat. In this sense, Johnnie Ray was a crucial link between the crooners of the postwar era and the rock 'n' roll stars of the later 1950s.

Country and Western Music

Country and western, the industry's new name for what used to be called hillbilly music, mushroomed in popularity after World War II. Although the South remained a lucrative area for touring performers, the wartime migration of millions of white Southerners meant that huge and enthusiastic audiences for country and western music had also been established in the cities and towns of Pennsylvania, Ohio, Michigan, and California. The postwar era saw the rapid spread of country music programming on the radio, and by 1949 over 650 radio stations were making live broadcasts of country performers. The continuing success of WSM's *Grand Ole Opry*, broadcast from Nashville, inspired a new generation of country music shows, including Shreveport's *Louisiana Hayride*, Dallas's *Saturday Night Shindig*, Boston's *Hayloft Jamboree*, and Los Angeles's *Hometown Jamboree*. As in the R&B field, dozens of independent record labels specializing in country music sprang up after the war, and Nashville, Tennessee, and Southern California began to assert themselves as centers for the production of country music. In 1950—when Capitol Records became the first major company to set up its country music operation in Nashville—it was estimated that country music accounted for fully one-third of all record sales nationwide.

HANK WILLIAMS AND THE BIRTH OF HONKY-TONK MUSIC

Hank Williams (1923–1953) was the most significant single figure to emerge in country music during the immediate post–World War II period. Williams wrote and sang many songs in the course of his brief career that were enormously popular with country audiences

Listening Guide   BLUEGRASS: BILL MONROE'S "IT'S MIGHTY DARK TO TRAVEL"

Written by Bill Monroe; performed by Bill Monroe and His Blue Grass Boys; recorded 1947

While some musicians sought to move country music onto the mainstream pop charts, others reached back into the musical traditions of the American South, refurbishing old styles to fit new circumstances. Although this "neotraditionalist" impulse took many forms, the most influential was probably the rise of **bluegrass music**, a style rooted in the venerable Southern string band tradition. The pioneer of bluegrass music was *Bill Monroe* (1911–1997), born in Kentucky. Monroe started playing music at a young age and was influenced by his uncle (a country fiddler) and a Black musician and railroad worker named Arnold Schulz, whose influence can be seen in the distinctive bluesy quality of Monroe's music. (As we saw in our discussions of Jimmie Rodgers and Bob Wills, the interaction between white and Black styles has long been an important aspect of country music.) In 1935 Bill formed a duo with his brother Charlie. The Monroe Brothers played throughout the southeastern United States, creating a sensation with

their vocal harmonies and virtuoso fiddle and guitar playing. In 1938 Bill started his own group, the Blue Grass Boys, and the following year joined the cast of the *Grand Ole Opry*.

The Blue Grass Boys' recording of "It's Mighty Dark to Travel," recorded in Nashville in 1947, is a classic example of bluegrass, a blend of Anglo-American string band music; traditional singing of the Appalachian Mountains; and influences from Black music, especially the blues. The instrumentation is typical of bluegrass groups: an acoustic quintet made up of fiddle, mandolin, banjo, guitar, and string bass. Unlike many postwar country bands, the Blue Grass Boys avoided amplified instruments, which added to the traditional feeling of the music.

The first seconds of "It's Mighty Dark to Travel" establish the virtuosity and high energy for which this group—and bluegrass music in general—is well known. The stringed instruments are all assigned well-defined

LISTENING GUIDE | "IT'S MIGHTY DARK TO TRAVEL"

TIME	FORM	LYRIC	DESCRIPTIVE COMMENTS
0:00	Introduction/Main Melody		Monroe's virtuoso mandolin playing featured both lightning fast melodic riffs and multistring chord work
0:13	Chorus	*It's mighty dark . . .*	Listen for Monroe's high tenor accompaniment to lead vocalist Lester Flatt
0:26	Instrumental		Fiddle with band accompaniment
0:39	Verse	*To me, she was a little angel . . .*	Sung by Flatt alone
0:52	Chorus		Listen for Monroe's "chopping" mandolin chords on the offbeat
1:05	Instrumental		Scruggs's three-finger style banjo playing was revolutionary, setting the bluegrass style

(continued)

Listening Guide   BLUEGRASS: BILL MONROE'S "IT'S MIGHTY DARK TO TRAVEL" *(continued)*

TIME	FORM	LYRIC	DESCRIPTIVE COMMENTS
1:18	Verse	*Many a night, we spoke . . .*	
1:30	Chorus		
1:43	Instrumental		Mandolin
1:57	Verse	*Travellin' down this lonesome highway . . .*	
2:09	Chorus		
2:22	Instrumental		Entire band, with fiddle and banjo most prominent
2:35	Chorus		Ends with brief syncopated chord sequence by the band

Singer, songwriter, and mandolin player Bill Monroe was the founder of bluegrass country music.

roles within the ensemble: for example, Bill Monroe's mandolin plays short, "chop-style" chords on the second and fourth beats of each measure, driving the music along; Earl Scruggs's highly syncopated, three-finger technique on the banjo interlocks with the rhythm of the other instruments; and the string bass provides steady support, playing on the first and third beats of each measure. The vocal performance, with Bill Monroe's tenor voice in the lead, is closely related to the "high lonesome" style popularized first by the Carter Family and then by hillbilly duos such as the Blue Sky Boys and the Monroe Brothers. But bluegrass is at its core a music for instrumentalists, featuring sections of flashy solo improvisation ("breakaways") rooted in the tradition of country fiddle contests and reinforced by the influence of Black music such as jazz.

Although bluegrass never really dominated the country charts—Bill Monroe himself was never able to score a Number 1 country hit—its unique blend of traditionalism and innovation has continued to inspire country musicians, and has played a large part in the recent flourishing of a large variety of roots-based music that is often grouped under the umbrella genre title of "Americana."

at the time; between 1947 and 1953 he amassed an astounding thirty-six Top 10 records on the country charts, including such Number 1 hits as "Lovesick Blues," "Cold, Cold Heart," "Jambalaya (on the Bayou)," and "Your Cheatin' Heart." All of these Number 1 hits—along with many other Williams songs—have remained long-term country favorites and are established "standards" of their genre. In addition, his songs were successfully covered by his contemporaries in mainstream pop, demonstrating the wide-ranging appeal of the new country material. "Cold, Cold Heart" helped launch the career of Tony Bennett when the young crooner scored a huge success with it in 1951 (Number 1 pop for six weeks).

Hank Williams reinvigorated for the postwar country audience the enduring myth of the hard-living, hard-loving rambler that had been established a generation earlier by Jimmie Rodgers (see Chapter 5). Although the details of Williams's life seem in retrospect to have custom-designed him for legendary status, it is important to realize that these *were* the actual facts of his life: born into crushing poverty in Alabama, this son of a sharecropper learned to make his way at an early age by performing on the street, learning a great deal from a Black street singer named Rufe "Tee-Tot" Payne. By the time he was sixteen, Williams, now called "the Singing Kid," had his own local radio show; shortly thereafter he formed a band, the Drifting Cowboys, and began touring throughout Alabama. Enormous success came to Williams by the time he was in his mid-twenties, but it did not come without problems. By 1952 he was divorced, had been fired from the *Grand Ole Opry* (for numerous failures to appear), and was seriously dependent on alcohol and painkilling drugs. He died on New Year's Day 1953 at age twenty-nine after suffering a heart attack in the back of his car while en route to a performance.

Williams affirmed the importance of religious traditions in country music by recording some gospel material. However, the fact that he recorded his sacred tunes under a pseudonym, rather than under his own name, ties him more closely to Black secular singers than most white artists. (Then again, his actual choice of pseudonym, "Luke the Drifter," links these records back to the rambler image projected by the bulk of Williams's secular work.)

A brief look at two of the most famous songs written and performed by Hank Williams will demonstrate his debts to country music traditions as well as the progressive elements in his music. "I'm So Lonesome I Could Cry" (1949) is a timeless lament that builds clearly on earlier models in both its words and its music, while "Hey, Good Lookin'" (1951) is an almost startling anticipation of the style that in the later 1950s would come to be called rockabilly.

"I'm So Lonesome I Could Cry" evokes the flavor of "old-timey" country music with its waltzlike triple meter and its straightforward strophic structure. (Its basic mood and musical ambience are somewhat reminiscent of Jimmie Rodgers's touching waltz-lament, "Dreaming with Tears in My Eyes"; see Chapter 5.) The lyrics too refer to traditional country images. The "wide open spaces" are evoked with images of birds, of the moon going behind the clouds, and of the "silence of a falling star" that illuminates the sky, while the presence of the "midnight train . . . winding low" affirms Williams's ties to the spirits of the ramblers who came before him. Against the steady rhythmic

Hank Williams with wife Audrey (to his right) performing on WSM radio.

backdrop of guitars and bass, the sound of the fiddle asserts Williams's kinship with earlier country music. However, the prominent steel guitar throughout helped create a sense of modernity for Williams's audience and assured listeners that the essence of his music would be a feeling of utter immediacy—a song for the here-and-now.

Like much of the finest rurally based music, Black and white, "I'm So Lonesome I Could Cry" is structured to capitalize on the regional characteristics of the singer-songwriter's performance style. The abundance of sustained vowel sounds placed on the downbeats of measures, as in "Hear that lonesome whippoorwill," or "The silence of a falling star," draws out the characteristic twang of Williams's accent and lends a particular expressivity to the actual *sound* of the lyrics that underlines their dark emotional content. Williams's drawl also leads him naturally to delay somewhat the full force of those vowel sounds, so that he seems rhythmically behind the beat. Again, this style beautifully reinforces the mournful essence of the song—as if it is a constant effort for the singer to rise to the high notes on those vowels, a technique that makes the fall in pitch that marks the end of every phrase seem that much more inevitable, and that much sadder. When he approaches the end of the song, the almost-break in Williams's voice as he sings "and as I wonder where you are" is heartbreaking; there seems to be no separation between the singer and the song, or between the sound of his country voice and the meaning of its expression. It's no wonder Williams evoked such a response in the burgeoning country music audience after World War II.

Along with a few of Williams's other records, the jaunty "Hey, Good Lookin'" was actually something of a minor crossover hit (Number 29 pop, Number 1 country for eight weeks in 1951). This popularity should not be surprising, given its danceable character and its pop-friendly thirty-two-bar AABA form borrowed from Tin Pan Alley models. With its prominent steel guitar and fiddle parts, not to mention the character of Williams's vocal, there's still no mistaking the record's basis in country music. What is most arresting here, however, is the specific targeting of a youthful audience. The lyrics address cars, dancing, and young romance, and the use of terms like "hot-rod Ford," "soda pop," "go steady," and "date book" create what would—about five years later—have been called a "teen-friendly" piece of material.

In a sense, "Hey, Good Lookin'" came a little too early, and Hank Williams of course died much too young. Had Williams been able to bring this same song, or something like it, to a savvy record producer in late 1955 or early 1956—a producer aware of the noise being made by the young Elvis Presley or Carl Perkins at the time—that cynical producer might have said something like this: "Hank, you've got something there. Please throw out those fiddles, though—too hillbilly. And replace the steel guitar with a regular electric guitar played R&B-style. Add some R&B-based drumming too, with strong backbeats. I think you'll have a hit rock 'n' roll record." And had Williams been interested, which is questionable, his name might well have been added to the rockabilly roster, perhaps even close to the top of it. As it is, Williams's early death leaves us pondering what might have been—but in any case, a song like "Hey, Good Lookin'" attests to the forward-looking character of his creativity.

Williams's success was part of a major new direction in postwar country and western music, **honky-tonk music**—sometimes called "hard country"—a style that conveyed the sound and ethos of the roadside bar or juke joint. During the Great Depression the oil fields of Texas and Oklahoma provided a lucrative (and rare) source of steady, well-paid work, attracting thousands of men from the American Southwest and farther afield. When Prohibition was repealed in 1933, the formerly illegal drinking establishments that serviced these men multiplied and became a major source of employment for country and western musicians. These honky-tonks, as the people who frequented them called them, provided relief from the daily pressures of work on the oilfields in the form of drinking and dancing. (The practice of going from bar to bar on a Saturday night is still called "honky-tonking.") By the postwar period thousands of these rowdy nightspots were sprinkled across the American Southwest and beyond, ranging from small, dimly lit dives to big, neon-lit roadhouses.

Country and western music, both recorded and performed live, was crucial to the profitability of honky-tonks. Many of them featured colorfully glowing (and loud) juke-boxes. In adjusting to the honky-tonk milieu, country musicians made a number of changes in their performance practices. First, many of the old-time songs about family and the church seemed out of place in the new setting. Musicians began to compose songs about aspects of life directly relevant to their patrons: family instability, the unpredictability of male-female relationships, the attractions and dangers of alcohol, and the importance of enjoying the present. When the rural past was referenced, it was usually through a veil of nostalgia and longing. Honky-tonk vocal styles were often directly emotional, making use of "cracks" in the voice and stylistic features from Black music such as melismas and blue notes.

Like urban blues musicians such as Muddy Waters, country musicians adapted traditional instruments and playing techniques to the rowdy atmosphere of the juke joint.

The typical instrumentation of a honky-tonk band included a fiddle, a steel guitar, a "takeoff" (lead) guitar, a string bass, and a piano. The guitars were electronically amplified, and the musicians played with a percussive, insistent beat (sometimes called "sock rhythm") that was well suited to dancing.

When today's musicians talk about playing "good old country music," they are most often referring to the postwar honky-tonk style rather than to the rural folk music of the South or the hillbilly recordings of the 1920s and 1930s. Honky-tonk stars such as Ernest Tubb, Hank Williams, Lefty Frizzell, Hank Snow, George Jones, and Webb Pierce dominated the country and western charts during the early and mid-1950s. Although their fortunes declined somewhat after the emergence of rock 'n' roll—and especially the appearance of a country-tinged variety of rock 'n' roll called rockabilly (see Chapter 8)—honky-tonk music remains the heart and soul of modern country music.

As you might expect, many of the pioneers of honky-tonk music were born in Texas. *Ernest Tubb* (1914–1984) began his career in the 1930s as a disciple of Jimmie Rodgers. By the 1940s he had developed into one of the first honky-tonk performers, singing in a deep baritone voice roughened by many years of singing in juke joints. Tubb was one of the first musicians to move toward a harder-edged country sound and to switch to amplified instruments, and he wrote some of the classic songs in the honky-tonk genre. His first big hit was "Walking the Floor over You" (released by Decca Records in 1941), which secured him a spot on the cast of the *Grand Ole Opry* and helped him to create a nationwide following. After the war Tubb recorded a series of honky-tonk classics, including "Slipping Around" (Number 1 country, 1949), often cited as the first country song to deal explicitly with marital infidelity.

Hank Thompson (1925–2007), a native of Waco, Texas, created a popular variation on honky-tonk music by mixing it with elements of western swing. Thompson, who began his career as "the Hired Hand," achieved his first success through his appearances on a Dallas radio show called *Cornbread Matinee*. In the late 1940s, after his discharge from military service, he formed a band called the Brazos Valley Boys and began performing in honky-tonks throughout the Southwest. His biggest hit was "The Wild Side of Life," which held the Number 1 position on the country charts for fifteen weeks in 1952. (The recording was made in Hollywood, a reflection of the burgeoning country music business in Southern California.) The song, composed by William Warren and Arlie Carter, was based on Warren's personal experiences with a "honky-tonk angel" who found the "glamour of the gay night-life" too hard to resist. It reflects two major themes of postwar honky-tonk music: the dislocations of urban working-class life and the transience of male-female relationships. The song relates how the "wild" woman could "never make a wife" to the man whom she left to pursue "the wild side of life." The song would inspire controversy in its implicit depiction of an extramarital affair, and, as we shall see, inspired a famous "answer song" (written in response to the original) recorded by Kitty Wells.

The melody of this song might seem familiar—it was adopted from Roy Acuff's prewar hit "Great Speckled Bird," discussed in Chapter 6. The same melody had a long history before Acuff fashioned it into a popular song, and it provides more evidence of the strong historical continuities that underpin country music, even during its periods of greatest change.

Although women were generally not able to adopt the footloose, hard-drinking persona of male stars like Lefty Frizzell and Hank Thompson, this does not mean that female singers were absent from the country charts of the early 1950s. In fact, it was during this period that the first female superstar of country music, *Kitty Wells* (1918–2012), rose to prominence. Born in Nashville, Tennessee, Muriel Dearson married a popular country entertainer named Johnny Wright and began appearing with him on the radio in 1938. (Her stage name was adopted from an old Southern parlor song called "Sweet Kitty Wells.") Like that of most other postwar country stars, her reputation was spread by network radio, particularly a series of appearances on the *Louisiana Hayride* show, which was second in popularity only to the *Grand Ole Opry*. Kitty Wells specialized in songs of love and betrayal, with titles like "Paying for That Back Street Affair" and "Whose Shoulder Will You Cry On," sung in a restrained, high-pitched, plaintive voice closely linked to the traditions of the Appalachian Mountains. While her stage image was that of a sweet, dignified country housewife, Kitty Wells was able to articulate a distinctively female perspective on the themes of honky-tonk music, paving the way for later stars such as Patsy Cline, Loretta Lynn, and Dolly Parton. Her hit records and radio appearances also helped to establish Nashville as a new center of the country music business.

Kitty Wells and fellow performers.

In 1952 Kitty Wells recorded her biggest hit, a pointed response to "The Wild Side of Life" titled "It Wasn't God Who Made Honky-Tonk Angels." (This recording is also representative of a fad then sweeping the country and R&B markets, the "answer" record.) The song was a critique of the male domination of urban beer hall culture, where the unattached "honky-tonk angel" was regarded as both a lure and a threat. This "woman's song" was written by J. D. Miller, a commercially astute male composer. (The two examples of female perspectives in R&B music we examined earlier in this chapter—"Mama, He Treats Your Daughter Mean" and "Hound Dog"—were also written by male songwriters. It was rare at the time for women to succeed as professional songwriters in the fiercely competitive, male-centered popular music industry.) The song's narrator is a betrayed woman whose bitter memories of a formerly happy married life are evoked by hearing Thompson's voice on the jukebox. The chorus gives a tart response to Thompson's critique of the wild honky-tonk angels; the singer scolds that "It wasn't God who made honky-tonk angels," noting that it took "married men [who] think they're still single" to cause "many a good girl to go wrong."

Wells's reserved, soulful style emphasizes the lyric content of the song, the melody and structure of which are modeled precisely on the original (and, in turn, upon "Great Speckled Bird"). "It Wasn't God Who Made Honky-Tonk Angels" was a historic recording, the first by a solo female performer to top the country and western charts. That the means of communication between the two singers is the jukebox, rather than a letter (the main medium for songs of heartbreak in an earlier era), suggests once again the central place of both the jukebox and country music in honky-tonk culture. This music functioned not only as entertainment but also as a repository for memory and emotion; it helped people to make sense of the sometimes-radical changes they were undergoing.

COUNTRY MUSIC GOES MAINSTREAM

As country music's core audience moved north, west, and upward into the urban middle class, the "mainstreaming" of country music continued apace. Pop artists such as Bing Crosby ("Sioux City Sue," Number 3 pop, 1946) and Tony Bennett ("Cold, Cold Heart," Number 1 pop, 1951) had huge chart successes with their adaptations of country material. Since the 1920s the New York–based music industry had underestimated—and often seemed embarrassed by—the popularity of popular styles based in Southern folk music. But by 1950, when a pop-style rendition of the country song "Tennessee Waltz" became the fastest-selling record in twenty-five years, the record company executives had no choice—country music was off the porch and sitting in the living room.

Patti Page (1927–2013), born in Oklahoma, sold more records than any other female singer of the early 1950s. She had success with love songs ("All My Love," Number 1 pop, 1950) and novelty items like "The Doggie in the Window" (Number 1 pop, 1953), but her biggest hit was a recording of "The Tennessee Waltz." Page's version of the song—previously recorded by one of its writers, *Grand Ole Opry* star Pee Wee King—held the Number 1 position on the pop charts for thirteen weeks and eventually went on to sell more than 6 million copies. In some ways this was a recording that pointed back toward the nineteenth century—a sentimental waltz song packed with nostalgic references to the South. However, the popular appeal of this record was also apparently boosted by two technological innovations: the use of multitrack tape recording, which allowed Page to sing a duet with herself, and the fact that this was one of the first songs to be issued as a 45 rpm single. "Tennessee Waltz" helped to make Mercury Records into a major label, spawned a rash of cover versions by other artists, and served notice that a pop-styled approach to country and western music could not only penetrate, but actually dominate, the mainstream.

In some ways, the range of country music styles during the postwar era resembles contemporaneous developments in rhythm & blues. There were country crooners, who specialized in a smooth, pop-oriented style; bluegrass musicians, who focused on the adaptation of traditional Southern music into a package suitable to the times; and honky-tonk musicians, who performed in a hard-edged, electronically amplified style and wrote songs about the trials and tribulations of migrants to the city and the gender roles and male/female relationships during a period of intense social change.

The rise of country crooners was not without precedent—in Chapter 5 we discussed Vernon Dalhart, the light-opera singer who in 1924 scored a big commercial success with his recording of "The Prisoner's Song," a Southern ballad sung in the pop style of the time. However, the stakes had risen considerably by the end of World War II as Southern-born country musicians watched pop stars reap huge profits covering country material. The later rise of "countrypolitan" music seems in retrospect an inevitable outcome of the growth of the country music industry and the mainstreaming of country music.

The most popular country crooner was **Eddy Arnold** (1918–2008), who not only dominated the country charts from 1947 to 1954 but also scored eleven Top 40 hits on the pop charts. Arnold began his career as a country singer on local radio shows in his native Tennessee and joined the cast of the *Grand Ole Opry* in the mid-1940s. In his early recordings, two key elements of his style are already evident: a smooth, warm baritone voice and a propensity for sentimental songs. Eddy Arnold's transformation from country singer ("The Tennessee Plowboy") into country-tinged crooner parallels that of Nat "King" Cole, who moved from jazz toward pop stardom at around the same time. If Cole's breakthrough as a singer of romantic love songs was his 1946 recording of "(I Love You) For Sentimental Reasons" (Number 1 pop, Number 3 R&B), Arnold's turning point came only a year later, with his recording of "Bouquet of Roses," which topped the country charts in 1947 and also crossed over into the pop market. The song itself, composed by Steve Nelson and Bob Hillard, combined the two-beat rhythm of country music with touches of Tin Pan Alley harmony and a sentimental lyric. More than the character of the song itself, however, the crossover success of this record was mainly due to its presentation, positioned midway between country and pop. In particular, Arnold's rich baritone voice had just a hint of rasp, his round pronunciation of vowels was colored with only the lightest touch of Tennessee dialect, and the orchestral accompaniment combined a typical country band of the period—electric guitars, including steel guitar, electric bass, drum set, and piano—with a string orchestra. It is easy to understand why this record provided a bridge between country music and the mainstream pop music audience. Despite his eventual induction into the Country Music Hall of Fame, many tradition-oriented country fans still view Arnold as a sellout, a country singer who turned his back on tradition. (This characterization bears more than a passing resemblance to the criticism of Nat "King" Cole's pop recordings by jazz fans. For his part, Eddy Arnold has always maintained that he listened to all kinds of music and was unaware that music was divided into categories.)

THE DECADE FOLLOWING World War II saw important changes in the popular music business, including the introduction of new technologies such as tape recording, the "covering" of rhythm & blues and country and western songs by mainstream pop artists, and the entertainment industry's increasingly sophisticated application of marketing techniques aimed increasingly at youth. All of these were preconditions for the rise of rock 'n' roll and the rapid transformation of American popular music that took place in the mid-1950s, the subject of our next chapter.

Key Terms

bluegrass music	feedback	payola
Chicago electric blues	honky-tonk music	rhythm & blues (R&B)
country and western	jump blues	Top 40 radio programming
cover version	magnetic tape recording	vocal harmony groups
distortion	melisma	

Key People

"Big Mama" Thornton	Hank Thompson	Patti Page
Bill Monroe	Hank Williams	Pete Seeger
Cecil Gant	Johnnie Ray	Rosemary Clooney
Charles Brown	Kitty Wells	Ruth Brown
Clyde McPhatter	Leroy Carr	Scrapper Blackwell
Damaso Perez Prado	Louis Jordan	Willie Dixon
Eddy Arnold	Milt Gabler	
Ernest Tubb	Muddy Waters (McKinley	
Frank (Francis Albert)	Morganfield)	
Sinatra	Nat "King" Cole	

Review Questions

1. What were the major developments and advancements in recording technologies during the postwar era?
2. How did the large-scale migrations from the rural South affect popular music after World War II?
3. What three significant new R&B styles developed in the postwar era?
4. How did folk music become a presence on the pop charts after World War II?
5. What new country music styles developed in the late 1940s/early 1950s, and who was responsible for popularizing them?
6. How did answer records like "It Wasn't God Who Made Honky Tonk Angels" give a voice to women in country music in the early 1950s?

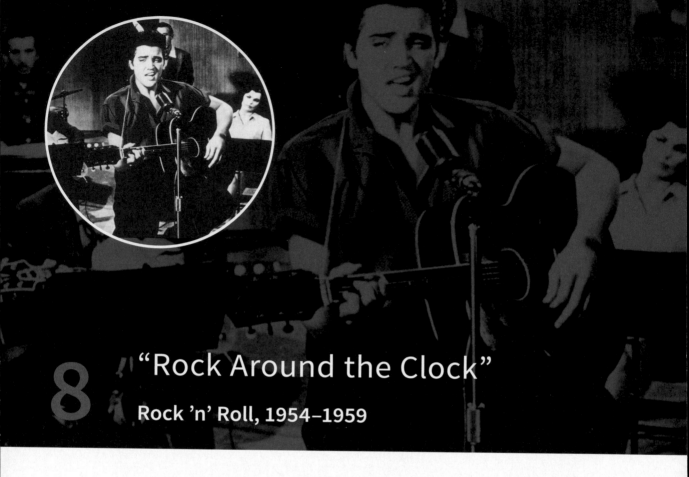

8 "Rock Around the Clock"
Rock 'n' Roll, 1954–1959

THE ADVENT OF ROCK 'N' ROLL IN THE MID-1950s BROUGHT ENORMOUS changes to American popular music, and eventually to world popular music—changes whose impact is still being felt today. Most significantly, styles that previously had remained on the margins of pop music from a marketing standpoint now began to infiltrate and eventually to dominate the center completely. Rhythm & blues and country music recordings were no longer necessarily directed to specialized and regionalized markets; they now began to be heard in significant numbers on mainstream pop radio, and many could be purchased in music stores nationwide that catered to the broadest general public.

The emergence of rock 'n' roll was surely an event of great significance in cultural terms. Because of its importance, we must be careful not to mythologize it or to endorse common misconceptions about it. In particular, the following issues demand our attention: first, rock 'n' roll was neither a "new" style of music, nor any single style of music; second, the era of rock 'n' roll does not mark the first time that music was written specifically to appeal to young people; and third, rock 'n' roll is certainly not the first American music to bring Black and white popular styles into close interaction. In fact, the designation "rock 'n' roll"—like "Tin Pan Alley," "hillbilly music," or "rhythm & blues"—was

Wurlitzer Jukebox,
c. 1950s.

introduced as a commercial and marketing term for the purpose of identifying a new target audience for musical products.

This new audience was dominated by those born into the so-called baby boom generation at the end of and in the years immediately following World War II. It was a much younger audience than had ever before constituted a target market for music, and it was a large audience that shared some specific and important characteristics of group cultural identity. These were kids growing up in the 1950s, a period of relative economic stability and prosperity, but also a period marked by a self-conscious return to "normalcy," as defined in socially and politically conservative ways, following the enormous destabilizing traumas of world war. In terms of the entertainment industry, this was the first generation to grow up with television as a readily available part of its culture;

this powerful new mass medium proved a force of incalculable influence and offered another outlet for the instantaneous nationwide distribution of music.

Yet the 1950s was also a period characterized by its own political and cultural traumas. Cold War tension between the United States and the Soviet Union fed an intense anticommunism in America that resulted in such controversial phenomena as congressional hearings concerning "un-American activities" and the blacklisting of many writers, musicians, and entertainment personalities who had been involved in suspect left-wing groups and actions in the 1930s, 1940s, and 1950s. During these years, children grew up amid fears induced by the introduction of atomic weapons and their further development by the American and Soviet—and eventually other—superpowers. Furthermore, new levels of racial awareness and tension in America emerged in the wake of the 1954 Supreme Court decision in the case of *Brown v. Board of Education*, which mandated the end of racial segregation in public schools.

Perhaps the most important distinguishing characteristic of all for adolescents during the 1950s was simply their identification by the larger culture itself as a unique generational group, even as they were growing up. Thus they quickly developed a sense of self-identification as teenagers (a category that was not necessarily limited to young people between the ages of thirteen and nineteen; many ten-, eleven-, and twelve-year-olds participated fully in "teen" culture). Naturally such a group had to have its own distinctive emblems of identity, including dance steps, fashions, ways of speaking, and music, from a young age. The prosperity of the 1950s gave these young people an unprecedented collective purchasing power, as the allowances of millions of kids went toward leisure and entertainment products geared especially to this generation's tastes and sense of identity. What resulted was an increasingly volatile give-and-take between, on the one hand, products and trends that were prefabricated for teens by the adult commercial culture, and, on the other hand, products and trends chosen and developed unpredictably by the members of the new generation themselves. Rock 'n' roll music was at the center of this give-and-take. It emerged as an unexpected musical choice by increasing numbers of young people in the early to mid-1950s; it then became a mass-market phenomenon exploited by the mainstream music industry in the later 1950s; and eventually it was to some extent reclaimed by these teenagers themselves in the 1960s as they grew old enough to make their own music and, increasingly, to assume some control of the production and marketing of it.

The Birth of Rock 'n' Roll

The term **rock 'n' roll** was probably first used for commercial and generational purposes by disc jockey *Alan Freed* (1922–1965). In the early 1950s Freed discovered that increasing numbers of young white kids were listening to and requesting the rhythm & blues records he played on his *Moondog Show* nighttime program in Cleveland—records he then began to call "rock 'n' roll" records. Freed also promoted concert tours featuring Black artists playing to a young, racially mixed audience as "rock 'n' roll revues." The term "rock 'n' roll" itself was derived from the many references to "rockin'" and "rollin'" (sometimes separately, sometimes together) that may be found in rhythm & blues songs and on race records dating back at least to the late 1920s. Among the relevant recordings that would have been known to Freed and his audience were the late 1940s rhythm & blues hit "Good Rockin' Tonight" (recorded by a number of different artists after first becoming a hit for its composer, Roy Brown) and the huge 1951 hit by the Dominoes mentioned in the previous chapter, "Sixty Minute Man" (which featured the lyric "I rock 'em, roll 'em, all night long, I'm a sixty-minute man"). "Rock" and "roll" are clearly associated in these and other songs with sexual implications, but as with the original associations with the word "jazz," these implications faded as "rock 'n' roll" increasingly came to refer simply to a type of music.

In 1954 Freed moved to station WINS in the larger New York radio market, taking the phrase "rock 'n' roll" with him to identify both the music he played and his target audience. Freed continued to promote African American musicians in the face of considerable resistance from society as a whole to the idea of racial integration. In 1957 a TV show sponsored by Freed was canceled after the Black teenage singer Frankie Lymon was shown dancing with a white girl. In 1958 Freed himself was arrested for anarchy and incitement to riot after a fight broke out at one of his rock 'n' roll concerts in Boston. In the early 1960s Freed was prosecuted for accepting payola—the illegal practice, common throughout the music industry, of paying bribes to radio disc jockeys in order to get certain artists' records played more frequently—while promoters like Dick Clark (who handled mainly white rock 'n' roll artists) escaped relatively unscathed. Freed was blackballed within the music business, and he died a few years later, a broken man.

Whatever his indiscretions, Alan Freed was clearly in the vanguard of an increasing number of disc jockeys, all over the country, who wished to capture the new, large audience of young radio listeners and potential record buyers, and who consequently embraced the term "rock 'n' roll" to refer to virtually any kind of music pitched to that audience. This new category included records that would previously have been marketed purely as rhythm & blues or as country and western, along with an expanding group of hybrid records that drew freely on multiple stylistic influences, including those associated with mainstream Tin Pan Alley–type music. Strange as it now seems, in the early heyday of rock 'n' roll Chuck Berry, Pat Boone, Fats Domino, *Ricky Nelson*, the Everly Brothers, and Elvis Presley were all lumped together as "rock 'n' roll singers"—meaning simply that they all had records being listened to and purchased

Disc Jockey Alan Freed in Cleveland.

by large numbers of teenagers. This was a period of remarkable heterogeneity on radio and the record charts, as all of the previously mentioned singers, along with the likes of Frank Sinatra and Patti Page, could be heard jostling each other on Top 40 radio stations and seen nudging each other on the pop charts. In the marketing confusion that resulted, rock 'n' roll records appeared on different, previously exclusive charts simultaneously; early in 1956, for example, Carl Perkins's "Blue Suede Shoes" and Elvis Presley's "Heartbreak Hotel" both made chart history by climbing to the upper reaches of the country and western, rhythm & blues, and pop charts all at the same time.

The purchase of rock 'n' roll records by kids in the 1950s proved a relatively safe and affordable way for kids to assert generational identity through rebellion against previous adult standards and restrictions of musical style and taste. (The original associations of the term "rock 'n' roll" with marginalized African American musical styles and sexually risqué lyrics obviously didn't hurt the sense of rebellion at all for those familiar with the associations—whether they were the kids themselves, or their parents!) Thus the experience of growing up with rock 'n' roll music became an early and defining characteristic of the baby boom generation. Rock 'n' roll records accompanied the boomers in their progress from preadolescence through their teenage years. It is consequently not surprising that this music increasingly and specifically catered to this age group, which by the late 1950s had developed its own distinctive culture (made possible by abundant leisure time and economic prosperity) with its own associated rituals: school and vacation (represented in rock 'n' roll songs such as "School Days" and "Summertime Blues"), fashions ("Black Denim Trousers and Motorcycle Boots" and "Itsy Bitsy Teenie Weenie Yellow Polka Dot Bikini"), social dancing ("At the Hop" and "Save the Last Dance for Me"), and courtship ("Teen-Age Crush," "Puppy Love," "A Teenager in Love," and "Poor Little Fool"). Some rock 'n' roll songs—for example, "Roll over Beethoven" and "Rock and Roll Is Here to Stay"—self-consciously announced themselves as emblems of a new aesthetic and cultural order, dominated by the tastes and aspirations of youth.

It would not be an exaggeration to say that the 1950s essentially invented the teenager as a commercial and cultural entity and that rock 'n' roll music, along with television and, to some extent, movies, played an essential role in this invention. Although popular music of all eras has reached out to young audiences through plentiful songs about love and courtship, the virtually exclusive emphasis on appealing to one particular, extremely young generation is what most distinguishes the phenomenon of rock 'n' roll from its predecessors. It is thus not surprising that teenagers themselves were recruited, with increasing frequency, as performers to market this music, beginning with the popular group Frankie Lymon and the Teenagers, who scored their first and biggest hit "Why Do Fools Fall in Love?" early in 1956, when lead singer Lymon himself was only thirteen years old, and continuing in the following years with such teenage performers as Paul Anka and Ricky Nelson. (The popularity of Nelson was closely linked to television; he was already well known to audiences as the younger son on *The Adventures of Ozzie and Harriet* show before he started making records.) The association of rock 'n' roll with adolescence and adolescents was so complete that in the 1960s, practitioners of the music who had grown out of their adolescent years and wanted to appeal to a maturing audience of their peers rechristened their music simply *rock*.

For all this appropriate emphasis on the generational culture of rock 'n' roll, we should not ignore that the shift in musical marketing away from primarily racial and regional considerations (and their associated class-related aspects) and toward primarily generational considerations had some unforeseen and extremely significant consequences that profoundly affected the American cultural landscape. There was a period in the later 1950s when much of the same popular music—rock 'n' roll records—was played for dances at primarily Black inner-city public schools, for parties at exclusive white suburban private schools, and for socials in rural settings catering to young people. This was a new kind of situation, especially in the society of the 1950s, which was in most respects polarized in terms of race, class, and region. In the preceding chapters of this book, we have seen how extensive the influences and interactions among supposedly exclusive groups of musicians (Black and white, rural and urban, upper and lower class) have been throughout the history of American popular music. But rock 'n' roll music seemed to offer a bridge connecting supposedly exclusive *audiences*. If you were young in the 1950s, no matter where you lived, no matter what your race or class, rock 'n' roll was *your* music. The important, if ultimately fragile, potential of popular music to create new connections and relationships among audiences in a highly fragmented society was first glimpsed on a large scale in the period of rock 'n' roll.

Cover Versions and Early Rock 'n' Roll

One of the most important precedents for the rise of rock 'n' roll was a commercial and musical phenomenon known as the cover version. In the broadest sense, this term simply refers to the practice of recording a song that has previously been recorded by another artist or group. However, practitioners, merchants, and scholars of popular music have usually used the term in a more restricted sense to refer to a version— sometimes an almost exact copy—of a previously recorded performance that often involves an adaptation of the original's style and sensibility and is usually aimed at cashing in on that original's success. Of course, the process of musical borrowing is no doubt as old as music itself. But this process takes on new significance when the element of financial profit is introduced and when issues of social inequality are involved. In such contexts, the influence of one tradition, style, or performer on another can also be seen as a kind of musical appropriation, and borrowing can become something more akin to stealing.

In Chapters 6 and 7 we noted a number of instances of cover versions, including Benny Goodman's "slicked-up" renditions of arrangements previously recorded by Fletcher Henderson's band and Bing Crosby's and Patti Page's pop versions of country and western songs. The practice of covering often worked in both directions, and country and rhythm & blues musicians sometimes recorded their own stylized renditions of Tin Pan Alley songs that had previously been popularized by pop crooners. However, the most notorious examples—and those most important for understanding the rise of rock 'n' roll in the mid-1950s—involved white performers covering the work of African American recording artists. This relationship was not simply between individual musicians but also between competing institutions, since the underlying motivation for covering a recording typically involved an attempt by the major record companies to capitalize on the musical discoveries of small independent record labels. The practice also represented a new stage in the evolution of white fascination with Black music, a theme that we have followed from the beginning of this book.

To better our understanding of this phenomenon, let's look at specific examples of cover versions. In 1947 a Black singer and pianist named Paula Watson recorded a song called "A Little Bird Told Me" for the independent label Supreme. Watson's version of the song, released in 1948, reached Number 2 on the R&B charts and made an impact on the pop charts, peaking at Number 6. This early crossover hit attracted the attention of Decca Records, which immediately issued a cover version of the song performed by a white singer named Evelyn Knight. Knight's version of the song reached Number 1 on the pop charts, in large part owing to the promotional power of Decca Records and the fact that white performers enjoyed privileged access to radio and television play.

The tiny Supreme label sued Decca Records, claiming that its copyright to the original had been infringed. In this case the crux of the matter was not the song per se—its author, Harvey Brooks, collected composer's royalties from both record companies. Rather, Supreme claimed that Decca had stolen aspects of the original recording, including its arrangement, texture, and vocal style. Although Evelyn Knight had indeed copied Paula Watson's singing precisely—to the degree that it fooled musical experts brought in as witnesses—the judge ultimately decided in favor of the larger company, ruling that musical arrangements were not copyrighted property and therefore did not enjoy legal protection. This decision affirmed the legal principle that the song (published in the form of sheet music) was a copyrightable form of intellectual property but individual interpretations or arrangements of a given song were not. This decision ensured the continuation of an older conception of music's legal status—focused on the written document—in an era when recordings, rather than sheet music, had become the dominant means of transmission. (Today, in the era of digital sampling, these questions continue to loom large in court cases concerning the ownership of popular music. In certain instances, specific aspects of a recorded performance have been deemed protectable by copyright; see Chapter 14.)

The "Little Bird Told Me" decision opened the floodgates for cover versions during the 1950s, for better or for worse. Let's take a closer look at three more examples of cover versions, each of which gives us a different perspective on the complex musical, economic, and social forces that converged to create rock 'n' roll in the mid-1950s.

Perhaps the most famous example of a mid-1950s cover version is the song "Shake, Rattle, and Roll," composed in 1954 by Jesse Stone, a Black producer and talent scout for Atlantic Records. (The song was actually published under the pseudonym Charles Calhoun.) "Shake, Rattle, and Roll" is a twelve-bar blues, with an a-a-b text scheme and a repeated section that functions like a chorus ("Shake, rattle, and roll . . ."). The original recording of the song, released by Atlantic in 1954, is in the jump blues R&B style. It features **Big Joe Turner** (1911–1985), a forty-three-year-old vocalist who had begun his career as a singing bartender in the Depression-era nightclubs of Kansas City and had sung with various big bands during the swing era. Turner was one of Atlantic's early stars, and his recording of "Shake, Rattle, and Roll" not only held the Number 1 position on the R&B charts but also crossed over to the pop charts, where it reached Number 22.

This crossover hit soon caught the attention of executives at Decca Records and of a former country and western bandleader named Bill Haley (see Box 8.1). Later in 1954 **Bill Haley and the Comets** recorded a rendition of "Shake, Rattle, and Roll" that was clearly indebted to Turner's original but also departed from it in significant ways. While the Atlantic recording features a band made up of veteran jazz musicians playing a medium-tempo shuffle rhythm, the Haley recording emphasizes guitars rather than saxophones and has a rhythmic feeling more akin to western swing than jump blues R&B. One of the most obvious differences between the two versions lies in the song's text. The original lyric, as written by Jesse Stone and embellished by Big Joe Turner, is full of fairly obvious sexual references. Presumably because these lyrics would have proved too wild for AM radio and offended many in the predominantly white pop music audience, Haley sang a bowdlerized (censored) version of the song. Stone's racy lyric "Well, you wear those dresses, the sun come shinin' through" becomes "Wearin' those dresses, your hair done up so nice" in Haley's version. Strangely Stone's even more suggestive verse beginning "I'm a one-eyed cat, peepin' in a seafood store" survived, although its final line was changed from "Well I can look at you, tell you ain' no child no more" to the tamer "I can look at you, tell you don't love me no more." That the opening line survived the censor's blade is surprising, since it is a fairly obvious double-entendre for the male and female sexual organs. The person charged with rewriting the lyric may have been a bit too square to catch the sexual reference, a fact that must have delighted those who knew the original version.

The other major difference between Turner's and Haley's versions of "Shake, Rattle, and Roll" is the level of profit generated by the two recordings. In fact, this is not the most egregious example of a white band and major record company reaping profits from a song originally recorded by Black musicians for an independent label, since both versions appeared on the pop charts, and each sold over a million copies. There are crucial differences between the two, however. While Big Joe Turner's version crossed over to the pop chart (and the expanding white teenage audience for Black popular music), reaching Number 22 on the pop charts, the majority of Atlantic's sales were nonetheless focused in the Black community (the song was Number 1 on the R&B charts). Haley's version reached Number 7 on the pop chart but did not appear on the R&B charts at all, indicating that Black audiences preferred Turner's jump band style to the country-tinged style of the Comets. Whereas Haley built on his early hit success, going on to become the first "king" of rock 'n' roll music, Turner was never again able to score a Top 40 pop hit or a Number 1 R&B hit. Atlantic sought to promote the middle-aged blues shouter to the teen audience for rock 'n' roll, but his time had passed. Turner himself claimed that "rock 'n' roll" was just another name for the same music he had always sung, but that he got "knocked down" in the traffic of a newly crowded scene.

The two versions of "Shake, Rattle, and Roll" represent a pivot point between early 1950s R&B and later 1950s rock 'n' roll. They are also a junction at which two popular musicians crossed paths: Big Joe Turner on his way down, and Bill Haley on his way up.

Listening Guide "SH-BOOM": A SONG AND ITS COVER VERSION

"Sh-Boom," original version written and performed by the Chords (Number 2 R&B, Number 5 pop, released 1954); cover version performed by the Crew Cuts (Number 1 pop for nine weeks, released 1954)

"Sh-Boom" is one of the most famous cover versions of the early rock 'n' roll era. In fact, its original recording by the Chords is often cited as one of the very first rock 'n' roll records. Certainly the Chords' "Sh-Boom" is a prime example of the rhythm & blues Black vocal group style and, as a Top 10 pop hit, was also one of the first records to demonstrate the huge appeal that this style could have to a mass audience. It is particularly significant that the Chords managed to place their record near the top of the pop charts in spite of a massively successful cover version of the tune by the white group the Crew Cuts. The Crew Cuts' "Sh-Boom" was one of the two biggest pop hits of 1954 and thus offers a particularly instructive example of the cover record phenomenon. A splendid irony underlying all this is the fact that the Chords' original "Sh-Boom" was in fact on the "flip" side of their own cover version (for the R&B market) of white pop singer Patti Page's hit "Cross over the Bridge"! If some discerning listeners and some enterprising disc jockeys hadn't turned the Chords' record over and enthused over the apparent throwaway number on the B-side, you wouldn't be reading these words right now.

The Chords' "Sh-Boom" also illustrates how the presence of unexpected elements in the arrangement and performance of a rather ordinary tune can help create an extraordinary and original pop record. Essentially, the song is a standard AABA love ballad whose sentimental lyrics and stereotypical chord changes would suggest, on paper, either a slow rhythm & blues ballad or some grist for a latter-day pop crooner's mill. However, the Chords made the striking decision to treat the song as an up-tempo number and to add some appropriate novel touches that really made this one stand out. Among these novel touches (see the following outline) are: an a cappella vocal introduction; the incorporation of brief passages of scat singing, borrowed from jazz, at strategic points in the performance; a long and sizzling instrumental break in the form of a saxophone solo—accompanied by the vocal group's rhythmic "doo-wop" nonsense syllables in the background—right in the middle of the record; and an unexpected ending on the term "sh-boom" itself, intoned by the group on an especially rich chord. This record anticipates the kind of unexpected syntheses from different musical styles that would come

to characterize the most inventive rock 'n' roll records. For example, the sax solo would have been typical of an up-tempo urban blues or dance-oriented R&B recording but would probably not have been expected in a recording with love ballad lyrics, while "doo-wop" vocal sounds—a standard part of R&B love ballads—were not typically paired with hot instrumental solos. The association made in the record between jazz-related scat vocal solos and the nonsense syllables of vocal group doo-wop, while logical, was also quite original.

There are novel touches in the Crew Cuts' recording as well that help account for its great popular success. As shown in the following outline, this version begins with scat singing. In the middle of the record, instead of a saxophone solo, there are two brief sections of group nonsense-syllable singing—each of which is punctuated by an isolated, loud, and humorous kettledrum stroke. Toward the end of the recording there are not one but two "false" endings. Arguably, all these effects tend to push this version into the category of a full-fledged novelty record (whereas the Chords' version comes across as an up-tempo R&B record with some novel aspects).

In terms of singing style, the Crew Cuts are crooners. The alternation between phrases in which a solo voice takes the lead and phrases that are sung by the full group produces some agreeable variety in their arrangement, but there is really no difference in vocal coloration between the solo and the group; that is to say, the group passages are, in effect, "crooning times four." In contrast, the Chords' vocal arrangement is typical of a rhythm & blues approach insofar as it exploits differences in vocal timbre among the group's members, as well as the opposition between solo and group singing. This opposition is heard most clearly in the B section (bridge) of the Chords' version, where the lead is taken by a solo bass voice that presents a strong contrast to the sound of the lead tenor heard in the first two A sections. Of course, the Chords' general approach throughout is rougher in sound than that of the Crew Cuts, underlining the much more aggressive rhythmic feeling of their recording as a whole. The overriding difference between the Chords' and the Crew Cuts' recordings of "Sh-Boom" has to do precisely with that rhythmic feeling: simply put, the former swings hard and the latter does not.

THE CHORDS' "SH-BOOM"		THE CREW CUTS' "SH-BOOM"	
TIME	LYRIC/COMMENT	TIME	LYRIC/COMMENT
0:00	INTRODUCTION (full group a cappella, then band enters)	0:00	INTRODUCTION (scat singing)
0:07	A (*Life could be a . . .*; tenor lead)	0:08	A (tenor lead)
0:22	Scat singing interlude	0:23	A (tenor lead)
0:29	A (*Life could . . .*; tenor lead)	0:37	B (tenor lead, then full group)
0:43	B (*Every time . . .*; bass lead)	0:52	A (tenor lead)
0:57	A (*Life could . . .*; full group)	1:07	Group "nonsense" singing (two sections, each the length of an A section, punctuated by kettledrum strokes)
1:11	Scat singing interlude		
1:22	Sax solo (with group "doo-wop" sounds in background; this is the length of two A sections)	1:37	B (full group)
1:53	A (full group; same words as first A section)	1:51	A (full group, then tenor lead; same words as first A section)
2:07	(Scat singing interlude, leading to sudden ending with the full group)	2:06	(Scat singing interlude, leading to first "false" ending, then to:)
		2:18	A (full group, then tenor lead; same words as the second A section)
		2:30	("False" fadeout leads to sudden loud conclusion with the full group singing "Sweetheart")

The Rock 'n' Roll Business

To understand the emergence of rock 'n' roll as a musical genre and a commercial category, it is important that we gain some understanding of the economics of the music business in the mid-1950s. The overall vitality of the American economy after World War II helped push the entertainment industry's profits to new levels. Sales of record players and radios expanded significantly after the war. Total annual record sales in the United States rose from $191 million in 1951 to $514 million in 1959.

This expansion was accompanied by a gradual diversification of mainstream popular taste and the re-emergence of independent ("indie") record companies whose predecessors had been wiped out twenty years before by the Great Depression. Most of these smaller companies—established by entrepreneurs in New York and Los Angeles, and in secondary centers such as Chicago, Cincinnati, Nashville, Memphis, and New Orleans—specialized in rhythm & blues and country and western recordings, which had begun to attract a national mass audience. This process was viewed with a mixture of interest and alarm by the directors of the "majors" (large record companies such as RCA Victor, Capitol, Mercury, Columbia, MGM, and Decca), which still specialized mainly in the music of Tin Pan Alley, performed by crooners. A few of the majors—such as Decca, which had already made millions from the sale of R&B and country records—did manage to produce some early rock 'n' roll hits. Other large record companies took a couple of years to react to the emergence of rock 'n' roll. RCA Victor, for example, scored a Number 1 hit in 1956 with Kay Starr's rendition of "Rock and Roll Waltz" (a song that described a teenager watching her parents try to dance to the new music, accompanied by music more akin to a ballroom waltz than to rock 'n' roll). But RCA also signed the **rockabilly** singer Elvis Presley and set to work transforming him into a Hollywood matinee idol and rock 'n' roll's first bona fide superstar. (The term "rockabilly"—a synthesis of rock 'n' roll and hillbilly—is used to refer to a style of music based in country traditions that also employs stylistic elements from rhythm & blues to a significant degree.)

The sales charts published in industry periodicals like *Billboard* and *Cashbox* during the 1950s chronicle changes in popular taste, the role of the indies in channeling previously marginal types of music into the pop mainstream, and the emergence of a new teenage market. The charts also reveal a complex pattern of competition among musical styles. As an example, let's have a look at the *Billboard* charts for July 9, 1955, when Bill Haley and the Comets' "Rock Around the Clock" became the first rock 'n' roll hit to reach the Number 1 position on the "Best Sellers in Stores" chart (see Box 8.1). This event is cited by rock historians as a revolutionary event, the beginning of a new era in American popular culture. However, two very different recordings, reminiscent of earlier styles of popular music, held the Number 1 positions on the jukebox and radio airplay charts on July 9: the Latin American ballroom dance hit "Cherry Pink and Apple Blossom White," by Perez Prado and His Orchestra, and "Learning the Blues," performed by the former big band crooner Frank Sinatra with the accompaniment of Nelson Riddle and His Orchestra. And lest we assume that this contrast in styles represented a titanic struggle between small and large record companies, it should be noted that all three of the records were released by majors (Decca, RCA Victor, and Capitol, respectively).

The record that pushed "Rock Around the Clock" out of the Number 1 position two months later was "The Yellow Rose of Texas," a nineteenth-century minstrel song that was performed in a deliberately old-fashioned sing-along style by the Mitch Miller Singers. Miller was the powerful director of the A&R department at Columbia Records and in that role had helped to establish the careers of pop crooners such as Doris Day, Tony Bennett, and Frankie Laine. He was also an archenemy of rock 'n' roll music and of its increasing influence on AM radio programming, which he derided as being geared to "the eight- to fourteen-year-olds, to the pre-shave crowd that make up twelve percent of the country's population and zero percent of its buying power" (Clarke 1995, 410).

An irony here is that Mitch Miller tried to enhance the popularity of his star crooners, throughout the early 1950s and beyond, by having them record songs and arrangements with a strong novelty component, as if to emphasize his own version of a contemporary (youthful?) flavor. A good example is Doris Day's "A Guy Is a Guy," a Number 1 song in 1952.

Doris Day (born Doris Mary Anne von Kappelhoff, in either 1922 or 1924, died in 2019) got her start as a big-band singer, and as a solo artist was regularly on the pop charts from the late 1940s through the late 1950s. "A Guy Is a Guy" has roots in British balladry, and indeed the opening two sections of the song suggest that it will be a strophic verse-and-chorus piece. These first sections prove, however, to be the first two "A" sections of an AABA structure; the addition of a bridge turns the song into a more traditional pop product. (An additional clue to the folk source of the song is the way in which the lyrics of the successive "A" sections convey a narrative story line, much in the manner of the old ballads, but here telling only a small-scale, mock-epic tale: the singer walks down the street, then walks to her house, and so forth.)

Doris Day's recording of "A Guy Is a Guy" demonstrates her warm and engaging singing style. She obviously doesn't take the song any too seriously; her performance embodies the vocal equivalent of a wink of her eye. The perky arrangement, with its upbeat tempo, its steady percussive "footsteps" portraying the walking described in the song's lyrics, and finally the church organ playing wedding music, complements perfectly Day's amused performance of the song. Lightweight it may be, but it's hard not to like it.

Mitch Miller even tried the novelty approach in the waning period of Frank Sinatra's contract with the Columbia label, having "The Voice" record a song like "Mama Will Bark" with the female television star Dagmar. It is not hard to understand Mitch Miller's anger over the domination of radio by Top 40 playlists—predetermined lists of records by a limited number of artists that were often backed up by bribes from record company officials to radio station personnel. One could see the free-form FM broadcasts of the late 1960s (see Chapter 10) and the rise of alternative stations in the 1980s and 1990s as similar reactions against the playlist concept. But Miller's refusal to recognize the teenage market was nothing if not shortsighted. A 1958 survey of the purchasing patterns of the 19 million teenagers in the United States at that time showed that they spent a total of $9 billion a year and strongly influenced their parents' choices of everything from toothpaste and canned food to automobiles and phonographs. And, of course, they bought millions and millions of records.

BOX 8.1 BILL HALEY AND "ROCK AROUND THE CLOCK" (1955)

Bill Haley (1925–1981) would seem an unlikely candidate for the first big rock 'n' roll star, but in the early 1950s this leader of various obscure western swing groups was seeking a style that would capture the enthusiasm of the growing audience of young listeners and dancers, and he accurately sensed which way the wind was blowing. He dropped his cowboy image, changed the name of his accompanying group from the Saddlemen to the Comets, and in 1953 wrote and recorded a song called "Crazy, Man, Crazy" that offered a reasonable emulation of dance-oriented Black rhythm & blues music. The record, released by

(continued)

BOX 8.1 BILL HALEY AND "ROCK AROUND THE CLOCK" (1955) (*continued*)

Bill Haley and the Comets clowning around, c. 1954.

1955, the first rock 'n' roll record to be a Number 1 pop hit. It stayed in the top spot for eight consecutive weeks during the summer of 1955 and eventually sold over 22 million copies worldwide.

"Rock Around the Clock," written by Max C. Freedman and Jimmy DeKnight, was actually recorded in 1954 and was not a big hit when first released. But then the record was prominently featured in the opening credits of the 1955 movie *Blackboard Jungle*, which dealt with inner-city teenagers and juvenile delinquency, and "Rock Around the Clock" quickly achieved massive popularity—and forged an enduring link that has connected teenagers, rock 'n' roll, and movies ever since. Bill Haley's claim to have "invented" rock 'n' roll deserves as little credibility as Paul Whiteman's claim a generation earlier to be the "King of Jazz." But, like Whiteman, Haley proved to be an important popularizer of previously marginalized musical sounds and ideas, and he paved the way for the widespread acceptance of many more creative artists working with rock 'n' roll.

a small indie label, rose as high as Number 12 on the pop charts. In 1954 the Comets were signed by Decca Records, where they worked in the studio with A&R man Milt Gabler. Gabler, who had produced a series of hit records with Louis Jordan and His Tympany Five (see Chapter 7), helped to push Haley's style further in the direction of jump band rhythm & blues—"I'd sing Jordan riffs to the group that would be picked up by the electric guitars and tenor sax," he later said.

As we have already mentioned, Bill Haley and the Comets recorded commercially successful cover versions of rhythm & blues hits in the mid-1950s, notably "Shake, Rattle, and Roll" (Number 7, 1954) and "See You Later, Alligator" (Number 6, 1956). But they attained their unique status in pop music history when their record of "Rock Around the Clock" became, in

"Rock Around the Clock" demonstrated the unprecedented success that a white group with a country background could achieve playing a twelve-bar blues song driven by the sounds of electric guitar, bass, and drums. It proved a portent of the enormous changes that were about to overtake American popular music and opened the floodgates for artists like Elvis Presley, Carl Perkins, and Buddy Holly. "Rock Around the Clock" also helped prepare a receptive mass audience for the sounds of rhythm & blues and for Black artists building on the rhythm & blues tradition. While the song was still at the top of the pop chart in 1955, Chuck Berry's trailblazing "Maybellene" made its appearance on the same chart and before long was itself in the Top 10.

Early Rock 'n' Roll Stars on the R&B Side

We will present the rhythm & blues–based side of rock 'n' roll using the three most prominent African Americans to be identified with the new music. Of the three, Chuck Berry was the songwriter/performer who most obviously addressed his songs to teenage America (white and Black) in the 1950s; Little Richard was the cultivator of a deliberately outrageous performance style that appealed to his audience on the basis of its strangeness, novelty, and sexual ambiguity; and Fats Domino's work most directly embodied the continuity of rhythm & blues with rock 'n' roll. As might be expected from this description, Domino was the earliest of the three to become an established performer (although he was slightly younger than Berry)—he cut his first rhythm & blues hit, "The Fat Man," in 1949 at the age of twenty-one. But all three crossed over to the pop charts and mainstream success within the first few months following the massive success of Bill Haley's "Rock Around the Clock" (see Box 8.1).

CHUCK BERRY

Charles Edward Anderson ("Chuck") Berry (1926–2017) burst precipitously onto the pop music scene with his first record, "Maybellene." It was a novel synthesis that did not sound precisely like anything before it, and it introduced listeners to an already fully formed style of songwriting, singing, and guitar playing that would exercise a primal influence on virtually all the rock 'n' roll to follow.

Berry was born in California but grew up in St. Louis, where he absorbed blues and rhythm & blues styles. He was one of the first Black musicians to consciously forge his own version of these styles for appeal to the mass market—and he was certainly the most successful of his generation in this effort. Like many other Black musicians,

Chuck Berry in 1959.

Berry also knew country music, and he found that his performances of country songs in clubs appealed strongly to the white members of his audience. He put this knowledge and experience to good use: "Maybellene" was distantly modeled on a country number called "Ida Red." Nevertheless, the primary elements of "Maybellene" trace their roots clearly to rhythm & blues: the thick, buzzing timbre of Berry's electric guitar (see Box 8.2); the blue notes and slides in both voice and guitar; the socking backbeat of the drum; and the form derived from twelve-bar blues structures.

What, then, made "Maybellene" sound so startlingly new? The explosive tempo, for one thing; while swing bands occasionally may have played for dancing at a tempo like this, no vocal-based rhythm & blues had ever gone at such a pace, because it's exceptionally hard to articulate words and have time to breathe when trying to sing at this tempo. But Berry pulls it off, articulating the words with clarity and remarkable force. This observation brings up another essential aspect of the record's novelty and appeal, which are the lyrics themselves. The lyrics to "Maybellene" provide an original and clever description of a lovers' quarrel in the form of a car chase, complete with a punning invented verb form (*motorvatin'*), humorous details ("Rain water blowin'" under the automobile hood, which is "doin' my motor good"), and a breathless ending in which the singer catches Maybellene in her Cadillac at the top of a hill—an ending that still leaves listeners room to imagine a wide range of sequels. And what could reach out to a young audience more effectively than a story featuring both cars and sex appeal?

In addition, we shouldn't miss the implied class distinction the lyrics make between Maybellene, in her top-of-the-line Cadillac Coupe de Ville, and the narrator, in his more humble, middle-class, but eminently functional "V-8 Ford." As he chases and finally catches the Cadillac (and Maybellene), there is a sense of the underdog's triumphing in the race, and the boastful claim of the first verse—that nothing could outrun his V-8 Ford—is vindicated. (Cars have long been an important status symbol in American culture, and African American culture is certainly no exception to this. A song recorded by Bessie Smith in 1928, a generation before "Maybellene," called "Put It Right Here [Or Keep It Out There]" described the singer's deadbeat lover as follows: "Once he was like a Cadillac, now he's like an old worn-out Ford." The concern with cars has persisted into contemporary rap music, with an early example being "Sucker M.C.'s," a 1983 hit by Run DMC.)

All the basic ingredients that would inform a string of successive, successful Chuck Berry records are present in "Maybellene." These elements became his trademarks: an arresting instrumental introduction for unaccompanied electric guitar; relentless intensity produced by a very fast tempo and a very loud volume level; formal and stylistic elements strongly related to earlier rhythm & blues music; and witty lyrics, clearly enunciated and designed to appeal to the lifestyle and aspirations of his young audience.

After the success of "Maybellene," Chuck Berry wrote and recorded other excellent rock 'n' roll songs that became more and more explicit celebrations of American teenage culture and its music. "Roll over Beethoven" (1956) praises rhythm & blues at the expense of classical music. "School Days" (Number 3 pop, Number 1 R&B, 1957) describes drudgery relieved by an after-school trip to the "juke joint," at which point the record becomes literally an advertisement for itself and an anthem for the music it represents: "Hail!

Listening Guide CHUCK BERRY'S "MAYBELLENE"

Music and lyrics by Chuck Berry (also credited to disc jockeys Russel Fratto and Alan Freed);[1] performed by Chuck Berry and His Combo; recorded 1955

Form

The form of "Maybellene" is clearly based on the twelve-bar blues. The chorus ("Maybellene, why can't you be true?") adheres to the traditional twelve-bar structure in every respect: three four-bar phrases, standard chord pattern, and even the three-line poetic arrangement in which the second line is a repetition of the first. But the verses, while twelve bars long, completely suppress chord changes, remaining on the "home" (or tonic) chord throughout while the voice delivers rapid-fire lyrics using brief, repetitive patterns of notes (see the accompanying chart). Ironically, by eliminating chord changes and restricting melodic interest in the verses, Berry turns what could have been a static, purely strophic form into something more dynamic. Instead of a string of standard twelve-bar blues stanzas, we hear an alternating verse-chorus structure that allows Berry to tell his story and build his record in a more exciting way.

The stripped-down music of the verses focuses all attention on their lyrics—which is appropriate, as it is the verses that relate the ongoing progress of the car chase. Their repetitive melodic formulas allow Berry to concentrate on articulating the densely packed words, with the continuous verbal activity more than compensating for the lack of musical variety. Actually, the verses build enormous tension, so that when the choruses at last bring some chord changes—basic as they are—there is a feeling of release and expansion. The pace of the lyrics also slows down momentarily for the choruses, which reinforces this effect of expansion and allows Berry to lean expressively on the crucial name "Maybellene." Yet, while the choruses provide variety and release, they also create tension of another sort, as they postpone the continuation of the story being told in the verses. This same effect is created on a larger scale by the instrumental break before the final verse: variety and release on the one hand (and an opportunity for Berry to showcase his considerable guitar chops), along with a real sense of

racing along down the highway, and tension and postponement of the story's climax on the other.

The manipulation of a limited set of musical materials to achieve maximal results of variety, novelty, and excitement is the essence of effective rock 'n' roll. "Maybellene" is an outstanding case in point. The formal issues discussed previously may seem either obvious or all but lost in the pure visceral intensity of the record, but the seamlessness of Chuck Berry's artistry should not blind us to the man's brilliance. Above all, "Maybellene" is a beautifully formed record, building inexorably from start to finish, where everything is made to count, without a single word or note wasted.

The Song/The Recording

In Chuck Berry's "Maybellene," the song is the recording. When people think of or cite "Maybellene," they are referring to Berry's original recording of it—the ultimate, and really the only important, source material. The culture of rock 'n' roll centered to an unprecedented extent on records: records played on the radio, records played at dances, records purchased for home listening. Studio recordings thus increasingly came to represent the original, primary documents of the music, often preceding and generally taking precedence over any live performances of the material. Baby boomers went to hear rock 'n' roll stars perform the hits they already knew from the records they had heard and bought; on the nationally broadcast television program American Bandstand, singers appeared without accompanying bands and lip-synched their songs while the records played in the background. The issuing of sheet music was becoming an afterthought, an ancillary to the recording. In many future discussions, consequently, we will be treating the song and the recording as one, rather than as separate entities.

The record opens arrestingly with the sound of Berry's hollow-body electric guitar playing a bluesy lick that literally sizzles with sonic energy. The impact of "Maybellene" is in no small part due to the infectious rhythmic groove and texture established by Berry and a gifted group of sidemen, including the great blues composer and bassist Willie Dixon, an integral part of Muddy Waters's recordings for Chess Records (see Chapter 7); Jerome Green, whose maracas were central to the Bo Diddley sound; and pianist Johnny Johnson, who may

1. In the early years of rock 'n' roll, the record market was fluid and unpredictable, and agents, promoters, distributors, and disc jockeys were often given (or would take) songwriting credits in exchange for the "favor" of pushing particular artists or records. There was nothing new in this practice; it just became much more widespread. In any case, it is doubtful that Fratto and Freed had anything substantial to do with the creation of "Maybellene," although they certainly helped it to be heard and to become popular.

(continued)

Listening Guide   CHUCK BERRY'S "MAYBELLENE" (continued)

well have played a role in the creation of Berry's songs. Some credit for the overall sound of the recording must also go to Phil and Leonard Chess, who in their years of recording Chicago blues musicians such as Muddy Waters and Howlin' Wolf had learned how to stay out of the way of a good recording. They sometimes offered advice but never tried to radically alter a musician's style for commercial effect.

Amid the numerous elements borrowed from rhythm & blues and urban blues, we may hear in "Maybellene" a prominent, very regular, and unsyncopated bass line, alternating between two notes on beats 1 and 3 of each bar. The rhythmic feel of this bass line is stylistically much more suggestive of country music than of anything typically found in rhythm & blues, and its presence here points to Berry's knowledge of country music and to what Berry himself has identified as the country origins of "Maybellene." As we shall see repeatedly, rock 'n' roll music is often based on a synthesis of widely diverse stylistic elements.

LISTENING GUIDE	"MAYBELLENE"		
TIME	**FORM**	**LYRIC**	**DESCRIPTIVE COMMENTS**
0:00	Instrumental introduction		Solo electric guitar "hook" establishes characteristic sound (suggesting auto horns) and tempo
0:04	Chorus	*Maybellene . . .*	Twelve-bar blues
0:17	Verse 1	*As I was . . .*	Twelve bars, without any chord changes; very fast pacing of lyrics
0:29	Chorus	*Maybellene . . .*	As before
0:41	Verse 2	*The Cadillac . . .*	As in verse 1
0:53	Chorus	*Maybellene . . .*	As before
1:05	Instrumental break		Two successive twelve-bar sections
1:30	Chorus	*Maybellene . . .*	As before
1:42	Verse 3	*The motor . . .*	As in verse 1
1:55	Chorus	*Maybellene . . .*	As before
2:07	Instrumental coda		Fades out

Hail! Rock 'n' roll! Deliver me from the days of old!" "Rock and Roll Music" (Number 8 pop, Number 6 R&B, 1957) articulates the virtues of its subject, as opposed to the limitations of "modern jazz" or a "symphony." "Sweet Little Sixteen" (Number 2 pop, Number 1 R&B, 1958) wittily describes the young collector of "famed autographs," coping with growing up ("tight dresses and lipstick"), for whom a rock 'n' roll show becomes—in her mind, at least—a national party where all the "cats" want to dance with her.

Berry's consummate statement on rock 'n' roll mythology is doubtlessly "Johnny B. Goode" (Number 8 pop, Number 2 R&B, 1958). Here he relates the story of a "country boy" who "never learned to read or write so well" but who "could play a guitar just like a-ringin' a bell." (Berry's autobiography states that the "country boy" was originally a "colored boy," but Berry opted to make his tale color-blind, recognizing the diversity of his audience and the potential universality of his myth.) The boy's mother predicts his coming success as a bandleader with his "name in lights, saying 'Johnny B. Goode tonight'"—and in this way one of pop music's greatest verbal puns embodies the dream of every teenager with a guitar and a wish to succeed as a rock 'n' roller (with parental approval and appreciation, no less)!

It cannot be known how many careers in music were inspired or encouraged by "Johnny B. Goode," but a list of pop musicians who have been obviously and singularly influenced by Chuck Berry would read like a who's who of rock stars from the 1960s and beyond. He is probably the only musician of his generation to be inescapably influential on three different, and essential, fronts: as a brilliantly clever and articulate lyricist and song-writer, as a fine rock 'n' roll vocal stylist, and as a pioneering electric guitarist. The mass adulation belonged to Elvis Presley, but the greatest influence on musicians unquestionably was made by Berry.

LITTLE RICHARD

The centrality of records to the culture of rock 'n' roll didn't negate the significance of live performances. Indeed, live performances disseminated via the new mass medium of television or on the movie screen bestowed a new significance on performers of rock 'n' roll music, and individual artists and vocal groups sought to cultivate visual characteristics or mannerisms that would set them apart from others and encourage listeners to remember them—and to go out and buy their records. Chuck Berry had his famous "duck walk" as a stage device. But no performer in the early years of rock 'n' roll was as visually flamboyant as Little Richard.

Little Richard in 1957.

"Little Richard" (Richard Wayne Penniman) (1932–2020) spent several lackluster years as a journeyman rhythm & blues performer before hitting the pop charts early in 1956 with his wild performance of the nonsensical song "Tutti-Frutti." Based on the twelve-bar blues, "Tutti-Frutti" alternated nonsense choruses ("Tutti-frutti, au rutti, a-wop-bop-a-loom-op a-lop-bam-boom!" and variants thereof) with nonspecific but obviously leering verses ("I got a gal named Sue, she knows just what to do"), all delivered by Little Richard in an uninhibited shouting style complete with falsetto whoops and accompanied with a pounding band led by Little Richard's equally uninhibited piano. In retrospect, it seems surprising that records like "Tutti-Frutti" and its even more successful—and more obviously salacious—follow-up, "Long Tall Sally" (see the Listening Guide in this chapter) got played on mainstream radio at all. It must have been assumed by programmers that Little Richard was a novelty act and that therefore nobody would pay attention to, or understand, the words of his songs. But teenage listeners in the 1950s certainly understood that Little Richard embodied the new spirit of rock 'n' roll music in the most extroverted, outrageous, and original way.

Any doubts on the matter would surely have been resolved by seeing Little Richard's performances in any of the three rock 'n' roll movies in which he appeared during the two years of his greatest popular success, 1956–1957: *Don't Knock the Rock, The Girl Can't Help It,* and *Mister Rock 'n' Roll.* Heavily made up, with his hair in an enormous pompadour, rolling his eyes, playing the piano while standing and gyrating wildly, Little Richard epitomized the abandon celebrated in rock 'n' roll lyrics and music. (Although new to his audiences, Richard's appearance and approach to performance had clear antecedents, going back to vaudeville and minstrelsy.) Both the sound of his recordings and the visual characteristics of his performances made Little Richard an exceptionally strong influence on later performers; the white rockabilly singer-pianist Jerry Lee Lewis was inestimably in his debt, and in the 1960s the English Beatles and the American Creedence Clearwater Revival—along with many other bands—played music whose roots could readily be traced back to Little Richard. Moreover, the lingering (and carefully crafted) ambiguity of Little Richard's sexual identity—available evidence suggests that he might best have been classified in the early days as an "omnivore"—paved the way for the image of performers such as David Bowie, Elton John, Prince, and Lady Gaga.

FATS DOMINO

Antoine "Fats" Domino (1928–2017), a singer, pianist, and songwriter, had been an established presence on the rhythm & blues charts for several years by the time he scored his first large-scale pop breakthrough with "Ain't It a Shame" in 1955 (Number 10 pop, Number 1 R&B). In this case, mainstream success was simply the result of the market's catching up with Domino; there is no significant stylistic difference between his earlier rhythm & blues hits and his rock 'n' roll bestsellers like "I'm in Love Again" and "I'm Walkin'." Domino himself remarked that he always played the same music, that they called it "rhythm & blues" first and "rock 'n' roll" later, and that it made no difference to him—although it surely did make a difference to him when the rock 'n' roll market catapulted his record sales into the millions and eventually made him the second biggest-selling recording artist of the 1950s, right behind Elvis Presley.

Listening Guide "LONG TALL SALLY"

Music and lyrics credited to Enotris Johnson, Richard Penniman, and Robert Blackwell; performed by Little Richard and unidentified band; recorded 1956

Our representative example of Little Richard's music is "Long Tall Sally." Like most of Little Richard's songs, this one is built on the twelve-bar blues. Like Chuck Berry and other artists who came out of rhythm & blues to seek pop stardom, Little Richard adapted the twelve-bar blues structure to reflect the more traditionally pop-friendly format of verse-chorus. Here, the first four bars of each blues stanza are set to changing words—verses—while the remaining eight bars, with unchanging words, function as a repeated chorus. This simple but surprisingly effective formal arrangement is reflected in both identical and varied ways in many rock 'n' roll songs of the period; for examples of variations on this structure, see the Listening Guides for Elvis Presley's "Don't Be Cruel" and for the Coasters' "Charlie Brown."

	LISTENING GUIDE	"LONG TALL SALLY"		
TIME	**FORM**	**LYRIC**	**DESCRIPTIVE COMMENTS**	
0:00	Verse 1	*Gonna tell Aunt Mary . . .*	Underlying rhythmic and chord structure is that of the twelve-bar blues, with the first four bars constituting the verse and the final eight bars the chorus; loud, flamboyant vocal style throughout	
0:05	Chorus	*Oh, baby . . .*		
0:16	Verse 2	*Well, Long Tall Sally . . .*	Twelve-bar blues pattern persists throughout the song	
0:21	Chorus	*Oh, baby . . .*		
0:32	Verse 3	*Well, I saw Uncle John . . .*		
0:37	Chorus	*Oh, baby . . .*		
0:47	Instrumental break		Two twelve-bar blues sections; intense saxophone solo reflects the mood of the vocal	
1:18	Verse 2	*Well, Long Tall Sally . . .*		
	Chorus	*Oh baby . . .*		
	Verse 3	*Well, I saw Uncle John . . .*		
	Chorus	*Oh baby . . .*		
1:49	Conclusion	*We're gonna have some fun tonight . . .*	Extended chorus-like section; twelve-bar blues structure	

Fats Domino and his band in a scene from the 1958 movie *the Big Beat*.

Domino was born in New Orleans and grew up bathed in the rich and diverse musical traditions of that city. His distinctive regional style best exemplifies the strong connections between rock 'n' roll and earlier pop music. Jazz, especially boogie-woogie (see Chapter 6), was a strong early influence on him, along with the rhythm & blues piano style of *Professor Longhair* (1918–1980; born Henry Roeland Byrd) and the jump band style of trumpeter Dave Bartholomew's ensemble. Bartholomew became Domino's arranger, producer, and songwriting partner, and their collaboration produced a remarkable string of consistently fine and successful records. Their "New Orleans" sound was also widely admired and imitated among musicians; Domino played piano on hit records by other artists, and Little Richard recorded in New Orleans to use the city's distinctive sidemen and thus try to capture some of the city's rock 'n' roll magic. (Little Richard's "Long Tall Sally" is modeled directly on Domino's "Ain't It a Shame," both in formal layout and musical arrangement.)

Given his strong links to tradition, it is not surprising that Fats Domino recorded a number of standards—in contradistinction to artists like Chuck Berry and Little Richard, who concentrated on novel songs and styles to appeal to their new audience. In fact, Domino's 1956 remake of "Blueberry Hill" proved to be his most popular record, reaching the Number 2 position on the pop charts and topping the R&B charts. "Blueberry Hill" was a Tin Pan Alley tune that had originally been a big hit in 1940 for the Glenn Miller Orchestra (with vocal by Ray Eberle). Domino preserved his own rhythm & blues–based style when performing "Blueberry Hill" and other standards, however, thus bringing a new kind of musical hybrid to mass-market attention, and with this phenomenon a new and important musical bridge was crossed. We might say that rather than crossing over himself, Domino made the music cross over to him. Smooth

Tin Pan Alley–style crooning and uninflected urban diction were replaced by Domino's rhythmically accented, full-throated singing in his characteristic New Orleans accent, and it certainly wasn't the sound of a sweet band backing him or shaping his own piano accompaniment. Another pop success for Domino was his rocking up-tempo version of "My Blue Heaven," which makes a striking and amusing contrast to Gene Austin's original recording (see Chapter 4).

Fats Domino, Little Richard, and Chuck Berry all achieved their successes recording on independent labels, thus demonstrating the great importance of the indies to the popularization of rock 'n' roll. Domino recorded for Imperial, a Los Angeles–based concern headed by Lew Chudd that also issued records by the important rhythm & blues electric guitar stylist Aaron "T-Bone" Walker. Little Richard was an artist for Specialty Records, Art Rupe's Hollywood label, which had on its roster such rhythm & blues stars as Percy Mayfield, Lloyd Price, and Guitar Slim, along with important African American gospel groups and soloists. Berry's records were issued on Chess, the Chicago label of the Chess brothers Leonard and Phil that also served as a home for an impressive list of blues-based artists like Muddy Waters, Howlin' Wolf, and Willie Dixon, along with other rock 'n' rollers like Bo Diddley and the Moonglows.

Early Rock 'n' Roll Stars on the Country Side

ELVIS PRESLEY

The biggest star of rock 'n' roll to come out of the country tradition—and arguably of the entire history of American popular music—was *Elvis Presley* (1935–1977). Presley was born in Tupelo, Mississippi, the only child of a poor family, and his musical taste was shaped at a young age by the white gospel music he heard at church, radio broadcasts of country music and rhythm & blues, and the popular crooners of the postwar era, especially Dean Martin. (At the age of eight Presley won a talent contest at a Mississippi county fair, singing an old country song called "Old Shep.") As a teenager he moved to Memphis, took a job as a truck driver, and nurtured his ambition to become a singing film star.

In 1954 Presley came to the attention of Sam Phillips, the owner of Sun Records, a small independent label in Memphis, Tennessee, that specialized in country and rhythm & blues recordings and had scored a few regional hits. Phillips teamed Presley with two musicians from a local country band called the Starlite Wranglers, *Scotty Moore* (b. 1931) on electric guitar and *Bill Black* (1926–1965) on string bass. Presley made a series of recordings with an R&B cover version on one side and a country song on the other. In essence, Sam Phillips was fishing with Elvis as bait, trying to see if he could develop a single artist who could sell to both white and Black audiences. In his early live appearances Elvis was billed as "the King of Country Bop," an attempt to indicate his idiosyncratic combination of Black and white influences.

When RCA Victor bought out Presley's contract from Sun in late 1955, at the then-extravagant price of $35,000, this mainstream major label set about consciously trying to turn the "hillbilly cat" into a mainstream performer without compromising the

The young Elvis Presley in action.

strength of his appeal to teenagers. They were assisted in this task by two major players. First, there was Presley's manager, Colonel Thomas Parker, who saw to it that Presley was seen repeatedly on television variety shows and in a series of romantic Hollywood films. Second was RCA's Nashville producer Chet Atkins, who ensured that Presley's records for the label were made in a pop-friendly style, according to Atkins's standards. (In the 1960s Atkins became the producer most credited with developing the "Nashville Sound" of pop-oriented country music; see Chapter 10.) This pair succeeded beyond anyone's expectations. Although Presley's television performances were denounced by authorities as vulgar because of the singer's hip-shaking gyrations, the shows were attended by hordes of screaming young fans and were admired on the screen by millions of young viewers. Presley's records racked up astronomical sales as he dominated the top of the pop charts steadily from 1956 on into the early 1960s, quickly establishing himself as the biggest-selling solo artist of rock 'n' roll, and then as the biggest-selling solo recording artist of *any* period and style—a title he still holds at the beginning of the twenty-first century!

Presley's extraordinary popularity established rock 'n' roll as an unprecedented mass-market phenomenon. His reputation as a performer and recording artist endured up to his death in 1977 at the age of forty-two and continues beyond the grave—Graceland, his home in Memphis, Tennessee, is now a public museum dedicated to his memory and is visited by upwards of 500,000 people annually. Presley gave strong performances and made fine records at many points throughout his career, and he starred in many movies. But it cannot

Listening Guide "MYSTERY TRAIN"

Original version written and performed by Junior Parker (no chart appearance, released 1953); cover version performed by Elvis Presley (Number 11 country and western, released 1953)

The last record that Elvis made with Sam Phillips—just before he signed with RCA Victor and went on to become a national celebrity—was a cover version of an R&B song called "Mystery Train," and it is this recording that we want to examine in some detail here. In 1953 **Herman "Little Junior" Parker** (1927–1971), a singer, songwriter, and harmonica player who was achieving some success with his rhythm & blues band Little Junior's Blue Flames, had recorded a tune called "Mystery Train" for Sam Phillips's Sun label. The song received little attention at the time of its release, but at some point the young Elvis Presley must have noticed it. Examining these two versions of "Mystery Train" will assist us in understanding the developing synergy between rhythm & blues and country music that led to the phenomenon called rock 'n' roll. It will also serve to underline the essential role of small independent record labels in disseminating "marginal" music and thus contributing to this synergy. Finally, it will help trace the origins of Elvis Presley's unique style, illuminating what Sam Phillips (who worked extensively with both Black and white artists during the heyday of Sun) had in mind when he made his oft-quoted, oft-paraphrased observation that if he could find a white man with "the Negro sound and the Negro feel," then he could become a millionaire.

"Mystery Train" as a composition is credited to Parker and Phillips, and, at least in its original version, it is structured as a strophic twelve-bar blues with one harmonic irregularity: some strophes begin on the subdominant chord rather than on the tonic, so that the first two four-bar phrases of these particular strophes are harmonically identical. Both Parker's original performance and Presley's cover version are individually fine recordings. What is most remarkable, however, is how different they are from one another. Although Presley obviously learned a great deal from listening to Parker and dozens of other fine rhythm & blues artists, Presley's "Mystery Train" is arguably less a traditional cover than a reconceptualization of the song—a reconceptualization that reflects both Presley's distinctive self-awareness as a performer and his emerging (if probably implicit) ideas regarding his listening audience and how to engage it.

Junior Parker's original "Mystery Train" is a darkly evocative record with obvious roots both in rural blues and in rhythm & blues traditions. The train was a favorite subject and image for country blues singers, and the

spare, nonlinear lyrics in Parker's song are clearly aligned with country blues traditions; this train is certainly "mysterious." In the first strophe, the "long Black train," with its "sixteen coaches" taking the singer's "baby" away, paints a funereal picture. By the time we reach the third and final strophe, the train is bringing "baby" back to the singer, and the mood has brightened. But that brightening is darkened by the certainty already communicated in the second strophe: the train that took her away will "do it again." Parker's "Mystery Train" articulates a pessimistic worldview characteristic of the blues by asserting that the singer may triumph over adversity, but only temporarily—that is to say, life is a cycle of misfortunes offering, at best, periodic relief, but no permanent reprieve. (Two out of the three verses portray "baby's" departure, while only one depicts her anticipated return.)

Parker's band constitutes a fairly typical rhythm & blues lineup for its time: electric guitar, acoustic bass, piano, drums, and saxophone. The "chugging" rhythm conveys a perfect sense of the train's steady, inexorable momentum. The saxophone is confined basically to long, low notes that evoke the train's whistle, while an additional atmospheric touch is added at the end of the recording: a vocal imitation of the sound of the train's brakes as it finally comes to a stop (an event marked by the concluding guitar chord and the cessation of the "chugging" rhythm).

Elvis Presley's "Mystery Train," recorded when the "hillbilly cat" was barely twenty years old, conveys a breathless sense of intensity, excitement, and even enthusiasm (listen to Presley's spontaneous-sounding, triumphant "whoop" at the end of the recording!) that makes for a totally different experience from that offered by Parker's rendition. The much faster tempo of the Presley record is of course a decisive factor, but it is only the most obvious of many reasons that may be cited for the essential transformation "Mystery Train" undergoes here. There is little, if any, attempt at naturalistic evocation of the train by Presley's band, which consists simply of electric guitar, acoustic guitar, acoustic bass, and drums. One might hear a trainlike rhythm in the pattern of the drumsticks, but the speed of the recording encourages one to imagine a roller coaster rather than a train (especially by 1955 standards). In fact, unlike Parker's record, Presley's version focuses on the singer rather than the train. Parker's protagonist seems ultimately at

(continued)

Listening Guide "MYSTERY TRAIN" (*continued*)

the mercy of the train, which has taken away his "baby" and will do so again, even if it occasionally brings her back. But Presley's vocal portrays a confident protagonist who projects control over his own future.

Presley's version presents significant alterations of Parker's original in the internal structuring of both the words and the music. In the lyrics to the second verse, Presley makes a crucial substitution, asserting that while the train took his "baby," "it never will again"! As if to emphasize this essential change, Presley repeats this second strophe, with its altered lyrics, at the end of his record, so that now there are a total of four verses, three of which look toward the return of his "baby" and only one (the first) emphasizing her departure. That departure now becomes a one-time occurrence, as the song assumes a linear narrative shape that it did not have in Parker's original version. Even more importantly, this revision of the lyrics expresses and underlines the singer's feeling of control over the situation—definitely not an attitude traditionally associated with the blues. (It would be hard to imagine Parker asserting that the train will never take his lover away again.) In Parker's "Mystery Train," the instrumental break occurs between the second and third verses, emphasizing and allowing the listener to ponder the singer's assertion that the train is going to take his "baby" again; arguably, this structural arrangement significantly colors our entire perception of the song. In Presley's version, by contrast, the instrumental break occurs after the third verse, leaving the singer's words "she's mine, all mine" resonating in the listener's ears.

While Parker's "Mystery Train" follows the standard format of twelve-bar blues in the rhythmic arrangement of all its phrases and strophes, Presley's version is highly irregular by comparison. Many of the phrases in Presley's "Mystery Train" are longer than they "should" be; if we attempted to notate his performance in terms of a twelve-bar blues paradigm, we would find ourselves constantly having to add "half-bar" extensions (two extra beats) to many phrases. Although there seems to be a general pattern formed by these extensions throughout the first three strophes, Presley breaks free of even this suggested pattern in his final strophe, extending one of the phrases even further than before while constricting another. (One of the truly remarkable things about this "Mystery Train" is that Presley's band was able to follow the apparent spontaneity, and consequent unpredictability, of his phrasing—especially given the breakneck speed of the performance.) Clearly, this singer is constrained by

nothing; the rhythmic freedom of the music itself is reflective of his apparently limitless confidence.

With all these differences, we still should not ignore Presley's obvious debts to the blues and rhythm & blues traditions represented by Parker's original composition and recording. It is not difficult to hear strong aspects of what Sam Phillips called "the Negro sound and the Negro feel" in Presley's performance: in particular, the strong regional accent and the frequency of blue notes and sliding between pitches. These characteristics are, of course, points of intersection between Black blues and white country traditions. What is important to understand is how Presley emphasized these common elements to form a style that sounded significantly "Blacker" (particularly to white audiences) than that of virtually any other white singer who had emerged in the post–World War II era. (Presley also incorporated some vocal effects more specifically associated with white traditions, especially the kind of rapid stuttering, "hiccuping" effect heard in lines like "comin' dow-hown the li-hine" or "she's mine, a-hall mine.") Even the kind of rhythmic freedom that we have observed in Presley's "Mystery Train" reflects practices common in African American music, although one would have to go back to country blues recordings to find anything comparably irregular, as most rhythm & blues records were tied to the kind of regularity in phrasing that was usually expected in music designed to be suitable for dancing.

Unlike the cover records we discussed previously, Elvis Presley's "Mystery Train" is unique because it is more aggressive and "raw" than the original on which it was modeled. But the freedom and rawness of Presley's version is not primarily in the service of a vision that seeks to return us to the original flavor and context of rural blues—far from it. Rather, Presley's "Mystery Train" is the expression of a young white singer who is looking with optimism toward an essentially unbounded future, flush with new possibilities for stylistic synthesis that would help assure both intensely satisfying personal expression and an unprecedented degree of popular success. Unlike Parker's "Mystery Train," which is the expression of a man working knowledgeably within a tradition that both defines and confines the outlines of his music and his worldview, Presley's "Mystery Train" offers a totally new kind of ride, a ride without preconceived limits or conditions. No wonder so many other young singers, and a remarkably large young audience, wanted to climb aboard!

Listening Guide "DON'T BE CRUEL"

Music and lyrics by Otis Blackwell and Elvis Presley;[2] performed by Elvis Presley, vocal and guitar, with the Jordanaires and backing instrumentalists; recorded 1956

Presley's biggest hit, "Don't Be Cruel," topped the charts for eleven weeks in the late summer and fall of 1956, eventually yielding pride of place to another Presley record, "Love Me Tender." "Don't Be Cruel" is based on the twelve-bar blues (see the following chart). Presley's vocal is heavy with blues-derived and country inflections; his regional accent is striking, and the occasional "hiccuping" effect ("baby, it's just you I'm a-thinkin' of") is associated particularly with rockabilly singers like Presley, Gene Vincent, and Buddy Holly. The strong backbeat throughout evokes rhythm & blues, while the repeated electric guitar figure at the opening is reminiscent of rhythmic ideas favored by western swing bands (and ultimately derived from boogie-woogie). Imposed on all these diverse and intense stylistic elements is a wash of electronic **reverb**—an attempt by the engineers at RCA's Nashville studios to emulate the distinctive (and decidedly low-tech) **slap-back** echo sound of Presley's previous recordings on Sun Records.

A sweetening sound is also incorporated into the song by the backing vocal group, the Jordanaires, whose precise bop,

Frank Sinatra and Elvis Presley on television together in 1960.

bops and crooning ahs and oohs are doubly rooted in white gospel music and in the most genteel, established mainstream pop style. Whether this odd amalgam is deemed to work as a source of stylistic enrichment, or whether listening to Presley and the Jordanaires together on this record seems like listening to the Chords and the Crew Cuts simultaneously performing "Sh-Boom" (see the earlier discussion of cover versions) will obviously be a matter of personal taste. It can never be

known how much the Jordanaires added—or if they added at all—to the appeal of this and many other records Presley made with them for RCA. But the commercial success of these records was unprecedented, and their mixture of styles was yet another indication of the extent to which the traditional barriers in pop music were falling down. (Major labels often tended to sweeten recordings by rock 'n' roll singers for the mass market, while the indies went for a rawer, more basic sound. For example, many of Jackie Wilson's rhythm & blues–based recordings for the Brunswick label—a

---

2. Presley, though not generally known as a songwriter, was credited as coauthor of a handful of his early hits for RCA.

(continued)

Listening Guide "DON'T BE CRUEL" (*continued*)

subsidiary of the major Decca—featured elaborately arranged backing choruses and orchestral arrangements.)

On the other side of "Don't Be Cruel" was Presley's version of "Hound Dog," a song that had been a major rhythm & blues hit in 1953 for Big Mama Thornton. Comparing Presley's cover of "Hound Dog" for RCA with the earlier cover he did for Sun of the rhythm & blues tune "Mystery Train" sheds further light on the shaping of Elvis's image for mainstream consumption. Whereas his rockabilly "Mystery Train" is noticeably faster, looser, and wilder than Junior Parker's original, his "Hound Dog" has lost some of its teeth—so to speak—as a result of the bowdlerization of the original words. Big Mama Thornton's version is full of sexual innuendo, making it clear that the term "hound dog" is being used

metaphorically, not literally ("Daddy, I know you ain't no real cool cat"; "You can wag your tail, but I ain't gonna feed you no more"; see the discussion in Chapter 7). Such sexual implications are gone in Presley's rendition, which seems to be literally about a pathetic mutt who is "cryin' all the time" and "ain't never caught a rabbit." With the lyrics cleaned up in this way for mass consumption, the undeniable passion of Presley's performance seems a bit over the top for the subject matter, turning the record into a kind of novelty song. But this certainly didn't bother the singer's audience, most of whom could not have been familiar with Thornton's original anyway; "Hound Dog" proved just about as popular as "Don't Be Cruel" itself, making the record what the industry called a "two-sided hit."

LISTENING GUIDE | "DON'T BE CRUEL"

TIME	FORM	LYRIC	DESCRIPTIVE COMMENTS
0:00	Instrumental intro		Repetitive guitar hook, strong backbeat (four bars long)
0:05	Verse 1	*If you know . . .*	Twelve-bar blues structure, arranged to suggest a verse-chorus pattern, with the first eight bars constituting the verse and the final four bars the chorus
0:16	Chorus	*Don't be cruel . . .*	
0:23	Verse 2	*Baby, if I made you mad . . .*	Twelve-bar blues structure, with an extension added (six bars in length) to the chorus
0:33(0:40)	Chorus + extension	*Don't be cruel . . . I don't want . . .*	
0:48	Verse 3	*Don't stop a-thinkin' of me . . .*	Twelve-bar blues, plus extension (as before)
0:59(1:05)	Chorus + extension	*Don't be cruel . . . Why should we . . .*	
1:13	Verse 4	*Let's walk up . . .*	Twelve-bar blues, plus extension (as before)
1:24(1:30)	Chorus + extension	*Don't be cruel . . . I don't want . . .*	
1:39 (1:50)	Concluding chorus + Additional extension	*Don't be cruel . . . Don't be cruel . . . I don't want . . .*	

be denied that Elvis Presley's principal importance as a musical influence and innovator—like that of Chuck Berry, Little Richard, and Fats Domino—rests upon his achievements during the early years of rock 'n' roll. In 1956 Presley cut a handful of records that literally changed the world for himself and for those around him, and the unbridled exuberance of his live performances at that time became the model for every white kid who wanted to move mountains by strumming a guitar, shaking his hips, and lifting his voice.

BUDDY HOLLY

Buddy Holly (Charles Hardin Holley) (1936–1959) offered an image virtually the opposite of Presley's intense, aggressive, suggestively sexual stage persona. Here was a clean-cut, lanky, bespectacled young man—obviously nobody's idea of a matinee idol, but one who certainly knew his way around a guitar and a recording studio. The Texas-born Holly began his career with country music but soon fell under the influence of Presley's musical style and success and formed a rock 'n' roll band called the Crickets.

Holly's first record in his new style, "That'll Be the Day," rose to Number 1 on the pop charts in late 1957 and established his characteristic and highly influential sound. "That'll Be the Day" combined elements of country, rhythm & blues, and mainstream pop in the kind of synthesis that typified rock 'n' roll in a general sense, but which nevertheless projected a distinctive approach and sensibility. Holly's vocal style, full of country twang, hiccups, and expressive blue notes, projected that mixture of toughness and vulnerability that forms the essence of both fine country singing and fine blues singing. The Crickets' instrumental lineup of two electric guitars (lead and rhythm), bass, and drums provided an intense support for Holly's voice, and during instrumental breaks, Holly's lead guitar playing was active, riff-based, and hard-edged in a way that reflected the influence of Chuck Berry. "That'll Be the Day" is structured like a typical pop song, alternating verses and choruses of eight bars each, but when it comes time to provide an instrumental break, the Crickets play a twelve-bar blues pattern. This approach works, because important aspects of both vocal and instrumental style throughout the record are based on blues- and rhythm & blues–derived elements. On some later records, like "Oh, Boy!" and "Peggy Sue," Holly used a twelve-bar blues structure for the song itself.

When he was twenty-two, Buddy Holly's career was tragically cut short by a plane crash that also claimed the lives of two other prominent rock 'n' roll personalities: the promising seventeen-year-old Chicano singer and songwriter Ritchie Valens, whose music proved to be an important stimulus for later Mexican American musicians like Carlos Santana and the members of the group Los Lobos (see the Listening Guide for "La Bamba" later in this chapter); and the Big Bopper (J. P. Richardson), who had achieved success with novelty records such at "Chantilly Lace." (This tragedy was the subject of Don McLean's famous record "American Pie," released in 1971.) A measure of Holly's influence on later pop music may be seen in the fact that the Beatles modeled their insect-based name, their four-piece instrumental lineup, and aspects of their vocal style on the Crickets—and through the Beatles, of course, that influence passed on to innumerable bands. Holly was also, like Chuck Berry, an important rock 'n' roll songwriter; in addition to the songs already mentioned, he wrote and recorded "Everyday," "Not Fade Away," "Rave On," and others, which became increasingly popular in the

Buddy Holly performs with the Crickets, c. 1957.

years after his death and were covered by rock bands. Furthermore, Holly's work with arrangements and studio effects looked forward to some of the recording techniques of the 1960s. He frequently used **double-tracking** on his recordings—a technique in which two nearly identical versions of the same vocal or instrumental part are recorded on top of one another, foregrounding that part so that it seems to come right out of the speaker at the listener—and some of his last records used orchestral strings.

Wild, Wild Young Women: Female Rock 'n' Roll Pioneers

While reading this completely male-dominated account of the early history of rock 'n' roll, it is only natural to ask: Where were the women? We have seen that there was a significant and occasionally empowered female presence both in rhythm & blues and in country music by the early 1950s (recall Big Mama Thornton's "Hound Dog" and Kitty Wells's "It Wasn't God Who Made Honky-Tonk Angels"); didn't some of this carry over into rock 'n' roll? Even the conservative mainstream pop music of the early to mid-1950s featured among its "big singers" strong female vocalists such as Doris Day, Patti Page, Jo Stafford, and Rosemary Clooney.

BOX 8.2 THE ELECTRIC GUITAR

It is almost impossible to conjure up a mental image of Chuck Berry—or Buddy Holly, or Jimi Hendrix—without an electric guitar in his hands. Certainly, one of rock 'n' roll's most significant effects on popular music was its elevation of the electric guitar to the position of centrality that the instrument still enjoys in most genres of popular music today. The development of the electric guitar is a good example of the complex relationship between technological developments and changing musical styles. Up through the end of World War II, the guitar was found mainly in popular music that originated in the South (blues and hillbilly music), and in various "exotic" genres (Hawaiian and Latin American guitar records were quite popular in the 1920s and 1930s). Because of its low volume, the acoustic guitar was difficult to use in large dance bands and equally difficult to record. Engineers began to experiment with electronically amplified guitars in the 1920s, and in 1931 the Electro String Instrument Company (better known as Rickenbacker) introduced the first commercially produced electric guitars. Laid across the player's knees like the steel or Hawaiian guitars used in country music and blues, these instruments were called "frying pans" because of their distinctive round bodies and long necks. By the mid-1930s the Gibson Company had introduced a hollow-body guitar with a new type of pickup—a magnetic plate or coil attached to the body of the guitar, which converts the physical vibrations of its strings into patterns of electric energy. This pickup later became known as the Charlie Christian pickup, after the young African American guitarist from Texas (1916–1942) who introduced the guitar into Benny Goodman's band and helped to pioneer the modern jazz style called bebop. Despite Christian's innovations with the Goodman band, few of the big swing bands incorporated the instrument into their ensembles, and none allowed it to play a prominent role.

The solid-body electric guitar was developed after World War II and was first used in rhythm & blues, blues, and country bands—the country musician Merle Travis (1917–1983) had one designed for him as early as 1946, and blues musicians such as T-Bone Walker (1910–1975) and Muddy Waters were also recording with electric guitars by the late 1940s. The first commercially produced solid-body electric guitar was the Fender Broadcaster (soon renamed the Telecaster), brainchild of Leo Fender and George Fullerton. This model, released in 1948, featured two electronic pickups, knobs to control volume and tone (timbre), and a switch that allowed the two pickups to be used alone or together, permitting the player to create a palette of different sounds. In 1954 Fender released the Stratocaster, the first guitar with three pickups, and the first with a "whammy bar" or "vibrato bar," a metal rod attached to the guitar's bridge that allowed the player to bend pitches with his right as well as his left hand. Fender's most successful competitor, the Gibson Company, released a solid-body guitar in 1952 that it christened the Les Paul, in honor of the popular guitarist who helped to popularize the new instrument and the use of multiple-track tape recording. The first widely popular electric bass guitar, the Fender Precision Bass, was introduced in 1951.

What is it about electric guitars that makes them such objects of fascination—sometimes bordering on fetishism—for musicians and fans alike? Like any kind of influential technology—say, the automobile or the phonograph—the meaning of the guitar is a complex matter. To begin with, the instrument came into the popular mainstream with a somewhat dubious reputation—perhaps a carryover from the medieval European association of stringed instruments with the Devil—and was long associated with the music of marginalized regions (the South, Latin America) and marginalized people (sailors and railway men, sharecroppers and hobos, Blacks, Latinos, and poor Southern whites). A lot of the put-downs aimed at young rock 'n' rollers by the mainstream music press of the 1950s ridiculed the guitar, suggesting that it was an instrument that anyone could play (if you believe that, we suggest that you take a few guitar lessons!). The electric guitar became a symbol of the energetic diversity that was elbowing its way into the mainstream of American popular music during this period. This feeling of excess and invasion was reinforced by the development of portable tube amplifiers, which, if pushed hard enough, could provide a dense, sizzling, and very loud sound, eventually augmented by special effects devices such as wah-wah pedals and "fuzz boxes," that was perfectly designed to drive parents and other authority figures nuts. In addition, the suitability of the guitar for use as a phallic symbol—a formerly male practice more recently appropriated by female rockers—has added to the instrument's aura of danger and excitement.

The truth of the matter is paradoxical. It is both correct and incorrect to claim that there were no female rock 'n' rollers comparable to the men we have been discussing. It is correct simply because, during the formative years of rock 'n' roll as a commercial phenomenon, women who aggressively embraced the new stylistic trends were a negligible presence on the charts. But it is incorrect because this lack of hit records doesn't mean that female rock 'n' roll artists didn't exist—far from it! The example of **Wanda Jackson**, probably the most remarkable of the pioneering rock 'n' roll women, illustrates the situation perfectly (see Box 8.3).

Among young women who could be viewed as stylistic "sisters" of Wanda Jackson was Virginia-born **Janis Martin** (1940–2007), barely sixteen years old when RCA Victor (Presley's own label) began promoting her as literally "the female Elvis" in 1956. Her teen-friendly records, like "My Boy Elvis" and her own composition "Drugstore Rock 'n' Roll," are energetic, thoroughly professional rockabilly and compare favorably with many big hits from the period. Yet Martin proved unable to make the hoped-for big impact, and by 1958—when what had been her secret marriage unavoidably became public knowledge as a result of her pregnancy—she had been dropped by RCA and quickly consigned to obscurity. **Jo Ann Campbell** (b. 1938 in Florida) was showcased by disc jockey Alan Freed as "the blonde bombshell" on his radio show, in his "rock 'n' roll revues," and in his movie *Go, Johnny Go!* (1959); in spite of this public exposure, such fine Campbell recordings as "Wait a Minute" and "You're Driving Me Mad," both of which exhibit the strong influence of rhythm & blues in their driving band arrangements, failed to achieve commercial success. **Lorrie (Lawrencine) Collins** (b. 1942 in Oklahoma, d. 2018) performed with her even younger brother Larry as the "Collins Kids" duo; their act became well known through television in the mid-1950s, and they also cut some scintillating rockabilly records for Columbia between 1956 and 1958. In particular, "Heartbeat" and "Mercy," both written by the Collins Kids themselves, feature the intense sound of Lorrie Collins's solo voice, but neither these nor any of their other recordings made the charts. Like Wanda Jackson, Martin, Campbell, and Collins all were gifted rock 'n' roll performers at a young (even very young) age, whose talents extended to the occasional writing of their own material, and who did not lack for publicity. Yet these three are so obscure today that neither the eleven-hundred-page *Rolling Stone Encyclopedia of Rock & Roll* nor the wide-ranging *Trouble Girls: The Rolling Stone Book of Women in Rock* so much as mentions any of them. In effect, these women—and who knows how many others like them?—have been written out of history. The phenomenon cries out for some larger explanation than multiple individual instances of bad luck.

Clearly the essential conservatism of the 1950s, politically and culturally, made it a particularly inauspicious time to be seen as a rebellious and empowered young woman. The rebellious, empowered young men of early rock 'n' roll proved controversial enough, and most teenagers of the period—both male and female—were happy admiring these men from a safe distance, and without wishing the rock 'n' roll attitude to cross the gender divide. The post–World War II ideal of domestic femininity proved to be extremely powerful and provoked no widespread and enduring challenges until the 1960s.

BOX 8.3 WANDA JACKSON

The Oklahoma-born Wanda Jackson (b. 1937), a multitalented singer, instrumentalist, and songwriter, had already achieved success in the country music field singing and touring with Hank Thompson (of "The Wild Side of Life" fame) when—still a teenager—she encountered Elvis Presley as the career of the "hillbilly cat" was just beginning to take off. Presley astutely sensed that Jackson would have a gift for performing rockabilly music, and he encouraged her to record in the style. Jackson's own rockabilly career began with "I Gotta Know" in 1956, a kind of transitional song that presented the unique pairing of breakneck, rocking verses with a moderately paced, country-waltz chorus. Following this record, between late 1956 and early 1958 Jackson recorded fierce performances of unapologetic rockers like "Hot Dog! That Made Him Mad," "Fujiyama Mama," "Let's Have a Party," and her own "Mean Mean Man," performances that established her as one of the most powerful and convincing rockabilly musicians of her time. In terms of pure energy, vocal charisma, aggressive sexuality, and stylistic mastery of both rhythm & blues and country elements, Jackson appears on these records as a performer who could readily go toe-to-toe (or pelvis to pelvis!) with Elvis Presley or any of the other major male rock 'n' rollers of this period.

"Hot Dog! That Made Him Mad" (1956) offers a fine example of Jackson staking a claim to be the "Queen of Rockabilly." The brief instrumental introduction, dominated by the electric guitar, establishes an emphatic danceable beat, but the instruments are literally stopped short by the force of Jackson's vocal entrance. This stop-time effect is employed at the beginning of each of the song's four strophes, and again toward the end of each strophe for Jackson's sizzling delivery of the title words. (Notice how aggressively she stretches out the word "hot"!) This arrangement allows the singer's vocal style and power to dominate the entire record. A final stop-time passage occurs at the conclusion of the recording when Jackson, in a leisurely free tempo, lingers over "he'll hug you and he'll kiss you, he'll squeeze you and he'll please you" in a manner allowing no doubt that here is a woman who understands exactly what she wants, and who has no hesitation about requiring it from her guy.

The female empowerment expressed in this song's lyrics, underlined in every way by Wanda Jackson's performance, goes beyond self-knowledge and self-assurance into an assertion of complete independence that might well have flustered a typical listener in the culturally and sexually conservative 1950s. The song's protagonist is unfazed even when her man threatens to leave; she will have this relationship on her own terms, or she's content not to have it at all! But there were relatively few listeners who actually got the chance to hear this strikingly unconventional record, simply because it wasn't played very much; "Hot Dog! That Made Him Mad" crossed too many stylistic and gender-based

Wanda Jackson.

(continued)

BOX 15.1 WANDA JACKSON (*continued*)

boundary lines for its time. (Interestingly, this song of female empowerment is credited to two male songwriters, Danny Barker and Don Raye.)

In the first flush of rock 'n' roll, one might have hoped that Wanda Jackson had everything possible going for her: she was an exceptional recording artist, a young and extremely photogenic woman, and an enthusiastic live performer who had the support of a major label (Capitol). Her records are rockabilly "classics" in every respect—except for one: none of them were hits! Following the modest showing of "I Gotta Know" on the country disc jockey chart (Number 15 in 1956, indicating that the record was getting some airplay on country music stations), Jackson vanished from all the charts for nearly four years. Capitol Records finally released "Let's Have a Party," originally an album track, as a single in 1960, two years after it was recorded, and Jackson scored her first entry on the mainstream pop chart with it—but it peaked at Number 37. By this time, however, Jackson's hopes for becoming a major rock 'n' roll star had understandably soured, and she was well on her way back to concentrating on more traditional-sounding country music—a style that enabled her to maintain some chart presence into the early 1970s.

If Wanda Jackson's story were unique, her lack of mainstream success could be attributed simply to the kind of "accidental" bad luck that all too frequently befalls very gifted people. And it must be granted that, in some respects, Jackson courted controversy. She embraced the implicit interracial character of rock 'n' roll to the extent of touring with an integrated band—a daring move for the time—and she refused to perform in any venues where her African American pianist, Big Al Downing, would face prejudicial treatment. (She also threatened, in the lyrics of "Fujiyama Mama," to "blow your head off" with nitroglycerine if you spoke ill of her!) Nevertheless, there were other talented candidates for a "female Elvis Presley" among young white Southern women in the 1950s, and each of them met an analogous fate.

Given the tenor of the times, an empowered *Black* female rock 'n' roll "idol" would have been even more unlikely—which is why African American women have played no part in this discussion. Only a few female Black artists, such as LaVern Baker and Sarah Vaughan, achieved even modest success on the pop charts during the early years of rock 'n' roll. In 1957 the Bobbettes, a group of five African American schoolgirls from New York's Harlem, seemed to come out of nowhere with an irresistible rock 'n' roll hit about their fifth-grade teacher, "Mr. Lee" (Number 6 pop, Number 1 R&B), after which the girls just as abruptly disappeared into oblivion.

The first woman who could be called a real recording "star" of the rock 'n' roll era is Italian American ***Connie Francis*** (b. 1938 as Concetta Rosa Maria Franconero in New Jersey), whose string of hit records only began in 1958 with her revival of a Tin Pan Alley tune from 1923, "Who's Sorry Now." Although Francis did occasionally perform bona fide rockers (such as "Stupid Cupid," Number 14 pop in 1958, and "Lipstick on Your Collar," Number 5 pop in 1959), her output overall is highly eclectic and best understood as that of a mainstream pop singer who appreciated the importance of appealing to the new young audience. Compared with someone like Wanda Jackson, Connie Francis—both on records and in her public image—seemed, if not demure, at least utterly unthreatening. By 1960 America was at last ready to embrace a young female recording artist with at least a somewhat feisty public image, and the teenage ***Brenda Lee*** (b. 1944 as Brenda Mae Tarpley in Georgia), who became known as "Little Miss Dynamite," was there to fill the bill with engaging rock 'n' roll songs like "Sweet Nothin's" (Number 4 pop, 1960) and "Rockin' Around the Christmas Tree" (Number 14 pop, 1960). Lee also recorded a large proportion of slow, sentimental love songs, but the real measure of just how far she was from being a true "female Elvis" may be taken by comparing any of her rock 'n' roll records to Wanda Jackson's "Fujiyama Mama," or even to Lorrie Collins's "Mercy."

The Latin Side of Rock 'n' Roll

Latin American music exerted an important influence on the popular genres that contributed to the rise of rock 'n' roll in the mid-1950s. The Latin tinge in rhythm & blues reflected the long-standing appreciation of Latin music in America's Black communities. Afro-Cuban music and its derivatives in the United States—including the rumba, the bolero, and the mambo—exerted a pervasive, if underrecognized, influence on R&B, an influence particularly evident in the work of musicians who grew up, played regularly, or recorded in New Orleans. The strongest Latin influences on country and western music came from Mexico and Mexican-American communities in the American Southwest. Western swing musicians such as Bob Wills and the Texas Playboys explicitly incorporated elements from Mexican mariachi music, and the influence of the *corrido* ballad song tradition is clear in hit recordings like Marty Robbins's "El Paso" (Number 1 on both the country and pop charts, 1960).

The Latin influence on rock 'n' roll is perhaps best exemplified by recordings made during the late 1950s in Los Angeles. The most popular of the musicians to emerge from the Los Angeles scene was Richard Valenzuela, who performed as **Ritchie Valens** (1941–1959) and was born in Pacoima, California, to working-class Mexican American parents. Although Valens's recording career lasted only eight months—cut short by the plane crash that also killed Buddy Holly and the Big Bopper—his recordings, released on the independent label Del-Fi Records, helped to create a distinctive Los Angeles rock 'n' roll sound. (Other such recordings included the Champs' Number 1 pop and R&B single, "Tequila" [1958], an instrumental number written by Mexican American drummer Danny Flores.)

Valens grew up surrounded by Mexican and country and western music but also listened keenly to rhythm & blues groups like the Drifters and rock 'n' rollers Buddy Holly, Bo Diddley, and Little Richard. His parents bought him a guitar, and he joined a local dance band, the Silhouettes, at sixteen. In 1958 Valens auditioned for Del-Fi owner Bob Keane and recorded his debut single, "Come On, Let's Go" (Number 42 pop, Number 27 R&B), at Gold Star Studios in Los Angeles. (This song was later covered by the Ramones, a punk rock band.) Valens's second recording date produced "Donna" and "La Bamba," hurriedly released on two sides of a 45 rpm single after a deejay played a test-pressing of the former song on a popular Los Angeles radio station. "Donna," which reached Number 2 on both the pop and R&B charts, was a classic teen love song written for a girl Valens knew in high school. Valens made a trip to New York in late 1958 to promote the record, appearing on Dick Clark's *American Bandstand* and Alan Freed's *Christmas*

Listening Guide RITCHIE VALENS'S "LA BAMBA"

Traditional Mexican folk song; adapted and performed by Ritchie Valens; recorded 1958

While his other recordings were excellent but conventional rock 'n' roll, Valens's most original contribution was the song "La Bamba" (Number 22 pop), an adaptation of a folk song from the Mexican region of Veracruz. To understand the creativity of his reworking of the song, we need to know a bit about the genre from which it sprang, a three-hundred-year-old tradition called "son jarocho."

Situated on Mexico's Caribbean coast, Veracruz is one of the historical centers of Afro-Mexican culture, and the region's music reflects a blend of Spanish, African, and Native American elements. Son jarocho is a fiery, up-tempo genre that alternates vocal refrains (estribillos) with rapid improvisational passages, accompanied by an ensemble of stringed instruments. The typical jarocho group consists of an arpa (a wooden harp) and

Ritchie Valens.

two smaller relatives of the guitar, the jarana and the requinto. The harpist usually plays a bass line with one hand and rapid melodic figures on the higher strings with the other hand, while the requinto adds improvisational lines complementing the harp and the jarana provides a vigorously strummed chordal accompaniment. Although jarocho groups play in a variety of social contexts—including tourist hotels—the genre is particularly associated with wedding ceremonies, at which the bride and groom together perform a subtle dance that symbolizes their unity.

Although the son jarocho was not as well known to American audiences as northern Mexican genres like mariachi, a number of musicians from Veracruz moved to Mexico City in the 1940s and made recordings and appeared in films that gained wider exposure for the tradition. This is very likely how the song "La Bamba" came to the attention of the young Ritchie Valens, living in a ranch house in the San Fernando Valley.

Compared to a more traditional rendition of "La Bamba," with its improvisation and dense interweaving of melodic-rhythmic patterns, Valens's version is much simpler and sparer in texture. The recording opens abruptly with a brief ascending line on the electric bass, followed by the rhythm guitar playing the basic chord pattern, which is soon doubled by the bass. The "La Bamba" pattern consists of a three-chord sequence heard later in thousands of other rock 'n' roll songs (e.g., "Twist and Shout"), and it became one of the most enduring riffs in popular music history, part of the repertoire of every aspiring rock 'n' roll guitarist or bassist.

After a mambo-like pause, Valens sings the traditional verses without any improvisation (more like a pop tune than a traditional son jarocho performance). The dance pulse, played by the great session drummer Earl Palmer, is reinforced by his use of a woodblock—reminiscent of the Cuban claves used in Latin dance music—to play a rhythm derived from the then-popular cha-cha-chá, a nonsyncopated rhythmic feel suitable for the driving rock 'n' roll groove. The rest of the two-minute, five-second recording—quite short for a 45 rpm single—follows this basic form, with an energetic guitar solo by Valens inserted in the middle.

"La Bamba" is unique among early rock 'n' roll records not only because of the source of the inspiration—a Mexican folk song—and because the lyric is exclusively in Spanish, but also because of the sonic texture of the recording, which is shaped by the unique tone qualities of the instruments used. The iconic opening rhythm guitar part is played by the renowned studio musician Carol Kaye on a large, hollow-bodied electric guitar. The Gibson Super 400 has what guitarists sometimes call a "woody" sound, here given a slightly "fuzzy" timbre by the distortion of the tube amplifier through which it is played. Valens plays his guitar solo on another hollow-bodied electric guitar, a Harmony H44 Stratotone.

The bass part is played on a Danelectro bass guitar, which had previously been used mainly in country and western recording sessions, often in combination with an acoustic string bass. (This combination was also used to great effect on Nancy Sinatra's 1966 Number 1 single "These Boots Are Made for Walkin'.") When played with a guitar pick, the Danelectro produces a slight percussive "click" on each note, and its thick, heavy sound gives the bass guitar in "La Bamba" a more immediate presence than is typical of early rock 'n' roll records.

Show, alongside his idols Chuck Berry and Bo Diddley. Tragically, "Donna"/"La Bamba" was the last of Valens's records to be released during his lifetime.

It is hard to know what impact Ritchie Valens might have exerted on the emergence of a Latin-influenced variant of rock 'n' roll had he not died so young. But his influence lives on, not least in the cover version of "La Bamba" performed by Los Lobos, a Chicano rock group formed in East Los Angeles in 1973. Their version of "La Bamba," featured in a semifictionalized film account of Valens's life (*La Bamba,* 1987), was a Number 1 pop single for three weeks in 1987.

Songwriters and Producers of Early Rock 'n' Roll

The relatively clear lines of division between songwriters and performers that characterized the world of mainstream pop music up to around 1955 no longer held up in the early years of rock 'n' roll's mainstream success. This is because the roots of rock 'n' roll lie with rhythm & blues and country music, areas of activity in which, as we have seen, performers often write their own songs and, conversely, songwriters frequently perform and record their own works. Of the five early rock 'n' roll stars we have discussed in detail, only Elvis Presley did not regularly write his own material. This diminishing importance of the independent songwriter represented another major shift brought about by the rock 'n' roll revolution. In time, it came to be expected that performers would be the composers of their own songs, and this expectation led to a correspondingly stronger identification of artists with specific material. Here lie the origins of the mystique of the pop music personality as a creative artist, rather than as merely an interpreter—a mystique that came into its own in the later 1960s.

None of this meant that important nonperforming songwriters ceased to exist, of course. As we shall see in the next chapter, the early 1960s actually saw a renewed emphasis on songwriting as an independent craft, at least prior to the heyday of songwriting bands like the Beatles and songwriter/performers like Bob Dylan. And with the increasing importance of the recording itself as the basic document of rock 'n' roll music, another behind-the-scenes job grew steadily in importance in the later 1950s and the early 1960s: that of the record producer. Producers could be responsible for many tasks, from booking time in the recording studio to hiring backup singers and instrumentalists and assisting with the engineering process. Essentially, though, the producer was responsible for the characteristic *sound* of the finished record, and the best producers left as strong a sense of individual personality on their products as did the recording artists themselves. When the producer and the songwriter were the same person (or persons), his or her importance and influence could be powerful indeed.

This was the case with the most innovative songwriting/producing team of the early rock 'n' roll years, *Jerry Leiber* (1933–2011) and *Mike Stoller* (b. 1933). Leiber and Stoller were not recording artists, but they were already writing rhythm & blues songs when they were teenagers. Eventually they wrote and produced many hits for Elvis Presley, and they did the same for one of the most popular vocal groups of this period, the Coasters. (They also produced and did occasional writing for the Drifters, and the elaborately produced orchestral sound of these records in the early 1960s was possibly even more influential than Leiber and Stoller's previous records had been in the later 1950s.) The team constructed what they called "playlets" for the Coasters, scenes from teenage life of the 1950s distilled into brilliantly funny rock 'n' roll records. Like many of the songs of Chuck Berry, the Coasters' hits were specifically about, and for, their intended audience. An examination of "Charlie Brown" will enable us to appreciate in detail this targeting of the teenage audience, along with the vocal artistry of the Coasters and the behind-the-scenes writing and production artistry of Leiber and Stoller.

Other Currents: The Standard and Folk Music in the Rock 'n' Roll Era

The advent of rock 'n' roll is often viewed as the death of Tin Pan Alley. It is easy to see why this would seem to be so. Country and rhythm & blues–based musical styles were moving to the center of the pop world from the peripheries, and Tin Pan Alley music represented the mainstream against which the baby boomers were rebelling: it was their parents' music. However, the Tin Pan Alley style proved versatile enough to survive, and even flourish, in a number of different guises during the early years of rock 'n' roll.

Fats Domino was not the only rock 'n' roller to successfully adapt standard songs to a rhythm & blues–based style. The procedure was a stock in trade of many Black vocal groups; the Platters virtually made a career of it, scoring Number 1 hits with "My Prayer" (1956), "Twilight Time" (1958), and "Smoke Gets in Your Eyes" (1959). These were all Tin Pan Alley tunes, dressed up with strong backbeats and a commanding, extroverted lead vocal, that were accepted by young listeners as rock 'n' roll ballads. From the country side, Elvis Presley included Tin Pan Alley standards in his performing repertoire from

Listening Guide "CHARLIE BROWN"

Music and lyrics by Jerry Leiber and Mike Stoller; performed by the Coasters with accompanying band (King Curtis, sax solo); recorded 1958

Basic Description

"Charlie Brown" presents an indelible portrait of a ubiquitous figure, the class clown. Although such a song topic would probably not have occurred to anyone prior to the 1950s, it certainly was an effective choice at a point when, for the first time ever, the biggest market of potential record buyers consisted of schoolchildren: junior high schoolers, high schoolers, and even elementary schoolers, each of whom probably knew a "Charlie Brown" in at least one of his or her classes. The specific time period and culture of the 1950s is evoked through a sparing but telling use of then-current slang terms like "cool" and "daddy-o."

From the first arresting vocal hook, "Fee fee, fie fie, fo fo, fum," the record brims with unrelenting high energy. Like Chuck Berry, the Coasters were adept at delivering a dense, cleverly worded text very clearly at a fast tempo. The intensity of the Coasters' vocal style owes much to rhythm & blues, although certain comic effects—like the low bass voice repeatedly asking, "Why's everybody always pickin' on me?" and "Who, me?" in the bridge—suggest roots going back to vaudeville routines. (The low bass voice was also a staple element of rhythm & blues group singing style; see the discussion of the Chords' "Sh-Boom" earlier in this chapter.) Several highly effective elements include the contrasts between passages that are essentially vocal solos (with occasional, minimal contributions by the rhythm instruments, at the start of each A section—see the accompanying chart), and the following passages in which the full band offers a steady accompaniment and the saxophone engages in call-and-response with the vocal group.

Form

"Charlie Brown" combines aspects of two different formal designs we have encountered in previous musical examples. The song reveals its mainstream pop roots in its overall AABA structure. However, the A sections are twelve-bar blues stanzas, which would not of course be typical of a Tin Pan Alley tune; furthermore, each A section divides the twelve bars into a little verse-chorus structure of the type we have seen in "Long Tall Sally" and "Don't Be Cruel." The song's most direct kinship is

with "Long Tall Sally": four bars of verse, followed by eight bars of chorus. The kinship is that much more marked because of an additional similarity between the two: in both "Charlie Brown" and "Long Tall Sally" the twelve-bar blues stanzas start off with vocal solos, and a continuous full accompaniment does not join in until the chorus portions at the fifth bar of the structure. The B section, in contrast, is eight bars in length, providing a harmonic and rhythmic release from the succession of blues structures.

The Song/The Recording

As songwriters, Leiber and Stoller always had an interest in mixing—even scrambling—elements derived from rhythm & blues music, which they knew well and loved, with elements derived from mainstream pop. This interest is evident in the form of "Charlie Brown" itself, as we have discussed, but it may also be seen in certain details. For example, the twelve-bar blues stanzas in the song are noticeably lacking in blue notes; Leiber and Stoller wrote a simple pop-oriented melody and just directed the bass singer to speak his solo line. But as producers, Leiber and Stoller brought in King Curtis, a Texas-born rhythm & blues saxophonist, to play on the record. In his twelve-bar instrumental break Curtis emphasized blue notes, jumping in front of and behind the beat in a syncopated manner evocative of stuttering (this style, as much indebted to country hoedown music as to R&B, was also used successfully by the country and western saxophonist Boots Randolph). Curtis's "yackety sax" sound links the Coasters' record to both rhythm & blues and country music and creates a humorous, goofy effect perfectly suited to the comic tale of Charlie Brown.

Apart from the sparkling clarity of the recording, there is only one prominent production effect in "Charlie Brown": the artificially high voices in the bridge on "Yeah, you!" This effect was produced by playing a tape of normal voices at double speed, a device that was popular on novelty records of this time. Here we see the modest beginnings of the kind of artificial studio effects that would be found on more and more records as producers more and more took advantage of increasingly sophisticated recording studios and techniques.

(continued)

Listening Guide "CHARLIE BROWN" (*continued*)

LISTENING GUIDE	"CHARLIE BROWN"		
TIME	**FORM**	**LYRIC**	**DESCRIPTIVE COMMENTS**
0:00	A (verse)	*Fee, fee, fie, fie . . .*	Twelve-bar blues stanza, divided into a four-bar verse (vocal solo) and an eight-bar chorus, with full accompaniment and call and response between the voices and the saxophone
0:08	Chorus	*Charlie Brown, Charlie Brown . . .*	
0:23	A (verse)	*That's him . . .*	As before
0:31	Chorus	*Charlie Brown . . .*	
0:46	B	*Who's always . . .*	Bridge section
1:01	A (verse)	*Who walks . . .*	As before
1:08	Chorus	*Charlie Brown . . .*	
1:24	Instrumental break		Twelve-bar blues stanza, constructed exactly like the A sections, but with the voices absent and the saxophone freely improvising over the rhythmic and chordal structure; blue notes are noticeable in the sax solo
1:46	Repetition of final A section		
2:09	Instrumental fade-out		

the beginning of his career with Sun Records, and in 1959 the country artist Carl Mann achieved a pop hit with his rockabilly version of "Mona Lisa," a song that had been a huge success in 1950 for Nat "King" Cole as a Tin Pan Alley–style ballad.

Furthermore, new songs in the old Tin Pan Alley style could be found on the pop charts even in the late 1950s, along with the new rock 'n' roll hits. In what might seem one of the unlikeliest musical success stories of the era, the young singer *Johnny Mathis* (b. 1935, the same year as Elvis Presley) began a career in 1957 as a latter-day crooner, releasing gentle pop ballads like "It's Not for Me to Say" and "Chances Are," and soon found himself a bestselling recording artist who appealed as much to the rock 'n' roll generation as he did to their parents. Mathis's widespread acceptance makes one hesitate to call his approach anachronistic and demonstrates again the fluidity of pop music styles and trends during this period.

Perhaps the most remarkable manifestation of Tin Pan Alley endurance may be found in the career and recordings of Frank Sinatra during the 1950s. Sinatra's status as *the* pop icon of the 1940s (see Chapter 7) seemed well on the wane in the opening years of the new decade; his records were no longer selling well, and by 1952 Columbia had allowed his contract to lapse. Reluctantly picked up by Capitol Records, Sinatra turned to the adult audience and to the new medium of the LP to reinvent himself, and he spectacularly revived his career. This feat involved a rethinking of the standard Tin Pan Alley repertoire, along with some novel ideas about the possibilities inherent in the pop album format.

Working with distinguished arranger/conductors like Billy May and Nelson Riddle, Sinatra conceived fresh interpretations of standards that reworked these old songs and, in some cases, brought new and unexpected meanings to them. One of the most famous examples of this is Sinatra's 1956 recording of "I've Got You under My Skin," a Cole Porter standard from the 1930s. The song most readily suggests a mood of acquiescence—of giving in to the condition of being obsessed by, and possessed by, another. But Sinatra's interpretation brings a novel and occasionally aggressive intensity to the song, as if the singer is surprised and even somewhat at war with his own newly discovered sense of vulnerability. This version uncovers new layers of richness and potential in a song that other singers and listeners might just have taken for granted in the 1950s, and Sinatra managed to do this with many of the standards he recorded during this decade. Furthermore, Sinatra presented these standards not as single records but in groups, in albums that were designed by him and his arranger/conductors as complete and integrated listening experiences, as opposed to essentially random collections of single songs. For example, "I've Got You under My Skin" was on the album *Songs for Swingin' Lovers*, on which Sinatra's distinctive interpretation of Cole Porter's standard clearly meshed with the active, worldly implications of the album's theme. Among other Sinatra albums from this period that present standards in thematically unified groups are *In the Wee Small Hours* (1955), a collection of world-weary "saloon" songs and *Come Dance with Me* (1959). Although the term did not come into common use until the mid-1960s, it is arguable that Sinatra's are the first real concept albums (see Chapter 10). Like the songs within them, these albums have themselves become "standards" of pop excellence and innovation.

Spurred by his new success as an album artist, Sinatra also sought out good new material in the Tin Pan Alley mold to re-establish a strong presence on the pop singles charts. Many of these songs came from movies—a medium through which Sinatra also reinvigorated his career in the 1950s by appearing successfully as a dramatic actor in nonmusical films, in addition to starring in musicals. One of Sinatra's major hits of this period, "Love and Marriage," which he introduced in 1955 on a television production of the Thornton Wilder play *Our Town*, found new life—and a new audience—as the theme song for another television show in the 1980s, the long-running comedy *Married with Children.* By this time, Sinatra, in his seventies, was himself the longest-running superstar in the history of American popular music.

As unlikely as it might seem, folk music also penetrated the charts in the later 1950s. One of the big hits of this period was "Tom Dooley," an adaptation of an old ballad song, at once a throwback to an earlier era and a harbinger of important currents in American popular music of the 1960s. Even as the taste of most young people was attracted to the electrified sounds of rock 'n' roll, the urban folk-pop tradition that had been pioneered by the Weavers in the early 1950s (see Chapter 7) continued to expand its appeal. The most popular of the folk groups was the **Kingston Trio**, composed of Dave Guard, Nick Reynolds, and Bob Shane. Formed in 1957, the group was named after the capital of Jamaica—a gesture in the direction of the Caribbean calypso-pop hits of **Harry Belafonte** and other folk singers of the mid-1950s. The group featured smooth, pop-style performances of folk songs and accompanied themselves on acoustic instruments (guitar, banjo, and string bass). In a sense the Kingston Trio—three bright, smiling, well-scrubbed young white men in collegiate sweaters—represented a neatened-up and depoliticized version of the Weavers. Operating in a middle zone between the abandon of Elvis Presley and the nostalgia of Frank Sinatra, they were able to appeal to many younger listeners while not scaring Mom and Dad.

While their music may have lacked the creativity and social engagement of the Weavers or later folk artists such as Bob Dylan, the Kingston Trio were responsible for keeping public interest in folk music alive through the late 1950s and early 1960s. In addition, their hit records represented a new trend in the record business, the hit LP. While only two of their single releases made it into the Top 10, the Kingston Trio dominated the sales of 33⅓ rpm LP albums. They had five Number 1 albums on the pop charts between 1958 and 1960 and fifteen Top 10 albums between 1958 and 1963, and four of their LPs stayed on the *Billboard* charts for over two years, an astonishing feat.

The Kingston Trio's only Number 1 hit single was their adaptation of "Tom Dula," a nineteenth-century American ballad about an innocent man hanged to death for allegedly murdering his girlfriend. The trio's adaptation of this old song, "Tom Dooley," reached Number 1 on the pop charts in 1958, sold more than 3 million copies, and was the most popular song on their debut LP, *The Kingston Trio*, which stayed on the *Billboard* album charts for over three and a half years. (The song even inspired a movie, *The Legend of Tom Dooley.*) The form of "Tom Dooley" should be familiar to you by now—it is a strophic ballad, with a series of verses telling a story and a chorus that comes back between the verses. There is a strange contrast between the grim tale told by the lyrics—that of a man waiting to be hanged—and the cheerful, upbeat tone of the trio's performance. When they sing, "Hang down your head, Tom Dooley, poor boy, you're bound to die," they almost sound happy about it. While the contrast between the content and style in this recording may strike you as a bit odd, this approach was an important element of the Kingston Trio's huge success in the late 1950s and early 1960s—they were optimistic, enthusiastic, and not given to deep philosophical exploration or political experimentation, just nice boys, and fun to sing along with in the bargain.

The Kingston Trio, c. early 1960s.

BOX 8.4 SINGLES VERSUS ALBUMS: A CASE OF NOT-SO-PARALLEL UNIVERSES

Frank Sinatra was among the first artists to creatively exploit the distinctive potential of the LP album as a medium for popular music and to engage the new audience that evidently existed for that medium. This audience was buying millions of albums a year by the mid-1950s. And while there was some commonality at the time between artists who topped the charts of bestselling single records and those who were the bestselling artists on the album charts, the discrepancies between those charts were more telling than the similarities. A very successful rocker like Elvis Presley could sell countless singles while also releasing successful albums. But the album charts of the late 1950s were dominated by the names of those who had only a minor presence (such as Harry Belafonte) or virtually no presence (such as Jackie Gleason, conductor and composer or arranger of instrumental albums) on the contemporaneous singles charts. Obviously there was a large and distinctive audience for their music—doubtless an audience consisting principally of those older than the teenagers buying rock 'n' roll records.

The central story of pop music in the later 1950s and beyond has become that of rock-based music. Rock 'n' roll was disseminated overwhelmingly by means of the 45 rpm single; as a result, the parallel story—of the flourishing of the LP and some of the most successful music popularized on albums—has tended to be minimized or even ignored. Rock-oriented artists only began to make truly creative use of an album's potential in the mid-1960s, with the Beatles and the Beach Boys leading the way (see Chapters 9 and 10). Still, the histories of popular music, including the present one, have always relied (with a few exceptions) basically on individual songs to identify trends and create a narrative. While this is the only possible way to tell the story before the advent of the LP, the situation clearly becomes more complicated from the 1950s on.

The importance of albums is invariably stressed by standard histories in the case of certain rock-era

(continued)

BOX 8.4 SINGLES VERSUS ALBUMS: A CASE OF NOT-SO-PARALLEL UNIVERSES
(continued)

artists whose undeniable influence far exceeds their achievement as producers of hit singles. Bob Dylan was never a major singles artist; Jimi Hendrix had a sole Top 20 single ("All Along the Watchtower," Number 20, 1968) among seven entries in the Top 100 singles charts; Joni Mitchell had only one Top 10 hit in her entire career ("Help Me," Number 7, 1974) and a mere eleven entries in the Top 100; Led Zeppelin was also a negligible presence on the singles charts, with one exception ("Whole Lotta Love," Number 4, 1970). It may well seem arbitrary, however, to cite artists like Dylan, Mitchell, and Led Zeppelin as major players in the history of pop music while failing to acknowledge the impact and achievements of top album sellers like Harry Belafonte or, more recently, **Barbra Streisand**. Belafonte, a folk singer of Jamaican and West Indian parentage who popularized calypso music in the mid-1950s, might seem to some no more than a product of his times, with little lasting influence. From another point of view, however, he appears as an early, underrecognized pioneer of "world music," who performed songs from around the globe (Jamaica, Israel, South Africa) and introduced the South African singer and activist Miriam Makeba to substantial American audiences. Streisand, for her part, has delighted audiences on Broadway, in movies, in concert, and on records for decades with her artistry as an exceptionally versatile pop singer; while in no sense an innovator, she is among

the bestselling album artists of all time and surely merits a mention in any history of popular music, as acknowledgment both of her and of her legions of faithful fans.

It should also be noted that the LP has functioned from its early days as a medium for certain very popular genres of music that have never been served well by singles, such as Broadway cast albums and movie soundtracks. The bestselling album charts have also served recently as a much better indicator than the pop singles charts of the size of the audience for country music. Five of the ten bestselling album artists of the 2000s are country singers: Toby Keith, George Strait, Kenny Chesney, Tim McGraw, and Alan Jackson, with Keith and Strait standing in second and third places, right behind Jay Z! Jazz and even classical music LPs have numbered among the bestsellers at times, which further enriches and complicates the picture. American classical pianist Van Cliburn had the top-selling album for seven weeks in 1958, when his recording of Tchaikovsky's Piano Concerto No. 1 became a "smash hit" after Cliburn won an international piano competition; the recording remained on the album charts for 125 weeks. While it is not possible for any history to be all-inclusive, it is important for authors (and their readers!) to articulate the awareness that history is a story that may always be told in many different ways.

THE RISE OF rock 'n' roll in the mid-1950s transformed the landscape of American popular music, further cementing the popularity of Southern-derived styles that were themselves derived from the blues and country music and transforming the teenager into both a marketing concept and a cultural icon. The dominance of youth culture—and of the music industry's sometimes clumsy attempts to interpret and shape it—was to become even more predominant during the following decade, as rock 'n' roll gave way to rock. In the next two chapters we will follow this story in some detail, from the emergence of a new generation of American teen pop stars and the onset of the so-called British Invasion through the rise of soul music and the musical experimentation of the late 1960s counterculture.

Key Terms

double-tracking	rockabilly	slap-back
reverb	rock 'n' roll	

Key People

Alan Freed	Connie Francis	Little Richard (Richard
Antoine "Fats" Domino	Doris Day	Wayne Penniman)
Barbra Streisand	Elvis Presley	Lorrie (Lawrencine) Collins
Big Joe Turner	Harry Belafonte	Mike Stoller
Bill Black	Herman "Little Junior"	Professor Longhair
Bill Haley and the Comets	Parker	Ricky Nelson
Brenda Lee	Janis Martin	Ritchie Valens (Richard
Buddy Holly (Charles	Jerry Leiber	Valenzuela)
Hardin Holley)	Jo Ann Campbell	Scotty Moore
Charles Edward Anderson	Johnny Mathis	Wanda Jackson
("Chuck") Berry	Kingston Trio	

Review Questions

1. Who was Alan Freed, and what was his contribution to rock 'n' roll?
2. Describe the career of Elvis Presley. Where did he begin his recording career? How did his public image and music evolve throughout his career?
3. Who were the female artists in rock 'n' roll during the 1950s? Why were they not as popular as their male counterparts?
4. In what ways did rock 'n' roll affect youth culture in America during the 1950s?
5. What role did producers and songwriters fill during the rock era? How was this role different from previous eras?

"Good Vibrations"

9 American Pop and the British Invasion, 1960s

FEW ERAS IN AMERICAN HISTORY HAVE BEEN AS DISRUPTIVE, controversial, and violent as the decade of the 1960s. The civil rights movement, the Vietnam War, and the assassinations of President John F. Kennedy and the Reverend Martin Luther King Jr. are events that still inspire impassioned debate among both historians and everyday citizens at the beginning of the twenty-first century. But one claim about the decade that could scarcely be contested is this: popular music played a role of unprecedented centrality and importance in defining the character and spirit of the 1960s. This is because the baby boom generation played a vital role in the essential political and cultural events of this period, and the boomers were a generation identified to a remarkable degree, by themselves and by others, with their own popular music: rock 'n' roll. As rock 'n' roll developed and changed with the times, eventually becoming "rock," it came increasingly to serve as an outlet for expression of the hopes and fears of a generation coming to terms with American politics, the racial climate in the country, and a controversial war in Southeast Asia.

The decade surely began innocently enough. In fact, the Number 1 song in the country at the turn of the decade—as the innovative, rockin' 1950s gave way to the revolutionary, rockin' 1960s—was an acoustic, deliberately old-fashioned cowboy ballad called

"El Paso," written and performed by the country singer Marty Robbins. This historically inconvenient fact is worth pausing over for a number of reasons. It reminds us of the extent to which popular views of history inevitably entail simplification and the neatening out of the complex and disorderly details that form much of the substance of life and culture in any period and place. It also reveals once again how diverse and unpredictable the pop music market continued to be in 1960 and beyond. Furthermore, the popularity of "El Paso" attests to the pull that country music—and not just rockabilly!—continued to exert on mainstream pop at this time. This is important, because the significant contributions of country music to mainstream American pop of the 1950s and 1960s tend to be largely underestimated and undervalued by most historians and critics. The sudden reemergence of country music as a major market force from the late 1980s onward came as a surprise only to those who had been ignoring the full picture for a long time. Country has surely gained commercial strength in recent decades, but since the first hillbilly recordings in the 1920s, it has never been absent from the pop scene.

The Early 1960s: Dance Music and "Teenage Symphonies"

The early 1960s are often described as a lackluster period in the development of American popular music, a time of relative stasis between the excitement of the early rock 'n' roll years and the coming of the *Beatles* to America in 1964. But at least three important trends emerged in the early 1960s. A new kind of social dancing developed, inspired by "The Twist" and a spate of other dance-oriented records that gave rock 'n' roll music for the first time a new and distinctive set of movements and social customs to accompany it. Members of the first generation to grow up with rock 'n' roll began to assume positions of power in the music industry as writers and producers, while the Tin Pan Alley system was reinvented for the new music and its new audiences at the **Brill Building** in New York, Gold Star Studios in Los Angeles, and the Motown headquarters in Detroit. Finally, new stylistic possibilities (and cultural contexts) for rock 'n' roll began to emerge out of California, spearheaded by the *Beach Boys*, whose leader, Brian Wilson, established a model for many to follow by becoming an innovative performer, writer, and producer all rolled into one.

THE TWIST

"The Twist" began its popular career inauspiciously, as the B-side of a 1959 single by the veteran rhythm & blues group Hank Ballard and the Midnighters. Ballard was convinced that he had written a smash hit with "The Twist," a teen-oriented rock 'n' roll song using a twelve-bar blues structure that celebrated a simple, hip-swiveling dance step that was gaining some popularity among young African Americans. But the decision-makers at Ballard's indie label, King, didn't agree and promoted the other side of the record, a perfectly fine but more old-fashioned rhythm & blues ballad called "Teardrops on Your Letter." This tune peaked at Number 89 on *Billboard*'s "Hot 100" chart (although both sides of the record enjoyed popularity among rhythm & blues fans) and then promptly disappeared from view—along with, one would have assumed, "The Twist." However, the dance named in Ballard's song continued its still somewhat obscure existence.

Meanwhile, somebody must have paid serious attention to that flip side of "Teardrops on Your Letter"—somebody with connections at another indie label, Parkway. Since Parkway was based in Philadelphia, its artists had particularly easy access to *American Bandstand*, the teen-oriented, nationally broadcast television show that originated in the same city. *American Bandstand* was all about dancing: rock 'n' roll records were played, and the camera showed the teenagers in the studio dancing to them. It was the perfect venue for promoting a new dance record and a new dance to the broad rock 'n' roll audience.

Parkway recording artist **Chubby Checker** was himself all of eighteen when he cut a cover of Hank Ballard's "The Twist" in 1960. (His real name was Ernest Evans; his stage name had in fact been suggested by the wife of *American Bandstand* host **Dick Clark** because of Evans's resemblance to a young Fats Domino.) This record was heavily promoted, and this time around, Ballard's conviction about the song proved justified: it reached the Number 1 position on the charts. Checker's version adhered so closely to the vocal inflections and arrangement of the original that Ballard (when interviewed for the 1993 documentary movie *Twist*) claimed he mistook it for his own record the first time he heard it on the radio!

Even more than the song, the dance itself caught the imagination of young people nationwide as they had the opportunity to observe it on *American Bandstand*. (In fact, Ballard's original recording also entered the pop charts at this time, swept there by the wave of enthusiasm engendered by the dance.) The twist was essentially an individual, noncontact dance without any real steps. Although it was generally done by a boy-and-girl couple facing one another, there was no inherent reason why it had to be restricted to this format; it could, at least hypothetically, be performed by any number of people, in any dance floor pattern, and in any gender combination. The twist was not the first noncontact, free-form dance to emerge in the history of American social dancing, but its enormous popularity signaled a sea change in the entire culture of popular dance. Against all apparent odds, it turned out to be much more than a passing novelty.

Soon adults of all ages, classes, and races were doing the twist along with the teenagers. In turn, the popularity and wide social acceptance of this free-form dancing brought rock 'n' roll music to a significantly broader audience than ever before: it was no longer just music for teenagers but an accepted fact of American social life. Clubs called discotheques, dedicated to the twist and other free-form dances that followed in its wake—the pony, the mashed potato, the monkey, and countless others—sprang up all over; one of the most famous, New York's Peppermint Lounge, gave its name to one of the biggest hits of early 1962, "Peppermint Twist," recorded by the club's house band, Joey Dee and the Starliters. Less than a year after it completed its first chart run, Chubby Checker's "The Twist" was back on the Hot 100 for another go-round and reached Number 1 a second time. (This feat has been accomplished by only two records in the history of the pop charts; that the other one is Bing Crosby's "White Christmas" gives some indication

In 1961, everybody did the twist! Teenagers on *American Bandstand*; Chubby Checker (center), with country singer Conway Twitty (left) and *American Bandstand* host Dick Clark.

of the extraordinary level of popularity of both the twist as a dance and "The Twist" as a record.) Live rock 'n' roll shows began to include female "go-go" dancers along with the singing acts; in the later 1960s these dancers also began to be featured, with or without their clothes, in clubs where recorded rock music was played.

The free-form dances that have accompanied, and in some cases inspired, so much of American popular music from the 1960s to the present thus all find their point of origin in the twist. The discotheques of the 1960s were the ancestors of the discos of the 1970s, and the spirit of bodily freedom represented by those institutions persisted in the mosh pits and related venues of the 1990s and beyond, to the "twerking" craze of the 2010s. Rock 'n' roll had found a social body language that matched the novelty of the music and the feeling of liberation that it celebrated.

It should come as no surprise that, in the wake of "The Twist," many other popular songs of the early 1960s were dance-oriented. To cite only a few representative examples: Chubby Checker recorded "Let's Twist Again" in 1961; teenager Dee Dee Sharp cut a duet with Chubby Checker, "Slow Twistin'," in addition to recording "Mashed Potato Time" (both 1962) and "Do the Bird" (1963); songwriter *Carole King* tapped her babysitter, sixteen-year-old Little Eva (Eva Narcissus Boyd), to record her song "The Loco-Motion" in 1962; and the Motown group the Miracles sang about "Mickey's Monkey" (1963). (As we will see in Chapter 11, the later disco craze of the 1970s inspired an analogous flood of dance-oriented songs. Popular music designed specifically for dancing remained popular through the 1980s into the 1990s; at the time of this writing, "dance" is treated by the music trade magazines as a separate and substantial genre of American and world pop music.) For the most part, the dance songs of the 1960s, like their later counterparts, were catchy and functional and tended to break no new ground musically or lyrically—which may account, at least somewhat, for the poor reputation of this period in many histories of American pop. Simple verse-chorus formats predominated. But if the songs were not in themselves novel or important, the new dance culture to which they contributed certainly was. And a few of these songs have retained the affection of a large public for a surprisingly long time: Chubby Checker joined with the rap group Fat Boys in a successful revival of "The Twist" (subtitled "Yo, Twist!") in 1988, and "The Loco-Motion" was a Number 1 song for the hard-rock group Grand Funk in 1974 and for the Australian singer Kylie Minogue in 1988.

PHIL SPECTOR

As we have seen, many teenagers achieved success as recording artists in the early years of rock 'n' roll. At the age of seventeen, *Phil Spector* (1940–2021) had a Number 1 record as a member of a vocal group called the Teddy Bears, whose hit song "To Know Him Is to Love Him" was also composed and produced by Spector. (The multitalented young man also played guitar and piano on the record, which was the first one he ever made!) It may initially seem surprising, then, that Spector elected not to follow the path of songwriting performers like Chuck Berry and Buddy Holly. Instead he emulated Jerry Leiber and Mike Stoller (see Chapter 8), with whom he apprenticed, and by the early 1960s Spector had established himself as a songwriter/producer, working behind the scenes of rock 'n' roll rather than in its spotlight. Spector must have sensed where the real power was emerging in this young music business: with the people who actually shaped the sounds of the records. The wisdom of his decision is reflected in the fact that his name today is probably better known, and certainly more widely revered among pop musicians, than that of Chubby Checker, Little Eva, and any number of young performers active in the early 1960s.

By the time he was twenty-one years old, Spector was in charge of his own independent label, Philles Records, and he brought a new depth of meaning to the phrase "in charge." Working with personally selected songwriters (and often serving as a collaborator in their writing) and with handpicked vocalists, instrumentalists, arrangers, and engineers, he supervised every aspect of a record's sound. Spector's level of involvement and obsession with detail became legendary; as a result, Philles record had a distinctive kind of sonority that is tied more closely to Spector's personal talents and vision than to the contributions of any other songwriters, technicians, or even the actual performers. That is to say, more than records by the Crystals or the

Phil Spector in 1965.

Ronettes, these are "Phil Spector records." Spector was the first American pop music producer to have had a CD box set issued under his own name; in fact, if you want to hear the hits of the Crystals or the Ronettes, you need to buy *Phil Spector: Back to Mono (1958–1969)*, a set of four compact discs issued in 1991.

The characteristic Philles sound was at once remarkably dense and remarkably clear, and it became known as the "wall of sound." Spector achieved this effect by having multiple instruments—pianos, guitars, and so forth—double each individual part in the arrangement and by using a huge amount of echo while carefully controlling the overall balance of the record so that the vocals were pushed clearly to the front. The thick texture and the presence of strings on these records led them to be called "teenage symphonies." A perfect example is "Be My Baby," to be discussed in detail shortly. However, Spector explored many different types of sound textures on his recordings, and a record like "Uptown," also discussed in the following Listening Guide, has a decidedly different and more intimate—while no less impressive—impact.

Philles Records helped establish a new and important model for the production and marketing of pop records. Many indie companies, mimicking the practice of major labels with earlier styles of pop music, rushed as many records as they could into the rock 'n' roll market, often without much thought for quality control, hoping for the occasional hit. In contrast, as would be expected from the description of his personality provided here, Phil Spector turned out an exceptionally small number of records, about twenty in a two-year period, an astoundingly large percentage of which were hits. Of course, the increasingly high profile of record producers through the later 1960s and up to the present (one need only recall the importance of George Martin's work with the Beatles) is a direct outgrowth of Spector's contribution and notoriety; a 1965 essay by the noted writer Tom Wolfe dubbed the then-twenty-four-year-old millionaire "the first tycoon of teen." And when today's bands labor painstakingly for a year or more over the studio production of a disc, they are demonstrating, knowingly or not, Spector's legacy at work.

It is also significant that Spector's own preferred recording venue was Gold Star Studios in Los Angeles; this choice was an early indication of the coming shift away from New York as the dominant power center of the pop music industry. The studio musicians with whom Spector worked regularly at Gold Star Studios came to be known as the "Wrecking Crew"; individually and collectively, they made essential contributions to a remarkable number of hit records from the 1960s on. Among the best known of these musicians are Hal Blaine, drummer; Carol Kaye, bassist; and Jack Nitzsche, arranger and percussionist.

Phil Spector preferred to work with vocal groups over individual artists (although he did do some work with soloists), and his output as a producer helped ensure, as a result of both its quality and its influence, that the early 1960s were a golden age for rock 'n' roll vocal groups. Spector's predilection for vocal groups—shared by many songwriters and producers at the time—was probably due to a couple of factors. The groups offered great potential for intricate and varied vocal textures, of course. But the groups also had a kind of anonymity, as far as the listening public was concerned: they had no star leaders known by name, and their personnel could be reduced, augmented, or otherwise altered at the will of the producer. The increased power of the producer in this situation was most likely the critical issue here. Cultural historians would also attach significance to the fact that the producers of vocal group rock 'n' roll in this period tended to be, like Phil Spector, male and white, while a large proportion of the most popular vocal groups were all-female (the so-called girl groups), and of these, a significant number were composed exclusively of African Americans. In effect, the increased specialization and resulting hierarchical arrangement of power and influence that occurred in an operation like Philles Records restored a Tin Pan Alley–like model to the creation and marketing of some of the most successful rock 'n' roll. The parallel even extends to the fact that a large number of the most important songwriters and producers of this period, including Spector himself, were Jews born in New York.

To list the songwriters with whom Spector worked is to list some of the most prodigious talents of the early 1960s, including the teams of Carole King and Gerry Goffin, *Barry Mann* and *Cynthia Weil*, and Jeff Barry and Ellie Greenwich. For these and many other aspiring songwriters of the time, New York's Brill Building (located at 1619 Broadway) and other nearby office buildings served as a base of operations, where they worked in little cubicles with pianos, all packed tightly together, turning out songs for large numbers of artists and (mostly indie) labels. Producers and label executives were constantly in attendance or close at hand, and these office buildings became quite literally rock 'n' roll's vertical Tin Pan Alleys. Successful songwriters often worked with a number of different artists, producers, and labels at the same time and consequently could hope to have several hits on the charts simultaneously; the regular work at a stable location and the promise of considerable royalty income made this type of work seem both more reliable and more potentially lucrative than that of performance. (Some of the Brill Building songwriters did perform occasionally on records, playing instruments, providing background vocals, and sometimes even doing a lead vocal, but this was not a regular thing. In the early 1960s the only one of this group to have a name as a recording artist was Neil Sedaka, who generally performed his own material; Carole King's performing career took off much later.)

Like Phil Spector, a large proportion of the Brill Building songwriters tailored their output toward vocal groups, and many of the resulting records remain classics of their period.

Songwriters at work in New York City's Brill Building: Barry Mann, Cynthia Weil, Carole King.

Listening Guide TWO PHIL SPECTOR PRODUCTIONS

"Be My Baby," composed by Phil Spector, Ellie Greenwich, and Jeff Barry; performed by the Ronettes; released 1963

"Uptown," composed by Barry Mann and Cynthia Weil; performed by the Crystals; released 1962

"Be My Baby" was one of the biggest hits among the many produced by Spector, and it remains a favorite to this day on oldies radio. With its employment of a full orchestral string section, pianos, an array of rhythm instruments, and a background chorus behind the lead vocal, it is an opulent "teenage symphony" and a fine illustration of Spector's "wall of sound" at full tilt. It is certainly the arrangement and production that give this record its individual and enduring character. As a composition, the song itself is a simple if effective vehicle, expressing the most basic romantic sentiments in a straightforward verse-chorus framework. But the listener is hooked immediately by an aggressive, distinctive rhythmic pattern on the solo drum that gives the record its beat from the get-go and draws us immediately into the song. (Notice also the spectacular effect achieved by the surprise recurrence of this drum introduction just before the final repetitions of the song's chorus; this sudden crack in the wall of sound has an explosive impact!)

"Uptown" is an earlier, very different Philles record (one of the first to be issued) that serves well to highlight another aspect of Spector's production talents. "Uptown" is a song quite unlike "Be My Baby," and Spector appropriately provided it with a highly individual arrangement and production. Although "Uptown" uses orchestral strings and percussion effects in as sophisticated a manner as "Be My Baby," the earlier song conveys a much more open, spacious feeling, as if illustrating in sound the relief experienced by the protagonist when he leaves work each evening and goes uptown.

"Uptown" deals with class inequalities and economic injustice; the fact that it does this gently makes it no less remarkable for 1962, when pop songs on such subjects were virtually nonexistent. (These subjects would have been regarded as appropriate for urban folk music at this time, but not for the pop market; see Chapter 10.) The hero of the song works downtown, where he "don't get no breaks," and it is only when he comes uptown in the evening to his lover's "tenement," where they "don't have to pay much rent," that he can feel like a "king" with the world "at his feet." The contrast between downtown and uptown is captured in the music as well. The downtown sections are in a minor key (also unusual for this period), while the uptown sections move to a major key. Note also the striking effect of the flexible tempo of the record's opening section, which helps establish the unusual atmosphere and functions as a kind of atypical hook by setting up a high degree of anticipation in the listener. The suspense is relieved when a steady tempo is established at the first occurrence of the word "uptown."

Spector recorded "Uptown" in New York. Given his own New York background, which he shared with the songwriters Mann and Weil, it is hard to escape the conviction that "Uptown" is indeed about New York, where uptown and downtown Manhattan exemplify the economic and class distinctions depicted in the lyrics. Furthermore, given the many "Spanish"-sounding features of this recording, one suspects that the specific uptown location is probably New York's Spanish Harlem, a largely Puerto Rican enclave that had gained pop music notoriety just a year before the release of "Uptown" through a song actually called "Spanish Harlem"—a Top 10 hit for Ben E. King that was cowritten by Phil Spector himself.

Several factors contribute to the general Latin feeling of "Uptown." (Like so much pop music, "Uptown" is concerned with the general evocation of an "exotic" locale, not with any kind of strict cultural accuracy. The "exotic" stylistic effects in "Uptown" are actually not specifically characteristic of Puerto Rican music at all.) The ornate guitar figures heard as accompaniment to the opening verse are obviously reminiscent of flamenco guitar style. The prominent use of castanets (also present in "Be My Baby," but only as part of the wall of sound, not as a specifically evocative presence) for percussion and the general rhythmic feeling of Latin American dance throughout the record (aspects of *baion* rhythm in the accompaniment and aspects of Cuban bolero rhythm in the song's melody) also contribute strongly to the exotic coloration of "Uptown." We dwell on this aspect because "Uptown" has to serve as the basic example here of an important trend—the incorporation of Latin American elements into the fabric of 1960s rock 'n' roll. The trend is also clearly evident in "Spanish Harlem" and in many records of the early 1960s by the Drifters (the most famous of which is "Save the Last Dance for Me").

The Drifters performed "Save the Last Dance for Me" by Doc Pomus and Mort Shuman (Number 1, 1960), "Up on the Roof" by Goffin and King (Number 5, 1963), and "On Broadway" by Mann and Weil and Leiber and Stoller (Number 9, 1963). The Shirelles were one of the first successful girl groups, and probably the most popular group in that category during the early 1960s; their best-remembered hit, "Will You Love Me Tomorrow?" (Number 1, 1961), was composed by Goffin and King. The list could go on and on. Talented hopefuls flocked to the Brill Building. In addition to those already mentioned, Neil Diamond also got his start as a writer there before becoming a super-star singer-songwriter in the late 1960s and 1970s.

Phil Spector retired from steady writing and production work in 1966 but periodically resurfaced to work on special projects that attracted his interest. The best-known of these involved the Beatles; he worked on the last album released by the group, *Let It Be* (1970), and then assisted individual members with solo albums in the early 1970s.

Berry Gordy and Motown

Meanwhile, in Detroit, *Berry Gordy Jr.* (b. 1929) was creating his own songwriting/producing/marketing organization along lines directly analogous to those used at Philles Records. But Motown (named after the "Motor town" or "Motor city" of Detroit, the automobile production capital of America) came to be a success story that surpassed even that of Philles; more importantly, it came to be the most stunning success story in the entire history of African American businesses in this country. Motown was not the first Black-owned record company by a long shot (see the discussion of Black Swan in Chapter 5). The intensity and duration of its commercial success (and it is still an important market presence at the time of this writing) may be attributed to the distinctive dual thrust of Gordy's vision.

First of all, he was determined to keep all of the creative *and* financial aspects of the business under African American control—which effectively meant under *his* control. This set-up worked because Gordy had an uncanny ability to surround himself with first-rate musical talent in all areas of the record-making process and to maintain the loyalty of his musicians for substantial periods of time. It also worked, of course, because Gordy had a shrewd head for business as well as for music, and this leads us to the second element of his visionary plan. Unlike the music of earlier Black-owned record companies, Motown's music was not directed primarily at Black audiences. Gordy unapologetically sought to make an African American pop music that was addressed to the widest possible listening public. The only segregation Gordy permitted his product was geared to age; like rock 'n' roll itself, Motown's music was designed to cut across divisions of race, region, and class, but it definitely was—as the label itself proclaimed—"the sound of young America."

It is almost as if Gordy launched his enterprise as a kind of counteroffensive against the expropriation of African American music and the exploitation of African American musicians that had been as much a part of the early history of rock 'n' roll as it had been of other periods in the development of American popular music. And the unique genius of Gordy—and of his entire Motown organization—was the ability to create a Black music aimed right at the commercial mainstream that somehow never evoked the feeling or provoked the charge of having sold out. With remarkably few exceptions, Motown recordings avoided direct evocations of earlier rhythm & blues forms and styles; twelve-bar blues patterns are strikingly rare in its records, as are the typical devices of doo-wop or anything suggestive of the 1950s sounds of Chuck Berry, Fats Domino, or Little Richard. Yet a generalized blues or gospel style remained a defining characteristic of Motown's performers; sometimes it could be very subtle, as is often the case with the records of William "Smokey" Robinson, and sometimes much more overt, as is the case with those of Martha Reeves. This style proved sufficient to give a definite African American slant to the pop-structured, pop-flavored songs that were characteristic of Motown.

Like Phil Spector, Berry Gordy Jr. started his career as a songwriter (he cowrote a number of pop and rhythm & blues hits performed by Jackie Wilson in the late 1950s), although unlike Spector, he did not perform on records. Motown, which began its operations in 1959 but at first grew very slowly, was reaching its commercial peak just at the point when Spector folded Philles in 1966. The Motown model was strikingly similar to that employed by Philles: tight quality control on all levels of creation and production and concentration on a small number of records to yield a high proportion of hits. It is impossible to determine direct influence, one way or the other, between the Philles and Motown organizations; rather, it seems to be a case of two remarkable talents having similar ideas and similar success at around the same time. However, Gordy's organization was noticeably larger in its scope and ambition than Spector's.

From the beginning, Gordy planned a group of labels rather than just one: records under the Motown, Tamla, Gordy, and Soul names were all issued from his Detroit headquarters, and each label boasted its own roster of hit makers. Furthermore, whereas Spector was essentially interested only in the records themselves, Gordy specifically chose and developed his recording artists to be charismatic and sophisticated live performers, complete with characteristic modes of dress and distinctive stage choreography—not to mention strict codes of onstage and offstage conduct that apparently were enforced quite vigorously. There were complaints about the iron hand with which Gordy ruled his roost, just as there were complaints about Spector's passion for control. But there can be no doubt that Gordy's active encouragement of his artists to be more than just recording acts made it possible for both individuals and groups from the organization to develop long-term careers. It is no accident that groups like the *Supremes* and the *Temptations* are significantly better known to a wide public than are the Crystals or the Ronettes—or that individuals like Smokey Robinson and Diana Ross were able to win the kind of name recognition that eventually enabled them to branch off from the groups with which they initially were associated (the Miracles and the Supremes, respectively) and to forge hugely successful solo careers. (The musical *Dreamgirls*, successful first as a Broadway show and then as a movie, presented a fictionalized account of the career of a Supremes-like singing group while capturing effectively the behind-the-scenes environment of a Motown-like organization.)

The Supremes (with Diana Ross in the middle) in the 1960s.

The Motown records of the early 1960s exemplify the rock 'n' roll trends of their time. Among the biggest of Motown's early hits were "Please Mr. Postman" by the Marvelettes (Number 1, 1961), a quintessential girl group record, and "Do You Love Me" by the Contours (Number 3, 1962), a hard-driving dance record that linked success in romance to the ability to perform currently popular dance steps such as the twist and the mashed potato. (The Contours' "Do You Love Me" found renewed chart success in 1988 on the strength of its prominent employment on the soundtrack of the movie *Dirty Dancing*, which is set in the early 1960s.) By the mid-1960s a more complex, occasionally lush sound came to characterize Motown's productions. Surely the Temptations' "My Girl" (see the associated Listening Guide) is as much a "teenage symphony" as any of Phil Spector's most elaborate offerings. Just like Spector, however, Motown never lost touch with a danceable beat, and although the Supremes'

"You Can't Hurry Love" (see the associated Listening Guide) has a much more sophisticated sound and arrangement than "Please Mr. Postman" from five years earlier, both records share an irresistible groove. Gordy's touch seemed never to falter, and his organization steadily increased its share of the hit record market throughout the 1960s; in the year 1970 alone, Motown and its affiliated labels placed sixteen records in the Top 10 and scored seven Number 1 records (out of the year's total of twenty-one Number 1 songs)!

Motown's headquarters in Detroit (which Gordy named "Hitsville, USA") served as a magnet for a spectacular array of talented individuals, some of whom did session work or even office work until they finally managed to get the attention of Gordy. Among performers, Gordy—like so many other producers—tended to favor vocal groups, although he did have important solo acts from early on, such as Marvin Gaye, Mary Wells, and Stevie Wonder, and did eventually glean some solo performers from the groups that they fronted. Significant Motown groups not yet mentioned include Martha (Reeves) and the Vandellas, Junior Walker and the All Stars, the Four Tops, Gladys Knight and the Pips, and the Jackson Five. The Jackson Five made their first record for Motown in 1969, when lead singer Michael was all of eleven years old, and their string of hits for the label helped assure Motown's fortunes well into the 1970s. Gordy's organization was also blessed with remarkable songwriting and production talent, and Gordy would often have his teams of songwriting producers compete for the privilege of working with particular hot recording acts. Among the most famous of these Motown writing/production teams were Eddie Holland, Lamont Dozier, and Brian Holland; Norman Whitfield and Barrett Strong; and Nickolas Ashford and Valerie Simpson. Smokey Robinson was unusual among the earlier Motown artists in being both a performer and a songwriter/producer; he furnished material not just to his own group, the Miracles, but also to Mary Wells, the Marvelettes, and the Temptations. Later on, in the 1970s, Marvin Gaye and Stevie Wonder also took on writing and production responsibilities for their own records.

Finally, but certainly not least important, Motown had a sterling house band, the so-called Funk Brothers, which was in every sense a match for Phil Spector's Wrecking Crew in ensuring that the highest level of instrumental musicianship was always present to back up and inspire the vocal performers. Bass player James Jamerson, drummer Benny Benjamin, and keyboardist Earl Van Dyke were among the most important contributors to the Motown sound. The documentary film *Standing in the Shadows of Motown* (2002) offers a fine, if ultimately sobering, history of these insufficiently celebrated musicians.

In 1971 Berry Gordy moved the Motown headquarters to Los Angeles, at last joining the "westward migration" that had been playing a major role in American pop music, and in American culture generally, since the early 1960s. We now turn our attention specifically to California, surf music, and Brian Wilson—who did more than any other single person to make California the new focus of America's rock 'n' roll mythology.

Listening Guide THE MOTOWN SOUND

"My Girl," composed and produced by Smokey Robinson and Ronald White; performed by the Temptations; released 1965

"You Can't Hurry Love," composed by Holland-Dozier-Holland; produced by Brian Holland and Lamont Dozier; performed by the Supremes; released 1966

"My Girl" is a moderate-tempo love ballad. As a composition, it is a song of sweetly conventional romantic sentiment in a straightforward verse-chorus form. But as a recording, it is lifted emphatically beyond the ordinary by virtue of the Temptations' thoroughly engaging performance and Motown's spectacular production values.

From the outset, the arrangement hooks the listener: a repeating solo bass motive establishes the beat, over which a lead guitar enters with a memorable melodic figure. (Both of these instrumental hooks are also used later on in the recording, so that they become firmly fixed in the listener's mind after one hearing of the song.) Then the drums and lead voice enter, followed subtly by background vocals; by the time the first chorus is reached, brass instruments are present in the accompaniment, to which are then added orchestral strings. The cumulative layering of sounds gives the song a sense of steadily increasing passion and intensity as the singer's words metaphorically detail his feelings for his "girl." There is a sumptuous instrumental interlude before the third (last) verse, dominated by the strings, which play a new melodic figure over the song's characteristic chord progressions. Then, as a final intensifying gesture, a dramatic upward key change takes place just before the concluding verse and chorus.

If "My Girl" showcases the brilliance of Motown's arranging and producing staff, "You Can't Hurry Love" demonstrates that Motown's writers could also come up with clever, innovatively structured pop songs. The description that follows conveys the intricacies of this Holland-Dozier-Holland composition, and is best understood with the Listening Guide chart close at hand. Nevertheless the most casual hearing of the record will affirm that—as with so much of the finest pop music—catchiness was absolutely not sacrificed to the cause of sophistication.

LISTENING GUIDE	"MY GIRL"		
TIME	**FORM**	**LYRIC**	**DESCRIPTIVE COMMENTS**
0:00	Introduction		Bass alone
0:05			Guitar enters playing the song's signature riff, accompanied by finger snaps
0:09	Verse	*I got sunshine . . .*	Lead vocalist enters along with full accompaniment, including drums
0:28	Chorus	*I guess . . . My girl . . .*	Horns are added to accompany vocalist; strings added; backup singers sing response to the vocalist
0:46	Verse	*I got so much honey*	Horns now answer vocal line
1:05	Chorus		
1:22	Instrumental	*Hoo . . . hoo*	Vocalist introduces; then guitar plays signature opening riff; finally strings enter as backup singers sing "Hey, hey, hey."
1:50	Verse	*I don't need no . . .*	Modulates up a key
2:09	Chorus		
2:27	Tag		Choral tag with backup vocalists singing "My girl" as lead singer repeats some of the verse lyrics; fades out

(continued)

Listening Guide THE MOTOWN SOUND (*continued*)

The opening A section of "You Can't Hurry Love" is extremely short, just half the length of each of the ensuing B and C sections. The function of this A section is at first unclear, both because of its brevity (Is it a kind of introduction? Or is it a very short verse?) and because of its similarity to the music of the B section; the basic chord progressions underlying both the A and B sections are virtually identical, even though their vocal melodies differ. The C section brings a striking chord change and another change of melody, which might initially suggest a kind of bridge section. But when A fails to return after C, and instead B and C alternate with one another, we seem to find ourselves in an unorthodox verse-chorus type of situation in which we hear the first verse (C) after the chorus (B) and in which the words of the chorus aren't always exactly the same. Just when a pattern seems to have been established, the A section unexpectedly returns with a vengeance. Instead of proceeding right to B, it is played twice through, creating a composite section that is now as long as either B or C. Then, in the most clever formal maneuver of all in this already complex song, an ambiguous section is inserted, in which the composers take advantage of the chord progression shared by A and B; with minimal melodic activity from the voice, which keeps "waitin'," we can't tell for sure which of the two sections we're actually hearing! The instruments tease us briefly here by playing the melodic motive associated with B, "You can't hurry love." But the voice holds back until we're at the top of the chord progression again, at which point it finally begins a proper, full repetition of B, toward the end of which the record fades out.

All this play with form would be just so much intellectual busywork if it didn't reflect on the meaning of the song. "You Can't Hurry Love" is a song about the importance of waiting. Formally, the song keeps us guessing—waiting for clarification of the functional relationships among the different sections. When the A section at last returns, it keeps us waiting extensively for B and its restatement of the song's essential message. On the level of detail, notice also in the second and third B sections how the lead vocalist avoids or postpones singing the words "You can't hurry love," again forcing the listener to wait. This makes the final B section that much more of a release of tension, as it behaves in an expected manner at last.

Like all the great Motown hits, "You Can't Hurry Love" submerges its many subtleties beneath an irresistible, pop-friendly surface. Maybe this is why you don't tend to find it, or other Motown records, the subject of discussion when matters turn toward innovative aspects of 1960s music. Still, any list of the significant music of this period that omits a record like "You Can't Hurry Love" is surely missing something important.

LISTENING GUIDE	"YOU CAN'T HURRY LOVE"		
TIME	**FORM**		**LYRIC**
0:00	Instrumental introduction		
0:07	A		*I need love . . .*
0:17	B: b		*You can't . . .*
0:27	b		*You can't . . .*
0:37	C		*But how many . . .*
0:57	B: b		*(You can't—) no . . .*
1:07	b		*How long . . .*
1:17	C		*No, I can't . . .*
1:37	B: b		*(You can't—) no . . .*
1:47	b		*You can't . . .*
1:57	Brief instrumental break		
2:00	A		*No, love, love . . .*
2:09	A		*For that soft . . .*
2:19	A or B?		*I keep waitin' . . .*
2:29	B: b		*You can't . . .*
2:39	b		*You can't . . .*

Brian Wilson and the Beach Boys

Brian Wilson (b. 1942) formed the Beach Boys with his two brothers, a cousin, and a friend in Hawthorne, California, in 1961. The band was achieving national chart hits within a year and thrived right through the period of the "British Invasion" to become not only the bestselling American group of the 1960s but probably the most nationally and internationally celebrated American rock group ever—and certainly the one with the longest history of chart success. (They scored a Number 1 hit as late as 1988, with "Kokomo.") As songwriter, arranger, producer, and performer, Brian Wilson was the guiding spirit of the Beach Boys during the first decade of the group's existence, when their artistic and commercial importance and influence were at a peak. Wilson's clear and stated model was Phil Spector, and Wilson worked regularly in the Los Angeles recording studios with many of the same musicians who graced Spector's productions. Unlike Spector, however, Wilson was always an essential performing presence on the records he wrote, arranged, and produced for the Beach Boys. Even after he stopped touring with the group in 1964, the sound of Wilson's clear, intense falsetto remained a defining element of the Beach Boys' studio recordings.

By participating significantly in the creation of beautifully produced "teenage symphonies" featuring vocal groups, Wilson and the Beach Boys obviously contributed to one of the central trends of the early 1960s. But if we wish to understand why their importance and influence went well beyond this, we have to look at even broader issues.

The Beach Boys, with Brian Wilson on bass guitar, center, c. 1963.

If we were to conceptualize a defining model for the career of a self-sustaining, trendsetting rock group of the 1960s, it would look something like this:

- Start out by demonstrating a mastery of the basic early rock 'n' roll ballad and up-tempo styles
- Create original material based on and extending those styles
- Eventually branch out totally beyond the traditional forms, sounds, and lyric content of rock 'n' roll to create something truly different and unique

The reference point that most people would use for constructing a model like this would probably, and understandably, be the career of the Beatles—the shape of their career is surely encapsulated by this description—or possibly that of one of the other "British Invasion" groups. But the group that first established this model, and did so with outstanding success, was the Beach Boys. The Beach Boys were in fact a clear and stated model for the Beatles, especially during both groups' remarkably productive and innovative years of 1965–1967.

In a sense, Brian Wilson was the first self-conscious second-generation rock 'n' roller. By this characterization we mean two things. First, that Wilson explicitly acknowledged his reliance on, and reverence for, his predecessors in the rock 'n' roll field by covering and quoting from their records. Second, that at the same time, Wilson carved out distinctive new ground by deliberately moving the lyrics and eventually the music of his own songs beyond the territory carved out by his predecessors and into novel areas that were of particular meaning to him, his time, and his place in America. (The Beatles, the Rolling Stones, and other bands of their kind were also self-conscious second-generation rock 'n' rollers in this sense, but it is important to realize that Brian Wilson was, in all essential respects, the first fully realized representative of this type of pop musician.)

Brian Wilson's place in America was, of course, Southern California, and that land of sun and surf was celebrated in song after song by the Beach Boys. These songs indelibly enshrined Wilson's somewhat mythical version of California in the consciousness of young Americans—to such an extent that still, for legions of pop music fans, merely the titles are sufficient to summon an entire state of mind: "Surfin' Safari," "Surfer Girl," "The Warmth of the Sun," "California Girls," and so forth. Wilson's vision was appealingly inclusive, even as it remained place-specific: "I wish they all could be California girls," he sang. (One also thinks of the opening lines of "Surfin' USA": "If everybody had an ocean, across the USA, then everybody'd be surfin' like Californ-i-ay.") Cars retained their importance to status and young romance in Wilson's California mythology, with the models suitably modernized and spruced up to serve the new time and place, as in "Little Deuce Coupe," "Little Honda," "Fun, Fun, Fun," and other songs.

A few examples may suffice to trace Wilson's journey from imitation through emulation to innovation. The Beach Boys' first Top 10 hit, the famous "Surfin' USA" (Number 3 pop, 1963), simply borrows the music of Chuck Berry's 1958 hit "Sweet Little Sixteen" as a setting for Brian Wilson's paean to California's—and America's—new beach craze. While the words are all new, they also embody an indirect homage to Berry's original lyrics, insofar as Wilson adopts Berry's idea of national celebration while changing its mode of expression from dancing to surfing. The many listeners who knew "Sweet Little Sixteen" encountered in "Surfin' USA" an unusual hybrid: musically, a cover record that shortened and simplified the form of Chuck Berry's original; lyrically, a tribute to the spirit of Berry that reworked and updated his approach to writing rock 'n' roll anthems to suit the requirements of a new time and place. The B-side of "Surfin' USA," "Shut Down," was a substantial hit as well. In "Shut Down," Wilson employed an established rock 'n' roll song form, the AABA pattern in which the A sections are twelve-bar blues structures (see the discussion of "Charlie Brown" in Chapter 8), to tell the story of a drag race between two high-powered automobiles. Needless to say, it is the singer's car that wins!

The Beach Boys' next hit, "Surfer Girl" (Number 7, 1963), reinvigorated the sound and spirit of a doo-wop ballad by infusing it with California beach content. "Fun, Fun, Fun," the group's first hit of 1964, evoked Chuck Berry again in an initially overt but ultimately more subtle way. The solo guitar introduction pulls its twelve-bar blues licks directly from Berry's "Roll Over Beethoven" and "Johnny B. Goode." But after paying its respects (or its dues?) to Berry in this way, the main body of the song pursues an original path. The song follows a strophic form, with newly composed music and words, and its sixteen-bar strophes have nothing to do with the structure of the blues—but everything to do with what Brian Wilson learned from Chuck Berry about how to write and perform rock 'n' roll anthems. That is to say, after acknowledging Berry by quoting his signature manner of beginning a record, Wilson surprises his listeners and proceeds to pay his mentor the best possible tribute: not by copying him, but by revealing how well his lessons have been absorbed. "Fun, Fun, Fun" turns imitation into emulation. With its rapid-fire, clearly articulated lyrics, which manage to compress a remarkable number of deeply resonant references to youth culture (fancy cars, car radios, fast driving, hamburger stands, schoolwork, parents, the pursuit of romance, and—naturally—fun) into two minutes' time, and its eminently catchy and danceable music, "Fun, Fun, Fun" is the kind of song Chuck Berry might have written had he been born sixteen years later in Southern California. (In the song "Do You Remember?"—an album track from the Beach Boys' *All Summer Long* [1964]—Berry is mentioned as "the greatest" of the early rock 'n' rollers to whom Brian Wilson pays tribute.)

By mid-1964 Wilson had moved past obvious emulation into a period of aggressive experimentation with his inherited styles and forms. "I Get Around," the Beach Boys' first Number 1 record, turns the up-tempo rock 'n' roll anthem into a thoroughly individual kind of expression; the song's adventurous chord changes and quirky phrase structure take it well beyond the boundaries of 1950s rock 'n' roll without ever sacrificing the immediate appeal and accessibility so essential to the genre. However, an album track like "The Warmth of the Sun" (from *Shut Down, Volume 2*, released in 1964), while clearly a descendant of the doo-wop ballad in sound, rhythm, and vocal texture, presents lyrics that probe the dissolution of young romance in a newly poignant and personal way, set to music that so enlarges the melodic and harmonic boundaries of the style that one quickly forgets the song's antecedents and focuses instead on its remarkable individuality. While it is questionable whether a song like "Warmth of the Sun" would have been successful as a single, it is unquestionable that songs like this were heard and

BOX 9.1 OTHER "SURF MUSIC"

The Beach Boys were not the only representatives of a distinctive "California sound" in the early 1960s. The popular duo Jan (Berry) and Dean (Torrence) worked with Brian Wilson and the Beach Boys on a number of mutual projects; Wilson in fact cowrote Jan and Dean's biggest hit, "Surf City" (Number 1, 1963). In addition, a highly influential style of guitar-dominated instrumental rock 'n' roll was pioneered in Southern California, principally by Dick Dale (b. 1937), who performed with his band, the Del-Tones. Dale employed a solid-body guitar, a high-wattage Fender amplifier, and lots of reverb to achieve the "wet" sound of what came to be known as "surf guitar." A characteristic device was Dale's rapid, descending tremolo—borrowed by a group called the Chantays to open their recording of what became the most famous surf instrumental, "Pipeline" (the title is a surfing term for the curl of a wave before it breaks). Sustained national recognition eluded Dick Dale in the 1960s, but it finally became his in the 1990s, when his 1962 recording of "Misirlou" was used as opening music for the hit film *Pulp Fiction*. The most successful instrumental group associated with surf rock was, paradoxically, a Seattle-based ensemble called the Ventures, who adopted aspects of the style after it became popular in California.

appreciated both by listeners and by those involved in the making of pop music and thus contributed significantly to the evolution of musical style. We can also see here the beginnings of a significant trend: namely, the increasing importance of album tracks, and eventually of albums themselves, in the development of adventurous popular music. Rock 'n' roll was on its way to becoming rock.

By 1965 Brian Wilson had achieved international acclaim as a composer and recording studio wizard who produced brilliant singles and albums, and the Beach Boys were being viewed as the most serious creative and commercial threat—in America *and* in England—to the dominance of the Beatles, whose American triumph in 1964 had turned the entire world of pop music upside down. Let us now catch up with the Beatles, whose music in its turn was providing Brian Wilson—and many, many others—with creative stimulation and challenges.

The Beatles, the British Invasion, and the American Response

By the time the Beatles had their first Number 1 record in America, "I Want to Hold Your Hand," which topped the charts at the beginning of February 1964, they were established stars in Great Britain and were widely known throughout Europe. Already in 1963, spurred by the mass adulation surrounding the group across the Atlantic that had come to be known as "Beatlemania," some small American indie companies had licensed Beatles recordings for stateside release—but the group's British hits did not catch on here at first.

Much ink has been spilled in conjecturing about the timing of the Beatles' remarkable success on American shores. Many historians of pop culture point to the impact of the assassination of President John F. Kennedy on November 22, 1963, claiming that as the new year began, young people were hungry for a change from the prevailing national mood of solemnity and the Beatles provided just the ticket in the form of something novel, "exotic," uplifting, and fun. This seems a convenient but facile explanation. A more practical, if also more cynical, one might be that the Beatles really "hit" in America only when a major label, Capitol (the American label officially linked to the Beatles' British label, EMI), launched a major promotional campaign behind the first Beatles single they chose to release here, "I Want to Hold Your Hand," and its accompanying album, *Meet the Beatles*. But outpourings of mass enthusiasm for entertainers were nothing new in the America of 1964; one thinks of the manias for Frank Sinatra in the 1940s and for Elvis Presley in the 1950s. Arguably the chief common element in these and other related phenomena in the entertainment business is their unpredictability.

Still, although America has retained a cultural fascination with things British throughout its history, American Beatlemania does represent the first time this degree

The Beatles on the Ed Sullivan Show in 1964. Left to right: Paul McCartney, George Harrison, Ringo Starr, and John Lennon.

of adulation was bestowed on nonnative pop musicians. America had been exporting its popular music to Great Britain, to Europe, and, increasingly, throughout the industrialized world with enormous success for a long time, but the impact of the Beatles in this country marked the significant beginning of an aggressively reciprocal process. Of course, the reciprocities involved here are deep and complex. As we have seen, American popular music, especially that of the twentieth century, is built on a complex amalgam of influences that may be traced to a variety of world sources. And the most direct, formative influences on the music of the Beatles themselves—and of countless other British bands of the 1960s—were those of 1950s American rock 'n' roll.

One immediate result of the Beatles' popularity in America was the unleashing of a flood of recordings by British bands on the American market (see Box 9.2), an astoundingly large number of which were successful. Although the impact of many of these "British Invasion" bands was short-lived, other groups have retained substantial, long-term importance in the pop culture of this country; one thinks particularly of the Rolling Stones, the Who, and the Kinks. Another immediate result was the formation—or adaptation—of American groups to mimic distinctive aspects of "British" style, which of course included fashion (particularly Beatles-style "mop-top" haircuts) and pseudo-English accents along with the musical characteristics that were supposed to evoke the Beatles or their countrymen. An extreme example of the effect of the British Invasion may be found in the career of the Walker Brothers, an American group that actually went to England in 1964 to record. They became popular in England and achieved some American hits—after being marketed here as a British Invasion band! (They weren't really brothers either.)

The close interconnections between American and British pop music that were established in the wake of the Beatles' stateside success continue to this day; among the most successful artists on the American charts in the 1990s, for example, were British acts like Eric Clapton, Elton John, Sting, and Oasis, and more recently Adele and Sam Smith have scored major American hits. Even more significantly, the British Invasion was the first of many developments that may be seen as indicative of an accelerating receptivity in America to *overt* pop music influences from all over the world. The Beatles themselves modeled such receptivity in their own embrace of influences from Indian music—first heard as a surface element in their employment of an Indian instrument, the *sitar*, in "Norwegian Wood" (a track from the 1965 album *Rubber Soul*) and later heard as a more profound influence on both the sound and structure of "Within You Without You" from *Sgt. Pepper's Lonely Hearts Club Band* (1967; see the discussion of this album in Chapter 10). At present, "world music" is important enough in the culture of American pop to represent a distinctive marketing category that is responsible for the sale in this country of increasing numbers of albums from international sources. The mingling of American and world popular musics, with all their attendant reciprocal influences, continues to accelerate.

This may seem a rather elaborate heritage to trace ultimately to one group, especially a group that had an American chart run of just over six years before they announced their disbandment. But the remarkable thing about the Beatles is that they proved truly worthy of the early adulation heaped upon them: up to the end of their career as a group, they continued to evolve in new and unexpected directions and to challenge themselves and their wide audience. They altered the character of pop music profoundly and bequeathed to popular culture a remarkably rich and complex inheritance.

We can trace the evolution of the Beatles using the model advanced for describing the career of the Beach Boys. The Beatles started out as a performing band modeled on Buddy Holly's group, the Crickets (see Chapter 8); after some initial shifts in personnel, they achieved a stable lineup by 1962 consisting of John Lennon and George Harrison (lead and rhythm guitars and vocals), Paul McCartney (bass and vocals), and Ringo Starr (drums and occasional vocals). During their extended pre-stardom period, the Beatles played at clubs in their home town of Liverpool and elsewhere—most famously in Hamburg, Germany—performing an imitative repertoire that centered on covers of songs by the American rock 'n' roll artists they most admired, such as Chuck Berry, Little Richard, Carl Perkins, and, naturally, Buddy Holly. (The country/rock 'n' roll duo the Everly Brothers also exercised a significant influence on the Beatles' group singing style.) Several such covers found their way onto early Beatles albums, once their manager Brian Epstein managed, after much difficulty, to get them a recording contract in 1962. A few of these cover recordings were also eventually chart hits for the Beatles in America, among them "Matchbox," a Carl Perkins tune (Number 17, 1964); and the Beatles' best-known cover record, "Twist and Shout" (Number 2, 1964), a rhythm & blues dance number composed by Phil Medley and Bert Russell that the Beatles doubtless learned from the 1962 hit recording by the Isley Brothers.

"Twist and Shout" was on the Beatles' first album, *Please Please Me*, released in Great Britain in 1963. By the time of this recording the Beatles were entering a period of emulation in which they wrote some of their own songs; *Please Please Me* contains six covers and eight original selections. The Beatles' chief songwriters were Lennon and McCartney, who, at least at first, worked as a team, but eventually Harrison began to contribute songs as well, and by the end of the Beatles' career even Starr had stepped in occasionally as a songwriter. This brings up an important point. Unlike the Beach Boys in the 1960s, whose creative center was unquestionably one member of the group, the Beatles throughout their prime years were a multiple-threat team. The many creative and performing abilities shared among the four Beatles allowed the group to achieve a wonderful collective synergy, a whole both greater than and different from the sum of its parts. (The after-the-fact proof of this statement may be seen in the four contrasting solo careers the individual members of the group enjoyed after the Beatles broke up in 1970.) The Beatles were also blessed with a sympathetic and encouraging producer in George Martin. Martin was sometimes called "the fifth Beatle" in acknowledgment of his increasingly essential role in the recording studio in the later 1960s, as the Beatles began to attempt more and more sophisticated arrangements and include electronic engineering effects on their recordings.

Four representative songs will serve well to chart the Beatles' career as songwriting performers from 1962 to 1966, the year that they quit touring, gave up live performance, and went on to become the world's first famous studio rock band. These

Listening Guide FOUR SONGS BY THE BEATLES, 1962–1966

"Please Please Me," written by John Lennon and Paul McCartney; performed by the Beatles; recorded 1962

"A Hard Day's Night," written by John Lennon and Paul McCartney; performed by the Beatles; recorded 1964

"Yesterday," written by John Lennon and Paul McCartney; performed by the Beatles (actually Paul McCartney, vocal solo, accompanied by guitar and string ensemble); recorded 1965

"Eleanor Rigby," written by John Lennon and Paul McCartney; performed by the Beatles, with accompanying string ensemble; recorded 1966

"Please Please Me" was recorded in late 1962. It was the Beatles' first Top 10 hit in Britain and was one of the songs unsuccessfully released in America in 1963. But indie label Vee-Jay re-released the single when "I Want to Hold Your Hand" began its rapid ascent on the American charts in early 1964, and before long "Please Please Me" was up in the Top 3 along with "I Want to Hold Your Hand" and another Beatles hit, "She Loves You," which had also initially been released in this country in 1963. (During a now-famous week in early April 1964 the Beatles achieved the unprecedented and still unique feat of having all of the top five records on the American charts for the week—an index of the intensity of American Beatlemania at the time.)

"Please Please Me," a fine example of the early Beatles' songwriting and performing, is a straightforward, up-tempo love song in a typical AABA form. The group sings and plays it crisply, energetically, and efficiently—once through the song, and it's over, in just two minutes' time.

Still, individualistic features in the song already point to the creative energy at work in the group. The lyrics contain some clever internal rhymes, as when "complainin'" is rhymed with "rain in [my heart]" at the beginning of the B section. The title itself plays with the word "please," using it both as an imperative and a verb. Effective rhymes and wordplay would become two trademarks of the Beatles' songwriting.

Musically, as shown in the first of the following charts, the A sections have their own distinctive internal form that proves a source of considerable interest. First there are two identical phrases (a, a) to set the poetic couplets that open these sections. These a phrases have a basically descending melodic motion over minimal chord changes. In the rather unexpected third phrase, b, for which the text consists simply of the repeated words "Come on, come on," the music becomes the focus of interest, with continuous chord changes and a steadily ascending melodic line that depicts the intensity that underlies the unchanging lyrics. With the final phrase, c,

a melodic high point is reached as the lyrics arrive at the words of the song's title, "Please please me," after which the melody descends once again and the harmony presents a conclusive **cadence**. The musical form of the A sections, a-a-b-c, also delineates the rhyme scheme in the four-line stanzas of the lyrics.

"A Hard Day's Night," a Number 1 hit in 1964, was the title song from the Beatles' first movie. It shares a few surface characteristics with "Please Please Me." The name of the song once again demonstrates wordplay in characterizing the work experience of those who do their "hard day's work" at night—such as members of a rock band. The overall form of the song is once again AABA. But the considerably more subtle and elaborate playing with formal characteristics and expectations clearly demonstrates the increasing sophistication of the Beatles' songwriting. And while the performance of the song is fully as energetic and engaging as that of "Please Please Me," some novel touches reveal the group's increasing attention to details of sound and arrangement.

In a sense, "A Hard Day's Night" may be heard as the Beatles' updating of the subject matter of "My Blue Heaven" (see Chapter 4): the delights of returning home to a rewarding domestic relationship. (It is not at all unthinkable that the Beatles knew "My Blue Heaven," especially since Fats Domino had revived it and made it a hit again—in rock 'n' roll style, of course—in 1956. Domino was very popular in Britain, and the Beatles eventually created an implicit tribute to his New Orleans style by writing and recording "Lady Madonna" in 1968. Domino appreciated the compliment and returned it by recording the song himself the same year.) Musically, "A Hard Day's Night" is clearly modeled on those AABA song forms in which the A sections are twelve-bar blues stanzas. But while the A sections are indeed twelve bars in length, have three four-bar phrases, and incorporate blue notes, they are not exactly traditional twelve-bar blues structures. In the lyrics, the Beatles begin by making a reference to the traditional a-a-b poetic stanza

LISTENING GUIDE | "PLEASE PLEASE ME" (1962)

TIME	FORM	LYRIC	DESCRIPTIVE COMMENTS
0:00	Instrumental introduction		As a hook, the lead guitar and harmonica play the melody of the first two phrases of A
0:08	A: a	*Last night . . .*	
0:15	a	*I know . . .*	Same melody line, new words
0:21	b	*Come on . . .*	Note steady chord changes, ascending melody
0:27	c	*Please please me . . .*	High point of melody comes on words of the title
0:35	A: a	*You don't . . .*	Same music as before, with new words for the first two lines of the stanza
	a	*Why do I . . .*	
	b	*Come on . . .*	
	c	*Please please me . . .*	
1:02	B: d	*I don't . . .*	Bridge section; new music
1:09	d'	*I do . . .*	Note change and extension at the end of this phrase, leading back to the final A
1:20	A	*Last night . . .*	Exact repetition of the opening A, with brief extension at the end

found in many blues, having the second line begin with the same words as the first (see the following chart). But that second line ends with different words, and the following A stanza features three completely independent lines. In the music of these A sections, the Beatles do not follow the traditional chord structure of twelve-bar blues. Other chords are used in addition to the traditional three (tonic, subdominant, and dominant—see the discussion of twelve-bar blues in Chapter 5), and the traditional chords do not always occur in the expected places. In particular, the usual chord change at the start of the second phrase (the move to the subdominant chord) is postponed to the start of the third and final phrase of the twelve-bar section. This yields an interesting result: although the lyrics to the A sections do not conform to the a-a-b pattern, the musical phrases do.

These musical alterations are not merely technical details, for they serve the meaning of the lyrics. It is the third line in each of the A stanzas that describes the trip home from work and the actual reuniting with the loved one. Thus it is entirely appropriate that the harmony should wait until this point to make its own anticipated move. (The harmony does return to the tonic at the expected point—in the eleventh bar—as the singer settles down with his lover at home and feels "all right" or "okay.")

Last, we may mention three aspects of the song's arrangement. The song begins literally with a bang: a loud, isolated guitar chord whose unexpected harsh dissonance is permitted to ring in the air before the song actually gets going. This is the most effective and efficient of hooks, and it also perfectly prepares the listener for the tense feelings described in the opening words of the song. Notice also the unique guitar timbre employed for the instrumental twelve-string guitar solo in the middle of the record, which allows this solo to stand out from the many other guitar sounds heard

(continued)

Listening Guide FOUR SONGS BY THE BEATLES, 1962–1966 (*continued*)

LISTENING GUIDE | "A HARD DAY'S NIGHT" (1964)

TIME	FORM	LYRIC	DESCRIPTIVE COMMENTS
0:00	Introductory guitar chord, then pause		Dissonance followed by open space creates anticipatory tension
0:03	A	It's been a . . . It's been a . . . But when . . .	Music and lyrics of A sections are modeled on twelve-bar blues patterns but introduce significant variations
0:24	A	You know . . . And it's . . . So why on earth . . .	Same music, new lyrics
0:44	B	When I'm home . . .	Bridge section; new music consisting of two similar phrases
0:58	A	It's been a . . .	Exact repetition of first A section
1:20	A	[Instrumental interlude] So why on earth . . .	Guitar solo for the first eight bars, then voices return for the last phrase (four bars) of the section
1:40	B	When I'm home . . .	As before
1:54	A	It's been a . . .	As before
2:21	Instrumental coda		Music fades out

elsewhere throughout the performance. The very end brings an unexpected instrumental coda as a solo guitar gently strums a repeating figure that fades out. The abrupt cessation of drums and accompanying chords underlines the relaxed character of this ending, which creates an effective counterbalance to the song's unnerving opening and surely signifies the final lifting of tension after the "hard day's night" and the settling in to the delights of being home.

"Yesterday," which reached the Number 1 position on the pop charts in 1965, may be the Beatles song with the most wide-ranging and enduring popularity; certainly it has been the one most performed by other artists, and its appeal cuts across generational and stylistic divides. The song comes across with a remarkable directness and simplicity, so natural in its verbal and melodic expression that it seems hardly to have been consciously composed. But, as we know from many previous examples of fine popular music, such an effect is difficult to achieve and almost invariably conceals much art.

As a composition, "Yesterday" obviously evokes Tin Pan Alley models. Musically, it employs a standard AABA form. Its lyrics pay homage to the time-honored theme of broken romance in a gentle, general, and straightforward manner, such that virtually anyone could understand and empathize, and virtually nobody could take offense. (One aspect of the song's appeal is that the feelings involved are utterly clear, whereas the specific situation remains vague enough to stimulate the imagination of many different listeners.) But the song may assert its kinship with Tin Pan Alley most tellingly in its emphasis on a distinctive and expressive melodic line, a line that fits the words beautifully. The melody is accompanied by equally expressive harmonies, which explore a wider range of chords than was typical for rock music at this time. The moderate tempo and the general avoidance of any intense rhythmic effects also distance "Yesterday" from the rock mainstream and edge it closer in spirit to Tin Pan Alley.

The Beatles' recording of "Yesterday" underlines the song's unexpected character in every way. The use of a solo voice throughout, the similarity of Paul McCartney's lyrical and unaffected style of delivery to Tin Pan Alley–style crooning, the choice of acoustic (rather than electric) guitar, the employment of orchestral string instruments to augment the accompaniment, the lack of any drums or percussion instruments, the prevailingly soft dynamic level—all these elements set the record apart from others of its time, including other records by the Beatles, as if to emphasize that this song is a deliberate venture into new musical territory. Although anyone who had been listening carefully to the Beatles knew by 1965 that they were capable of writing beautifully melodic love ballads (such as "And I Love Her" and "If I Fell," both from the Beatles' 1964 movie *A Hard Day's Night*), "Yesterday" was designed to—and did—make listeners really sit up and take notice. Maybe the Beatles were more than just a good old rock 'n' roll band, or even more than a good new rock band. Maybe they were just something else entirely.

As you listen to "Yesterday," try to notice some of the artistry that went into the creation and performance of this famous song. Each of the A sections begins with an isolated, essential word that serves as a decisive hook into the story (see the following chart); these single opening words are set to foreshortened musical phrases (one bar in length, as opposed to the standard two bars) that function equally as focusing hooks. The ascending gestures in the melody always depict the receding past ("all my troubles . . ."), while the immediately following descending gestures always bring us back down to earth in the present ("Now it looks . . ."). The lyrics to the bridge section reveal again the Beatles' adeptness at internal rhyming ("go" and "know," "wrong" and "long"). And the final word in the bridge, "yesterday," links this B section effectively to the final A, which begins with the same word. In terms of the arrangement, we can admire how withholding the entrance of the orchestral strings until the second A section makes their arrival a wonderfully rich, intense surprise that goes splendidly with the word "suddenly."

"Eleanor Rigby," a Number 11 pop hit in 1966, was not quite the smash hit the preceding three songs were. Actually, it was issued as the B-side of "Yellow Submarine," a novelty number that went to the Number 2 position on the charts; it is a tribute to the impact of

LISTENING GUIDE | "YESTERDAY" (1965)

TIME	FORM	LYRIC	DESCRIPTIVE COMMENTS
0:00	Brief introduction: acoustic guitar vamp		
0:05	A	*Yesterday . . .*	Guitar accompaniment continues
0:22	A	*Suddenly . . .*	String ensemble joins the guitar; fuller sound
0:40	B	*Why she . . .*	Bridge section; new music, consisting of two similar phrases
0:49		*I said . . .*	
0:59	A	*Yesterday . . .*	
	B		
	A		
	Brief coda		Voice hums the closing melodic phrase of A, accompanied by the strings

(continued)

Listening Guide FOUR SONGS BY THE BEATLES, 1962–1966 (*continued*)

"Eleanor Rigby" that it made the charts at all, let alone that it reached nearly as high as the Top 10.

"Eleanor Rigby" is a startling song right from the outset. Without any preparation, the voices enter with a high, loud cry of "Ah," accompanied by an active string ensemble (composed of violins, violas, and cellos). Orchestral strings in popular forms are traditionally associated with soothing music—an association exemplified by a song like "Yesterday"—but here they are confined to steady, repeated chords and brief rhythmic figures, assuming functions much like those of the rhythm guitar and drums in a more typical rock configuration. The harmony is equally dislocating. The song opens on a big major chord, but after the initial vocal phrase it settles onto an unexpected minor chord. These two chords alternate throughout the song, and they are in fact the only two chords used. The restriction of the chordal vocabulary (which beautifully suits the story of repression told by the song); the oscillation between two chords that do not share a traditional harmonic relationship; and the fact that it is the second, minor chord (rather than the opening major chord) that proves to be the central focus (or tonic) of the song as a whole are all factors that contribute strongly to the unique atmosphere of "Eleanor Rigby."

The subject matter of the song, loneliness, is not in itself an unusual one in pop music, but "Eleanor Rigby" looks at loneliness and a lack of human connection from a uniquely philosophical, even spiritual, viewpoint rather than a romantic one. Eleanor Rigby and Father McKenzie, introduced in two separate verses of the song, remain isolated from both one another and other people in their lives—even in death. Only Father McKenzie is even aware of Eleanor's passing; they "meet" in the third and final verse only in a graveyard that finalizes their nonrelationship, and the "good" Father can only wipe dirt from his hands as he walks away from the site of Eleanor's burial. As the lyrics say so succinctly and eloquently, "No one was saved." This is somber stuff indeed, and it is to the Beatles' credit that the song conveys its despairing message in an efficient and utterly unsentimental way, which of course maximizes the effect.

Apart from the striking introduction, the form of the song suggests that of the traditional folk ballad, with verses that tell a developing story alternated with a repeated chorus (see the following chart). By the mid-1960s the urban folk revival had already been in full swing for years (see Chapter 10), so it was not surprising to see the Beatles laying claim to the folk ballad form as they continued to expand their musical horizons. What was, and remains, surprising is their unique take on this tradition. The ballad form was conventionally used as a means of telling a large-scale, dramatic, and often tragic story. (See the adaptation of ballad form in the sentimentally tragic "After the Ball," discussed in Chapter 2.) Many of the urban folk performers, such as Bob Dylan, adapted the form in their original songs to serve the same kind of dramatic purpose. In "Eleanor Rigby," however, *nothing* happens in the lives of the protagonists. And that, the Beatles tell us, is the source of this tragedy.

The bowed strings take over the role of a strumming guitar in the "ballad" of "Eleanor Rigby," paradoxically giving the song a much harder edge. As you listen, notice the slight variations in the string parts from verse to verse and even in the repetitions of the chorus; they help maintain interest in the emerging story.

A few more musical details deserve mention here. The phrase structure of the verses is distinctive: a long initial phrase (of four bars), "Eleanor Rigby . . .", is answered by a very short (one-bar) phrase: "Lives in a dream." The consistent, atypical, extreme asymmetry of these paired phrases gives the song an unquiet quality of continual incompletion—especially since the shorter phrases are left to hang melodically at a relatively high point, without any conventional feeling of resolution. This is a perfect musical illustration of the incompleteness that characterizes the lives being described. (In a sense, this kind of phrase structure is the reverse of that used in "Yesterday," in which the opening phrase of each section is foreshortened while the ensuing phrases blossom out to traditional lengths.) Also notice how the second phrase in the chorus goes higher than the first, making the question it asks even more intense and insistent.

Finally, the Beatles find extremely imaginative uses for their introductory material later on in the song,

LISTENING GUIDE | "ELEANOR RIGBY" (1966)

TIME	FORM	LYRIC	DESCRIPTIVE COMMENTS
0:00	Introduction	Ah, look at...	Voices and strings enter at once
0:07		Ah, look at...	Exact repetition
0:14	Verse 1: a	Eleanor Rigby...	Solo voice, accompanied by strings marking each beat with a chord; unusual phrase structure creates a striking effect
0:23	a	Waits...	
0:31	Chorus: b	All the lonely...	Second phrase of chorus changes the melody to go higher than the first phrase
0:39	b'	All the lonely...	
0:45	Verse 2: a	Father McKenzie...	As before
0:54	a	Look at him...	
1:03	Chorus: b	All the lonely...	
1:10	b'	All the lonely...	
1:17	Introduction recurs	Ah, look at...	As before
1:24		Ah, look at...	
1:31	Verse 3: a	Eleanor Rigby...	As before
1:39	a	Father McKenzie...	
1:48	Chorus: b	All the lonely...	As a conclusion, the melody and lyrics of the introduction are sung in counterpoint against the melody and lyrics of the chorus, and then strings bring the song to an abrupt ending.
1:55	b'	All the lonely...	

demonstrating again their originality and mastery of form. Just at the point when two successive verse-chorus sections have us convinced that we are listening to a straightforward strophic form, the introduction is unexpectedly brought back. This reappearance underlines the song's theme and helps set off the crucial third verse. Then, at the very end, the final chorus is rendered climactic rather than simply repetitive because the introduction's words and melody are sung simultaneously with it in **counterpoint**, bringing the song full circle. There is nothing left to say, and the strings bring "Eleanor Rigby" to a quick, brusque conclusion.

four songs demonstrate their development from emulators to innovators; the final phase of their career will be discussed in the next chapter. From very early on, the Beatles' original songs showed considerable individuality and creativity in dealing with the inherited materials of rock 'n' roll. By 1965, when the appropriately titled "Yesterday" was released, they had revealed an ability to emulate Tin Pan Alley as well as American rockers. And with "Eleanor Rigby" in 1966, the Beatles achieved a song that was—and is—truly "beyond category," a song that helped certify their new status as not only the most popular band in the history of rock 'n' roll but also the most innovative one.

The Beatles and their music have been discussed in such detail in this book simply because the impact of their popularity and originality on American popular music has been incalculable; the group was *the* central fact of American pop culture in the 1960s. Brian Wilson viewed them as his principal rivals in the creation of innovative pop music, and even Motown's Temptations acknowledged, in their own hit song "Ball of Confusion," that "the Beatles' new record's a gas"! Thus the Beatles are an essential part of the history of American pop—or, put another way, with the arrival of the Beatles on our shores and on our charts, American pop music became unavoidably international.

BOX 9.2 **OTHER BRITISH INVASION BANDS**

It was not only the Beatles' immense popularity but also the wide-ranging and eclectic character of their musical output that made their influence on American pop so great. No other 1960s band—British or American—had the range or reach of the Beatles. The other British Invasion acts that did make a long-term impact in America started as the Beatles did: with firm roots in American rhythm & blues and rock 'n' roll. But the Rolling Stones, the Animals, the Who, the Kinks, and Eric Clapton all remained closer to these roots, on the whole, during their careers than the Beatles did. Indeed, it was just at the point that the Beatles became a studio band and began producing music that was essentially uncategorizable, like "Eleanor Rigby" and many of the songs on the album *Sgt. Pepper's Lonely Hearts Club Band* (see Chapter 10) that the Rolling Stones—who to this day play international live tours—began to call themselves the "World's Greatest Rock 'n' Roll Band." Regardless of one's feelings about that claim, there is no doubt that of all the British Invasion acts other than the Beatles, the Rolling Stones have had the greatest cumulative influence in America.

The Rolling Stones excelled in presenting covers and original songs of an intense, gritty, and often dark character. They cultivated an image as "bad boys," in deliberate contrast to the friendly public image projected by the Beatles. Their most famous hit record is perhaps "(I Can't Get No) Satisfaction" (Number 1, 1965), composed by band members Mick Jagger and Keith Richards; with its memorable buzzing guitar "hook," its unrelenting beat, and its unabashedly self-oriented and ultimately sexual lyrics, the song perfectly exemplifies the distinctive low-down, hard-rocking essence both of the Rolling Stones themselves and of their music. The Rolling Stones experimented occasionally in the later 1960s with unusual instrumentation and unconventional forms, as did virtually every other major British and American group—one had, after all, to keep up with the Beatles in some sense. But while a record like "As Tears Go By" (Number 6, 1966) is undeniably affecting and effective, its gently somber atmosphere and employment of orchestral strings render it a highly atypical Stones opus. The ultimate importance of the Rolling Stones lies in the power and longevity with which they kept—and continue to keep—the spirit of basic rock 'n' roll alive. (As late as 1986, the group achieved a Top 10 hit with "Harlem Shuffle," their faithful remake of a neglected American rhythm & blues hit from 1964 by Bob and Earl.)

It is obviously impossible to do justice in this book to the Rolling Stones or to many other important British acts of the 1960s and beyond—although we will return to the Stones for a while in Chapter 11. While the importance of these artists to the stylistic development of American pop may not be extensive, their presence on the American and world pop music landscape has been, and continues to be, a formidable one.

Meanwhile, Back in California . . .

While the other Beach Boys were out on tour, Brian Wilson was preparing his response and challenge to the Beatles, whose late 1965 album *Rubber Soul* had particularly inspired him, in the form of an elaborately produced and strikingly unconventional album called *Pet Sounds*. Less a work of rock 'n' roll than a nearly symphonic cycle of songs, *Pet Sounds* charts a progression from youthful optimism ("Wouldn't It Be Nice" and "You Still Believe in Me") to philosophical and emotional disillusionment ("I Just Wasn't Made for These Times" and "Caroline, No"). Released in mid-1966, *Pet Sounds* was arguably rock's first **concept album**—that is, an album conceived as an integrated whole, with interrelated songs arranged in a deliberate sequence. (The listening sequence was obviously easier to mandate in the days of LPs with two numbered sides that were played on phonographs without remote controls.) *Pet Sounds* was a modest seller compared to some other Beach Boys albums, but it had an enormous impact on musicians who heard it. With its display of diverse and unusual instrumentation, including orchestral wind instruments as well as strings; its virtuosic vocal arrangements, showcasing the songs' advanced harmonies; and its occasional formal experiments, exemplified by the AABCC form of the remarkable instrumental "Let's Go Away for Awhile," the album was state-of-the-art pop music in every sense, designed to push the boundaries of what had been considered possible. Its historical importance is certified by Paul McCartney's affirmation that *Pet Sounds* was the single greatest influence on the Beatles' landmark 1967 album *Sgt. Pepper's Lonely Hearts Club Band* (see next chapter).

Wilson furthered his experimentation with the late 1966 single "Good Vibrations," which reached Number 1 on the charts and has remained probably the Beach Boys' most famous song (see the following Listening Guide). By this time, Wilson was also at work on an album to be called *Smile*. Eagerly anticipated for many months, *Smile* was abandoned in 1967, and the collapse of what was evidently a strikingly novel and ambitious project—even by Wilson's exceptionally high standards—marked the onset of a decline in his productivity and achievement from which he has only recently recovered. Material from the *Smile* sessions occasionally surfaced on later albums and CD compilations by the Beach Boys, hinting at how unprecedented and stunning the album was intended to be. The promise of *Smile* was finally fulfilled when Wilson returned to and completed the project in 2004.

Latin Sounds in 1960s Pop: A Tall Man, a Tanned Girl, and a Taste of Honey

By 1960 the mambo dance craze had run out of steam, and the use of romantic Latin themes in Hollywood and on Broadway, common in earlier decades, had also subsided considerably. Although there were local Latin music scenes in cities such as Miami and San Antonio, both the recording and the mass distribution of Latin-influenced popular music were still mainly centered in the media capitals of New York and Los Angeles.

Listening Guide "GOOD VIBRATIONS"

Music by Brian Wilson, lyrics by Mike Love; produced by Brian Wilson; performed by the Beach Boys with instrumental accompaniment; recorded 1966

Basic Description

"Good Vibrations" may well be the most thoroughly innovative single from the singular decade of the 1960s. Virtually every aspect of the record is unusual, from the vocal arrangement to the instrumentation and the chordal vocabulary to the overall form. Beginning with a gentle, unaccompanied sigh in a high solo voice right at the outset (which might be an anticipation of the opening word "I" but could also be just the sighing sound "ah"), "Good Vibrations" establishes a unique world of sounds, textures, and feelings.

Probably the only remotely conventional thing about the song is its lyrics, with their admiring references to the beloved's "colorful clothes," hair, perfume, smile, and eyes. But there is something otherworldly about the lyrics as well—at least when they claim, "I don't know where, but she sends me there," or when they refer to "a blossom world," not to mention the "good vibrations" themselves. Notice also the extensive periods on the recording where lyrics are of secondary importance, or of no importance at all: the C section, the following instrumental transition, and the concluding "variations on B" section (see the accompanying chart). These are in no sense secondary or unimportant portions of the record itself; it is just that here *sound* becomes more significant than *sense* (literally speaking)—or better, here the sound *becomes* the sense of the song. The sound is the way in which Wilson musically communicates the sensuous experience that is the essential subject matter of "Good Vibrations."

FORM

There is no name for the form of "Good Vibrations"; it is as individual and distinctive as everything else about this recording. The best way to follow it is with the listening chart. The formal freedom is that much more effective because Wilson sets the listener up at first to expect a straightforward, predictable verse-chorus form with his initial ABAB pattern—since the lyrics to A change but those to B remain the same—and then goes on to present the unexpected. The C section could seem at first like a bridge, but instead of any return to A we get totally new material in D. In fact, the A music never returns at all, which is probably the second most surprising thing about this formal structure. The most surprising thing is that Wilson somehow manages to make this unconventional form work so effectively.

It works because of subtle interconnections that are established among the different musical sections. The C section has overlapping vocal textures that are reminiscent of the vocal textures in the B sections, even though the specific music and the words are different. In the unexpected D section, the organ and percussion accompaniment maintains a kinship with the A sections, which also prominently feature those instruments. In addition, the clear presence of the words "good vibrations" in the D section provides a textual link between it and the preceding B sections, as well as tying D to the concluding section, which we here call "variations on B."

This final section requires a few comments. Its relationship with the earlier B sections is textually and musically obvious, but it is also clear that this is not a literal repetition, nor is it the kind of slight modification that would mandate a B' label. Rather, Wilson is taking verbal, musical, and textural ideas from his B material and arranging them in new ways to create a section that sounds evolutionary rather than stable. We could borrow a term from classical music and call this a kind of "development" of the ideas; "development" is a term rarely, if ever, needed to describe formal sections of popular songs, but then most popular songs do not behave like "Good Vibrations." (Wilson employs one particularly sophisticated musical device here. At the beginning of the "variations on B" section he plays the characteristic chord progression of the earlier B sections, but in reverse order, starting on the final chord and ending on the opening chord. This approach allows him to proceed by then taking the opening chord again and playing the chords in the original order—but with new, textless vocal parts. The material is constantly in flux.) Remarkably, the song fades out while immersed in this development section, never having returned to its point of origin or to any other stable reference point. In a way, this is a perfect ending for a record so thoroughly liberated from traditional formal constraints.

THE SONG/THE RECORDING

As a composition, "Good Vibrations" boasts memorable melodic hooks and a wide and colorful palette of chords. Both the high opening minor-key melody of the A section (which first ascends, and then descends) and the major-key bass line "I'm pickin' up good vibrations" of the B section (which first descends, and then ascends) are instantly memorable tunes—and beautifully contrasting ones. Consequently, they serve as effective landmarks for the listener who is journeying for the first time through this complex musical landscape. The D section offers a new but equally memorable melody. Some details of the harmony are indicated on the following chart, for those who may wish to follow them.

The instrumentation of "Good Vibrations" is perhaps the most unusual ever employed on a hit record. Organ, flutes, solo cello, and colorful percussion instruments are all in evidence, clearly differentiating the sound of this recording from anything commonly associated with rock 'n' roll. But the ultimate exotic touch is provided by the

LISTENING GUIDE	"GOOD VIBRATIONS"			
TIME	**FORM**	**LYRIC**	**DESCRIPTIVE COMMENTS**
0:00	A	*I love the colorful clothes . . .*	High solo voice, with delicate, high-range accompaniment of organ, flutes, and eventually percussion; minor key
0:26	B	*I'm pickin' up good vibrations . . .*	Bass voice enters, accompanied by cello, theremin, and percussion, then rest of group comes in with overlapping vocal parts; major key
0:51	A	*Close my eyes, she's somehow closer now . . .*	As before
1:16	B	*I'm pickin' up good vibrations . . .*	As before; formal structure up to this point suggests verse-chorus form
1:42	C		Steadily building tension expressed by subtle humming that builds to more vocal activity; no stable key
		I don't know where, but she sends me there . . .	
2:14	Brief instrumental transition		Organ and percussion
2:22	D	*Gotta keep those lovin' good vibrations happenin' with her . . .*	Solo voice, then group, with organ accompaniment; the line of text repeats, then fades out while organ finishes the section
2:54	Transition	*Aah!*	
2:57	Variations on B	*I'm pickin' up good vibrations . . .*	Full group texture with overlapping vocal parts; major key; then voices drop out, leaving cello and theremin, which are joined by percussion before fading out; no stable key

(continued)

Listening Guide "GOOD VIBRATIONS" (continued)

theremin—the whirring, sirenlike, otherworldly instrument that appropriately illustrates the "good vibrations" in the B sections. (There is some question about whether the recording actually employed a theremin or a somewhat different instrument that sounds very much like one. But such questions are not of great significance to listeners; the exotic effect is certainly achieved!) Notice how Wilson also uses the voices of the Beach Boys as an additional choir of sound colors, pitting solo against group sounds, high voices against low, and so forth. Some prominent details of both the instrumental and vocal parts are indicated in the descriptive comments on the listening chart.

"Good Vibrations" was an extremely costly recording to produce in terms of both time and money. Wilson tried out many different instrumental and vocal arrangements and a number of different formal schemes, committing hours and hours of rehearsal time to tape before he finally settled on the version we can hear today on record—which is actually a composite of several tapes made at various times. Thus, "Good Vibrations," which Brian Wilson called his "pocket symphony," is an important milestone in the developing history of rock production, as well as a landmark hit record of the 1960s.

Despite the seeming downturn in mainstream popular appetite for Latin American music during the 1960s, three distinct tributaries of Latin influence on mainstream popular music emerged between 1962 and 1966, one centered on the East Coast and two on the West Coast.

In New York City, musicians from Cuba, Puerto Rico, and elsewhere in Latin America began to create a fusion of rumba and mambo with Black American popular music. Variously termed **bugalú** or **Latin soul**, this music pushed its way onto the pop charts in 1963. The biggest hit was "Watermelon Man," recorded by ***Ramon "Mongo" Santamaria*** (1917–2003), which stayed on the charts for eleven weeks in 1963, peaking at Number 10. Born in Cuba, Santamaria made his reputation in New York as a virtuoso *conguero* (conga drum player) in the bands of mambo masters Perez Prado and Tito Puente (see Chapter 7). "Watermelon Man," composed by the jazz pianist Herbie Hancock, is a sixteen-bar blues that Hancock has said was inspired by his childhood memories of the cries of a watermelon vendor in the streets of Chicago. The style of the performance is a fusion of R&B and jazz (sometimes called soul jazz) with a medium-tempo cha-cha-chá dance rhythm and a pop hook. The instrumentation blends the jazz combo and Latin *conjunto* traditions: a trumpet, two saxophones, and a rhythm section of piano, string bass, drum set, conga, timbales, and *guiro* (a ridged gourd, scraped with a stick).

Another important development of the early 1960s was the rise to mass popularity of the Brazilian genre bossa nova. The bossa nova (Portuguese for "new trend") was a blend of samba rhythms, a sophisticated Brazilian tradition of song composition (recall our discussion of "Brazil" in Chapter 6), and the West Coast style of modern jazz, which emphasized relaxed tempos, sophisticated harmonies, and a cool, cerebral emotional

Listening Guide   "EL WATUSI"

By Ray Barretto and his Charanga Moderna; recorded in 1962

For an example of a Latin soul record more closely aligned with Latin American music in its style and substance, we turn to "El Watusi," by Ray Barretto and his Charanga Moderna. *Ray Barretto* (1929–2006) was a New York–born musician and bandleader of Puerto Rican descent who had played conga in a number of the leading mambo bands during the 1950s. "El Watusi," a 1962 recording that reached Number 17 on both the pop and R&B charts the following year, was based on the *charanga*, a genre that rose to popularity in New York's Latin dance scene during the early 1960s. The term *charanga* refers to an energetic style of dance, its accompanying music, and the ensemble that plays it, typically combining Afro-Cuban percussion with flute and violins. Barretto's version of "El Watusi" featured this instrumentation. In musical terms, it fell squarely within the *charanga* framework, with the violins playing a repeated montuno pattern and the solo flute improvising throughout, a texture punctuated by resonant hand claps that land on the last beat of each eight-beat cycle (that is, just before the downbeat).

The recording also features improvised verbal banter between Barretto and one of his fellow musicians, who plays the role of a seven-foot-tall, 169-pound homely fellow from Havana, nicknamed "Watusi." Throughout the course of the recording Barretto abuses his adversary in *Nuevayorquino* (New York Puerto Rican) street slang, making this recording a Latino ancestor of hip-hop, which was pioneered in New York a decade later by African American, Puerto Rican, and Caribbean American youth. (Latin records also played an important, if underrecognized, role as source material for the multiple turntable "breaks" created by early hip-hop DJs; see Chapter 12.)

Barretto's single was an immediate hit in the Latin American community of New York, but the record's pop chart success came somewhat later, largely as a result of a new dance craze called the Watusi. Although the Watusi—a shuffling step with alternating arm movements—bore no resemblance whatsoever to the *charanga* danced by Barretto's fans in East Harlem, and the text of Barretto's song does not even mention the

Ray Barretto lays down the beat.

(continued)

Listening Guide "EL WATUSI" (continued)

Watusi dance, the mainstream popularity of "El Watusi" was apparently boosted by its association with the Watusi dance. Interestingly, two R&B songs completely unrelated to Barretto's also scored big hits during the dance craze: the Vibrations' "The Watusi," which reached Number 13 on the R&B and Number 25 on the pop charts in 1961, and "The Wah Watusi" by the Philadelphia vocal group the Orlons, which hit Number 2 on the pop and Number 5 on the R&B charts in 1962. Few songs performed entirely in Spanish have ever reached the Top 20 in the United States ("La Bamba" being one obvious exception), and so this is a good example of the effect that popular dance can have on the fate of a record coming from outside the pop mainstream.

atmosphere. The instrumentation of a typical bossa nova group consists of nylon-stringed acoustic guitar, played with the fingers rather than a plectrum, plus piano, string bass, and drum set. The drum set is played in a distinctive style derived from samba music, characterized by a continuous pulsation that the drummer plays with one hand on the closed high-hat cymbal (mimicking the role of the tambourine in a samba band) while tapping the snare drum's metal rim in a 3-3-4-3-3 pattern with the other (a pattern related to that of the Cuban clave).

The musician most often credited with initiating bossa nova is the guitarist and singer *João Gilberto* (1931–2019). The first recording of the genre was made in 1958, a version of the song "Chega de Saudade" ("Enough of Longing"), composed by *Antônio Carlos Jobim* (1927–1994) and lyricist Vinícius de Moraes, and performed by the singer Elizete Cardoso, with Gilberto on guitar. A subsequent version of the song, featuring Gilberto's intimate, breathy singing, was boosted both in Brazil and internationally by its inclusion in the soundtrack of the 1959 film *Black Orpheus*.

Jazz musicians from California, including the guitarist Charlie Byrd (1925–1999) and saxophonist *Stan Getz* (1927–1991), became passionately interested in bossa nova—which is not surprising, given its affinities with West Coast jazz—and made a series of recordings back in the United States, including *Jazz Samba*, a Number 1 album in 1962, and *Getz/Gilberto*, which reached Number 2 in 1963. The latter album yielded the biggest hit of the bossa nova era, the single "The Girl from Ipanema" (Number 5 pop, 1964), sung by Gilberto's wife, Astrud, with Stan Getz on tenor saxophone. The cool, emotional tone of the song (composed by Jobim and de Moraes), combined with the delicacy of Gilberto's voice and the sensual imagery of the lyrics, which describe a young woman walking along Rio de Janeiro's Ipanema beach, made the song a symbol of cultural sophistication for millions of American listeners.

During the mid-1960s, bossa nova became a staple of the repertoire of jazz musicians and singers, including Ella Fitzgerald and Frank Sinatra; Sinatra recorded an album with Antônio Carlos Jobim in 1967. A few Brazilian groups were able to sign recording and touring contracts in the United States. The most successful of these was Brasil '66, led by the pianist Sergio Mendes, whose biggest hit was a bossa nova–inflected version of the Burt Bacharach ballad "The Look of Love" (Number 4 pop, 1968). By the late 1960s, the bossa nova's status as an exciting new thing had been eclipsed by the rise of rock music. However, even if recordings like "The Girl from Ipanema" were relegated to the clichéd role of "elevator music," it is worth noting that later musicians—including David Byrne and Paul Simon—saw the music of Brazil, including the bossa nova, as a rich source of creative inspiration and an important part of the globalizing future of American popular music.

The influence of Mexican music on the pop mainstream was in general less direct during the early 1960s, but a major exception may be found in the widely popular music of **Herb Alpert** (b. 1935) and the Tijuana Brass. In 1962 Alpert, a Los Angeles–born trumpet player and songwriter, and his business partner Jerry Moss founded an independent label called A&M (for Alpert and Moss) Records. Alpert had been working in the music business since 1957, making some recordings under the name Dore Alpert and producing tracks for the surf duo Jan & Dean. His prior songwriting credits (with partner Lou Adler) included the Sam Cooke hit "Wonderful World" (Number 12 pop, Number 2 R&B, 1960), better known by its first line, "Don't know much about history." A&M Records started small—"We had a desk, piano, piano stool, a couch, coffee table, and two phone lines," Moss recalled of the early days, when the label's office was located in Alpert's garage (Holden 1987).

As it turned out, the company's first release was a big hit. The single "The Lonely Bull (El Solo Toro)" sold 700,000 copies and reached Number 6 on the pop singles charts in 1962. As Alpert recounted it:

> The idea behind the song, which was composed by a writer named Sol Lake, was to capture the feeling Jerry [Moss] and I both had while watching the same bullfight in Tijuana. Jerry thought up the name Tijuana Brass. It was just a name without a concept. In fact, it didn't occur to me to make more records that sounded like that until people who heard "The Lonely Bull" assumed that the Tijuana Brass was a quasi-mariachi band. (Holden 1987)

"The Lonely Bull" is an instructive example of the Tijuana Brass's "Ameriachi" sound. The recording opens with crowd sounds recorded at a bullfight, an *audio verité* experience meant to temporarily relocate the listener to Mexico. (It is worth noting that the Tijuana Brass, a band named after a Mexican border town, in fact had no Latino members. Alpert was fond of introducing the band as comprising "three pastramis, two bagels, and an American cheese.") In addition to Alpert's adaptation of the two-trumpet harmonies common in mariachi music, the piece as a whole is a hybrid of several styles. The form, AABA with a few extra measures thrown in here and there for interest, is straight out of Tin Pan Alley, while the rhythmic feel is a medium-tempo bolero—more Cuban than Mexican in inspiration—with a rock 'n'

Herb Alpert and the Tijuana Brass, c. 1965.

roll–style backbeat on the snare drum. The electric guitar solo that occurs twice in the arrangement, positively dripping with reverb, is reminiscent of the themes of so-called spaghetti westerns, Italian-made cowboy films popular in the early 1960s. Though it may seem simple at first listening, "The Lonely Bull" is in fact layered with pop music references, craftily arranged into a two-minute, nineteen-second experience.

"The Lonely Bull" was the first of a long string of hit singles and albums. Between 1965 and 1968, the Tijuana Brass enjoyed extraordinary—indeed almost unparalleled—success, placing ten albums in the *Billboard* Top 10, six of which reached Number 1 on the album charts. As time went on, Alpert shifted away from the imitation mariachi style that characterized his band's early recordings toward an accessible, horn-driven pop sound that incorporated Latin grooves, Dixieland jazz, Brill Building–style songwriting, and, on the rare occasions when he sang, crooning. He applied this sensibility to a wide variety of material, including Tin Pan Alley classics such as "I've Grown Accustomed to Her Face" and "I'm Getting Sentimental Over You," Burt Bacharach ballads ("Don't Go Breaking My Heart"), Beatles songs ("All My Loving"), bossa novas ("Desafinado" and "The Girl from Ipanema"), R&B hits ("Spanish Harlem"), soul jazz ("Work Song"), film themes ("Zorba the Greek," "Third Man Theme," "Casino Royale"), and Broadway songs ("America," "Mame," and "Cabaret").

Listening Guide   "A TASTE OF HONEY"

By Herb Alpert and the Tijuana Brass, recorded 1965

One of the biggest singles for the Tijuana Brass was their version of "A Taste of Honey" (Number 7 pop, 1965), from the Broadway show of the same name (1960; made into a film, 1961). The single appeared on the album *Whipped Cream & Other Delights*, which featured an attractive female model apparently clothed only in mountains of whipped cream. (The degree to which this arresting image contributed to the album's enormous success—eight weeks at Number 1, 185 weeks on the charts overall—is perhaps best left to scholars of the visual, rather than the musical, arts.)

After a slow introduction, played by trombone and electric guitar with marimba and mandolin accompaniment, the pulse is established for three measures on the bass drum—one of the most iconic moments in any pop recording of the 1960s—and the band launches into a medium-tempo, swinging groove (sometimes called a "shuffle"). The form includes an A section and a B section, with the former being fourteen bars in length (4 + 4 + 2 + 4) and the latter consisting of four bars in

tempo and a two-measure phrase that slows the tempo to a virtual halt. Then, as at the beginning, the bass drums kick in again for three measures, and we're off.

Blend Alpert's economical, almost terse phrasing on the trumpet with the smooth flow of the rhythm section; pour into the mold of a beautifully balanced pop arrangement; mix in some exotic instrumental colorations (marimbas and mandolins); bake in a state-of-the-art recording studio with talented engineers, a hallmark of A&M Records productions; slather with whipped cream; and you have one of the most memorable recordings of the 1960s, an example of how creative (and delicious) "easy listening" music can be. In 2006 A&M Records released a digitally "rewhipped" version of the tracks from the 1965 album *Whipped Cream & Other Delights*. This new album offered a tribute to Herb Alpert's talent and tenacity by a new generation of musicians—including the multiethnic Los Angeles–based band Ozomatli, named after an ancient Mexican deity.

LISTENING GUIDE | "A TASTE OF HONEY"		
TIME	**FORM**	**DESCRIPTIVE COMMENTS**
0:00	Introduction	Free rhythm, melody on trombone and electric guitar, with mandolin and marimba backing
0:21	Pause	Bass drum plays pulse for 3 measures
0:26	A	Trumpet plays main melody; 14 measures
0:46	A	Repeats; 14 measures
1:07	B	4 measures in tempo (trumpet with marimba), followed by 2 measures, slowing down toward the end (with mariachi-like horns in the background)
1:24	Pause	Bass drum (3 measures)
1:28	A	As before
1:49	B	Trumpet improvises on melody for 4 bars; then slows down as before
2:06	Pause	Bass drum
2:11	Transition	4 measures (first two lines of melody), marked by key change
2:16	A	Extended to 18 measures (with first phrase of last line repeated twice, then ends with brief piano figure)

BY THE MID-1960s the transition from rock 'n' roll to rock music was well under way as a result of the influence of performers such as the Beach Boys, the Beatles, and Bob Dylan. In the following chapter we will follow American popular music into the culturally and politically turbulent period of the late 1960s, tracing the development of country and western, soul music, and the urban folk movement, the rise of psychedelia and the counterculture, and the diversification of rock—now positioned at the center of the popular mainstream—into dozens of subcategories and specialized audiences.

Key Terms

Brill Building	cadence	counterpoint
bugalú	concept album	Latin soul

Key People

Antônio Carlos Jobim	Chubby Checker	Ramon "Mongo"
Barry Mann	Cynthia Weil	Santamaria
Beach Boys	Dick Clark	Ray Barretto
Beatles	Herb Alpert	Stan Getz
Berry Gordy Jr.	João Gilberto	Supremes
Brian Wilson	Phil Spector	Temptations
Carole King		

Review Questions

1. Describe the "British Invasion" by the Beatles in 1964. How did they influence American popular music? Include a description of the Beatles' music and the songwriting talents of Paul McCartney and John Lennon, and describe two or three representative songs.
2. What made the decade of the 1960s one of the most disruptive, controversial, and violent eras in American history?
3. Who was Phil Spector? Discuss the "wall of sound" and Spector's studio recording techniques.
4. What was Motown? Who founded it, and why did it proclaim itself "the sound of young America"?
5. What were the unique, groundbreaking elements in the Beach Boys' recording of "Good Vibrations"?

"Blowin' in the Wind"

Country, Soul, Urban Folk, and the Rise of Rock, 1960s

10

IN CHAPTER 8 WE STRESSED THE INTEGRATION OF COUNTRY AND RHYTHM & blues–based styles into the mix that came to be known as rock 'n' roll. Rhythm & blues was an obvious influence on virtually all the music discussed in Chapter 9. While the country influences on 1960s rock 'n' roll were far less obvious, they remained present as well. In particular, the Beatles' close harmony singing owed no small debt to the model of the Everly Brothers—and thus to the whole history of country's "high lonesome" duo and group sounds. One of the Beatles' chart-making cover recordings was in fact "Act Naturally," a song issued on the B-side of "Yesterday" that had originally been a Number 1 hit on the country charts in 1963 for Buck Owens.

However, this mention of the country charts brings us to the fact that the pre–rock 'n' roll distinctions among genres and audiences did not simply collapse after 1955, although the situation was much more fluid than it had been. One still finds much significant popular music that did not cross over into the mainstream during the late 1950s and 1960s, even though eclectic influences were everywhere present on the pop charts. Artists and records that appealed to select or regional audiences were much less likely to find their way onto the pop charts than those that managed to cut across such distinctions. Listeners to pop- and rock-oriented radio stations in New York City or Detroit

could probably have gone through the whole decade of the 1960s totally unaware of performers like Buck Owens or Merle Haggard. Yet these performers—along with many
others who would not have been heard on these urban radio stations, such as George
Jones, Sonny James, Webb Pierce, Kitty Wells, and Loretta Lynn—were the bread and
butter of country stations in the southern and western parts of the United States during
this same period. Thus we find the striking anomaly that, among all the artists just
mentioned, only one achieved a national Top 40 pop hit during the entire decade, and
he did so only once: Buck Owens's "I've Got a Tiger by the Tail" got up to Number 25 on
the pop charts in 1965. Yet the same record occupied the Number 1 spot on *Billboard*'s
country charts for five weeks and was just one of twenty-one Number 1 country songs
for Owens during the decade. Sonny James had twelve Number 1 country hits during
this same period, Merle Haggard had seven, and the list goes on.

But the anomalies don't end there. Those same listeners in New York or Detroit
might in turn have heard rhythm & blues–oriented music on their radios that, while
popular locally, failed to make much of a dent in the national pop charts. Although
Motown's records had no trouble crossing over—they were, as we have seen, designed
to do so—a record like Freddie Scott's "Are You Lonely for Me," issued on the small
Shout label, could hold the Number 1 spot on *Billboard*'s R&B chart for four weeks in
1967, while climbing no higher than Number 39 (and then for one week only) on the
pop chart.

Just how much weight should be given to all this chart data is, of course, a justifiable
question. But regardless of the actual numbers, it seems clear that such data does reflect
some clear and persistent divisions among markets and audiences for popular music, divisions that had at least something to do with racial and ethnic factors, geographical location, and distance from major urban centers. The especially large differences between
the country and the pop charts for much of the 1960s might have resulted to a certain
extent from some inherent bias on the part of the data collectors toward the large radio
stations and record retailers centered in the big cities of the North.[1] But these differences
also reflected the authentic and increasingly wide gulf between the lingeringly rural
cultures of the South and Southwest and the urban cultures that dominated much of
the North. (The feeling of separateness that characterized much of the country audience
was articulated memorably in Merle Haggard's controversial 1969 recording "Okie from
Muskogee"—a critique of the late 1960s **counterculture** that may or may not have been
made with deeply serious intent—that rose to Number 1 on the country and Number
41 on the pop charts.) In spite of all these factors, country music did have a much wider
impact on the pop music of the 1960s than is generally acknowledged.

---

1. Such a bias would also help explain the relatively much greater congruence between the R&B and
pop charts during this time, as R&B is a largely urban (albeit not exclusively Northern) music. The
R&B and pop charts were getting close enough to each other that *Billboard* over-optimistically dropped
the separate R&B charts for a little over a year, from late 1963 to early 1965; thereafter, the R&B charts
resumed their appearance. Significantly, when *Billboard* changed its methods of gathering data in the
early 1990s to rely on electronically generated data of actual record sales and radio play instead of reports
from selected outlets, the presence of country records on the pop charts increased dramatically.

Many of the younger country artists at this time, while not directly embracing the rockabilly styles of Elvis Presley or Buddy Holly, wanted to update the sound of their honky-tonk roots. Starting with a basis in the ballad style of Hank Williams—taking, we might say, a song like "I'm So Lonesome I Could Cry" instead of "Hey, Good Lookin'" as their point of orientation (see the discussion of Hank Williams in Chapter 7)—they opted for a newly sophisticated approach to the vocal presentation and instrumental arrangement of country music that came to be known as **countrypolitan**, a fusion of "country" and "cosmopolitan." Nashville was at the center of this development, and the style was also often called the "Nashville Sound." Among its most important manifestations were the recordings of Patsy Cline.

Patsy Cline and the Nashville Sound

Patsy Cline (1932–1963) began her career as a hit maker in 1957 with her recording of "Walkin' after Midnight," which was indicative of her future achievements and importance insofar as it was successful on both the country (Number 2) and the pop charts (Number 12). Such crossover success from country to pop was of course not uncommon in the fluid record market of 1957. But it was note-

worthy when Cline achieved even greater crossover success in 1961, at a time of vastly increasing segregation between the country and pop markets. Her two big hits of that year, "I Fall to Pieces," which reached Number 1 on the country and Number 12 on the pop charts, and "Crazy" (Number 2 country, Number 9 pop) reflected a particular kind of sensibility: these were ballads of broad appeal, in no sense "teen" records, performed by Cline in a manner that, while sophisticated in phrasing and articulation, had sufficient hints of rural and bluesy inflections to show where her roots lay. The crooning background voices gave these records a pop sheen, while the high-register piano remained evocative of the honky-tonk origins of this type of music. Cline continued to be a significant presence on both the country and the pop charts until her premature death in a plane crash in early 1963.

Other recordings of the early 1960s that demonstrated the crossover appeal of the Nashville Sound were those of Jim Reeves and Floyd Cramer. A ballad like Reeves's "He'll Have to Go" (Number 2 pop, Number 1 country—for fourteen weeks!—in 1960) demonstrates a mixture of elements similar to that

Country and pop star Patsy Cline, c. 1958.

which made Cline's records so successful. Reeves possessed a fine, full, deep baritone voice that was particularly well suited for mainstream pop appeal. Floyd Cramer was a Nashville session pianist who combined his honky-tonk-derived style with orchestral strings to produce the huge instrumental hit "Last Date" (Number 2 pop, Number 11 country, 1960).

The impact of the Nashville Sound on 1960s pop is clear if we consider certain records by artists not primarily identified with country music. Connie Francis and Brenda Lee, the two most popular female vocalists of the early 1960s, depended mainly on the young rock 'n' roll audience for their reputation and record sales, and both certainly made up-tempo records obviously addressed to the new teenage audience (such as Francis's 1962 hit "Vacation" and Lee's 1960 smash "Sweet Nothin's"). But Connie Francis's two biggest hits, "Everybody's Somebody's Fool" and "My Heart Has a Mind of Its Own"—both of which made it to Number 1 on the pop charts in 1960—betray a significant Nashville Sound influence, and Brenda Lee's own biggest hit, the 1960 Number 1 song "I'm Sorry," shows that influence even more transparently. Indeed, "I'm Sorry," with its strings and crooning chorus backing Lee's mournful and blues-inflected vocal performance, features a type of sound that has been prominent on the country charts for much of the latter part of the twentieth century. These mainstream pop hits by Francis and Lee may well have paved the way for Patsy Cline's crossover successes in 1961.

The records made by rock 'n' roller Elvis Presley from 1960 on (after he returned from a tour of duty in the U.S. Army) reflected an increasingly eclectic set of influences, but the Nashville Sound is especially prominent among them. Good illustrations of this influence would be his 1961 hit "Can't Help Falling in Love" and his 1965 recording of "Crying in the Chapel," originally a country (and R&B) hit in 1953.

It might seem initially surprising that the Nashville Sound's influence extended into rhythm & blues in the early 1960s, but given the constant interchanges between white and Black musicians throughout the history of American popular music, this really shouldn't strike us as unexpected. Two hits by Solomon Burke, "Just Out of Reach (Of My Two Open Arms)" (Number 24 pop, Number 7 R&B, 1961), and "Cry to Me" (Number 44 pop, Number 5 R&B, 1962) sound for all the world like country records performed by a Black vocalist, and a large number of similar-sounding records were made in the wake of their success, both by Burke and by other artists associated with rhythm & blues. By the later 1960s the career of Charley Pride—an African American who set out to appeal principally to the country audience—was in full swing; by 1983 Pride had racked up an astonishing twenty-nine Number 1 country hits (none of which even dented the rhythm & blues charts), thus illustrating once again how color-blind music and its audiences really can be, at least some of the time.

Ray Charles and Soul Music

Despite Pride's success, the most remarkable and unexpected synthesis of country with rhythm & blues elements was probably achieved by Ray Charles. Charles's achievement looms so large in the history of American popular music that we must stop here to consider his career in some detail.

"The Genius," Ray Charles, performing
c. early 1960s.

Ray Charles (1930–2004), born Ray Charles Robinson, was a constant presence on
the rhythm & blues charts during the 1950s, but major crossover success eluded him
until 1959, which is why we have not grouped him with early African American rock
'n' roll stars like Chuck Berry, Little Richard, and Fats Domino. In any case, Charles
was never interested in being typecast as a rock 'n' roller, and he never consciously addressed his recordings to the teen market—or to any obviously delimited market, for
that matter. Characteristically, as soon as he established himself as a mass market artist
with the stunning blues-based and gospel-drenched "What'd I Say" (Number 6 pop,
Number 1 R&B, 1959), he immediately sought new worlds to conquer; his next record
was a highly individual cover of Hank Snow's 1950 hit "I'm Movin' On," one of the biggest country records of all time. Within a year, Charles had achieved his first Number
1 pop hit with his version of the old Tin Pan Alley standard "Georgia on My Mind"
(by Stuart Gorrell and Hoagy Carmichael), which also made it to Number 3 on the

rhythm & blues chart. But Charles's most astounding success was with his version of country artist Don Gibson's "I Can't Stop Loving You," which brought Charles's unique take on country music to the top spot on both the pop and the rhythm & blues charts (Number 1 pop for five weeks, Number 1 R&B for ten weeks) in 1962 and gave him the biggest hit record of that entire year.

Ray Charles was certainly not the first artist to assay many different genres of American popular music, and he was of course only one of many to achieve remarkable crossover success. What is it then that made his career so distinctive and made him such a universally admired pop musician—by audiences, critics, and other musicians—that the appellation "genius" has clung to his name for decades, as if he had been born to the title?

Part of it is the astounding range of talents Charles cultivated. He was a fine song-writer, having written many of his early rhythm & blues hits, including classics of the genre like "I've Got a Woman" and "Hallelujah I Love Her So." He was also a highly skilled arranger and an exceptionally fine keyboard player who was fluent in jazz as well as mainstream pop idioms. And above all he was an outstanding vocalist, with a timbre so distinctive as to be instantly recognizable and an expressive intensity that, once heard, is difficult to forget. But this still is not the whole story. Charles's most characteristic recordings are not only distinguished, individual statements but also unique and encompassing statements about American popular music style.

After a period of imitation, during which he emulated the pop-friendly vocal and instrumental approach of Nat "King" Cole and the King Cole Trio (see Chapter 7), Ray Charles established a style that immediately expressed his interest in synthesis. Charles's first Number 1 rhythm & blues recording, "I've Got a Woman" (1954), is an obviously secular song based on gospel models, performed by Charles in a manner clearly related to gospel vocal stylings. Although Black gospel music had long been an influence for various aspects of secular "race" records and rhythm & blues (see Chapters 5 and 7), arguably nobody before Charles had brought the sacred and secular idioms into such a direct and intimate relationship; by the time of "Hallelujah I Love Her So" (Number 5 R&B, 1956) he was expressing the connection in the song's very title! Needless to say, some people were scandalized by this explicit connection. The final portion of "What'd I Say," in which Charles shouts and groans in call and response with a female chorus to produce music that simultaneously evokes a wild Southern Baptist service and the sounds of a very earthly sexual ecstasy, was banned on many radio stations in spite of the record's status as a national hit.

Although the term **soul music** would not enter the common vocabulary until the later 1960s, it is clearly soul music that Ray Charles was pioneering in his gospel-blues synthesis of the 1950s. He is now widely acknowledged as the first important soul artist, and his work proved to be an incalculable influence on James Brown, Aretha Franklin, Curtis Mayfield, Otis Redding, Sly Stone, and innumerable others. When Charles went on to record Tin Pan Alley and country material in the 1960s, far from leaving his soul stylings behind, he brought them along to help him forge new, wider-ranging, and argu-ably even braver combinations of styles.

When Charles recorded "Georgia on My Mind," he did not attempt to turn the Tin Pan Alley standard into a rhythm & blues song (the way Fats Domino did with "My Blue Heaven"). Neither did he remake himself into a crooner (the way Elvis Presley often did when performing mainstream pop-oriented material). Rather than using the jump band group that had backed him on most of his earlier records—and then perhaps adding some superficial sweetening with strings and crooning background chorus— Charles wholeheartedly embraced the Tin Pan Alley heritage of the song and presided over a sumptuous arrangement of it that included orchestral strings and accompanying chorus and virtually outdid Tin Pan Alley itself in its elaborateness and unrestrained sentiment. But against this smooth and beautifully performed backdrop (Charles always insisted on the highest musical standards from all people involved in his performances), Charles sang "Georgia on My Mind" as if he were performing a deeply personal blues. While the original words, melody, and phrasing of the song were clearly conveyed, Charles employed an intense and sometimes rough-edged vocal timbre, used constant syncopation, and selectively added shakes, moans, and other improvised touches ("I said-a, Georgia") to reflect what was at this point his natural, individual vocal approach, rooted in gospel and blues. In a similar vein, he occasionally provided jazz-based fills in his piano part between vocal phrases to evoke call and response within his own performance, while the backing chorus echoed his words at strategic intervals, producing call and response between them and Charles himself.

The result of all this was an extraordinary and unprecedented juxtaposition of and dialog between styles within a single recording. And, as the preceding description indicates, this was no haphazard jumble of different elements; instead, the different parts combined in a way that seemed both expressive and utterly purposeful. In effect, Ray Charles did more than reinterpret "Georgia on My Mind"; he virtually reinvented the song for a new generation of listeners and left his mark on the song permanently. It seems only appropriate that in 1979 his recording was named the official song of the state of Georgia.

In 1962 Charles cast his stylistic net still wider, producing a concept album called *Modern Sounds in Country and Western Music* that stands as a milestone in the history of American popular music. When Charles first announced to his record company that he wanted to do an album of country songs, the project was derisively labeled "Ray's folly"; it was thought that he would lose his audience. Charles was not a man to be crossed, however, and he persevered, with the result of course that he enlarged his audience even further—far beyond anyone's expectations. By this point, Charles was aggressively and creatively playing with stylistic mixtures, and the album essentially redrew the map of American popular music, both appealing to and challenging fans of radically different genres.

Every song on *Modern Sounds in Country and Western Music* was transformed from its origins into something rich and strange. The Everly Brothers' "Bye, Bye, Love" and Hank Williams's "Hey, Good Lookin'" became big band shouts that bookended the album, while other songs received orchestral treatments worthy of the best Tin Pan Alley arrangements—or of Charles's own "Georgia on My Mind." It's hard to think of any major aspect of American pop that isn't represented, or at least evoked, somewhere on this amazingly generous record, which weaves a tapestry of stylistic and historical associations that reach across space, time, and race to build radically new bridges. The enormously popular "I Can't Stop Loving You" merges aspects of country, Tin Pan Alley, gospel, and blues, and even (as in "Georgia") a hint of jazz piano. Here Charles engages in stylistic call and response with the large background chorus, personalizing the lyrics that they sing in smooth, massed harmony. The deliberateness of this dialog is clearly revealed toward the end of the record by Charles's seemingly offhand, but illuminating, aside to the chorus: "Sing the song, children" (a remark that also confirms, as if there could be any doubt, exactly who's in charge here).

Although Ray Charles's many country-oriented records of the 1960s did extremely well on both the pop and the rhythm & blues charts, they did not register on the country charts of the time. Perhaps Charles's genre-bending approach was a bit too exotic for the typical country music fan. Still, these records were heard and deeply appreciated by many country musicians. We can take the word of no less an authority than Willie Nelson, who is quoted in the booklet accompanying the Ray Charles box set *Genius & Soul*: "With his recording of 'I Can't Stop Loving You,' Ray Charles did more for country music than any other artist." Charles finally did crack the country charts in the 1980s with some of his later efforts in the genre.

Ray Charles remained active almost until his death, performing and recording in all the many genres (and mixed styles) of which he was a seasoned master. In summarizing an astounding career that steadfastly resists summarizing, we might paraphrase what Jerome Kern reportedly said about Irving Berlin: this man has no "place" in American music; he *is* American music! Or perhaps we can leave the last word to Charles himself (as quoted by Quincy Jones in the booklet accompanying *Genius & Soul*): "It's all music, man. We can play it all."

Sam Cooke, the "King of Soul"

Sam Cooke (1931–1964), another of soul music's pioneers, began his career as a gospel singer with a group called the Soul Stirrers. Cooke began to explore secular music in 1956, initially recording under the pseudonym "Dale Cooke" out of concern that his gospel music audience would question the sincerity of his Christian beliefs if they discovered he was also singing nonreligious music. Cooke's fear proved to be well founded, and he was ultimately forced to choose between the two worlds. He chose secular music, and the gospel community never completely accepted him again.

Cooke thus moved from a self-selected community that prided itself on its high moral standards to the wider, grittier world of popular music, and he ultimately combined the two influences into a whole that directed the power of older traditions into new forms. From the gospel point of view, Cooke was debasing sacred music by using its style to sing songs about romance, partying, and secular politics. But from the pop point of view, Cooke was bringing a spiritual perspective *to* soul and rock 'n' roll music.

In many ways, Cooke's struggle was very similar to that which Bob Dylan was just beginning to face in the folk world (as we will see later in this chapter), and in fact he often covered Dylan's song "Blowin' in the Wind" in concert. Eventually, this piece inspired Cooke to write his most political song, "A Change Is Gonna Come," which he openly described as a response to "Blowin' in the Wind."

Though not primarily viewed as a "political" artist today, Sam Cooke's career set the stage for later expressions of politics in both soul and rock music. Beyond "A Change Is Gonna Come," Cooke's politics resided more in his life than in his songs. His devotion to the African American community was manifest in his admiration for Malcolm X and his friendship with Muhammad Ali (both highly controversial figures in the early 1960s). His commitment to Black self-determination was also apparent in the way he conducted his business. Rather than trust music in-dustry insiders, Cooke took great pains

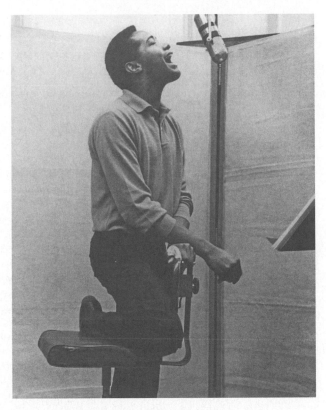

Sam Cooke in the recording studio, c. 1959.

to control every aspect of his career himself, an approach that was highly unusual for an African American artist in the late 1950s and early 1960s. (One of the few others to accomplish this was Ray Charles.) Cooke was shot and killed on December 11, 1964, by Bertha Franklin, the manager of the Hacienda Motel in Los Angeles, after he burst into her office in pursuit of another woman who had just fled from his room. The precise details of the incident remain in dispute to the present day.

James Brown and Aretha Franklin

Among the many significant artists whose names became linked with the concept of soul music in the 1960s, James Brown and Aretha Franklin may be selected as represen-tative. Like Ray Charles, Brown and Franklin had multidecade careers as exceptionally popular performers; in fact, Joel Whitburn's *Top R&B Singles, 1942–1995* lists Brown and Franklin as the top two rhythm & blues artists of this entire time period. Both Brown (known as "Soul Brother Number One") and Franklin (known as "Lady Soul") brought experience with gospel singing to bear upon their performances of secular material.

Listening Guide "YOU SEND ME" AND "A CHANGE IS GONNA COME"

"You Send Me," written and performed by Sam Cooke; recorded 1957

"A Change Is Gonna Come," written and performed by Sam Cooke; recorded 1964

"You Send Me," Sam Cooke's first pop hit, was recorded in Los Angeles and released in 1957 on the independent label Keen Records. At the time, Sam and the other members of the Soul Stirrers were under contract with another Los Angeles–based independent label, Specialty Records. In 1956 Sam Cooke had written to Specialty's owner, Art Rupe, asking his permission to record "some popular ballads for one of the major recording companies" (Guralnick 2005, 131). Rupe agreed but insisted that the recording—"Loveable," a thinly disguised secular cover version of one of the Soul Stirrers' biggest gospel hits—instead be released by Specialty. It was the release of this record that caused such great consternation in the gospel music community, and it was a major influence on Sam's decision, only four months later, to jump into the pop field with both feet.

"You Send Me" was produced by Robert "Bumps" Blackwell, who had achieved success for Specialty Records a few years before as the producer and co-writer of Little Richard's hits "Good Golly Miss Molly" and "Long Tall Sally." According to eyewitnesses, Art Rupe stormed into the recording session, objecting to Blackwell's decision to use a white vocal group as backing for Sam Cooke's singing and pushing for a less pop-oriented sound that was more firmly grounded in rhythm & blues. Blackwell held his ground, resigned from Specialty Records, and decamped for a new label called Keen Records, taking Sam Cooke with him. To Art Rupe's great consternation, "You Send Me" shot straight to the top of both the pop and the R&B charts, selling almost 2 million copies for Keen Records and establishing Sam Cooke as a major pop star. Although "You Send Me" was written by Sam Cooke, the copyright to the song was registered in the name of his brother, L. C. Cook, so that Rupe could not claim publishing royalties. (The fact that Rupe, a white label owner, took a position on behalf of a sound more closely related to rhythm & blues while Blackwell, an African American producer and songwriter, opted for a "whiter," more commercial sound illustrates how important it is not to assume a straightforward link between social identity and musical style, particularly when business interests are at stake.)

In its style and form, "You Send Me" is designed to appeal to a broad audience. The recording opens with Cooke gently singing the single word "Darling," followed, a breath later, by the entrance of a small and subdued rhythm section (comprising acoustic string bass, electric guitar, and drums, which are played in a quiet, subtle manner with wire brushes rather than wooden sticks) and a lush vocal background. "You Send Me" fits firmly within the framework of popular romantic songs of the time and is a good example of the classic AABA Tin Pan Alley form that we discussed in Chapter 4.

So what separates this record from literally hundreds of others like it being released at the time? The answer is self-evident: Cooke's voice and, by extension, his personality. Simultaneously self-deprecating and confident, his gentle yet emotionally intense performance fits squarely within the framework of romantic crooning, while selectively drawing upon aspects of his gospel experience, particularly in his use of melisma (a technique in which a single word or syllable of text is stretched out over multiple pitches). It is Cooke's supple, agile voice—not the song, not the band, and not even the "angelic" vocal chorus—that sent millions of listeners to their local record stores in search of this recording and inspired Coral Records (a subsidiary of the major record company Decca) to record a Top 10 cover version of the song by the white pop singer Teresa Brewer within months of its initial release.

"A Change Is Gonna Come" is generally regarded as Sam Cooke's greatest song, and although it did not rise as high on the pop and R&B charts as many of his earlier singles, the song has gained in popularity and stature in the decades since its release. ("A Change Is Gonna Come" is ranked Number 12 on *Rolling Stone's* list of the "500 Greatest Songs of All Time" and Number 3 in the webzine *Pitchfork's* "Greatest Songs of the 60s.") Although it was first recorded in December 1963, the single version was not released until a year later, just a few weeks after Cooke's death.

According to Cooke's biographer, Peter Guralnick, the song was inspired not only by Bob Dylan's song "Blowin' in the Wind" but also by Cooke's experiences while on tour, including a conversation with sit-in demonstrators in Durham, North Carolina, and his arrest in Shreveport, Louisiana, for attempting to check into a racially segregated motel. The centrality of Cooke's personal experiences to the lyric of "A Change Is Gonna Come" is indicated by his decision to write it in the first person, creating a testimony of the sort common in the gospel music tradition.

The recording opens with a majestic orchestral introduction, complete with eleven strings, five brass, and tympani—an arranging strategy that, through its association with classical music, announces the seriousness of what is to follow—and then Sam Cooke begins to sing his story:

> I was born by the river, in a little tent,
> Oh, and just like the river, I've been a-runnin' ever since

In keeping with the lyric, the song's chorus seems to flow seamlessly from the verse:

> It's been a long, a long time coming,
> But I know a change go'n come, oh yes it will

According to his close friend and business partner J. W. Alexander, Cooke reported that the song came to him whole-cloth, as if he had dreamed it: "He was very excited, and when he finished it, he explained it to me—his reason behind the lyrics. Like, 'I don't know what's up there beyond the sky'—it's like somebody's talking about I want to go to heaven, really, but then who knows what's really up there? In other words, that's why you want justice on earth" (Guralnick 2003, 18). Other verses of the song resonate with Cooke's first-hand experience of racial discrimination ("I go to the movie and I go downtown, somebody keep tellin' me, don't hang around") and with the drowning death of his eighteen-month-old son just a few months prior ("There have been times that I thought I couldn't last for long, but now I think I'm able to carry on").

Listening to the eloquence of "A Change Is Gonna Come," its emotional force redoubled by Cooke's impassioned performance, it is easy to understand how this song was adopted as an anthem of the 1960s civil rights movement in the years following his death. In 1964 Cooke donated the use of the recording for an album benefiting Martin Luther King's Southern Christian Leadership Conference, and director Spike Lee used the song at a critical point in the 1992 biographical film *Malcolm X*.

In so doing, they each developed an intense, flamboyant, gritty, and highly individual approach to the singing of pop music, and their approaches represented distinctive analogs to the "soul" style of Ray Charles.

JAMES BROWN

If Charles employed "soul" as an avenue of approach to the most diverse kinds of material, *James Brown* (1933–2006) revealed different tendencies virtually from the beginning. His first record, "Please, Please, Please" (Number 5 R&B, 1956), which Brown wrote himself, is indicative: while the song is in the general format of a strophic 1950s R&B ballad, Brown's vocal clings obsessively to repetitions of individual words (the title "please," or even a simple "I") so that sometimes the activity of an entire strophe centers around the syncopated, violently accented reiterations of a single syllable. The result is startling and hypnotic. Like a secular version of a transfixed preacher, Brown shows himself willing to leave the traditional notions of verbal grammar, and even meaning, behind in an effort to convey a heightened emotional condition through the effective employment of rhythm and vocal timbre, animating repetitive ideas. Later on, Brown would leave the structures of 1950s R&B far behind and eventually would abandon chord changes entirely in many of his pieces. By the later 1960s a characteristic Brown tune like "There Was a Time" (Number 3 R&B, Number 36 pop, 1968) offered music that focused almost exclusively on the play of rhythm and timbre, in the instrumental parts

James Brown, the "Godfather of Soul," on stage c. 1970s.

as well as in the vocal. While the singer does tell a story in this song, the vocal melody is little more than informal reiterations of a small number of brief, formulaic pitch shapes; the harmony is completely static, with the instrumental parts reduced to repeating riffs or held chords. But this description does the song scant justice—when performed by Brown and his band, its effect is mesmerizing. James Brown's fully developed version of soul is a music of exquisitely focused intensity, devoted to demonstrating the truth of the saying "less is more."

In the politically charged "Say It Loud—I'm Black and I'm Proud," which reached Number 1 on the R&B and Number 10 on the pop charts in 1968, Brown pares his vocal down to highly rhythmic speech, backed once again by a harmonically static but rhythmically active accompaniment. Although the term would not be in use for at least a decade, "Say It Loud—I'm Black and I'm Proud" is for all intents and purposes a rap number, a striking anticipation of important Black music to come (both in its musical style and in its emphasis on the Black experience as subject matter) and a telling illustration of Brown's pivotal role in the history of pop culture generally. In the wake of the urban folk movement of the early 1960s and the subsequent wave of folk rock (which we will discuss shortly), in which white singers presented themselves as spokespeople for the political and social concerns of their generation, Brown led Black musicians in assuming a comparable role for the Black community, especially in the time of enormous unrest and political instability that followed the assassination of the Reverend Martin Luther King Jr. in 1968. For his constructive contributions to the politics of his time, Brown was publicly honored by both Vice President Hubert Humphrey and President Lyndon Johnson. Thus soul musicians came to be seen not merely as entertainers but also as essential contributors to—and articulators of—African American life and experience—a view that was held by both the Black community and the national political leadership alike.

From the late 1960s through the disco music of the 1970s, from the beginnings of rap on through the flowering of hip-hop in the 1990s, no other single musician proved to be as influential to the sound and style of Black music as James Brown. His repetitive, riff-based instrumental style, which elevated rhythm far above harmony as the primary source of interest, provided the foundation on which most of the dance-oriented music of this entire period has been based. His records have been **sampled** repeatedly by hip-hop artists—which is not surprising, given his achievement as a pioneer of rap style.

Brown's focus on rhythm and timbre, and in particular the complex, interlocking polyrhythms present in many of his songs, have been cited as demonstrating his strong conceptual links with African music styles. Certainly, the minimization or elimination of chord changes and the consequent deemphasis on harmony makes Brown's music seem, both in conception and in actual sound, a lot less "Western" in orientation than a good deal of the African American music that preceded it. However, this quality in Brown's work resonated with many aspects of African American culture in the late 1960s and the 1970s, when there was a marked concern with the awareness of African "roots." One could argue that the acceptance and wide influence of the "non-Western" aspects of Brown's music helped provide a foundation for the recent explosion of interest in world music of many sorts, which was such a significant and distinguishing characteristic of the cultural scene of the 1980s and 1990s.

One additional and fascinating aspect of Brown's work is the relationship it suggests to the "minimalist" music of avant-garde "art music" composers, such as Philip Glass and Steve Reich, that was developing simultaneously if independently in the late 1960s in New York. This music was also based on repetitive rhythmic patterns that deemphasized traditional harmonic movement. There is no issue of direct influence here, one way or the other. But it could be argued that only old cultural habits and snobbery have kept James Brown out of discussions of minimalism in scholarly forums and journals.

As influential as his recordings were and are, Brown was above all an artist who exulted in and excelled at live performance, in which his acrobatic physicality and remarkable personal charisma added great excitement to the vocal improvisations he spun over the ever-tight accompaniment of his band. A typical Brown show ended with the singer on his knees, evoking once again the intensity of the gospel preacher as he exhorted his "congregation," "Please, please, please!" Although he was not the first pop artist to release a "live" album, Brown's *Live at the Apollo*, recorded in concert at the famed Apollo Theater in Harlem in late 1962, proved an important pop breakthrough both for him and for the idea of the concert album, as it reached the Number 2 position on the *Billboard* chart of bestselling albums in 1963 and remained on that chart for well over a year. In particular, the album allowed the listener to experience without interruption an example of one of Brown's remarkable extended "medleys," in which several of his songs were strung directly together, without dropping a single beat, to produce a cumulative effect of steadily mounting excitement. Many pop artists since have released "live" albums—in fact, the "live" album has become virtually an expected event in the recording career of any artist with a significant following—but few have matched the sheer visceral thrill of James Brown's *Live at the Apollo*.

Listening Guide "PAPA'S GOT A BRAND NEW BAG"

Composed by James Brown; performed by James Brown and the Famous Flames; released 1965

"Papa's Got a Brand New Bag" was Brown's first Top 10 pop hit and the biggest R&B hit of his entire career (Number 8 pop, Number 1 R&B). It is an excellent representative example of the music of James Brown, as it is a record that, in a sense, looks both forward and back in his career. In terms of its form, the song uses the time-tested twelve-bar blues pattern as its basis, breaking up the pattern after two strophes with an eight-bar bridge section (a device we have also seen before, the roots of which go back to "St. Louis Blues") before continuing with further blues-based stanzas. In terms of subject matter, the song's lyrics obviously recall the dance-oriented rock 'n' roll songs of the early 1960s, as the singer praises "Papa's"—presumably Brown's—ability to do the jerk, the fly, the monkey, the mashed potato, the twist (naturally), and even the "boomerang" (Brown's dancing was a legendary aspect of his live shows). However, the title tells us that "Papa's Got a Brand *New* Bag," and even if the song itself looks toward the past in its form and its lyrics, Brown's actual recording sounds nothing like a typical blues-based R&B record of its time or a typical teen-oriented dance song. Instead, the record looks forward to the riff-dominated records by Brown and

others that would virtually define dance-oriented soul music in the later 1960s and the 1970s.

The critical factor here is the repeating instrumental riff, which embodies a kind of call-and-response pattern as two strong, short, rhythmic "stabs" on successive beats are answered by a four-note figure in the horn section of the band, landing on an accented final note (da-da-da-*dum*). This riff is used for all of the twelve-bar blues stanzas in "Papa's Got a Brand New Bag." The pitches change slightly to accommodate the chord change at the fifth bar of these stanzas (see the discussion of twelve-bar blues in Chapter 5). But the really arresting event occurs at the tenth bar, where the instrumental accompaniment stops entirely for a few beats, creating a passage of what jazz musicians call stop time. This moment produces enormous tension, and after Brown completes his next vocal phrase, the lead guitar bursts back in with an aggressive pattern of rapidly strummed chords that prepares the return of both the riff and the rhythm section. Thus the listener's attention is directed away from the harmonic changes in the twelve-bar blues pattern and more toward events defined by rhythm: the presence or absence of the riff, and stop time as opposed to rhythmic continuity. Even the

LISTENING GUIDE	"PAPA'S GOT A BRAND NEW BAG"		
TIME	**FORM**	**LYRICS**	**DESCRIPTIVE COMMENTS**
0:00	Introduction		Brief introduction, consisting of a single chord played by the horns
0:03	Verse	*Come here sister . . .*	Twelve-bar blues; Brown sings the verse; prominent accent notes played by the saxophone
0:20		*Papa's got . . .*	Instruments drop out; Brown sings the final line of the verse; followed by rhythmic guitar chords and chord by horns
0:24	Verse	*Come here mama . . .*	Twelve-bar blues
0:47	Bridge	*He's doing the Jerk . . .*	Eight bars; background riff continues
1:01	Verse	*Come here sister . . .*	Repeats first verse
1:24	Verse	*Oh papa! . . .*	Twelve-bar blues again
1:46		*Come on . . .*	Fades out

sense of a separate bridge section is downplayed considerably on this recording, as the harmony remains fairly static throughout the bridge (whereas typically it would wander and change more rapidly than elsewhere), while a slightly different—but nonetheless clearly related—three-note horn riff is heard in every bar.

When listening to "Papa's Got a Brand New Bag," then, one experiences musical shaping created more emphatically by rhythmic patterns than by chord changes or melodic lines. In terms of the sound and the groove of the recording, we are here well on our way toward the minimization or even elimination of chord changes that would characterize much of Brown's later work. It is this aspect of the record that is so arrestingly novel and that represents such a significant discovery on Brown's part. James Brown's "Papa's Got a Brand New Bag" is worthy of its title and its enduring popularity. In 1965 it represented an enormous flying leap into the future of soul, a musical analogy to Brown's own daring acrobatic leaps onstage.

ARETHA FRANKLIN

Like Ray Charles and James Brown, *Aretha Franklin* (1942–2018) underwent a long period of "apprenticeship" before she achieved her definitive breakthrough as a pop star in 1967. After a commercially lackluster career as a Columbia Records artist from 1960 to 1966, during which time she recorded a mixture of Tin Pan Alley standards and unremarkable rhythm & blues material, she went over to Atlantic Records. Atlantic, an indie label with a long history of R&B success, knew what to do with Franklin. Atlantic producers Ahmet Ertegun and Jerry Wexler encouraged her to record strong material well suited to her spectacular voice and engaged seasoned and empathetic musicians to back her up (usually the Muscle Shoals Sound Rhythm Section, based in Alabama). The rest, as they say, is history. Beginning with "I Never Loved a Man (The Way I Love You)" (Number 1 R&B, Number 9 pop, 1967), Franklin produced an extraordinary and virtually uninterrupted stream of hit records over a five-year

Aretha Franklin on stage, c. 1972

period that included thirteen million-sellers and thirteen Top 10 pop hits. Although the later 1970s and early 1980s witnessed a decline in Franklin's status as a top hit maker, she was never completely absent from the charts, and the mid-1980s saw a resurgence of her popularity, with hits like "Freeway of Love" (Number 1 R&B, Number 3 pop, 1985) and a duet with George Michael called "I Knew You Were Waiting (For Me)" (Number 1 pop, Number 5 R&B, 1987). In the 1990s Franklin was still a presence on the R&B, pop, and pop album charts. Her continuing iconic status is reflected by the fact that she was chosen to sing at the inauguration of President Barack Obama in 2009.

Unlike Ray Charles and James Brown, Franklin literally grew up with gospel music; her father was the Reverend C. L. Franklin, the pastor for a large Baptist congregation in Detroit and himself an acclaimed gospel singer. Aretha Franklin's first recordings, made at the age of fourteen, were as a gospel singer, and she occasionally returned to recording gospel music even in the midst of her career as a pop singer—most spectacularly with the live album *Amazing Grace*, which was actually recorded in a Los Angeles church in 1972. *Amazing Grace* built on Franklin's established popularity to introduce legions of pop music fans to the power of gospel music. The album was a Top 10 bestseller and the most successful album of Franklin's entire career, selling over 2 million copies. This performance was filmed, and the movie *Amazing Grace* finally was released in 2018. The movie is of uneven visual and audio quality, and some selections are clearly abridged or missing entirely; nevertheless it is a remarkable document, revealing the singer in all her glory. It is a privilege to be able to see, as well as hear, the ecstasy, intensity, and reverence that possessed Aretha Franklin when she returned to her musical and spiritual roots in gospel.

What is most important about Aretha Franklin is the overwhelming power and intensity of her vocal delivery. Into a pop culture that had almost totally identified female singers with gentility, docility, and sentimentality, her voice blew huge gusts of revisionist fresh air. When she demanded "respect" (see the following Listening Guide) or exhorted her audience to "think about what you're trying to do to me" (in the hit recording "Think" of 1968, which she cowrote), the strength of her interpretations arguably moved her songs beyond the traditional realm of personal intimate relationships and into the larger political and social spheres. Especially in the context of the late 1960s, with the civil rights and Black power movements at their heights, and the movement for women's empowerment undergoing its initial stirrings, it was difficult not to hear large-scale ramifications in the records of this extraordinary African American woman. Although Aretha Franklin did not become an overtly political figure in the way that James Brown did, it may be claimed that she nevertheless made strong political and social statements just through the very character of her performances.

Directly tied to this issue is the fact that Franklin was not only a vocal interpreter on her records but also—like Charles and Brown—a major player in many aspects of their sound and production. She wrote or cowrote a significant portion of her repertoire (an involvement going back to her early days at Columbia). In addition, Franklin is a powerful keyboard player; her piano is heard to great advantage on many of her recordings. Finally, she also provided vocal arrangements, which were colored by the call and response of the gospel traditions in which she was raised.

Listening Guide "RESPECT"

Composed by Otis Redding; performed by Aretha Franklin; recorded 1967

"Respect" was for Franklin both her first Number 1 pop hit and the biggest R&B hit (also Number 1) of *her* entire career. Merely by recording "Respect," Aretha took a daring step. The song had already been a significant hit for its composer, Otis Redding, in 1965 (Number 4 R&B, Number 35 pop); by covering it, Franklin was, in a sense, going head to head with one of the most impressive and powerful soul singers of the day—and on his home turf, so to speak, by taking on a song he had written for himself. But the implications of Franklin's cover extend well beyond this, because Redding's song is a demand for "respect" from one's lover, and by putting the song in a woman's voice Franklin radically shifts the sense of who is in control in the relationship. In her version, it is *she*—the woman—who has "what you want" and "what you need," not to mention "money" as well! And Franklin makes a telling change in the lyrics of the second verse. In Redding's original, he acknowledges

that his woman might do him wrong, yet it's all right with him so long as she only does so "while I'm gone." But Franklin tells her lover that "I ain't gonna do you wrong while you're gone" (presumably his doing *her* wrong is not even in question), but only "'cause I don't wanna." It could not be clearer just who is holding all the cards in Franklin's version!

Of course, none of Franklin's play with the gender issues implicit in "Respect" would have any effect if it weren't for the overwhelming power and assurance with which she delivers the song and makes it her own. Each strophe of the song builds effectively to the crucial word "respect," at which point the backing group joins in call and response with Franklin. But Franklin is also careful to structure her entire performance around a steadily building intensity, so that the listener hears something much more than a song with four identical verses. By the time we reach the third verse, she is improvising variants

LISTENING GUIDE	"RESPECT"		
TIME	**FORM**	**LYRICS**	**DESCRIPTIVE COMMENTS**
0:00	Introduction		Riff played on guitar accompanied by horns
0:10	Verse 1	*What you want . . .*	Aretha shouts with "oohs" from backup singers
0:21		*Respect . . .*	Aretha leads, with backup singers singing "Just a little bit . . ."
0:30	Verse 2	*I ain't gonna . . .*	
0:41		*Respect . . .*	
0:51	Verse 3	*I'm about to give you . . .*	
1:03		*Just a . . . just a*	
1:11	Instrumental		Sax solo with horn chords; new harmonic pattern
1:28	Verse 4	*Ooh, your kisses . . .*	
1:40		*Re-re-re-re . . .*	
1:50	Break	*R-E-S-P-E-C-T*	Aretha spells out the lyrics with stoptime accompaniment
1:57	Coda	*Sock it to me . . .*	Repeats several times, followed by call-and-response, then fade out

(continued)

Listening Guide "RESPECT" (continued)

on the basic melody, and the call and response is varied as well ("just a, just a, just a, just a, just a, just a, just a, just a—just a little bit"). After this section a brief but completely unexpected instrumental break, with totally unexpected chords new to the song, raises the emotional temperature in preparation for the final strophe. The last time around, Franklin reaches her highest note yet in the song on "All I want you to *do* for me," and the backing group matches her new intensity with its own new response: "re-re-re-re-re-re-re-re-re-*spect*." Then, instead

of ending, this final verse is extended with a stop time solo for Franklin, after which the group responds with a shot heard 'round the world ("sock it to me, sock it to me, sock it to me") and the record fades with Franklin and her backing singers trading shout for shout.

After the daring and achievement of this recording, Aretha Franklin never had to demand "respect," at least from musicians and audiences, again. It was hers wherever and whenever she brought her great and insightful gifts of song.

BOX 10.1 TIN PAN ALLEY *STILL* LIVES! DIONNE WARWICK AND THE SONGS OF BURT BACHARACH AND HAL DAVID

We saw in Chapter 9 how the Tin Pan Alley model for the creation and marketing of popular music was adopted for rock 'n' roll by 1960s labels like Philles and Motown. Furthermore, performers based in Tin Pan Alley traditions, both older (Frank Sinatra and Tony Bennett) and younger (Johnny Mathis), continued to command substantial audiences throughout the 1960s. However, arguably the most remarkable testament to the resilience of the Tin Pan Alley aesthetic in the 1960s was the extensive series of hit songs written for singer **Dionne Warwick** (b. 1940) by composer **Burt Bacharach** (b. 1928) and lyricist Hal David. In Warwick, the two songwriters found a distinctive young African American vocalist who, despite a training in gospel music that might have more typically prepared her for a career as an R&B-oriented performer, was willing to cultivate more of a crooning approach to performance that proved perfect for the convincing delivery of their work. (This is not to say that Warwick couldn't shout soulfully when needed, as any listener who has enjoyed the explosive endings of "Anyone Who Had a Heart" and "Promises, Promises" can affirm.)

The kinship of the Bacharach-David songs to Tin Pan Alley models is the result of a number of factors. David's lyrics are almost always intelligent and adult-oriented, and they can exhibit a

cleverness of structure and rhyme that is reminiscent of Ira Gershwin or Cole Porter (as in "Do You Know the Way to San Jose"). Bacharach's music generally owes little to rock in terms of direct influence; its emphasis is placed instead on melodic and harmonic sophistication of a nature that clearly links him to the tradition of someone like George Gershwin (as may be heard in songs like "Alfie" and "Promises, Promises," in particular). Yet Bacharach is not an imitator, and therein lies his importance and achievement. His use of minor keys—in songs like "Walk On By" and "The Look of Love"—is noteworthy, but perhaps most distinctive is Bacharach's way of incorporating highly original phrasing and rhythms into his songs. His novel rhythms are not those of rock but rather are related to complexities of meter found more often in modernistic art music or the jazz of a rhythmic innovator like Dave Brubeck than in pop song. (The chorus section of "I Say a Little Prayer" may serve as a good example of Bacharach's rhythmic gifts; a listener attempting to count out the patterns here will have a pleasantly dizzying experience!)

Every virtue of the Bacharach-David songs is emphasized in Dionne Warwick's elegant recordings of them, as Warwick is both melodically expressive and rhythmically precise, while articulating the lyrics with clarity and intensity. These recordings are among the glories of 1960s music. Although the Bacharach-David team provided excellent material to other artists as well ("What the World Needs Now Is Love," recorded by Jackie DeShannon, and "One Less Bell to Answer," performed by the Fifth Dimension, are two famous and outstanding examples), and although Dionne Warwick also found success with songs by other writers, a certain synergic magic was undeniably lost when the singer and the songwriters parted company early in the 1970s.

In other words, Franklin not only symbolized female empowerment in the sound of her records but also actualized female empowerment in the process of making them. By the time she recorded a tune called "Sisters Are Doin' It for Themselves" (with Eurythmics) in 1985, she was, in effect, telling a story that had been personally true of her for a long time. But in the 1960s female empowerment was something quite new and important in the history of pop music. And neither its novelty nor its importance was lost on the rising generation of female singer-songwriters, such as Laura Nyro, Joni Mitchell, and Carole King, whose ascent to prominence began directly in the wake of Aretha Franklin's conquest of the pop charts.

The Broadway Musical in the Age of Rock

A review of the most successful and influential Broadway shows of the period 1955–1967 would yield scant evidence that rock 'n' roll even existed—with a single exception. That exception is *Bye Bye Birdie* (1960; music by Charles Strouse, lyrics by Lee Adams), a parody of the teenage culture of its time that employs rock 'n' roll music only incidentally and not at all seriously—in fact, the musical was originally conceived as a vehicle for high school performance. (The "hero" of the show, Conrad Birdie, was obviously modeled on Elvis Presley.) Otherwise, Broadway shows continued in the Rodgers and Hammerstein mold of the serious musical with well-integrated plot, characters, and songs, and their music reflected basically the heritage and aesthetics of earlier Broadway styles. Few individual chart hits resulted, but major bestselling albums were made by Broadway casts and from the soundtracks of movie adaptations.

   This is not to say that sophisticated and occasionally innovative scores were lacking on Broadway at this time. Leonard Bernstein's music for *West Side Story* (1957) made striking use of modern jazz and Latin American elements, and the accompanying lyrics by Broadway newcomer Stephen Sondheim introduced a brilliant and witty "voice" to American song. The film of *West Side Story* (1961) became a smash hit, and its soundtrack album sat at Number 1 on the bestselling album charts for an astounding fifty-four weeks in 1962–1963, not only making it a statistical phenomenon of the 1960s, but also granting it the distinction of the album that held the top spot longer than any other album released to date! *Fiddler on the Roof* (1964; music by Jerry Bock, lyrics by Sheldon Harnick) took as its seemingly unpromising subject the people of a small

Russian Jewish village around the turn of the twentieth century and exhibited a strong Jewish folk influence in its songs. The result was the longest-running musical up to that time (3,242 performances of the original Broadway production), a show beloved by a wide and diverse public, a bestselling Broadway cast album (Number 7 in 1964; 206 weeks on the charts), and a successful movie (1971) with a bestselling soundtrack album of its own (Number 30 in 1972; 90 weeks on the charts).

Rock music finally arrived on Broadway with *Hair* (1968; music by Galt MacDermot, lyrics by Gerome Ragni and James Rado), which rather self-consciously proclaimed itself "The American Tribal Love-Rock Musical." An overt celebration of the late 1960s counterculture, *Hair* brought political controversy, nudity, drug use, and amplified instruments to the Broadway stage, and the resulting buzz sustained the musical for a run of 1,750 performances. Its embrace of rock styles also made *Hair* a significant source of big hit singles, an anomalous situation at the time that remains unusual to this day, although there has been no lack of attempts—both successful (*Jesus Christ Superstar* and *Godspell*, both 1971) and unsuccessful—to mount musicals with rock scores on Broadway. While the original cast album of *Hair* was itself a big hit (Number 1 for thirteen weeks in 1969; 151 weeks total on the bestselling album charts), the big hit singles were made by other artists in 1969: "Hair" by the Cowsills (Number 2 pop), "Good Morning Starshine" by Oliver (Number 3 pop), "Easy to Be Hard" by Three Dog Night (Number 4 pop), and, most memorably, the medley "Aquarius/Let the Sunshine In" by the Fifth Dimension (Number 1 pop for six weeks, and the top hit of the year). *Hair* was clearly a product of its time, and a most savvy and successful one, but surprisingly it was revived to much acclaim in New York in 2008, after which the production toured the country. Whether this revival attests to the musical's continuing relevance or simply to widespread nostalgia for the 1960s remains an unresolved and perhaps unresolvable issue.

Urban Folk Music in the 1960s: Bob Dylan

Urban folk music continued to flourish during the early days of rock 'n' roll and into the 1960s. We have not yet discussed this genre because, to a large extent, it followed an independent course through the early 1960s, remaining an acoustic guitar–based music aloof from the new styles and large-scale changes that characterized much of the pop music of this time. In the early 1960s it was even fashionable for urban folk performers to look down their noses at rock 'n' roll as "unserious"; the dour liner notes to the hugely successful first album by Peter, Paul and Mary (1962) exhorted readers, "No dancing, please!" But by 1967 electric instruments and drums had joined Peter, Paul and Mary's acoustic guitars, and they were in the pop Top 10 singing (somewhat ironically, but with a firm bid for continuing relevance) "I Dig Rock and Roll Music"! The individual most responsible for this shift was not Peter or Paul or Mary, but the man who had written their biggest acoustic hit, "Blowin' in the Wind" (Number 2 pop, 1963). He was also the man who, virtually single-handedly, dragged urban folk music—with some people kicking and screaming—into the modern era of rock. His name was Bob Dylan.

Bob Dylan (b. 1941 as Robert Zimmerman) first established himself as an acoustic singer-songwriter in New York City's burgeoning urban folk scene. The early 1960s was a period of explosive growth for acoustic urban folk music. The baby boomers were reaching college age, demonstrating increasing cultural and political interests and awareness, and they represented an expanding audience both for traditionally based folk music and for newly composed "broadsides" on the issues of the day (such as the Cold War with the Soviet Union, the testing and stockpiling of nuclear arms, and racial bigotry). Encouragement and a sense of history were provided by elder statesmen of the urban folk scene, such as Pete Seeger and the Weavers, whose careers in turn were reinvigorated by the thawing of the political climate after the blacklisting days of the 1950s (see Chapter 7) and by the enthusiasm of younger folk performers and their audiences. By 1962 even the extremely popular Kingston Trio (see Chapter 8)—whose acoustic folk repertoire almost always stayed within the bounds of safe traditional material or the occasional novelty number—ventured to record Pete Seeger's poignant antiwar song "Where Have All the Flowers Gone," unexpectedly scoring a pop hit with it (Number 21). This success attests to the increasing politicization of the urban folk movement and its audiences at this time; the success of "Where Have All the Flowers Gone" doubtless helped pave the way for that of "Blowin' in the Wind" the following year.

Bob Dylan as urban folk singer (1963) and as folk rocker, in 1966.

Bob Dylan's contemporaries in the urban folk scene included such gifted performers as Joan Baez and Judy Collins, and such talented songwriters as Tom Paxton and Phil Ochs. But Dylan stood out early for two basic reasons. First was the remarkable quality of his original songs, which reflected from the beginning a strong gift for poetic imagery and metaphor and a frequently searing intensity of feeling, sometimes moderated by a quirky sense of irony. Second was Dylan's own style of performance, which eschewed the deliberate and straightforward homeliness of the Weavers, the smooth and pop-friendly approach of the Kingston Trio and Peter, Paul and Mary, and the lyrical beauty of Joan Baez and Judy Collins in favor of a rough-hewn, occasionally aggressive vocal, guitar, and harmonica style that demonstrated strong affinities to rural models in blues and earlier country music. Dylan's performance style was sufficiently idiosyncratic in the context of the urban folk scene to keep him from being truly pop-marketable for years; his early songs were introduced to Top 40 audiences by other, smoother performers. Still, it may be claimed that Dylan's own performances serve the distinctive intensity of his songs more tellingly than the inevitably sweeter versions of other singers.

Bob Dylan the songwriter was introduced to many pop fans through Peter, Paul and Mary's recording of his "Blowin' in the Wind," and to this day the song remains probably Dylan's best-known work. The opening strophe clearly reveals Dylan's gift for concise, evocative, and highly poetic lyric writing, the ability to suggest much with a few finely turned images.

The verse begins with three successive questions that build in specificity and intensity. The first question ("How many roads . . .") could imply many different things having to do with maturity and experience. The image of the "white dove" in the second question ("How many seas . . .") is one traditionally associated with peace. With the third question ("How many times . . ."), the subject of war becomes inescapable, and it becomes clear that Dylan is asking, in three different ways, just what it will take, and how long it will take, before humankind develops the maturity to put a stop to wars. What makes the song so poignantly effective, though, is that Dylan leaves the answer—and even the issue of whether there *is* an answer—up to us, and in our hands: the phrase "The answer is blowin' in the wind" returns to the deliberate, thoroughgoing ambiguity of the opening question. This structure effectively sets up the two additional strophes of the song, which are similarly structured as three increasingly pointed questions followed by the same ambiguous answer. Dylan's avoidance of any specific political agenda in "Blowin' in the Wind" is typical of many of his best protest songs and is actually a source of their strength, as it helps ensure their continuing relevance despite changes in the political climate. In any case, the questions posed in "Blowin' in the Wind" surely—if unfortunately—ring with a resonance not limited by the time and place of the song's creation.

As is the case with many of the finest folk songs, whether traditional or newly composed, the melody of "Blowin' in the Wind" provides a simple, functional, and immediately memorable setting for the words. In this strophic form, notice how Dylan's melody makes each of the three questions hang unresolved; a final feeling of cadence in the melody is delayed until we reach the "answer" on the last word of each strophe.

It is illuminating to compare the Peter, Paul and Mary recording of "Blowin' in the Wind" with Dylan's own performance as heard on his second album, *The Freewheelin' Bob Dylan* (1963). The folk trio performs the song with a touching sincerity and simplicity; the various questions posed in the lyrics are sung by different numbers and combinations of voices, at varying levels of intensity, while the "answer" is always provided by Mary's gentle solo sound. One might initially find Dylan's rendition monochromatic in comparison. But his syncopation of the melodic line—a performance approach utterly lacking in the Peter, Paul and Mary interpretation—throws rhythmic weight on the most pointed words in the song (such as, in the opening stanza, "*before* they're *forever* banned") and the resulting feeling of angularity, reinforced by the intense and rough-hewn timbre of Dylan's voice, arguably presses the listener to ponder the lyrics that much more seriously.

In addition to writing impressive topical songs like "Blowin' in the Wind," Dylan quickly distinguished himself as a composer of more intimate but highly original songs about human relationships. One hesitates to call a song like "Don't Think Twice, It's All Right" (also on *The Freewheelin' Bob Dylan,* and also a Top 10 single for Peter, Paul and Mary—their follow-up hit to "Blowin' in the Wind") a "love song," however. Dylan himself is quoted regarding this song in the liner notes to the *Freewheelin'* album: "A lot of people make it a sort of a love song—slow and easy-going. [Was he thinking of a performance like Peter, Paul and Mary's?] But it isn't a love song. It's a statement that maybe you can say to make yourself feel better." Dylan's gift for irony, to which we have previously referred, is exemplified memorably in the lyrics of "Don't Think Twice, It's All Right," which reveal that the singer and his partner "never did too much talkin'."

Clearly, this situation is not "all right" at all, and the blunt realism underlying Dylan's view of romantic relationships, as expressed in this song and many others, sounded a refreshingly original note in a pop landscape where the typical treatment of relationships was still that reflected in a song like "Be My Baby," and where a relationship crisis might be represented by a date's inability to do the twist or the mashed potato. Dylan's own performance of "Don't Think Twice, It's All Right" does the song full justice by conveying a deep, underlying sense of personal injury.

We have been stressing the innovative character of Dylan's songwriting, but he maintained important ties with folk traditions as well. Many of his original compositions were modeled, implicitly or explicitly, on the musical and poetic content of pre-existing folk material. For example, one of his most famous protest songs, "A Hard Rain's A-Gonna Fall," is clearly based on the old English ballad "Lord Randall"; both employ a strophic pattern, in which each strophe opens with a pair of questions addressed by a mother to her son, followed by the son's answer or answers, and ending always with the same concluding line. Even the melodic lines of "Lord Randall" and "A Hard Rain's A-Gonna Fall" are distinctly similar. But Dylan is never merely a mimic, and "A Hard Rain's A-Gonna Fall" introduces a highly original structural device that has no parallel in "Lord Randall": its strophes are of widely varying lengths, depending on the number of times the third melodic phrase is repeated to changing words. (The son offers anywhere from five to twelve answers to the individual questions posed by his mother.)

The concept of the "variable strophe," as we might call it, is found in a number of Dylan's finest songs, notably "Mr. Tambourine Man" and—as we shall see shortly—"Like a Rolling Stone."

The year 1965 was a pivotal one in Bob Dylan's career, the year in which he moved from his role as the most distinctive songwriter among American urban folk artists to that of an undeniable influence on the entirety of American popular culture. We may cite four major events that proved decisive in this extraordinary development: the release of an album, the release of two hit singles (one by the Byrds and one by Dylan himself), and a live performance.

Early in 1965 Dylan released his fifth album, *Bringing It All Back Home*, in which acoustic numbers demonstrating Dylan's now-familiar style shared disc space with songs using electric guitar and drums. In addition to adumbrating a radical shift in Dylan's sound, the album featured several songs that carried Dylan's flair for intense and unusual poetic imagery into the realm of the surreal. One such song, "Mr. Tambourine Man," which Dylan performed in an acoustic style, was covered by the fledgling California rock group the Byrds; their truncated version of "Mr. Tambourine Man," adapted to fit the customary length for radio play, soared remarkably to Number 1 on the pop charts in June 1965, thus becoming the first landmark folk-rock hit. The Byrds' combination of Dylan's lyrics and melody with a musical accompaniment that included tambourine (naturally), drums, and their own trademark electric Rickenbacker twelve-string guitar sound was unique, memorable, and—obviously, if unexpectedly—marketable. The lesson was not lost on Dylan himself, who returned to the recording studio early in the summer with a rock band to cut his own breakthrough single, "Like a Rolling Stone." This six-minute, epic pop single, which made it to Number 2 on the charts, certified that a sea change was taking place in American popular culture. (See the detailed discussion of this song in the following Listening Guide.) As if to affirm that there would be no turning back, Dylan then appeared at the famous Newport Folk Festival in late July with an electric band. Many folk purists were appalled by this assault on their home turf, and Dylan the "rock star" was received with controversy, to say the least. (Dylan returned afterward to play acoustic numbers.) But he had the last laugh, of course, as it was not long before many other urban folk artists had followed his lead into the electric wonderland of rock music.

From our latter-day vantage point, all the fuss about Dylan's "going electric" can seem quite silly. We have seen that the entire history of American popular music has been a story of influences, interactions, and syntheses among its various streams. The steadily increasing popularity of both urban folk music and rock 'n' roll in the early 1960s made it inevitable that these two supposedly independent styles would eventually interact with one another, and even fuse to some extent. But the boost given to this fusion by the fact that the most individual and creative of the young urban folk artists, Bob Dylan, was the first to promote it—and to promote it aggressively and enthusiastically at that—should not be underestimated.

From Dylan's own point of view, he was probably just following a model already well established by performers in the genres of blues and country music, genres to which his personal performing style had always demonstrated obvious ties. Rural blues artists like Muddy Waters and Howlin' Wolf had long ago made their way to the city and developed electric blues, just as country artists like Bob Wills and Hank Williams had developed the western swing and honky-tonk styles (see Chapter 7). And these newer blues-and country-based styles had themselves played an essential role in the 1950s synthesis that is called rock 'n' roll. Why, then, was such a shock wave produced by the concept of Bob Dylan as a rock 'n' roll star?

The impact of this transformation probably had to do with the differing cultural roles assigned by most people to urban folk music on the one hand and rock 'n' roll on the other. Urban folk in the early 1960s was an increasingly topical, political, and socially conscious music. Even the singing of traditional folk songs often carried with it a subtext of political identification—with labor, with the poor, with minority groups and other peoples seen as oppressed, with a movement for international peace and understanding—that depended on the nature and origins of the particular songs chosen. Thus the words of songs were of paramount importance in urban folk music, and their acoustic guitar accompaniments enabled those words to be heard clearly. Besides, acoustic guitars were easily portable, readily accessible, and presented no elaborate barrier between performers and audiences. It was a relatively simple matter to bring an acoustic guitar along to a political meeting or demonstration, and to set it up and play it there when and if the occasion presented itself, which surely cannot be said of rock 'n' roll band equipment. And, of course, rock 'n' roll was identified—even, perhaps especially, by those who enjoyed it—as a "fun" music, a music to accompany dancing and other socializing, whose lyric content was by definition light, amusing, sometimes clever, and often generic, but virtually never serious.

By the mid-1960s changes within rock 'n' roll were already in the wind, as evidenced by the music of the Beatles and the Beach Boys. But Bob Dylan's electric style and other manifestations of folk rock had the effect of an enormous injection of growth hormones into the pop music scene. Suddenly, it was all right—expected, even—for rock 'n' roll to be as "adult" as its baby boomer audience was now becoming itself, and rock 'n' roll abruptly grew up into rock. Pop records on serious subjects, with political and poetical lyrics, sprang up everywhere; before long, this impulse carried over into the making of ambitious concept albums, as we shall see. The later 1960s flowered into a period of intense and remarkable innovation and creativity in pop music. (Of course, the pressure to be adult and creative also inevitably led to the production of a lot of pretentious music as well.)

Dylan was, naturally, the main man to emulate. In the summer and fall of 1965 it seemed that almost everybody was either making cover records of Dylan songs or producing imitations of Dylan's songs and style. For example, both the Byrds and the pop singer Cher were on the charts during the summer with competing versions of Dylan's "All I Really Want to Do," and the first Number 1 pop hit of the fall was the politically charged, folk-rock "Eve of Destruction," composed by the Los Angeles songwriter P. F. Sloan in an obviously Dylanesque style, complete with variable strophes, and sung in a gruff Dylanesque voice by Barry McGuire, who had been a member of the acoustic urban folk group the New Christy Minstrels.

Despite the popularity of "Like a Rolling Stone" and a few singles that followed, Bob Dylan never really established himself as primarily a "singles artist." Rather, he was the first important representative of yet another pop phenomenon: the rock musician whose career was sustained essentially by albums. (Among the many prominent figures who have followed in these particular footsteps are Frank Zappa, Joni Mitchell, Led Zeppelin, and the Grateful Dead.) Every single Bob Dylan album except his very first one has appeared on *Billboard* magazine's "Top Pop Albums" chart. Although his influence was at its peak in the 1960s—and one way to measure that peak is to remember that Dylan was the choice of the then-new *Rolling Stone* magazine for president of the United States in 1968!—Dylan has continued to be a widely admired and closely followed artist into the next century. Never content to be pigeonholed or to fall into a predictable role as elder statesman for any particular movement or musical style, Bob Dylan has over the course of his career produced a distinctive, heterogeneous, and erratic output of albums that, taken together, represent a singular testament to the spirit of pop music invention. Among these albums may be found examples of country rock (*Nashville Skyline*, 1969), what would later be termed "Christian rock" (*Slow Train Coming*, 1979, and *Saved*, 1980), and even latter-day forays back into traditional acoustic folk material (*Good as I Been to You*, 1992, and *World Gone Wrong*, 1993)—along with many examples of the folk-rock approach that initially sealed his place in the pantheon of American music.

In 1997, Dylan was awarded a Kennedy Center Honor by then-president Bill Clinton. In the first decades of the twenty-first century, he released a series of highly acclaimed albums drawing on a diverse range of sources, from folk and blues to even Tin Pan Alley, including *"Love and Theft"* (2001), *Modern Times* (2006), and *Tempest* (2012). Meanwhile, he released the autobiographical book *Chronicles, Volume One* in 2004, and a year later came filmmaker Martin Scorsese's documentary *No Direction Home*, first aired on PBS. Confounding critics and fans yet again, Dylan recorded three cover albums of vintage Tin Pan Alley songs in the mid-2010s, including the three-CD *Triplicate* (2017). Just when it seemed as if Dylan's career as a songwriter had come to an end, the year 2020 saw the appearance of his 2-CD set *Rough and Rowdy Ways*, consisting entirely of newly composed material. Here were ten Dylan originals, most of them lyrically complex and musically ambitious, including the epic "Murder Most Foul," the longest album track of his entire career (just under seventeen minutes!), a somber rumination centered upon the assassination of President Kennedy in 1963.

In 2016, Dylan was awarded the Nobel Prize in Literature, provoking controversy once more when he did not acknowledge the award immediately and did not attend the award ceremony in Sweden. He did express his gratitude, however, and produced a Nobel Lecture, later published, in which he urged people to *listen* to his lyrics as essential elements of his songs, not to regard them only as "literature" to be read on a page. (Aspects of Bob Dylan's later career are explored further in the Chapter 15 box "Popular Musicians Who Endured, and Endure.")

Listening Guide "LIKE A ROLLING STONE"

Composed and performed by Bob Dylan (with unidentified instrumental accompaniment); recorded 1965

Basic Description

"Like a Rolling Stone" is one of a handful of watershed recordings in the history of American popular music. It effectively put an end to existing restrictions on length, subject matter, and poetic diction that had exercised a controlling influence on the creation of pop records. Although other recordings had mounted some challenges to these restrictions before Dylan cut "Like a Rolling Stone," no other pop record had attacked them so comprehensively or with such complete success. After the huge acceptance of "Like a Rolling Stone," literally nothing was the same again.

In discussing the impact of this recording, its sheer *sound* must not be neglected. "Like a Rolling Stone" has an overall timbre and a sonic density that were unique for its time, owing to the exceptional prominence of *two* keyboard instruments—organ and piano—that dominate the texture even more than the electric guitars, bass, and drums. And the distinctive sound of Dylan's vocal cuts aggressively through this thick instrumental texture like a knife. It is difficult to say which was more influential on the future sound of rock: the keyboard-dominated band, or Dylan's in-your-face vocal style, which was positioned on the cutting edge between rhythmic speech and pitched song.

The density of sound and the aggressiveness of the vocal style are clearly suited to this fierce song about a young woman's fall from a state of oblivious privilege into one of desperation. The lyrics range from the bluntest realism to the kind of novel surrealistic imagery that Dylan was pioneering in many of his lyrics at this time.

The chorus that concludes each strophe is typical of Dylan insofar as it provides no resolution or answers; instead, it hurls a defiant question at the song's protagonist—and at the listener:

"How does it feel . . .?"

Doubtless, for many of those in Dylan's audience, who were reaching adulthood and venturing out on their own for the first time, this question possessed a profound and pointed relevance.

Form

"Like a Rolling Stone" reveals its roots in Dylan's acoustic folk style in a number of ways, the most obvious of which relate to form. Like "Blowin' in the Wind" and many of Dylan's other early compositions, "Like a Rolling Stone" falls into a strophic verse-chorus pattern (see the following chart). But the strophes in "Like a Rolling Stone" are extremely long; it is as if every formal aspect present in "Blowin' in the Wind" has been enlarged to create an effect of great intensity and expansion. In the strophes of "Blowin' in the Wind," each verse consists of three questions, which are followed by the "answer" of the chorus. Each of the questions, as well as the "answer," is eight bars long, resulting in a rather typical thirty-two bar formal unit. In "Like a Rolling Stone," however, the verse portions alone are forty bars in length. In the chorus portions, Dylan employs his "variable strophe" idea on a small scale but to considerable effect: the chorus in the first strophe is twenty bars long (five four-bar phrases), while in succeeding strophes the chorus expands to twenty-four bars in length (*six* four-bar phrases, the result of an additional repetition of a musical phrase, accompanying added words).

This formal expansion is necessary to accommodate the song's poetic content. The remarkable thing is that "Like a Rolling Stone" feels denser, not looser, than "Blowin' in the Wind." Obviously, the lyrics are packed more tightly in an eight-bar phrase of "Like a Rolling Stone" than they are in a comparable eight-bar phrase of "Blowin' in the Wind." The combination of greater verbal density (note the internal rhymes in the line quoted above, which are not atypical of "Like a Rolling Stone" and add considerably to the effect) with overall formal expansion creates an ongoing, coiled-spring intensity that is even more marked because Dylan's choruses in "Like a Rolling Stone" don't even afford the listener the comfort of an ambiguous "answer"; they only ask questions. Poetically, "Like a Rolling Stone" takes the question-answer format of "Blowin' in the Wind" and turns it on its head.

The Song/The Recording

In a strophic form, it is obviously the lyrics that must supply a sense of continuing development. Each succeeding strophe of "Like a Rolling Stone" widens its focus as the alienation of the protagonist from her earlier realm of privilege becomes more and more marked and painful. The opening strophe basically describes

(continued)

Listening Guide "LIKE A ROLLING STONE" (continued)

the protagonist and her behavior. The second strophe mentions the school she used to attend, and the third refers to "the jugglers and the clowns" who entertained her and the "diplomat" with whom she consorted. In the final strophe, we are given a wide-angle picture of "all the pretty people" who are "drinkin', thinkin' that they got it made"—a party at which the protagonist is no longer welcome.

Dylan's music serves its purpose of reinforcing the tension embodied in the content of the lyrics. We have already discussed this tension in terms of the overall sound of the recording, but here, notice also how every phrase in the verse portions ends with a sense of melodic incompletion, keeping the tension alive. This structural element is also shared by "Blowin' in the Wind." And, again as in the earlier song, a cadence is reached only in the chorus portions—although this arguably has an ironic effect in "Like a Rolling Stone," since the words offer no sense of completion whatsoever at these points. (Dylan's recording of "Like a Rolling Stone" fades out rather than actually concluding—like a typical rock 'n' roll song—while his "Blowin' in the Wind" comes to a formal ending, like a typical acoustic folk song.)

One further connection with acoustic folk traditions in the recording of "Like a Rolling Stone" lies in the fact that this record is, for all intents and purposes, simply a document of a live studio performance, exhibiting minimal, if any, editing or obvious "production" effects. Dylan has remained true to this kind of sound ideal throughout his recording career, eschewing the highly produced sound typical of so much 1960s (and later) rock.

At a duration of six minutes, "Like a Rolling Stone" was by far the longest 45 rpm pop single ever released up to that time. Dylan's record company knew they were making history; the time "6:00" was emblazoned on the label in huge black numerals, demanding as much attention as the title of the song and the name of the artist! At first, some record stations pared the song down to conventional length by playing only the first two of its four strophes. But before long the complete single was being heard widely on national radio, and an important barrier in pop music had been broken. By the end of the 1960s, pop singles lasting over seven minutes had been made—the Beatles' "Hey Jude" (1968), the biggest chart hit of the entire decade, clocked in at seven minutes, eleven seconds.

LISTENING GUIDE | "LIKE A ROLLING STONE"

TIME	FORM	LYRICS	DESCRIPTIVE COMMENTS
0:00	Instrumental introduction		Note the double-keyboard sound of organ and piano
0:12	Strophe 1: Verse	*Once upon a time . . .*	
1:00	Chorus	*How does it feel . . .*	
1:34	Strophe 2: Verse	*You've gone to the finest school . . .*	
2:23	Chorus (expanded)	*How does it feel . . .*	Note the additional phrase, which makes the chorus even longer than in strophe 1
3:02	Strophe 3: Verse	*You never turned around . . .*	
3:51	Chorus (expanded)	*How does it feel . . .*	As in strophe 2
4:31	Strophe 4: Verse	*Princess on the steeple . . .*	
5:19	Chorus (expanded)	*How does it feel . . .*	As in strophe 2, followed by record fading out

BOX 10.2 SIMON AND GARFUNKEL

Perhaps nothing illustrates the changes wrought by the phenomenon of folk rock so well as the story of Simon and Garfunkel's first hit record, "The Sounds of Silence." In early 1965 **Paul Simon** and Arthur Garfunkel were an urban folk duo with a fine acoustic album to their credit, *Wednesday Morning, 3 a.m.*, that was causing no excitement whatsoever in the marketplace. When folk rock hit the scene mid-year and Bob Dylan went electric, Simon and Garfunkel's producer, Tom Wilson—who was also the producer for Bob Dylan's records at the time—had a bright idea. He took one of Simon's original compositions from the *Wednesday Morning* album, a highly poetic song about urban alienation called "The Sound of Silence"; overdubbed a rock band accompaniment of electric guitars, bass, and drums onto the original recording; speeded it up very slightly; changed the title for some reason to "The Sounds of Silence"; and released it as a single—all without Simon or Garfunkel's prior knowledge or permission! The duo found little to complain about, however, as they found themselves with a Number 1 pop hit on New Year's Day 1966. Needless to say, they never looked back. Simon and Garfunkel became one of the most enduringly popular acts ever to perform in a folk-rock style. Although the duo broke up in 1970 (they have occasionally reunited for special occasions), their songs and albums continue to be popular to this day.

We will meet Paul Simon again later on, as he is among the few singer-songwriters to come to prominence in the 1960s who arguably achieved his creative peak considerably later on. To say this is not to denigrate Simon's work with Simon and Garfunkel, which includes such memorable and varied songs as "A Hazy Shade of Winter," "America," and "Bridge over Troubled Water"; it is simply to claim that these earlier compositions would probably not lead one to suspect that Simon would eventually go on to produce such adventurous works of world music as *Graceland* and *The Rhythm of the Saints* (see Chapter 13).

Folk rockers Paul Simon (left) and Art Garfunkel performing, c. 1966.

The Counterculture and Psychedelic Rock

The unanticipated entrance of folk rock into the wide arena of American popular culture coincided, as we have seen, with the development of increasingly innovative approaches to rock 'n' roll itself (exemplified most forcefully in the work of the Beatles and the Beach Boys in 1965–1966). Both of these phenomena were abetted, of course, by the maturation into early adulthood of the baby boomer audience, as well as the maturation of many of those actually making the music. This was also a period of increasing political restlessness and ferment in the United States. America's engagement in the Vietnamese civil war was steadily escalating, while the civil rights movement was challenging the persistence of racial segregation and inequality everywhere on the home front. There were many who sensed a relationship between these two volatile political issues, linking what they viewed as external colonialism—an inappropriate involvement with the affairs of a so-called Third World country—with internal colonialism—the systematic oppression of minority peoples and cultures within the United States itself. This connection was made more apparent to many because of the large proportion of African American soldiers serving in the U.S. forces in Vietnam.

The youth audience for pop culture was directly implicated in the politics of the Vietnam War, as all young American men between the ages of eighteen and twenty-six were eligible to be drafted into the armed forces and increasing numbers of them were as time went by. Antiwar groups and organizations began to multiply, attracting large numbers of young—especially college-aged—men and women. In addition, a significant number of young people were involved in various ways with the many organizations, demonstrations, and legal initiatives that formed the civil rights movement.

In the later 1960s the meeting of the culture surrounding new rock music with the political and social discontents that largely defined the era resulted in a famous, if slippery, phenomenon: the emergence of what was called the counterculture. This was never the kind of systematic, highly organized movement that many liked to claim it was at the time (and later on). Although the mythical typical member of the counterculture was a young rock music fan who supported the civil rights movement and opposed the Vietnam War, it is important to remember that many older folks opposed the Vietnam War as well, and that many of these probably had no special fondness for the new rock music; that many young rock music fans were apolitical, or even supporters of conservative political agendas; and that many of the same movements that promulgated utopian visions of a new, more just social order excluded most women and people of color from leadership positions. In other words, although the notion of a counterculture provides us with a convenient label for the more innovative, rebellious, and radical aspects of 1960s musical, political, and social culture taken all together, it is inevitably a simplification, and unless we are careful, it may involve us in a number of dubious historical fictions. What is probably most significant here, for our purposes, is to note that rock music—the unruly 1960s child of unruly 1950s rock 'n' roll—was an essential part of the definition of the counterculture, which demonstrates once again the remarkable degree of identification between the baby boomer generation and the music they chose to make and hear.

Along with rock music and radical politics, the counterculture developed its own characteristic jargon, fads, and fashions: long hair for both women and men, beards, beads, "peasant," "Eastern," and tie-dyed shirts, and blue jeans. The slang terms most often associated with hippies—"groovy," "far out," "stoned," and so on—were mainly derived from Black English, a continuation of a historical pattern that goes back to nineteenth-century minstrelsy. In addition, the counterculture's fascination with "exotic" cultures—as reflected in the popularity of Indian classical music, Nehru jackets, and African dashikis—also has deep historical roots. At the same time, a distinctive openness and sense of freedom regarding sexual activity also emerged, encouraged to no small extent by the successful development and marketing of the first birth-control pills for women.

Many members of the counterculture were members of the American middle class, born into families that were predominantly white, Christian, or Jewish, and financially solvent. It is thus understandable that the rebellious attitude of young people during the late 1960s—as during earlier periods—focused as much on a critique of the values and social habits of the middle-class family as it did on resistance to government policies or the operations of big industry. This critical attitude toward bourgeois values and outlooks was perhaps quintessentially embodied in the concept of communal living, regarded as an antidote to the psychological pathologies of the nuclear family. (Some prominent San Francisco rock bands, including the Grateful Dead, actually were communes.) These communitarian values were embodied in large, loosely bounded public events called "be-ins," which emphasized informal musical performance, spontaneity, and camaraderie. This communal "let it all hang out" ethos spilled over into the large concert venues where rock music was typically played in the late 1960s, including San Francisco's Avalon Ballroom and the Fillmore West. The countercultural commitment to antiestablishment values included a variety of anarchist and libertarian philosophies. This commitment was correlated with a rejection of both the romanticism of mainstream pop music and the commercial motivations of the big corporations that marketed pop music. (Ironically, some rock bands associated closely with the counterculture—including the Jefferson Airplane—had enough business savvy to secure lucrative contracts with major labels. Some of the biggest record corporations, such as Columbia Records, actually promoted themselves as specializing in countercultural music.)

The issues surrounding free love—or liberated sexuality—in the 1960s have become so controversial and mythologized that straightforward discussion of them is still nearly impossible. In fact, the sexual mores of the period had surprisingly little direct effect on the style or substance of pop music. Surely there was much intricate and newly poetic probing of the emotional nature of relationships in the song lyrics of the era, owing chiefly to the influence of Dylan and other folk rockers. But apart from isolated, and slightly later, examples (one could cite "Love the One You're With," a hit for both Stephen Stills and the Isley Brothers in 1971, or "The Pill," a 1975 recording by country star Loretta Lynn), the sexual revolution of the 1960s seems not to have been significantly documented in the music of the time. Of course, it could also be claimed that sexuality has been at least an implicit subject in most of the popular love songs of any period—we could go back to "My Blue Heaven," where "baby makes three" (see Chapter 4)—and that consequently there was little need to change the basic character of love song lyrics in the 1960s to accommodate a new generation. Presumably, everybody who needed to know knew what was being sung about when a singer pleaded "I want you," whether that singer was Elvis Presley in the culturally conservative 1950s ("I Want You, I Need You, I Love You," 1956) or Bob Dylan in the culturally radical 1960s ("I Want You," 1966).

Similarly, the contemporary dilemma of drug use in American society—including the abuse of drugs by very young people—makes it hard to provide a simple, unambiguous evaluation of the counterculture's relationship to intoxicants and recreational chemicals. The vulgar catchphrase used to sum up the counterculture's attitude toward such things was "sex, drugs, and rock and roll"; instead of (or in addition to) the alcohol of their parents' generation, many young people in the 1960s came to favor psychedelic substances, particularly marijuana and LSD (lysergic acid diethylamide, or "acid"). Unquestionably there was lots of drug use by both musicians and their audiences in the later 1960s. Many recordings and concerts were experienced by "stoned" young people; at least some of those recordings and concerts were probably intended by the musicians to be experienced in that way, and some of the musicians involved made the music while stoned themselves. There is, for example, no possible dispute about the subject matter of a song with a title like "Don't Bogart That Joint." But when questioned about the Beatles' song "Lucy in the Sky with Diamonds," whose title and psychedelic imagery were widely assumed to be connected to LSD, John Lennon replied that the song had been inspired by a picture drawn by his four-year-old son that the little boy had himself called "Lucy in the sky with diamonds" and disclaimed any connection between the song and drugs. (Of course, one could choose to be skeptical about Lennon's statement as well; the point is that there is no absolute "truth" that can be determined here.) Certainly the flamboyant, colorful visual effects used on rock music posters and record jackets and in the light shows at rock concerts were to some degree modeled on the experience of tripping. In the end, however, it is not easy to pin down the degree to which the characteristic openendedness of many rock music performances—including the hours-long musical explorations of bands like Jefferson Airplane and the Grateful Dead—is directly attributable to drug use.

In order to put the drug culture of the 1960s into perspective, it is necessary to remember a number of things. The use and abuse of alcohol, marijuana, cocaine, heroin, and other drugs has formed a part of the culture of musicians and their audiences in this country for a very long time. The pressures and doldrums of a performer's life have led many musicians to use stimulants, depressants, and intoxicants of various kinds, and unhealthy dependencies have naturally resulted all too frequently, prematurely snuffing out some of the brightest lights in America's musical history. (A partial list would include jazz great Charlie Parker, Hank Williams, Elvis Presley, Janis Joplin, and Jimi Hendrix, among many others.) Furthermore, the venues in which pop music is heard live are most commonly those in which the legal—and sometimes illegal—consumption of intoxicants forms an essential aspect of the audience's "good time." In this connection, it is important to recall that during the era of Prohibition (1919–1933), the manufacture and sale of alcoholic beverages were illegal in the United States. Thus many adults who were nonplussed by younger people's consumption of illegal marijuana and LSD in the 1960s had doubtless themselves enjoyed the new pop music and jazz of the 1920s and early 1930s to the accompaniment, in speakeasy clubs or at home, of illegal bootleg liquor.

An appropriate perspective on the drug use of the 1960s would also take into account that many participants in the counterculture, including musicians and members of the rock audience, were not involved with drugs. Furthermore, along with the pleasure-seekers who sought only to enjoy themselves and follow fashion while repeating the slogans of the time about "mind expansion" and "turning on," there were those who were quite seriously seeking alternatives to the prevailing American bourgeois lifestyle and may have employed hallucinogens such as peyote, psilocybin mushrooms, and LSD carefully and sparingly as an aspect of spiritual exploration (in a manner akin to that found in certain non-Western cultures—there was, for example, a good deal of interest in Indian culture among members of the counterculture, some of it superficial and trendy but some of it assuredly serious). In the end, it appears that the value of psycho-active substances depends on the context and manner of their use, and we can conclude that the drug culture of the 1960s was, at various times, both an enabler and a destroyer of musical creativity. Interviews with rock musicians of the late 1960s—now senior citizens—are notable for their lack of nostalgia regarding drug use.

It was, and is, easy to poke fun at stereotypical images of the counterculture. Frank Zappa, assuredly a participant in the counterculture (and reportedly a non–drug user), wrote a savagely satirical song in 1967 called "Who Needs the Peace Corps?" that tar-geted "phony hippies" and their "psychedelic dungeons." Yet the greatest virtue of the 1960s counterculture, for all its naïveté and excesses, may be that it gave birth to and encouraged some innovative and remarkable creative manifestations, among which are certainly the works of Zappa himself. We will now look at a few of these creative reflec-tions of, and influences on, the "age of psychedelia."

Sgt. Pepper's Lonely Hearts Club Band

Summer 1967 was the so-called Summer of Love, when many young participants in the newly self-aware counterculture were following the advice of a pop hit that told them to head for San Francisco (whose Haight-Ashbury district was already a legend-ary center of countercultural activity), wearing flowers in their hair. But the group celebrations called "love-ins" were not limited to San Francisco. In fact, a sense of participation in the counterculture was readily available that summer to anyone who had a phonograph and the spending money to purchase the Beatles' new album, *Sgt. Pepper's Lonely Hearts Club Band*, as revolutionary a work of pop musical art as had ever been made.

The countercultural ambience of *Sgt. Pepper* was obvious in a number of ways. The unprecedented and now-famous album cover, a wild collage of faces and figures surrounding the four Beatles dressed in full formal band regalia, pictured a number of people from many different time periods who were associated with aspects of the counterculture: Karl Marx, Oscar Wilde, Marlon Brando, James Dean, and Bob Dylan. (The figure of a young girl off to the side was dressed in a sweater that read "Welcome the Rolling Stones"!) The song that opened the second side of the record, "Within You Without You," was the most profound of the Beatles' attempts to evoke the sound and spirit of Indian music: it featured Indian instruments (sitar and tabla, in lieu of guitars

The famous *Sgt. Pepper* cover showing the Beatles surrounded by dozens of earlier "stars," including wax figures of the group from their early days.

and Western drums); unusual meters and phrase structures; and deeply meditative, philosophical lyrics. The lyrics to a number of other songs had what could easily be interpreted as drug references, for those so inclined. We have already mentioned "Lucy in the Sky with Diamonds," but among other examples noted at the time were "With a Little Help from My Friends," which features the repeated line "I get high with a little help from my friends," and the concluding song "A Day in the Life," which ends the album with the famous line "I'd love to turn you on." Furthermore, the record had many musical sounds and sound effects that could be—and were—interpreted as psychedelic in inspiration. Among the most celebrated of these are the electronically distorted voices in "Lucy in the Sky with Diamonds" and the chaotic orchestral sweep upward that occurs twice in "A Day in the Life."

Arguably more important than any specific countercultural references in *Sgt. Pepper* was the way in which the album was structured to invite its listeners' participation in an implied community. The record is a clearly and cleverly organized performance that reflects an awareness of, and actually addresses, its audience. The opening song, "Sgt. Pepper's Lonely Hearts Club Band," formally introduces the "show" to come and acknowledges the listener(s) with lines like "We hope you will enjoy the show" and "You're such a lovely audience, we'd love to take you home with us." This song is reprised, with different words ("We hope you have enjoyed the show") as the penultimate selection on the album, after which the "performance" ends and the performers return to "reality" with "A Day in the Life" ("I read the news today, oh boy"). Yet even in this final song, the continued presence of the listener(s) is acknowledged, at least implicitly, with the line "I'd love to turn you on."

The Beatles' brilliant conceit of *Sgt. Pepper* as a "performance" is evident even before the music begins: the opening sounds on the record are those of a restless audience. Audience sounds of laughter and applause are heard at schematic points in both the initial presentation and the reprise of the song "Sgt. Pepper's Lonely Hearts Club Band." Yet this is clearly not a recording of an actual live performance. Virtually every song on the album features a unique instrumental arrangement significantly different from that of the songs that precede and follow it—in other words, the songs are arranged to provide maximum variety and contrast on a record album, not as a practical sequence for a live performance situation. Even more obviously, the album is full of studio-produced effects, the most spectacular of which are the sound collage that actually overlaps the ending of "Good Morning Good Morning" with the reprise of "Sgt. Pepper's Lonely Hearts Club Band," and the explosively distorted final chord of "A Day in the Life," which very gradually fades out over the duration of about forty-five seconds. In the employment of these effects, and in many other aspects of the album, the hand of producer George Martin is clearly evident.

There is a profound irony in the fact that the first album made by the Beatles after they decided to abandon live performing and assume an identity solely as a recording act is an album that, in effect, mimics and creatively reimagines the concept of performing before an audience. This irony would, of course, not be lost on Beatles fans, who were well aware of the group's highly publicized decision, and who had to wait longer for this album than for any previous one by the group. (More than nine months separated the release of *Sgt. Pepper* from that of the Beatles' immediately preceding album, *Revolver*—a long time in those days.) But *Sgt. Pepper* in turn so widened and enriched the idea of what a rock album could be that, it could be argued, the gain at least somewhat balanced the loss of the Beatles as a touring group.

Rock 'n' roll had always communicated to its widest audience by means of records. *Sgt. Pepper* simply turned that established fact into the basis for brilliantly self-conscious artifice. When the Beatles sang "We'd love to take you home with us" in the opening song of the album, they must have done so with ironic recognition of the fact that it was actually their audience that takes them home—in the form of their records. As we have already attempted to show, everything about *Sgt. Pepper* is inclusionary: it posits the rock album as the creator of an audience community, a community for which that album also serves as a means of communication and identity. In fact the album achieved unprecedented success in reaching a large community, even by the Beatles' standards: it sold 8 million copies and remained on *Billboard*'s album charts for more than three years.

The most historically significant fact about *Sgt. Pepper* is the way in which it definitively redirected attention from the single-song recording to the record album as the focus of where important new pop music was being made. That *Sgt. Pepper* was conceived as a totality, rather than as a collection of single songs, is apparent in many ways, but most indicative perhaps was the unprecedented marketing decision not to release any of the songs on the album as singles. (The singles gap was filled by the Beatles' release of "All You Need Is Love" in the summer of 1967, a song that would only later be collected on an album.) *Sgt. Pepper* was not the first concept album, but it was the first album to present itself to the public as a complete and unified marketing package, with a distinctive and interrelated collection of parts, all of which were unavailable in any other form; these parts include not just the songs on the record itself, but also the cover art and the inside photograph of the Beatles in their band uniforms, the complete song lyrics printed on the back of the album jacket (a first, and a precedent-setting one), the extra page of "Sgt. Pepper cut-outs" supplied with the album, and even (with the earlier pressings) a unique inner sleeve to hold the record that was adorned with "psychedelic" swirls of pink and red coloring!

Sgt. Pepper did for the rock album what Dylan's "Like a Rolling Stone" had done for the rock single. It rewrote all the rules, and things were never the same again. Countless albums appearing in the wake of *Sgt. Pepper* imitated aspects of the Beatles' tour de force, from its cover art to its printed lyrics to its use of a musical reprise, but few could approach its real substance and achievement. To their credit, the Beatles themselves did not try to imitate it but went on to other things, continuing to produce innovative music on albums and singles until they disbanded early in 1970. As of the present writing, interest in the Beatles continues unabated; their three anthology collections (on both discs and videos) of previously unreleased material have all been recent bestsellers, and in 2000 a new compilation of their top-selling singles, entitled simply *1*, was released and proved extremely popular. The release of the Beatles' catalog on iTunes in 2010 was so successful that 2 million songs were sold in the first week. In 2015, their catalog was finally released to streaming services.

Their Satanic Majesties: The Rolling Stones after *Sgt. Pepper*

The relationship between the public images of the Beatles and the Rolling Stones—initially a marketing strategy pitting the adorable, witty mop-tops against their rougher, more streetwise cousins—took on an added dimension in December 1967 when the Stones released their "answer" to *Sgt. Pepper*, the album *Their Satanic Majesties Request*. *Their Satanic Majesties* reached Number 2 on the album charts but was widely panned as a pretentious and overambitious attempt to outdo the Beatles. In the years that followed, the Stones turned more and more to their ultimate inspiration—the blues and rhythm & blues that they had heard and attempted to master as youths—while continuing to cultivate the dark image suggested by the album's title.

The thick, guitar-centered sound texture that fans now associate with the Rolling Stones—and that was a template for hard rock bands that followed them—wasn't fully realized until the late 1960s. In 1968 the band's guitarist, Keith Richards, began to use open tunings, in which a guitar is tuned so that a chord may be played without fretting, or pressing down, any of the strings. This technique—used most commonly in blues and folk music—contributed greatly to the sound of hit singles like "Honky Tonk Women" and "Brown Sugar" (Number 1 singles in 1969 and 1971, respectively).

The morally ambiguous and even malevolent image of the Rolling Stones was intensified by the release of songs like "Street Fighting Man" and "Sympathy for the Devil" (both on the 1968 album *Beggars Banquet*). This association between the Stones and rock 'n' roll, violence, and Satanism was reinforced by the film *Gimme Shelter* (1970), which documented a free concert at the Altamont Speedway in California the previous December, at which members of the Hell's Angels motorcycle gang, who had been hired to provide security for the event, killed a young Black man named Meredith Hunter. Mick Jagger's desperate pleas to the audience to "keep cool" and "relax," captured in the film, did nothing to dispel the impression that the Rolling Stones were ultimately responsible for the outbreak of violence at Altamont, and for putting a definitive end to the era of peace and love, symbolized by the Woodstock Festival just four months earlier.

The controversy surrounding *Gimme Shelter* and the subsequent convictions of Mick Jagger and Keith Richards on drug charges seem only to have increased the appetite of Rolling Stones fans. Between 1971 (*Sticky Fingers*) and 1981 (*Tattoo You*) all eight of the Stones' studio albums reached the top of the American charts. In 1986, the group achieved a Top 10 hit with "Harlem Shuffle," their faithful remake of a neglected American rhythm & blues hit from 1964 by Bob and Earl.

However, while both their new releases and back catalog continue to sell well in the age of the digital download, the Rolling Stones remain, first and foremost, a live band. The album *Steel Wheels* (1989) reached Number 3 on the charts, but the record was far overshadowed in economic terms by its supporting tour, which grossed over $140 million and set a new watershed for box office records. The huge concert earnings that have been generated by the Stones over the last two decades are an indication of the increasing importance of live performance revenues over sales of recordings, and attendance at a Rolling Stones concert today remains a badge of honor for many rock fans. The international "A Bigger Bang" tour (2005–2007) was the highest grossing rock tour of its time, generating well over half a billion dollars in receipts. In 2016, the group toured Latin America—including an historic performance in Havana, Cuba—and returned to their roots with *Blue & Lonesome*, their first album devoted entirely to cover versions of blues songs, which debuted at Number 4 on the pop album charts. This meant that the Rolling Stones had scored a record thirty-seven Top 10 albums in the course of their career, an accomplishment unequaled by any other artists in popular music history.

San Francisco Rock: Jefferson Airplane, Janis Joplin, and the Grateful Dead

During the late 1960s an "alternative" rock music scene, inspired in part by the Beatles' experimentalism, established itself in San Francisco. The city had already long been a center for artistic communities and subcultures, including the "beat" literary movement of the 1950s, a lively urban folk music scene, and a highly visible and vocal gay community. "Psychedelic rock," as the music played by San Francisco bands was sometimes called, encompassed a variety of styles and musical influences, including folk rock, blues, "hard rock," Latin music, and Indian classical music. In geographical terms, San Francisco's psychedelic music scene was focused on the Haight-Ashbury neighborhood, center of the hippie movement.

A number of musical entrepreneurs and institutions supported the growth of the San Francisco rock music scene. Tom Donahue, a local radio DJ, challenged the mainstream Top 40 AM pop music format on San Francisco's KYA and later pioneered a new, open-ended, and eclectic broadcasting format on FM station KMPX. (Donahue is the spiritual forefather of today's alternative FM formats, including many college stations.) The foremost promoter of the new rock bands—and the first to cash in on the music's popularity—was Bill Graham. Graham, a European immigrant who had worked as a taxi driver to support his business studies, began staging rock concerts in San Francisco in 1965. For one of his first rock concerts Graham rented a skating rink, which he later renamed the Fillmore. The Fillmore—renamed the Fillmore West when Graham opened the Fillmore East in New York City—was a symbolic center of the counterculture, and psychedelic posters advertising its concerts are today worth thousands of dollars. Other individuals built professional careers out of the job of creating psychedelic atmosphere for rock concerts: Chet Helms, for example, was responsible for developing the multimedia aesthetic of light shows at the Fillmore and the Avalon Ballroom.

Jefferson Airplane was the first nationally successful band to emerge out of the San Francisco psychedelic scene. Founded in 1965, the Airplane was originally a semi-acoustic folk-rock band that performed blues and songs by Bob Dylan. Eventually they began to develop a louder, harder-edged style with a greater emphasis on open forms, instrumental improvisation, and visionary lyrics. Together, the Quicksilver Messenger Service, the Grateful Dead, and Jefferson Airplane formed one of the original triumvirates of San Francisco "acid rock" bands, playing at the Matrix Club (center of the San Francisco alternative nightclub scene), larger concert venues such as the Avalon Ballroom and the Fillmore, and communal outdoor events such as happenings and be-ins. In late 1965 the Airplane received an unprecedented $20,000 advance from RCA, one of the largest and most powerful corporations in the world. (Despite the anticommercial rhetoric of the counterculture, this event was responsible for sparking off the formation of dozens of psychedelic bands in the Bay Area eager to cash in on the Airplane's success. Parallels to this seemingly paradoxical link between countercultural values and the good old profit motive may sometimes be observed in connection with today's "alternative" music movements.) The Airplane's 1967 LP *Surrealistic Pillow* sold over a million copies, reaching Number 3 on the pop album charts and spawning two Top 10 singles. The biggest celebrity in the group was vocalist *Grace Slick* (b. 1939), who—along with Janis Joplin—was the most important female musician on the San Francisco scene.

Jefferson Airplane were introduced to a national audience by their recording of "Somebody to Love," which reached Number 5 on the national pop charts in 1967. "Somebody to Love" exemplifies the acid rock approach, which is marked by a dense musical texture with plenty of volume and lots of electronic distortion. (The process of making hit singles encouraged the band to trim its normally extended, improvised performances down to a manageable—and AM radio–friendly—three minutes.)

The song itself, which originated in an act of familial composition by Grace Slick, her husband, and her brother-in-law, exemplifies the tendency of late 1960s rock musicians to compose their own material. (Another paradox of the psychedelic rock movement was that it combined the urban folk musicians' emphasis on communal creativity with the influential rock-musician-as-artist ideology represented in the work of the Beatles, Bob Dylan, and Brian Wilson.)

Grace Slick's only serious competition as queen of the San Francisco rock scene came from *Janis Joplin* (1943–1970), the most successful white blues singer of the 1960s. Born in Port Arthur, Texas, Joplin came to San Francisco in the mid-1960s and joined a band called Big Brother and the Holding Company. Their appearance at the Monterey Pop Festival in 1967 led to a contract with Columbia Records, eager to cash in on RCA's success with Jefferson Airplane and the growing national audience for acid rock. Big Brother's 1968 album *Cheap Thrills*—graced with a cover design by the underground comic book artist Robert Crumb—reached Number 1 on the pop charts and included a Number 12 hit single (the song "Piece of My Heart," a cover version of a 1960s R&B hit by Erma Franklin).

Joplin's full-tilt singing style and directness of expression were inspired by blues singers such as Bessie Smith and the R&B recordings of Big Mama Thornton. (Joplin rediscovered Big Mama in the late 1960s and helped to revive her performing career.) She pushed her voice unmercifully, reportedly saying that she would prefer a short, exceptional career to a long career as an unexceptional performer. Although her growling, bluesy style made her an icon for the mainly white audience for rock music, Joplin was not a success with Black audiences, and she never managed to cross over to the R&B charts.

One of Joplin's most moving performances is her rendition of the George and Ira Gershwin composition "Summertime," written in 1935 for the American folk opera *Porgy and Bess*. Although this recording was criticized for the less-than-polished accompaniment provided by Big Brother and the Holding Company, Joplin's performance is riveting. She squeezes every last drop of emotion out of the song, pushing her voice to the limit, and creating not only the rough, rasping tones expected of a blues singer but also multipitched sounds called multiphonics. The impression one retains of Janis Joplin—an impression reinforced by listening to her recordings—is actually that of a sweet, vulnerable person, whose tough exterior and heavy reliance on drugs functioned as defense mechanisms and armor against life's disappointments.

No survey of the 1960s San Francisco rock scene would be complete without mention of the Grateful Dead, a thoroughly idiosyncratic band—actually as

Janis Joplin performing, c. 1967.

much an experience or institution as a band in the usual sense—whose career spanned more than three decades. (Although it is often stated that the Grateful Dead were not a commercially successful band, eight of their LPs reached the Top 20, including 1987's *In the Dark*, which held the Number 9 position on *Billboard*'s album charts.) "The Dead," as they are known to their passionately devoted followers, grew out of a series of bands involving *Jerry Garcia* (1942–1995), a guitarist, banjoist, and singer who had played in various urban folk groups during the early 1960s. This shifting collective of musicians gradually took firmer shape and in 1967 was christened the Grateful Dead.[2] The Dead helped to pioneer the transition from urban folk music to folk rock to acid rock, adopting electric instruments, living communally in the Haight-Ashbury district, and participating in public LSD parties ("acid tests") before the drug was outlawed. (These experiences were chronicled in Tom Wolfe's book *The Electric Kool-Aid Acid Test*.)

In musical terms, it is hard to classify the Grateful Dead's work. For one thing, their records do not for the most part do them justice. The Dead were the quintessential "live" rock band, specializing in long jams that wander through diverse musical styles and grooves and typically terminate in unexpected places. The influence of folk music— prominent on some of their early recordings—was usually just below the surface, and a patient listener may expect to hear a kind of "sketch-map" of American popular music— including folk, blues, R&B, and country music, as well as rock 'n' roll—with occasional gestures in the direction of African or Asian music. Their repertoire of songs was huge; in any given live performance, one might have heard diverse songs from different periods in the band's existence. (This means that each performance was also a unique musical version of the band's history, at least for those who had studied it.)

If the Grateful Dead were a unique musical institution, their devoted fans— "Deadheads"—were a social phenomenon unparalleled in the history of American popular music. Traveling incessantly in psychedelically decorated buses and vans, setting up camp in every town along the tour, and generally pursuing a peaceful mode of coexistence with local authorities, hardcore Deadheads literally lived for their band. While it has been pointed out that much of the satisfaction of this mobile/communal lifestyle has to do with the creation of a special social ethos, there can be no denying that the core source of appeal for serious Deadheads was the band's music. They taped the band's performances—and were often encouraged to do so, something quite unusual in the popular music business—and then circulated these tapes (called bootlegs), building up extensive lists that chronicle every concert the band ever played. There are now entire sites devoted to this purpose on the internet, with precise descriptions of the repertoires played at particular concerts and statistical breakdowns of the frequency of certain songs and certain sequences of songs. Although other popular musicians have certainly inspired adoration—Frank Sinatra, Elvis Presley, and the Beatles come immediately to mind—the devotion of Deadheads remains truly unique.

---

2. Many stories circulate about the origin of the band's name. It appears that in actuality the phrase "the grateful dead" was something Jerry Garcia happened upon accidentally in a reference book, and it refers to a motif found in a cycle of folk tales (Meriwether, 2007, xiii).

Jerry Garcia died in 1995—partly as a result of longtime drug and alcohol use—and the remaining members of the band have gone their separate ways. Periodically, however, the survivors assemble to hit the road together, with their huge entourage in tow. And although in the span of more than three decades the band placed only one single in the Top 40 ("Touch of Gray," a Number 9 pop hit in 1987), the thirty-odd albums recorded by the Grateful Dead continue, year by year, to sell hundreds of thousands of copies to one of the most loyal audiences in the history of American popular music. And the Grateful Dead phenomenon is even reflected in areas other than music and music-related merchandise; Ben & Jerry's wildly popular "Cherry Garcia" ice cream is marketed as an "edible tribute to guitarist Jerry Garcia & Grateful Dead fans everywhere."

The Doors and "Light My Fire"

One of the most controversial rock bands of the 1960s, the **Doors**, was formed in Los Angeles in 1965 by keyboardist Ray Manzarek and singer Jim Morrison (both film students at UCLA), with the addition of John Densmore on drums and guitarist Robby Krieger. The Doors adopted their name from philosopher Aldous Huxley's 1954 book *The Doors of Perception*, which detailed Huxley's experiences with the hallucinogen mescaline, derived from the peyote cactus. The group never added a bass player, and their sound was dominated by Manzarek's ornate electric organ playing and Morrison's deep baritone voice and poetic, often obscure lyrics.

The Doors soon landed a steady gig as the house band at the Whisky a Go Go nightclub on Sunset Boulevard, where they opened for folk-rock acts such as Buffalo Springfield and the Turtles. They were signed by Elektra Records in 1966 and recorded their eponymous first album, featuring the hit single "Light My Fire," the following year. (Elektra, an independent label specializing mainly in folk acts, also signed a number of important rock bands, including Detroit-based proto-punk bands the MC5 and the Stooges.) *The Doors* went to Number 2, where it got stuck behind the immovable *Sgt. Pepper*.

So much attention has been focused on the persona of "Lizard King" Jim Morrison—whose Dionysian lifestyle, controversial lyrics, and early demise reinforced his potency as a symbol of countercultural rebellion—that it is easy to overlook the strictly musical impact of the group's early recordings. Although other songs on *The Doors* more explicitly challenged prevailing norms of content and taste—including "The End," a psychedelic, introspective twelve-minute meditation on the end of a romance that squeezes in an explicit reference to the Oedipal myth—it was "Light My Fire," cowritten by Krieger and Morrison and distinguished by Ray Manzarek's classically inspired introduction and solo on the Vox electric organ, that had the greatest impact on the way that rock music was experienced and consumed in the late 1960s.

At six minutes and fifty seconds in length, the original version of the song was deemed too long for AM radio airplay, which was then still largely limited to three-minute singles (despite the success of Dylan's six-minute "Like a Rolling Stone"). Elektra

Records issued the original single with part of the instrumental break excised, and it shot to Number 1 on the pop charts, staying there for three weeks. Once "Light My Fire" was established as a hit, a number of Top 40 stations began to play the longer version of the song from the album, figuring that it made sense to use a hit record to hold a listener's attention for almost seven minutes of airtime. As more AM stations put the long version of "Light My Fire" into their top-three rotation, sales of *The Doors* album took off. From the perspective of the record industry, this was a potential gold mine, since albums were much more profitable than singles. The record companies began to more actively promote rock albums on radio, particularly on the still-emerging progressive FM stations, which were willing to experiment with playing extended material by emerging artists. This was a crucial development in the economy of rock music.

BOX 10.3 "CLOUD NINE": THE MOTOWN RESPONSE TO PSYCHEDELIA

With its gaze always fixed firmly on the commercial mainstream, the Motown organization was never one that could directly be associated with the conception of a counterculture. But Motown was also "the sound of young America," and Berry Gordy Jr. was savvy enough to realize that completely ignoring the influence of artists like Bob Dylan and the Beatles on the rock audience would relegate Motown's music to the dreaded realm of the irrelevant and unhip. Sure enough, the Supremes' Summer of Love hit in 1967, "Reflections," opened with the sounds of a strange, repeated electronic beep, followed by an explosion. After this hat tip to psychedelia, the record proceeded in a style basically identical to that of the Supremes' earlier efforts—except for the occasional recurrence of the strange beep.

A more thoroughgoing, serious attempt by Motown to respond to currents in the counterculture is represented by the late 1960s and early 1970s records of the Temptations. Producer Norman Whitfield, who cowrote songs for the Temptations with Barrett Strong, actually caused some controversy within the Motown organization when he came up with "Cloud Nine" in late 1968. The "cloud nine" of the song, where "you can be what you want to be" and "you're a million miles from reality," is obviously a drug reference, but the context is far removed from that of blissful, mind-expanding psychedelia; the reality of the song is that of the urban slums, where people turn to drugs out of desperation. The gritty depiction of slum life in the lyrics of

"Cloud Nine" related the song much more closely to the spirit of socially conscious urban folk rock than to that usually associated with psychedelia. The sound of the record was also quite novel for Motown, with distorted electric guitars and echo-like effects setting off a vocal arrangement that made a point of contrasting the varied vocal timbres and ranges represented among the members of the Temptations. In effect, "Cloud Nine" represented a new kind of hybrid for Motown, one that fused elements of the new rock and folk rock with the potent synthesis of pop and rhythm & blues that had always characterized its music. (A parallel may be drawn with the music being developed at this same time by the San Francisco–based interracial "psychedelic soul" group Sly and the Family Stone, which was attempting a similar kind of complex fusion. This group was headed by the African American songwriter/producer Sylvester Stewart.)

The success of "Cloud Nine" (Number 6 pop, Number 2 R&B) established the marketability of Whitfield's new approach and led, naturally enough, to other hit records by the Temptations along analogous lines, like "Run Away Child, Running Wild," "Psychedelic Shack," "Ball of Confusion (That's What the World Is Today)," and "Papa Was a Rollin' Stone." Other Motown acts also made their contributions to the organization's hipper image; 1970 brought Edwin Starr's protest song "War"—another Whitfield-Strong composition that reached Number 1 on the pop charts—and a record by the Supremes called "Stoned Love."

Guitar Heroes: Jimi Hendrix and Eric Clapton

The 1960s saw the rise of a new generation of electric guitarists who functioned as cultural heroes for their young fans. Their achievements were built on the shoulders of previous generations of electric guitar virtuosos—Les Paul, whose innovative tinkering with electronic technology inspired a new generation of amplifier tweakers; T-Bone Walker, who introduced the electric guitar to R&B music in the late 1940s; urban blues musicians such as Muddy Waters and B. B. King, whose raw sound and emotional directness inspired rock guitarists; and early masters of rock 'n' roll guitar, including Chuck Berry and Buddy Holly. Beginning in the mid-1960s, the new guitarists—including Jimi Hendrix, Eric Clapton, Jimmy Page, Jeff Beck, and the Beatles' George Harrison—took these influences and pushed them further than ever before in terms of technique, sheer volume, and improvisational brilliance.

Jimi Hendrix (1942–1970) was the most original, inventive, and influential guitarist of the rock era, and the most prominent African American rock musician of the late 1960s. His early experience as a guitarist was gained touring with rhythm & blues bands. In 1966 he moved to London, where, at the suggestion of the producer Chas Chandler, he joined up with two English musicians, bassist Noel Redding and drummer Mitch Mitchell, eventually forming a band called the Jimi Hendrix Experience. The Experience first appeared in America in 1967 at the Monterey Pop Festival, where Hendrix stunned the audience with his flamboyant performance style, which involved playing the guitar with his teeth, and behind his back, stroking its neck along his microphone stand, pretending to make love to it, and setting it on fire with lighter fluid and praying to it. (This sort of guitar-focused showmanship, soon to become commonplace at rock concerts, was not unrelated to the wild stage antics of some rhythm & blues performers. Viewing the Hendrix segment of the documentary film *Monterey Pop*, it is clear that some people in the self-consciously hip and mainly middle-class white audience were shocked and therefore delighted by Hendrix's boldness.)

Jimi Hendrix's creative employment of feedback, distortion, and sound-manipulating devices like the wah-wah pedal and the fuzz box, coupled with his fondness for aggressive dissonance and incredibly loud volume all represented important additions to the musical techniques and materials available to guitarists. Hendrix was a sound sculptor who consciously explored the borderline between traditional conceptions of music and noise, a pursuit that links him in certain ways to composers exploring electronic sounds and media in the world of art music at around the same time. (One of the most famous examples of Hendrix's experimentation with electronically generated sound was his performance of the American national anthem at the Woodstock Festival in 1969. Between each phrase of the melody, Hendrix soared into an elaborate electronic fantasy, imitating "the rockets' red glare, the bombs bursting in air," and then landing precisely on the beginning of the next phrase, like a virtuoso jazz musician. This performance was widely perceived as an antiwar commentary, although Hendrix had himself served in the U.S. Army as a paratrooper.) All of these cited characteristics, along with any number of striking studio effects, may be heard

Jimi Hendrix in performance.

on the first album by the Experience, *Are You Experienced?* (1967), and particularly on its famous opening cut, "Purple Haze."

In one limited sense, "Purple Haze" is a strophic song with clear roots in blues-based melodic figures, harmonies, and chord progressions. But to regard the extraordinary instrumental introduction, the guitar solo between the second and third strophes, and the violently distorted instrumental conclusion all as mere effects added to a strophic tune is really to miss the point. In fact, it could be argued that the strophic tune serves as a mere scaffolding for the instrumental passages—but at the very least, the effects are equal in importance to the elements of the tune itself. The radical character and depth of Hendrix's contribution may be seen in the extent to which he requires us to readjust our thinking and terminology in an effort to describe appropriately what constitutes the real essence of his song. When we add in the impact of the lyrics, with their reference to "blowin' my mind" and lines like "'scuse me while I kiss the sky," it is easy to see why Hendrix became an iconic figure for the counterculture, as well as a role model for rock musicians.

It is emblematic of how far Hendrix had strayed from his rhythm & blues roots in music like "Purple Haze" that neither this song, nor any other released by Hendrix as a single, ever made a dent in the R&B charts. Hendrix was not a singles artist in any case, and his real kinship was with the new rock audience that viewed the record album as its essential source of musical enlightenment. In a sense, this approach made him a new kind of crossover artist. His audience rewarded him by elevating all of the five albums he designed for release in his all-too-brief lifetime into the Top 10.

We have noted that Hendrix's notoriety as a creative force first developed in England, and this was no accident. On the one hand, it was arguably difficult for an African American musician who neither fit into nor cared much about popular definitions of Black musical style to find acceptance in the American popular music scene. Furthermore, Hendrix's road to success in London was also paved by a thriving British pop culture scene that included boutiques, nightclubs, and youth movements such as the "mods"—who wore elaborate clothing reminiscent of centuries-old fashions and listened to American soul music—and the "rockers"—leather-jacketed rock 'n' roll fans. As we have seen, British youth seized upon American popular music with a passion during the 1960s, and a key part of this fascination was focused on the electric guitar.

Eric Clapton (b. 1945) was the most influential of the young British guitarists who emerged during the mid-1960s. Influenced by the blues recordings of Robert Johnson and B. B. King, he first attracted notice as a member of the Yardbirds, a band that had little pop success but served as a training ground for young guitarists, including Clapton, Jeff Beck, and Jimmy Page (later a member of Led Zeppelin). Clapton soon began to attract the adulation of young blues and R&B fans, largely as a result of his long, flowing, blues-based guitar solos. (The most common graffiti slogan in mid-1960s London was "Clapton is God," an index of his popularity.) From 1966 to 1968 Clapton played in a band called Cream, featuring the drummer Ginger Baker and bassist Jack Bruce. Cream, the first in a line of rock "power trios" that formed during the late 1960s and early 1970s, exerted a major influence on early heavy metal music (see Chapter 11). Their performances were more akin to avant-garde jazz than to pop music, using "songs" as quickly discardable pretexts for long, open-ended improvised solos. Cream took the United States by storm in the late 1960s, selling millions of LPs in the space of three years and placing two singles in the Top 10. Following the band's end, Clapton formed a short-lived "super group" with Stevie Winwood called Blind Faith.

Clapton's career as a solo artist started off strong in 1970 with the Number 18 single, "After Midnight." That same year saw the release of the album *Layla and Other Assorted Love Songs* by Derek and the Dominoes, a blues-rock band assembled by Clapton. Most of the tracks on the album, including the title song "Layla" (Number 10 pop, 1972), also featured the work of the brilliant guitarist Duane Allman (see Chapter 11). In 1974, Clapton returned to the pop charts with a cover version of Bob Marley's reggae song "I Shot the Sheriff" (see Chapter 12 for a comparison of these two versions of the song).

In the following decades, Clapton's work varied in quantity and quality, partly due to a longtime struggle with drug and alcohol addiction. He returned to the spotlight in

Listening Guide "CROSSROADS"

Written by Robert Johnson; performed by Cream; recorded 1968

Although it is difficult to summarize the work of a master improviser using a single recording, Cream's version of Robert Johnson's "Cross Road Blues," retitled "Crossroads" and recorded live at the Fillmore West in San Francisco, does convey a sense of the power and passion of Eric Clapton's guitar playing. Although this song represents the deep respect that many rock guitarists hold for Robert Johnson, the 1936 and 1968 recordings are in many ways light-years apart. In stylistic terms, Cream's performance is more indebted to postwar urban blues and R&B than to the Delta blues. Johnson's complex guitar accompaniment has been reduced to a single powerful riff, played in unison by the electric guitar and bass guitar, and projected by a veritable wall of amplifiers. Clearly, the recordings of Robert Johnson were an inspiration and not a direct musical model for young guitarists like Clapton.

Still, there is at least one similarity between the musical challenges faced by the two master guitarists, playing some thirty years apart: both men's performances are highly exposed, with Johnson playing solo and Clapton playing with only bass and drum set accompaniment. This

exposure has the effect of focusing attention on the guitarist and requiring that he play more or less constantly to keep the performance moving. Clapton's approach to this task involves not only the application of highly developed technical skills but also the use of electronic feedback, which allows him to sustain long notes and create flowing streams of shorter notes. The performance opens with Clapton singing a few strophes of Johnson's song before launching into an escalating series of improvised twelve-bar choruses. This is "busy" music, designed to showcase the virtuosity of the performers, and Baker and Bruce play constantly throughout, driving Clapton along to higher and higher emotional peaks. Although some rock critics regard Cream as an example of the self-indulgence and showiness of some late-1960s rock music, there can be no disputing that Clapton, Baker, and Bruce both upped the technical ante for rock musicians and paved the way for later guitar-focused bands. They also helped to establish the importance of the concert as a venue for experiencing rock music—hardcore fans argued that unless you heard Clapton play live, you hadn't really heard him at all.

BOX 10.4 ROOTS ROCK: CREEDENCE CLEARWATER REVIVAL

In 1969, a year when the influence of the counter-culture seemed to have reached new heights—as demonstrated by widespread domestic political turmoil on the one hand, and the Woodstock music festival's attraction of nearly half a million fans on the other—the pop charts were ruled by **Creedence Clearwater Revival**. This seems initially like another of pop music's great historical ironies. Creedence was a deliberately old-fashioned rock 'n' roll band, consisting of two guitarists, a bass player, and a drummer, which performed both original material and 1950s rock 'n' roll tunes in a musical style essentially untouched by the psychedelic era: no exotic instruments, no unusual or extended guitar

solos, no studio effects, and no self-conscious experimentation with novel harmonies, rhythms, or song forms. Creedence was one of the all-time great singles bands, turning out a spate of incredibly catchy, up-tempo two- to three-minute pop records that cut right through all the psychedelic haze and scored major hits for the group, one after the other. Given these songs' lack of pretension, they were as effective as live performance vehicles as they were as pop recordings. In addition, the albums put out by Creedence were all huge sellers, despite—or perhaps because of—the fact that they were essentially just old-fashioned collections of great singles.

Creedence Clearwater Revival restored to rock music a sense of its roots at precisely the point when the majority of important rock musicians seemed to be pushing the envelope of novel possibilities as far and as rapidly as they could. Creedence was in no sense a reactionary phenomenon, however; the group's choice of the word "revival" was an astute one. The many original songs in their repertoire, all written by lead singer and guitarist John Fogerty, possessed solid musical virtues, and several of them also reflected a decidedly up-to-date political awareness (such as "Bad Moon Rising" and "Fortunate Son") that nevertheless was not tied to any specific agenda (much like the awareness found in Bob Dylan's lyrics). In fact, Creedence's best songs have arguably stood the test of time better than a lot of other music from the 1960s that might have seemed much more adventurous and relevant at the time.

Creedence Clearwater Revival was the first widely successful "roots" rock 'n' roll band. Perhaps owing to their extraordinary popularity, many other

Creedence Clearwater Revival, with John Fogerty (far right), c. 1970.

roots artists have appeared as rock has continued to evolve. But Creedence set the standard in this realm, and it is one that has yet to be approached by anyone else.

1992 with a performance on MTV's *Unplugged* series and the subsequent release of the *Unplugged* live album and the single "Tears in Heaven" (Number 2, co-written with Will Jennings), which together garnered six Grammy awards. During the 1990s and 2000s, Clapton scored a scattering of pop hits (including "My Father's Eyes," which earned him a Grammy in 1999), and maintained his connection with the American blues tradition, recording a duet album with his long-time hero B. B. King in 2000. Although health issues have recently impacted him, Clapton celebrated his 70th birthday in 2015 with two sold-out performances at Madison Square Garden, followed by a seven-night residency at London's Royal Albert Hall, where he had debuted with the Yardbirds some fifty years earlier. The durability of the brilliant British guitarist, regularly ranked among the very greatest musicians in rock history, was confirmed in 2016 by the release of his twenty-third studio album, entitled *I Still Do*.

DURING THE SECOND half of the 1960s, the popular music favored by many young Americans took on a harder-edged, more emphatic tone. African American soul musicians re-emphasized the gritty, down-to-earth side of rhythm & blues and made its political dimensions more explicit. A new generation of musicians—raised on a diet of blues, R&B, urban folk music, and rock 'n' roll—helped to create rock, the loud, unruly, and increasingly profitable child of the music pioneered by Chuck Berry, Elvis Presley, and others in the 1950s.

In Chapter 11 we will follow rock music's transformation from an experimentalist, countercultural movement into a profit-making center of the American entertainment industry. It was during the 1970s that the tension between commercialism and authenticity that characterizes rock music right up to the present day arose in a clear form. In addition, the 1970s saw the first appearance of rock 'n' roll nostalgia, a sign both that the baby boomers were aging and that rock music had begun to develop a sense of its own history.

Key Terms

counterculture	sampled
countrypolitan	soul music

Key People

Aretha Franklin	the Doors	Jimi Hendrix
Bob Dylan	Eric Clapton	Patsy Cline
Burt Bacharach	Grace Slick	Paul Simon
Creedence Clearwater Revival	James Brown	Ray Charles
Dionne Warwick	Janis Joplin	Sam Cooke
	Jerry Garcia	

Review Questions

1. What is soul music? What are the essential elements of a song that make it "soul"? In other words, what are the "sounds of soul"?
2. Describe the Nashville Sound. What significant artists were involved in producing this sound?
3. Who was Bob Dylan? Why was his music so important in the development of the popular styles of the 1960s?
4. What artists came from the San Francisco rock music scene in the 1960s?
5. Describe the impact and importance of Jimi Hendrix and Eric Clapton.

The 1970s

Rock Music, Disco, and the Popular Mainstream

ONE OF THE MOST PERVASIVE STEREOTYPES ABOUT THE 1970s—FAMOUSLY captured in novelist Tom Wolfe's label "The Me Decade"—has to do with a shift in the values of young adults away from the communitarian, politically engaged ideals of the 1960s counterculture and toward more materialistic and conservative attitudes. While this generalization should be taken with a large grain of salt, it is undeniable that the early 1970s did see a kind of turning inward in American culture. The majority of Americans had grown weary of the military conflict in Vietnam, which drew to a close with the U.S. withdrawal from Saigon in 1975. Around the same time, popular attention focused increasingly on domestic problems, including the 1973 oil crisis and economic inflation, which threatened the financial security of millions of Americans. If the assassination of President Kennedy in 1963 had robbed many Americans of a certain political idealism, the Watergate hearings—viewed by millions on television—and the subsequent resignation of President Nixon in 1974 occasioned a growing cynicism about politics.

Meanwhile, the ideological polarization of the late 1960s continued unabated, and popular music remained a favorite target of conservative politicians and commentators, much as it had been during the jazz and rock 'n' roll "scares" of the 1920s and 1950s. It is interesting that in 1970, just as America was taking a conservative turn, hippie dress and slang, psychedelic imagery, and rock music had begun to enter the cultural mainstream of AM radio, network television, and Hollywood movies. (This suggests an analogy to the 1920s, when the Jazz Age was born in a period of strong political conservatism.) In the early 1970s the market for popular music became focused on two main categories of consumers: a new generation of teenagers, born in the late 1950s and early 1960s; and adults aged twenty-five to forty, who had grown up with rock 'n' roll and were looking for more mature (i.e., more conservative) material. Nostalgic fare such as the film *American Graffiti* (1973), the Broadway musical and film *Grease* (1972 and 1978, respectively), and the popular television series *Happy Days* used early rock 'n' roll—now nearly twenty years old—to evoke the so-called Golden Age of 1950s America, before the Kennedy assassination, the invasion of the Beatles, the rise of the counterculture, and the escalating social conflicts of the late 1960s.

If many Americans wished that the 1960s would just go away, others mourned the decade's passing. For rock fans, the end of the counterculture was poignantly symbolized by the deaths of Jimi Hendrix (1970), Janis Joplin (1970), and Jim Morrison (1971), and by the breakup of the Beatles, who, more than any other group, inspired the triumphs (and excesses) of rock music. On December 31, 1970, Paul McCartney filed the legal brief that was to formally dissolve the business partnership of the Beatles. For many rock fans, the demise of the "Fab Four" was incontrovertible proof that the 1960s were dead and gone. But this closing of an era certainly didn't mean that rock music itself was moribund. If in the late 1960s rock was the music of the counterculture, defined by its opposition to the mainstream of popular music, by the 1970s rock had helped to redefine the popular mainstream, becoming the primary source of profit for an expanding and ever more centralized entertainment industry.

During the 1970s the music industry reached new heights of consolidation. Six huge corporations—Columbia/CBS, Warner Communications, RCA Victor, Capitol-EMI, MCA, and United Artists-MGM—were responsible for over 80 percent of record sales in the United States by the end of the decade. Total profits from the sale of recorded music reached new levels—$2 billion in 1973 and $4 billion in 1978—in part owing to the increasing popularity of pre-recorded tapes. (The eight-track cartridge and cassette tape formats had initially been introduced during the mid-1960s, and their popularity expanded rapidly during the early 1970s. By 1975 sales of pre-recorded tapes accounted for almost one-third of all music sales in the United States.)

However, the music industry had also become increasingly risky. During the 1970s the industry came to depend on a relatively small number of million-selling ("platinum") LPs to turn a profit. A small number of "multiplatinum" superstars—including Paul McCartney, Elton John, and Stevie Wonder—were able to negotiate multimillion-dollar contracts with the major record companies. Unable to compete in this high-end market, small independent labels of the sort that had pioneered rock 'n' roll in the 1950s accounted for only about one out of every ten records sold in the early 1970s. (The energy crisis of 1973, which created a shortage of polyvinyl chloride, the petroleum-based substance from which tapes and discs were made, also helped to drive many small record companies out of business.) Yet, as we shall see in Chapter 12, the indies came back to exert an important musical influence in the second half of the decade, introducing new genres such as punk rock, funk, and reggae.

Like other big businesses, the record industry was increasingly impelled to present more choices (or at least to create the impression of choice) for its customers. This imperative led to the emergence of dozens of specialized types of popular music—middle of the road (MOR), easy listening, adult contemporary, singer-songwriters, country pop, soft soul, urban contemporary, funk, disco, reggae, oldies, and lots of subgenres of rock music, including country rock, folk rock, soft rock, hard rock, pop rock, heavy metal, southern rock, jazz rock, blues rock, Latin rock, art rock, glam rock, punk rock, and so on—each with its own constellation of stars and target audience. Record stores were organized in more complex patterns, with dozens of distinct categories listed on the labels of record bins.

In contrast, however, the Top 40 playlist format, based on nationally distributed, pre-taped sequences of hit songs, increasingly dominated the AM radio airwaves, resulting in a diminished range of choices, at least for AM radio listeners. By the mid-1970s most AM radio stations relied heavily on professional programming consultants, who provided lists of records that had done well in various parts of the country. Throughout the decade, these radio playlists grew more and more restricted, making it difficult for bands without the backing of a major label to break into the Top 40.

While some hard rock or progressive rock bands were able to get singles onto Top 40 radio, the primary medium for broadcasting rock music was FM radio. During the 1970s the number of FM radio stations in the United States increased by almost a thousand, and the popularity of FM—with its capability for high-fidelity stereo broadcasting—surpassed that of AM radio. The eclectic, free-form FM programming of the late 1960s—in which a DJ might follow a psychedelic rock record with a jazz or folk record—became restricted mainly to community- or college-based stations situated at the left end of the dial (where many such stations remain today). Seeking to boost their advertising revenues, many FM stations moved to a format called AOR (album-oriented rock), aimed at young white males aged thirteen to twenty-five. The AOR format featured hard rock bands such as Led Zeppelin and Deep Purple, and art rock bands like King Crimson; Emerson, Lake, and Palmer; and Pink Floyd. AOR generally excluded Black artists, who were featured on a radio format called urban contemporary. (The only exceptions to this rule seem to have been Marvin Gaye, Stevie Wonder, and Sly and the Family Stone, whose music transcended the boundary between soul and rock.) Although these changes led to greater economic efficiency, the definition of rock as white music and the increasingly strict split between Black and white popular music formats reflected the general conservatism of the radio business and of the music industry as a whole.

A survey of *Billboard* charts during the 1970s reveals a complex picture in which the various traditions discussed throughout this book—Tin Pan Alley, Black popular music (now called "soul"), and country music—continued to intermingle with one another, as well as with rock music. The commercial mainstream, as defined mostly by AM radio, featured a variety of styles, each designed to reach a mass audience. Among the major styles of the 1970s were:

- Singer-songwriters, a cross between the urban folk music of Peter, Paul and Mary and Bob Dylan and the commercial pop style of the Brill Building tune-smiths (e.g., Carole King, Paul Simon, James Taylor)[1]
- Pop rock, an upbeat variety of rock music (e.g., Elton John, Paul McCartney, Rod Stewart, Chicago, Peter Frampton)
- Soft soul, a slick variety of rhythm & blues, often with lush orchestral accompaniment (e.g., Barry White, the O'Jays, the Spinners, Al Green)
- Disco, a new form of dance music in the mid- to late 1970s characterized by elaborate studio production and an insistent beat (e.g., *Donna Summer*, *Chic*, the Village People, the Bee Gees)
- Country pop, a style of soft rock that is lightly tinged with country music influences (e.g., John Denver, Olivia Newton-John, Kenny Rogers, the early Eagles)
- Adult contemporary, an extension of the old crooner tradition, with varying degrees of rock influence (e.g., Barbra Streisand, Neil Diamond, Roberta Flack, the Carpenters)
- Bubblegum, cheerful songs aimed mainly at a preteen audience (e.g., the Jackson Five, the Osmonds)

It deserves attention that, among other significant mainstream trends of the decade, the 1970s also saw the beginnings of "oldies radio," which played hits of the 1950s and early 1960s. This development is a further instance of the nostalgic tendencies that characterized the period—tendencies also symbolized by the renewed popularity of Elvis Presley, who scored more than twenty Top 40 hits during the 1970s, and of Chuck Berry, who charted his first Number 1 pop record in 1972, the double-entendre song "My Ding-a-Ling."

It is worth taking a moment to consider what the mainstream environment of the 1970s meant for African American musicians, who had, after all, provided much of the inspiration for new forms of popular music. By the mid-1970s older soul and R&B stars such as Aretha Franklin and James Brown, though still popular among Black listeners, found it more difficult to penetrate the pop- and rock-dominated Top 40 charts. (However, both Franklin and Brown staged big comebacks during the 1980s.) Atlantic Records, a pioneer in the field of R&B and soul music, increasingly turned its attention to grooming and promoting white rock acts such as Led Zeppelin. Motown Records continued to score successes on Top 40 radio and the pop singles charts with artists such as Diana Ross (who left the Supremes to become a solo act in 1970), the "soul bubblegum" group Jackson Five, the Spinners, and Marvin Gaye. Nevertheless, Motown no longer enjoyed its former dominance of the crossover market.

---

1. Of course, performing artists can and did write their own material in all kinds of styles, but singer-songwriters were most frequently identified with the style indicated here.

Many of the Black performers featured on the AM radio airwaves and Top 40 charts specialized in the smooth, romantic, soft soul style previously discussed. One of the most commercially successful forms of soul music during the 1970s was the so-called Philadelphia Sound, produced by the team of Kenny Gamble and Leon Huff and performed by groups such as the O'Jays ("Love Train") and Harold Melvin and the Blue Notes ("If You Don't Know Me by Now"). These groups had a great deal of crossover success in the 1970s, regularly scoring Top 10 hits on the pop charts and the soul (the equivalent of the old R&B) charts. In retrospect, it does seem that much 1970s soul music was less assertive in its lyrics and its rhythms than its 1960s counterpart, and some observers have suggested that this was a strategic counterreaction on the part of radio stations and record companies to the racial violence that had erupted on the streets of Watts, Detroit, and Newark during the late 1960s.

Watching today's cable television advertisements for collections of "classic seventies hits," one could come to the conclusion that rock music had by 1970 pushed the old Tin Pan Alley songwriting tradition off the map entirely. That would be inaccurate, however, for the first Number 1 single of the 1970s was a throwback to the Brill Building era of the early 1960s (see Chapter 9), a sprightly and thoroughly escapist pop song entitled "Raindrops Keep Fallin' on My Head," performed by former country singer B. J. Thomas. This record—which stayed on the charts for nearly six months, in no small part owing to its being featured in the soundtrack of a popular film, *Butch Cassidy and the Sundance Kid*—was composed by Hal David and Burt Bacharach, third-generation Tin Pan Alley songwriters (see Box 10.1), and the song was shopped around to various other singers (including Bob Dylan!) before Thomas was chosen to record it. (Interestingly, the song was a crossover hit, with a cover version by the Black soul singer Barbara Mason reaching Number 38 on the R&B charts in 1970.) Several Number 1 singles of the 1970s—such as Roberta Flack's "Killing Me Softly with His Song" (1973), Debby Boone's "You Light Up My Life" (1977), Barbra Streisand's film theme "The Way We Were" (1973), and her romantic duet with Neil Diamond on "You Don't Bring Me Flowers" (1978)—attest to the continuing popularity of an approach to composing and performing songs that was directly derived from the Tin Pan Alley tradition. All of these recordings are representative of the "adult contemporary" style of 1970s pop. Although rock critics tend to regard most "soft rock" and "adult contemporary" as the musical equivalent of pond scum, there is no denying their mass popularity throughout the 1970s.

Singer-Songwriters: Carole King, Joni Mitchell, James Taylor

The career of *Carole King* (b. 1942) in the 1970s illustrates, perhaps better than any other example could, the central prominence of singer-songwriters during this period. King had been an important songwriter for more than a decade (in the 1960s, she wrote many hits with Gerry Goffin, her husband at that time; see Chapter 9) but was virtually unknown as a performer until she released the album *Tapestry*, from which the single "It's

Too Late" was drawn, in 1971. The astounding popularity of both the single and the album established Carole King as a major recording star. In the aftermath of King's success as a performer, relatively few songwriters were content to remain behind the scenes; it came to be expected that most pop songwriters would want to perform their own material—and, conversely, that most pop singers would want to record material that they had written themselves. Just the same, few singer-songwriters at this time were able to achieve the degree of success won by King. "It's Too Late" held the Number 1 spot for five weeks, and even its flip side, "I Feel the Earth Move"—also a cut from *Tapestry*—proved popular in its own right and was frequently played on the radio. (Both songs remained long-term favorites of King's fans.) *Tapestry* itself was an unprecedented hit. It was the Number 1 album for fifteen weeks, and remained on the charts for nearly six years.

Carole King was approaching the age of thirty when she recorded "It's Too Late." Clearly she was far from being the teenager who had written such songs as "Will You Love Me Tomorrow?" and "Take Good Care of My Baby" for a market consisting principally of other teenagers; King had matured, and her audience had matured along with her. "It's Too Late" is clearly an *adult* relationship song, written from the point of view of someone who has long left behind teenage crushes, insecurities, and desperate heartbreak. The singer describes the ending stage of a significant relationship with a feeling of sadness, but also with a mature philosophical acceptance that people can change and grow apart, and an understanding that this does not represent the end of the world for either of them.

The music of "It's Too Late" also reflects King's maturity. Her acoustic piano is the song's backbone, and it leads us through a sophisticated progression of relatively complex chords that portray a musical world far removed from the harmonic simplicity of early rock 'n' roll. When, toward the end of the substantial instrumental interlude preceding the final verse of the song, the saxophone enters to play a melody, the context evokes a kind of light jazz, rather than earlier rock. (The recording as a whole epitomizes the kind of sound that came to be known—fortunately or otherwise—as "soft rock.") Like the words of the song, the sound of its music was clearly geared toward an audience of maturing young adults. It is equally clear that such an audience was out there and more than ready to appreciate a recording like this one.

Joni Mitchell (b. 1943) began her career as a songwriter, placing hit songs like "The Circle Game" with Tom Rush and "Both Sides Now" with Judy Collins. She began recording on her own in 1968, and reached her greatest success in the 1970s with her unique brand of confessional songs. Perhaps her best-known album is *Blue* (1971). It consists of a cycle of songs about the complexities of love. The album is carefully designed to create a strong emotional focus, which is in turn clearly related to the autobiography of the singer herself. In some ways *Blue* is a culmination of the tendency inherent in the folk-rock and singer-songwriter genres toward self-revelation. Even the most optimistic songs on the album—"All I Want," "My Old Man," and "Carey"—have a bittersweet flavor. Some—such as "Little Green," about a child given up for adoption, and the concluding track "The Last Time I Saw Richard"—are delicate yet powerful testimonials to the shared human experience of emotional loss. The sound of the LP is spare and beautiful, focusing on Mitchell's voice and acoustic guitar. This is a case in which studio technology is used to create a feeling of simplicity and immediacy.

James Taylor (b. 1948) has had perhaps the most successful long-running career of the 1970s era singer-songwriters. He had great initial success with his 1970 album *Sweet Baby James*, which produced hit singles, including the Number 3 hit "Fire and Rain." The album had great influence on folk rockers and even country stars; Garth Brooks named his first child "Taylor" in honor of his favorite songwriter. Taylor's attractive tenor voice, nostalgic subject matter, and finger-picked guitar style have all contributed to his success; and his longevity as a recording artist was confirmed by the release in 2015 of *Before This World*, Taylor's first Number 1 pop album, more than forty-five years after *Sweet Baby James* entered the charts.

Country Music and the Pop Mainstream

During the 1970s, country and western music—now generally just called "country"—became a huge business, reaching out to young and middle-class listeners while at the same time reinforcing its traditional Southern and white working-class audience base. In 1974 the Grand Ole Opry moved from the run-down Nashville theater where it had been broadcasting since 1941 into a multimillion-dollar facility, complete with a 110-acre theme park called "Opryland." The national weekly magazines *Newsweek* and *Time* ran sympathetic cover stories on country stars Loretta Lynn and Merle Haggard (see Box 11.1); three country music shows were featured on network television in the early 1970s (*The Glen Campbell Goodtime Hour*, *The Johnny Cash Show*, and *Hee-Haw*); and eventually Hollywood films such as *Nashville* (1975) and *Coal Miner's Daughter* (1980, a depiction of Loretta Lynn's life story) helped to broaden country's audience and ameliorate long-standing stereotypes of country fans as "rednecks." The generally conservative mood of the country—reflected in Richard Nixon's landslide victory over George McGovern in the 1972 presidential election—helped to reinforce country's popularity among the American middle class.

The country-pop crossover of the 1970s—an updated version of the success enjoyed by Patti Page and Eddy Arnold during the 1950s (see Chapter 7)—was accomplished by a new generation of musicians, many of whom had developed their careers in the fields of pop, urban folk music, and rock 'n' roll. During the mid-1970s a number of records reached the Number 1 position on both the pop and the country charts—Charlie Rich's ballad "The Most Beautiful Girl" (1973); John Denver's "Thank God I'm a Country Boy" (1975); Glen Campbell's rendition of "Rhinestone Cowboy" (1975); and the truckers' anthem "Convoy," recorded by C. W. McCall in 1975 in the midst of nationwide fuel shortages and a Teamsters Union strike. The last record helped to spread the popularity of citizens band (CB) radio, part of a more general "redneck chic" movement in which millions of middle-class Americans adopted Southern working-class cultural practices.

These "country pop" stars came from diverse musical and social backgrounds. *Glen Campbell* was born in Arkansas in 1936, and died of Alzheimer's disease in 2017.

He worked with western swing bands in the Southwest as a teenager and moved to Los Angeles in 1958, where he developed a career as a studio session guitarist and vocalist. Starting in the late 1960s he had a string of crossover hits on the country and pop charts, including "Gentle on My Mind" (1967), "By the Time I Get to Phoenix" (1967), and "Wichita Lineman" (1968). In 1969 he began hosting his own network television series, and his genial, laid-back style helped to expand his national popularity. *Charlie Rich* (1932–1995), the "Silver Fox," was also born in Arkansas. Rich was a talented jazz and blues pianist whose career started as part of the stable of rockabilly performers at Sam Phillips's Sun Records. By the 1960s he had switched to the pop-oriented country-politan style, and he scored a series of Number 1 crossover hits during the mid-1970s, winning the Country Music Association's Entertainer of the Year award in 1974. At the following year's CMA awards ceremony, Rich announced the country-tinged pop singer John Denver as his successor for Entertainer of the Year and demonstrated his distaste by setting fire to the envelope. Many in the traditional audience for country music despised Denver and his pop-oriented hit records even more than Charlie Rich did.

The dichotomy between pop performers who capitalized on the popularity of country music and established country musicians who moved toward the pop mainstream is well illustrated by the careers of two female recording stars of the 1970s: *Olivia Newton-John* and *Dolly Parton*. Newton-John was born in England in 1948 and grew up in Australia. During the mid-1970s she scored a series of Top 10 country pop crossover hits—"Let Me Be There," "If You Love Me (Let Me Know)," and "Have You Never Been Mellow"—and in 1974 won the Country Music Association's award for Female Singer of the Year. After the awards ceremony, a group of veteran country musicians met to form a new association—the Association of Country Entertainers—dedicated to resisting the perceived invasion of pop singers like Olivia Newton-John and John Denver, who were eager to capitalize on country's burgeoning popularity but ambivalent about identifying themselves too exclusively with the genre. The suspicions of hard-core country fans seemed justified when in the late 1970s Newton-John abandoned country music to jump on the oldies rock 'n' roll bandwagon, appearing in the film *Grease* and on its bestselling soundtrack album (1978). In fairness, however, it must be noted that pop opportunists such as Newton-John and Denver played a major role in widening the national audience for country music during the 1970s.

At about the same time that Newton-John was moving out of country music, Dolly Parton, an established country music star, was making her first major inroads into pop. Born in the hill country of Tennessee in 1946, Parton began recording at the age of eleven, moved to Nashville in 1964, and built her career through regular appearances on country music radio and television programs, including the Grand Ole Opry. Parton's flexible soprano voice, songwriting ability, and carefully crafted image as a cheerful sex symbol combined to gain her a loyal following among country fans. (Parton succeeded Olivia Newton-John as the CMA's Female Singer of the Year in 1975 and 1976, and later on, in the 1980s, was the first female country musician to host her own national television series.) Although she scored a series of Number 1 hits on the country charts during this period, it was not until the late 1970s that Parton was able to get a record into the

BOX 11.1   **HARDCORE COUNTRY: MERLE HAGGARD AND THE BAKERSFIELD SOUND**

"Hardcore country" singer Merle Haggard (left) and Kris Kristofferson on stage together in 2011.

During the 1970s, as country music became a multimillion-dollar business dominated by various blends of country and pop music, some musicians returned to the straightforward, emotionally direct approach of postwar honky-tonk musicians like Hank Williams and Ernest Tubb (see Chapter 7). The "back to the basics" spirit of so-called hardcore country is perhaps best captured in the recordings of **Merle Haggard** (1937–2016), born near Bakersfield, California. The son of migrants from Oklahoma (the "Okies" whose lives formed the basis for John Steinbeck's novel *The Grapes of Wrath*), Haggard wandered from place to place as a child, spending time in a series of juvenile homes and reform schools. When as a nineteen-year-old he began serving three years for burglary in San Quentin Prison, it did not appear that Merle Haggard had much of a future.

However, Haggard's talents as a musician and songwriter and a newfound gift for being in the right place at the right time eventually bailed him out. In the early 1960s, after his release, Haggard worked odd jobs around Bakersfield, playing at night in local honky-tonks. Bakersfield was at precisely this moment emerging as the center of a distinctive style of country music, an outgrowth of the rockabilly style of the 1950s (see Chapter 8). Defined by a spare, twangy sound, electric instrumentation, and a strong backbeat, the "Bakersfield Sound" stood in direct opposition to the slickness of much Nashville country music. Popularized by musicians like Haggard and Buck Owens, this Bakersfield country became one of the most influential country genres of the late 1960s, reviving the spirit of postwar honky-tonk and setting the stage for subsequent movements such as country rock and outlaw country.

In 1965 Haggard scored a Top 10 country hit with the song "(My Friends Are Gonna Be) Strangers," which established the name for his band (the

(continued)

> **BOX 11.1 HARDCORE COUNTRY: MERLE HAGGARD AND THE BAKERSFIELD SOUND** (*continued*)
>
> Strangers) and led to a recording contract with Capitol Records. In the late 1960s Haggard capitalized on his experience as a convict to write songs about life outside the law (e.g., "The Fugitive," a Number 1 country hit in 1967). An important aspect of Haggard's work as a songwriter is his commitment to chronicling the lives and attitudes of everyday people in gritty, realistic language. The central character of many Haggard songs is a white male worker, struggling to achieve the comfort and security of middle-class life. Hardworking, beer-drinking, patriotic, and politically conservative, this character's voice is perhaps most famously heard in Haggard's 1969 recording of his song "Okie from Muskogee," which reached Number 1 on the country charts and Number 41 on the pop
>
> charts and garnered him an invitation to Richard Nixon's White House.
>
> Although this song alienated many liberal listeners who had previously lauded Merle Haggard as a "poet of the common man" and therefore expected him to share their own political sentiments, there is no denying that Haggard's songs reflected the real concerns and aspirations of millions of Americans, particularly migrants from the South who were struggling to support their families through the shifting economic climate of the 1970s. Songs like "If We Make It Through December" (Number 1 country, Number 28 pop in 1973) captured the real-life dilemmas of working-class Americans struggling to create secure lives for their families in a hostile world.

Top 40 pop charts. (Her rendition of "Here You Come Again"—written by veteran Brill Building composers Barry Mann and Cynthia Weil—reached Number 3 on the pop and Number 1 on the country charts in 1977.) Between them, Olivia Newton-John and Dolly Parton illustrate the extremes of the 1970s' country–pop continuum—one a pop performer seeking to capitalize on the rising popularity of country music, and the other a country singer seeking to maintain her loyal following in that market while extending her appeal to a wider audience.

John Denver (1943–1997), born John Henry Deutschendorf, got his start in the 1960s as part of the urban folk movement (as a member of the Chad Mitchell Trio), and the sound of the acoustic guitar remained a prime element of many of the records he made as a solo artist in the 1970s. Several of his early hits, including his first two Top 10 records ("Take Me Home, Country Roads" and "Rocky Mountain High," from 1971 and 1972, respectively) were "country" records more in terms of their subject matter than in terms of their actual musical style, which might best be described as an urban folk style flavored with some pop elements. By the time he achieved his third Number 1 hit with "Thank God I'm a Country Boy" in 1975, however, Denver was obviously going all-out to portray himself as a country artist musically as well as thematically. In this he was obviously successful, insofar as he was a significant presence on the country charts as well as on the pop charts in the mid-1970s.

Throughout the 1970s it was fashionable in certain hip circles to praise the virtues and alleged simplicity of rural life. Country-flavored pop and rock music was popular during this period, as is demonstrated by much of the recorded output of the Eagles. Obviously a recording like John Denver's "Thank God I'm a Country Boy" both partook

John Denver on stage in the mid-1970s.

of and benefited from this trend, even if John Denver himself was generally not regarded as being particularly hip by the standards of the day.

"Thank God I'm a Country Boy" is a cut taken from Denver's live album *An Evening with John Denver*, which documented his concert performances in Los Angeles during the summer of 1974. Although live albums were commonplace by this time, live singles were still relatively uncommon; however, the sense of immediacy and spontaneity so essential to the character and appeal of this recording obviously results directly from the presence of an actual, enthusiastic concert audience. The opening, in which Denver sings unaccompanied except for the rhythmic hand clapping of his audience, captures something of the ambience of a real country dance party. The rural flavor of Denver's vocal of course adds to this impression; it should be noted that Denver came by this flavor naturally, having been raised in the South and the Southwest. When the instruments enter on the second verse of the song, the fiddle-led ensemble directly evokes the general sound and feeling of the old-time acoustic country string bands. The lyrics also make continual reference to the fiddle as a marker of country culture, and the second verse even mentions directly the classic country fiddle tune "Sally Goodin."

A cynic might call a recording like "Thank God I'm a Country Boy" an example of "country lite," and certainly there is no trace of hardship in the lyrics' description of "life on a farm," where things are "kinda laid back" and "life ain't nothin' but a funny, funny riddle"; the joyful music and singing also lie quite a distance from the "high lonesome" sound of much early country and bluegrass music. Still, even if this record is regarded as the musical equivalent of a city dweller's Sunday drive into the country (and we should remember that it was recorded in Los Angeles), John Denver and his accompanying musicians make the drive an exhilarating one, and there is no trace of condescension either in their deliberate evocation of country style or in the singer's exuberant delivery of the song's message.

COUNTRY-ROCK: THE EAGLES

While country music was increasingly emulating the sounds and styles of mainstream pop, a group of rock musicians were attracted to performing country-styled music. Among the leaders of this movement was singer/songwriter Gram Parsons, a Boston-bred folksinger who became attracted to the honky-tonk music of the 1950s. Parsons joined the Byrds to record the highly influential 1968 album, *Sweetheart of the Rodeo*, consisting mostly of country covers. He would then form the Flying Buritto Brothers with Byrds' bass player Chris Hillman and multi-instrumentalist Bernie Leadon. Leadon would in turn form one of the most influential of all the country-rock bands, the Eagles, which eventually went beyond its countryish roots.

California in the 1970s retained the central position in American popular culture that it had attained during the 1960s, and if the Beach Boys epitomized the culture of Southern California in the earlier decade, then the *Eagles* were the group that most obviously inherited that distinction. Indeed, the close association of this Los Angeles–based group with the Golden State was so well established at the time of their peak popularity (1975–1980) that it lent particular authority to their ambitious saga of "Hotel California"—the million-selling single from the extraordinarily successful album of the same name (which today has sold in excess of 16 million copies).

The Eagles serve as an excellent case in point to illustrate the accelerating ascendancy in importance of albums over singles during the 1970s. When the Eagles issued their first compilation of singles in album form, *Eagles/Their Greatest Hits, 1971–1975*, the album achieved sales far beyond those of all its hit singles taken together; it was, in fact, the first recording to be certified by the Recording Industry Association of America (RIAA) as a million-selling ("platinum") album, and it went on to sell more than 29 million copies.

Starting out in 1971 with feet firmly planted in what was called "country rock," the Eagles had moved from laid-back tunes like "Take It Easy" and "Peaceful Easy Feeling," and songs that evoked traditional western imagery like "Desperado" and "Tequila Sunrise" to harder-hitting material like "One of These Nights" by 1975. "Hotel California" was the fourth of their five Number 1 singles, and it introduced a new, complex, poetic tone into the Eagles' work. Indeed, of all the many songs under consideration here, "Hotel California" sounds closest to an ambitious late 1960s record. This association is due to several factors. Its length, its minor-key harmonies, and its rather unusual overall shape (with extended guitar solos at the *end* of the record) all contribute to the effect, but surely it is the highly metaphorical lyrics that establish the most obvious kinship with the songwriting trends of the 1960s.

The tone of "Hotel California," however, is pure 1970s. The hotel is peopled by a disillusioned group of trendsetters, who maintain superficial relationships. The female protagonist is portrayed as valuing material possessions ("Her mind is Tiffany twisted. She got the Mercedes bends") over relationships ("She got a lot of pretty, pretty boys, that she calls friends"). When the visitor asks the hotel captain to bring up some wine, he is told, "We haven't had that spirit here since 1969," a pun on the word "spirit" (meaning feeling or attitude as well as an alcoholic drink). Finally, as the last verse ends, the fleeing visitor is told by the "night man" at the door that "you can check out any time you like, but you can never leave." As if to illustrate all the implications of this memorable line, the song does not proceed to the now-expected chorus ("Welcome to the Hotel California," whose pop-friendly major-key music assumes an increasingly ironic edge as the record progresses) nor does it fade out quickly. Instead, "you can never leave" become the final words we hear, and the Eagles launch into lengthy guitar solos—over the chords of the verses, not those of the chorus—as if to underline our "stuck" situation and eliminate any sound that remotely suggests "welcoming." California, that sun-blessed beacon to the generation of peace and love in the 1960s, has here become a sinister trap for those who have no place left to go.

Rock Comes of Age

During the 1970s rock music, the brash child of rock 'n' roll, diffused into every corner of the music industry. Influenced by the Beatles, Bob Dylan, Brian Wilson, and Jimi Hendrix, many progressive rock musicians had come to view themselves as *Artists* and their recordings as works of *Art*. While this attitude occasionally led to self-indulgence, some musicians used the medium of the long-playing record album to create innovative and challenging work. At the same time, the music industry moved to co-opt the appeal of rock music, creating genres like pop rock and **soft rock** that were designed to appeal to the widest possible demographic and were promoted on Top 40 radio and television. Musicians as diverse as Led Zeppelin, Stevie Wonder, Elton John, Carole King, Pink Floyd, Paul Simon, Neil Diamond, Crosby, Stills, and Nash, the Rolling Stones, Frank Zappa and the Mothers of Invention, and Santana were promoted by record companies under the general heading of rock music. Even Frank Sinatra, unabashedly hostile to rock music, tried his hand at a Beatles song or two.

SOFT/POP ROCK

By the 1970s the British Invasion of the 1960s had turned into a long-running "British occupation" of the American pop charts as numerous artists from across the Atlantic achieved hit singles and albums in the United States on a regular basis. No artist illustrates this trend better than *Elton John* (b. 1947 as Reginald Kenneth Dwight), named in Joel Whitburn's *Top Pop* books as "the #1 pop artist of the 70s" in America. "Crocodile Rock," which was released late in 1972 and topped the charts in February 1973, was the first of six Number 1 hits for John during this decade. The song was a featured single on his album *Don't Shoot Me I'm Only the Piano Player*, the second of seven consecutive million-selling Number 1 albums for John during this same period.

Like Carole King and Stevie Wonder, Elton John was a keyboard-playing singer-songwriter; the sound of John's piano is essential to the character of "Crocodile Rock"

Elton John in 1975 on his "Captain Fantastic" Tour.

and to many of his other hits. Lyricist Bernie Taupin was John's songwriting partner not only for "Crocodile Rock" but for all of John's major hits of the 1970s.

"Crocodile Rock" (1972) reveals how thoroughly Elton John had assimilated the basic sounds and feelings of American rock 'n' roll while still incorporating his own personal touch. The song capitalizes in a savvy way on the nostalgia that seemed to be sweeping the pop music landscape at the time of its release. In late 1972 Chuck Berry and Ricky Nelson were both back in the Top 10 for the first time in many years, while Elvis Presley was enjoying the last Top 10 hit of his career ("Burning Love"), which was also his biggest hit in a long time. This was also the period when aging baby boomers began to flock to rock 'n' roll "revival" shows in which artists from the 1950s and early 1960s (frequently vocal groups with old names but lots of new faces) appeared to play their original, now "classic," hits. (Note the sly reference to the old Bill Haley hit "Rock Around the Clock" in the opening verse of "Crocodile Rock.")

Not insignificantly, just a year before "Crocodile Rock" hit Number 1, the singer-songwriter Don McLean made an enormous impact with his own Number 1 hit "American Pie"—a record whose subject matter was nostalgia for the early years of rock 'n' roll and the conviction that something of great innocence and promise had been lost amid the tumult and violence that marked the end of the 1960s.

Like "American Pie," "Crocodile Rock" deals with nostalgia and the sense of loss, but in a much more lighthearted fashion, emphasizing the happy memories ("I remember when rock was young, me and Susie had so much fun") over the unhappy present ("But the years went by and rock just died"); in fact, the second verse ends up affirming the persistence of remembered joy ("But they'll never kill the thrills we've got"), and the final verse is simply a return back to the first, "When rock was young." Musically, the flavor is clearly that of an upbeat teenage dance song, and even though there never actually was a famous rock 'n' roll dance called the "crocodile," the song may be deliberately evoking the memory of other "animal" dances, like the monkey. The chord progressions of "Crocodile Rock" obviously recall those of early rock 'n' roll songs without duplicating them exactly, and an element of novelty is added in the wordless part of the chorus with the kazoo-like sound of John's Farfisa organ.

No single record could be cited to represent an artist's entire career when the artist's musical output has been as substantial and as varied as that of Elton John. But "Crocodile Rock" can surely serve as a representation of John's characteristic good humor, and of the way in which he typically is able to link commercial smarts with musical intelligence. John was a veritable hit-making machine through the 1970s, from his first top ten U.S. hit "Your Song," written and performed in the soft singer-songwriter style then popular, and he thereafter alternated slower ballads ("Daniel"; "Candle in the Wind") with harder rocking numbers like "Saturday Night's Alright for Fighting." As of 2013, he had sold over 300 million records worldwide. John remains a strong concert draw and has extended his writing beyond his own recordings to score musicals for stage and screen.

AFRICAN AMERICAN MUSICIANS AND ROCK

There were some important exceptions to the general popular appeal of rock music. Record sales in Black communities, as reflected in the *Billboard* soul charts during the 1970s, do not suggest much interest in rock music. (The Rolling Stones managed to get only one of their singles onto the *Billboard* Top 40 soul chart during the decade, and multiplatinum rock acts such as Led Zeppelin, Deep Purple, and Pink Floyd made no dent whatsoever.) Although the Monterey and Woodstock rock festivals had featured performances by African American artists, the promise of rock music as a zone of interracial interaction seemed to have largely vanished by the early 1970s. Many of the white rock stars who had formed their styles through exposure to earlier styles of blues and R&B seemed to have little interest in contemporary Black popular music of the 1970s. As one critic put it in 1971, "Black musicians are now implicitly regarded as precursors who, having taught the white men all they know, must gradually recede into the distance" (Morse 1971, 108).

While there was no clear successor to Jimi Hendrix in the decade following Woodstock—that is, no single artist who could champion the presence of Black musicians in rock music—we can point to a number of interestingly diverse interactions between soul music and rock. Several prominent Black musicians—Sly Stone, Stevie Wonder, Marvin Gaye, and George Clinton—were able to connect long-standing aspects of African American musical traditions with elements from rock, including the notion of the musician as an artistic mastermind and of the LP record album as a work of art. In addition to their intrinsic importance, the varied work of these musicians paved the way for later artists such as Prince and Michael Jackson.

Stevie Wonder (b. 1950) was perhaps the most commercially successful of this group to cross over into mainstream rock while still maintaining a strong African American sound. He was a highly successful singer and songwriter during his teenage years with Motown in the 1960s. But he established a new benchmark of achievement for a pop music figure in 1971 when, at the age of twenty-one, he negotiated a new contract with Motown that guaranteed him full artistic control over all aspects of his music. As a master of all trades—singer, songwriter, multi-instrumentalist, arranger, and producer—Wonder was able to use this control to his utmost advantage, and he made all his subsequent recordings his own to a degree that has rarely been approached by other artists in the field. We can hear the results of this control on an incredibly tight cut like "Superstition," on which Wonder plays most of the instruments (synchronizing the performance by **overdubbing** several tracks on the recording tape) to accompany his own singing of his own composition. "Superstition" was the first featured single from the album *Talking Book*, which also achieved tremendous popularity.

"Superstition" blends elements borrowed from different aspects of African American musical traditions and adds its own distinctive flavorings to the mix. The use of a repeated syncopated riff over an unchanging chord as the song's hook—a riff heard right from the outset, and which persists throughout all three verse sections of the song—obviously reflects the influence of James Brown's brand of late 1960s soul music (see Chapter 10). This also gives the record a much harder edge than was typical of the soft soul style of the era. Wonder gives this music his own inflection through his employment of the electric keyboard instrument called the Clavinet—a novelty at the time—to play the riff. (Throughout the early 1970s, Wonder was a pioneer in the use of new electronic instruments, including **synthesizers**, in pop music.)

The chorus section ("When you believe . . .") introduces chord changes that are suggestive of blues influence; taken as a whole, the large verse-chorus unit of the song may be heard as an expanded variant of the twelve-bar blues in terms of both phrase structure and harmonic vocabulary. (The persistence and flexibility of blues traditions in American popular music remains a source of wonder.) This blues coloring in "Superstition" is another factor that differentiates this recording from one representative of soft soul, which only rarely would reflect such obvious blues elements. The lyrics, however, take a thoroughly modern, sophisticated stand ("Superstition ain't the way"). As a result, in "Superstition," Stevie Wonder successfully fused something old and something blue with the borrowed and the new to create an irresistible pop hit.

THE RISE OF THE ROCK CONCERT AND THE CONCEPT ALBUM

Early rock festivals such as Monterey (1967) and Woodstock (1969), regarded as the crowning moment of the 1960s counterculture, had by the early 1970s mutated into highly profitable mass-audience concerts that were held in civic centers and sports arenas across the country. In 1973 the British hard rock group Led Zeppelin (see the Listening Guide in this chapter) toured the United States, breaking the world record for live concert attendance set by the Beatles during their tours of the mid-1960s. A whole series of bands that sprang up in the early 1970s (such as Styx, Journey, Kansas, REO Speedwagon, ZZ Top, Rush, and others) tailored their performances to the concert context—touring the country with elaborate light shows, spectacular sets, and powerful amplification systems, all of which were transported in caravans of semi trucks—creating the phenomenon that has come to be known as "arena rock." For most rock fans, the live concert was the peak of the musical experience—you hadn't really heard Led Zeppelin, it was said, until you'd heard and seen them live (and spent a little money on a poster or T-shirt imprinted with the band's image). Of course, the relationship between rock stars and their devotees at these concerts was anything but intimate. Nonetheless, the sheer enormity, sound, and spectacle of a rock concert helped to create a visceral sensation of belonging to a larger community, a temporary city formed by fans.

The 1960s recordings such as the Beach Boys' *Pet Sounds* (1966), the Beatles' *Sgt. Pepper's Lonely Hearts Club Band* (1967), and the Who's "rock opera" *Tommy* (1969) established the idea of the record album as a thematically and aesthetically unified work instead of simply a collection of otherwise unrelated cuts. By the early 1970s the twelve-inch high-fidelity LP had become the primary medium for rock music.

What makes a rock album more than a mere collection of singles? Let's start with a basic fact about the medium: its capacity. A twelve-inch disc, played at 33⅓ rpm, could accommodate more than forty minutes of music, with over twenty minutes per side. In the 1950s and early 1960s little creative use was made of this additional real estate—most rock 'n' roll era LPs consist of a few hit singles interspersed with a lot of less carefully produced filler. During the second half of the 1960s rock musicians began to treat the time span of the LP as a total entity, a field of potentiality akin to a painter's canvas. They also began to put more effort into *all* of the songs on an album, and to think of creative ways of linking songs together to create an overall progression of peaks and valleys. (Of course, old habits die hard, and most progressive rock albums still used songs, each approximately three to six minutes in length, as basic building blocks.)

The development of studio technology also encouraged musicians to experiment with novel techniques. High-fidelity stereo sound, heard over good speakers or headphones, placed the listener in the middle of the music (and the music in the middle of the listener!) and allowed sound sources to be "moved around." The advent of sixteen-, twenty-four-, and thirty-two-track recording consoles and electronic sound devices allowed musicians—and the record producers and studio engineers with whom they worked—to create complex aural textures and construct a given track on an LP over a period of time, adding and subtracting (or "punching in" and "punching out") individual instruments and voices. Innovations in the electronic synthesis of sound led to instruments like the Mellotron, which could imitate the sound of a string orchestra both in the studio and at live performances.

The musical response to the opportunities provided by these technological changes varied widely. Some rock bands became famous for spending many months (and tons of money) in the studio to create a single rock "masterpiece." A few multitalented musicians, such as Stevie Wonder and Edgar Winter, took advantage of multitracking to play all of the instruments on a given track. Other musicians reacted against the dependence on studio technology, recording their albums the old-fashioned way, with little overdubbing. (As we shall see, when punk rock arose in the late 1970s as a reaction against the pretentiousness of studio-bound progressive rock, musicians insisted on doing recordings in one take to create the sense of a live performance experience.) Studio technology could even be used to create the impression that it was not being used, a technique used in recording many folk rock albums.

Although the ideas of creating some sort of continuity between the individual tracks and creating an inclusive structure that could provide the listener with a sense of progression were shared widely, rock musicians took a range of approaches to achieving these aims. One way to get a sense of this range is to listen to a handful of classic rock LPs from the early 1970s.

Some rock albums are centered on a fictitious character whose identity is analogous to that of one or more musicians in the band. Perhaps the best-known example of this strategy is *The Rise and Fall of Ziggy Stardust and the Spiders from Mars* (1972), the creation of "glam rock" pioneer **David Bowie** (1947–2016). (Glam—short for glamour—rock emphasized the elaborate, showy personal appearance and costuming of its practitioners.) In this case, the coherence of the album derives more from the imaginative and magnetic persona of the singer and his character than from the music itself. As Bowie put it, "I packaged a totally credible plastic rock star," an alien who comes to visit earth and becomes first a superstar and finally a "Rock 'n' Roll Suicide," perishing under the weight of his own fame. Much of the LP's effect was connected with the striking image of Bowie playing the role of Ziggy, decked out in futuristic clothing and heavy facial makeup, a sensitive rocker, sexy in an androgynous, cosmic way. The *Ziggy Stardust* concert tour was a theatrical tour de force, with special lighting effects and spectacular costumes, that set the standard for later rock acts ranging from "new wave" bands like the Talking Heads (see Chapter 12) to hard rockers like Kiss. Bowie's unique ability to create quasi-fictional stage personae and change them with every new album was a precedent for the image manipulation of 1980s stars like Michael Jackson, Prince, and Madonna, and has also exerted a significant influence on the LGBTQ artists of the twenty-first century.

Dark Side of the Moon (1973), an album by the British rock band **Pink Floyd**, is based on the theme of madness and the things that drive us to it—time, work, money, war,

David Bowie performing as Ziggy Stardust, 1973.

and fear of death. The LP opens with the sound of a beating heart, followed by that of a ticking clock, a typewriter, a cash register, gunfire, and the voices of members of Pink Floyd's stage crew discussing their own experiences with insanity. The album's feeling of unity is related to its languid, carefully measured pace—most of the songs are slow to midtempo—as well as its musical texture and mood. In terms of style, the progression moves from spacey, neo-psychedelic sound textures to jazz- and blues-influenced songs and then back to psychedelia. The sound of the record, produced by Alan Parsons, is complex but clear, and interesting use is made of sound effects, as in the song "Money," in which sampled sounds of clinking coins and cash registers are treated as rhythmic

BOX 11.2 **ALBUM ART**

If the rock LP was a container for music, it was also an art object in its own right. LP dust jackets often featured a printed version of the lyrics and a range of highly imaginative designs. Covers conveyed a

Andy Warhol's cover for the Rolling Stones' album *Sticky Fingers*, 1971.

lot, not only about a rock group's physical appearance, but also about their aesthetic aims and personality. Some showed concert photos of the artists at work; Jimi Hendrix's *Band of Gypsys* (1970) and Deep Purple's *Made in Japan* (1973) were bestselling examples. Others revealed some aspect of the musicians' private lives; the eponymous LP *Crosby, Stills & Nash* (1969) has a cover photo of the three folk rock musicians lounging on an old sofa on the front porch of a house, while the inside of Marvin Gaye's *What's Going On* (1971) contains a photo collage of his family. The cover art for Joni Mitchell's album *Blue* (1971) reflects the introspective mood of her songs. The sexuality of rock stars was often emphasized in these designs, as on the Rolling Stones' quadruple-platinum LP *Sticky Fingers* (1971), which featured a close-up photograph of the crotch of a pair of blue jeans, complete with a working zipper! Tapping into the sexual fantasies of the young male audience for rock music, other covers, particularly of hard rock and heavy metal albums, featured scantily clad women in suggestive poses. Alternative models of sexuality also found their way onto album covers, with the most

Brain Salad Surgery cover, 1973, designed by H. R. Giger.

notorious example being David Bowie's *Diamond Dogs* (1975), which featured an androgynous Bowie-canine creature with its genitals exposed. (The cover created a furor and was soon yanked from the shelves of record stores and replaced with a tamer alternative.)

Record companies often gave dust-jacket artists wide latitude to invent visual analogs to the music inside. The cover of *Brain Salad Surgery* (1973), a Top 10 LP by the art rock band Emerson, Lake, and Palmer, was designed by the Swiss artist H. R. Giger, who went on to create the nightmarish creature in the film *Alien*. The Latin rock band Santana's second LP, *Abraxas* (1970), presented a colorful psychedelic rendering of the fusion of European and African cultural influences. Even reissues of oldies from the 1950s and 1960s were given imaginative treatments, as on the Drifters' *Greatest Recordings* album cover (1971), which took an old publicity photo and turned it into a psychedelic image. Finally, some album designs featured a minimalist approach, with the prototypical example being *The Beatles* (1968), whose stark white cover earned it the nickname "The White Album."

accompaniment. (This achievement is particularly impressive when we recall that 1973 was before the advent of digital recording techniques.)

If there was ever an antidote to the notion that popular music must be cheerful and upbeat in order to be successful, *Dark Side of the Moon* is it. This meditation on insanity stayed on the *Billboard* Top LPs charts for over fourteen years, longer than any other LP in history, and has sold an estimated 45 million copies worldwide. In recent years, various mythologies have grown up around *Dark Side of the Moon*. For example, it is claimed that the album can be synchronized with the 1939 film *The Wizard of Oz*. Many people maintain that if you start the album up after the MGM lion's third roar you will discover some amazing synchronicities. (For example, the song "Brain Damage" begins playing just as the Scarecrow starts to sing "If I Only Had a Brain.") Whatever the merit of these claims, it is clear that Pink Floyd's album continues to exert a powerful, if somewhat dark, fascination upon millions of rock fans.

A final example of the theme album is **Marvin Gaye**'s bestselling LP *What's Going On* (1971), which fused soul music and gospel influence with the political impetus of progressive rock. The basic unifying theme of this album is social justice. The title track, inspired by the return of Gaye's brother from Vietnam, is a plea for nonviolence, released during the peak of antiwar protests in the United States. Other songs focus on ecology, the welfare of children, and the suffering of poor people in America's urban centers. Gaye (1939–1984) cowrote the songs and produced the album himself, supporting his voice—overdubbed to sound like an entire vocal group—with layers of percussion, strings, and horns. Once again, the producer's consideration of the overall sound texture of the album had a great deal to do with its aesthetic effect and commercial success.

Motown owner Berry Gordy initially didn't want to release *What's Going On* because he thought it had no commercial potential. This was a rare case of misjudgment on Gordy's part; the album reached Number 2 on the LP charts and generated three Number 1 singles on the soul charts, all of which crossed over to the pop Top 10: the title song, "Mercy Mercy Me (The Ecology)," and "Inner City Blues (Make Me Wanna Holler)." Two other tracks, "Wholy Holy" and "Save the Children," inspired hit cover versions by Aretha Franklin and Diana Ross. But the significance of this album, and of Marvin Gaye's commitment to a socially responsible aesthetic vision, surpasses any measure of commercial success. Along with Stevie Wonder and Sly Stone, Marvin Gaye showed that soul and R&B albums could exhibit artistic coherence that transcended the three-minute single; bridged the divides among AM Top 40, FM album-oriented radio, and the soul music market; and held open the possibility that popular music might still have something to do with social change, as well as money-making and artistic self-expression.

A strategy that was fairly unusual in rock music was the adoption of elements of large-scale structure from European classical music. The live album *Pictures at an Exhibition* (1971), recorded by the art rock band Emerson, Lake, and Palmer, adopts its main themes and some of its structural elements from a suite of piano pieces by the Russian composer Modest Mussorgsky (1839–1881). This was a canny choice, since Mussorgsky's composition—inspired by a walk through an art gallery—consists of a sequence of accessible, reasonably short, easily digestible "paintings," a parallel with the song format of much popular music. Some sections of the LP are reorchestrations of the original score (making prominent use of Keith Emerson's virtuosity on organ and synthesizer); others are improvisations on the borrowed materials; and still others are new songs by the band, musing on ideas in the music. The album concludes with "Nutrocker," a rock 'n' roll version of Tchaikovsky's *Nutcracker Suite*.

In the end, however, rock music is less centrally concerned with large-scale architectural structures than with the immediate experience of musical texture, rhythmic momentum, and emotional intensity. Many of the most effective rock albums do not have an overarching structural logic, a story to tell, or a single organizing image, but rather find their unity in a visceral cohesion of musical style, texture, and attitude. *Exile on Main Street* (1972), now often cited as the best album ever recorded by the Rolling Stones, received decidedly mixed reviews when it first came out because of its impenetrable sound and the inaudibility of its lyrics. The cover art for the LP—a photographic collage of freaks and misfits—represented a new trend that moved away from standard photos of artists or groups (see Box 11.2). It seemed designed to repel many in the Stones' loyal audience, who had followed the band since their early days as the slightly nasty counterpart of the Beatles. In *Exile on Main Street* we have an album—actually a double album, containing two LPs and eighteen songs—that is held together by its texture (dense, dark, guitar-based rock 'n' roll); its rough, unpolished studio sound (reminiscent on some tracks of Elvis Presley's early work with Sun Records); and its bad attitude (personified by the sneering, mumbling Mick Jagger). The material is strongly oriented toward the Stones' musical roots, as it consists mainly of blues-based rockers like "Rocks Off," "Shake Your Hips," and "Tumbling Dice," with a few examples of country and folk music influence ("Sweet Virginia" and "Sweet Black Angel").

Exile on Main Street was recorded in the basement of guitarist Keith Richards's home in France—where the Stones were living in tax exile at the time—and Jagger's voice is purposefully buried in the mix, under the gritty guitars, bass, drums, and the occasional horn section. (Producer Jimmy Miller was largely responsible for creating the LP's cohesive sound palette.) The overall impression is one of bleakness and desolation, a reflection of the Stones' mental state at the time. The band's abuse of drugs and alcohol was so intense that members have since wondered aloud how they ever got the record made. *Exile on Main Street* is at once an apotheosis of the Stones' image as bad boys and a tip of the hat to the influences that formed their style, including urban blues, soul, and country music.

LED ZEPPELIN AND HEAVY METAL

By the early 1970s the British hard rock band Led Zeppelin, formed in London in 1968, was well on its way to becoming the most profitable and influential act in rock music. "Zep," as its fans called it, was made up of Jimmy Page, a brilliant guitarist who had honed his skills as Eric Clapton's successor in a pioneering British band called the Yardbirds; John Bonham, who established the thunderous sound of heavy metal drumming; John Paul Jones, who provided the band's solid bottom, doubling on electric bass and organ; and Robert Plant, whose agile high tenor voice established the norm for subsequent heavy metal singers. Zeppelin's sledgehammer style of guitar-focused rock music drew on various influences, including urban blues, San Francisco psychedelia, and the virtuoso guitar playing of Jimi Hendrix. Although Led Zeppelin is usually associated with the heavy textures and extremely loud volume of their hard rock repertoire, their recordings also included another important stream—an interest in folk music, and particularly the traditions of the British Isles.

Robert Plant (left) and Jimmy Page of Led Zeppelin, c. 1970

Listening Guide   "STAIRWAY TO HEAVEN"

Music and lyrics by Jimmy Page and Robert Plant, performed by Led Zeppelin (recorded 1971)

"Stairway to Heaven" is Led Zeppelin's most famous recording, and it reflects certain unique features of the band's musical approach, as well as its position vis-à-vis the commercial mainstream of pop music. To begin with, the song presents us with a fascinating marketing strategy that at first glance is quite perverse, but is actually quite brilliant. Although "Stairway to Heaven" was the most frequently requested song on FM radio during the 1970s, the eight-minute track was never released as a single. In other words, to own a copy of "Stairway to Heaven," you had to buy the album. Of course, that task could prove difficult for the uninitiated consumer, since the band insisted on an album cover that bore neither the name of the album, nor the name of the band, nor even the name of the record company. (Atlantic Records was horrified by this design, but the band held the master tapes for the album hostage, and the record company had no choice but to go along with their strategy.) Driven in part by the popularity of "Stairway to Heaven," the LP *Led Zeppelin IV* reached the Number 2 position on the *Billboard* Top LP charts and stayed on the charts for five years, eventually selling 23 million copies.

"Stairway to Heaven" has been called the anthem of heavy metal music, a genre that developed out of hard rock in the 1970s and achieved mainstream success in the 1980s (see Chapter 13; other examples of early proto-metal bands include Deep Purple and Black Sabbath). What accounts for this recording's tremendous commercial success and its ability to ignite the imaginations and inspire the loyalty of millions of fans? To begin with, "Stairway" skillfully juxtaposes two dimensions of Led Zeppelin's musical persona: the bone-crushing rock band, known for inspiring riots and dismantling hotel rooms, and the folk music aficionados steeped in a reverence for ancient English and Celtic mythology. Although these two sensibilities might seem diametrically opposed, the twin musical threads of sonic aggression and acoustic intimacy run through the entire history of heavy metal. (Most heavy metal albums include at least one "ballad," a term that in this context usually implies the use of acoustic guitar.) For many fans in Zeppelin's predominantly young, male audience, the combination of rock physicality and folk mysticism in "Stairway to Heaven" created something

akin to a sacred experience. The somewhat inscrutable song text, composed by singer Robert Plant during a rehearsal, is also an important source of the recording's attraction. Both Plant and Jimmy Page were at the time exploring the writings of the noted English mystic Aleister Crowley—into whose house Page eventually moved—and reading scholarly tomes like *Magic Arts in Celtic Britain*, which Plant later said influenced the lyrics for "Stairway." The text's references to mythological beings—the May Queen and the Piper—and rural images—paths and roads, rings of smoke through the forest, a songbird by a brook, the whispering wind—help to create a growing mood of mystery and enchantment.

Although the basic building blocks of "Stairway to Heaven" are straightforward four- and eight-bar phrases, the overall arrangement is quite complex in formal terms (see the following chart). The song contains three main sections. The first section alternates two eight-measure phrases, which we call A and B. The basic form of this section is thus ABABAA' (with the last subsection being an abridged version of A). The second section reverses the order of the phrases and inserts a brief, one-measure-long linking phrase (which we call X). The form of this section is thus BAXBAXB. The third section, which takes up almost half of the total eight minutes of recording time, introduces a new (though closely related) chord progression and melody, which we call C.[2] The first part of the third section has the form CXBCX. After a one-measure pause, this is followed by an instrumental fanfare that propels us into Jimmy Page's guitar solo. Robert Plant's voice then re-enters, and there is an extended vocal section that uses the harmonies from phrase C. The arrangement concludes with an instrumental phrase, which slows down and becomes much quieter in the last two measures. The track concludes quietly, with Robert Plant repeating the key line of the text: "And she's buying a stairway to heaven." The arrangement of "Stairway to Heaven" is constructed to create a continuous escalation in density, volume, and speed. (The tempo increases from around seventy-two beats per minute at the opening of the recording to

---

2. Throughout "Stairway to Heaven," the harmonies circle around a set of closely related chords, including A minor, C major, and F major, giving the performance an additional sense of continuity.

eighty-four beats per minute (bpm) at the beginning of the third section, peaking at around 98 bpm during the guitar solo. This substantial, though gradual, increase in speed is crucial to the overall impact of the recording.)

If "Stairway" seems complex in purely structural terms, this may be because the logic of its organization is fundamentally emotional and metaphoric. The recording can itself be seen as an analog of the heavenly stairway, springing from the rural, mythological past (symbolized by acoustic instruments); soaring on jet-powered wings of metal; and finally coming to rest on a high, peaceful plateau. Similarly, the outer cover of the original album juxtaposes the sepia image of a peasant with that of a modern skyscraper rising over the formerly rustic landscape. The inner jacket portrays a mysterious hooded figure standing atop an icy peak with a staff and a lantern, looking down at a bell-bottomed seeker of knowledge who struggles to reach the top. Also included inside the album's dust jacket are the lyrics to "Stairway to Heaven" and a set of mystical symbols, or runes, one of which inspired the informal name for the album, "ZOSO." In seeking to understand what a recording like "Stairway" meant to its fans, the analysis of musical form must be coupled with a consideration of its other expressive dimensions, including the song text and the graphic design of the album on which it appeared.

LISTENING GUIDE	"STAIRWAY TO HEAVEN"		
TIME	**FORM**	**LYRIC**	**DESCRIPTIVE COMMENTS**
Section 1			
0:00	A (8 measures)		Six-string acoustic guitar; double-tracked recorder (flute) duet enters in measure 5; slow tempo (72 beats per minute)
0:26	B (8 measures)		Guitar and recorders continue
0:53	A (8 measures)	*There's a lady . . .*	Vocal enters
		When she gets there . . .	
1:21	B (4 measures)	*Ooo . . .*	
		And she's buying . . .	
1:33	A (8 measures)	*There's a sign . . .*	
		In a tree . . .	
2:01	A' (4 measures)		Six-string guitar and recorders continue
Section 2			
2:14	Instrumental		Twelve-string guitar, soft electric guitar, electric piano; intensity increases, tempo slightly faster (80 bpm)
	B (8 measures)	*Oooo, It makes . . .*	
		Oooo, It makes . . .	
2:38	A (8 measures)	*There's a feeling . . .*	
		In my thoughts . . .	
	X (1 measure)		One-measure instrumental linking section; electric guitar becomes more dominant

(*continued*)

Listening Guide "STAIRWAY TO HEAVEN" (*continued*)

TIME	FORM	LYRIC	DESCRIPTIVE COMMENTS
3:07	B (8 measures)	*Oooo, It makes . . .*	Texture thickens, volume and tempo increase slightly
		Oooo, really makes . . .	
3:29	A (8 measures)	*And it's whispered . . .*	
		And a new day . . .	
	X (1 measure)		Instrumental linking section
3:57	B (8 measures)		Slight crescendo, slight tempo increase; drums enter at end, leading us into next section

Section 3

TIME	FORM	LYRIC	DESCRIPTIVE COMMENTS
4:19	C (8 measures)	*If there's a bustle . . .*	New minor chord progression; electric guitar, twelve-string acoustic guitar, plus electric bass and drum set; tempo faster (84 bpm)
		Yes there are . . .	
	X (1 measure)		Instrumental linking section
4:45	B (8 measures)	*And it makes . . .*	
5:07	C (8 measures)	*Your head . . .*	
		Dear lady . . .	
	X (2 measures)		Instrumental linking section, plus one-measure pause
5:35	D (8 measures)		Instrumental fanfare using chords from C; tempo speeds up, leading us into next section
5:56	Guitar solo (20 measures)		Chord pattern continues; tempo faster (ca. 98 bpm); multitracked guitar plays supporting pattern under solo (last 8 measures)
6:44	C (18 measures)	*And as we . . .*	
		There walks . . .	
		How everything . . . The tune . . .	
		To be a rock . . .	
7:27	C (8 measures)		Instrumental section; tempo slows down, intensity decreases
7:46	B (3 measures)	*And she's buying . . .*	Solo voice (tempo rubato)

SANTANA: A LATIN VOICE IN ROCK

If rock was quintessentially defined for many listeners by white bands like Led Zeppelin, Pink Floyd, and the Rolling Stones, the San Francisco–based group Santana reveals a nascent trend within rock music toward multicultural engagement. The band was led by Mexican guitarist **Carlos Santana** (b. 1947), who began his musical career playing guitar in the nightspots of Tijuana. As a kid he was exposed to the sounds of rock 'n' roll, including the music of Mexican American musicians such as Ritchie Valens, whose version of the folk song "La Bamba" had broken into the *Billboard* Top 40 in early 1959 (see Chapter 8). Santana moved to San Francisco at age fifteen, where he was exposed to other forms of music that were to play a profound part in shaping the style and sensibility of his own music: jazz, particularly the experimental music of John Coltrane and Miles Davis; salsa, a New York–based style of Latin dance music strongly rooted in Afro-Cuban traditions; and, in the late 1960s, San Francisco rock, including artists as diverse as Janis Joplin, Jimi Hendrix, and Sly and the Family Stone (see Chapter 10).

Carlos Santana, c. early 1980s.

Listening Guide "OYE COMO VA"

Music and lyrics by Tito Puente, performed by Santana (recorded 1971)

We will take a closer look at the LP version of "Oye Como Va," since it allows the band to stretch out a bit and best illustrates certain features of Santana's style. To appreciate what goes into a recording like "Oye Como Va," we must consider not only the instrumentation—essentially a guitar-bass-keyboards-drums rock band plus Latin percussion—but also the recording's "mix," that is, the precise tonal quality, balancing, and positioning of sounds recorded on various tracks in the studio. (*Abraxas* was coproduced by the band and Fred Catero, whose straightforward approach to studio production can also be heard on early LPs of the jazz rock band Chicago.) Santana's instantly recognizable sound focused on the fluid lead guitar style of Carlos Santana and the churning grooves created by the drummer (Mike Shrieve), the bass player (Dave Brown), and two Latin percussionists (Jose Areas and Mike Carabello). The rhythmic complexity of "Oye Como Va"—essentially an electrified version of an Afro-Cuban dance rhythm—required that the recording be mixed to create a "clean" stereo image so that the various instruments and interlocking rhythm patterns could be clearly heard. Listening over headphones or good speakers, you should be able to hear where the various instruments are positioned in the mix. The electric bass is in the middle, acting as the band's rhythmic anchor; the guitar and keyboards are placed slightly to the left and right of center, respectively, and are thus kept out of each other's way; and the percussion instruments (including the *güiro*, a ridged gourd scraped with a small stick; timbales, a set of two drums played with flexible sticks; *agogo*, a metal bell; and congas, hand-played drums) are positioned even farther out to the left and right.

The track opens with the electric bass and Hammond B-3 organ—one of the most characteristic sounds of 1970s rock music—playing the interlocking pattern that functions as the core of the groove throughout the recording. (In a salsa band, this two-measure pattern would be called the *tumbao*.) In the background we hear someone say "Sabor!" ("Flavor!"), and at the end of the fourth measure the timbales and *agogo* enter, bringing in the rest of the instruments at the beginning of the fifth measure. At this point all of the interlocking repeated patterns—bass, organ, bell, scraper, and congas—have been established. The signature sound of Carlos Santana's guitar enters in the ninth measure,

as he plays a two-measure melodic theme four times. This is followed by the first of four sections in which the whole band plays a single rhythmic and melodic pattern in unison (in the following chart we call these sections B and B', respectively). Throughout the track, the rhythm functions as the heart of the music. As if to remind us of the importance of this deep connection with Afro-Latin tradition, all of the other layers are periodically stripped away, laying bare the pulsing heart of the music.

At the most general level, we can make a few observations about how the four minutes and seventeen seconds of "Oye Como Va" are organized. The whole arrangement is 136 measures in length; out of that total only sixteen measures (about 12 percent) are devoted to singing, which in this context seems almost a pretext for the instrumental music. In general, song lyrics are less important than the musical groove and texture in most of Santana's early recordings. (The lyric for this song consists of a short phrase in Spanish, repeated over and over, in which the singer boasts about the potency of his "groove" to a brown-skinned female dancer.)

Taking away the other obviously precomposed elements—the guitar melody (phrase A), the unison figures played by the whole band (B, B', and the call-and-response figure after the first guitar solo), and the other interlude sections—we find that nearly half of the recording (sixty-six measures) is devoted to improvised solos by the guitar and organ. The other elements of the arrangement—including the dramatic group crescendos that lead into the last two solos—seem designed to support improvisation. In essence, then, "Oye Como Va" is a vehicle for instrumental solos, more like a jazz performance than a Top 40 pop song. (Of course, it is precisely the solos that Columbia Records chose to cut when they edited the track for AM radio airplay.) In particular, Carlos Santana's solos on "Oye Como Va" provide us with a good example of the work of a talented rock improviser. Rather than playing torrents of fast notes to show off his guitar technique (which was and remains considerable), Santana uses the electric guitar's ability to sustain notes for long periods of time to create long, flowing melodic lines that gradually rise in intensity, lifting the whole band with him. In live performance, of course, Santana and other instrumental soloists could stretch out for much more than four and a half minutes. If the soft side of rock often worked within the restricted time format imposed by Top 40 radio, progressive rock bands such as Santana, the Allman Brothers, and the Grateful Dead kept alive the notion of extended, open-ended performance, an important part of the legacy of the San Francisco rock scene of the late 1960s (see Chapter 10).

TIME	FORM	LYRIC	DESCRIPTIVE COMMENTS
0:00	Groove (8 measures)		The basic rhythm is established on organ, electric bass, and (from the fifth measure) percussion
0:16	A (8 measures)	|	The guitar states a two-measure melodic phrase four times (with minor embellishments)
0:31	B (4 measures)	|	A unison figure, played by the whole band
0:38	C (8 measures)	*Oye como va...*	Vocals (two four-measure phrases)
0:53	B′ (2 measures)		Instrumental; unison figure appears again (first half only)
0:57	Guitar solo (20 measures)		Extended solo by Carlos Santana
1:34	Interlude (6 measures)		Call-and-response exchange between guitar and band
1:45	Groove (4 measures)		Stripped down to the basics again
1:53	Interlude (8 measures)		Suddenly quieter; organ and guitar play chord pattern; gradual crescendo
2:08	Organ solo (22 measures)		
2:48	Groove (4 measures)		One more time!
2:56	B′ (2 measures)		Unison figure again (first half only)
3:00	C (8 measures)	*Oye como va...*	Vocals (two four-measure phrases)
3:14	Interlude (4 measures)		Instrumental; suddenly quieter, then crescendo
3:22	Guitar solo (24 measures)	|	Another solo by Carlos Santana
4:06	B (4 measures)		Unison figure again, functioning as a tag

LISTENING GUIDE | "OYE COMO VA"

Around 1968 Santana put together a group of middle- and working-class Latino, Black, and white musicians from varied cultural backgrounds. The band's eponymous first album, *Santana*, released in 1969, reached Number 4 on the Top LPs chart, in large part due to the band's spectacular performance in the film and soundtrack LP of *Woodstock*.

In 1970 Columbia Records released Santana's second LP, which firmly established both the band itself and a strong Latin American substream within rock music. *Abraxas* held the Number 1 position on the LP charts for six weeks, spent a total of eighty-eight weeks on the charts, and sold over 4 million copies in the United States alone. The album also produced two Top 40 singles: "Black Magic Woman" (Number 4 pop in 1970), originally recorded by the English blues rock band Fleetwood Mac; and the infectious "Oye Como Va" (Number 13 pop, Number 32 R&B in 1971), composed by the New York–based Latin percussionist and dance music king Tito Puente. These two singles, which had a great deal to do with the success of the album, were shorter versions of the tracks found on the LP. (This was a typical strategy, given the duration of tracks on many rock LPs.) Tying blues, rock, and salsa together in one multicultural package, *Abraxas* also featured less commercial tracks such as "Gypsy Queen" (composed by jazz guitarist Gabor Szabo) and the impressionistic "Singing Winds, Crying Beasts."

SOUTHERN ROCK

At the end of Chapter 10 we discussed the "roots rock" band Credence Clearwater Revival, who, despite their strategic use of Southern accents and imagery, hailed from northern California. The late 1960s and early 1970s also saw the rise to national popularity of bands actually from the American South, playing regional variants on the basic rock band formula. The most important of these groups, the ***Allman Brothers Band***, helped to reconnect the generative power of the blues to both the mainstream of rock music and the open-ended instrumental improvisations of modern jazz and San Francisco "jam bands" such as the Grateful Dead.

The Florida-born brothers Duane and Gregg Allman began gigging with various bands in the early 1960s. In 1969 they joined with guitarist Dickey Betts, bassist Berry Oakley, and drummers Butch Trucks and Jai Johanny (Jaimoe) Johanson to form the Allman Brothers Band, featuring Duane on lead guitar and Gregg on organ, piano, and lead vocals. A sought-after session musician both before and during his tenure with the band, Duane Allman recorded with soul music stars such as Aretha Franklin and Wilson Pickett, and he collaborated with Eric Clapton on the celebrated 1970 album *Layla and Other Assorted Love Songs*. Working out of Macon, Georgia, the Allman Brothers Band achieved their artistic and commercial breakthrough in 1971 with the release of *At Fillmore East*, often cited by critics as one of the best live rock albums ever made.

The Allman Brothers Band's performances in the leading concert venues of the day, their use of rock music technology, and their celebrity status marked them as contemporary artists. At the same time, their style was rooted in Southern folk music, including songs, rhythms, and textures derived from African American tradition; the use of instruments such as harmonica (or "blues harp"); and playing techniques like "bottleneck guitar," in which the severed neck of a bottle—or a substitute made of plastic or metal—is slid over a finger on the guitarist's left hand, allowing him to glide smoothly over the individual tones of the scale and thus create long, swooping melodic lines. The blues were central to the Allman Brothers' sound and sensibility, and "Statesboro Blues," composed by the Georgia-born blues musician Blind Willie McTell (1898–1959), became one of their signature tunes, often used to open concerts. At the same time, the *At Fillmore East* album also features relatively lengthy, open-ended improvisations on original compositions such as "In Memory of Elizabeth Reed" and "Whipping Post." *At Fillmore East* established Duane Allman's stature as a rock guitarist; in 2003, *Rolling*

Stone magazine ranked him Number 2 on their list of the one hundred greatest guitarists of all time, second only to Jimi Hendrix.

For the first half of the 1970s, and despite the tragic deaths of Duane (1971) and bassist Berry Oakley (1972) in eerily similar motorcycle accidents, the Allman Brothers Band was among the most influential rock groups in America. Their incorporation of elements of blues, rhythm & blues, and jazz (and, increasingly, country music) and their powerful, extended live "jams" helped to alter the norms of concert performance. While other rock groups, such as the Grateful Dead and Cream, were known for their onstage jamming, when the Allman Brothers stretched a song out for a half hour or more, they were capable of achieving peaks of collective musical creativity that surpassed any band of their era. At the same time, they established the genre of **Southern rock**, paving the way for other bands from the Deep South, including the Marshall Tucker Band, Lynyrd Skynyrd, and the Charlie Daniels Band.

Before moving on, it is important that we address the political implications of a genre that defined itself as proudly—and often defiantly—"Southern." In expressing this pride, many Southern rock bands, intentionally or unintentionally, presented a view of the South that was, at best, insensitive to African American history and, at worst, simply racist. Such sentiments could be seen in everything from the use of Confederate iconography in album packaging and stage sets to a general conflation of the idea of the rock rebel with that of the Southern rebel to specific song lyrics. Perhaps the most famous instance of this association is a musical exchange between the Southern rock band Lynyrd Skynyrd and Canadian-born rock musician Neil Young, whose song "Southern Man" (Number 4 in 1970) depicts the racist treatment of Blacks in the American South ("I saw cotton and I saw Blacks, tall white mansions and little shacks. Southern Man, when will you pay them back?"). Lynyrd Skynyrd's "Sweet Home Alabama" (Number 8, 1974), was a direct rejoinder to this charge:

> *Well I heard mister Young sing about her* [Alabama]
> *Well, I heard ol' Neil put her down*
> *Well, I hope Neil Young will remember*
> *A Southern man don't need him around, anyhow*

Although Lynyrd Skynyrd's lead singer, Ronnie Van Zant, has argued that the lyrics of "Sweet Home Alabama" are more ambiguous than is generally recognized, there can be little doubt about the association of much Southern rock with whiteness and conservative social values. At the same time, it is equally true that, musicologically speaking, Southern rock is built almost entirely on a foundation of African American tradition, from the blues and soul apparent in its lead vocals and musical forms to the gospel influence on its backup vocals and the impact of jazz on its harmonized guitar lines and long, improvised solos.

In fact, the Allman Brothers Band—arguably the definitive representative of the Southern rock genre—openly declared their indebtedness to and admiration for Black musicians as varied in approach as Willie Dixon, Ray Charles, and jazz great John Coltrane. And, as previously mentioned, before forming the band Duane Allman had recorded extensively with many of the major African American soul artists of the era, as had drummer Jai Johanny Johanson, who was himself African American. Ultimately, the simple fact is that when it comes to race, Southern rock contains many contradictions. Regardless of how—or even if—one chooses to resolve those contradictions, one thing is clear: the stereotypical association of certain genres of music with certain social values and attitudes (and certain "kinds of people") rarely tells the whole story.

JAZZ ROCK

While Southern rock was unified by its shared regional roots, **jazz rock** was a more loosely defined category that included commercially successful collaborations between jazz and rock musicians—such as the groups Blood, Sweat & Tears and Chicago—and a variety of hybrid styles that melded rock aesthetics and instrumentation with the harmonic and rhythmic complexity and improvisational virtuosity of contemporary jazz. Some of these groups and their recordings are typically mentioned in the context of jazz history, whereas others are more common to discussions of the development of rock music.

The most influential and, for many listeners, startling example of a fusion between jazz and rock music was Miles Davis's album *Bitches Brew*, released in 1970. *Miles Davis* (1926– 1991) began his career in the late 1940s playing trumpet with modern jazz pioneers such as Charlie Parker and for much of the 1950s and 1960s played a critical role in the evolution of jazz—leading a variety of bands, pushing the evolution of the music along at critical junctures, and helping to bring to prominence younger musicians who themselves became leading innovators of modern jazz (including the brilliant saxophonist John Coltrane).

Somewhat parallel to the reaction of traditionalist folk music fans to Bob Dylan's embrace of rock music in the mid-1960s, many jazz aficionados were confounded and even alienated by *Bitches Brew*, which combined the exploratory spirit of avant-garde jazz with sonic textures and funky grooves inspired by the music of Jimi Hendrix and Sly Stone. The double album made a vivid visual impression, designed around a surrealistic Afrocentric painting by German artist Mati Klarwein, whose work adorned Santana's *Abraxas* album as well (also released in 1970). To make *Bitches Brew*, Miles Davis assembled a roster of thirteen musicians—including the pianists Joe Zawinul and Chick Corea, saxophonist Wayne Shorter, guitarist John McLaughlin, and the Brazilian percussionist Airto Moreira—most of whom went on to play major roles in the evolution of jazz rock, performing in bands such as Weather Report, Mahavishnu Orchestra, and Return to Forever. The ensemble for *Bitches Brew* was larger than the norm for contemporary jazz groups or rock bands and was centered on a rhythm section of two drummers, two keyboardists, and two bassists (electric and acoustic), who together created shifting rhythmic grooves and textures.

The musicians were brought together for three days in the studio and were given only minimal instructions: an indication of the tempo that Davis wanted, a musical gesture or melody, and sometimes impressionistic suggestions of the desired mood or tone. As Davis himself described the process:

> I would direct, like a conductor, once we started to play, and I would either write down some music for somebody or would tell him to play different things I was hearing, as the music was growing, coming together. While the music was developing I would hear something that I thought could be extended or cut back. . . . After it had developed to a certain point, I would tell a certain musician to come in and play something else.[3]

---

3. See "The making of *Bitches Brew*," by Paul Tingen, *Jazz Times* 31 (May 2001): 49.

Davis worked closely on *Bitches Brew* with record producer and composer Teo Macero, who kept the tape running continuously throughout the recording sessions, and worked with the trumpeter to shape the final product by cutting, splicing, and rearranging the music and adding post-production studio effects. (It has been suggested that Macero's decades-long creative relationship with Miles Davis was not unlike producer George Martin's work with the Beatles.) This fluid process—akin to "free jazz" improvisation and the open-ended jamming of the Grateful Dead, but with two "authors" firmly in charge of the final recorded product—yielded a recording that didn't fit either the jazz or the rock paradigms of the time, and that still sounds fresh and challenging today. Extraordinarily, for a double album that contained more than one hundred minutes of highly experimental music, *Bitches Brew* reached Number 4 on the R&B album chart and Number 35 on the pop album chart, and was Miles Davis's first recording to be certified a platinum record (indicating sales of half a million units).

Of the various bands that inhabited the rock-oriented, AM radio–friendly side of jazz rock in the early 1970s, **Chicago** (who changed their name from Chicago Transit Authority in response to threatened legal action by the real CTA) achieved the greatest long-term popularity and commercial success. In 2002, Chicago's hit singles were assembled together on a two-disc set, and the album debuted in the Top 40, giving the band the distinction of having had chart albums in five consecutive decades.

Today Chicago is best known for anthemic love songs such as "If You Leave Me Now" (1976), "Hard to Say I'm Sorry" (1982), and "Look Away" (1988), all of which reached Number 1 on both the pop and the adult contemporary charts. But in their early days the band specialized in a harder-edged style that fused the guitar-centered sound of rock with a three-piece horn section that could play R&B-style riffs and improvise in the manner of jazz musicians. They honed their chops as the house band at Los Angeles's Whisky a Go Go nightclub, following in the footsteps of the Doors. In 1968 they were heard by Jimi Hendrix, who, on the strength of guitarist Terry Kath's playing, hired them to open for him and Janis Joplin on a European tour. The band was signed by Columbia Records in 1969, and their first album (*Chicago Transit Authority*) reached the Top 20, without the benefit of a hit single.

"25 or 6 to 4" (Number 4 pop in 1970), was the highest-charting track from Chicago's second album (*Chicago II*) and is a good example of their earlier, more rock-oriented approach. "25 or 6 to 4" is part of a twelve-song suite entitled *Ballet for a Girl from Buchannon*, an indication of the band's artistic ambitions that was very much in tune with rock albums of the time. The track opens with guitarist Terry Kath playing the song's signature riff, a series of five descending chords. (The muffled, distorted sound of the chords was created with the use of a foot-operated electronic device called a fuzz box.) This chord sequence is repeated with the addition of drums, followed by the entry of the horn section, which plays a tightly organized sequence of unison and contrapuntal melodic lines that is dominated by the trombone sound of James Pankow. The song consists of a series of verses sung by bassist Peter Cetera (the voice on many of Chicago's later hit singles) and a chorus sung in harmony. The sound and attitude of this recording place it clearly within the category of rock music; whether this music is more accurately described as jazz rock or as "rock music with horns" is in the end an academic matter.

It has been argued that the rock sound of Chicago's early recordings is primarily attributable to the presence of the guitarist and singer Terry Kath, who died of an apparently accidental self-inflicted gunshot wound in 1978. Kath was a talented musician, admired by contemporaries such as Hendrix and Eric Clapton, and his solo on the album version of "25 or 6 to 4" provides an example of his virtuosic technique, his command of scales not commonly used by rock guitarists, and his adept use of a device called a wah-wah pedal, which approximates the acoustic characteristics of a human voice saying "wah." (One of the most popular wah-wah pedals of the early 1970s was called "Cry Baby," an evocation of the sound of an infant wailing.) Kath's playing is melodically inventive and unpredictable, and uses the continuous sound created by electronic distortion to soften and blur the attack of his guitar pick so that the notes form a smooth, flowing chain of sound that builds gradually in intensity. In a parallel to the Doors' "Light My Fire," which was initially edited for AM airplay by cutting out Ray Manzarek's organ solo, Terry Kath's solo on the album version of "25 or 6 to 4," which is about seventy-six seconds in length (accounting for over one-quarter of the duration of the entire track), was truncated drastically in the single version that received the most airplay on AM Top 40 radio. (Singing is almost invariably favored over instrumental improvisation in the creation of three-minute pop singles. The album version of "25 or 6 to 4" was, however, favored on the more free-form format of FM radio.) Terry Kath's death was a watershed moment for Chicago, which in the years to follow achieved commercial success by moving away from rock music toward a smoother "adult contemporary" sound.

"Night Fever": The Rise of Disco

The **disco** era—roughly 1975 to 1980—represented the rise of a massively popular alternative to rock music. Unlike most rock music, disco was centrally focused on social dancing, including couple-based dances such as the hustle and choreographed line dances that hearkened back to nineteenth-century ballroom dances such as the quadrille. Disco music also represented a reaction against two of the central ideas of album-oriented rock: the LP as art and the rock group as artists. Disco deemphasized the importance of the band—which, in disco music, was usually a shifting concatenation of professional session musicians—and focused attention on the producers who oversaw the making of recordings, the DJs who played them in nightclubs, and a handful of glamorous stars who sang with the backing of anonymous studio musicians and often had quite short-lived careers. Disco also rejected the idea of the rock album as an architecturally designed collection of individual pieces. Working night after night for audiences who demanded music that would keep them dancing for hours at a stretch, DJs rediscovered the single, expanded it to fill the time frame offered by the twelve-inch long-playing vinyl disc, and developed techniques for blending one record into the next without interruption. (These turntable techniques paved the way for the use of recordings in popular genres of the 1980s and 1990s, such as hip-hop, house, and techno.)

The term "disco" was derived from "discotheque," a term first used in Europe during the 1960s to refer to nightclubs devoted to the playing of recorded music for dancing.

Listening Guide "LOVE'S THEME"

Written by Barry White, performed by the Love Unlimited Orchestra, conducted by Barry White (released 1973)

A dizzying upward sweep in the strings, the pulse kicks in—subtly at first, but becoming progressively stronger—and a downward lunge on the keyboard ushers in "Love's Theme," one of the biggest instrumental hits of the 1970s. The Love Unlimited Orchestra, a forty-piece studio ensemble, was the brainchild of *Barry White* (1944–2004), a multitalented African American singer, songwriter, arranger, conductor, and producer who had already enjoyed a string of solo vocal hits by the time that "Love's Theme" hit the Number 1 spot on the pop chart in February 1974. Originally formed to back the female trio Love Unlimited—yet another of White's projects as a writer and producer—the Love Unlimited Orchestra also played on some of White's solo recordings, in addition to having hit instrumental records under its own name. ("Love's Theme" was featured on *Rhapsody in White*, the cleverly titled Top 10 album by the Love Unlimited Orchestra.)

The instrumental pop hit, which reached its pinnacle as a genre during the swing era (see Chapter 6), never totally died out during the early years of rock 'n' roll or during the emergence of rock in the 1960s. In fact, as we have seen, instrumental virtuosity on the electric guitar became one of the defining elements of late 1960s and 1970s rock. Still, "Love's Theme" represented a different kind of instrumental for the 1970s. Guitar pyrotechnics play no part in the arrangement, although the use of the "scratch" guitar sound as a recurring percussive element throughout the recording does constitute a nod to the more advanced guitar styles of the period cultivated by artists such as Jimi Hendrix. Instead, the emphasis in "Love's Theme" is on two things: danceability on the one hand, and the sweet sound of string-dominated melody on the other. Its successful synthesis of these two elements, which might seem at first to be unlikely bedfellows, is one of the strikingly original—and very influential—aspects of this record.

The danceability of "Love's Theme" made it one of the earliest disco-styled hits, as it quickly became a favorite in dance clubs. This recording was the first in a long line of instrumental, or largely instrumental, disco records. These records followed the lead of "Love's Theme" insofar as they typically presented a similar combination of a strong beat with an elaborate arrangement featuring bowed string instruments; examples include the Number 1 hits "TSOP (The Sound of Philadelphia)" by MFSB (which topped the charts later in 1974), "The Hustle" by Van McCoy and the Soul City Symphony (1975), and "Fly, Robin, Fly" by Silver Convention (also 1975). In addition, the lush arrangement of "Love's Theme," featuring a melody designed to take full advantage of the way orchestral string instruments can hold long notes, links this instrumental in a general way to the sound of soft soul, a popular genre in the later 1960s and throughout the 1970s, exemplified by languid or mid-tempo love songs with similarly "romantic" arrangements. (Examples include recordings by the Delfonics, the Spinners, the Stylistics, and Barry White himself as a solo vocalist.) In a sense, "Love's Theme" has it both ways: it's a love ballad for instruments with a double-time dance beat. The steady, syncopated dance groove keeps the string sounds from spilling over into sentimentality, while the smooth string melody prevents the dance pulse from seeming overly mechanical or depersonalized.

While listening to "Love's Theme," it is a relatively simple matter to pick out the tune's basic AABA structure—yet another testament to the remarkable durability of this formal arrangement. Note how the bridge section (B) is slightly longer than the others and how effective this extension of the bridge is as we wait for the return of A.

Barry White was best known for his full, deep voice, which he could employ to great and seductive effect, not only in actually singing his love songs, but also in the spoken introductions he sometimes provided for them (as in his 1974 Number 1 solo hit "Can't Get Enough of Your Love, Babe"). Still, the single biggest hit record with which White was associated remains "Love's Theme," and in terms of the long-range impact of its sound on the pop music market, it may also be his most influential recording. It is no accident that the track that leads off *The Disco Box*, a four-CD compilation of the dance-oriented music of the 1970s and early 1980s (issued by Rhino in 1999), is "Love's Theme."

By the mid-1970s clubs featuring an uninterrupted stream of dance music were increasingly common in the United States, particularly in urban Black and Latino communities, where going out to dance on a weekend night was a well-established tradition, and in the increasingly visible gay communities of cities such as New York and San Francisco. The rise of disco and its invasion of the Top 40 pop music mainstream were driven by several factors: the inspiration of Black popular music, particularly Motown, soul, and funk; the rise in popularity of social dancing among middle-class Americans; new technologies, including synthesizers, drum machines, and synchronized turntables; the role of the Hollywood film industry in promoting musical trends; and the economic recession of the late 1970s, which encouraged many nightclub owners to hire disc jockeys rather than live musicians.

By the late 1970s disco had taken over the popular mainstream, owing in large part to the success of the film *Saturday Night Fever* (1977), the story of a working-class Italian kid from New York who rises to become a championship dancer. *Saturday Night Fever*—shot on location at a Brooklyn discotheque—strengthened interest in disco stars like Donna Summer and Gloria Gaynor. The film also launched the second career of the Bee Gees, an Australian group known theretofore mainly for sentimental pop songs like "Lonely Days" (a Number 3 pop hit from 1970) and "How Can You Mend a Broken Heart" (Number 1 in 1971). The Bee Gees reinvented themselves by combining their polished Beatle-derived vocal harmonies with strong, repetitive rhythms played by Miami studio musicians, creating a mix that appealed both to committed disco fans and to a broader pop audience; their songs from the *Saturday Night Fever* soundtrack, such as "Stayin' Alive" and "Night Fever," were among the most popular singles of the late 1970s. At a more general level, *Saturday Night Fever* also helped to link disco music and dancing to a traditional American cultural theme: upward mobility. Spreading from the urban communities where it first took root, disco dancing offered millions of working-class and middle-class Americans, from the most varied of cultural and economic backgrounds, an access to glamour that hadn't been experienced widely since the days of the grand ballrooms.

The strict dress codes employed by the most famous discotheques implied a rejection of the torn T-shirt and jeans regalia of rock music, and the reinstatement of notions of hierarchy and classiness—if you (and your clothes) could pass muster at the velvet rope, you were allowed access to the inner sanctum. Walking through the front door of a disco in full swing was like entering a sensory maelstrom, with thundering music driven by an incessant bass pulse; flashing lights and mirrors on the ceiling, walls, and floor; and—most important—a mass of sweaty and beautifully adorned bodies packed onto the always limited space of a dance floor. For its adepts, the discotheque was a shrine to hedonism, an escape from the drudgery of everyday life, and a fountain of youth. (The death throes of this scene are evocatively rendered in the 1998 film *The Last Days of Disco*.)

A few examples must suffice here to give a sense of how thoroughly disco had penetrated popular musical taste by the late 1970s. One important stream of influence involved a continuation of the old category of novelty records, done up in disco style. A band called Rick Dees and His Gang of Idiots came out of nowhere to score a Number

John Travolta in an iconic pose from the hit film *Saturday Night Fever*, 1977.

1 hit with the goofy "Disco Duck" (1976), followed by the less successful zoo-disco song "Dis-Gorilla" (1977). The Village People—a group built from scratch by the French record producer Jacques Morali and promoted by Casablanca Records—specialized in over-the-top burlesques of gay life and scored Top 40 hits with songs like "Macho Man" (Number 25, 1978), "Y.M.C.A." (Number 2, 1978) and "In the Navy" (Number 3, 1979). For those who caught the inside references to gay culture, the Village People's recordings were charming, if simple-minded, parodies; for many in disco's new mass audience, they were simply novelty records with a disco beat. Morali's double-entendre strategy paid off—for a short while in the late 1970s, the Village People were the bestselling pop group in North America.

For a few years everyone seemed to be jumping on the disco bandwagon. Barbra Streisand teamed up with disco artists, including the Bee Gees' Barry Gibb, who produced her multiplatinum 1980 album *Guilty*, and Donna Summer, with whom she made the single "No More Tears" (Number 1 in 1979). Disco met the surf sound when Bruce Johnston of the Beach Boys produced a disco arrangement of "Pipeline," which had been a Number 4 instrumental hit for the Chantays back in 1963. Even hard rock musicians like the Rolling Stones released disco singles (such as "Miss You," Number 1 in 1978). On the other side of the Atlantic a genre called Eurodisco developed, featuring prominent use of electronic synthesizers and long compositions with repetitive rhythm tracks that were designed to fill the entire side of an LP. (This sound, as developed by bands like Germany's

Kraftwerk, was to become one important root of techno.) And Black musicians, who had provided the basic material of which disco was constructed, were presented with new audiences, opportunities, and challenges. Motown diva Diana Ross scored several disco-influenced hits (e.g., "Love Hangover," Number 1 in 1976, and "Upside Down," Number 1 in 1980). James Brown, who was knocked off the pop charts by disco music, responded in the late 1970s by promoting himself as the "Original Disco Man." (His R&B hit "It's Too Funky in Here," released in 1979, is a clear gesture in this direction.)

Few styles of popular music have inspired either such passionate loyalty or such utter revulsion as disco music, and it is worth taking a few moments to consider the negative side of this equation. If you were a loyal fan of Led Zeppelin, Pink Floyd, and other album-oriented rock groups of the 1970s, disco was likely to represent a self-indulgent, pretentious, and vaguely suspect musical orientation. The rejection of disco by rock fans reached its peak during a 1979 baseball game in Chicago, where several hundred disco records were blown up and a riot ensued. (This mass passion is reminiscent of the burnings of Beatles records organized during the 1960s by fundamentalist Christian preachers.) After all, disco is only music—what on earth could inspire such a violent reaction?

Some critics connect the antidisco reaction of the 1970s with the genre's links to gay culture. The disco movement initially emerged in Manhattan nightclubs such as the Loft and the Tenth Floor, which served as social gathering spots for homosexual men. According to this interpretation, gays found it difficult to get live acts to perform for them. The disc jockeys who worked at these clubs responded to the demands of customers by rummaging through the bins of record stores for good dance records, often coming up with singles that had been successful some years earlier in the Black and Puerto Rican communities of New York.

That disco was to some degree associated in the public imagination with homosexuality has suggested to some observers that the phrase "Disco Sucks!"—the rallying cry of the antidisco movement—evinces a strain of homophobia among the core audience for album-oriented rock: young, middle- and working-class, and presumably heterosexual white men. Certainly disco's associations with a contemporary version of ballroom dancing did not conform to contemporary models of masculine behavior. The tradition of dancing to prefigured steps, or to music specifically designed to support dancing, which had found its last expression in the early 1960s with dance crazes like the twist, had fallen out of favor during the rock era. It may therefore have seemed to many rock fans that there was something suspect—even effeminate—about men who engaged in ballroom dancing.

Still, it can safely be assumed that the audience for album-oriented rock wasn't entirely straight, and that heterosexuals did patronize discos with large homosexual clienteles, at least in the big cities. The initial rejection of disco by many rock fans may have had as much to do with racism as with homophobia, since the genre's roots lay predominantly in Black dance music. In addition, the musical values predominant among rock fans—including an appreciation of instrumental virtuosity, as represented in the guitar playing of Jimi Hendrix, Eric Clapton, or Jimmy Page—would not have inclined them to view disco positively, since the genre relied heavily on studio overdubbing

Listening Guide   THREE DISCO HITS

"Love to Love You Baby," written by Pete Bellotte, Giorgio Moroder, and Donna Summer, performed by Donna Summer (recorded 1975)

"Bad Girls," written by Joseph Esposito, Edward Hokenson, Bruce Sudano, and Donna Summer, performed by Donna Summer (recorded 1979)

"Good Times," written by Bernard Edwards and Nile Rodgers, performed by Chic (recorded 1979)

The archetypal early disco hit is Donna Summer's "Love to Love You Baby" (Number 2 pop, Number 3 R&B in 1976), recorded in Germany and released in the United States by Casablanca Records, the independent label that also released LPs by Parliament/Funkadelic (see Chapter 12). "Love to Love You Baby" reflects the genre's strong reliance on the musical technologies of the mid-1970s and the central importance of the record producer in shaping the sound texture of disco recordings. Producer Giorgio Moroder's careful mix takes full advantage of multitrack recording technology (which allows Summer's voice to appear in several places at the same time); clear stereo separation of instruments; keyboard synthesizers with the ability to play more than one note at a time and imitate other musical instruments; and electronic reverb, which plays a crucial role in establishing the spatial qualities of a recording. At seventeen minutes long, the original recording is much longer than the usual pop single and was produced specifically for use in discotheques, where customers demanded unbroken sequences of dance music. (The version that made the *Billboard* singles charts was edited down to under five minutes in length in order to fit the framework of Top 40 radio.) The performance is clearly seductive in intent, an impression created not only by the lyrics themselves but also by Summer's languorous and sexy whispers, moans, and growls. (This impression is reinforced by the nicknames bestowed on Donna Summer at the time by the popular music press, including "First Lady of Lust" and "Disco's Aphrodite.")

The recording opens with an intake of breath and Summer's voice singing the hook of the song ("Ahhhh, love to love you baby") in an intimate, almost whispering voice, accompanied by the gentle sound of a closed hi-hat cymbal (a pair of cymbals opened and closed by the drummer's left foot). The next sounds we hear are the electric guitar, played with a wah-wah pedal (which allows the guitarist to change the timbre of his instrument), and the bass drum, playing a solid four-to-the-bar beat. The core elements of early disco music are thus presented within the first few measures of the recording: a sexy, studio-enhanced female voice and a rhythm track that is anchored by a hypnotic, steady pulse. The overall arrangement is made up of two basic phrases, which are alternated but always return to the hook. Working with his then-state-of-the-art multitrack recording board, Giorgio Moroder gradually builds up layers of sound texture and then strips them away to reveal the basic pulse of the music. Dance-oriented music dominated the American pop charts in the late 1970s. The titles of the Number 1 pop records from the end of 1977 through the summer of 1979 would read, with few exceptions, like a track listing for a "Disco's Greatest Hits" album. Disco's spectacular hold on the Number 1 spot

Donna Summer on stage, c. mid-1970s.

(continued)

Listening Guide THREE DISCO HITS (*continued*)

ended with two splendid examples of the genre: "Bad Girls," performed by Donna Summer, and "Good Times," performed by Chic. A brief consideration of the similarities shared by these records and the differences between them will offer us a useful look at the essential characteristics, as well as the diversity, of disco music.

What Makes Both These Records "Disco"?

1. *The BEAT!* This is dance music, of course, and the pounding beat defines the music as disco. Indeed, the beat is established immediately on both "Bad Girls" and "Good Times," and it never lets up, persisting right through the fade-outs that end these recordings. The beat constitutes the essential hook on all disco records. It is characteristic of disco that every pulse is rhythmically articulated by the bass and/or the drums. There is no such thing as stop time in this music, and the signature *thump!—thump!—thump!—thump!* of disco creates and maintains an irresistible dance groove that means disco dancers literally never have to skip a beat. Consequently, although there are many changes in the musical texture during "Bad Girls," the rhythm never lets up, regardless of whatever other instruments or vocal parts enter or leave the mix. The fact that there are only slight alterations in texture throughout "Good Times" helps ensure that attention remains focused on the rhythm itself, and the minimal feel of this particular recording offers an excellent example of how hypnotic a basic rhythm-propelled track can be.

2. *A steady, medium-fast tempo.* Like most social dance music, disco recordings maintain an unvarying tempo throughout. Above and beyond this obvious characteristic, however, the tempos of most disco records tend also to be fairly similar to one another in order to accord with the active dance styles preferred by the patrons of discotheques. The tempo of "Bad Girls" is slightly faster than that of "Good Times," but obviously the same kinds of steps and body movements would fit both records equally well. Recordings intended for use in discotheques often bore indications of their tempos in the form of beats per minute (bpm) to assist the club disc jockeys in arranging relatively seamless sequences of dance numbers; if the DJ had an adjustable-speed turntable, it was possible to adjust the tempos of individual records slightly so that the dance beat wouldn't vary at all from

one to the next, so that even when the song changed, the dancers still would never have to skip a beat.

3. *Straightforward, repetitive song forms.* Given their emphasis on dancing, it would obviously be pointless for disco records to employ complex, intricate song forms of the kind developed by some artists in the late 1960s and the 1970s. Such niceties suggest an entirely different kind of listening environment and, if they weren't just missed entirely by disco fans, might prove distracting and even annoying on the dance floor. Both "Bad Girls" and "Good Times" are clearly based on a verse-chorus kind of form. Furthermore, the chorus is heard first in both, a structure that serves a number of purposes. Each song's chorus begins with the title words ("Bad girls," "Good times"), identifying the song immediately and functioning as a concise and extremely effective verbal and musical hook. Counting the initial statement, the chorus in each of these recordings is heard a total of three times, which results in a readily accessible, repetitive structure that assures memorability.

4. *Straightforward subject matter and lyrics.* No Dylanesque imagery or poetic obscurities, please—again, for obvious reasons. There is no doubt about what either "Bad Girls" or "Good Times" is about. This is not to say that the lyrics of disco songs are without interest, however; see the following discussion, especially in reference to "Bad Girls," in the next section.

5. *Limited harmonic vocabulary.* In essence, the harmony of "Good Times" simply oscillates between two chords, with the change occurring on the downbeat of every other measure. "Bad Girls" has only a slightly wider harmonic vocabulary, but it too gives the sense of being built around two basic, alternating chords much of the time; these two chords underlie the entire chorus and do not shift when the choruses give way to the verses. Both records thus achieve a highly focused, almost hypnotic, effect in the harmonic realm that is analogous to—and abets—their virtually obsessive rhythmic character. (The conceptual debt that recordings of this type owe to the late 1960s music of James Brown should be obvious; see Chapter 10.)

It is important to note that these five characteristics—emphasis on the beat, steady, relatively fast tempo, avoidance of formal complexity, direct lyrics, and a limited chordal vocabulary—clearly do not apply only to typical disco music. They also would serve well in describing much typical early rock 'n' roll. The point to be made here is that in the context of album-oriented rock, the output of singer-songwriters, and several other manifestations of 1970s pop music, the "return to basics" (that is, the return to danceable music) with a new twist that disco represented came across to many as both novel and refreshing. It is also important to emphasize here that disco music proved, in certain ways, to be forward-looking. The most immediate example of this is the fact that the chords and rhythmic patterns of "Good Times" were borrowed wholesale for the instrumental backing for the single that broke rap music into the commercial mainstream for the first time: "Rapper's Delight," by the Sugar Hill Gang (see Chapter 12).

Some Distinguishing Characteristics of "Bad Girls" and "Good Times"

We have already noted the greater textural variety of "Bad Girls." Donna Summer's lead vocal, responding voices, brass instruments, and even a police whistle appear, disappear, and reappear—sometimes expectedly, sometimes not—over the course of the recording, creating a feeling that is evocative of the action, excitement, and occasional unpredictability of a busy street scene. It also seems appropriate that "Bad Girls" is more elaborate from a formal point of view than "Good Times." The verse sections of "Bad Girls" fall into two distinct parts, with the second part marked by a pause in the vocals and the interjection of short, accented chords on the brass instruments. In addition, after the third and final verse, a coda appears in place of the expected concluding chorus. In this coda, the lead vocalist at last abandons her position as an observer of the scene and actually joins the "bad girls" with a shout of "Hey, mister, have you got a dime?"—acting, in effect,

upon her earlier realization (in the third verse) that she and the "bad girls" are "both the same," even though the others are called "a different name."

The vocal styles used in the two recordings are decidedly different. Donna Summer's emphatic, expansive style clearly derives from roots in R&B and gospel; her background, like that of so many African American pop stars, included church singing. Summer's personal intensity solicits our involvement in and concern with the story of the "bad girls." In short, "Bad Girls" is a brilliantly performed pop record that is enhanced by an elaborate and clever production. Yet the question suggests itself: Can any recording so irresistibly danceable, with such an upbeat rhythmic feeling, really convey a downbeat social "message"—especially about an issue as thorny and complex as prostitution? Won't people be too busy dancing to notice? And doesn't it sound as if these "bad girls" are really just out for—and having—"good times"?

In a way, the inverse situation applies to "Good Times." This apparently carefree anthem is intoned by a small group of voices singing in unison in a clipped, unornamented, basically uninflected kind of style that comes across as intentionally depersonalized. Is there ultimately something just a little too mechanistic about the voices, and the accompanying obsessive chords and rhythms, in these "good times"? Some rock critics have suggested that the song has an ironic edge to it, and they could certainly support this idea by pointing to those occasional darker phrases that pop up in the lyrics like momentary flickering shadows: "A rumor has it that it's getting late" and "You silly fool, you can't change your fate." However, it might also be claimed that those looking for hidden depths in a song like "Good Times" are those who have simply lost the ability to enjoy a superb party record.

and consisted mainly of fairly predictable patterns designed for dancing. The fact that millions of sports fans of all descriptions today enthusiastically mimic the movements of a popular—and, for some listeners, explicitly gay—disco recording like the Village People's multimillion-selling single "YMCA" complicates the picture even further. Although disco cannot simply be identified as "gay music," there is no doubt that the genre's mixed reception during the late 1970s provides additional evidence of the transformative effect of marginalized musical styles and communities on the commercial mainstream of American popular music.

ALTHOUGH THE SEVENTIES are often portrayed as a time of corporate consolidation and conservatism in popular music, these were only two dimensions of a much more complex story. In the next chapter we will examine a number of developments that extend a pattern we have discerned in earlier periods: the continual refreshing of popular music by performers and styles situated at the margins of the commercial mainstream. In the creativity and energy of genres such as progressive country, reggae, punk, funk, and early rap music, we will find affirmation both of changes in the business of music and of deep continuities underlying the history of American popular music.

Key Terms

disco	overdubbing	Southern rock
jazz rock	soft rock	synthesizers

Key People

Allman Brothers Band	David Bowie	Joni Mitchell
Barry White	Dolly Parton	Marvin Gaye
Carlos Santana	Donna Summer	Merle Haggard
Carole King	Eagles	Miles Davis
Charlie Rich	Elton John	Olivia Newton-John
Chic	Glen Campbell	Pink Floyd
Chicago	John Denver	Stevie Wonder

Review Questions

1. What makes a rock album more than a collection of singles?
2. What changes occurred in the recording industry in the 1970s?
3. What was the "Philadelphia Sound"?
4. What was the relationship between country music and the pop mainstream during the 1970s?
5. What contributed to the popularity of disco?

Outsiders' Music

Progressive Country, Reggae, Salsa, Punk, Funk, and Rap, 1970s

12

ALTHOUGH THE 1970S ARE OFTEN DESCRIBED AS A PERIOD OF STYLISTIC conservatism and corporate consolidation in popular music, the decade also fostered music that did not fit neatly into the frameworks of Top 40 radio, album-oriented rock, or the Nashville Sound. The genres we will be discussing in this chapter arose, for the most part, as a response to the conservatism of the music industry; the exception is reggae music, which came from completely outside this commercial mainstream. Each of these genres embodied in its own way the contradictions built into the popular music industry and the complex processes by which the mainstream and the margins of popular music are continually redefined.

The Outlaws: Progressive Country Music

During the late 1960s and early 1970s, mainstream country music was dominated by the slick Nashville Sound, the hardcore country of artists like Merle Haggard, and various blends of country and pop promoted on AM Top 40 radio (see Chapter 11). But a new generation of country musicians at this time began to embrace the music and attitudes that had grown out of the 1960s counterculture. **Progressive country**, as this movement came to be known, was inspired by the honky-tonk and rockabilly amalgam of Bakersfield country music; the singer-songwriter genre (especially the work of Bob Dylan); and the country rock style of musicians like Gram Parsons, who was a member of the Byrds for a brief time in the late 1960s. In general, progressive country performers wrote songs that were more intellectual and liberal in outlook than those of their contemporaries and were more concerned with testing the limits of the country music tradition than with scoring hits. Many of the movement's key artists—such as Willie Nelson, Kris Kristofferson, Tom T. Hall, and Townes Van Zandt—were not polished singers by conventional standards, yet they wrote distinctive, individualistic songs and had compelling voices. These artists developed a sizable cult following, and progressive country began to inch its way into the mainstream, usually in the form of cover versions. Tom T. Hall's "Harper Valley PTA" was a Number 1 pop and country hit for Jeannie C. Riley as early as 1968, while Sammi Smith took Kris Kristofferson's "Help Me Make It Through the Night" to the top of the country charts and into the pop Top 10 in 1971.

One of the most influential figures in the progressive country movement was *Willie Nelson* (born in Texas in 1933). Nelson had already developed a successful career as a professional songwriter when he left Nashville to return to Texas in 1971. (His song "Crazy" had been a Top 10 country and pop hit for Patsy Cline in 1961.) He settled in Austin, a university town and home to one of the most energetic and eclectic live music scenes in the country. At "cosmic cowboy" venues such as the Armadillo World Headquarters, and on Austin radio station KOKE-FM, a movement that fused country music and countercultural sensibilities was already well underway. Nelson fit right into the Austin scene, letting his hair and beard grow long and donning a headband, an earring, jogging shoes, and blue jeans (one of the few markers of cultural identity shared by rednecks, cowboys, and hippies!). Singing in an unpolished, almost conversational voice—an approach that had frustrated his attempts to gain success as a recording artist in Nashville—Willie Nelson bridged the gap between rock and country without losing touch with his honky-tonk roots. In the summer of 1971 he organized the first of a series of outdoor festivals that included older country musicians (e.g., Roy Acuff and Earl Scruggs) as well as younger musicians who were experimenting with a blend of country and rock music. These "picnics," closer in ethos to Woodstock than to the *Grand Ole Opry*, brought thousands of rock fans into the fold of country music and prepared the way for Nelson's ascendance as the pre-eminent male country music star of the 1980s.

Willie Nelson's initial rise to national fame came in the mid-1970s, through his association with a group of musicians collectively known as "the Outlaws." The centerpiece of the Outlaws was another Texas-born musician, *Waylon Jennings* (1937–2002). Jennings began his career as a musician and disc jockey and in 1958 joined Buddy Holly's rock 'n' roll group the Crickets. In the early 1960s he set up shop at a nightclub in Phoenix, Arizona, where the clientele included businessmen, college students, and cowboys, a diverse audience that encouraged him to develop a broad repertoire. In 1965 he was signed by RCA Victor and relocated to Nashville. Although RCA producer Chet Atkins—who had remolded Elvis into a pop star in 1956—attempted to push him in the direction of the countrypolitan sound popular at the time, Jennings resisted these

Willie Nelson performing in 2004.

efforts, eventually winning substantial leeway in his choice of material. (His early 1970s LPs included Beatles songs such as "Norwegian Wood" and "You've Got to Hide Your Love Away.")

While he chose to remain close to the music industry in Nashville rather than return to Texas, Jennings cultivated an image as a rebel, and in 1972 recorded an album called *Ladies Love Outlaws*. On the cover he appeared in "bad guy" dress, complete with a black cowboy hat and a six-shooter. The commercial potential of the outlaw image was soon recognized by music publicists in Nashville, who lost no time turning it into a commercial term. The Outlaws were never a cohesive performing group; in fact, the label "outlaw country" was largely a product of the record industry's search for a way to capitalize on the overlap between audiences for rock and those for country music.

In 1976, after musicians such as Willie Nelson and Waylon Jennings had begun to receive substantial radio airplay, RCA Victor released a compilation of their early 1970s recordings entitled *Wanted: The Outlaws*. This LP included a mix of material, ranging from a version of the country music classic "T for Texas," first recorded under the title "Blue Yodel" by Jimmie Rodgers in 1927, to a cover of an Elvis Presley hit ("Suspicious Minds"), and even

Listening Guide "Blue Eyes Crying in the Rain"

Red Headed Stranger (concept album), Willie Nelson, recorded 1975
"Blue Eyes Crying in the Rain" (Fred Rose) recorded by Willie Nelson, 1975

One of the ideas that progressive country musicians adopted from rock music during the 1970s was that of the concept album. The central medium for the transmission of country music during the 1970s was still the individual song, and although some country LPs sold well, 45 rpm singles remained the bread and butter of the industry. During the mid-1970s, however, progressive country musicians began to create albums unified around a single theme or dramatic character. Perhaps the best example of this trend is Willie Nelson's album *Red-Headed Stranger* (1975), which sold over 2 million copies and reached Number 28 on *Billboard*'s Top LPs chart. (*Billboard* had no separate LP charts for country or soul music, since these genres were assumed by definition to be singles-oriented.) *Red-Headed Stranger* included Nelson's first big crossover hit as a singer, rather than as a songwriter—"Blue Eyes Crying in the Rain," Number 21 pop and Number 1 country—and established the notion of the country concept album. The song, originally recorded by Roy Acuff in 1947, was written by Nashville music publisher Fred Rose, who also was Hank Williams' manager.

Of course, the technique of telling stories through song had long been part of the Anglo-American ballad tradition, one of the main taproots of country music. In putting together *Red-Headed Stranger*, a meticulously crafted song cycle outlining the saga of a broken-hearted cowboy, Nelson stuck close to the traditional time limit of three minutes per song, alternating songs with shorter bits of material that established the narrative context (for example, dance music to give us the feeling of a turn-of-the-century saloon in Denver). The musical accompaniment—acoustic guitar, electric guitar, mandolin, piano, harmonica, electric bass, and drums—is strikingly spare and restrained, and some tracks use only acoustic guitar and piano (played by Nelson's sister). The jacket sleeve featured excerpts from the lyrics, accompanied by paintings of the red-headed stranger in the various scenarios portrayed by the songs.

The album opens with the song "Time of the Preacher," which sets the stage for the cycle and establishes the main characters (the "lady" and the "man") and the lady's infidelity that inspires the man to hunt her down. In the next song, only a minute and a half in length, Nelson adopts the first-person voice of the jilted cowboy, who discovers his wife's infidelity—"I couldn't believe it was true." This is followed by a reappearance of the "Time of the Preacher" song, which functions throughout the album as a thematic refrain, connecting the various songs. As the story unfolds, we observe the red-headed stranger tracking down his wife and her lover, shooting them dead in a tavern, and riding off on his black stallion. As in rock concept albums based on a dramatic character—say, *The Rise and Fall of Ziggy Stardust and the Spiders from Mars*—the line dividing the fictional persona in the song and the musician who sings the song is thin indeed. The album cover of *Red-Headed Stranger* portrays Nelson in cowboy dress, with a beard and long, ragged, red-tinted hair, an image clearly intended to reinforce the longtime Nashville songwriter's public image as an outlaw musician.

"Blue Eyes Crying in the Rain," with its simple ABAB song form and sparse accompaniment, offers a fine introduction to Willie Nelson's distinctive vocal style. He has an atypically high voice for country music, and he employs its very individual timbre to achieve expressive effects. Nelson can sing very softly; notice the tender feeling conveyed when he suddenly retreats to a near-whisper on the words "never meet again," and later as he concludes the final phrase of the song. He also allows himself a subtle vibrato that may be heard when he sings the words "blue" and "rain." Nelson's unconventional voice might have delayed his making a strong impact as a singer early in his career, but once he began to gain popularity as a vocalist, that very unconventionality made him instantly recognizable to a larger and larger audience. That audience in turn rewarded him increasingly for both his songwriting and his singing.

| LISTENING GUIDE | "BLUE EYES CRYING IN THE RAIN" | | |
TIME	FORM	LYRIC	DESCRIPTIVE COMMENTS
0:00	Brief introduction		Acoustic guitar alternating bass part and chords
0:04	A	*There in twilight . . .*	Nelson's voice enters; guitar accompaniment continues
0:35	B	*Love is like . . .*	Soft chords on accordion accompany voice
0:53		*Through the ages . . .*	Accordion drops out
1:07	A		Electric guitar enters, playing the melody of the A section; accompanied by acoustic guitar and electric bass
1:42	B	*Someday when we . . .*	Accordion re-enters; overdubbed vocal harmony on 2nd line
1:58		*In a land . . .*	Solo voice with accordion and acoustic guitar; song concludes with brief instrumental tag

to Willie Nelson's humorous song "Me and Paul," in which the country singer compares his problems on the road to those of rock star Paul McCartney. The album was a huge success—it reached the Top 10 on *Billboard*'s Top LPs chart, soon became the first platinum country music LP, and eventually sold over 2 million copies. Although the Outlaws—like most "alternative" music movements—had a commercial dimension, they did represent a heartfelt rebellion against the conservatism of the country music establishment. Their approach found common ground in the past and the future of country music; managed to briefly challenge country pop's hold on the charts in the mid-1970s; and paved the way for later alternative country artists such as k.d. lang, Dwight Yoakam, and Lyle Lovett.

"I Shot the Sheriff": The Rise of Reggae

Reggae—a potent mixture of Caribbean folk music and American rhythm & blues—was the first style of the rock era to originate in the so-called Third World. The popularity of reggae in America may be related both to earlier "exotic" music crazes—the Argentine tango and the Cuban rumba—and to the coming world beat movement of the 1980s and 1990s. Born in the impoverished shantytowns of Kingston, Jamaica, reggae first became popular in the United States in 1973 after the release of the Jamaican film *The Harder*

They Come and its soundtrack album. (This is yet another example of the importance of film as a medium for promoting popular music, exemplified by the Hollywood musicals of the 1930s and the rock 'n' roll films of the 1950s.) During the 1970s a handful of Jamaican musicians—notably Bob Marley and Jimmy Cliff—achieved a measure of commercial success in the United States, while numerous American and British rock musicians—including Eric Clapton, Paul Simon, the Police, and Elvis Costello—found inspiration (and profit) in the style. In addition, rap music of the 1980s was strongly influenced by Jamaican "dub," a branch of the reggae tradition in which verbal performances are improvised over pre-recorded musical accompaniments.

Reggae music was itself a complex composite of influences, some of them from the United States. The history of reggae thus gives us an opportunity to examine not only the burgeoning interest of American musicians in "world music" but also the influence of American forms on local music elsewhere, a fascinating story that mainly lies outside the scope of this book. The roots of reggae lie in the Jamaican equivalent of country music, a genre called *mento*. A mixture of Jamaican folk songs, church hymns, sailor's shanties, and Cuban influences, mento arose in rural Jamaica during the late nineteenth century. By World War II, the genre had lost its popularity among the thousands of young Jamaicans who were migrating to the capital city of Kingston. (Today's tourist resorts on Jamaica's north coast are among the last places where mento can be heard.) During the 1940s and early 1950s swing bands from the United States—including those of Benny Goodman, Count Basie, and Glenn Miller—became popular in the dance halls of Kingston. Jamaican musicians formed what they called "road bands," local swing bands that toured from town to town playing public dances.

Starting in the 1950s American rhythm & blues—broadcast by powerful radio stations in Miami and New Orleans—became popular among youth in Kingston. Migrant Jamaican workers in Costa Rica, Panama, Cuba, and the United States brought back the hit recordings of American artists such as Louis Jordan and Fats Domino, and local entrepreneurs set up portable sound systems to play R&B records for dances and parties, driving the road bands out of business. In the 1960s a shortage of U.S. records encouraged some sound system operators to set up their own recording studios in Kingston. Some of these men—including Coxsone Dodd and Leslie Kong—became leading producers in the Jamaican popular music business.

During the 1960s a succession of new popular genres emerged out of the intersection of Jamaican folk music and American rhythm & blues. The first of these was **ska** (an onomatopoeic term derived from the style's typical sharp offbeat accents). The instrumentation of ska bands was derived from R&B, with a rhythm section of piano, bass, guitar, and drums and a horn section made up of some combination of brass instruments and saxophones. Ska music was usually played at fast tempos, with the bass playing a steady four-beat pattern and the piano, guitar, and drums emphasizing the backbeats. The singing on ska records was strongly influenced by R&B, ranging from rougher blues-influenced styles to romantic crooning. The biggest star of Jamaican ska was Don Drummond, a trombonist and leader of a band called the Skatalites. The Skatalites also worked as a studio band, backing many of the most popular singers of the time and exerting a substantial influence on the youth culture of Kingston, particularly when several members of the band joined the Rastafarian religious movement.

It is worth taking a moment here to discuss the Rastafarian movement, since it is such a prominent theme in reggae music. Rastafarianism was founded by Josiah Marcus Garvey (1887–1940), a Jamaican writer and political leader who inspired a "Back to Africa" repatriation movement among Black Americans in the 1920s. Before leaving Jamaica for the United States in 1916, Garvey wrote, "Look to Africa for the crowning of a Black king; he shall be the redeemer," a phrase that was taken quite literally as prophecy by Garvey's followers. In 1930, when Haile Selassie (whose name, translated, means "Power of the Trinity") was crowned king of the African nation of Ethiopia, preachers in Kingston saw this event as confirmation of Garvey's prediction and proceeded to scrutinize the Old Testament in search of passages that supported the authenticity of Selassie's divinity. The Rastafarians' reinterpretation of the Bible focused on passages that dealt with slavery, salvation, and the apocalyptic consequences that would eventually be visited upon the oppressors (collectively referred to as Babylon). Rastafarianism became associated with a unique set of cultural practices, including special terminology (for example, "I-and-I" is substituted for "we"), the use of marijuana (*ganja*) as a sacramental herb, and the wearing of a distinctive hairstyle called "dreadlocks."

The Rastafarian movement spread rapidly through an extensive network of neighborhood churches and informal prayer meetings, where music and dance were used to "give praise and thanks" (*satta amassanga*) and to "chant down Babylon." In the mountainous interior of Jamaica, where communities of escaped slaves called "maroons" had been living since the nineteenth century, Rastafarian songs and chants were mixed with an African-derived style of drumming called *burru* to create a heavier, slower sound. This style in turn fed back into urban popular music, resulting around 1966 in an updated version of ska called **rock steady**. Rock steady was considerably slower in tempo than ska, reflecting the aforementioned influence of *burru* drumming, and some of its leading exponents—notably Alton Ellis, who had the first big rock steady hit in 1966—began to record songs with social and political content.

The main patrons of rock steady were the Rude Boys, a social category that included anyone against "the system": urban Rastas, thugs hired by competing political parties, and lower-class youth generally. An informal and unruly Jamaican youth movement, the Rude Boys increasingly came into conflict with the Jamaican police, and media coverage of their exploits helped to create the image of romantic outlaw heroes. The film that initiated reggae music's popularity in the United States, *The Harder They Come* (1972), was in fact a thinly disguised biography of one such ghetto hero (Vincent Martin, a.k.a. Rhygin', a Jamaican outlaw of the early 1960s). Bob Marley's song "I Shot the Sheriff" is about a young man who is persecuted by the local sheriff and then accused of murdering both the sheriff and his deputy in cold blood.

Under the influence of Rastafarian religiosity and Rude Boy street politics, a new genre called reggae took shape in Kingston during the late 1960s. (The word "reggae" is derived from "raggay," a Kingston slang term meaning "raggedy, everyday stuff.") In musical terms reggae was a further extension of the evolution from ska to rock steady. In reggae music the tempo is slowed down even more, creating wide spaces between notes, allowing the music to breathe, and emphasizing the polyrhythmic heritage of Afro-Jamaican traditions. Each instrument in a reggae band has its own carefully defined role to play. The heart of reggae music consists of "riddims," interlocking rhythmic patterns played by the guitar, bass, and drums. The guitar often plays short, choppy chords on the second and fourth beats of each measure, giving the music a bouncy, up-and-down feeling. The bass-drum combination is the irreducible core of a reggae band, sometimes called the "riddim pair." (The most famous of these pairs are the brothers Aston and Carlton Barrett, who played in Bob Marley's band; and Sly Dunbar and Robbie Shakespeare, who have appeared on literally hundreds of reggae recordings and the LPs of rock artists such as Bob Dylan, Mick Jagger, and Peter Gabriel.) This musical mixture was further enlivened by the influence of contemporary Black American popular music, particularly the soul recordings of James Brown and Aretha Franklin. Political messages were central to reggae music—while ska musicians of the early 1960s, like their American R&B counterparts, sang mainly about love and heartbreak, the most popular reggae artists focused their attention on issues such as social injustice and racism.

The film *The Harder They Come* featured reggae songs by a number of the most popular Jamaican musicians. The star of the film, and the vocalist on the title track of the soundtrack LP, was *Jimmy Cliff* (b. 1948). Like Ivan, the outlaw character he portrayed in the film, Cliff was only a teenager when he left the rural Jamaican town of St. James for the city of Kingston. Cliff arrived in Kingston in 1962 and made his first record within a year. Working with the producer Leslie Kong, he recorded a series of Jamaican Top 10 hits during the mid-1960s. While performing at the 1964 World's Fair in New York City, Cliff met Chris Blackwell of the English independent label Island Records, who convinced him to move to London. After working as a backup singer and scoring a few hits on the European charts, he returned to Jamaica in 1969 and recorded the song "Many Rivers to Cross," which inspired the director Perry Henzel to offer him the lead role in *The Harder They Come*. Although the film did not reach the mass audience commanded by many Hollywood movies, it did create a devoted audience for reggae music in the United States, particularly among young, college-educated adults who were attracted by the rebellious spirit of the music and its associations with Rastafarianism and *ganja* smoking. (The film played for seven years straight at a movie theater in Boston, Massachusetts, sustained mainly by the enthusiasm of that city's large student population.)

Jimmy Cliff's 1972 recording of "The Harder They Come" exemplifies the reggae style of the early 1970s: a moderate tempo, strong guitar chords on the second and fourth beats of each measure, R&B-influenced singing, and a gritty lyric about the individual's struggle against oppression.

Although Cliff was the first Jamaican musician to gain recognition in the United States, his contemporary *Bob Marley* (1945–1981), leader of the Wailers, quickly surpassed him in popularity. A national hero in his native Jamaica, Marley was reggae's most effective international ambassador. His songs of determination, rebellion, and faith, rooted in the Rastafarian belief system, found a worldwide audience that reached from America to Japan and from Europe to Africa. The son of a British naval officer who deserted his family when Bob was six years old, Marley migrated to Kingston from the rural parish of St. Ann at the age of fourteen. His early career reflects the economic precariousness of the music industry in a Third World country. After making a few singles for the Chinese-Jamaican producer Leslie Kong, Marley formed the Wailers in 1963 and signed with Coxsone Dodd's studios. Following a long period with little financial success (including a year in which Marley was forced to take up factory work in Wilmington, Delaware), the Wailers signed with the producer Lee Perry, who added the masterful bassist-and-drummer "riddim pair" of Aston and Carlton Barrett to the group.

In 1972 Chris Blackwell, who had launched Jimmy Cliff's international career, signed Bob Marley and the Wailers to Island Records and advanced them the money to record at their independent Tuff Gong studio in Jamaica. Marley's recognition abroad was boosted by the success of Eric Clapton's cover of "I Shot the Sheriff," from the Wailers' second LP for Island Records. The Wailers' first major concert in the United States took place in 1974 in Boston, where for the prior year and a half over a thousand young people a day had been viewing *The Harder They Come*. Between 1975 and 1980 Marley recorded six bestselling LPs for Island Records, including *Rastaman Vibration*, which reached Number 8 on the *Billboard* Top LPs charts in 1976. Wounded in a politically motivated assassination attempt in 1976, Marley died of cancer in 1981 at the age of thirty-six. His appeal and popularity, both in America and worldwide, has only grown in the years since his death: the 1984 compilation *Legend* has sold over 15 million copies in the United States alone.

Bob Marley.

THE POPULARIZATION OF REGGAE

Although the majority of American listeners became conscious of reggae as a distinctive musical style only with the steadily increasing popularity in this country of Bob Marley and the Wailers in the mid- to late 1970s, there are individual instances long before this of Jamaican music appearing on the American charts. In fact, among the many imported hits during the British Invasion year of 1964 was a ska-flavored recording by the Jamaican teenager Millie Small called "My Boy Lollipop," which climbed all the way up to Number 2 on *Billboard*'s list of top singles. In 1968 Johnny Nash, an African American pop singer who established a recording studio in Jamaica, had a Top 5 hit with the reggae-influenced "Hold Me Tight," and 1969 saw the American success of two reggae records by Jamaican artists: "Israelites" by Desmond Dekker and the Aces (Number 9 pop), and "Wonderful World, Beautiful People," by Jimmy Cliff (Number 25 pop).

Both Johnny Nash and Jimmy Cliff went on to bigger things in the early 1970s. Nash hit the Number 1 spot for four weeks in 1972 with another reggae-flavored tune, "I Can See Clearly Now." Nash wrote this song himself (he had also authored "Hold Me Tight"), but he endowed it with a sense of Jamaican authenticity by arranging for members of the Wailers to provide his instrumental support on the track. He then followed this up with a cover of Bob Marley's "Stir It Up" (Number 12 pop, 1973). As for Jimmy Cliff, his starring role in *The Harder They Come* introduced both him and the Jamaican music scene to a significant American audience previously unaware of both. (We might recall here the significance of another movie, *Blackboard Jungle*, in popularizing another music from the margins—rock 'n' roll—in 1955; see Chapter 8.) In a fine illustration of the reciprocal relationships that tend to characterize so much of pop music history, Cliff returned to the charts for the first time in many years, and hit the American Top 20 for the first time in the early 1990s with nothing other than his own cover of Nash's "I Can See Clearly Now" (Number 18 pop, 1994), which was also featured in a movie, *Cool Runnings*.

Surely the best-known cover version of any reggae number is Eric Clapton's million-selling recording of Bob Marley's "I Shot the Sheriff," a Number 1 hit in 1974 that appears on Clapton's Number 1 album from the same year, *461 Ocean Boulevard*. Clapton's name on the label, along with his easygoing vocal delivery, doubtless helped to propel the single to the top of the charts; considered in terms of the song's lyrics and music, "I Shot the Sheriff" seems an unlikely 1970s hit. It is clearly a political song, but for anyone not thoroughly versed in contemporary Jamaican politics, its precise significance is difficult to grasp. This is an example of a "coded" lyric, reminiscent of the coded blues lyrics (see Chapter 5) that communicate something extra to members of a specific group who are attuned to its message. Furthermore, the music of the song is appropriately dark in color, with a predominance of minor chords.

It is instructive to compare Clapton's version with Bob Marley's own recording of "I Shot the Sheriff," which may be found on the 1973 album *Burnin'* and on compilations issued after Marley's death in 1981. Marley's version sounds much more insistently rhythmic and intense than Clapton's. Actually, Marley's tempo is only a hairbreadth faster than Clapton's, but the greater prominence of both bass and percussion in Marley's recording emphasizes the distinctive "riddims" of Jamaican reggae and creates the illusion of a considerably faster performance. (The recording closes with just the bass guitar and drums—the heartbeat of reggae—played by the riddim pair of Aston and Carlton Barrett.) In addition, the high range of the Wailers' voices creates a strong element of urgency that is lacking in the Clapton recording. Marley and the Wailers add small but effective and apparently spontaneous variations in the vocal lines of the successive verses of this clearly structured verse-chorus song, giving a sense of familiarity and freedom with the material that also has no real counterpart in the cover version. And there is of course no substitute for the Jamaican patois (a dialect of English with strong African influence) in Marley's original ("Ev'ry day the bucket a-go-a well; one day the bottom a-go drop out"). It is to Clapton's credit, however, that he doesn't even try to mimic Marley's rendition of a Jamaican proverb about the eventual triumph of the oppressed (instead he sings, "Every day the bucket goes to the well, but one day the bottom will drop out").

In sum, Clapton made an effective 1970s pop single out of Marley's "I Shot the Sheriff" by smoothing out its sound. The traditional rock backbeat (in which the drums emphasize the second and fourth beats of the four-beat measures), clearly heard on Clapton's recording, ties it to the rock mainstream, while the basic rhythmic character of Marley's version (in which all the beats are much more evenly emphasized and the syncopated patterns imposed over them are brought strongly forward) is decidedly outside that mainstream. It may seem ironic to find a hero of the 1960s counterculture like Eric Clapton cast in the role of mainstream popularizer for a new marginal music in the 1970s, but the history of American popular music is full of such ironies, as one decade's rebel becomes the next decade's establishment.

The Rise of Salsa Music

Latin American influence on mainstream popular music appeared to wane during the early 1970s as rock music consolidated its dominance in the popular music marketplace. In the aftermath of the *bugalú* movement, which had mixed Latin styles with African American R&B and jazz, and despite a few successful attempts at melding the mambo with guitar-based rock music (e.g., Santana's "Oye Como Va"; see Chapter 11), most Latin musicians in New York City returned to the *típico* (traditional) sound of Cuban dance music, rooted in the *son montuno* form.

In his pioneering book *The Latin Tinge*, John Storm Roberts quotes Louie Ramirez, a successful dance band arranger, who speaks about the Latin music scene in New York in the early 1970s:

> If it's not *típico*, [they say] it's no good. It's a thing like, "let's progress, but at the same time let's keep it *típico!*" But *típico* music is two chords. It's soul, but

> musically it's primitive! Aretha Franklin's drummer told me, "You know, in the
> fifties and sixties you guys were doing some heavy things. Now you're kind of
> like calypso [tourist] bands!" (Roberts 1998, 187)

Perhaps in response to the musical conservatism that Ramirez bemoaned, by the mid-1970s a rhythmically charged, harmonically advanced style of music was coming into its own in the dance clubs of New York. The genre was being called **salsa**, or "[hot] sauce," a verbal metaphor for the intensity, passion, and rhythmic flow of well-played dance music that had long been in circulation among Latin American musicians. Like "jazz," "swing," and "rock 'n' roll," salsa was at once an aesthetic sensibility, a genre classification, and a marketing label. One of salsa's most widely cited origin myths credits the introduction of the term to Izzy Sanabria, publisher of *Latin New York* magazine, who played an important role in promoting the music during the 1970s.

Another important factor in the emergence of salsa music was the rise of independent Latin-oriented record companies. The most successful of these was Fania Records, founded in 1964 by the Dominican Republic–born bandleader Johnny Pacheco and an Italian American lawyer named Jerry Masucci. In the early 1970s Masucci, a capable though famously tough businessman, began promoting a group called the Fania All-Stars, which included Pacheco, master conga player Ray Barretto (see Chapter 9), trombonist and arranger Willie Colón, and singer-songwriter Rubén Blades, with frequent guest appearances by established stars like the bandleader and timbalist Tito Puente and the Cuban-born singer Celia Cruz. Masucci booked the superstar group into a series of increasingly capacious venues; in 1973 they presented a concert for forty-four thousand fans at Yankee Stadium, followed the next year by a concert in the central African country of Zaire as a lead-up to the notorious "Rumble in the Jungle" heavyweight title fight between Muhammad Ali and George Foreman, and then in 1976 by a return appearance in Yankee Stadium. (Documentary footage of these performances is included in the films *Nuestra Cosa* [*Our Latin Thing*], released in 1972, and *Salsa*, released by Columbia in 1976.)

In musical terms, salsa music was an extension of the experimental blend of Latin ballroom dance music, Afro-Cuban rumba drumming, and modern jazz that was forged by Mario Bauza, Machito, and Dizzy Gillespie back in the 1940s (see Chapter 6). As Bauza himself suggested, "What they call *salsa* is nothing new. When Cuban music was really in demand the kids didn't go for it. Now they call it *salsa* and they think it belongs to them. It's good as a gimmick" (Roberts 1998, 188). While Bauza's emphasis on musical continuities (and the commercial function of musical genres) makes sense, salsa can also be viewed as a product of the stylistic and ideological tension between *típico* roots and modernist experimentalism, Latino community identity and urban cosmopolitanism.

The two most influential figures of early salsa were **Eddie Palmieri** (b. 1936) and **Willie Colón** (b. 1950), both born to Puerto Rican immigrant parents in New York City. Palmieri's musical development was influenced by his older brother, the pianist and

Willie Cólon on stage in 2010.

bandleader *Charlie Palmieri* (1927–1988), who began playing with Tito Puente's mambo band in the late 1940s and had a key role in the Latin music of the 1960s. Eddie's approach to the piano was strongly shaped by modern jazz of the 1950s and 1960s, and his breakthrough albums *Sentido* (1973) and *Sun of Latin Music* (1974) juxtaposed his deep knowledge of the stylistic history of Latin music with various experimental moves, including solo piano preludes influenced by the style of Miles Davis's pianist McCoy Tyner and the incorporation of tape-based sound effects. Working with musically sophisticated arrangers, Eddie Palmieri's band pushed the compositional and harmonic limits of Latin dance music while always maintaining a connection to the *típico* style. As Palmieri himself put it:

> I can use the same phrasing as the old groups use, and I could extend it, and build master structures around it—make it with such high-tension chords that everybody would blow their minds—but the phrasing would not disrupt the rhythmic patterns. Rhythm is your foundation. (Roberts 1998, 189)

Willie Colón, fourteen years Palmieri's junior, grew up during the *bugalú* era and was less directly influenced by the Cuban *típico* style. His distinctive approach to salsa music added touches of West African, Panamanian, Colombian, and Brazilian music as well as Puerto Rican styles such as *jíbaro* ("country") songs, which were accompanied with the *cuatro* (a small ten-stringed guitar); and the *plena*, an African-influenced narrative song genre with percussion accompaniment. Like Eddie Palmieri, Colón gave the trombone a lead role in the horn section of his band. His first album, *El Malo* (*The Bad Dude*), released by Fania in 1967, helped to create an image of Colón as a tough, streetwise guy—an impression reinforced by his band's restlessly energetic, gritty sound, an alternative to the more polite flute-and-violins texture of the then still-popular *charanga* (see the discussion of "El Watusi" in Chapter 9). The popularity

Rubén Blades.

of Colón's band was reinforced by a series of excellent lead singers, including **Hector Lavoe** (1946–1993), who became an icon of Nuyorican (New York Puerto Rican) immigrant identity during the 1970s, and **Rubén Blades** (b. 1948), the son of a middle-class family in Panama (with a Cuban father and a Colombian mother) who had attended Harvard Law School.

Blades got his start in the music trade as a stock boy at Fania Records and soon rose to become one of the label's biggest stars. A gifted singer-songwriter, film actor, and political activist, Blades is best known for a series of story-songs that capture the feel of life in a neighborhood *barrio* populated with memorable characters. His composition "Pedro Navaja" ("Pedro the Knife"), included on the album *Siembra* (released by Fania Records in 1977), never appeared on the pop music charts in the United States, but it is the most popular song to emerge from the salsa movement of the 1970s, in large part because it drew upon the experience of millions of people living in urban neighborhoods throughout Latin America.

"Psycho Killer": 1970s Punk and New Wave

During the 1970s the first "alternative" movements emerged within rock music. Although rock had begun as a vital part of the 1960s counterculture, by 1975 it had come perilously close to occupying the center of popular taste, a development that left some young musicians feeling that its rebellious, innovative potential had been squandered by pampered, pretentious rock stars and the major record companies that promoted them. The golden age of **punk rock**—a "back to basics" rebellion against the perceived artifice and pretension of corporate rock music—lasted from around 1975 to 1978, but both the musical genre and the sensibility with which it was associated continue to exert a strong influence today on alternative rock musicians. **New wave** music, which developed alongside punk rock, approached the critique of corporate rock in more self-consciously artistic and experimental terms. (The term "new wave" was soon picked up by record companies themselves, who began using it in the late 1970s to refer to pop-influenced performers such as Blondie.) Although the initial energy of the punk and new wave scene was largely expended by the start of the 1980s, young

Listening Guide "PEDRO NAVAJA"

Written by Rubén Blades, performed by Willie Colón and Rubén Blades (recorded 1977)

Conceived as an homage to the song "Mack the Knife" (originally from *The Threepenny Opera* by Kurt Weill and Bertolt Brecht), "Pedro Navaja" ("Pedro the Knife") tells the story of the violent demise of a street tough who attacks a prostitute. As Navaja stabs her, the woman defends herself by shooting him with a handgun. Both of them die on the spot, and their bodies are soon discovered by a drunk, who searches them, empties their pockets, and stumbles off. As he weaves down the street, the drunk sings an out-of-tune refrain that is immediately adopted as the call-and-response *coro* (chorus) of the montuno section that follows.

The arrangement, by Luis "Perico" Ortiz, provides a sophisticated musical framework for the narrative portrait of "Pedro Navaja." The track begins with an instrumental introduction in which the sound of police sirens place us directly in the gritty urban environment of the *barrio*. The instruments enter one after another to accompany Blades's voice: congas during the first verse, bongó and timbales during the second, bass and piano on the third, and finally a four-trombone brass section on the fourth verse. When the trombones enter, the key rises, ratcheting up the dramatic and musical intensity—a strategy that Ortiz repeats on the sixth, eighth, and ninth choruses before launching us into the montuno section.

Because its lyric is so central to the enormous impact that this song had on audiences throughout Latin America (including Latin New York), it is worth presenting in its entirety. (See Dashboard for a complete line-by-line English translation of "Pedro Navaja.")

The scene opens with Rubén Blades describing the young street tough Pedro the Knife walking down the streets of the *barrio* with an easy, sinister gait. He is a striking figure, sporting a shiny gold tooth, dark sunglasses, a stylish wide-brimmed hat, and state-of-the-art sneakers (in case he needs to flee from trouble). Pedro keeps his hands deep inside his coat pockets so that no one can see which hand is holding the knife. Down the street he sees a prostitute step into a tenement to drink. An unmarked police car glides slowly by, and Pedro smiles, his gold tooth lighting up the street. Suddenly the woman emerges from the tenement onto the deserted street, and Pedro runs silently toward her. As he stabs her in the chest, laughing, she shoots him with a gun that she carries in her purse for protection. Fatally wounded, Pedro falls to the sidewalk, and the woman, who is also dying, says, "I thought my luck was bad, but you are worse off, you are nothing." There follows a great silence, during which no one comes out to see what has happened, no one asks questions, no one cries—until a drunk stumbles up, pockets the gun, the knife, and the money, and weaves down the street singing the song's existentialist moral: "Life gives you surprises, surprises give you life, oh God." Blades sings this last, pivotal line in a slurred manner, inhabiting the character of the drunkard who has been unexpectedly blessed by serendipity.

After a three-measure instrumental transition, the call-and-response-dominated montuno section of the arrangement begins, with the band singing the refrain. Blades improvises a series of solo vocal responses, including traditional proverbs ("He who lives by the sword, dies by the sword" and "He who laughs last, laughs best"), the tagline from a popular television police drama ("There are 8 million stories in New York City"), and literary references ("As in a Kafka novel, the drunkard turned at the corner").

The call-and-response montuno form is interrupted by an instrumental section, in which the piano plays a harmonically complex five-measure pattern and the trombones join in with a unison melody. (All the while, police sirens are wailing in the background, reminding us of the dramatic context.) The next sixteen measures of the arrangement feature the voices singing a soaring melodic line that alternates with trombone riffs. The band then sings the phrase "I like to live in America," adopted from Leonard Bernstein's Broadway musical *West Side Story*. This edgy, sarcastic reference to mass media portrayals of daily reality in New York City's Latino neighborhoods—all the more pointed given the pointless street corner tragedy described in Blades's song—is followed by a dissonant melodic pattern in the trombones.

The rest of the arrangement carries on in much the same manner, alternating the call-and-response montuno section with the varied instrumental material that we have just discussed. As the recording fades, we

(continued)

Listening Guide "PEDRO NAVAJA" (*continued*)

hear a television newscaster speaking in Spanish: "In New York City two people were found dead. Early this morning the lifeless bodies of Pedro Barrio and Josefina Wilson, of unknown address . . ."

The combination of gritty realism, cinematic imagery, literary and pop culture references, an air of knowing fatalism, a well-crafted arrangement (grounded in the old Afro-Cuban *son montuno* form) and an irresistible groove made "Pedro Navaja" an instant transnational classic, an iconic representation of the spirit, sophistication, and community orientation of the best salsa music of the 1970s.

LISTENING GUIDE | "PEDRO NAVAJA"

TIME	LYRIC	DESCRIPTIVE COMMENTS
0:00		Instrumental introduction (with sound of police sirens)
0:18		Conga with sirens
0:28	*Por la esquina del viejo . . .*	Conga continues, with whistling and other sound effects behind the vocalist, who half-chants the lyrics
0:51	*Usa un sombrero . . . .*	Timbales and bongó drums enter
1:13	*Como a tres cuadras . . .*	Bass and piano enter; vocalist begins to sing more melodic line; sound effects dropped
1:35	*Un carro pasa muy despacito . . .*	Harmonized trombones enter; key rises half-step; vocalist continues to develop a more melodic approach to the lyrics
2:16	*Mira pa' un lado . . .*	Key rises another half-step; piano chord accents at end of third line of each verse
2:58	*Y Pedro Navaja . . .*	Key rises another half-step
3:18	*Y Pedro Navaja . . .*	Key rises another half-step
3:59	*Y tropezando se fue . . .*	On final line, vocalist changes timbre of his voice to indicate irony
4:20		Chorus repeats last line, with lead vocalist improvising over it; instrumental continues
4:41		Continuing instrumental part with piano playing rhythmic chord riff; return of sirens; horns play melodic riffs; chorus sings la-las in exchange with horns
5:25		Chorus quotes line from *West Side Story* (*I like to live in . . .*) followed by horn flourish; then return to singing final line with vocalist riffing above
5:57		Piano plays block chord riff with police sirens; horn riffs; chorus sings "la-las"
6:34		Quote from *West Side Story* repeated; continued vocal on last line of verse
7:13		Newscaster speaks over final trumpet riffs

musicians inspired by the raw vigor and minimalism of this movement went on to create distinctive regional music scenes in Los Angeles, Minneapolis, and Seattle, as well as Athens, Georgia, and elsewhere.

Punk was as much a cultural style—an attitude defined by a rebellion against authority and a deliberate rejection of middle-class values—as it was a musical genre. The contrarian impulse of punk culture is evoked (and parodied) in the song "I'm Against It," recorded by the Ramones in 1978, in which the vocalist gave a long list of things he "don't like" from "sex and drugs" to "waterbugs," "ping-pong," and "Burger King," concluding "All I care about is me." This is reminiscent of the motorcycle gang leader played by Marlon Brando in the archetypal teen rebellion film *The Wild One* (1954). When asked by a young woman, "What are you rebelling against?" the Brando character responds, "Whaddaya got?"

Punk was in fact both the apotheosis and the ultimate exploitation of rock 'n' roll as a symbol of rebellion, a tradition that began in the 1950s, when white teenagers gleefully co-opted the energy and overt sexuality of Black rhythm & blues to annoy their parents, and continued through the 1960s with songs like the Who's youth anthem "My Generation" ("Why don't you all just f-f-fade away?"). To many of its fans, punk rock represented a turn toward the authentic, risk-taking spirit of early rock 'n' roll and away from the pomposity and self-conscious artistry of album-oriented rock. However, like all alternative styles of popular music, punk rock was rife with contradictions.

To begin with, if punk was explicitly against the standards of traditional commercial fashion, it was also a fashion system in its own right, with a very particular look: torn blue jeans, ripped stockings, outfits patched with ragged bits of contrasting materials, and perhaps a safety pin through the cheek. If some punk musicians framed their challenge to established authority in terms of progressive social values, others flirted with fascist imagery, attaching Nazi swastikas to their clothing and associating with the racist "skinhead" movement. Many in the punk movement—including musicians, fans, and those rock critics who championed the music—saw punk as a progressive response to the conservatism of the record industry. Yet the nihilism of much punk rock—the music's basic "I don't give a f—" stance—posed a crucial question that still resonates in today's alternative rock music: Is it possible to make music that is "authentic" or "real" while at the same time loudly proclaiming that you don't care about anything?

In musical terms, punk rock turned progressive rock—with its artistic aspirations and corporate backing—on its head. As the drummer for the Ramones, widely regarded as the first punk rock band, put it:

> We took the rock sound into a psychotic world and narrowed it down into a straight line of energy. In an era of progressive rock, with its complexities and counterpoints, we had a perspective of non-musicality and intelligence that took over from musicianship. (Laing 1985, 23)

Punk was a stripped-down and often purposefully "nonmusical" version of rock music that was in some sense a return to the wildness of early rock 'n' roll stars like

Jerry Lee Lewis and Little Richard, but with lyrics that stressed the ironic or dark dimensions of human existence: drug addiction, despair, suicide, lust, and violence. As David Byrne, the leader of the new wave band Talking Heads, put it (on the PBS television series *Rock & Roll*):

> Punk . . . was more a kind of do-it-yourself, anyone-can-do-it attitude. If you only played two notes on the guitar, you could figure out a way to make a song out of that, and that's what it was all about.

Punk rock and its more commercial cousin, new wave, took shape in New York City during the mid-1970s. One of the predecessors of punk rock was an American musical institution called the **garage band**, which was typically a neighborhood operation made up of young men who played mainly for themselves, their friends, and the occasional high school dance. A few of these local groups went on to enjoy some commercial success, including the Los Angeles–based Standells (whose "Dirty Water" was a Number 11 pop hit in 1966), the Mysterians, who hailed from the industrial town of Flint, Michigan (and whose "96 Tears" went to the top of the charts in the same year), and Portland, Oregon's Kingsmen, best known for their cover version of the 1950s R&B song "Louie, Louie" (Number 2 pop in 1963). The rough-and-ready, do-it-yourself attitude of the garage bands, which were somewhat akin to a rock 'n' roll–based folk music movement, paved the way for punk rock.

Three groups, none of them very successful in commercial terms, are frequently cited as ancestors of 1970s punk music, as well as of later genres such as new wave, hardcore, industrial, and alternative rock: the Velvet Underground, the Stooges, and the New York Dolls. The Velvet Underground, a New York group, was promoted by the pop art superstar Andy Warhol, who painted the famous cartoonlike image of a banana on the cover of their first LP. Their music was rough-edged, chaotic, extremely loud, and deliberately anticommercial, and the lyrics of their songs focused on topics such as sexual deviancy, drug addiction, violence, and social alienation. The leaders of the Velvet Underground were singer and guitarist *Lou Reed* (1942–2013)—who had worked previously as a pop songwriter in a Brill Building–style "music factory"—and *John Cale* (b. 1942), a viola player active in the avant-garde art music scene in New York who introduced experimental musical elements into the mix, including electronic noise and recorded industrial sounds.

If the Velvet Underground represented the self-consciously experimentalist roots of 1970s new wave music, the Stooges, formed in Ann Arbor, Michigan, in 1967, were the working-class, motorcycle-riding, leather-jacketed ancestors of punk rock. The lead singer of the Stooges, Iggy Stooge (a.k.a. *Iggy Pop*, born James Osterburg in 1947), was famous for his outrageous stage performances, which included flinging himself into the crowd, cutting himself with beer bottles, and rubbing himself with raw meat. Guitarist Ron Asheton has described the Stooges' approach:

> Usually we got up there and jammed one riff and built into an energy freak-out, until finally we'd broken a guitar, or one of my hands would be twice as big as the other and my guitar would be covered in blood. (Palmer 1995, 263)

The Stooges' eponymous first album (1969), produced by the Velvet Underground's John Cale, created a devoted if small national audience for the band's demented "garage band" sound. A good example of the sensibility that underlay much of the Stooges' work—the depression of unemployed Michigan youth caught in the middle of a severe economic recession—is the song "1969," which evokes a world light-years distant from the utopianism of the hippie movement and the Woodstock Festival, held that same summer. The song's protagonist laments that 1969 will be "another year with nothing to do," just like the year before and presumably all the following years.

Another band that exerted a major influence on the musical and visual style of the punk rock movement was the New York Dolls, formed in New York City in 1971. Dressed in fishnet stockings, bright red lipstick, cellophane tutus, ostrich feathers, and Army boots, the all-male Dolls were an American response to the English glam rock movement, typified by the reigning master of rock gender bending, David Bowie (see Chapter 11). Their professional career began inauspiciously—at a Christmas party in a seedy welfare hotel in

Patti Smith in performance in 1979.

Manhattan—but by late 1972 they had built a small and devoted following. Although the New York Dolls soon succumbed to drug and alcohol abuse, they did establish certain core features of punk antifashion and helped to create a new underground rock music scene in New York City.

The amateur energy of garage band rock 'n' roll, the artsy nihilism of the Velvet Underground, the raw energy and abandon of the Stooges, and the antifashion of the New York Dolls converged in the mid-1970s in New York City's burgeoning club scene. The locus of this activity was a converted folk music club called CBGB & OMFUG ("Country, Bluegrass, Blues & Other Music for Urban Gourmandizers"), located in the run-down Bowery area of Manhattan; the club remained in business until 2006. The first rock musician to perform regularly at CBGBs was *Patti Smith* (b. 1946), a New York–based poet, journalist, and singer who had been experimenting with combining the spoken word and rock accompaniment. In 1975 Smith began a stint at CBGBs, establishing a beachhead for punk and new wave bands, and signed a contract with Arista, a new label headed by Clive Davis, the former head of Columbia Records. Her critically acclaimed album *Horses* reached Number 47 on the *Billboard* charts in 1976. (Smith has enjoyed a longer career than many of her punk cohorts; most recently, she has distinguished herself as an author with two award-winning memoirs of her life and career, *Just Kids* (2010) and *M Train* (2015).) Other influential groups who played at CBGBs during the mid-1970s included Television (whose lengthy instrumental improvisations were inspired by the Velvet Underground and avant-garde jazz saxophonist Albert Ayler), Blondie, and the Voidoids (whose songs featured the alienated lyrics and howling voice of lead singer Richard Hell, one of the original members of Television).

The first bona fide punk rock band was the *Ramones*, formed in 1974 in New York City. The Ramones' high-speed, energetic, and extremely loud sound influenced English punk groups such as the *Sex Pistols* and the Clash and also became a blueprint for 1980s hardcore bands in Los Angeles. Although they projected a street-tough image, all of the band's members were from middle-class families in the New York City borough of Queens. The band—not a family enterprise, despite their stage names—consisted of Jeffrey Hyman (a.k.a. Joey Ramone) on vocals, John Cummings (Johnny Ramone) on guitar, Douglas Colvin (Dee Dee Ramone) on bass, and Tom Erdelyi (Tommy Ramone) on drums. The band's first manager, Danny Fields, had previously worked with the Stooges and Lou Reed and thus had a good sense of the Ramones' potential audience.

Taking the stage in blue jeans and black leather jackets—a look calculated to evoke the sneering, rebellious ethos of 1950s rock 'n' rollers—the Ramones began playing regularly at CBGBs in 1975. By the end of the year they had secured a recording contract with Sire Records, an independent label that signed a number of early punk groups. Their eponymous debut album was recorded in 1976 for just over $6,000, an incredibly small amount of money in an era of expensive and time-consuming studio sessions. The album gained some critical attention and managed to reach Number 111 on the *Billboard* album charts.

Later that year the Ramones staged a British Invasion in reverse. Their concerts in English cities, where their records had already created an underground sensation, were attended by future members of almost every important British punk band, including the Sex Pistols (see Box 12.1), the Clash, and the Damned. In 1977 the Ramones scored

The Ramones, c. 1977.

a UK Top 40 hit with the song "Sheena Is a Punk Rocker" (Number 81 U.S.), which announced that the center of the rock 'n' roll universe had shifted from the beaches of Southern California to the Lower East Side of Manhattan.

The Ramones' music reflected their origins as a garage band made up of neighborhood friends. As the guitarist Johnny Ramone phrased it in an interview with the popular music scholar Robert Palmer:

> I had bought my first guitar just prior to starting the Ramones. It was all very new; we put records on, but we couldn't figure out how to play the songs, so we decided to start writing songs that were within our capabilities. (Palmer 1995, 274)

These songs had catchy, pop-inspired melodies; were played at extremely fast tempos; and generally lasted no more than two and a half minutes. (In live performances, the Ramones managed to squeeze twelve or thirteen songs into a half-hour set.) The band's raw, hard-edged sound was anchored by a steady barrage of notes played on drums, bass, and guitar. Johnny Ramone rarely if ever took a guitar solo, but this makes sense when you consider the band's technical limitations and the aesthetic goal of rejecting the flashy virtuosity of progressive rock music, with its extended and sometimes self-indulgent solos.

The song "I Wanna Be Sedated," from the band's fourth album, *Road to Ruin* (1978), is a good example of the Ramones' style and their mordant—one is tempted to say twisted—sense of humor:

> *Twenty-twenty-twenty-four hours to go, I wanna be sedated*
> *Nothin' to do and nowhere to go-o-o, I wanna be sedated*
> *Just put me in a wheelchair, get me to the show*
> *Hurry hurry hurry, before I gotta go*
> *I can't control my fingers, I can't control my toes*
> *Oh no no no no no*
> *Ba-ba-bamp-ba ba-ba-ba-bamp-ba, I wanna be sedated*
> *Ba-ba-bamp-ba ba-ba-ba-bamp-ba, I wanna be sedated*

The song text's images of drug-induced insanity (and its putative antidote, drug-induced paralysis) are juxtaposed with a catchy pop melody and Beach Boys–like chorus, a combination that affirms Joey Ramone's early description of the band's style as "sick bubble-gum music."

It is, in fact, hard to know how seriously to take the Ramones. Although they played alongside self-consciously "cutting-edge" bands like the Patti Smith Group and Television, the Ramones identified themselves as a band that was "able to just play and be song-oriented and sound great, people who play real rock 'n' roll." Nonetheless, some of their recordings did provide grim "news flashes" on the facts of life in many working-class and middle-class homes during a period of severe economic recession. The song "I Wanted Everything" (1978) is a kind of punk counterpart to Merle Haggard's hardcore country song "If We Make It Through December" (1973; see Chapter 11)—sung, however, by a dispossessed son rather than a struggling father. The stark realism of this tale of a good boy gone wrong is reminiscent of the work of Bruce Springsteen, often regarded as a working-class rock 'n' roll hero of the 1980s (see Chapter 13), and suggests that American punk rock was not a totally nihilistic movement.

If the Ramones and the Sex Pistols epitomized punk rock's connections to the rebellious energy of early rock 'n' roll, another band, Talking Heads, represented the more self-consciously artistic and exploratory side of the alternative rock scene of the mid-1970s. Talking Heads was formed in 1974 by **David Byrne** (born in Scotland in 1952), Chris Frantz, and Tina Weymouth, who met as art students at the Rhode Island School of Design. They first appeared at CBGBs in 1975 as the opening act for the Ramones, though they attracted a somewhat different audience, made up of college students, artists, and music critics. In 1976 they were signed to a recording contract by Sire Records, and their first album, *Talking Heads: 77*, achieved critical acclaim and broke into the Top 100 on the *Billboard* album charts. The band's style reflected their interest in an aesthetic called minimalism, which stresses the use of combinations of a limited number of basic elements—colors, shapes, sounds, or words. This approach was popular in the New York art music scene of the 1960s and 1970s, as represented in the work of composers such as Steve Reich, Terry Riley, and Philip Glass, who made use of simple musical patterns that were repeated and combined in various ways. The Talking Heads' instrumental arrangements fused this approach with the interlocking, riff-based rhythms pioneered by African American popular musicians, particularly James Brown (see the following discussion of funk music). Clarity is another important aspect of the minimalist aesthetic,

David Byrne with Talking Heads.

BOX 12.1   "THE END OF ROCK 'N' ROLL": THE SEX PISTOLS

We have already mentioned the impression made by the Ramones on musicians in the United Kingdom, an "American Invasion" that began some twelve years after the Beatles stormed New York City. The English stream of punk rock bubbled up during the summer of 1976, an unusually hot summer and a high point of unemployment, inflation, and racial tension in cities like London, Birmingham, Manchester, and Liverpool. In England, more than the United States, punk rock was associated with a mainly white working-class youth subculture. More explicitly political and less artsy than some of the New York bands, groups like the Sex Pistols, the Clash, and the Damned succeeded in outraging the British political establishment and the mainstream media while at the same time achieving a modicum of commercial success in the late 1970s.

The most outrageous—and therefore famous—punk band was the Sex Pistols, formed in 1975 in London. They were the creation of Malcolm McLaren, owner of a London antifashion boutique called Sex that specialized in leather and rubber clothing. (McLaren had begun his career in the music business in 1974, when he unsuccessfully managed the short-lived New York Dolls.) Upon his return to London, McLaren conceived the idea of a rock 'n' roll band that would subvert the pop music industry and horrify England's staid middle class. Glen Matlock (bass), Paul Cook (drums), and Steve Jones (guitar) were regular customers at the shop, and they were looking for a singer. McLaren introduced them to John Lydon, a young man who hung around listening to the jukebox at Sex and had never sung in public before. (Lydon's inconsistent approach to personal hygiene led Steve Jones to christen him **Johnny Rotten**, a stage name that stuck.) The Sex Pistols got their first gigs by showing up and posing as the opening band. Given the nature of Johnny Rotten's stage act—sneering and screaming obscenities at the audience, commanding them to applaud, and throwing beer on them when they didn't—it is perhaps not surprising that they were banned from many nightclubs.

The trajectory of this band's rapid ascent and implosion is complex, and we can present only a summary here. EMI Records, England's biggest and most conservative label, signed the Sex Pistols for around $60,000 in 1976, releasing their first single, "Anarchy in the UK," in December. The single was a Top 40 hit in the UK but was withdrawn from record shops after Rotten uttered an obscenity during a television interview. At an annual meeting of shareholders in December 1976, the chairman of EMI, Sir John Read, made the following statement (as recorded in the December 7 formal Report of the EMI General Meeting):

> Sex Pistols is the only "punk rock" group that EMI Records currently has under direct recording contract and whether EMI does in fact release any more of their records will have to be very carefully considered. I need hardly add that we shall do everything we can to restrain their public behavior, although this is a matter over which we have no real control.

The uproar that resulted from the on-air obscenity caused EMI to terminate the Sex Pistols' contract in January 1977, and all but five out of twenty-one dates on a planned concert tour of the United Kingdom were promptly canceled. In March the bassist Glen Matlock was replaced by John Ritchie, a nonmusician friend of John Lydon, who went by the stage name **Sid Vicious**. The American label A&M Records then signed the Pistols for over $200,000, only to fire them the very next week. In May Virgin Records signed them and released their second single, "God Save the Queen (It's a Fascist Regime)." Despite being banned from airplay, the song went to Number 2 (cited as a blank on the UK charts). The band was featured in a 1978 film called *The Great Rock 'n' roll Swindle*, a title that some critics thought captured perfectly the essence of the band's exercise in manipulation. The Sex Pistols broke up that same year during their only U.S. tour, a tour undertaken to support the release of their only studio album, *Never Mind the Bollocks, Here's the Sex Pistols* (1977). In 1979 Sid Vicious was imprisoned in New York on charges of stabbing his girlfriend to death, and he died of a heroin overdose while out on bail. In 1986 the surviving members of the group sued Malcolm McLaren for cheating them out of royalties and were awarded around $1.5 million. Though they did not represent "the end of rock 'n' roll," the Sex Pistols did manage to do away with themselves quite efficiently.

and the Talking Heads' songs were generally quite simple in structural terms, with strong pop hooks and contrasting sections marked off by carefully arranged changes in instrumental texture.

In their visual presentation and stage demeanor, the Talking Heads were from another universe than the other CBGBs bands—they dressed in slacks, sweaters, and vests, projecting the image of cerebral but nerdy college students. David Byrne's stage demeanor was described by reviewer Michael Aron for the November 17, 1977, issue of *Rolling Stone* magazine:

> Everything about him is uncool: his socks and shoes, his body language, his self-conscious announcements of song titles, the way he wiggles his hips when he's carried away onstage (imagine an out-of-it kid practicing Buddy Holly moves in front of a mirror).

Just as the punk rockers' antifashion became a new kind of fashion, so David Byrne's studied awkwardness established a new kind of cool, one still much in evidence on college campuses today.

Rather like David Bowie's Ziggy Stardust, the character projected in "Psycho Killer"—tongue-tied, nervous, emotionally distant, and obsessively intellectual—provided David Byrne with a durable stage persona. In a review of the 1984 Talking Heads concert film *Stop Making Sense*, one critic remarked on Byrne's ability to project "a variant on his basic 'Psycho Killer' self for each song; he demonstrates over and over that a public self is a Frankenstein self, a monster put together from bits and pieces of image tissue." Throughout the late 1970s and 1980s Talking Heads recorded a series of critically acclaimed albums, most of which reached *Billboard*'s Top 40 and achieved either gold or platinum status. This commercial success can be partially attributed to the accessibility of Talking Heads' music, which mixes in influences from rhythm and blues, funk, and West African music with its complexly interlocking but catchy poly-rhythmic patterns. David Byrne went on to become a major figure in the world beat movement of the 1980s and 1990s, introducing American audiences to recording artists from Africa, Brazil, and the Caribbean.

"Tear the Roof off the Sucker": Funk Music

Punk rock was a reaction against the pretentiousness of progressive rock and its multimillionaire superstars, hidden behind designer sunglasses, limousine windows, and mansion walls. **Funk music** represented yet another back-to-basics impetus: the impulse to dance. Most album-oriented rock music was aimed at a predominantly white male audience and was designed for listening rather than dancing. (Although rock fans certainly engaged in free-form movement, the idea of organized social dancing was anathema to both the "do your own thing" ethos of the counterculture and the "high art" aspirations of some rock musicians.) In urban Black communities across America, however, dance remained a backbone of social life, a primary means for transmitting traditional values and generating a sense of novelty and excitement. And for the first

Listening Guide   "PSYCHO KILLER"

Music and lyrics by David Byrne, Chris Frantz, Tina Weymouth; performed by Talking Heads; recorded 1977

The center of attention on most Talking Heads recordings is David Byrne's trembling, high-pitched voice and eclectic songwriting. Byrne often delivers his lyrics in a nervous, almost schizophrenic stream-of-consciousness voice, like overheard fragments from a psychiatrist's office. A good example of this approach—as well as the only single from the Heads' first LP to appear on the singles charts (peaking at Number 92)—is the song "Psycho Killer," inspired by Norman Bates, the schizophrenic murderer in Alfred Hitchcock's film *Psycho*. Although it now seems like an ironic commentary on mass media portrayals of the "serial killer," this song had a darker, more immediate resonance when it was released in 1977, during the Son of Sam killing spree in which a deranged man shot thirteen people in New York City.

The recording opens with Tina Weymouth's electric bass playing a simple riff reminiscent of mid-1970s funk (see the following section) or disco music. She is soon joined by two guitars that play crisply articulated, interlocking chord patterns. David Byrne's voice enters in the thirteenth bar, enunciating the lyrics in a half-spoken, half-sung style over a simple melody that uses only a few pitches and stays mainly on the tonic note. The first verse (A^1) gives us a glimpse into the psychosis of the narrator. This verse is followed by two statements of the chorus (B), which references the title of the song, dips abruptly and somewhat schizophrenically into a second language (French), and ends with a stuttered warning to the listener.

The chorus blends into a four-bar vocal interlude, with Byrne's voice leaping up an octave and emitting a distressed "Ay yai yai yai," and a two-bar instrumental section that reestablishes the basic groove. In the

second verse (A^2), Byrne shifts from singing to speech, becoming more agitated as he expresses his anger at people who talk a lot, despite having nothing to say, and at his own inability to communicate with others.

The chorus (B) is repeated two more times, followed by the interlude, and then by a new section (C), in which Byrne struggles to confess his crime in an awkward, strangled variant of French:

Ce que j'ai fais, ce soir la [The things I did on that night]
Ce qu'elle a dit, ce soir la [The things she said on that night]
Réalisant mon espoir [Achieving my hope]
Je me lance vers la gloire . . . Okay [I hurl myself toward glory . . . Okay]

Eventually Byrne switches back into English, focusing obsessively on a single pitch and revealing more of his character's motivation for committing an unspecified though presumably horrific act:

We are vain and we are blind
I hate people when they're not polite

After the final repetitions of the "Psycho Killer" chorus (B) and interlude, the band moves into a concluding twenty-four-bar instrumental section (or coda), in which the basic groove is elaborated with distorted textures, wavering pitches on the guitars, strange vocal sounds from Byrne, and the panning of one guitar back and forth from left to right speaker, like the unanchored movement of a madman's thoughts. The last sound we hear is the squeal of feedback from one of the microphones, fading into silence and darkness.

LISTENING GUIDE	"PSYCHO KILLER"		
TIME	FORM	LYRIC	DESCRIPTIVE COMMENTS
0:00	Introduction (12 measures)		Bars 1–4: The electric bass plays a simple two-bar pattern twice
0:08			Bars 5–8: The bass drum enters with a steady pulse, and the electric guitar plays sustained chords

(continued)

Listening Guide "PSYCHO KILLER" (*continued*)

TIME	FORM	LYRIC	DESCRIPTIVE COMMENTS
0:17			Bars 9–12: The second electric guitar enters, completing the basic groove; the two guitars play choppy, rhythmically interlocking chords (in a style inspired by James Brown)
0:24	A¹ (8 measures)	*I can't seem to face up . . .*	Vocal enters; simple melody, centered on tonic pitch; instrumental accompaniment is based on interlocking riffs
0:40	B (8 measures)	*Psycho Killer, Qu'est-ce que c'est? . . .*	New harmonies, sustained chords on guitar mark beginning of chorus; bass and drums continue pulse
0:55	B (8 measures)	*Psycho Killer, Qu'est-ce que c'est? . . .*	Repeated lyrics
1:10	Interlude (6 measures)	*Oh . . . Ai yai yai yai yai*	Byrne sings nonsense syllables, repeated four times, and makes muffled vocal sounds in background; bass, drums, and guitars play basic groove for last two bars
1:22	A² (8 measures)	*You start a conversation . . .*	Byrne moves from singing into speech mode; uses vocal quality to evoke psychotic persona
1:38	B (8 measures)	*Psycho Killer . . .*	
1:54	B (8 measures)	*Psycho Killer . . .*	Repeated lyrics
2:09	Interlude (2 measures)	*Oh . . . Ai yai yai yai yai*	First part only
2:13	C (20 measures)	*Ce que j'ai fais, ce soir la . . .*	Rhythm section plays marchlike pulse in unison for first eight bars, while Byrne speaks the lyrics; guitar plays sustained chords (four bars)
2:29		*Je me lance, vers la gloire . . .*	Rhythm section reestablishes basic groove (four bars); groove continues (four bars)
2:41	Interlude	*Ai yai . . .* *We are vain . . .*	
2:52	B (8 measures)	*Psycho Killer . . .*	
3:07	B (8 measures)	*Psycho Killer*	Repeated lyrics

TIME	FORM	LYRIC	DESCRIPTIVE COMMENTS
3:23	Interlude (4 measures)	*Oh . . . Ai yai yai yai yai*	Byrne sings nonsense syllables, makes vocal sounds in background
3:30	Coda (24 measures)		Bass, drums, and guitars elaborate on basic groove for last twenty-four bars, building in intensity; last eight bars feature stereo effect, with guitar moving back and forth from left to right speaker

time since the twist craze of the early 1960s, funk music—and its commercial offspring, disco—brought this intensive focus on dancing back into the pop mainstream.

The word "funky"—probably a fusion of the eighteenth century English word funky, meaning old or musty smelling, and the (Central African) KiKongo term *lu-fuki,* connotating body odors associated with exertion—was already in wide use by New Orleans jazz musicians during the first decade of the twentieth century. Today "funky" carries the same ambivalent meaning that it did a century ago—strong odors (particularly those related to sex) and a quality of earthiness and authenticity that is quintessentially expressed in music. If the concept of soul symbolized the spiritual, uplifting side of Black consciousness, then funk was its profane and decidedly down-to-earth counterpart.

By the early 1970s the term "funk" was being used as a label for a genre of popular music characterized by strong, dance-oriented rhythms; catchy melodies; call-and-response exchanges between voices and instruments; and a heavy reliance on repeated, rhythmically interlocking patterns. Most funk bands, echoing the instrumentation of James Brown's hits of the late 1960s, consisted of a rhythm section (guitar, keyboards, electric bass, and drums) and a horn section, which effectively functioned as part of the rhythm section and occasionally supplied jazz-influenced solos. Although funk music was initially targeted mostly at the predominantly urban Black audience for soul music, funk groups such as Kool and the Gang and the Ohio Players were able to score Number 1 pop hits during the 1970s. Funk represented a vigorous reassertion of African American musical values in the face of soft soul's dominance of the R&B/pop crossover market, and it paved the way for the more commercialized sounds of disco music in the mid-1970s.

As we have suggested, James Brown was one of the prime inspirations for funk musicians. During the early 1970s Brown continued to score successes with dance-oriented hits, including "Super Bad" (Number 13 pop, Number 1 R&B in 1970), "Hot Pants (She Got to Use What She Got to Get What She Wants)" (Number 15 pop, Number 1 R&B, 1971), "Get on the Good Foot" (Number 18 pop, Number 1 R&B, 1972), and "The

Payback" (Number 26 pop, Number 1 R&B, 1974). Brown's ranking on the pop charts declined gradually throughout this period, however, in large part owing to competition from a new generation of musicians who played variations on the basic style he had established the decade before. This approach—the core of funk music—centered on a strong rhythmic momentum or groove, with the electric bass and bass drum often playing on all four main beats of the measure; the snare drum and other instruments playing equally strongly on the second and fourth beats (the backbeats); and interlocking ostinato patterns distributed among other instruments, including guitar, keyboards, and horns.

Another important influence on 1970s funk music was the group Sly and the Family Stone, an interracial "psychedelic soul" band whose recordings bridged the gap between rock music and soul music. *Sly Stone* (Sylvester Stewart) was born in Dallas, Texas, in 1944 and moved to San Francisco with his family in the 1950s. He began his musical career at the age of four as a gospel singer; went on to study trumpet, music theory, and composition in college; and later worked as a disc jockey at both R&B and rock-oriented radio stations in the San Francisco Bay Area. Sly formed his first band (the Stoners) in 1966 and gradually developed a style that reflected his own diverse musical experience: a blend of jazz, soul music, San Francisco psychedelia, and the socially engaged lyrics of folk rock. The Family Stone's national popularity was boosted by their fiery performance at the Woodstock Festival in 1969, which appeared in the film and soundtrack album *Woodstock*.

Between 1968 and 1971 Sly and the Family Stone recorded a series of albums and singles that reached the top of both the pop and the soul charts. Recordings like "Dance

Sly Stone, c. 1970.

to the Music" (Number 8 pop, Number 9 R&B, 1968); the double-sided hit singles "Everyday People"/"Sing a Simple Song" (Number 1 pop, Number 1 R&B, 1969) and "Thank You (Falettinme Be Mice Elf Again)"/"Everybody Is a Star" (Number 1 pop, Number 1 R&B, 1970); and their last big crossover hit, "Family Affair" (Number 1 pop, Number 1 R&B, 1971) exerted a big influence on funk music. The sound of the Family Stone was anchored by the electric bass of Larry Graham—positioned prominently in the studio mix—and by an approach to arranging that made the whole band, including the horn section, into a collective rhythm section.

By 1973 funk music had burst onto the pop music scene, pushed to the top of the charts by a large and heterogeneous audience that was united by their thirst for rhythmically propulsive dance music. Crossover gold records such as Kool and the Gang's "Jungle Boogie" (Number 4 pop, Number 2 R&B, 1973) and "Hollywood Swinging" (Number 6 pop, Number 1 R&B, 1974), the Ohio Players' "Fire" (Number 1 pop, Number 1 R&B, 1974) and "Love Rollercoaster" (Number 1 pop, Number 1 R&B, 1975), and the multimillion-selling "Play That Funky Music" (Number 1 pop, Number 1 R&B, 1976) by the white band Wild Cherry were played constantly on AM radio and in nightclubs and discotheques. These bands kept the spirit and style of James Brown and Sly Stone alive, albeit in a commercialized and decidedly nonpolitical manner. The image of Black "funkmasters" dancing in Afro hairdos, sunglasses, and brightly colored clothing on television shows like *American Bandstand* and *Soul Train* occasionally came uncomfortably close to racial stereotyping. Certainly, the record industry's packaging of Black "authenticity"—as symbolized by strongly rhythmic, body-oriented music—had a great deal to do with the sudden crossover success enjoyed by bands such as Kool and the Gang and the Ohio Players (who had struggled for success as an R&B band since 1959). However, if the success of funk music in the mainstream pop market capitalized to some degree upon long-standing white American fantasies about Black culture, white funk bands such as Wild Cherry and the Average White Band were also able to place records in the R&B Top 10.

Although they did not share the huge commercial success of the groups just mentioned, the apotheosis of 1970s funk music was a loose aggregate of around forty musicians (variously called Parliament or Funkadelic) led by *George Clinton* (a.k.a. Dr. Funkenstein). Clinton (b. 1940), an ex-R&B vocal group leader and songwriter, hung out with Detroit hippies, listened to the Stooges, and altered his style (as well as his consciousness) during the late 1960s. Enlisting some former members of James Brown's band (among them bassist William "Bootsy" Collins and saxophone player Maceo Parker), he developed a mixture of compelling polyrhythms, psychedelic guitar solos, jazz-influenced horn arrangements, and R&B vocal harmonies. Recording for the independent record company Casablanca (also a major player in the field of disco music), Parliament/Funkadelic placed five LPs in the *Billboard* Top 40 between 1976 and 1978, two of which went platinum.

The band's reputation was in substantial measure based on their spectacular concert shows, which featured wild costumes and elaborate sets (including a huge flying saucer called the "Mothership"), and their innovative concept albums, which expressed an alternative Black sensibility, embodied in a patois of street talk, psychedelic imagery, and science fiction–derived images of intergalactic travel. George Clinton took racial and musical stereotypes and played with them, reconfiguring Black popular music as a positive moral force. On his albums, Clinton wove mythological narratives of a primordial conflict between the "Cro-Nasal Sapiens" (who "slicked their hair and lost all sense of the groove") and the "Thumpasorus People," who buried the secret of funk in the Egyptian pyramids and left earth for the Chocolate Milky Way under the wise leadership of "Dr. Funkenstein." Parliament concerts featured a cast of characters such as "Star Child" (a.k.a. "Sir Lollipop Man"), the cosmic defender of funk; and "Sir Nose D'VoidOf Funk," a spoof of commercialized, soulless, rhythmically challenged pop music and its fans. Clinton's blend of social criticism, wacky humor, and psychedelic imagination is perhaps best captured in his revolutionary manifesto for the funk movement: "Free Your Mind, and Your Ass Will Follow."

"Give Up the Funk (Tear the Roof off the Sucker)," from the million-selling LP *Mothership Connection*, was Parliament's biggest crossover single (Number 5 R&B, Number 15 pop, 1976). It exemplifies the band's approach to ensemble style, known to fans as "P-Funk": heavy, syncopated electric bass lines, interlocking rhythms underlain by a strong pulse on each beat of each measure, long, multisectioned arrangements featuring call-and-response patterns between the horn sections and keyboard synthesizer, R&B-styled vocal harmonies, and verbal mottoes designed to be chanted by fans ("We want the funk, give up the funk; We need the funk, we gotta have the funk"). Arranged by Clinton, bass player Bootsy Collins, and keyboardist Bernie Worrell, the recording is constructed out of these basic elements, which are alternated and layered on top of one another to create a series of shifting sound textures while remaining anchored in the strong pulse of bass and drums.

Clinton and other former Parliament/Funkadelic musicians continued to tour and record throughout the 1980s, but public and critical disdain for 1970s popular culture—especially disco and the dance-oriented music that preceded and inspired it—had a negative impact on the band's fortunes. During the early 1990s the rise of funk-inspired rap (e.g., Dr. Dre) and rock music (e.g., the Red Hot Chili Peppers) established the status of George Clinton and his colleagues as one of the most important—and most frequently sampled—forces in the recent history of Black music. In 1997 Clinton and fifteen other members of Parliament/Funkadelic were inducted into the Rock and Roll Hall of Fame. Discovered by a new generation of listeners, Clinton is still active as of this writing (including a 2015 performance with Mark Ronson, Mary J. Blige, and Grandmaster Flash at the Glastonbury Festival, and an appearance on Kendrick Lamar's album *To Pimp a Butterfly* [see Chapter 15]).

"Rapper's Delight": The Origins of Hip-Hop

Of all the genres of popular music surveyed in this book, none has spurred more vigorous public debate than rap music. Rap has been characterized as a vital link in the centuries-old chain of cultural and musical connections between Africa and the Americas, as the authentic voice of an oppressed urban underclass, and as a form that exploits long-standing stereotypes of Black people. In fact, each of these perspectives has something to tell us about the history and significance of rap music. Rap is indeed based on principles ultimately derived from African musical and verbal traditions. Evidence of these deep continuities may be found in features familiar throughout the history of African American music: an emphasis on rhythmic momentum and creativity; a preference for complex tone colors and dense textures; a keen appreciation of improvisational skill (in words and music); and an incorporative, innovative approach to musical technologies. Much rap music does constitute a cultural response to oppression and racism, serving as a system for communication among Black communities throughout the United States ("Black America's CNN," as rapper Chuck D once put it) and as a source of insight into the values, perceptions, and conditions of people living in America's beleaguered urban communities. And finally, although rap music's origins and inspirations flow from Black culture, the genre's audience has become decidedly multiracial, multicultural, and transnational. As rap has been transformed from a local phenomenon based in a few neighborhoods in New York City to a multimillion-dollar industry and a global cultural phenomenon, it has grown ever more complex and multifaceted.

Rap initially emerged during the 1970s as one part of a complex cultural phenomenon called hip-hop. **Hip-hop culture**, forged by African American, and Caribbean American youth in New York City, included distinctive styles of visual art (graffiti), dance (an acrobatic solo style called breakdancing and an energetic couple dance called the freak), music, dress, and speech. Hip-hop was at first a local phenomenon, centered in certain neighborhoods in the Bronx, the most economically devastated area of New York City. Federal budget cuts caused a severe decline in low-income housing and social services for the residents of America's inner cities during the mid-1970s. By 1977, when President Carter conducted a highly publicized motorcade tour through New York's most devastated neighborhoods, the South Bronx had become, as the *New York Times* put it, "a symbol of America's woes."

The youth culture that spawned hip-hop can on one level be interpreted as a response to the destruction of traditional family- and neighborhood-based institutions and the cutting of funding for public institutions such as community centers, as well as an attempt to lay claim to—and, in a way, to "civilize"—an alienating and hostile urban environment. The young adults who pioneered hip-hop styles such as breakdancing, graffiti art, and the performance of rap music at nightclubs and block parties and in city parks often belonged to informal social groups called "crews" or "posses," each of which was associated with a particular neighborhood or block. It is important to understand that hip-hop culture began as an expression of local identities. Even today, many multiplatinum rap recordings, marketed worldwide, are filled with inside references to particular neighborhoods, features of the urban landscape, and social groups and networks.

If hip-hop music was a rejection of mainstream dance music by young Black and Puerto Rican listeners, it was also profoundly shaped by the techniques of disco DJs. The first celebrities of hip-hop music—*Kool Herc* (Clive Campbell, b. 1955 in Jamaica), *Grandmaster Flash* (Joseph Saddler, b. 1958 in Barbados), and *Afrika Bambaataa* (Kevin

Donovan, b. 1960 in the Bronx)—were DJs who began their careers in the mid-1970s, spinning records at neighborhood block parties, gym dances, and dance clubs and in public spaces such as community centers and parks. These three young men—and dozens of lesser-known DJs scattered throughout the Bronx, Harlem, and other areas of New York City and New Jersey—developed their personal styles within a grid of fierce competition for celebrity and neighborhood pride. As Fab Five Freddy, an early graffiti artist and rapper, put it:

> You make a new style. That's what life on the street is all about. What's at stake is honor and position on the street. That's what makes it so important, that's what makes it feel so good—the pressure on you to be the best . . . to develop a new style nobody can deal with. (George 1985, 111)

The disco DJ's technique of "mixing" between two turntables to create smooth transitions between records was first adapted to the hip-hop aesthetic by Kool Herc, who had migrated from Kingston, Jamaica, to New York City at the age of twelve. Herc noticed that the young dancers in his audiences responded most energetically during the so-called breaks on funk and salsa records, brief sections where the melody was stripped away to feature the rhythm section. Herc responded by isolating the breaks of certain popular records—such as James Brown's "Get on the Good Foot"—and mixing them into the middle of other dance records. These rhythmic sound collages came to be known as "breakbeat" music, a term subsequently transferred to breakdancing, the acrobatic solo performances improvised by the young "b-boys" who attended hip-hop dances.

Another innovation helped to shape the sound and sensibility of early hip-hop: the transformation of the turntable from a medium for playing recorded sound into a playable musical instrument. Sometime in the mid-1970s Kool Herc began to put two copies of the same record on his turntables. Switching back and forth between the turntables, Herc found that he could "backspin" one disc (i.e., turn it backward, or counterclockwise, with his hand) while the other continued to play over the loudspeakers. This technique allowed him to repeat a given break over and over by switching back and forth between the two discs and backspinning to the beginning of the break. This technique was refined by Grandmaster Flash, who adopted the mixing techniques of disco DJs, particularly their use of headphones to synchronize the tempos of recordings and thus create smooth transitions from one dance groove to the next. Using headphones, Flash could more precisely pinpoint the beginning of a break by listening to the sound of the disc being turned backward on the turntable. Flash spent many hours practicing this technique and gained local fame for his ability to "punch in" brief, machine gun–like segments of sound.

A new technique called "scratching" was developed by Flash's young protégé, Theodore, who broke away and formed his own hip-hop crew at the tender age of thirteen. In 1978 Theodore debuted a new technique that quickly spread through the community of DJs. While practicing backspinning in his room, Theodore began to pay closer attention to the sounds created in his headphones as he turned the disc counterclockwise. He soon discovered that this technique yielded scratchy, percussive sound effects, which could be punched in to the dance groove. At first Theodore wasn't sure how people would react:

Grandmaster Flash, left rear, and the Furious Five after being inducted into the Rock & Roll Hall of Fame during ceremonies in New York, 2007.

> The Third Avenue Ballroom was packed, and I figured I might as well give it a try. So, I put on two copies of [James Brown's] "Sex Machine" and started scratching up one. The crowd loved it. . . . They went wild. (Hager 1984, 38)

The distinctive sound of scratching became an important part of the sonic palette of hip-hop music; even in the 1990s, after digital sampling had largely displaced turntables as a means of creating the musical textures and grooves on rap records, producers frequently used these sounds as a way of signaling a connection to the "old school" origins of hip-hop.

Although all DJs used microphones to make announcements, Kool Herc was also one of the first DJs to recite rhyming phrases over the breakbeats produced on his turntables. Some of Herc's "raps" were based on a tradition of verbal performance called "toasting," a form of poetic storytelling with roots in the trickster tales of West Africa. The trickster—a sly character whose main goal in life is to defy authority and upset the normal order of things—became a common figure in the storytelling traditions of Black slaves in the United States, where he took on additional significance as a symbol of cultural survival and covert resistance. After the Civil War the figure of the trickster was in part supplanted by more aggressive male figures who became the focus of long, semi-improvised poetic stories called "toasts." The toasting tradition frequently focused on "bad men": hard, merciless bandits and spurned lovers who vanquished their enemies, sometimes by virtue of their wits, but more often through physical violence (see our discussion of the song "Stagolee" in Chapter 1).

Although the toasting tradition had largely disappeared from Black communities by the 1970s, it continued to flourish in prisons, where Black inmates found that the old narrative form suited their life experiences and present circumstances. One of the main sources for the rhymes composed by early hip-hop DJs in the Bronx was the album *Hustler's Convention* (1973), by Jala Uridin, leader of a group of militant ex-convicts known as the Last Poets. *Hustler's Convention* was a compelling portrait of "the life"—the urban underworld of gamblers, pimps, and hustlers—comprising prison toasts with titles like "Four Bitches Is What I Got" and "Sentenced to the Chair." The record, featuring musical accompaniment by an all-star lineup of funk, soul, and jazz musicians, became enormously popular in the Bronx and inspired Kool Herc and other DJs to compose their own rhymes. Soon DJs were recruiting members of their posses to serve as verbal performers, or "MCs" (an abbreviation of the term "master of ceremonies"). MCs played an important role in controlling crowd behavior at the increasingly large dances where DJs performed and soon became more important celebrities than the DJs themselves. If DJs are the predecessors of today's rap producers—responsible for shaping musical texture and groove—MCs are the ancestors of contemporary rappers.

Until 1979 hip-hop music remained primarily a local phenomenon. The first indication of the genre's broader commercial potential was the twelve-inch dance single "Rapper's Delight," recorded by the Sugar Hill Gang, a crew based in Harlem. This record, which popularized the use of the term "rapper" as an equivalent of MC, established Sugar Hill Records—a Black-owned independent label based in New Jersey—as the predominant institutional force in rap music during the early 1980s. The recording recycled the rhythm section track from Chic's "Good Times" (see Chapter 11), played in the studio by session musicians usually hired by Sugar Hill to back R&B singers. The three rappers—Michael "Wonder Mike" Wright, Guy "Master Gee" O'Brien, and Henry "Big Bank Hank" Jackson—recited a rapid-fire succession of rhymes, typical of the performances of MCs at hip-hop dances.

The text of "Rapper's Delight" alternates the braggadocio of the three MCs ("My name is known all over the world/by all the foxy ladies and the pretty girls . . .") with descriptions of dance movements, exhortations to the audience, and humorous stories and references. One particularly memorable segment describes the consternation of a guest who is served rotting food by his friend's mother, seeks a polite way to refuse it, and finally escapes by crashing through the apartment door. The record, which reached Number 4 on the R&B chart and Number 36 on the pop chart, introduced hip-hop to millions of people throughout the United States and abroad. The unexpected success of "Rapper's Delight" ushered in a series of million-selling twelve-inch singles by New York rappers, including Kurtis Blow's "The Breaks" (Number 4 R&B, Number 87 pop, 1980); "Planet Rock," by Afrika Bambaataa and the Soul Sonic Force (Number 4 R&B, Number 48 pop, 1982); and "The Message," by Grandmaster Flash and the Furious Five (Number 4 R&B, Number 62 pop, 1982).

Listening Guide   "THE MESSAGE"

Written by Sylvia Robinson, Ed Fletcher, and Melle Mel; performed by Grandmaster Flash and the Furious Five; recorded 1982

While most of the early hip-hop crossover hits featured relatively predictable party-oriented raps, "The Message" established a new (and, in the end, profoundly influential) trend in rap music: social realism. In a recording that links the rhythmic intensity of funk music with the toast-derived images of ghetto life exemplified in *Hustler's Convention*, "The Message" is a grim, almost cinematic portrait of life in the South Bronx. The rap on the first half of the recording was cowritten by Sylvia Robinson, a former R&B singer and co-owner of Sugar Hill Records, and Ed "Duke Bootee" Fletcher, a sometime member of the Furious Five. (Resident Sugar Hill percussionist Fletcher composed the musical track using a Roland 808 digital drum machine and keyboard synthesizer, embellished with various studio effects.) On top of the stark, cold electronic groove Duke Bootee intones the rap's grim opening hook: "It's like a jungle sometimes, makes me wonder how I keep from goin' under." The sudden sound of glass shattering (produced on the drum machine) introduces a rhythmically complex and carefully articulated performance that alternates the smooth, slyly humorous style of Grandmaster Flash with the edgy, frustrated tone of MC Melle Mel:

> *Don't push me 'cause I'm close to the edge*
> *I'm tryin' not to lose my head, ah huh huh huh huh*

The two MCs—Melle Mel in particular—time their performances with great precision, speeding up and slowing down, compressing and stretching the spaces between words, and creating polyrhythms against the steady musical pulse. The lyric alternates between the humorous wordplay typical of hip-hop MC performances and various images of desperation—threatening bill collectors, a homeless woman "living in a bag," violent encounters in Central Park, a young child alienated by deteriorating public schools. The relationship between the grim reality of ghetto life and the tough-minded

humor that is its essential antidote is summed up by Melle Mel's humorless quasi-laugh: "Ah huh huh huh huh."

The second half of "The Message"—a *Hustler's Convention*-style toast written and performed by Melle Mel—paints an even more chilling picture, an account of the life and death of a child born into poverty in the South Bronx:

> *A child is born with no state of mind*
> *Blind unto the ways of Mankind*

This recitation is followed by the sound of the Furious Five—MCs Cowboy, Kidd Creole, Rahiem, Scorpio, and Mel—meeting and greeting on a street corner to discuss the evening's plans. Suddenly a police car screeches up and officers emerge, barking orders at the young Black men. "What are you, a *gang*?" one of the policemen shouts. "Nah, man, we're with Grandmaster Flash and the Furious Five." Flash enters from one side to defend his friends: "Officer, officer, what's the problem?" "You're the problem," the cop shouts back. "Get in the car!" We hear the car driving away with the Furious Five in custody, arrested evidently for the crime of assembling on a street corner, and the track quickly "fades to black."

A whole stream within the subsequent history of rap music can be traced to this gritty record, ranging from the explicitly political raps of KRS-One and Public Enemy to the "gangsta" style of Los Angeles MCs like N.W.A., Snoop Doggy Dogg, and Tupac Shakur. As the first honest description of life on the streets of the nation's urban ghettos in the 1980s to achieve wide commercial circulation, "The Message" helped to establish canons of realness and street credibility that are still vitally important to rap musicians and audiences. And the issues addressed in this striking recording most assuredly have not gone away.

ON THE ONE HAND, the popular music of the 1970s provides rich evidence of the continuing vitality of venerable musical forms and techniques—including the African-derived polyrhythms of funk music, reggae, and early rap music, the twelve-bar blues form in rock music, and the European American ballad form in country music—and of the capacity of marginalized communities and musical traditions to revitalize the commercial mainstream of popular music. On the other hand, the 1970s also saw the consolidation of corporate control over the production of musical products on an unprecedented worldwide scale. By the close of the decade, a handful of major transnational companies were responsible for the majority of record sales in both America and worldwide and were busy swallowing up smaller companies. At the same time that the major record companies sought to make the market more predictable, however, the audience for popular music fragmented into dozens of specialized taste communities, creating a complex musical landscape bound to elude the predictive efforts of even the most experienced record producer or corporate CEO. The margins and the mainstream, corporate control and consumer unpredictability, ancient traditions and new technologies—these are the themes that will now carry us into the decades of the 1980s and 1990s, as we continue our journey through the history of American popular music.

Key Terms

funk music	progressive country	salsa
garage band	punk rock	ska
hip-hop culture	reggae	
new wave	rock steady	

Key People

Afrika Bambaataa	Iggy Pop	Rubén Blades
Bob Marley	Jimmy Cliff	Sex Pistols
Charlie Palmieri	John Cale	Sid Vicious
David Byrne	Johnny Rotten	Sly Stone
Eddie Palmieri	Kool Herc	Waylon Jennings
George Clinton	Lou Reed	Willie Colón
Grandmaster Flash	Patti Smith	Willie Nelson
Hector Lavoe	Ramones	

Review Questions

1.   Describe progressive country. Who were its key artists?
2.   What was reggae and where did it come from? From what musical styles did it evolve?
3.   What nonmusical elements were associated with punk?
4.   Discuss hip-hop culture, both its musical and its nonmusical aspects.
5.   What techniques did DJs develop in early hip-hop and rap music?

TIMELINE: 1980—TODAY

MAJOR EVENTS IN U.S. HISTORY	YEAR	IMPORTANT LANDMARKS IN AMERICAN POPULAR MUSIC
 Ronald Reagan is elected president of the United States, reflecting a national turn toward conservative cultural values	1980	
IBM introduces the personal computer (PC)	1981	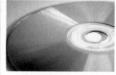 MTV debuts
	1982	• "The Message" (recorded by Grandmaster Flash and the Furious Five) introduces social realism to rap • Michael Jackson's *Thriller* is released and goes on to become the bestselling album ever worldwide • *The Phantom of the Opera* opens on Broadway to become its longest-running musical
United States invades Grenada	1983	• First CDs (compact discs) offered for sale • MIDI (musical instrumental digital interface) introduced

MAJOR EVENTS IN U.S. HISTORY	YEAR	IMPORTANT LANDMARKS IN AMERICAN POPULAR MUSIC
		• Bruce Springsteen's *Born in the U.S.A.* launches him to a new level of success
	1984	• Prince achieves his greatest success with the album/film *Purple Rain* • NYU student Rick Rubin founds Def Jam Records, operating it out of his dorm room; the label would become a major force in hip-hop
The Iran/Contra Affair reveals the Reagan administration's secret plan to arm the Contra rebels from profits made selling arms to Iran	1986	• Paul Simon's *Graceland* establishes the pop potential of world music • Run DMC's version of "Walk This Way" becomes a major hit, launching rap as a pop phenomenon and revitalizing the career of Aerosmith
 The Simpsons debuts as a cartoon feature on TV's *Tracy Ullman Show*	1987	
	1988	• *Yo! MTV Raps* debuts and demonstrates the popular market for hip-hop videos • *It Takes a Nation of Millions to Hold Us Back* by Public Enemy transforms rap from party music to a form of social protest
	1989	• Madonna releases "Express Yourself" and "Like a Prayer," two of her most controversial videos • *Straight Outta Compton* by N.W.A (Niggaz With Attitude) launches gangsta rap
	1990	The term "world music" is introduced as a pop music category by *Billboard* magazine

MAJOR EVENTS IN U.S. HISTORY	YEAR	IMPORTANT LANDMARKS IN AMERICAN POPULAR MUSIC
		• *Metallica* debuts at number one on the pop charts, confirming the mainstream appeal of heavy metal
• The Soviet Union collapses, ending the Cold War • Operation Desert Storm forces Iraq to withdraw from Kuwait	1991	• Nirvana releases the single "Smells Like Teen Spirit" and the album *Nevermind*, with the result that "alternative" music achieves massive mainstream success
Bill Clinton elected president	1992	
	1994	• Queen Latifah's "U.N.I.T.Y." brings a new, female-empowered message to rap • Johnny Cash releases his *American Recordings* album produced by Rich Rubin, relaunching his career
O.J. Simpson found not guilty of murdering his ex-wife and her boyfriend at the end of a highly publicized trial in Los Angeles	1995	• DVDs (digital video discs) introduced • Latina star Selena is murdered by a fan, inspiring an outpouring of grief in the Tex-Mex community
	1996	Rap star Tupac Shakur is murdered, a casualty of the East Coast–West Coast rap rivalries; his rival, the Notorious B.I.G., is killed a year later
 The Hale-Bopp comet makes its closest orbit to earth	1997	MP3 technology introduced on the Internet, enabling the easy transfer and downloading of sound files
	1998	*The Miseducation of Lauryn Hill*, a classic blend of rap, reggae, and R&B, is released
Bill Clinton is acquitted in his impeachment trial by the U.S. Senate	1999	
	2000	• The soundtrack for the film *O Brother, Where Art Thou?* spawns a revival for roots-country music • Pandora Internet Radio, which offers listeners suggestions for music they might like based on their selections, launches

MAJOR EVENTS IN U.S. HISTORY	YEAR	IMPORTANT LANDMARKS IN AMERICAN POPULAR MUSIC
 • 9/11 terrorist attacks destroy the World Trade Center in New York and damage the Pentagon in Washington • United States invades Afghanistan	2001	 • Apple introduces the iPod • Napster.com, a music file-sharing site, is shut down by a record industry lawsuit
Wal-Mart becomes the largest corporation in the world	2002	• Britney Spears tops *Forbes* magazine's list of most powerful celebrities, the youngest pop star ever to reach this peak (at age twenty) • The reality competition *American Idol* debuts; singer Kelly Clarkson is the first winner
United States attacks Iraq over the alleged presence of weapons of mass destruction	2003	MySpace, a popular social networking site often used by musicians to promote themselves, is launched
	2004	 Facebook is launched by Mark Zuckerberg and his associates out of Harvard; it eventually becomes the leading social network site
 Hurricane Katrina devastates New Orleans	2005	• "Podcast" named word of the year by the *New Oxford American Dictionary* • Digital sales of music included for the first time in *Billboard* singles and albums charts • Kanye West criticizes the government's reaction to Hurricane Katrina, saying "George Bush doesn't care about black people."

MAJOR EVENTS IN U.S. HISTORY	YEAR	IMPORTANT LANDMARKS IN AMERICAN POPULAR MUSIC
 Barack Obama elected first African American president of the United States	2008	• Taylor Swift's *Fearless* (2008) spawns eleven Hot 100 hit singles • Spotify is launched in Sweden as a streaming music service supported by advertising
A major oil spill in the Gulf of Mexico occurs when British Petroleum's Deepwater Horizon oil rig leaks oil for three months	2010	
	2011	 *The Voice*, a vocal competition that focuses on the singer's performances rather than their visual appeal, premieres on NBC
• The Supreme Court rules that the Patient Protection and Affordable Care Act (known by friends and foes as Obamacare) is constitutional • "Superstorm" Sandy devastates the East Coast of the United States	2012	
• Boston marathon bombed by two homegrown terrorists • Black Lives Matter founded in response to the acquittal of Trayvon Martin's murderer	2013	Kanye West and Jay Z both release major new albums, *Yeezus* and *Magna Carta Holy Grail* (respectively)
• Russia invades the Ukraine • Ebola outbreak in Africa	2014	
	2015	• Taylor Swift's video for "Blank Space" becomes the most-watched video ever by a female artist on its release, beating Katy Perry's "Dark Horse," the previous record holder that was released a month earlier. Both had over 1 billion views. • *Hamilton* premieres on Broadway. The sung-and-rapped musical, written by Lin-Manuel Miranda, tells the story of founding father Alexander Hamilton and its cast features predominantly actors of color.

MAJOR EVENTS IN U.S. HISTORY	YEAR	IMPORTANT LANDMARKS IN AMERICAN POPULAR MUSIC
• Donald J. Trump elected forty-fifth president of the United States	2016	• Beyoncé releases *Lemonade*, a landmark all-music-video album • Beyoncé and Adele both nominated for song and record of the year by the Grammys; Adele wins record of the year
	2017	"Despacito," by Luis Fonsi with Daddy Yankee, becomes the first video to reach 3 billion views on YouTube
	2019	Lil' Nas X sets records for 19 weeks at Number 1 on Billboard Hot 100 with "Old Town Road," becomes first openly LGBTQ+ artist to win a CMA
• COVID-19 declared a global pandemic, becoming one of the deadliest viral events in history • Donald J. Trump defeated in his bid for re-election; Joseph R. Biden, Jr. becomes the forty-sixth president of the United States • The killings of George Floyd in Minneapolis and Breonna Taylor in Louisville lead to the summer uprisings in protest of police brutality and racial violence	2020	 Billie Eilish becomes the second artist (following Christopher Cross) to sweep the 4 major Grammy categories (New Artist, Song of the Year, Record of the Year, Album of the Year)
• On January 6, a violent mob attacks the U.S. Capitol building in an ultimately unsuccessful attempt to stop the certification by Congress of the 2020 presidential election	2021	Taylor Swift releases "Fearless (Taylor's Version)" the first of six planned re-recordings of her back catalog in order to gain rights to the master tapes

The 1980s

13 Digital Technology, MTV, and the Popular Mainstream

FROM THE VIEWPOINT OF THE AMERICAN MUSIC INDUSTRY, THE 1980S began on a sour note. Following a period of rapid expansion in the mid-1970s, 1979 saw an 11 percent drop in annual record sales nationwide, the first major recession in the industry in thirty years. Profits from the sale of recorded music hit rock bottom in 1982 ($4.6 billion), down half a billion dollars from the peak year of 1978 ($5.1 billion). The major record companies—now subdivisions of huge transnational conglomerates— trimmed their staffs, cut back expenses, signed fewer new acts, raised the prices of LPs and cassette tapes, and searched for new promotional and audience-targeting techniques. The pattern of relying on a small number of multiplatinum artists to create profits became more pronounced in the 1980s. By the middle of the decade, when the industry began to climb out of its hole, it was clear that the recovery was due more to the spectacular success of a few recordings by superstar musicians—Michael Jackson, Madonna, Prince, Bruce Springsteen, Whitney Houston, Phil Collins, Janet Jackson, and others—than to any across-the-board improvement in record sales.

A number of reasons have been adduced for the crash of the early 1980s: the onset of a national recession brought on by the laissez-faire economic policies of the Reagan administration; competition from new forms of entertainment, including home video, cable television, and video games; the decline of disco, which had driven the rapid expansion of the record business in the late 1970s; and an increase in illegal copying ("pirating") of commercial recordings by consumers with cassette tape decks. In 1984 sales of pre-recorded cassettes, boosted by the popularity of the Sony Walkman personal tape player and larger portable tape players called "boom boxes," surpassed those of vinyl discs for the first time in history. The introduction of digital audio tape (DAT) in the early 1990s and writable compact discs (CD-Rs) at the end of the decade provided consumers with the ability to make near-perfect copies of commercial recordings, a development that prompted the music industry to respond with new anticopying technologies.

The 1980s also saw the rise of technologies that revolutionized the production of popular music. The development of digital sound recording led to the introduction of the five-inch compact disc (CD) and the rapid decline of the vinyl disc. The sounds encoded on a compact disc are read by a laser beam and not by a diamond needle, meaning that CDs are not subject to the same wear and tear as vinyl discs. The first compact discs went on sale in 1983, and by 1988 sales of CDs surpassed those of vinyl discs for the first time. Although CDs cost about the same as vinyl LPs to manufacture, the demand for the new medium allowed record companies to generate higher profits by pricing them at thirteen dollars or more, rather than the eight or nine dollars charged for LPs. Digital technology also spawned new and more affordable devices for producing and manipulating sound—such as drum machines and sequencers, and samplers for digital sampling—and the musical instrument digital interface (MIDI) specification, which standardized these technologies, allowing devices produced by different manufacturers to "communicate" with one another. Digital technology—which was both portable and relatively cheap—and the rapid expansion of the personal computer (PC) market in the early 1990s allowed musicians to set up their own home studios and stimulated the growth of genres like hip-hop and techno, both of which rely heavily on digitally constructed sound samples, loops, and grooves. For the first time, satellite technology allowed the worldwide simultaneous broadcast of live concerts, and the development of fiber optics allowed musicians in recording studios thousands of miles apart to work together in real time.

Deregulation of the entertainment industry led to an explosion in the growth of cable television, one byproduct of which was the launching of **Music Television (MTV)** in 1981. MTV changed the way the industry operated, rapidly becoming the preferred method for launching a new act or promoting the latest release of a major superstar. (The advent of videos designed to promote rock recordings is often traced to the band Queen's mock-operatic hard rock extravaganza "Bohemian Rhapsody," released in 1975. However, such early music videos were essentially advertisements for the sound recordings and were not viewed as products that might be sold on their own merits.) Although the first song broadcast on MTV bore the title "Video Killed the Radio Star" (recorded by the Buggles), it is more accurate to say that MTV—and its spin-off VH-1, which was aimed at an older, twenty-five- to-thirty-five-year-old audience—worked synergistically with radio and other media to boost record sales and create a new generation of rock superstars. It also strongly influenced the direction of popular music in the early 1980s, sparking what has been called a second British Invasion by promoting English artists such as the Eurythmics, Flock of Seagulls, Adam Ant, Billy Idol, and Thomas Dolby. (In July 1983 eighteen of the singles in *Billboard*'s Top 40 chart were by English artists, topping the previous record of fourteen that was set in 1965 during the first British Invasion.) By the mid-1980s the impact of MTV had been felt throughout the music industry.

MTV's relentless focus on white rock artists reminded many critics of the exclusionary practices of album-oriented rock radio in the 1970s. Out of more than 750 videos shown on MTV during the channel's first eighteen months, only about twenty featured Black musicians (a figure that includes racially mixed bands). At a time when Black artists such as Michael Jackson and Rick James were making multiplatinum LPs, they could not break into MTV, which put Phil Collins's cover version of the Supremes' "You Can't Hurry Love" into heavy rotation but played no videos by Motown artists themselves. Executives at MTV responded to widespread criticism of their policy with the argument that their format focused on rock, a style played by few Black artists. Of course, this was a tautological argument—the restrictive format of MTV was the cause, and not merely a byproduct, of the problem.

The mammoth success of Michael Jackson's *Thriller*, released by Columbia Records in 1982, forced a change in MTV's essentially all-white rock music format. The three videos made to promote the *Thriller* LP through three of its hit singles—"Billie Jean," "Beat It," and "Thriller"—set new standards for production quality, creativity, and cost and established the medium as the primary means of promoting popular music. "Thriller"—a musical horror movie directed by John Landis, who had previously made the feature film *An American Werewolf in London*—metamorphosed into a sixty-minute home video entitled *The Making of Michael Jackson's Thriller* that comprised the original fifteen-minute video and lots of filler material, including interviews with the star. *The Making of Michael Jackson's Thriller* sold 350,000 copies in the first six months, yet MTV still refused to air Jackson's videos. Finally, after Columbia Records threatened to ban its white rock groups from performing on MTV, the channel relented, putting Jackson's videos into heavy rotation. (*Thriller* will be discussed in more detail later; for now we will simply note that Jackson did not share the segregationist sentiments of MTV executives, going out of his way to include white rock stars such as Paul McCartney and Eddie Van Halen on his LP.)

The process of corporate consolidation (sometimes called "horizontal integration"), which has emerged at intervals throughout the history of American popular music, once again reared its head during the late 1980s and early 1990s. To a greater extent than ever before, record labels could no longer be considered stand-alone institutions but were rather subdepartments of huge transnational corporations. By 1990 six corporations collectively controlled over two-thirds of global sales of recorded music: the Dutch Polygram conglomerate (owner of Mercury, Polydor, Island, A&M, and other labels); the Japanese corporations Sony (Columbia Records) and Matsushita (MCA and Geffen Records); the British firm Thorn (EMI, Virgin, Capitol); the German Bertelsmann conglomerate (BMG and RCA Records); and Time-Warner, the only American-based corporation in this list (Warner, Elektra, and Atlantic Records). Similarly, the American market for recorded music now had to be seen as part of a wider global market that transcended national borders. In 1990 the largest market for recorded music in the world was the United States, which, at $7.5 billion, accounted for approximately 31 percent of world trade, followed at some distance by Japan (12 percent), the United Kingdom and Germany (9 percent each), and France (7 percent). Even in the United States, however, the record company executives concerned themselves to an unprecedented degree with global sales and promotion.

This move toward global corporate consolidation of the music business was accompanied by a further fragmentation of the marketplace for popular music and the creation of dozens of new musical genres, marketing categories, and radio formats. Some of these categories were more novel than others, but all bore some relationship to musical forms of the past. Country music continued its six-decade journey from the margins to the center of popular taste, becoming the bestselling musical genre in the United States and boasting such rock- and pop-influenced country superstars as Garth Brooks, Clint Black, and Reba McEntire. During the 1980s rock music, which had undergone a process of fragmentation in the early 1970s, sub-divided into a hundred specialized genres and subgenres, some with huge audiences (adult contemporary and heavy metal), and others supported by smaller but devoted groups of fans (hardcore, thrash, and techno, the respective children of punk rock, heavy metal, and Eurodisco). Rap music, which emerged during the mid-1970s from the hip-hop culture of Black, Latino, and Caribbean American youth in New York City, had by the late 1980s grown into a multimillion-dollar business. During the 1990s the relationship between the center and the periphery of the music business—and between mainstream and marginalized types of music—became even more complicated, with self-consciously anticommercial genres like gangsta rap, speed metal, and grunge reaching the top of the *Billboard* LP and singles charts and generating huge profits for the music industry, and musicians from Latin America (Ricky Martin) and francophone Canada (Celine Dion) ranking among the most profitable superstars in the United States at the end of the second millennium.

The core themes that we have traced throughout this book—the intimate relationship between social identity and musical style; the links among music, economics, and technology; and the interaction of various streams of musical tradition—were just as evident at the close of the twentieth century as they were at its inception. Nevertheless, much has changed over the past hundred years: old, deep patterns of American musical culture have been profoundly shaped by the advent of new technologies and institutions, new social movements, and profound shifts in the self-definition and values of musicians and their audiences. In this chapter we will begin our consideration of the popular music of the 1980s and 1990s with a look at the changing nature of the musical mainstream.

Digital Technology and Popular Music

During the 1980s new technologies—including digital tape recorders, compact discs, synthesizers, samplers, and sequencers—became central to the production, promotion, and consumption of popular music. These devices were the fruit of a long history of interactions between the electronics and music industries and between individual inventors and musicians.

Analog recording—the norm since the introduction of recording in the nineteenth century—transforms the energy of sound waves into either physical imprints (as in pre-1925 acoustic recordings) or electronic waveforms that closely follow (and can be used to reproduce) the shape of the sound waves themselves. **Digital recording**, on the other hand, samples the sound waves and breaks them down into a stream of numbers (0s and 1s). A device called an analog-to-digital converter does the conversion. To play back the music, the stream of numbers is converted back to an analog wave by a digital-to-analog converter (DAC). The analog wave produced by the DAC is amplified and fed to speakers to produce the sound. There have been many arguments among musicians and audiophiles over the relative quality of the two technologies: initially, many musicians found digital recording too "cold" (perhaps a metaphor for the process itself, which disassembles a sound into millions of constituent bits). Today, however, almost all popular recordings are digitally recorded.

Synthesizers—devices that allow musicians to create or "synthesize" musical sounds—began to appear on rock records during the early 1970s, but their history begins much earlier. One important predecessor of the synthesizer was the Theremin, a sound generator named after Leon Theremin, the Russian inventor who developed it in 1919. This instrument used electronic oscillators to produce sound, and its pitch was controlled by the player waving his or her hands in front of two antennae. The Theremin was never used much in popular music, although its familiar sound can be heard in the soundtracks of 1950s science fiction films such as *The Day the Earth Stood Still*, as well as on the Beach Boys' 1966 hit "Good Vibrations."

Another important stage in the interaction between scientific invention and musical technology was the creation of the Hammond organ in 1935 by the inventor Laurens Hammond. The sound of the Hammond B-3 organ became common on jazz, R&B, and rock records (e.g., Santana's "Oye Como Va"), and its rich, fat sound is frequently sampled in contemporary popular music. The player can alter the timbre of the organ through control devices called "tone bars," and a variety of rhythm patterns and percussive effects have been added over the years. Although the Hammond organ is not a true synthesizer, it is certainly a close ancestor.

In the early 1970s the first synthesizers aimed at a mass consumer market were introduced. These devices, which used electronic oscillators to produce musical tones, were clumsy and limited by today's standards, but their characteristic sounds are viewed with some nostalgia and are often sampled in contemporary recordings. The first synthesizers to be sold in music stores alongside guitars and pianos were the Minimoog, which had the limitation of being able to play only one pitch at a time, and the Arp synthesizer, which could play simple chords. The Synclavier, a high-end (and expensive) digital synthesizer, was introduced to the market in 1976. The more affordable Prophet-5, introduced in 1978, was an analog synthesizer that incorporated aspects of digital technology, including the ability to store a limited number of sampled sounds.

The 1980s saw the introduction of the first completely digital synthesizers—including the widely popular Yamaha DX-7—that were capable of playing dozens of "voices" at the same time. The Yamaha DX-7 was made possible by the discoveries of computer music researcher and composer John Chowning (b. 1934), who did much of his work at Stanford University's Center for Computer Research in Music and Acoustics. The MIDI specification, introduced in 1983, allowed synthesizers built by different manufacturers to be connected to and communicate with one another, introducing compatibility into a highly competitive marketplace. Digital **samplers**—for example, the Mirage keyboard sampler, introduced by Ensoniq in 1984—were capable of storing both pre-recorded and synthesized sounds. (The latter were often called "patches," a nostalgic reference to the wires or "patch cords" that were used to connect the various components of early synthesizers.) Digital **sequencers**, introduced to the marketplace at around the same time, are devices that record musical data rather than musical sound and allow the creation of repeated sound sequences (loops), the manipulation of rhythmic grooves, and the transmission of recorded data from one program or device to another. **Drum machines** such as the Roland TR-808 and the Linn LM-1—which are almost ubiquitous on 1980s dance music and rap recordings—rely on "drum pads" that can be struck and activated by the performer, and which act as a trigger for the production of sampled sounds (including not only conventional percussion instruments but also glass smashing, cars screeching, and guns firing).

Digital technology has given musicians the ability to create complex 128-voice textures, create sophisticated synthesized sounds that exist nowhere in nature, and sample and manipulate any sound source, creating sound loops that can be controlled with great precision. With compact, highly portable, and increasingly affordable music equipment and software, a recording studio can be set up literally anywhere—in a basement, or even on a roof. As the individual musician gains more and more control over the production of a complete musical recording, distinctions between the composer, the performer, and the producer sometimes melt down entirely.

Certain contemporary genres make particularly frequent and effective use of digital technologies, particularly rap/hip-hop and various genres of electronic dance music (electronica or techno, now commonly known as EDM). The technology of digital sampling allows musicians to assemble pre-existing sound sources and cite performers and music from various styles and historical eras. During the 1980s musicians began to reach back into their record collections for sounds from the 1960s and 1970s. It has been suggested that this practice reflects a more general cultural shift toward a "cut-and-paste" approach to history in which pop music cannibalizes its own past. However, it is worth remembering that while the technology is new, the idea of recycling old materials (and thereby selectively reinventing the past) is probably as old as music itself.

Some interesting legal dilemmas are connected with the widespread use of digital sampling. American intellectual property law has always made it difficult to claim ownership of a groove, style, or sound—precisely those things that are most distinctive about popular music, like the timbre of James Brown's voice, the electric bass sound of Parliament/Funkadelic's Bootsy Collins, or the distinctive snare drum sound used on many of Phil Collins's hit recordings (a sound constructed in the studio out of a combination of sampled and synthesized sources). In recent years these issues have become the center of many lawsuits, in which musicians and producers claim that their sound has been stolen by means of digital sampling. George Clinton has responded to the wholesale sampling of his albums by rap musicians by releasing a collection of sounds and previously unreleased recordings called *Sample Some of Disc, Sample Some of D.A.T.* The collection comes with a copyright clearance guide and a guarantee that users will only be "charged per record sold, so if your single flops, you won't be in the red."

Of course, no technology is inherently good or evil—it's what humans do with their tools that counts. On the one hand, many musicians mourn the replacement of acoustic musical instruments—and the physical discipline and craft involved in mastering them—by machines. Others tout the democratization of popular music made possible by more affordable technologies. And still others point out that no matter how good the technology, only a small percentage of musicians are able to gain access to the powerful corporations that control the music industry. The odds that a musician will succeed have not changed much, precisely because almost everyone now has access to the new technology. While high-quality demonstration tapes ("demos") used to be a luxury available to only those musicians who could afford to rent a professional recording studio, now every kid on the block has a demo.

The Pop Mainstream of the 1980s: Some Representative Hits

By the 1980s the single 45 rpm disc, introduced back in 1949, had begun to decline as a primary medium for distributing popular music, displaced first by LPs, then tape cassettes, and still later CDs and music videos. However, it still remained true that, as one record company executive put it, "nobody goes around humming albums." Individual songs remained the basic unit of popular music consumption in the 1980s, and in this section we will look at four hit singles, each of which reached the Number 1 position on the pop charts during the decade. Taken as a group, they give us a sense of the diversity of styles embraced by the mass audience for popular music, ranging from country-tinged pop ballads to rock and R&B fusions, from synth pop (the predecessor of techno music) to heavy metal.

COUNTRY-POP CROSSOVER: "LADY" (KENNY ROGERS)

The blend of country and pop music that had helped to create huge crossover hits for Nashville during the 1970s continued apace throughout the following decade, paving the way for country music's spectacular invasion of the mainstream during the 1990s. Texas-born *Kenny Rogers* (1938–2020)—a veteran of folk pop groups such as the New Christy Minstrels and the First Edition, as well as the star of made-for-TV movies such as *The Gambler* and *Coward of the County*—was one of the main beneficiaries of country pop's increasing mainstream appeal. As a renegade from pop music, Rogers was not considered authentic by conservative country music fans, but he did receive a number of awards from the Country Music Association, including Male Vocalist of the Year in 1979. From 1977 to 1984 he sold an estimated $250 million worth of records, including a total of six gold (sales of over 500,000) and twelve platinum albums.

The song "Lady" appeared on *Kenny Rogers's Greatest Hits*, the bestselling country album of the 1980s, and was the tenth bestselling single of the entire decade. In addition, it was one of very few singles during the decade to appear on all of the major *Billboard* charts, topping the pop (Hot 100), adult contemporary, and country charts and reaching Number 42 on the rhythm & blues chart. Only a few other recordings in the history of American popular music accomplished this feat, including Elvis Presley's "Hound Dog" and "Don't Be Cruel" (1956). In style and sensibility, however, Rogers's performance of "Lady" is light years away from Presley's crossover hits. Whereas Presley found common ground between the blues and country music that were part of the musical heritage of the South, Rogers was first and foremost a creature of the pop mainstream, and more particularly of a category called "adult contemporary," which did not even exist as a marketing category in 1956 and mainly encompassed romantic songs aimed at a twenty-five-to-forty-five-year-old audience.

"Lady" was written and produced by another superstar of the 1980s, *Lionel Richie*. Richie (b. 1949), a former member of a vocal R&B group called the Commodores, is an African American singer and songwriter whose career overarches conventional genre boundaries. Although his own big hits of the 1980s were soul-tinged variants of adult contemporary music, Richie also placed two singles in the country Top 40 during the 1980s and was the composer of "Sail On," a song covered by a number of prominent country artists. (In the mid-1980s Richie became one of the few Black musicians admitted to the Country Music Association during a period when country and Black popular music had less overlap than ever before.)

"Lady" is a sentimental song that has much in common with popular songs of the nineteenth century, such as Stephen Foster's "Jeanie with the Light Brown Hair" (see Chapter 2). The song has a verse-chorus structure and uses the image of a knight in shining armor, derived from the Crusades of the Middle Ages, to profess the singer's deep and undying love. Lionel Richie, who produced the recording, followed a strategy of keeping it simple, avoiding "gimmicks," and foregrounding Rogers's sincere delivery of the lyrics.

The musical accompaniment for Rogers's husky voice is delicate, opening with a solo acoustic piano and only gradually introducing additional layers of orchestration—an oboe, strings, and a suggestion of pedal steel guitar (evocative of country music). Finally, just as the chorus arrives, the whole rhythm section joins in, energetically supporting the emotional climax of the whole song. This structure repeats with the same pattern of quiet reflection giving way to the more explicitly emotional chorus, which is repeated at the end.

In many ways "Lady" seems a throwback to the pre-rock era: a soft and sentimental song, couched in a determinedly bland arrangement calculated both to create an air of intimacy and to offend as few people as possible. The crossover success of

"Lady" is particularly interesting in that it took place in the 1980s, a period when the country and R&B charts each overlapped frequently with the pop charts but rarely with each other. By the early 1980s it may have been that the one thing that country music and soul fans had in common was the old tradition of the romantic "torch song." Teaming with another "countrypolitan" star Dolly Parton in 1983, Rogers showed again that this type of song had strong appeal with the hit "Islands in the Stream." It reached number 1 on the Billboard Hot 100 (pop song) chart, which was highly unusual for a "country" record. However, afterwords Rogers mostly had success on the country charts and as a performer. He announced his retirement from performing in 2015.

ROCK MEETS R&B: "WHAT'S LOVE GOT TO DO WITH IT" (TINA TURNER)

By the time *Tina Turner* (born Annie Mae Bullock in 1939 in Tennessee) recorded "What's Love Got to Do with It" she had been in the popular music limelight for over twenty years. Her recording debut took place in 1960 as a member of the Ike and Tina Turner Revue. Tina's husband, Ike Turner, had begun his recording career much earlier, as a performer on Jackie Brenston's "Rocket 88" (1951), sometimes credited as the first rock 'n' roll record. Ike and Tina scored big crossover hits during the 1960s with "A Fool in Love" (Number 2 R&B, Number 27 pop, 1960), "It's Gonna Work Out Fine" (Number 2 R&B, Number 14 pop, 1961), and a gold record version of Creedence Clearwater Revival's 1969 hit "Proud Mary" (Number 4 pop, Number 5 R&B, 1971).

Tina Turner in action, 1990.

As recounted in her 1986 bestselling autobiography, *I, Tina*, Tina Turner eventually tired of the abusive behavior of her husband, leaving him in 1976 to start her own career. The first years were tough, but by 1981 the Rolling Stones and Rod Stewart, old fans of the Ike and Tina Revue, had hired her as an opening act on their concert tours. In 1983 she was offered a contract by Capitol Records. Her first album, entitled *Private Dancer* (1984), reached Number 3 on the album charts, stayed in the Top 40 for seventy-one weeks, spawned five hit singles, and eventually went on to attain worldwide sales in excess of 11 million copies. In succeeding years Turner continued to build her career, releasing a series of platinum albums and appearing in movies such as *Mad Max Beyond Thunderdome* (1985). In 1993 a film version of her autobiography was produced, entitled *What's Love Got to Do with It*, which featured Turner's last Top 10 hit, "I Don't Wanna Fight." Through the 1990s and into the twenty-first century, Turner enjoyed greater success in Europe both as a recording and touring artist. In 2005, President George W. Bush awarded her a Kennedy Center Honor.

The crossover hit "What's Love Got to Do with It" (Number 1 pop, Number 2 R&B, 1984) stayed on the charts for twenty-eight weeks and earned Grammy Awards in 1984 for Best Female Pop Vocalist, Song of the Year, and Record of the Year. Turner did not like the song at first and did not hesitate in conveying this sentiment to Terry Britten, its coauthor and producer of the *Private Dancer* album. "[Terry] said that when a song is given to an artist it's changed for the artists," Turner reminisced. "He said for me to make it a bit rougher, a bit more sharp around the edges. All of a sudden, just sitting there with him in the studio, the song became mine" (Wynn 1985, 132).

The lyric of "What's Love Got to Do with It" sets up an ambivalent relationship between the overwhelming sexual attraction described in the verses and the singer's cynicism about romantic love, derided in the song's chorus as a "secondhand emotion." This dynamic in the song's text is reinforced by the musical accompaniment. Though the tempo remains fairly constant (a relaxed pace of ninety-eight beats per minute), the instrumental arrangement alternates between the rich, continuous texture, dominated by flute- and stringlike synthesizer sounds, that underlies the verses and a more bouncy, reggae-like groove established by the electric bass and guitars on the chorus, the lyrics of which begin with the song's title.

The whole arrangement itself is carefully constructed—an eight-bar instrumental introduction, an unusual thirteen-bar verse ("You must understand . . .") comprising seven- and six-bar sections (A), an eight-bar chorus (B), another verse (A) ("It may seem . . ."), and finally another chorus (B). The middle point of the arrangement in structural terms is a synthesizer solo of seven and a half bars that uses the harmonies of the chorus (B'). This is followed by an eight-bar section (C) with new harmonies, where the singer reveals her fear of heartbreak more explicitly ("I've been taking . . ."). The arrangement concludes with three repetitions of the chorus (minus one bar, thanks to the early entrance of the chorus each time through), fading away at the very end.

For many in her audience, the character in this song—an experienced, cynical, and yet still vulnerable woman—was Turner herself, a case in which the boundary between the public and private lives of a recording artist seems to have dissolved almost entirely. (In the case of a David Bowie or—as we shall discuss—Madonna, a sense of ironic distance between the celebrity image and the individual behind it is carefully maintained. In Tina Turner's case, this distinction between image and identity is much less certain.) The combination of poignancy and toughness projected in Turner's recordings and live performances was linked by her fans to the details of her biography and helps to explain her appeal as the first Black woman to attain major status in the predominantly white male field of arena rock music.

THE RISE OF SYNTH-POP: "SWEET DREAMS" (EURHYTHMICS)

"Sweet Dreams (Are Made of This)," a Number 1 single from the early 1980s, exemplifies one of the directions dance music took in the postdisco era. With its heavy reliance on electronically synthesized sounds, sequenced loops, and what has been described as a cool or austere emotional tone, "Sweet Dreams" points the way toward later technology-centered music styles such as techno. Like some of the most successful techno groups of the 1990s (see Chapter 14), *Eurythmics* consisted of a core of only two musicians—the singer *Annie Lennox* (b. 1954 in Scotland) and keyboardist and technical whiz *Dave Stewart* (b. 1952 in England).

Eurythmics' first chart appearance in the United States came with the release of their second album, *Sweet Dreams (Are Made of This)*, in 1983. The title track was released as a single soon after the album rocketed to Number 2 on the English charts, and shortly afterward climbed to Number 1 on the American charts. The popularity of "Sweet Dreams (Are Made of This)" in the United States was boosted enormously by a video produced to promote the record, which was placed into heavy rotation by the fledgling MTV channel. In particular, the stylishly androgynous image of Annie Lennox—a female David Bowie in a business suit and close-cropped orange hair—is often identified as an important ingredient of the Eurythmics' success.

"Sweet Dreams" is a good example of commercial new wave music of the early 1980s, an outgrowth of the 1970s new wave/punk scene promoted by the major record labels. It also exemplifies a more specific genre label that began to be used about this time: **synth-pop**, the first type of popular music explicitly defined by its use of electronic sound synthesis. Although synth-pop declined sharply in mainstream popularity by the end of the 1980s, it helped to establish the centrality of the synthesizer in popular dance music, and has continued to exert a strong influence on the EDM and LGBTQ musical scenes.

"Sweet Dreams" is built around a hypnotic digital loop: a repeated pattern established abruptly at the beginning of the record, as though the listener were dropped

Eurythmics.

into the flow of a synthetic river of sound. A booming, steady pulse, synthesized on a digital drum machine and reminiscent of disco music, underlies the melodic portion of the loop. Annie Lennox's singing alternates between an R&B- and soul-influenced melismatic style and the flatter, more deadpan tone that she adopts on the verses. The verses themselves consist of two four-line blocks of text, sung by Lennox in overdubbed harmonies. The singer seems to be expressing an unsettling and titillating combination of cynicism, sensuality, and—in the chorus—hope for the future.

Some lines of the text ("Some of them want . . .") hint darkly at sadomasochistic relationships, suggesting that the singer's sophistication has perhaps been won at some emotional cost. In the call-and-response chorus—which uses multitracking technology to alternate Lennox as lead singer with Lennox as choir—the mood changes, and the listener is exhorted to "hold your head up," while the multitracked voices urge us to keep "movin' on."

Combined with Lennox's carefully cultivated sexual ambiguity—in a subsequent music video, "Who's That Girl," she plays both male and female characters and ends up kissing herself/himself—the lyrics and musical textures of "Sweet Dreams" suggest a sophisticated, even world-weary take on the nature of love, far removed from the naïve romanticism of Kenny Rogers's recording of "Lady."

Finally, although "Sweet Dreams" is sometimes regarded as an example of the emerging technological sophistication of the early 1980s, the recording was made under less than optimal conditions. The studio rented by Stewart was a dingy, V-shaped warehouse attic that lacked any of the amenities of a professional studio (such as acoustical tiles or isolation booths for recording separate instrumental tracks). The duo's equipment was rudimentary—an eight-track tape recorder and a cheap mixer, two microphones, an early version of a digital drum machine available in England at the time, and a handful of old sound effects devices. "It sounded so sophisticated," reported Stewart in a 1983 feature in *Billboard*, "but often we had to wait for the timber factory downstairs to turn off their machinery before we could record the vocals." In fact, not all of the instrumental sounds on the recording are electronic in origin: the clinking counterpoint under the chorus of "Sweet Dreams" was played on milk bottles pitched to the right notes by filling them with different levels of water. In this sense "Sweet Dreams" both hearkens back to the "do it yourself" ethic of 1970s punk and new wave music and points forward to the experiments of 1990s techno musicians, who often introduced natural environmental sounds into their recordings.

The Eurythmics ended in 1990, with Lennox pursuing a successful solo career. While she maintained her formidable vocal style and gripping appearance, her later recordings were in the more traditional rock and pop-ballad mode, with less emphasis on highly produced, synthesized backing tracks. Stewart meanwhile continued to work as a producer along with issuing solo projects and working on film and television soundtracks.

METAL IN THE MAINSTREAM: "JUMP" (VAN HALEN)

Heavy metal music, pioneered in the late 1960s and early 1970s by bands such as Led Zeppelin and Deep Purple, went into a period of relative decline during the late 1970s, partly as a result of the disco craze. By the early 1980s most hit singles—particularly those promoted on MTV—were oriented more toward postdisco dance music played on keyboard synthesizers than toward the electric guitar virtuosity of heavy metal bands. The music industry tended to ignore heavy metal music, regarding it and its core audience of adolescent white males as something of an embarrassment.

During the 1980s, however, heavy metal came back with a vengeance. A slew of metal albums topped the singles and album charts, ranging from the pop metal sounds of bands like **Van Halen**, Bon Jovi, Mötley Crüe, and Def Leppard to the harder sound of speed metal bands such as Metallica, Slayer, Anthrax, and Megadeath. One of the most important moments in the mainstreaming of heavy metal was the release of Van Halen's album *1984*, which featured the Number 1 pop single "Jump."

"Jump" was in some ways a remarkable departure from standard heavy metal practice. To begin with, its main instrumental melody is played on a synthesizer rather than an electric guitar. This may seem like a minor detail, but it was an important symbolic and aesthetic issue for hardcore metal fans, many of whom highly value the technical virtuosity of guitarists like **Eddie Van Halen** (1955–2020). From this perspective, the keyboard synthesizer (like disco music) is viewed as a somewhat questionable, perhaps even effeminate, instrument. As Philip Bashe, an expert on heavy metal music, has put it, the fact that Eddie Van Halen played the bombastic opening theme of "Jump" on a synthesizer rather than a guitar was "a brave test of the Van Halen audience's loyalty" (Bashe 1985, 137). The success of the single was boosted by its corresponding music video, which was shot in home-movie style and featured the athletic prowess and oddball sense of humor of David Lee Roth—at that time Van Halen's lead singer.

On "Jump," the song itself (in the conventional sense of words-plus-melody) is not a core focus of attention for the musicians or their listeners. (Eddie Van Halen, when asked by an interviewer what his mother would think of the lyrics to his band's songs, said that he had no idea at all what they were!) The text of "Jump"—a casual come-on to a girl from a guy leaning against a jukebox—seems almost an afterthought, apart, perhaps, from the clever "Go ahead and jump!" hook phrase, which sounds rather as though David Lee Roth were counseling the object of his affections to jump off a high ledge, rather than into his arms. The notion of love as a risk-taking act—so strongly portrayed in Tina Turner's "What's Love Got to Do with It"—is present here as well, though from a decidedly male point of view.

The chief significance of a recording like "Jump," however, lies not in the song per se but in the musical textures created by the band and the studio engineer and in the sensibility that they evoke. As we have mentioned, one of the main points of attraction for heavy metal fans is the virtuosity of the genre's master guitarists, a tradition that they trace back to pioneers such as Jimi Hendrix and Led Zeppelin's Jimmy Page. Eddie Van Halen, widely recognized as a primary innovator in electric guitar performance, is famous for developing widely used techniques ("pull-offs" and "tapping") and for performing various operations on his guitars and amplifiers to modify their sound.

Although "Jump" relies heavily on the keyboard synthesizer for its effect, the sounds generated by Eddie Van Halen are in fact closely analogous to his guitar style. In particular, he uses the synthesizer to create something akin to "power chords," two-note combinations that, when played at high volume on an electric guitar, create the massive, distorted, bone-crunching sound associated with heavy metal bands. "Jump" opens with a synthesized power chord, as if to announce right from the beginning that the sheer sound of the music is more important than the specific instruments used to produce it. Thick textures and a strong pulse played on keyboards, bass, and drums propel us through the first two verses of the song. The arrival of the chorus is marked by a sudden opening up, in which the synthesizer plays long, sustained chords; the electric guitar plays a sizzling counterpoint to the vocal melody; and the drums and bass play an interesting irregular rhythmic pattern that first suspends the beat and then, after four bars, unleashes it with even greater energy. After another verse-and-chorus section, we are transported into the midst of a virtuoso guitar solo that uses Eddie Van Halen's famed techniques. The guitar solo is followed by a longer synthesizer solo, which develops an elaborate melodic improvisation that closely parallels the style of Van Halen's guitar playing.

Although some hardcore metal fans criticized Van Halen for moving away from the guitar-centered model of heavy metal musicianship, the band succeeded in introducing synthesizers into the genre and helping to spread metal's popularity to a larger and more diverse audience. In 1983 only 8 percent of records sold in the United States were heavy metal; a year later that total had risen to 20 percent, making metal one of the most popular genres of popular music. This process was continued further in 1986 when the pop metal band Bon Jovi released the album *Slippery When Wet*, which held the Number 1 spot for eight weeks and went on to sell over 12 million copies worldwide. By the end of 1986 MTV had launched *Headbangers' Ball*, a show designed specifically for metal fans, which soon became the most-watched show on the channel. In the late 1980s heavy metal music accounted for around half of the Top 20 albums on the *Billboard* charts on any given week.

BOX 13.1 MTV AS HIT-MAKER: PETER GABRIEL'S "SLEDGEHAMMER" (1986)

Peter Gabriel (b. 1950 in England) first achieved celebrity as a member of the art rock group Genesis. After leaving Genesis in 1976, Gabriel released four solo albums, all of them titled Peter Gabriel. Partly in an effort to clear up the consumer confusion that followed in the wake of this unusual strategy, he gave his next album a distinctive, if brief, title: So. So was an interesting and accessible amalgam of various musical styles that reflected Gabriel's knowledge of new digital technologies; his budding interest in world music (see Chapter 14); and his indebtedness to Black music, particularly R&B and the soul music of the 1960s. The album peaked at Number 2 on the Top LPs chart, sold 4 million copies, and produced Gabriel's bestselling single "Sledgehammer" (Number 1 pop, Number 61 R&B, 1986).

"Sledgehammer" features a horn section led by the trumpet player Wayne Jackson, who, as a member of the Memphis Horns, had played on many of the biggest soul music hits of the 1960s (e.g., "Knock on Wood," "Soul Man"). Jackson had deeply impressed sixteen-year-old Peter Gabriel during an appearance with the Otis Redding Soul Revue at a London R&B club in 1966. Gabriel described "Sledgehammer" as "an attempt to recreate some of the spirit and style of the music that most excited me as a teenager—60s soul. The lyrics

(continued)

BOX 13.1 MTV AS HIT-MAKER: PETER GABRIEL'S "SLEDGEHAMMER" (1986) (*continued*)

of many of those songs were full of playful sexual innuendo and this is my contribution to that song-writing tradition. It is also about the use of sex as a means of getting through a breakdown in communication" (Bright 1999, 267).

The lyrics to "Sledgehammer"—packed with double entendres about sledgehammers, big dippers, steam trains, the female "fruitcake," and the male "honeybee"—are in fact a G-rated variant of the sexual metaphors that have long been a part of the blues tradition (compare, for example, Blind Lemon Jefferson's 1926 recording of "That Black Snake Moan," discussed in Chapter 5).

The formal building blocks of "Sledgehammer" are twelve-bar and eight-bar sections, with the former predominating in the first half of the arrangement. While most pop music recordings are eager to establish the beat or groove as quickly as possible, "Sledgehammer" opens with an exotic touch, a digital keyboard sample of a Japanese flute called the shakuhachi as a hint of Gabriel's wide-ranging musical interests. The funk-influenced groove—with

the snare drum producing strong backbeats; the keyboard bass landing strongly on the first beat of each measure; and the guitar playing a bouncy, upbeat pattern similar to ska—is introduced by the horn section, backed by synthesizers. After eight bars the horns drop out and the rhythm takes four measures to establish the groove that will carry us through the rest of the recording.

Following the introduction, Peter Gabriel sings two verses (beginning with the lines "You could have a steam train" and "You could have a big dipper"), each of which is twelve bars in length. Though his intent to evoke the blues form seems clear, he does not strictly observe the AAB lyric form of the classic blues (that is to say, he does not repeat the first line of the text in the verses). In addition, he dispenses with the traditional approach to blues harmonies, staying on the tonic chord for a full eight measures, moving to a related chord (which musicians call the relative minor) for two bars, and then returning to the tonic for the last two bars. (Although many traditional blues linger on the tonic chord in a manner

Peter Gabriel looks relaxed with recording technology, 1987.

similar to this, they rarely if ever move to the relative minor chord, a harmony more in keeping with Tin Pan Alley music.)

After singing two of these twelve-bar verses, Gabriel moves to the eight-bar chorus ("I want to be your sledgehammer"). Once again, the song takes an interesting turn in harmonic terms, shifting from the major key of the verse to a minor key based on the same tonic note. (More precisely, the B section begins on a chord closely related to the tonic major and then shifts to the tonic minor chord itself.) Listen closely for the shift between the A and the B sections and see if you can hear the different color or feeling of the harmonies.

The arrangement continues with a four-bar instrumental section that takes us back to the major-key harmonies of the verse; another verse ("Show me 'round your fruitcakes"), shortened to eight instead of twelve bars; and two presentations of the chorus ("I want to be your sledgehammer"). The last section of the arrangement begins with a keyboard synthesizer solo and relies on a minor-key harmonic pattern closely related to that of the chorus, moving back and forth between the tonic minor chord and another closely related chord. Finally, a series of eight-bar sections ("I will show for you") are heard, in which Gabriel's vocal phrases alternate with a choir of gospel-style singers. The arrangement reaches a peak here, with Gabriel improvising solo phrases against the responses of the choir ("Show for me, Show for you"). Gabriel's attempt to "recreate some of the spirit and style" of 1960s soul music may be successful precisely because he does not try to produce an exact copy of the Black musical styles that inspired him. Rather, he uses fundamental elements such as the twelve-bar blues form, call-and-response singing, strong funk-derived polyrhythms, and an R&B-style horn section as the basis for a performance that reflects his own musical experience and taste, including references to world music and harmonies that take the blues in new directions.

The success of "Sledgehammer" was in no small part due to the massive exposure it received on MTV in the mid-1980s. The video version of "Sledgehammer" was an eye-catching, witty, and technically innovative work that pushed the frontiers of the medium. It won nine MTV awards (more than any video in history), including Best Video and the prestigious Video Vanguard Award for career achievement in 1987, and was ranked the fourth-best video of all time in a 1999 retrospective aired on MTV. The making of the video, which combined stop-motion techniques and live action, required Gabriel to spend eight painful sixteen-hour days lying under glass with his head supported by a steel pole. (Aardman Animations, the outfit that produced the "Sledgehammer" video, went on to work on the Wallace and Gromit videos and the talking car ads aired by Chevron in the late 1990s.)

One key to the success of any music video is the relationship it establishes between the sound of the original recording (which, except in the case of live concert videos, is always made first) and the flow of visual images. The video of "Sledgehammer"—directed by Steven Johnston—opens with enlarged microscopic images of human sperm cells impregnating an egg, which develops into a fetus to the accompaniment of the exotic sound of the synthesized flute. As the groove is established, we see Gabriel's face in close-up, moving to the groove and wiggling his eyebrows, ears, and mouth in time to the music. The stop-motion technique—in which the camera is halted and restarted in order to create the illusion of inanimate objects moving under their own power—creates a jerky stop-start effect that establishes a kind of parallel reality and is carefully coordinated to match the rhythms of the music. The lyrics of the song are also reflected in the video images: when Gabriel sings "You could have a steam train," a toy locomotive circles his head on miniature tracks; when he sings "You could have a bumper car bumping, this amusement never ends," two smiling (and singing) bumper cars appear next to his ears, mountains of popcorn pile up behind him, and his hair turns to pink cotton candy. After a series of stop-motion sequences featuring everything from singing fruits and vegetables to dancing furniture, Gabriel is transformed into a "starman" and walks off into the night sky. Thus the video takes us from the microscopic origins of life to the vastness of the galaxy, with many diverting stops in between. As Gabriel himself admitted some years later, although the recording of "Sledgehammer" would probably have done well on its own, the ambitious and highly creative video of the song, played endlessly on MTV, introduced "Sledgehammer" to millions of Americans who might otherwise never have purchased a Peter Gabriel record.

A Tale of Three Albums

A brief look at three multimillion-selling albums of the 1980s will help document the variety of styles that characterized this period. Each of these albums represents the biggest commercial success of its artist's solo career. *Thriller*, in fact, ranks as the top-selling album in history as of this writing, having achieved worldwide sales in excess of 60 million copies, and it was the Number 1 album for thirty-seven weeks during 1983.

In the case of Michael Jackson, *Thriller* was the zenith of a career as a solo artist that had been gathering momentum throughout the 1970s, even while Jackson continued to be a pivotal member of the tremendously successful group the Jackson 5 (which changed its name to the Jacksons after its departure from the Motown organization in 1976, a move that caused no substantial interruption in its long-running success story). *Thriller* was state-of-the-art pop music, an album dedicated not so much to breaking new ground as to consolidating Michael Jackson's dominance of the contemporary pop scene by showcasing his versatility as a performer of a stylistically wide range of up-to-date material.

Like Jackson, Paul Simon got his start in the 1960s as a member of a group, in this case the famous folk rock duo Simon and Garfunkel (see Box 10.2). When Simon branched off toward a productive solo career in the 1970s, however, the duo disbanded. In 1986 *Graceland* revived Simon's career, which had seemed to be in decline in the early 1980s (his two preceding albums had neither the critical nor the commercial success that greeted most of his work of the 1970s); with its employment of African musicians, African music, and (occasionally) African subject matter, along with other "exotic" touches, the album suddenly thrust Simon into the forefront of the new category called world music.

In contrast, the depiction of adult working-class Americans whose better days are behind them presented in Bruce Springsteen's *Born in the U.S.A.* seemed more concerned with this country's past, and the album's music is drenched appropriately in Springsteen's typical roots-based rock sound. The glitzy, consciously "modern" sound and production values of *Thriller* clearly were not for Springsteen; neither was he trying in any way to change the basic direction of his career or his music, as Simon was with *Graceland*. In *Born in the U.S.A.* Springsteen was simply continuing to make the kind of music, and to voice the kinds of concerns, that had characterized his career from its beginning in the 1970s. The unexpected mega-success of the album (it sold over 15 million copies, whereas the best-selling album among Springsteen's previous efforts—*Born to Run* from 1975—had sold less than 5 million) took the artist himself somewhat by surprise and left him anxious to ascertain whether his newly enlarged audience was truly understanding the less-than-cheerful messages he wished to convey, as we shall see.

THRILLER *(MICHAEL JACKSON, 1983)*

In fashioning *Thriller*, **Michael Jackson** (1958–2009) worked with the veteran producer Quincy Jones to create an album that achieved boundary-crossing popularity to an unprecedented degree. At a time when the pop music audience seemed to be fragmenting

Michael Jackson shows off his dance moves.

to a greater extent than ever before, *Thriller* demonstrated a kind of across-the-board appeal that established new and still unduplicated heights of commercial success. In a sense, Jackson here revived the goal that had animated his old boss at Motown, Berry Gordy Jr. (see Chapter 9): to create an African American–based pop music that was aimed squarely at the mainstream center of the market. That Jackson met his goal in such a mind-boggling fashion proved conclusively that there indeed still was a mainstream in the pop music market of the early 1980s, and that Jackson had positioned himself unquestionably in the center of it.

To accomplish this task, Jackson had to be more than just "the sound of young America" (to quote Motown's memorable phrase from the 1960s). It is of course true that teenagers, preteens, and young adults made up a substantial portion of the 1980s market. But members of the baby boom generation, along with the many men and women who came to maturity during the 1970s, were also still major consumers of pop music. And age was far from the only basis on which segmentation of the audience seemed to be taking place; fans of soft rock, heavy metal, funk, and new wave music, for instance, appeared to want less and less to do with one another. A disturbing subtext of this fragmentation was a tendency toward increasing resegregation along racial lines of the various audiences for pop. Heavy metal and new wave fans—and bands—were overwhelmingly white, while funk and the emerging genre of rap were associated with Black performers and listeners.

Thriller represented an effort to find ways to mediate among the various genres of early 1980s pop music, to create points of effective synthesis from the welter of apparently competing styles, and to bridge the divides—actual or potential—that separated different segments of the pop music audience. Jackson confronted the racial divide head-on by collaborating with two very popular, and very different, white artists: ex-Beatle Paul McCartney joined Jackson for a lyrical vocal duet on "The Girl Is Mine," while Eddie Van Halen of the heavy metal group Van Halen contributed the stinging guitar solo on the intense "Beat It." Both of these radically different songs, along with two others on *Thriller*, were written by Jackson himself; his versatility and his gift for crossing genres extended also into the domain of songwriting. It is also clear that "The Girl Is Mine" and "Beat It" were fashioned to attract different segments of the white audience. The mere presence of Paul McCartney was a draw for many listeners who had been fans of the Beatles in the 1960s, as well as for those who admired McCartney's 1970s band Wings; as a song, "The Girl Is Mine" combines a gentle melodic flow with a feeling of rhythmic vitality, effectively echoing the virtues of the best Beatles and Wings ballads. "The Girl Is Mine" captured this essentially soft rock ambience—and its audience—especially well: its single release held the Number 1 spot on *Billboard*'s Top Adult Contemporary chart for four weeks. Moreover, "The Girl Is Mine" had sufficient crossover appeal to top the R&B chart (in this period called "Hot Black Singles") for three weeks as well. As the first single to come out of the *Thriller* album, "The Girl Is Mine" demonstrated immediately how well Michael Jackson's new music could break down preconceptions about marketability.

"Beat It," in contrast, has nothing to do with soft rock and was a gesture obviously extended to "metal-heads," who must have been struck by the novelty of a collaboration between a celebrated heavy metal guitarist and an African American pop icon. But this door also could, and did, swing both ways. "Beat It" joined "The Girl Is Mine" on the list of Number 1 Black singles in 1983.

Much of *Thriller* consists of up-tempo, synthesizer- and bass-driven, danceable music that occupies a (probably conscious) middle ground between the heavy funk of an artist like George Clinton and the brighter but still beat-obsessed sound that characterized many new wave bands (of which Blondie would be a good example). Perhaps the outstanding—and, in this case, unexpected and highly original—example of the album's successful synthesis of diverse stylistic elements may be found in the title song.

"Thriller" starts out depicting a horror movie scene, which eventually turns out to be on the television screen being watched by two lovers, providing them with an excuse for cuddling "close together" and creating their own kind of thrills. In a conclusion that pairs an old white voice with a new Black style, horror movie star Vincent Price comes from out of nowhere to perform a "rap" about the terrors of the night. (This "rap" describes some typical horror film situations, but its language is occasionally spiced up with current pop-oriented slang—as when Price refers to "the funk of forty thousand years.")

In the early years of long-playing records, the pop music album was typically a collection of individual songs, several (and sometimes all) of which had previously been released as singles. In our discussions of the 1960s and 1970s, we have remarked on the steadily increasing importance of the album over the single as pop artists began more and more to conceive of the album as their principal creative medium. *Thriller* is a unique landmark in this evolutionary process. *Thriller* is not a concept album—unless the "concept" is to demonstrate that an album can be made to engender hit singles, rather than vice versa. Out of the nine songs on *Thriller*, seven were released as singles, one by one, starting with "The Girl Is Mine" (the only one to be released prior to the album itself), and all seven were Top 10 hits. (Both "Billie Jean" and "Beat It" were Number 1 pop hits; these two and "Thriller" sold over 2 million copies each as singles, while "The Girl Is Mine" was a million-selling single. The only songs from *Thriller* that were not turned into hit singles are "Baby Be Mine" and "The Lady in My Life.")

Visual media both old and new played a significant role in the *Thriller* saga. In May 1983 Jackson appeared on the television special *25 Years of Motown* and introduced what came to be known as his "moonwalk" dance while performing "Billie Jean"; the performance was a sensation and doubtless added to the continuing popularity of the album. By this time, the videos for *Thriller* songs that Jackson had made were being shown regularly on MTV. Jackson's embrace of the relatively new medium of music video reflected his foresight in realizing its potential. While bringing his work to the attention of yet another segment of the music public, his videos in turn helped boost the power and prestige of MTV itself, because they were so carefully, creatively, and elaborately produced. Since Jackson was the first African American artist to be programmed with any degree of frequency on MTV, *Thriller* thus contributed to the breakdown of yet another emerging color line in pop culture. (Significantly, in the video of "Beat It," Jackson is seen breaking up a racially charged gang fight.)

BORN IN THE U.S.A. *(BRUCE SPRINGSTEEN, 1984)*

Throughout the 1970s **Bruce Springsteen** (b. 1949) forged a progressively more successful career in pop music while continuing to cast both his music and his personal image in the light of the rebellious rock 'n' rollers of the 1950s and the socially conscious folk rockers of the 1960s. Springsteen's songs reflected his working-class origins and sympathies, relating the stories of still young but aging men and women with dead-end jobs (or no jobs at all) who are looking for both romance and excitement in the face of repeated disappointments while seeking meaningful outlets for their seething energies and hopes in an America that seems to have no pieces of the American dream left to offer them. Some of the song titles from his first few albums are indicative: "Born to Run," "Darkness on the Edge of Town," "Hungry Heart," "Racing in the Street," "Wreck on the Highway," and so on. Springsteen performed with his E Street Band, and their music was characterized by a strong, roots-rock sound that emphasized his connections to 1950s and 1960s music. The band even included a saxophone—virtually an anachronism in the pop music of this period—to mark the link with the rhythm & blues and rock 'n' roll of earlier eras. (In this connection, it is worth noting that one of the songs on *Born in the U.S.A.*, "Cover Me," is based on a twelve-bar blues progression. Twelve-bar blues form was also all but an anachronism in the mainstream pop music of the 1980s,

Bruce Springsteen is born in the U.S.A.

but it was part of Springsteen's musical heritage and style, and his continuing employment of this form represented another obvious homage to the roots of rock.) Still, the emphasis in Springsteen's music was predominantly on the traditional rock ensemble of guitars, bass, and drums, with keyboard instruments occasionally used prominently.

The album immediately preceding *Born in the U.S.A.* represented a departure for Springsteen: *Nebraska* (1982) featured him in a solo, "unplugged" setting that underlined the particular bleakness of this collection of songs. Consequently, many fans may have celebrated *Born in the U.S.A.*, which brought back the E Street Band with an actual as well as a symbolic bang, as a kind of "return to form" for Springsteen. Certainly the album is dominated by up-tempo, rocking songs, with Springsteen shouting away in full voice and grand style and the band playing full tilt behind him. Nevertheless, listening to the record (or tape or CD) with the album's lyric sheet in hand, it is hard to see how anybody could have regarded *Born in the U.S.A.* as anything other than a typically dire commentary by Springsteen on the current state of the union. The album's title single, "Born in the U.S.A.," tells the story of a returning Vietnam veteran unable to get a job or rebuild his life, and its despairing message is characteristic of most of the songs on the album.

But maybe many people weren't listening to the words. In the wake of this album's rapid and enormous popularity, Springsteen found himself and his band on tour playing to huge, sold-out stadiums where—given the amplification levels and the crowd noise—most people probably couldn't even *hear* the words. Confronted with hordes of fans waving American flags and the exploitation of his image in the presidential election year of 1984 by political forces for which he had little sympathy, Springsteen periodically found himself having to explain that he was not associated with "feel-good" politics or uncritical "America first" boosterism. Was Springsteen a victim of his own success, forced into a stadium rock culture that ill served the purpose and meaning of his songs? (Had rock music gained the world, so to speak, only to lose its soul?) Or was there actually some fundamental dichotomy between Springsteen's message and the energetic, crowd-pleasing music in which he was couching it?

There is of course no objectively "correct" answer to such questions. But when listening to *Born in the U.S.A.* as a recording and as a whole, Springsteen's sincerity seems as apparent as his intensity, and it is hard not to sense and be affected by the album's prevailing dark ambience. In a general way, *Born in the U.S.A.* is a concept album: a series of musical snapshots of working-class Americans, all of whom seem to be somewhere around Springsteen's age (he turned thirty-five the year he released this album, the same age as his protagonist in the song "My Hometown"), many of whom face economic or personal difficulties, and all of whom sense the better times of their lives slipping into the past. In the album's original LP form, each of the two sides starts out with a strong, aggressive song and winds down to a final cut that is softer in sound but, if anything, even darker in mood. The first side ends with the low-key but eerie "I'm on Fire," whose protagonist seems about to explode from the weight and pain of his own "bad desire"; in terms of the listening experience, the spooky urgency of this song appears to speak to the cumulative hard luck and frustration of all the different characters described in the songs of side one. Side two starts off with an extroverted rebound in musical energy expressed in the cry of "No Surrender." But disillusionment and resignation come to characterize the songs on this side of the record as well, until the "fire" image reappears strikingly in the penultimate song, "Dancing in the Dark." Finally "My Hometown" concludes the album; Springsteen, his voice drained of energy, sings of the decay of his place of birth and of possibly "getting out" with his wife and child, heading toward—it isn't clear what. In this poignant finale, Springsteen comes as close as any pop artist ever has to embracing and conveying an authentically tragic vision.

Amazingly, "My Hometown" was a major hit as a single recording, reaching Number 6 on the pop chart in early 1986 (and Number 1 on the adult contemporary chart). It was the last of seven consecutive singles to be culled from the album, all of which became Top 10 pop hits; in this respect, *Born in the U.S.A.* followed in the footsteps of *Thriller* as an album that spawned a parade of hit singles. The album itself sold over 15 million copies, as we have already noted, and stayed on the album charts for over two years. Like Michael Jackson, Springsteen produced a series of music videos to go with several of these singles, which ultimately proved popular in their own right and further enhanced the popularity of the album. Thus Springsteen stayed abreast of the changing music scene at the same time that he tried to speak, through his songs, to the values and attitudes that for him lay at the core of all that was worthwhile and enduring in rock.

After the great success of *Born in the U.S.A.* and the following tour, Springsteen again changed directions, producing the more introspective *Tunnel of Love* (1987), foregoing the harder rocking accompaniment of the E Street Band. He formally broke up the band two years later. Springsteen's career has continued to vary between moments of addressing broad cultural moments (such as 2002's *The Rising*, inspired by the September 11 attacks, which reunited him with the E Street Band) and more personal material. Like the Grateful Dead and Bob Dylan, he has built a dedicated fan base through successful tours. In 2016, he published his autobiography, *Born to Run,* and was awarded the Presidential Medal of Freedom by Barack Obama.

GRACELAND *(PAUL SIMON, 1986)*

Paul Simon's interest in music that was not indigenous to the United States manifested itself in his songs long before he recorded *Graceland*. When he was still singing with Art Garfunkel, Simon (b. 1941) recorded "El Condor Pasa," a song that paired his own lyrics with a backing instrumental track based on an old Peruvian folk melody, performed in "native" style by a group called Los Incas. "El Condor Pasa" appeared on the 1970 Simon and Garfunkel album *Bridge over Troubled Water* and was released as a single that same year. Beginning his solo career in the 1970s, Simon continued to pull on diverse musical traditions, including the Latin-tinged hit "Me and Julio Down by the School Yard" (1972) and "Loves Me Like a Rock" (1973) that drew on American gospel music. These songs were indicative of the path that Simon would later pursue much more systematically and thoroughly in *Graceland*, an album in which many of the songs present Simon's vocals and lyrics over an accompaniment performed in South African style by South African musicians.

A considerable portion of the music for *Graceland* was actually recorded in South Africa, a decision that resulted in some awkward political problems for Simon. Like *Born in the U.S.A.*, this album became a focus of political attention for fans, skeptics, and, with reluctance, its creator. At the time, a United Nations boycott on performing and recording in South Africa was in effect as part of an international attempt to isolate and ostracize the government of that country, which was still enforcing the widely despised policy of apartheid (separation of the races). Simon could not deny that he broke the boycott, but he claimed that he was in no sense supporting the ideology of the South African government by making music with Black South Africans on their native soil. In fact, the success of *Graceland* helped bring Black South African musicians and styles to a much wider and racially more diverse audience than they had ever been able to reach before, both within South Africa itself and in America and many other parts of the world. It could be argued that through his racially integrated music, Simon ultimately made a forceful statement about the virtues of free intermingling and cultural exchange. In any case, Simon came to a mutual understanding with the United Nations and the opponents of apartheid in relatively short order, and he stopped performing in South Africa until apartheid was dismantled several years later.

A truly "global" album from a geographical point of view, *Graceland* was recorded in five different locations on three different continents: in addition to Johannesburg, South Africa, tracks were cut in London, England, New York City, Los Angeles, and Crowley, Louisiana. Many of the selections on the album combine elements that were recorded

The Graceland tour with Paul Simon and Ladysmith Black Mambazo, 1987.

at different times in different places, but others are the result of sessions in which all the participants were present in the same place at the same time. While Simon flew to South Africa to work on several songs with musicians there, at another time he brought South African musicians to New York to work with him, and on yet another occasion Simon and the South African vocal group Ladysmith Black Mambazo recorded together in London.

What ultimately distinguishes *Graceland* from earlier forays into world music, whether by Simon or by other pop musicians, is the extent to which the album explores the concept of collaboration—collaboration among artists of different races, regions, nationalities, and ethnicities, and thus in turn collaboration among diverse musical styles and approaches to songwriting. This dynamic provides a conceptual basis for *Graceland*, to be sure, but Simon's album is quite different from the usual concept album. There is certainly no explicit or implicit story line that connects the songs, nor is there any single, central subject that links them all together—unless one is willing to view collaboration itself (primarily *musical* collaboration but also, in two instances, collaboration on lyrics as well) as the album's "subject matter." But the idea of an album designed to explore collaboration seems a perfectly logical, if unusual, concept to embrace in understanding *Graceland*.

The various approaches to the concept of collaboration that are found among the songs on *Graceland* run a gamut from "Homeless," in which both the words (in Zulu and English) and the music were cowritten by Simon and Joseph Shabalala of Ladysmith Black Mambazo, to a track like "I Know What I Know," in which Simon added his own lyrics and vocal melody to pre-existing music (originally not written for Simon) by General M. D. Shirinda and the Gaza Sisters. In the case of "Homeless," the song makes a unified and gently poignant impression; the images of poor people could refer to South Africa or America or both, and the slow-moving, harmonious vocal music encourages us to take their plight seriously. In "I Know What I Know," in contrast, Simon deliberately makes no attempt to match the tone of his lyrics to the culture or implied locale of the original South African music. Instead, the lyrics seem to portray an encounter between two worldly-wise and cynical people at an upper-crust cocktail party, and their mood and subject both stand in remarkable, ironic contrast to the jubilant, uninhibited sound of the danceable South African instrumental music and the Gaza Sisters' backing voices. The result is a virtual embodiment, in both words and sounds, of a profound clash of cultures—as if the characters typical of Simon's earlier, sophisticated urban songs of late twentieth-century anxiety (such as those found on the 1975 album *Still Crazy After All These Years*) were suddenly dropped into the middle of a busy South African village on a day of celebration.

That the uneasy mismatch of music and lyrics in "I Know What I Know" is neither accidental nor careless on Simon's part is signaled by the presence on the album of songs that, occupying a middle ground between "Homeless" and "I Know What I Know," make cultural diversity an aspect of both their stated subject matter and their music. The third verse of "You Can Call Me Al" describes a man who is uncomfortable in a foreign culture, unable to speak the language of this "strange world" and surrounded by its "sound." The "sound" here is produced by a group of Black South African musicians playing with Simon and American session musicians in New York City; significantly, the multicultural group is joined on this cut by Morris Goldberg, who (Simon's liner notes pointedly inform us) is a white South African emigrant based in New York, and who contributes a striking pennywhistle solo. Members of this same diverse ensemble also play on "Under African Skies," the verses of which actually shift location from Africa to Tucson, Arizona, and back again. Here Simon is joined in vocal duet by Linda Ronstadt—a singer hailing from Tucson, Arizona.

The meanings and implications of both the music and the words of *Graceland* can be allusive and elusive, often seeming to change color or shift in midphrase. Yet the lilt of Simon's melodies and the dynamic rhythms provided by his diverse collaborators keep the album from ever sounding "difficult" or arcane. It is to Simon's credit that he never attempts to sound like anybody but himself, nor does he require his fellow musicians to adapt their style to his; this embrace of difference is why the songs on *Graceland* are true collaborations—and such unusually successful ones. In the largest sense, one might say that *Graceland* is "about" the joys, complexities, and perplexities of living in an increasingly diverse, multicultural world. (This is a subject that also informs the words and music of Simon's next album, *The Rhythm of the Saints*, released in 1990.)

That one need not venture to other continents, or even to other countries, to find "other" cultures is a point made by the last two songs on *Graceland*: "That Was Your Mother," in which Simon is joined by the Louisiana-based zydeco band Good Rockin' Dopsie and the Twisters; and "All Around the World, or The Myth of Fingerprints," in which Simon plays with Los Lobos, the well-known Mexican American band from Los Angeles. On both of these selections, the prominent use of accordion and saxophone creates aural links with the sounds of South African ensembles that appear on other songs from *Graceland*, demonstrating musically that the world is indeed a shrinking place. (Conversely, Simon remarks in his liner notes how the South African instrumentalists he recorded in Johannesburg for the title song produced a sound that reminded him in certain ways of American country music.) At the end, then, Paul Simon comes home, only to find himself still, and always, a musical "citizen of the world."

Graceland, although not exactly the kind of smash-hit album that both *Thriller* and *Born in the U.S.A.* were (it never hit Number 1 on the album chart), eventually sold over 5 million copies. As the Grammy Award winner for Album of the Year in 1986, it spectacularly revived Simon's then-flagging career and garnered a great deal of attention, not only for Simon himself, but also for many of the musicians who played on the album with him. *Graceland* did not prove to be a major source of hit singles, but a concert video featuring much of its music, taped in Africa with African musicians, became very popular. More than any other, it is the album responsible for introducing a wide audience to the idea of world music, and for this reason alone the importance and influence of *Graceland* should not be underestimated.

Simon's career never again reached its height of success as he achieved on *Graceland*, but he continued to explore an expanded musical vocabulary on albums ranging from the follow-up record, *The Rhythm of the Saints* (1990), featuring South

BOX 13.2 BROADWAY IN RECENT TIMES

The 1970s were a time of transition and economic stress for Broadway, as they were for New York City generally. Although the age of the integrated Rodgers and Hammerstein–style musical seemed largely to have passed, no dominant trend emerged successfully to replace it. The rock musical, exemplified by *Hair*, proved to be an occasional rather than a systematic phenomenon, although musical styles influenced by rock and contemporary pop music began to appear in Broadway scores more regularly. An example of this phenomenon is the music for Stephen Sondheim's *Company* (1970); while certainly not a "rock musical," *Company* demonstrates Sondheim's absorption and distinctive adaptation of the popular music idioms of the time (including rock).

Company inaugurated a decade of extraordinary productivity and diverse achievement for Sondheim, who had begun composing very sophisticated music for his own words after beginning his Broadway career (with *West Side Story*) as solely a writer of lyrics. Sondheim's 1970s shows included *Follies* (1971), which referred both in its plot and in its musical idiom to the revue-style musicals of the 1920s and 1930s; the operetta-like *A Little Night Music* (1973); and finally, in 1979, the unique "musical thriller" *Sweeney Todd, the Demon Barber of Fleet Street*. Sondheim remains to this day the most critically acclaimed, and arguably the most influential, Broadway composer of recent times. Yet his success with the theater going public has always been modest, exemplified by the relatively short runs of his shows on Broadway, which were accompanied usually by a failure to earn back the investments made in producing them. This paradox illuminates well the complex and economically fragile state of affairs that characterized Broadway during this period. (One might compare the situation of Sondheim on Broadway to that of Chuck Berry in rock music: a crucial, innovative figure whose long-term impact vastly exceeds any statistical measures of his "popularity.") Sondheim's musicals yielded only one significant pop hit, "Send in the Clowns" from *A Little Night Music* (a chart success for Judy Collins in both 1975 and 1977), but the songs from his musicals have constituted the bread and butter of many nightclub and cabaret singers for several decades now.

Three factors help account for Broadway's recent success in extricating itself from the doldrums. One is the emergence of what might be termed the "mega-musical," a high-impact spectacle of staging and sound that is musical theater's rough equivalent to arena rock. The second is the increasing number of successful revivals of older musicals, a phenomenon that sometimes seems (or threatens) to be turning Broadway into its own kind of "oldies" act. The final factor, clearly related to the second, is the development and proliferation of "jukebox musicals," revue-type shows fashioned around a specific repertory of older popular music; together with the numerous revivals, this type of show is making Broadway into a kind of living museum of "classic" American pop music.

The mega-musical typically involves continuous (or virtually continuous) singing, eschewing spoken dialogue; anthem-like individual songs designed to be instantly hummable and memorable, delivered with pop-style vocals; and self-consciously elaborate staging that is fashioned to wow the audience. This format is well represented in the work of Andrew Lloyd Webber, a British composer who has become the ruling "king" of the musical theater of Broadway and London's West End—if not of world musical theater. (In a sense, Webber is Elvis Presley to Sondheim's Chuck Berry.) Webber's mega-hits on Broadway include *Evita* (1979), *Cats* (1982), and *The Phantom of the Opera* (1988), the last of which is Broadway's longest-running show to date. The original cast album of *Phantom* became a multiplatinum seller. The mega-musical truly came into its own with the stunning popularity of *Les Misérables*, an adaptation of the novel of the same name by nineteenth-century French author Victor Hugo. This show, with music by Claude-Michel Schönberg and French words by Alain Boublil, actually originated in France and was translated and adapted for a wildly popular London production before it premiered on Broadway in 1987. Its Broadway run of 6,680 performances is indicative of its impact, which has been worldwide and continues to be felt in the form of frequent revivals.

Broadway revivals of previously successful musicals are nothing new, but they began to appear with increasing frequency in the later 1980s and into the subsequent decades as it became obvious that potential audiences who might balk at purchasing the increasingly expensive tickets for new and unproven shows would willingly spend—often lavishly—to see a "proven" item. Among the most acclaimed examples we may cite here are the revival of Cole Porter's 1934 hit *Anything Goes* in 1987 (784 performances), the revival of Kern and Hammerstein's 1927 classic *Show Boat* in 1994 (946 performances), and the 2003 revival of the Bernstein-Comden-Green show *Wonderful Town*, which ran for 497 performances—nearly matching the original 1953 run of 559 performances. A phenomenon related to the popularity of revivals is the proliferation of successful movie adaptations for Broadway; among the most celebrated and best known are *Beauty and the Beast* (1994; 5,461 performances) and *The Lion King* (1997; still playing on Broadway at the time of this writing, and currently the third longest-running show in Broadway history), both stage adaptations of animated film musicals from Disney studios. (The movie soundtrack for *The Lion King* was the bestselling album for ten weeks in 1994 and went on to sell over 11 million copies.)

Finally, the jukebox musical takes us full circle from the loosely structured Broadway shows of the 1920s and 1930s, which served frequently as showcases to introduce potential hit songs (see the section on Broadway and Tin Pan Alley in Chapter 4). In a twist of the formula, the jukebox musical uses long-established hit songs to draw audiences into potential Broadway hit shows fashioned (often quite loosely) around those songs. Early examples from the 1970s are *Bubbling Brown Sugar* (1976; 766 performances), an "all-Black" revue presenting songs from the 1920s and 1930s, and the even more successful *Ain't Misbehavin'* (1978; 1,604 performances), which was essentially a live concert of songs composed by or associated with the great jazz pianist and singer Fats Waller (1904–1943). Significantly, both of these shows originated in small New York theaters off Broadway and surprised many when they proved to be major Broadway hits. The jukebox musical embraced the rock era emphatically with the outstandingly successful *Smokey Joe's Cafe* (1995; 2,036 performances), a show fashioned around the hit songs of Jerry Leiber and Mike Stoller (see Chapter 8) that currently stands as the longest-running Broadway revue in history. Among those that followed in its wake in the new millennium are *Mamma Mia!*, based on the many hits by the Swedish rock group ABBA (the show was also made into a popular movie); and *Jersey Boys*, based on the hits and career of the Four Seasons, an extremely popular singing group from the 1960s. Both of these musicals offer basic story lines in order to provide greater coherence than that usually present in a revue.

The greatest impact achieved by any recent musical is surely that achieved by Lin-Manuel Miranda's *Hamilton: An American Musical*. The most unlikely premise—a historically astute recounting of the career of Alexander Hamilton (1757–1804), one of the "Founding Fathers" of the United States and its first treasury secretary, told via a hip-hop score—resulted in a runaway smash hit that opened in 2015 and is still playing to sold-out houses at the time of this writing. In 2016 *Hamilton* won the Pulitzer Prize for Drama, eleven Tony awards (including Best Musical), and the Grammy for Best Musical Theater Album. *Hamilton* was not the first hip-hop musical, but its extraordinary success would seem to open the door to many future attempts to employ the hip-hop style and aesthetic to the venerable genre of the American musical.

American percussionists and rhythms, through his unsuccessful Broadway musical, *The Capeman* (1998), which drew on New York's Latino musical cultures, and a collaboration with sonic artist/producer Brian Eno for *Surprise* (2006). In 2011, he released the song "Getting Ready for Christmas Day" which included samples from a 1941 recording by Reverend J. M. Gates, a legendary preacher/performer, who can be heard interacting with his congregation. In 2016, his album *Stranger to Stranger* was released, debuting at Number 3 on the top pop album charts.

"Baby I'm a Star": Prince, Madonna, and the Production of Celebrity

The production of celebrity may be as central to the workings of the American music industry as the production of music itself. In the 1910s and 1920s Irene and Vernon Castle were made into national figures through a combination of theater tours, silent film appearances, magazine stories, and mass-produced "how-to" guides to ballroom dancing. In the 1930s and 1940s crooners such as Bing Crosby and Frank Sinatra were turned into media stars through increasingly sophisticated promotional techniques involving sound film, network radio, and print media. During the postwar years network television became an indispensable tool for the promotion of popular music and the production of celebrity—it is, for example, hard to imagine the careers of Elvis Presley or the Beatles without the initial boost provided by network television appearances.

By the 1980s the "star-making machinery behind the popular song" (to quote a lyric by singer-songwriter Joni Mitchell) had grown to unprecedented proportions. Since the profitability of the music industry depended on the sales generated by a relatively limited number of multiplatinum recordings, the coordination of publicity surrounding the release of such recordings was crucial. The release of a potential hit album—and of those individual tracks on the album thought to have potential as hit singles—was cross-promoted in music videos, television talk show appearances, Hollywood films, and newspaper, magazine, and radio interviews, creating the overall appearance of a multifront military campaign run by a staff of corporate generals.

The power of mass-mediated charisma is rooted in the idea that an individual fan can enter into a personal relationship with a superstar via images and sounds that are simultaneously disseminated to millions of people. The space between the public image of the star and the private life and personality of the musician who fills this role is where the contemporary industry of celebrity magazines, television exposés, "unauthorized" biographies, and paparazzi flourishes, providing fans with provocative tidbits of information concerning the glamour, habits, and character traits of their favorite celebrities. This field of popular discourse is dominated by certain well-worn narratives. In what is perhaps the most common of these story lines, the artist, born into humble circumstances, rises to fame; is overtaken by the four demons of greed, power, lust, and self-indulgence; falls into a deep pit (of despair, depression, drug addiction, or alcoholism); and then repents of his or her sins and is accepted (in a newly humbled status) by the media and millions of fans. Some celebrities manage to flaunt convention and maintain their "bad boy" or "bad girl" image throughout their careers, while others are portrayed as good-hearted and generous (if a bit bland) from the get-go. Of course, these story lines are as much about the fans themselves—and the combination of admiration and envy they feel toward their favorite celebrities—as about the particular musicians in question.

While stars such as Bing Crosby, the Beatles, and Bob Dylan played a key role in shaping their own public image, the 1980s saw the rise of a new breed of music superstar who was particularly adept at manipulating the mass media and stimulating public fascination with their personal characteristics, as well as with their music. Certainly, no analysis of celebrity in late twentieth-century America would be complete without discussion of *Madonna* and *Prince*. Like their contemporary Michael Jackson, Madonna Louise Veronica Ciccone and Prince Rogers Nelson were born in the industrial north of the midwestern United States during the summer of 1958. (All three of these 1980s superstars were only six years old in 1964, when the Beatles stormed America, and they were not yet in their teens during the first Woodstock Festival.) Despite the proximity of their geographical origins, Ciccone and Nelson followed quite distinctive career paths. To begin with, Ciccone was a dancer and photographic model who moved into music almost by accident, while Nelson had been making music professionally since the age of thirteen as an occasional member of his father's jazz trio. Madonna first emerged out of New York's thriving dance club scene, while Prince's career developed in the regional metropolis of Minneapolis, Minnesota. Madonna's hit recordings—like most pop recordings—depended on a high degree of collaborative interaction among the singer, the songwriter(s), the producer, the recording engineers, studio session musicians, and others. But many of Prince's hit recordings, inspired by the early 1970s example of Stevie Wonder, were composed, produced, engineered, and performed solely by Nelson himself, many at his own studio in Minneapolis (Paisley Park, Inc.).

Despite these obvious differences, however, Madonna and Prince have much in common. Both are self-conscious authors of their own celebrity, creators of multiple artistic alter egos, and highly skilled manipulators of the mass media. Both experienced a meteoric rise to fame during the early 1980s and were dependent on mass media such as cable television and film. And both Madonna and Prince have sought to blur the conventional boundaries of race, religion, and sexuality and have periodically sought to rekindle their fans' interest by shifting shape, changing strategy, and coming up with new and controversial songs and images. Early, sexually explicit recordings by Madonna and Prince played a primary role in stimulating the formation of the Parents' Music Resource Center (PMRC), a watchdog organization founded in 1985. During the second half of the 1980s, the PMRC—bolstered by its alliance with the Parent/Teachers Association (PTA)—pressured the recording industry to institute a rating system parallel to that used in the film industry. Although popular musicians ranging from Frank Zappa to John Denver argued against the adoption of a ratings system, the industry began to place parental warning labels on recordings during the late 1980s.

MADONNA

From the late 1980s through the 1990s Madonna's popularity was second only to that of Michael Jackson. Between 1984 and 1994 Madonna scored twenty-eight Top 10 singles, eleven of which reached the top spot on the charts. During the same ten-year period she recorded eight Top 10 albums, including the Number 1 hits *Like a Virgin* (1984), *True Blue* (1986), and *Like a Prayer* (1989). Over the course of her career, Madonna has sold in excess of 50 million albums and has been one of the most reliable sources of profit for Warner Entertainment, corporate owner of the Sire record label, for which she records. She also paved the way for female dance music superstars of the 1990s and beyond, such as Paula Abdul and Britney Spears.

Madonna recalls Marilyn Monroe in her "Material Girl" video, 1985.

As a purposefully controversial figure, Madonna has tended to elicit strongly polarized reactions. A 1987 *Rolling Stone* readers' poll awarded her second place for Best Female Singer and first place for Worst Female Singer. (In the same poll she also scored third place for Best-Dressed Female and first place for Worst-Dressed Female.) Jacques Chirac, the president of France, once described Madonna as "a great and beautiful artist," while the political philosopher Camille Paglia asserted that she represented "the future of feminism." The author Luc Sante's distaste for Madonna (as articulated in his 1990 article for the *New Rebooklic*, "Unlike a Virgin") was based largely on aesthetic criteria:

Madonna . . . is a bad actress, a barely adequate singer, a graceless dancer, a boring interview subject, a workmanlike but uninspired (co-)songwriter, and a dynamo of hard work and ferocious ambition.

Other observers are ambivalent about Madonna, perhaps feeling as the satirist Merrill Markoe once put it: "I keep trying to like her, but she keeps pissing me off!"

(Sexton 1993, 14). In the academic field of popular culture studies, scholars have created a veritable cottage industry out of analyzing Madonna's social significance, variously interpreting her as a reactionary committed to turning back the advances of feminism, a postmodern performance artist, a politically savvy cultural subversive, and a "container for multiple images." Whatever one's view of these various characterizations, the fact that it is difficult to find anyone who (a) has never heard of Madonna, or (b) harbors no opinion of her at all, is an indication that her career strategy has by and large been very effective.

Born Madonna Louise Veronica Ciccone into an Italian American family in Bay City, Michigan, Madonna moved to New York City in 1977, worked as a photographic model, studied dance, and became a presence at Manhattan discotheques such as Danceteria, where DJ Mark Kamins played her demo tapes. (It was Kamins who introduced Madonna to executives at Sire Records, the label of the Ramones and Talking Heads, and who in 1982 produced her first dance club hit, "Everybody.") In 1983 Madonna's breakthrough single "Holiday" (Number 16 pop, Number 25 R&B) established certain elements of a distinctive studio sound that was rooted in the synth-pop dance music of the early 1980s (see the discussion of "Sweet Dreams (Are Made of This)" earlier in this chapter). In addition, Madonna took a page from Michael Jackson's book, enlisting the services of manager Freddie DeMann, who had guided Jackson's career in the years leading up to the mega-success of 1982's *Thriller*. DeMann oversaw the production of Madonna's first two music videos, "Borderline" and "Lucky Star," the latter of which featured glimpses of the young star's navel, setting a precedent for subsequent, ever more explicit sexual provocations. The choice of Freddie DeMann also points toward an important aspect of Madonna's modus operandi—the ability to enlist a collaborative network of talented professionals, including producers, recording engineers, designers, and videographers.

In 1984 her second album—*Like a Virgin*, produced by Nile Rodgers, who was involved with the writing and production of a number of disco era hits, including Chic's "Good Times" (see Chapter 11)—shot to the top of the album charts, eventually selling more than 10 million copies. The album spawned a series of hit singles: "Like a Virgin" (Number 1 for six weeks in 1984 and early 1985), "Material Girl" (Number 2 in 1985), "Angel," and "Dress You Up" (both Number 5 in 1985). *Like a Virgin* was promoted on MTV through a series of videos and formed the basis for an elaborately staged concert tour (the "Virgin Tour"), all carefully coordinated as part of a campaign to establish Madonna as a national celebrity. In 1985 Madonna also played a leading role in the film *Desperately Seeking Susan*, receiving generally positive reviews. In an industry in which women are often treated as attractive but essentially noncreative "objects," Madonna began early on in her career to exert an unusual degree of control, not only over her music (writing or cowriting many of the songs on her early albums and playing an active role in the production process), but also over the creation and promulgation of her media image. Even seemingly uncontrollable events—like the ubiquitous tabloid accounts of her tempestuous and short-lived marriage to actor Sean Penn—seemed only to feed Madonna's growing notoriety.

During the second half of the 1980s Madonna began to write and record songs with deeper—and more controversial—lyric content. These included "Papa Don't Preach" (1986), in which a pregnant young woman declares her determination to keep her baby and urges her father to lend his moral support; "Open Your Heart" (1986), the video version of which portrays Madonna on display at a sleazy peep show attended by dozens of men; "Express Yourself" (1989), in which she appears alternatively as a cross-dressing figure, dominating a tableau of male industrial workers, and as a submissive female stereotype, crawling under a table with a collar around her neck; and "Like a Prayer" (1989), the video of which included images of group and interracial sex, burning crosses, and an eroticized Black Jesus. (This last video was censured by the Vatican and caused the Pepsi-Cola Corporation to cancel a lucrative endorsement deal with Madonna.)

The controversy and commercialism ante was upped even further in 1992 with the publication of *Sex*, a 128-page coffee-table book featuring photographs of nude and S&M-garbed Madonna and other celebrities, and the synchronized release of the album *Erotica*, which peaked at Number 2 on the *Billboard* album chart and produced five major hit singles. The year 1994 saw the release of a warmer and more subtly sexual album, *Bedtime Stories*, which spawned "Take a Bow," her biggest single hit ever (Number 1 for seven weeks in 1994). Toward the end of the 1990s Madonna once again redefined her public image, winning a Golden Globe award for her leading role in the film *Evita* (1996, a movie version of the Andrew Lloyd Webber musical) and releasing an album of love ballads (*Something to Remember*, 1996) aimed at a more mature audience.

Beginning with the 1998 album *Ray of Light* (which debuted at Number 2 on the album charts) and continuing through *Confessions on a Dance Floor* (2005, a Number 1 album with three tracks that reached the top of the hot dance music/club play charts; the following global tour reached 1.2 million fans and grossed over $193.7 million), Madonna has pursued a back-to-basics strategy, returning to the disco-derived synth-pop sound and the core audience that launched her career in the early 1980s. The artist returned to more R&B-influenced flavors on her 2008 album, *Hard Candy*, collaborating with younger artist/producers like Pharell Williams, and in 2012 released *MDNA*. Both debuted in Billboard's Top Ten album charts. She released the "more personal" album *Rebel Heart* in 2015, addressing issues of sexism and ageism in society. In 2016, she was named Billboard's Woman of the Year; in her acceptance speech, she pointedly attacked the music industry and society in general for its attitudes toward women.

Madonna has frequently challenged the accusation—leveled at her by critics on both the left and the right—that her recordings, videos, and concert productions reinforce old, negative stereotypes of women. In a 1991 interview Madonna responded to these criticisms:

I may be dressing like the typical bimbo, whatever, but I'm in charge. You know, I'm in charge of my fantasies. I put myself in these situations with men, you know, and everybody knows, in terms of my image in the public, people don't think of me as a person who's not in charge of my career or my life, okay? And isn't that what feminism is all about, you know, equality for men and women? And aren't I in charge of my life, doing the things I want to do? Making my own decisions? (Sexton 1993, 286)

Listening Guide "LIKE A VIRGIN"

Written by Billy Steinberg and Tom Kelly; performed by Madonna; released 1984

The core dichotomy of Madonna's public persona—the innocent, emotionally vulnerable, cheerful girl versus the tough-minded, sexually experienced, self-directed woman—was established in the hit single that propelled her to superstar status: "Like a Virgin" (Number 1 pop, Number 9 R&B, 1984). "Like a Virgin" was not written by Madonna herself but by a pair of male songwriters, Billy Steinberg and Tom Kelly. As Steinberg himself put it, this is not a song about a virgin in any narrowly technical sense—rather, it is about the feeling that someone who has grown pessimistic about love gets from a new relationship. (We have already encountered this theme in Tina Turner's rendition of "What's Love Got to Do with It.") "Like a Virgin" is a good example of the mileage that Madonna and her producer, Nile Rodgers, were able to get out of a fairly simple set of musical elements.

The form of "Like a Virgin" is straightforward. After a four-bar instrumental introduction that establishes the dance groove, there is an eight-bar verse, which we call A¹ ("I made it through the wilderness . . ."); a ten-bar version of the verse with somewhat different harmonies, which we call A² ("I was beat, incomplete . . ."); and a chorus featuring the hook of the song, which we call B ("Like a virgin . . ."). The only additional structural element is an eight-bar interlude near the middle of the arrangement. The basic structure of the recording is thus

A¹A²B
A¹A²B
Eight-bar interlude
A²BBB (etc., with a gradual fade out)

As in much popular music, the timbre, texture, and rhythmic momentum of "Like a Virgin" are more important to the listener's experience than the song's structure. The studio mix—overseen by Madonna's longtime collaborator Shep Pettibone—is clean, with clear stereo separation, heavy reliance on synthesized sound textures, and the singer's voice strongly foregrounded over the instruments. (As on many dance-oriented hit singles of the 1980s, the characteristic lead guitar sound of rock music is absent here.) Synthesizers are indispensable to the overall effect of this recording—this is a studio sound that simply could not have been created

ten years before. Throughout the recording, however, the producer and engineers are careful not to make the instrumental parts too busy or complex, so that Madonna's voice remains the undisputed center of the listener's attention.

As we have discussed, Madonna's persona on recordings and videos and in concert depends on the ironic manipulation of long-standing stereotypes about women. Her vocal style in "Like a Virgin" reflects this aspect of her persona clearly and deliberately, ranging from the soft, intimate breathiness associated with Hollywood sex symbols like Marilyn Monroe to the throaty, tougher sound of 1960s singers like Ronnie Spector, the lead singer on the Ronettes' "Be My Baby." (The contrast between these two vocal personas is reinforced in the video version of "Like a Virgin" by an alternation between images of one Madonna as a bride, dressed in white and about to be taken to bed by her groom, and another Madonna, dressed in a tight black skirt and top and blue tights who dances sexily in a gondola moving along the canals of Venice.) During the verses Madonna uses a breathy, somewhat reedy "little girl" voice, occasionally interspersing the words with little squeals, sighs, and intakes of breath at the ends of phrases. Throughout the recording, she shifts back and forth between the two personas of the innocent virgin and the experienced, worldly-wise woman, each of which is signified by a distinctive set of vocal timbres.

Of course, how a song's lyrics are interpreted is strongly influenced by their musical setting and the visual images that accompany the words and music in a video or live concert. When Madonna revived "Like a Virgin" for her 1990 *Blonde Ambition* tour, the song was placed in a more complex and provocative context, with Madonna clad like an ancient Egyptian princess, reclining on a huge bed, and framed on either side by Black male dancers wearing cone-shaped brassieres. Whatever one's interpretation of the sexual and religious symbolism of Madonna's performances and its relationship to her own experience growing up as a Catholic, it is clear that she has a talent for recycling her repertoire in controversial and thought-provoking ways.

Madonna's rhetorical question pulls us into the middle space between the public image and the private life: between the international superstar Madonna and Madonna Louise Veronica Ciccone, a talented and ambitious Italian American woman from the suburbs of industrial Detroit. Throughout her career, Madonna Ciccone has released tidbits of information about her private life, attitudes, and values that invite her fans (and her detractors) to imagine what the woman behind the "star-making machinery" is "really" like.

PRINCE

Between 1982 and 1992 Prince (a.k.a. the Artist) placed nine albums in the Top 10, reaching the top of the charts with three of them (*Purple Rain* in 1984, *Around the World in a Day* in 1985, and *Batman* in 1989). During the same decade he placed twenty-six singles in the Top 40 and produced five Number 1 hits. Over the course of his career, Prince sold over 80 million albums, making him one of the most popular music superstars of the last three decades. More importantly, Prince was one of the most talented musicians ever to achieve mass commercial success in the field of popular music.

Prince Rogers Nelson was born in Minneapolis, Minnesota, the child of parents who migrated from Louisiana to the North and identified themselves as African Americans while acknowledging a mixed-race heritage that includes Italian and Native American ancestry. Prince stated that growing up in a middle-class Minneapolis neighborhood exposed him to a wide range of music, and that his early influences included everything from James Brown and Santana to Joni Mitchell. As he testified in a 1985 interview on MTV:

> I was brought up in a black-and-white world and, yes, Black and white, night and day, rich and poor. I listened to all kinds of music when I was young, and when I was younger, I always said that one day I would play all kinds of music and not be judged for the color of my skin but the quality of my work.

When he was seven his mother and father separated, and Prince spent much of his adolescence being shunted from one home to another. Various statements by Prince suggest that the instability of that period in his life and the ambivalence of his relationships with his estranged parents have formed the source material for some of his best-known songs.

One of the first things that strike listeners about Prince's career is his amazing productivity. Throughout the 1980s and 1990s, when most superstars were releasing an album every two or three years, Prince's output averaged over an album per year. During the 1980s he composed, performed, and recorded more than seventy-five songs each year. Only about three hundred of these songs have been released, but the studio vault at Paisley Park is said to contain more than one thousand unreleased songs that constitute more than ten thousand hours of material. Prince's compositions have been recorded by a wide range of artists, including George Clinton, Miles Davis, Joni Mitchell, Madonna, Bonnie Raitt, Celine Dion, and Alicia Keys. In addition to recordings released under his own name, Prince developed a variety of satellite projects—groups or artists who have served in part as outlets for his music (for example, the Time, Apollonia 6, and Sheila E).

In stylistic terms, Prince's recorded output has encompassed a wide range of musical inspirations, from funk music and guitar-based rock 'n' roll to urban folk songs, new wave, jazz, and psychedelic rock. Although the dominant impression of Prince's musical approach is that of a thoroughgoing open-mindedness, he also from the very beginning of his career sought to exert tight control over his music, its marketing, and its distribution. He owned his own studio (Paisley Park Studios, in Minneapolis) and produced his own recordings, played most of the instruments on his recordings, and worked for years to maintain control over the master tapes recorded in his studio.

Prince's musical and commercial breakthrough came with the release of his third album, *Dirty Mind*, which reached Number 7 on the R&B album charts in 1980. Recorded in his home studio, with Prince himself playing almost all of the instruments, *Dirty Mind* introduced a captivating new fusion of soul, synth-pop, and new wave sensibilities juxtaposed with a hard-edged rock sound that centered on his virtuoso guitar work. A number of the tracks were explicitly sexual in content, establishing Prince's controversial public image as an exuberant and graphic eroticist. He followed this recording with a double album titled *1999* (1982), which demonstrates his musical range even more clearly, presenting songs that range from pop ("Little Red Corvette") and rock 'n' roll ("Delirious") to the apocalyptic dance-club funk—"Everybody's got a bomb, we could all die any day / But before I'll let that happen, I'll dance my life away"—that is embodied in "1999," the album's eponymous title track (Number 12 pop, 1983).

During the mid-1980s, it was an album track (never released as a single) that did the most to reinforce Prince's reputation for controversy. "Darling Nikki," from the *Purple*

Prince in a scene from *Purple Rain*, 1987.

Rain album, was the first recording ever to receive a Parental Advisory warning from the Parents' Music Resource Center (PMRC), founded by Tipper Gore in 1985, and was attacked by the Trinity Broadcasting Network and preacher Jimmy Swaggart as "pornographic" and "satanic."

Prince's commercial success was accompanied by an increasing frustration with Warner Brothers, the corporation that had produced and promoted his early albums. By the early 1990s, he had entered into a protracted struggle with the company, going so far as to appear in public with the word "slave" written on his cheek. (During this period he is reported to have coined the deathless credo, "If you don't own your masters, your masters own you.") In 1993 Prince changed his name to a visual symbol (the Love Symbol) that combined male and female elements, leading wags in the press to dub him "The Artist Formerly Known as Prince" or simply "The Artist." A 1993 press release explained his motivations for this decision:

> Prince is the name that my mother gave me at birth. Warner Bros. took the name, trademarked it, and used it as the main marketing tool to promote all of the music that I wrote. The company owns the name Prince and all related music marketed under Prince. I became merely a pawn used to produce more money for Warner Bros. . . . I was born Prince and did not want to adopt another conventional name. The only acceptable replacement for my name, and my identity, was the Love Symbol, a symbol with no pronunciation, that is a representation of me and what my music is about.

After he separated from Warner Brothers in 1995, it seemed to many fans and critics that The Artist turned away from his formerly open musical stance toward a more introspective and self-indulgent approach. The triple album *Emancipation* (1996), released on his own independent label, NPG Records, reached Number 6 on the R&B and Number 11 on the pop album charts. However, only two singles from *Emancipation* reached the Top 20, and it has been argued that Prince's desire to release material that had been held up by Warner Brothers out of fear of overexposing him simply led him to unleash too much music for fans to digest in one meal.

The Artist spent the next decade making a series of lesser-selling albums that ranged all over the stylistic map, from a four-disc set of outtakes and unreleased material (*Crystal Ball*, 1998) to a collection of instrumental studio jams (*N.E.W.S.*, 1999) and an eclectic musical celebration of his newfound spiritual commitment to the Jehovah's Witnesses movement (*Rainbow Children*, 2001). By the late 1990s he was releasing his own music exclusively and extensively on his NPG label, and he became one of the first artists to sell his own music via the Internet. In 2000 he readopted the name Prince, although his relationship to all but the most loyal of his fans continued to deteriorate when he sued a nonprofit fan-operated website in 2002, charging them with copyright infringement.

In the years preceding his untimely death in 2016, Prince returned to the charts in an astonishing fashion. Beginning in 2004 he released a trio of albums—*Musicology* (Number 3 pop, R&B, and Internet), *3121* (Number 1 pop, R&B, and Internet, 2006), and

Planet Earth (Number 1 R&B, Number 3 pop and Internet, 2007)—that resurrected the blend of funky jams, sensuous grooves, and hard rock guitar that had initially launched his career, re-establishing his place at the top of the charts. A national "Greatest Hits" tour, combined with performances at the Grammy Awards and the Rock & Roll Hall of Fame induction ceremony (2004) and as the headliner on *Saturday Night Live* (2006) and in the halftime show for Superbowl XLI (2007), reignited the loyalty of fans who had been turned off by his seeming lack of focus during the previous decade and brought Prince's music to an even wider and, importantly, younger audience. His last official albums were released in 2015 (*Hit n Run Phase One* and *Hit n Run Phase Two*). A year later, he died of an apparent drug overdose from prescription pain killers. Like Jimi Hendrix before him, Prince left behind a large cache of unreleased recordings, said to be being prepared for release.

As this summary of his career suggests, descriptions of Prince's personality in the popular press have presented a series of opposing images: he was a flower child and a dictator; a male chauvinist who can form close personal relationships only with women; an intensely private person and a shrewd self-promoter; a sexual satyr and a steadfastly pious man who dedicated many of his albums to God. These discussions of Prince draw many comparisons with earlier figures in the history of popular music: the extroverted and sexually ambiguous rock 'n' roll star Little Richard, the guitar virtuoso Jimi Hendrix, the groundbreaking and idiosyncratic bandleader Sly Stone, and the brilliant songwriter and multi-instrumentalist Stevie Wonder. Prince was critical of the tendency of journalists and record company publicists to identify him only with Black artists. In response to the question "What do you think about the comparisons between you and Jimi Hendrix?" he responded, "It's only because he's Black. That's really the only thing we have in common. He plays different guitar than I do. If they really listened to my stuff, they'd hear more of a Santana influence than Jimi Hendrix" (Karlen 1985).

Prince's British biographer Barney Hoskyns christened Prince "the Imp of the Perverse," referring to his apparent delight in confounding the expectations and assumptions of his audience, music critics, and the record industry. Certainly, Prince's relationship to the "star-making machinery" of the entertainment industry was as complex as his racial identity, sexual orientation, and musical style. As a public celebrity, Prince occupied a middle ground between the hermitlike reclusiveness of Michael Jackson and the exuberant exhibitionism of Madonna. Throughout his career, he granted few press interviews yet for the most part managed to keep himself in the limelight. Perhaps the best example of Prince's skill at manipulating the boundary between the public and the private are the film and soundtrack album *Purple Rain* (1984), which established him as a pop superstar. *Purple Rain* was the bestselling album of 1984, bumping Bruce Springsteen's *Born in the U.S.A.* out of the top position on *Billboard*'s pop album chart, holding the Number 1 position for twenty-four weeks, and producing five hit singles, including "When Doves Cry," "Let's Go Crazy," and "Purple Rain." Since 1984 the album has sold more than 13 million copies, making it one of the bestselling albums of all time. The film did reasonably well at the box office, although it did not succeed in establishing Prince as a matinee idol. Reviews varied widely: some critics regarded the film as a self-indulgent, poorly written, and badly acted attempt to promote a music album, while *Rolling Stone* numbered it among the best rock movies ever made. The film and the album were cross-promoted by Warner Entertainment, which spent $3.5 million for television ads, and by MTV, which ran footage from the celebrity-packed premiere party in Hollywood. The single of "When Doves Cry" was released a few weeks before *Purple Rain* appeared in theaters and helped to boost the film's popularity, which in turn helped several other songs on the soundtrack to reach the Top 40.

The plot and characters of *Purple Rain* draw heavily on the details of Prince's life, both personal and professional. Prince stars as "the Kid," a young, gifted musician struggling to establish himself in the nightclub scene of Minneapolis. His main competition in the musical arena is Morris Day, the real-life leader of one of Prince's satellite projects, the Time. The Kid is attracted to a beautiful young singer named Apollonia (another of Prince's real-life protégés), who in the film is also being pursued by Morris Day. The Kid's parents—the only characters in the film portrayed by professional actors—are to some degree based on Prince's own mother and father. Another subplot has to do with the Kid's inability to accept creative input from the musicians in his band, the Revolution. The film concludes on a relatively upbeat note as the Kid adopts one of his father's compositions, incorporating a rhythm track created by members of the Revolution, and creates the song "Purple Rain," which wins over his audience, the band, Apollonia, and even Morris Day.

As with any semiautobiographical work, it is not easy to draw boundaries between the fictional character (the Kid), the celebrity persona (Prince), and the private individual (Prince Rogers Nelson). The character of the Kid—talented, self-absorbed, obsessed with exerting control over his music and his career, troubled by family conflicts and an inability to sustain intimate relationships—seems consonant with the accounts offered by Prince's family and professional associates of the artist's own personality. Apart from the Academy Award–winning soundtrack, a major source of the film's attraction for Prince's fans no doubt lies in the idea that it acts as a form of public psychoanalysis, providing a tantalizing opportunity to catch a glimpse of the "man behind the curtain." If *Purple Rain* is a film with genuinely confessional aspects, it is also a product of the increasingly sophisticated marketing strategies applied by entertainment corporations during the 1980s.

If "Like a Virgin" can be interpreted as a musical analog to Madonna's "split personality," "When Doves Cry" may represent an even more complex set of psychological relations between the public persona and the private personality of a pop superstar. In a 1996 television interview, Prince Rogers Nelson revealed that he, like millions of other children, had created an alternative personality, an imaginary companion who not only had helped him through the dislocations of his youth but also continued to offer him guidance as an adult. It may not be too much of a reach to suggest that the "multiple Princes" of "When Doves Cry"—a song that wears its Oedipal heart on its sleeve, so to speak—are not only an experiment in musical polyphony but also a conscious representation of the continuous inner dialogue that shaped Prince's career. (In interviews, Prince described how his "spirit" has advised him to change course, abandon projects,

Listening Guide   "WHEN DOVES CRY"

Written, performed, and produced by Prince; released 1984

"When Doves Cry"—a last-minute addition to the *Purple Rain* soundtrack—is an unusual pop recording in a number of regards. To begin with, the album track runs almost six minutes, a length that, although not without precedent, was much longer than the typical Top 40 hit of the 1980s. (A shortened version was released as a single.) Pop music recordings of the 1980s—such as Madonna's "Like a Virgin"—were typically the product of collaboration among the singer, songwriter(s), producer, studio engineers, session musicians, and others. "When Doves Cry," in contrast, is essentially the work of a single person: Prince wrote the song, produced the recording, sang all of the vocal parts, and played all of the instruments, including electric guitar, keyboard synthesizers, and the Linn LM-1 digital drum machine. The lyric of "When Doves Cry," with its striking imagery and psychoanalytical implications, certainly does not conform to the usual formulas of romantic pop songs. In addition, this recording crosses over the boundaries of established pop genres, fusing a funk rhythm with the lead guitar sound of heavy metal, the digitally synthesized and sampled textures of postdisco dance music, and the aesthetic focus and control of progressive rock and the singer-songwriter tradition. In this sense it is a good example both of Prince's desire to avoid being typecast as a traditional R&B artist and of the creative eclecticism that led music critics to come up with labels such as "dance rock," "funk rock," or "new wave funk" to describe his music.

The instrumentation of "When Doves Cry" is also somewhat unusual, as it lacks a bass part. Usually the bass helps to establish the tonality (or key) of a given piece of music and combines with the drums to provide the rhythmic bedrock of a recording. Prince's decision to "punch out" (exclude) the bass track that he had already recorded—apparently a spur-of-the-moment experiment during the process of mixing—gives the recording an unusually open feeling. In addition, his composition avoids the tendency, pronounced in many rock and pop recordings, to establish a clear distinction between a verse and a chorus, each having its own distinctive melody and harmonies. "When Doves Cry" does use the verse-and-chorus form, but the melody and supporting harmonies are almost identical in the two sections,

making the distinction between them much less fixed. While many pop recordings use the verse-chorus structure to build to a final climax that is followed by a relatively rapid fade-out, the musical intensity of "When Doves Cry" rises and falls continuously, creating a complex succession of peaks and valleys. (One critic has interpreted this "ebbing and flowing of pleasure" as embodying a female rather than male pattern of sexual excitement and has connected this musical approach to Prince's embrace of female qualities in his own personality.) Finally, the studio mix is also unusual, being relatively spare and dry and quite unlike the lush, reverb-laden studio sound of most 1980s dance music recordings (including Madonna's hit singles). Prince does use studio effects such as echo and digital processing, but they are lightly controlled and focused.

The arrangement of "When Doves Cry" can be divided into two major sections. Section 1, about three and a half minutes in length, is basically a presentation of the song with its alternation of verse (A) and chorus (B). Section 2 consists of a series of eight-bar phrases in which the background texture is subtly varied while instrumental solos (guitar and keyboard synthesizer), sung phrases (both solo and overdubbed in harmony), and other vocal effects (breathing, screaming, sighing, groaning) are sometimes juxtaposed or layered on top of one another and other times alternated one after the other. Perhaps the best analogy for the overall effect of this recording is that of a woven material, made up of patches of subtly shifting textural effects and tone colors, held together by the strong threads of a funk-derived dance groove, and strung on a formal loom made up of eight-bar sections. This is a recording that rewards repeated listening, not least because one musician has created every sound that you hear throughout.

"When Doves Cry" opens abruptly with a virtuoso burst of lead guitar, establishing from the very first moment Prince's mastery of the hard rock idiom. (We could say that Prince was able to do for himself what Michael Jackson needed Eddie Van Halen's help to accomplish on his *Thriller* album.) As the main dance groove is established on the Linn LM-1 digital drum machine, the guitar plays five more bars. We then hear a strange yet recognizably human sound, a pattern

(continued)

Listening Guide "WHEN DOVES CRY" (continued)

created by running Prince's voice through a digital processor and turning it into a repeating loop. As the keyboard synthesizer introduces a chord pattern that interlocks rhythmically with the drum machine (completing the basic groove that will carry us through most of the recording), Prince's voice moves across the stereo space of the recording from left to right and then fades out. Only sixteen bars into the recording, it is clear that this is not your typical pop single.

The first half of the arrangement (Section 1) begins by placing equal weight on the verse and the chorus material (sixteen bars each) and then gradually de-emphasizes the verse (A), which finally disappears altogether (see the following chart). The chorus is always followed by an eight-bar groove section in which the underlying dance rhythm produced by the drum machine and the synthesizer is brought to the fore. The presentation of the song, with its weakly contrasted verse-chorus structure, makes full use of studio technology, as well as Prince's remarkable abilities as a singer. In the first verse he sings alone in a middle-register voice. The second verse introduces a second copy of Prince, another middle-register voice that overlaps slightly with the first one; as this

verse concludes, the two Princes sing together, first in unison and then in overdubbed harmony. In the chorus ("How can you . . .") these two voices are joined by a third, low-register, growling voice; eventually ("Maybe you're . . ."), we are presented with four Princes singing in harmony with one another, plus a fifth Prince who interjects solo responses.

The second half of "When Doves Cry" (Section 2) presents an even more complex palette of timbral and textural variations, playing with combinations of the drum machine–synthesizer groove, sustained orchestral sounds, instrumental solos (including a keyboard solo that resembles eighteenth-century music), and an astonishing variety of vocal timbres. If you listen closely you should be able to distinguish as many as a dozen unique voices in the studio mix, positioned to the left, right, and center, some heavily modified by digital technology and others closer to the natural sound of Prince's singing voice. In addition to the complex patterns of harmony and call-and-response singing, Prince uses a variety of vocal effects, including a James Brown–like scream, rhythmic breathing, sighs, and groans. These sounds lend a sense of physical intimacy to the recording and enhance its aura of sexuality.

LISTENING GUIDE | "WHEN DOVES CRY"

TIME	FORM	LYRIC	DESCRIPTIVE COMMENTS
0:00	Introduction		Lead guitar solo, no accompaniment
Section 1			
0:03	Groove (8 measures)		Dance tempo established on drum machine; guitar stops at end of bar 5; digitized loop of Prince's voice enters in bar 6 (L side)
	Groove (8 measures)		Keyboard synthesizer enters, playing main riff; Prince's voice loop moves left to right and then fades (bars 1–4)
	A (8 measures)	*Dig if you will . . .*	Keyboard drops out; solo voice and drum machine only
	A (8 measures)	*Dream if you can . . .*	Second solo voice enters (overlaps with first voice); two voices combined (overdubbed), bars 5–8; vocal harmony in bars 7–8 ("They feel the heat")
	B (8 measures)	*How can you . . .*	New vocal timbre added (growling bass voice); solo voice responds in bar 4 ("So cold"); new synthesizer pattern added (offbeats)

TIME	FORM	LYRIC	DESCRIPTIVE COMMENTS
	1 measure		
	8 measures	*Maybe you're . . .*	More overdubbed voices added; four-part vocal harmony; solo voice responds in bar 4 ("She's never satisfied")
1:34	Groove (8 measures)		Drum machine and keyboard synthesizer
1:50	A (8 measures)	*Touch . . .*	Vocal sounds in background (groans, sighs)
2:05	B (8 measures)	*How can you . . .*	New vocal timbre added (bass voice, growling); vocal responses in harmony
	1 measure		
2:20	8 measures	*Maybe you're . . .*	More overdubbed voices added; four-part vocal harmony
2:35	Groove (8 measures)		Drum machine and keyboard synthesizer; voices drift in and out (high falsetto timbre); vocal harmony riff (bars 6–7)
2:50	B (8 measures)	*How can you . . .*	Synthesized string sounds added in background; four-part vocal harmony with solo voice responses
	1 measure		
3:05	8 measures	*Maybe you're . . .*	Four-part vocal harmony with solo voice responses
Section 2			
3:20	Interlude (8 measures)	*When doves cry . . .*	Synthesizer riff drops out; drum machine plus synthesized string sounds; Prince's "voices" overlap
	Groove (8 measures)		Groove re-established; lead guitar solo begins; solo and duet voices drift in and out

NOTE: The single version of the song fades out and ends at this point

	Groove (8 measures)		Guitar solo; solo and duet voices drift in and out
4:06	Groove (8 measures)		Guitar solo; solo and duet voices drift in and out; James Brown–style scream begins bar 5
	Groove (8 measures)		Guitar solo ends; vocal sounds float over the groove (breathing, sighs, screams, groans)
4:37	Groove (8 measures)		Vocal sounds float over groove
	Groove (8 measures)		Stop time in rhythm section with vocal harmony response; keyboard solo begins bar 5
	Groove (8 measures)		Keyboard solo continues with vocal riff background; groove re-established in bar 5
	Groove (8 measures)	*When doves cry . . .*	Prince's "voices" overlap; synthesized strings
	Groove (4 measures)	*Don't cry . . .*	Prince's "voices" overlap
	Coda		Rising melodic pattern on keyboard; synthesized strings in background

and even alter his name.) In its rich layering of instrumental textures and vocal personalities, "When Doves Cry" imparted to the public image of Prince a complexity and psychological depth that is in fact not typical of mass-media celebrities. And in the process, it established his reputation as one of the most creative and influential musicians of the 1980s.

THE DECADE OF the 1980s saw important shifts in the music business, starting with a precipitous decline in record sales unprecedented since the Great Depression, the introduction of digital technologies, including samplers and the compact disc, the increasing reliance of corporations on a small number of multiplatinum albums by megastars that were promoted through the new medium of music video, and the continued splintering of the market for popular music into dozens of specialized audiences and genres. In Chapter 14 we will follow the development of alternative music movements such as hip-hop, hardcore, alternative rock, techno, and world beat from the 1980s into the 1990s, paying particular attention to conflicts over authenticity and commercialism (or "keeping it real" versus "selling out").

Key Terms

analog recording	Music Television (MTV)	synth-pop
digital recording	samplers	
drum machines	sequencers	

Key People

Annie Lennox	Kenny Rogers	Peter Gabriel
Bruce Springsteen	Lionel Richie	Prince
Dave Stewart	Madonna	Tina Turner
Eddie Van Halen	Michael Jackson	Van Halen
Eurythmics	Paul Simon	

Review Questions

1. What new technologies of the 1980s changed the sound of popular music?
2. How did MTV influence the promotion of popular music during the 1980s?
3. What gave Michael Jackson's *Thriller* across-the-board appeal and contributed to the album's unprecedented commercial success?
4. How is the concept of collaboration manifested in Paul Simon's album *Graceland*?
5. How did Madonna court controversy to build her career as a pop superstar?
6. What makes Prince one of the most creative and influential artists of the 1980s?

"Smells Like Teen Spirit"

Hip-Hop, Alternative Music, and the Entertainment Business

14

DURING THE FIRST DECADES OF THE TWENTIETH CENTURY THE MARKET for popular music was clearly divided into a stylistic core—Tin Pan Alley love songs and ragtime- and jazz-influenced dance music, with the occasional touch of Latin American exoticism—and a periphery, which included types of music that came to be known as race music, hillbilly music, and ethnic music. By the end of the twentieth century, it had become almost impossible to sustain a clear-cut dichotomy between the center of American popular music and its margins.

For one thing, the most economically successful popular music (in terms of record sales and radio airplay) no longer presented a coherent stylistic thumbprint. The bestselling albums of the 1990s featured an extraordinary variety of artists, ranging from "adult contemporary" divas such as Celine Dion, Janet Jackson, and Mariah Carey (the biggest-selling pop and R&B recording artist of the decade) to country music stars like Clint Black, Reba McEntire, Shania Twain, and Garth Brooks (the biggest-selling male artist of the decade); the R&B vocal quartet Boyz II Men; gangsta rappers such as Snoop Doggy Dogg, Tupac Shakur, and the Notorious B.I.G.; hard rock and heavy metal bands like Aerosmith and Metallica; punk-influenced alternative rock bands such as Nirvana, Pearl Jam, and the Red Hot Chili

Peppers; the confessional "alternative singer-songwriter" Alanis Morissette; and hugely popular, lush, romantic soundtrack albums for films such as *The Bodyguard* (1993) and *Titanic* (1996). Albums by new artists became very successful as the record companies sought to identify and promote a new generation of pop superstars (in the process spending hundreds of millions of dollars on recording deals in the hope of repeating the ever-elusive Michael Jackson phenomenon). Five of the annual bestselling albums of the 1990s were in fact debut albums by previously unknown artists: Mariah Carey's eponymous debut album (1991); *The Sign* by the Swedish Eurodisco group Ace of Base (1994); the Southern blues rock album *Cracked Rear View* by Hootie and the Blowfish (1995); Alanis Morissette's angst-ridden *Jagged Little Pill*, the bestselling album of the entire decade (1996); and *Spice* (1997), by pop icons the Spice Girls.

While the music business and the music public continued to seek out and welcome novelty, as they have done throughout the history of American popular culture, established older artists like Bob Dylan, Joni Mitchell, and Paul Simon continued their hold on the devotion of many fans and occasionally were even able to expand their fan base to include new, younger listeners. Dylan, for example, initiated something of a late-career renaissance with his highly regarded 1997 album *Time Out of Mind* (which was followed by the similarly successful *"Love and Theft"* in 2001 and *Modern Times* in 2006). But few artists have ever experienced the kind of resurgence accomplished by *Johnny Cash* with his series of "American Recordings" beginning in 1994. Cash (1932–2003) had begun his career in the mid-1950s as one of the rockabilly stars of Sun Records, was acclaimed as a country artist throughout the 1960s and 1970s, and had served as the host and star of the television variety series *The Johnny Cash Show*. By the 1980s, however, he seemed well past his prime commercially, and well-known rap producer Rick Rubin's signing of Cash to the former's American Recordings label in the early 1990s appeared initially to be, at best, a rather eccentric move on the part of both.

Conventional wisdom was proved wrong once again as Cash's five "American Recordings" (the last released posthumously) proceeded to garner critical raves and popular attention. Cash's inclusion on these albums of contemporary rock material—interpreted in his own distinctive way—along with the more expected country-oriented and traditional folk repertoire attracted the attention and approval of a new generation and brought Cash renewed fame and respect. Two years after his death, the release of the extremely popular biopic *Walk the Line* (named after one of Cash's earliest and most enduring hits, "I Walk the Line") brought the story of Johnny Cash's life and the sound of his music to many additional millions of people and cemented his now unquestionable status as an icon of American music.

Although the singles market as a whole continued to shrink during the 1990s, the decade did produce a number of the bestselling singles in history, including "One Sweet Day," an R&B-flavored love song by Mariah Carey and Boyz II Men, which held the Number 1 position for a record sixteen weeks in 1995; "Candle in the Wind 1997," retro-rocker Elton John's multiplatinum tribute to the late Princess Diana; and a Latin novelty number called "The Macarena," which swept the nation in a matter of weeks in 1996, inspiring a dance fad and supplementing the repertoire of songs performed by audiences at massive sporting events (a diverse corpus that also includes "Take Me Out to the Ballgame," composed in 1908 by Tin Pan Alley songwriters Albert von Tilzer and Jack Norworth; "We Will Rock You," by the 1970s arena rock band Queen; and the Village People's disco hit "Y.M.C.A.").

Taken as a whole, then, the popular music of the 1990s included a jumble of old and new styles: slick pop and R&B, rock-influenced country music, and rough-edged, in your-face alternative rock and rap music. It is these last two categories on which we wish to focus in this chapter. Throughout this book we have traced the relationship between mainstream popular music—the music that in any given era attracts the broadest audience, receives the widest dissemination via the mass media, and generates the bulk of profits for the music industry—and varieties of music that originate on the margins of the musical economy, where survival is predicated on patronage from particular regional or ethnic communities. Many of the strongest influences in the history of popular music have come from people historically excluded from power, wealth, and social mobility, including African Americans, the working class, rural Southerners, and immigrant communities. More recently, ironically, the very notion of outsider, alternative, or marginal music has itself become a means of promoting music to a mass audience hungry for novelty, excitement, and a sense of authenticity.

In this chapter we will examine a group of genres and styles that originated outside the mainstream in one way or another. First, we will look at hip-hop and its transformation from a local outgrowth of minority youth culture in New York City into a multimillion-dollar global industry. Then, in the second half of the chapter, we will examine the concept of **alternative music**, a term that is used across a wide range of popular genres, including rock, rap, adult contemporary, dance, folk, and country music. We will begin this half of the discussion with a consideration of alternative rock, which emerged as a more or less underground movement in the early 1980s, combined the rebellious spirit and youth appeal of rock 'n' roll with the nihilism of punk rock, and during the 1990s led to the confounding spectacle of vociferously anticommercial artists playing at corporate-sponsored rock festivals and releasing multiplatinum albums for major record companies. We will then examine the meaning of the term "alternative" as it is applied to other genres, including urban folk music (e.g., Ani DiFranco), hip-hop (e.g., Lauryn Hill), and country music (e.g., k.d. lang), and we will take a brief look at the development of postdisco electronic dance music (EDM). Finally, our focus will turn to one of the few truly novel developments of the 1980s and 1990s: the emergence of so-called world music, or world beat, a heterogeneous category that encompasses artists from Africa, the Near East, and Asia—the ultimate margins of the American music industry and the American musical imagination. Although this category covers a great diversity of musical styles, we will focus on two examples of collaboration between American and non-Western artists.

Each of these musical genres or movements—hip-hop, alternative music, EDM, world music—exemplifies the tensions and contradictions created when music is marketed to a mass audience specifically on the basis of its difference from or opposition to the popular mainstream, and, taken as a whole, they give us a glimpse of the diversity and complexity of American popular music at the beginning of the twenty-first century.

Hip-Hop Breaks Out (1980s–1990s)

In Chapter 12 we examined the origins of rap music and hip-hop culture in New York City during the mid-1970s. By the early 1980s million-selling records like "Rapper's Delight" (1979) and "The Message" (1982) had created opportunities for New York rappers to perform at venues outside their own neighborhoods and thereby widen their audience. They also alerted the major record companies to the commercial potential of hip-hop, eventually leading to the transition from the twelve-inch dance single as the primary medium for recorded rap (an inheritance from disco) to the rap album.

The mid-1980s saw a rapid acceleration of rap's movement into the popular mainstream. In 1983 the jazz fusion musician Herbie Hancock collaborated with DJ Grandmixer DST on "Rockit," which made the R&B Top 10 and was played frequently on the still-young MTV channel. The following year, the popular soul singer Chaka Khan invited Melle Mel to provide a rap introduction for her hit single "I Feel for You," an adaptation of a Prince song that went to Number 1 on the R&B and Number 3 on the pop charts.

The year 1986 saw the release of the first two multiplatinum rap albums, *Raising Hell* by **Run DMC** (which reached Number 3 on the *Billboard* Top Pop Albums chart and sold over 3 million copies) and *Licensed to Ill* by the Beastie Boys (Number 1 for seven weeks, with over 10 million copies sold). That neither Run DMC nor the Beastie Boys hailed from the Bronx indicates the expanding appeal of rap music in the New York area. The key to the commercial success of these albums, however, was the expansion of the *audience* for hip-hop music, which now included millions of young white fans who were attracted by the transgressive, rebellious sensibility of the genre. Both *Raising Hell* and *Licensed to Ill* were released on a new independent label called Def Jam, cofounded in 1984 by the hip-hop promoter Russell Simmons and the musician-producer Rick Rubin. During the 1980s Def Jam took up where Sugar Hill Records left off, cross-promoting a new generation of artists, expanding and diversifying the national audience for hip-hop, and in 1986 becoming the first rap-oriented independent label to sign a distribution deal with one of the "Big Five" record companies, Columbia Records.

Run DMC—a trio consisting of the MCs **Run** (Joseph Simmons, b. 1964) and **DMC** (Darryl McDaniels, b. 1964), and the DJ *Jam Master Jay* (Jason Mizell, 1965–2002)—was perhaps the most influential act in the history of rap music. Simmons, McDaniels, and Mizell were college-educated Black men, raised in a middle-class neighborhood in the borough of Queens. Working with Russell Simmons (Run's older brother) and producer Rick Rubin, they established a hard-edged, rock-influenced style that was to profoundly influence the sound and sensibility of later rap music. Their raps were intricate and rhythmically skilled, with Run and DMC weaving their phrases together and sometimes

Run DMC, (from left) Reverend Run (Joseph Simmons), Darryl McDaniels, Jam Master Jay (Jay Mizell), January 1986.

even completing the last few words of one another's lines. The "beats" produced by Rubin and Jam Master Jay were stark and powerful, mixing digitized loops of hard rock drumming with searing guitar sounds from heavy metal. Run DMC was the first rap group to headline a national tour and the first to appear on MTV. They popularized rap among the young, predominantly white audience for rock music, gave the genre a more rebellious image, and introduced a unique sartorial style—hats, gold chains, and untied Adidas sports shoes with fat laces—to millions of young Americans. The now famil-iar connection between rap music and athletic wear was established in 1986 when the Adidas corporation and Run DMC signed a $1.5 million promotional deal.

The Beastie Boys, the rap trio whose album *Licensed to Ill* topped the pop charts a few months after the release of *Raising Hell*, were the first commercially successful white act in hip-hop. Like Run DMC, their recordings were produced by Rick Rubin and released on Def Jam Records, and they benefited greatly from the distribution deal signed by Russell Simmons with industry giant Columbia Records. Although they re-ceived a great deal of criticism for ripping off a Black style, it is perhaps more accurate to suggest that their early recordings represent a fusion of the youth-oriented rebel-liousness of hardcore punk rock—the style that they began playing in 1981—with the sensibility and techniques of hip-hop. In 1985 the Beastie Boys were signed by Def Jam Records, appeared in *Krush Groove*—one of the first films to deal with hip-hop culture—and toured as the opening act for both Madonna and Run DMC. The following year *Licensed to Ill*, their first album, sold 720,000 copies in six weeks and thereby became

Listening Guide "WALK THIS WAY"

Written by Joe Perry and Steven Tyler, performed by Run DMC with Perry and Tyler (from Aerosmith); recorded 1986

The creative and commercially successful synergy between rock music and hip-hop pioneered by Def Jam Records and Run DMC is well illustrated in "Walk This Way" (Number 4 pop, Number 8 R&B, 1986), the million-selling single that propelled *Raising Hell* nearly to the top of the album charts. "Walk This Way," a collaboration between Run DMC and the popular hard rock group Aerosmith, was a cover version of a song written and previously recorded by Aerosmith. (Aerosmith brought a large portion of the hard rock audience to the table, having sold over 60 million albums since the early 1970s.) The recording opens with a sample of rock drumming from the original recording, which is interrupted by the sound of a turntable scratching and the main riff of the song, played by Aerosmith's guitarist Joe Perry. Run and DMC trade lines of the song's verses in an aggressive, shouted style that matches the intensity of the rock rhythm section. The chorus ("Walk this way, talk this way . . .") is performed by Aerosmith's Steven Tyler, who sings the lyrics in a high, strained voice, a timbre associated with heavy metal music. As the track progresses, Run, DMC, and Tyler combine vocal forces in the interest of collective mayhem, and the recording ends with a virtuoso guitar solo by Joe Perry.

The video version of "Walk This Way"—the first rap video to be put into heavy rotation by MTV—gives visual substance to the musical image of a tense conversation between the worlds of hard rock and rap, unified by the sizzling textures of hip-hop scratching and hard rock guitar, the contrasting but similarly aggressive vocal timbres of Run DMC and Steven Tyler, and the over-the-top male braggadocio of the song's text. (The lyrics to "Walk This Way," with their references to horny cheerleaders and high school locker room voyeurism, suggest that one of the few things shared by the predominantly male audiences for rap and rock was a decidedly adolescent approach to sex.)

The video opens with Run DMC performing in a small sound studio. The amplified sound of turntable scratching penetrates a wall that separates this intimate but restricted musical world from that of a hard rock concert being held on the stage of a huge arena. Disturbed by the noise, the members of Aerosmith use their guitars to punch a hole in the wall, through which Run DMC run onto the stage of the concert and basically take over the show. Initially met with scowls from Tyler and Perry, the rappers succeed in winning them over, and the video ends in discordant harmony, with the huge, largely white crowd cheering. It is difficult to think of a more explicit (or more calculated) acting out of the process of Black-white crossover in the history of American popular music, and the video of "Walk This Way" doubtless played a pivotal role in the mainstreaming of rap music. (Run DMC was not the first rap group to incorporate textures and grooves from rock music. Early hip-hop DJs Kool Herc and Afrika Bambaataa regularly used breaks from groups like the Rolling Stones and Led Zeppelin.)

LISTENING GUIDE	"WALK THIS WAY"		
TIME	**FORM**	**LYRIC**	**DESCRIPTIVE COMMENTS**
0:00	Instrumental Introduction		Digital sample of drums from 1975 Aerosmith recording, with "scratching" turntable sounds
0:09			Main riff on electric guitar
0:17	Verse	*Now there's a back seat lover . . .*	Run and DMC perform the lyrics in rap style
0:35	Instrumental		Main guitar riff

TIME	FORM	LYRIC	DESCRIPTIVE COMMENTS
0:45	Verse	*See-saw swingin'* . . .	Rapping resumes, with a bit of rock-style harmonizing at the end of each line
1:04	Chorus	*Walk this way* . . .	Tyler performs the chorus, Run and DMC respond
1:22	Instrumental		Brief electric guitar solo
1:32	Instrumental		Main guitar riff
1:40	Verse	*School girl sleazy* . . .	Run and DMC rapping, ends with brief "stop time" where instruments drop out
1:58	Instrumental		Main guitar riff
2:07	Verse	*See-saw swingin'* . . .	Run DMC and Steven Tyler perform lyrics together, alternating parts of lines; symbolic fusion of rap and rock
2:25	Chorus	*Walk this way* . . .	Tyler performs the chorus, Run and DMC respond
2:44	Instrumental		Guitar solo; Tyler screams in background
2:52	Instrumental		Electric guitar riff with added guitar sounds in the background; on third repetition, guitar solo begins. Continues through several repetitions until the song fades out

Columbia Records' fastest-selling debut album up to that point. The most popular track on the album, the Top 10 frat-boy anthem "(You Gotta) Fight for Your Right (to Party)" (a hit in 1987), established the Beastie Boys' appeal for the most rapidly expanding segment of the rap audience, young white males. After leaving Def Jam Records in 1988, the Beastie Boys continued to experiment with combinations of rap, heavy metal, punk, and psychedelic rock, and they scored a series of critical and commercial successes in the 1990s, culminating with the release of their 1998 album *Hello Nasty*.

By 1987 a series of million-selling singles had proven rap's commercial potential on the pop and R&B charts; these hits included rap ballads (L. L. Cool J's "I Need Love," Number 1 R&B, Number 9 pop, 1987), women's rap (Salt-N-Pepa's "Push It," Number 19 pop, Number 28 R&B, 1987), humorous party records (Tone-Lōc's "Wild Thing," Number 2 pop, Number 3 R&B, 1987), and rap specifically targeted at a young adolescent audience ("Parents Just Don't Understand" by D.J. Jazzy Jeff and the Fresh Prince, the single that established the career of actor Will Smith, which reached Number 12 on the pop and

Number 10 on the R&B charts in 1988). A number of the small independent labels that had sprung up to feed the growing demand for hip-hop music—Jive Records, Cold Chillin' Records, Tommy Boy Records, and Priority Records—followed the lead of Def Jam, signing distribution deals with the multinational entertainment conglomerates.

If 1986 and 1987 saw the emergence of new markets for hip-hop music, 1988 brought possibly an even more important milestone: the launching of MTV's first show dedicated entirely to hip-hop music. Hosted by hip-hop raconteur Fab Five Freddy Braithwaite, *Yo! MTV Raps* immediately attracted the largest audience in the network's history and was soon being broadcast on a daily basis. The mass popularity of rap was also reflected in the appearance of *The Source*, the first magazine devoted solely to hip-hop music and fashion. Over the subsequent decade *The Source* became the largest-selling music periodical in America, surpassing by a wide margin even such long-established publications as *Rolling Stone*. In 1988 the National Academy of Recording Arts and Sciences added a rap category to the Grammy Awards, and *Billboard* added a rap singles chart. This mainstreaming of rap music had a number of interesting consequences. While some rappers and producers focused their energies on creating multiplatinum crossover hits, others reacted against the commercialism of "pop rap," re-animating the tradition of social realism that had informed recordings like "The Message" and creating a more hardcore sound that paradoxically ended up generating some of the biggest crossover hits of all.

The tradition of socially engaged rap that chronicled the declining fortunes of urban Black communities received its strongest new impetus from the New York–based group **Public Enemy**. Founded in 1982, Public Enemy was organized around a core set of members who met as college students, drawn together by their interest in hip-hop culture and political activism. The standard hip-hop configuration of two MCs—**Chuck D** (Carlton Ridenhour, b. 1960) and **Flavor Flav** (William Drayton, b. 1959)—plus a DJ—**Terminator X** (Norman Lee Rogers, b. 1966)—was augmented by a "Minister of Information," **Professor Griff** (Richard Griffin, b. 1960), and the Security of the First World (S1W), a cohort of dancers who dressed in paramilitary uniforms, carried Uzi submachine guns, and performed martial arts–inspired choreography.

The release of Public Enemy's second album in 1988—*It Takes a Nation of Millions to Hold Us Back*—was a breakthrough event for rap music. The album fused the trenchant social and political analyses of Chuck D—delivered in a deep, authoritative voice—with the streetwise interjections of his sidekick Flavor Flav, who wore comical glasses and an oversized clock around his neck. Their complex verbal interplay was situated within a dense, multilayered sonic web created by the group's production team, the Bomb Squad (Hank Shocklee, Keith Shocklee, and Eric "Vietnam" Sadler). Tracks like "Countdown to Armageddon" (an apocalyptic opening instrumental track taped at a live concert in London), "Don't Believe the Hype" (a critique of white-dominated mass media), and "Party for Your Right to Fight" (a parody of the Beastie Boys' hit "[You Gotta] Fight for Your Right [to Party]" from the previous year) turned the technology of digital sampling to new artistic purposes and effectively insisted that rap music continue to engage with the real-life conditions of urban Black communities.

Listening Guide "NIGHT OF THE LIVING BASEHEADS"

Written by Hank Shocklee, Eric Sadler, and Chuck D; performed by Public Enemy; recorded 1988

"Night of the Living Baseheads" illustrates the moral authority and musical complexity of many of Public Enemy's recordings. The lyrics for "Night of the Living Baseheads" combine images of corpselike zombies with a commentary on the crack cocaine epidemic that was sweeping through America's inner cities during the 1980s. The track opens with the voice of the Black nationalist leader Khalid Abdul Muhammad, sampled from one of his speeches:

> Have you forgotten that once we were brought here, we were robbed of our names, robbed of our language, we lost our religion, our culture, our God? And many of us, by the way we act, we even lost our minds.

With these words still ringing in our ears, we are suddenly dropped into the middle of a complexly textured groove. The lead MC of Public Enemy, Chuck D, opens with a verbal explosion, a play on words derived from hip-hop slang.

In hip-hop argot the term "dope" carries a double meaning: it can function as a positive adjective that is broadly equivalent to older terms such as "cool," "hip," or "funky"; or as a reference to psychoactive drugs ranging from marijuana to the new, more devastating drug being critiqued by Chuck D here, crack cocaine. The rhetorical tactic of announcing the arrival of a compelling performance (a "dope jam") and thereby laying claim to the listener's attention is common in rap recordings. Chuck D takes this opening gambit and plays with it, redefining the term "dope jam" as a message about drug use and its effects on the Black community. At the end of each stanza of his rap, Chuck D uses another pun, based on the homonyms "bass" (the deep, booming tones favored by rap producers) and "base" (a shorthand reference to "freebase," or crack cocaine).

Chuck D presents a chilling snapshot of the effects of crack on the human body ("Some shrivel to bone, like comatose walkin' around"), and uses the bass/base pun to draw a contrast between the aesthetics of hip-hop and the devastating scourge of crack cocaine ("please don't confuse this [base] with the sound [bass]"). After this first occurrence, the bass/base homonym returns periodically in a syncopated, digitally sampled loop that punctuates the thickly layered sonic texture created by the Bomb

Squad. Chuck D goes on to scold Black drug dealers for victimizing members of their own community ("Shame on a brother when he dealin' [drugs on] the same block where my [Oldsmobile] 98 be wheelin'"). A sampled verbal phrase ("How low can you go?") is used as a rhythmic and rhetorical device to set up the final sequence of Chuck D's rap, which concludes with the story of a crack addict, a former hip-hop MC fallen on bad times.

The grim message of "Night" is enveloped in a jagged and stark sonic landscape, layered with fractured words and vocal noises, bits and pieces of music and other sounds sewn together like a crazy quilt. The producers incorporated digital samples from no fewer than thirteen different recorded sources, among them an early twelve-inch rap single, several soul music records, a gospel music group, a glam rock record, and the sound of drums and air-raid sirens. In musical terms, "Night of the Living Baseheads" is like a complex archaeological dig, a site richly layered with sonic objects, the cumulative meaning of which depends on the cultural and musical expertise of the listener.

Although rap is often regarded primarily as a verbal genre, a recording like "Night of the Living Baseheads," with its carefully constructed pastiche of sampled sound sources, compels us to consider rap as music. Hank Shocklee has argued vociferously for a broader conception of music and musicianship:

> Music is nothing but organized noise. You can take anything—street sounds, us talking, whatever you want—and make it music by organizing it. That's still our philosophy, to show people that this thing you call music is a lot broader than you think it is. (Rose 1994, 82)

This philosophy is similar to that expressed by certain art music composers throughout the twentieth century who used tape recorders, digital technology, and elements of noise in their works. But it could be argued that the most extensive and creative use of the technology of digital sampling has been made in dance music—hip-hop, R&B, and EDM—rather than in contemporary art music composition. Rather than creating

(continued)

Listening Guide "NIGHT OF THE LIVING BASEHEADS" (continued)

a cold, disembodied form of self-expression—as many critics of the new technologies had feared—digital technology in pop music has often been used to create communal experiences on the dance floor. However, some critics bemoan what they see as a lack of creativity in much contemporary rap music, referring to the practice of sampling as "artistic necrophilia" and the end product as "Memorex music." Whatever one's position on these matters, Public Enemy's "Night of the Living Baseheads" stands as a pioneering example of the creative and social potential of digital sound technologies.

Flavor Flav and Chuck D of Public Enemy perform live on their 2007 tour.

Commercialization, Diversification, and the Rise of Gangsta Rap (1990s)

The expanding nationwide appeal of rap music during the late 1980s and early 1990s followed a familiar pattern. At the same time that some artists moved toward the pop mainstream, developing styles that blended the verbal cadences of rap and the techniques of digital sampling with R&B-derived dance rhythms and vocal styles, a variety of alternative rap styles emerged that reflected the attitudes, experiences, and dialects of particular segments of the hip-hop audience. Interestingly, these marginal variants of hip-hop—especially so-called **gangsta rap**—ended up generating millions and millions of dollars in profits for the record industry.

The year 1990 was a watershed year for the mainstreaming of hip-hop. *MC Hammer* (Stanley Kirk Burrell, b. 1962), a rapper from Oakland, California, hit the charts in March of that year with *Please Hammer Don't Hurt 'Em,* which held the Number 1 position for twenty-one weeks and sold over 10 million copies. Hammer's celebrity was boosted by music videos that highlighted his impressive abilities as a dancer, his appearances in corporate soft drink advertisements, and even by a short-lived children's cartoon show called *Hammerman.* At the height of his popularity, Hammer was attacked by many in the hip-hop community for his lack of skill as a rapper and for pandering to a mass audience. There can be no denying that Hammer's success pushed rap fully into the mainstream, continuing a trend started in the mid-1980s by Run DMC and the Beastie Boys. At the same time, Hammer's pop-friendly rap style opened the door for an artist widely considered hip-hop's icon of "wackness" (weakness), the white rapper *Vanilla Ice* (Robert Van Winkle, b. 1968 in Florida). Ice's first album, *To the Extreme* (1990), monopolized the Number 1 position on the Billboard 200 pop album chart for sixteen weeks in early 1991, selling 7 million copies in the United States. In hip-hop culture, a performer's credibility is correlated by fans not only with musical and verbal skill but also with the degree to which the artist in question possesses "street knowledge," that is, firsthand experience of the urban culture that spawned rap music. When it was discovered that Van Winkle, raised in reasonably comfortable circumstances in a middle-class neighborhood, had essentially invented a gangster persona for himself—a form of misrepresentation known in hip-hop parlance as "perpetrating"—many fans turned their backs on him. It is undeniable that race was also a factor in the rejection of Vanilla Ice, for he was widely regarded as being merely the latest in a long line of untalented white artists seeking to make a living off the fruits of Black creativity. Yet some white rappers and producers—for example, the Beastie Boys—have managed to gain acceptance as legitimate hip-hop artists, largely by virtue of their ability to forge a distinctive style within the parameters of an African American tradition.

WEST COAST RAP

By the late 1980s a number of distinctive regional variations on the formula of hip-hop music were well established in cities such as Philadelphia, Cleveland, Miami, Atlanta, Houston, Seattle, Oakland, and Los Angeles. The music critic Nelson George noted this process of regionalization as follows:

> The rap that'll flow from down South, the Midwest, and the West Coast will not, and should not, feel beholden to what came before. Just as hip-hop spit in the face of disco (and funk too), non–New York hip-hop will have its own accent, its own version of b-boy wisdom, if it's to mean anything. (George 1998, 132)

During this period Southern California became a primary center of hip-hop innovation, supported by a handful of independent labels and one of the few commercial AM stations nationwide to feature hip-hop programming (KDAY).

The sound of "new school" West Coast rap differed from "old school" New York hip-hop in a number of regards. The edgy, rapid-fire delivery of Melle Mel and Run DMC remained influential but was augmented by a smoother, more laid-back style of rapping. The dialects of Southern California rappers, many of them the children of migrants from Louisiana and Texas, also contributed to the distinctive flavor of West Coast rap. And if the verbal delivery of West Coast rap was sometimes cooler, the content of the MCs' recitations themselves became angrier, darker, and more menacing, the social commitment of Public Enemy supplanted by the outlaw swagger of artists such as *Ice-T* (Tracy Marrow, b. 1958), who in 1987 recorded the theme song for *Colors*, Dennis Hopper's violent film about gang–police warfare in South Central Los Angeles. Both the film and Ice-T's raps reflected ongoing changes in Southern California's urban communities, including a decline in industrial production, rising rates of joblessness, the continuing effects of crack cocaine, and a concomitant growth of drug-related gang violence.

The emergence of West Coast gangsta rap was heralded nationwide by the release of the album *Straight Outta Compton* by *N.W.A* (Niggaz With Attitude). While rap artists had previously dealt with aspects of urban street life in brutally straightforward terms, N.W.A upped the ante with recordings that expressed the gangsta lifestyle and were saturated with images of sex and violence straight out of the prison toast tradition. The nucleus of the group was formed in 1986 when *O'Shea "Ice Cube" Jackson* (b. 1969), the product of a middle-class home in South Central Los Angeles, met *Andre "Dr. Dre" Young* (b. 1965), a sometime member of a local funk group called the World Class Wreckin' Cru. Jackson and Young shared an interest in writing rap songs, an ambition that was realized when they teamed up with *Eric "Eazy-E" Wright* (1973–1995), a former drug dealer who was using the proceeds of that occupation to fund a record label, Ruthless Records. Soon the three began working together as N.W.A, eventually adding DJ Yella (Antoine Carraby) and MC Ren (Lorenzo Patterson) to the group.

When the group started work on their second album, *Straight Outta Compton*, the idea of establishing a distinctive West Coast identity within hip-hop was clearly in their minds. As MC Ren put it in a 1994 interview in the *Source*:

> When we did N.W.A . . . New York had all'a the bomb groups. New York was on the map and all we was thinking, man—I ain't gonna lie, no matter what nobody in the group say—I think we was all thinking about making a name for Compton and LA. (George 1998, 135)

Released in 1989, the album was more than a local success, selling 750,000 copies nationwide even before N.W.A started a promotional tour. The album's attitude, sound, and sensibility were clearly indebted to earlier hip-hop recordings— particularly Public Enemy's *It Takes a Nation of Millions to Hold Us Back*, released the year before—but were in some ways unlike anything heard before, featuring tracks with titles like "F— tha Police" and "Gangsta Gangsta," which were underlain by a soundtrack that mixed the sound of automatic weapon fire and police sirens with samples from funk masters such as George Clinton and James Brown; a bouncy drum machine–generated dance groove called new jack swing; and high-pitched, thin-sounding synthesizer lines. The raps themselves were harrowing, egocentric accounts of gang life, hearkening back to the bleakest aspects of the prison toast tradition. The cover of the CD—in which the posse stares implacably down at and holds a gun to the head of the prospective purchaser—reinforced the aura of danger, one of the main appeals of the group for the young suburban audience that pushed the album to multiplatinum sales. N.W.A was the subject of a well-received "biopic" in 2015, named after their breakthrough album.

The acrimonious breakup of N.W.A beginning in 1989 had the effect of disseminating the group's influence over a wider territory. During the 1990s Ice Cube went on to make a series of platinum albums totaling almost 6 million in sales, including the brilliant *AmeriKKKa's Most Wanted* (Number 19 on the album charts in 1990), a more explicitly political album recorded in New York with Public Enemy and the Bomb Squad; and *The Predator*, which reached Number 1 in 1992. Eazy-E sold over 5 million albums in the 1990s, all released on his Ruthless Records label, and MC Ren sold one million copies of his *Kizz My Black Azz* (Number 12 in 1992). But the most influential and economically successful member of N.W.A turned out to be Andre Young (Dr. Dre), who founded an independent record label called Death Row Records, cultivated a number of younger rappers, and continued to develop a distinctive hip-hop production style that was christened "G-Funk" in homage to the P-funk style developed in the 1970s by George Clinton and was often sampled on Dre's productions. Dr. Dre's 1992 album *The Chronic*—named after a particularly potent strain of marijuana—which was released on Death Row and distributed by major label Interscope, sold over 3 million copies and introduced his protégé, **Snoop Doggy Dogg** (Calvin Broadus, b. 1972 in Long Beach).

While the conflation of gangsta rhetoric and reality at least temporarily boosted the sales of rap recordings, it also had terrible real-life consequences, as the matrix of conflict between posses—one source of the creative energy that gave birth to hip-hop in the 1970s—turned viciously in on itself during the mid-1990s. Such conflicts—evoked constantly in gangsta rap—can develop at many levels: between members of the same posse ("set trippin'"), between posses representing different neighborhoods, between gangs of different ethnicities (e.g., between Chicano and Black gangs in Los Angeles), between larger organizations (e.g., national gangs like the Crips, Hoods, and Black Gangster Disciples), and between entire cities or regions of the country.

EAST VERSUS WEST COAST RAP

The mid-1990s saw the violent eruption of conflicts between East and West Coast factions within the hip-hop business. Standing in one corner was Marion "Suge" Knight, CEO of Los Angeles–based Death Row Records, and Death Row's up-and-coming star *Tupac (2Pac) Shakur* (1971–1996). In the other corner stood the producer and rapper *Sean "Puffy" Combs* (also called Puff Daddy or P. Diddy, 1969–), CEO of the New York–based independent label Bad Boy Records, and the up-and-coming star the *Notorious B.I.G.* (Christopher

Listening Guide "WHAT'S MY NAME?"

Written by George Clinton, Gary Shider, Snoop Dogg, and David Spradley; produced by Dr. Dre; performed by Snoop Doggy Dogg; recorded 1993

Snoop's soft drawl and laid-back-but-lethal gangster persona were featured on his album *Doggystyle* (1993), which made its debut at the top of the album charts. The million-selling single "What's My Name?"—a so-called "clean" remix of the opening track on the *Doggystyle* album—gives us a sense of Snoop Doggy Dogg's prowess as a rapper and of Dr. Dre's distinctive G-funk production style. (Like many rap recordings intended to cross over to the pop charts, "What's My Name?" was released on the album in its original, unexpurgated version and as a "clean" version on a single designed for radio airplay and mass distribution. We will analyze the remix here, which reached Number 8 on the *Billboard* Hot 100 singles chart in 1993.)

Although the track opens with a dense, scratchy sample reminiscent of a Public Enemy/Bomb Squad recording—actually a brief sequence from an old Parliament track, looped to create a syncopated pattern—the texture soon shifts to a smoother, more dance-oriented sound. A relaxed, medium-tempo dance groove is established by a drum machine and keyboard synthesizers (including a weighty and sinuous keyboard bass part), over which a digitally processed, nasal-sounding human voice floats, singing a melismatic phrase:

Eee-yi-yi-yi-yi-yah, the Dogg Pound's in the hou-ouse

A treble choir enters, repeating the phrase "Snoop Doggy Dogg" in soul music style, and is answered by the sampled voice of George Clinton intoning "Da Bomb" (a phrase commonly used to describe compelling grooves and other pleasurable experiences). After this brief mood-setting introduction, Snoop's drawling, laconic voice enters:

From the depths of the sea, back to the block [the neighborhood]
Snoop Doggy Dogg, funky as the, the, the Doc [Dr. Dre]
Went solo on that ass, but it's still the same
Long Beach is the spot where I served my cane [sold my cocaine]

These two stanzas immediately establish Snoop's local identity, his indebtedness to his mentor Dr. Dre, and his street credibility. He then explodes into a rapid-fire, percussively articulated sequence of tongue-twisting wordplay:

Follow me, follow me, follow me, follow me, but you betta not slip
'Cause Nine-trizzay's the yizzear [1993's the year] *for me to fizzup my grip* [increase my wealth]
So I ain't holdin nuttin' back
And once again I got five on the twenty sack [put five dollars down on a twenty-dollar bag of marijuana, i.e., I'm back in the game]

Snoop declares his arrival in no uncertain terms, asserting that 1993 is the year for him to make a major impact on the scene, musically and otherwise. He then shifts to a more threatening posture—aided by Dr. Dre's interjection of an automatic weapon–like sound effect:

SNOOP: *It's like that and as a matter of fact*
DR. DRE: *rat-tat-tat-tat*

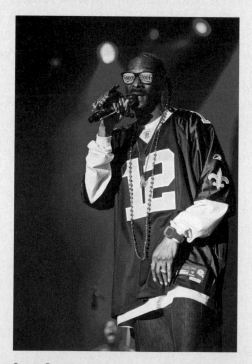

Snoop Dogg.

SNOOP: *'Cause I never hesitate to put a fool on his back* [imitating Muhammad Ali]

DR. DRE: *Yeah, so peep out the manuscript* [pay close attention to the words]

You see that it's a must we drop gangsta sh—[talk gangster talk]

SNOOP: *Hold on, wha's my name?*

The treble choir re-enters, introducing a bit of hip-hop history: a melodic line from Parliament's "Give Up the Funk (Tear the Roof off the Sucker)" (see the discussion of this recording in Chapter 12). Then Snoop continues to add verbal layers to his gangsta persona, boasting about his potential for lethal violence, referring to himself as "Mr. One Eight Seven"—a reference to the California penal code for homicide—and departing the scene of a bloody massacre by disappearing mysteriously into the night ("I step through the fog and I creep through the smog").

The following interlude between verses introduces a digitally processed voice chanting "Bow-wow-wow, yippieyo-yippie-yay," a sly reference to cowboy films and the 1988 action movie *Die Hard*, whose star Bruce Willis popularized the catchphrase, "Yippee kai yay, motherf***er." References to cowboys and country music are not unknown in rap music; for example, Seattle-based rapper Sir Mix-A-Lot's "Buttermilk Biscuits," recorded in 1988, is a parody of square dance music. In the third and final section, Snoop moves on to another favorite subject, his sexual potency. He begins with a catchphrase that goes back to the South Bronx origins of hip-hop and MCs like Kool Herc and Grandmaster Flash:

Now just throw your hands way up in the air
And wave them all around like ya just don't care

Read as words on a page, divorced of their musical context, "What's My Name?" is simply an updated version of "Stagolee," the traditional African American ballad about a powerful Black desperado of prison toast fame (see Chapter 12). But the commercial success of "What's My Name?" had as much to do with the musical groove and texture of the recording as with the content and flow (rhyme and rhythm) of Snoop Doggy Dogg's verbal performance. "What's My Name?" is in fact a club dance record, more than half of which is taken up by instrumental music or singing. (It could be argued that most of the people who bought this record could not have interpreted portions of the text in any case, given the heavy use of local references and gang jargon.) Judged from the viewpoints of sound texture, tone color, or historical references, this recording is obviously less musically complex than Public Enemy's "Night of the Living Baseheads." Dr. Dre's G-funk sound, while indebted to the innovations of Public Enemy's production team, the Bomb Squad, has an entirely different aesthetic and commercial goal. Dre's approach to the use of digital sampling is much less ambitious than Public Enemy's: he uses here only three pre-recorded sources—George Clinton recordings from the 1970s and early 1980s—and generally seems to aim for a clean, crisp studio sound. (The less ambitious use of digital samples may have to do with the court cases discussed in Box 14.1, which by the mid-1990s made it much more difficult for hip-hop producers to experiment with pre-recorded sources.) Despite its controversial verbal content, "What's My Name?" is a quintessential pop record, bristling with hooks, catchy melodies, riffs, and verbal mottoes, organized around a medium-tempo groove and carefully calibrated for dance club consumption.

Wallace, also called Biggie Smalls, 1972–1997). By the time the stranger-than-fiction scenario played itself out at the end of the 1990s, Tupac Shakur and Christopher Wallace had been shot to death; Suge Knight, already on parole for a 1992 assault conviction, was reincarcerated after an attack on two rappers in a Las Vegas casino and had come under federal investigation for racketeering; Interscope, a subdivision of Time Warner Entertainment, had severed its formerly lucrative promotion and distribution deal with Death Row Records; Tupac Shakur's mother had sued Death Row for the rights to her dead son's tapes; and Dr. Dre and Snoop Doggy Dogg, Death Row's biggest stars, had severed ties with the label. In January 1998 Snoop told the *Long Beach Press-Telegram* that he was leaving Death Row Records because he feared for his life:

> I definitely feel my life is in danger if I stay in Death Row Records. That's part of the reason why I'm leaving. . . . There's nothing over there. Suge Knight is in jail, the president; Dr. Dre left and 2Pac is dead. It's telling me that I'm either going to be dead or in jail or I'm going to be nothing.

Chillingly, both 2Pac and the Notorious B.I.G. had recorded prophetic raps that ended with the narrator speaking from the grave rather than standing in bloody triumph over his victims. (True to the logic of the popular music business, these voices were commercially promoted in highly profitable posthumous albums with titles like *Life After Death*, *Born Again*, *Still I Rise*, and *Here After*.)

Since the late 1980s the highly stylized narratives of gangsta rap have provided a chronicle of the dilemmas faced by urban communities—poverty, drug addiction, and violence—from a first-person, present-tense viewpoint. The recordings of artists like Ice-T, N.W.A, Snoop Doggy Dogg, 2Pac Shakur, and the Notorious B.I.G. combine a grim, survivalist outlook on life with a gleeful celebration of the gangster lifestyle. This celebratory nihilism, propelled by funk-derived, digitally sampled grooves and surrounded in the video versions of rap recordings with a continual flow of images of hip-hop fashion, champagne, expensive cars, and scantily clad women (characterized as "bitches" and "hos"), provokes an understandable ambivalence toward gangsta rap on the part of observers genuinely sympathetic to the plight of people struggling for economic and cultural survival in America's cities. How, such critics ask, could a genre of music that presents itself as being committed to "keeping it real" so deeply indulge itself in the escapism of consumer capitalism and the exploitation of women as sex objects?

Part of the answer may lie in the fact that rap music is a part not only of African American culture but also of American culture as a whole. Rap reflects the positive qualities of American culture—its creative energy, regional diversity, and technological acumen—just as it expresses American society's dark side: the obsession with guns and violence, the preoccupation with material wealth and status symbols, and long-standing traditions of racism, homophobia, and sexism. (And, as a number of observers have pointed out, folk tales of Black outlaws like Stagolee have always existed in dialog with popular images of white gangsters like Capone and Dillinger and violent Hollywood films like *Little Caesar*, *Scarface*, and *Natural Born Killers*.)

On the one hand, rap has provided an unvarnished view of the dystopia that characterizes many urban communities—what the prominent African American cultural critic Cornel West has called "the lived experience of coping with a life of horrifying meaninglessness, hopelessness, and lovelessness . . . a numbing detachment from others and a self-destructive disposition toward the world" (West 1993, 14). On the other hand, it is also clear that gangsta recordings, promoted by huge entertainment corporations to a predominantly white mass audience, may have served inadvertently to reinforce old and pernicious stereotypes of Black masculinity that date back to the knife-toting dandy of the nineteenth-century minstrel show. Perhaps this is what Chuck D was referring to when in 1998 he told an interviewer, "Ten years ago, I called rap music Black America's CNN. My biggest concern now is keeping it from becoming the Cartoon Network."

BOX 14.1 HIP-HOP, SAMPLING, AND THE LAW

As we have seen, the tradition of incorporating beats from secondary sources is as old as hip-hop itself. However, the increasing sophistication and affordability of digital sampling technology had, by the late 1980s, made it possible for rap producers to go much further, weaving entire sound textures out of pre-recorded materials. This development triggered some interesting court cases, as some of the artists being sampled sought to protect their rights.

In 1989 the Miami-based rap group 2 Live Crew released a song called "Pretty Woman," which borrowed from the rock 'n' roll hit "Oh, Pretty Woman" (Number 1 pop, 1964) written by Roy Orbison and William Dees. Although 2 Live Crew had tried to get permission from the music publisher of the song, Acuff-Rose Music, to make a rap version of it, permission had been denied. A lawsuit ensued over rapper Luther R. Campbell's (a.k.a. Luke Skyywalker's) raunchy send-up of the tune, and Campbell took the position that his use of the song was a parody that was legally protected as a fair use. The Supreme Court recognized the satirical intent of Campbell's version and held that 2 Live Crew's copying of portions of the original lyric was not excessive in relation to the song's satirical purpose.

Although the 2 Live Crew decision upheld the rights of rap musicians and producers to parody pre-existing recorded material, control over actual digital sampling tightened during the 1990s as a result of a few well-publicized court cases. In 1991 the 1960s folk rock group the Turtles sued the hip-hop group De La Soul for using a snippet of the Turtles' song "You Showed Me" on a track called "Transmitting Live from Mars." The Turtles won a costly out-of-court settlement. That same year, up-and-coming hip-hop artist Biz Markie recorded a track that sampled the sentimental pop song "Alone Again (Naturally)," a Number 1 pop hit for the Irish songwriter Gilbert O'Sullivan in 1972. O'Sullivan was not pleased and pursued the case, eventually forcing Warner Brothers to remove Biz Markie's album from the market until the offending track was removed from the album. These decisions sent a chill through the rap music industry and encouraged producers to be less ambitious in their use of sampled materials. As the hip-hop historian Nelson George phrases it, "The high-intensity sound tapestries of Public Enemy have given way to often simple-minded loops of beats and vocal hooks from familiar songs—a formula that has grossed [MC] Hammer, Coolio, and Puff Daddy millions in sales and made old R&B song catalogs potential gold mines" (George 1998, 95).

Today it is common for hip-hop producers to license the material that they sample, which can add greatly to the cost of production. In a 2004 interview, Hank Shocklee of 2 Live Crew commented on the effect this had on hip-hop recordings:

It wouldn't be impossible [to record *It Takes a Nation of Millions* today]. It would just be very, very costly. The first thing that was starting to happen by the late 1980s was that the people were doing buyouts. You could have a buyout—meaning you could purchase the rights to sample a sound—for around $1,500. Then it started creeping up to $3,000, $3,500, $5,000, $7,500. Then they threw in this thing called rollover rates. If your rollover rate is every 100,000 units, then for every 100,000 units you sell, you have to pay an additional $7,500. A record that sells two million copies would kick that cost up twenty times. Now you're looking at one song costing you more than half of what you would make on your album.

QUEEN LATIFAH

Queen Latifah (b. 1970) was not the first nationally popular female hip-hop artist—that honor belongs to the all-female rap crew Salt-N-Pepa, who scored a string of hits in the late 1980s and reached the peak of their commercial success with the release of the album *Very Necessary* (Number 4 pop, 1994). There can be no doubt, however, that Queen Latifah is the most important woman in the early history of hip-hop, in terms of both her commercial success and her effectiveness in establishing a feminist beachhead on the male-dominated field of rap music. Latifah provided an alternative to the misogynist

Queen Latifah.

braggadocio of gangsta rappers like Snoop Doggy Dogg, while her strong R&B-influenced voice and assertive persona evoked earlier rhythm & blues and soul artists such as Big Mama Thornton and Tina Turner.

Born in inner-city Newark, New Jersey, Dana Elaine Owens received the nickname Latifah—an Arabic word signifying "gentle" or "pleasant"—from a cousin at the age of eight. She began rapping in high school, and in college participated in Afrika Bambaataa's Native Tongues collective, a group dedicated to raising the political consciousness of hip-hop. Her debut album on Tommy Boy Records, *All Hail the Queen* (1989), reached Number 6 on the R&B album chart and spawned the hit single "Ladies First" (Number 5 rap, 1990), a direct challenge to the putative supremacy of male rappers.

All Hail the Queen, with its R&B, reggae, and house music influences, gave an early indication of Latifah's talent and musical range. However, her second album (*Nature of a Sista*, 1991) failed to crack the R&B Top 20, and Tommy Boy Records decided not to re-sign her contract. After a hiatus—motivated in part by the death of her brother in a motorcycle accident—she signed with Motown Records and in 1993 released *Black Reign*, which earned a gold record. Dedicated to her brother and featuring her biggest hit single, "U.N.I.T.Y.," it reached Number 7 on the R&B charts, crossed over to the pop Top 40, and won a Grammy for Best Solo Rap Performance.

Queen Latifah established a precedent for sustainable hip-hop careers—an antithesis to the live-fast, die-young ethos of gangsta rap. Following her early success as a recording artist, she appeared on television and in films, including the acclaimed movie musical *Chicago* (2002), which garnered her Best Supporting Actress nominations from both the Screen Actors Guild and the Hollywood Foreign Press Association. In 2004 she demonstrated her musical versatility once again, releasing an album of Tin Pan Alley and soul standards backed with big band and strings. *The Dana Owens Album* broke the Top 20 on both the pop and R&B album charts and presaged a whole new set of commercial and artistic opportunities for the queen of hip-hop, including a role in the film version of *Hairspray* (2007); her appearance that same year as an HIV-positive woman in the film *Life Support*, for which she won Golden Globe and Screen Actors Guild awards; the starring role in the biopic *Bessie* (2015), in which she portrayed the "empress of the blues," Bessie Smith; and as Executive Producer of the hit MTV slasher series *Scream* (2019–).

Listening Guide "U.N.I.T.Y."

Written by Queen Latifah and Kier "Kay Gee" Gist; released 1994

"U.N.I.T.Y." opens with a sample of jazz tenor saxophone with guitar, string bass, and drum set accompaniment and then moves into a slow, sultry, reggae-influenced groove that is anchored by a window-rattling bass riff and digitized snare drum backbeat. The reggae association is continued in the opening chorus, which Latifah performs in a languorous Jamaican patois, interrupted by more aggressive responses in an American dialect. The hypnotic flow of the music—with the "old school" jazz saxophone reappearing periodically—supports the chorus's idealistic message, that Black men and women should treat one another with love and respect:

> Uh, U.N.I.T.Y., U.N.I.T.Y. that's a unity
> U.N.I.T.Y., love a Black man from infinity to infinity

Then Queen Latifah launches into her rap, abandoning the Jamaican dialect entirely and squaring off and dropping rhythmic accents into her speech like a boxer jabbing at her opponent:

> Instinct leads me to another flow
> Every time I hear a brother call a girl a bitch or a ho'
> (music halts briefly)

In her next verse, Latifah tightens the narrative focus, describing an abusive relationship with a man:

> I guess I fell so deep in love I grew dependency

The overall musical structure of the track is straightforward, alternating the "U.N.I.T.Y." chorus with a series of rapped verses. On this track, as in so many hip-hop recordings, the focus is on the verbal performance, and the music functions to set the mood, create a temporal flow, and (through digital sampling) evoke a range of associations. Queen Latifah's performance counterpoises her smoldering indignation over the abuse of women by men with a more empathetic and optimistic approach. (This dialectic is emphasized in the music, which plays off the assertive, even pugilistic, quality of Latifah's rapping against the laid-back, sensuous feeling of the bass-heavy groove and the hauntingly mellow jazz saxophone bathed in reverb.) If "U.N.I.T.Y." is a threat, delivered in the most straightforward terms, it is also a plea for civility and the healing power of love.

EMINEM

Another artist who embodied the increasingly blurred line between rock and hip-hop at this time was *Marshall "Eminem" Mathers* (b. 1972 in Missouri). Raised by a single mother, Mathers spent much of his youth in a lower-middle class, predominantly African American neighborhood in Detroit. Initially inspired by an Ice-T track from the 1984 movie *Breakin'*, he honed his rapping skills at open-mic contexts at clubs on West Seven Mile Road, the epicenter of Detroit's local hip-hop scene.

Coming to prominence in 1999 with *The Slim Shady LP*, an expanded major-label re-release of an earlier independent album, Eminem was the first white rapper to enjoy substantial mainstream success while also being accepted by the hip-hop community. While initially this was largely due to the credibility he gained by being produced by Dr. Dre (of N.W.A), it quickly became clear that Eminem was a skilled and dedicated hip-hop artist in his own right. Particularly impressive were Eminem's extraordinary rhythmic sensibility and ability to use the *sound* of his words as musical elements.

He was also adept at the use of compound rhymes, a skill he attributed to the influence of underground New York emcees such as Lord Finesse and Big L. In his lyrics, Eminem explored his own identity and experiences in a way that connected with multiple demographics simultaneously. Rather than renouncing his whiteness, he embraced it as a symbol of working-class Midwestern anxiety. The reality of that equation for a huge segment of American society is something that had rarely, if ever, been addressed in hip-hop music.

Eminem's position as a superstar was cemented by his hugely successful third album: *The Marshall Mathers LP* (2000), which won the Grammy Award for Best Rap Album and was, until the release of Adele's *25* (2015), the fastest-selling album by a solo artist in the history of American popular music. This was followed by the multiplatinum albums *The Eminem Show* (2002)—which again took the Best Rap Album Grammy—and *Encore* (2004), which extended Eminem's reputation for controversy with tracks mocking Michael Jackson and President George W. Bush. Eminem's success has extended into the second decade of the twentieth century, with his Number 1 albums *Recovery* (2010), which included four simultaneous Top 20 singles, making him the first artist to accomplish that feat since the Beatles, and *The Marshall Mathers LP 2* (2013), which earned his seventh Best Rap Album Grammy, and featured an appearance by the emerging artist Kendrick Lamar. In 2015, he released a ten-disc box set of vinyl records that looked back over his recording career, and included the soundtrack of *8 Mile*, the 2002 film that marked Eminem's emergence as an actor, and is today widely regarded as a hip-hop classic.

Widely accepted within the hip-hop community, excoriated by critics across the political spectrum for lyrics that have at times evoked violent, sexist, and homophobic images and sentiments, and massively successful in the commercial arena, Eminem is a unique figure in the history of rap music. He is not the only white performer to achieve commercial success in the genre, as the best-selling recordings of artists as varied in style and reputation as Vanilla Ice, the Beastie Boys, and, more recently, Macklemore and Ryan Lewis attest. Eminem's ability to be both a rap and rock star simultaneously was aided tremendously by the fact that he was one of the first—arguably *the* first—rapper to be consistently played on rock radio, a fact that would be hard to attribute to anything other than his race. At the same time, Eminem's music did embrace intensely personal themes that were unusual for hip-hop. The idea that pop music should serve in a sense as therapy for the artist, as a way to exorcise his most intimate demons, was something that was much more closely associated with rock music—and the "rock star" approach—than it was with hip-hop. In a larger sense, the question of the degree to which Eminem drew on hip-hop approaches as compared to rock is beside the point. What's important is that it seemed not to matter either to him or to his fans. His ability to ignore those genre boundaries yet still be successful is, of course, a reflection of his personal talent and skill in positioning himself culturally, but it is also reflective of the decreasing significance of these boundaries in the first place.

EDM: Dance Music in the Digital Age

During the 1980s, following on the heels of disco and paralleling the emergence of hip-hop, new forms of up-tempo, repetitive dance music developed in the club scenes of cities such as New York, Chicago, and Detroit, cross-fertilized by developments in London, Düsseldorf, and other European cities. These styles, which can generally be traced to early 1980s genres such as garage and house music and are loosely lumped together under the broad term **electronic dance music (EDM)**, are in fact quite varied. This genre encompasses literally dozens of subcategories, including techno, jungle, drum 'n' bass, funky breaks, tribal, 'ardcore, gabba, happy hardcore, trance, trip-hop, acid jazz, electro-techno, intelligent techno, ambient, and ever-more subtly defined sub-subcategories (ambient house, dark ambient, ambient breakbeat, ambient dub, and so on), each patronized by a loyal group of fans. As Simon Reynolds puts it in his book *Generation Ecstasy*:

> For the newcomer to electronic dance music, the profusion of scenes and sub-genres can seem at best bewildering, at worst willful obfuscation. Partly, this is a trick of perspective: kids who've grown up with techno feel it's *rock* that "all sounds the same." The urgent distinctions rock fans take for granted—that Pantera, Pearl Jam, and Pavement operate in separate aesthetic universes—makes sense only if you're already a participant in the ongoing rock discourse. The same applies to dance music: step inside and the genre-itis begins to make sense. (Reynolds 1998, 7)

In essence, EDM is the musical dimension of a whole youth culture, within which arguments about the difference between good music and bad music are informed by a set of shared assumptions and shared knowledge of the genre's history. EDM culture is focused on DJ/producers, who, unlike disco and hip-hop DJs, often attempt to remain anonymous, operating their equipment in the dark behind a web of wiring. (Most EDM "groups"—such as the Orb, Orbital, Prodigy, Moby, and Daft Punk—are in fact solo acts, or teams of two or three DJs.)

The main venues for EDM are dance clubs and semipublic events called **raves** that are partly modeled on the be-ins of the 1960s counterculture. A controversial aspect of raves—which started in England in the late 1980s and spread, in a more limited fashion, to the United States soon thereafter—is the prevalent use by participants of a psychoactive drug called "ecstasy" (MDMA), which creates visceral sensations of warmth and euphoria. Matthew Collin, a British journalist who has written extensively about the drug-rave-music connection that emerged in his country in the 1980s, has described the drug's sensation:

> The world had opened up all around, the blank warehouse somehow changed into a wonderland designed just for us, glistening with a magic iridescence that I couldn't see earlier. New world. New sound. New life. Everything felt so right. A huge, glowing, magical *yes*. (Collin 1997, 3)

Unfortunately, this *yes* eventually mutated into a resounding *no*, for one of the documented long-term effects of MDMA is an alteration of brain chemistry that makes it harder and harder to get high, leading to severe depression. To compound this ambiguity, ecstasy was banned by the FDA in the United States, which drove the drug underground, exacerbated the problem of more dangerous drugs being circulated in the guise of ecstasy, and led to a number of fatal overdoses. In any case, by the mid-1990s increasing numbers of DJs and fans had rejected the use of ecstasy. As one insider put it, "The *music* drugs the listeners."

The roots of **techno** are often traced to the Detroit area, home of Motown, the Stooges, and George Clinton. During the early 1980s a group of young, middle-class African American men living in the predominantly white suburban town of Belleville developed a style of EDM that techno pioneer Derrick May likened to the sound that would be produced if George Clinton and Kraftwerk were stuck in an elevator with just a sequencer. Detroit techno was grounded in a different cultural scene than that which had spawned the Motown sound; young men like May and Juan Atkins were obsessed with symbols of class mobility, Italian fashions, and European disco recordings, and they developed a style that featured futuristic imagery; samples from European records; and a dry, minimalist sound that was underlain by a subliminal funk pulse.

At around the same time a genre called **house music** (named after the Warehouse, a popular gay dance club) was developing in Chicago. The Chicago house scene was pioneered by Frankie Knuckles, a DJ from New York who worked at the Warehouse from 1979 until 1983. Knuckles introduced New York turntable techniques to Chicago, manipulating disco records to emphasize the dance beat—the drums and bass—even more strongly. Many house recordings were purely instrumental, with elements of European synth-pop, Latin soul, reggae, rap, and jazz grafted over an insistent dance beat. By the mid-1980s house music scenes had emerged in New York and London, and in the late 1980s the genre made its first appearances on the pop charts under the names of artists like M|A|R|R|S and Madonna.

In the 1990s EDM began to diversify into the dozens of specialized subcategories mentioned earlier. These branches were often distinguished by their relative "hardness," a quality connected with the tempo or beats per minute of recordings. Some forms of EDM were influenced by punk rock, others by experimental art music, and still others by Black popular music such as funk and hip-hop. The sensual and emotional tone of the music also varied widely, from the stark, futuristic sound of Belgian gabba and the energetic funkiness of jungle to the world music influences of tribal and the otherworldly sonic atmospheres of ambient. Although EDM started as an underground genre for live dancing, EDM recordings were increasingly licensed as the soundtracks for technologically oriented television commercials and films. By the late 1990s, EDM artists such as Orbital, Moby, and the UK-based duo the Prodigy, whose 1996 track "Firestarter" reached Number 30 on the U.S. *Billboard* charts, were scoring big international hits. EDM producers rose to celebrity status a decade later, with Skrillex, David Guetta, and Calvin Harris charting huge hits by collaborating with A-list pop singers.

Alternate Currents

In the 1990s the marketplace for popular music continued to metastasize into hundreds of named genres, each correlated with a particular segment of the audience. From jangle pop to trip hop, psychobilly to thrashcore, the decade saw a splintering of genres that exceeded anything previously experienced in the history of American popular music. While many of these styles sprang from the ground up, as it were, nurtured by local audiences, regional networks of clubs, and low-profit independent labels, the entertainment industry had by this time refined its ability to identify such "alternative" genres and their specialized audiences.

By the end of the 1990s, almost every major genre had sprouted an alternative subcategory. According to the *All Music Guide* (www.allmusic.com), a widely consulted internet guide to popular music, the range of alternative genres included alternative dance (including techno, which often forms its own category, and groups such as Pop Will Eat Itself and Everything but the Girl), adult alternative pop/rock (e.g., Alanis Morissette, Dave Matthews Band), alternative country (e.g., k.d. lang, Dwight Yoakam, Lyle Lovett), alternative country rock (e.g., Uncle Tupelo, the Jayhawks), alternative contemporary Christian music (e.g., Sixpence None the Richer, Jars of Clay), alternative metal (e.g., Rage Against the Machine, Korn, Limp Bizkit), alternative rap (e.g., De La Soul, Arrested Development, Lauryn Hill), and a variety of styles broadly lumped under the heading of alternative pop/rock (e.g., R.E.M., Sonic Youth, Living Colour, Soundgarden, Nirvana, Nine Inch Nails, Red Hot Chili Peppers, Phish, and many other groups). Some artists classified under the "alternative pop/rock" rubric sound similar to each other, whereas others seem to have come from different musical planets entirely. Some record for small independent labels, while others sign contracts with major record companies. Some have a strong social, moral, or political outlook—either right-wing or left-wing—that shapes their music, and others do not. And to all these subcategories, still others could be added, such as "alternative singer-songwriters" (e.g., Sinéad O'Connor, Ani DiFranco, Tracy Chapman). What, then, defines them all as "alternative" musicians?

Our difficulty in coming up with a one-size-fits-all definition of "alternative music" stems partly from the use of this term to advance two different, and often conflicting, agendas. On the one hand, the term "alternative"—like the broadly equivalent terms "underground" and "independent"—is used to describe (and positively valorize) music that, in one regard or another, challenges the status quo. From this perspective alternative music is fiercely iconoclastic, anti-commercial, and anti-mainstream; it is thought by its supporters to be local as opposed to corporate, homemade as opposed to mass-produced, and genuine as opposed to artificial.

On the other hand, an entirely different sense of the term underlies the music industry's use of "alternative" to denote the choices available to consumers via record stores, radio, cable television, and the internet. This sense of the term is bound up with the need of the music business to identify and exploit new trends, styles, and audiences. In an interview conducted during the late 1980s, a senior executive for a major record company revealed that "there's a whole indie section [of our company. There are] . . . kids—that will only buy records that are on an indie label . . . which is why we sometimes concoct labels to try and fool them" (Negus 1992, 16).

The notion of a huge entertainment corporation cooking up a fake independent record label to satisfy an audience hungry for musical expressions of authenticity and rebellion may seem a bizarre contradiction at first glance. From our long-term historical perspective, however, we can see this institutional development as the culmination of a decades-old trend within the music business. In the days before rock 'n' roll, genres such as race music, hillbilly music, and ethnic music were predominantly the bailiwick of small, independently owned and operated record labels. By the 1980s and 1990s, however, the major record companies had fully internalized the hard lesson of rock 'n' roll and had come to view independent labels as the functional equivalent of baseball farm teams: small, specialized, close-to-the-ground operations perfectly situated to sniff out the next big thing. In an era when most so-called independent labels are distributed, promoted, and even owned outright by huge entertainment corporations, it became difficult to sustain a purely economic definition of alternative music as music that doesn't make money. To put it another way, the fact that a band's music, song lyrics, appearance, and ideological stance are anticommercial doesn't mean that they can't sell millions of records and thereby help to generate huge corporate profits.

ALTERNATIVE ROCK: 1980s–1990s

In the wake of punk rock's collapse—symbolized by the breakup of the Sex Pistols in 1978 (see Chapter 12)—a number of distinctive streams of "indie rock" or "underground rock" bubbled up in cities and towns across the United States. Strong underground rock scenes developed in towns such as Boston, Massachusetts; Athens, Georgia; Ann Arbor, Michigan; Minneapolis, Minnesota; Austin, Texas; San Francisco, California; and Seattle, Washington. Many of these communities are home to large populations of college students and student-programmed college radio stations, both key ingredients for a regional underground scene. Starting out as local phenomena, supported by small but devoted audiences, touring within regional networks of clubs, and releasing recordings on tiny, hand-to-mouth independent labels, bands such as Sonic Youth, R.E.M., the Dead Kennedys, and Nirvana came to symbolize the essence of indie rock—local, anticommercial, guitar-based music blending the abrasive, do-it-yourself sensibility of 1970s punk with the thick, heavy sonic textures of heavy metal. In general, underground rock bands maintained a defiant stance toward the conformity and commercialism of the music industry. They were committed to songwriting that explored taboo issues (drug use, depression, incest, suicide); interested in social and political movements such as environmentalism, abortion rights, and AIDS activism; and identified with unconventional (and soon merchandised) styles of self-presentation that included "dressing down" in torn jeans, flannel shirts, and work boots. Despite their avowed opposition to mainstream rock music, genres such as indie rock, hardcore, and thrash were supported by a predominantly white, middle- and working-class, male audience.

As time wore on, some of these groups went on to achieve commercial success on an international scale, signing deals with major record companies and moving toward a more pop-influenced sound. Others, driven by the ideology of authenticity through nonconformity, remained small, intensely local, and close to their fan base. For the underground bands who made it big—leading to the emergence of alternative rock as a marketing category around 1990—there were many contradictions to face, not least the problem of maintaining an outsider identity as their albums rose to the top of the *Billboard* charts, received Grammy Awards, and were promoted on the mainstream mass media. For many of these groups, the sensation of being on the inside looking out was new and unnerving. For a few musicians, it proved fatal.

The most influential indie rock bands of the 1980s were **R.E.M.** (formed in 1980 in Athens, Georgia) and New York's **Sonic Youth** (formed in 1981). While both bands were influenced by the 1970s New York punk scene, they developed this musical impetus in different directions. R.E.M.'s reinterpretation of the punk aesthetic incorporated aspects of folk rock—particularly a ringing acoustic guitar sound reminiscent of the 1960s group the Byrds—and a propensity for catchy melodic hooks. Touring almost constantly and releasing a series of critically acclaimed and increasingly profitable albums on the independent label IRS, R.E.M. gradually grew from its roots as a regional cult phenomenon to command a large national audience. This process culminated in the release of *Document*, the band's first Top 10 album, in 1987. In 1988 R.E.M. signed a $10 million, five-album agreement with Warner Brothers, becoming one of the first underground bands of the 1980s to receive such a deal. By 1991, when alternative rock seemed to many observers to have suddenly erupted onto the pop music scene, R.E.M. had already been working steadily for over ten years to develop its idiosyncratic sound. That year the band released the album *Out of Time*, which shot to Number 1 on the album chart, sold 4 million copies, generated two Top 10 singles, and won a Grammy Award for Best Alternative Music LP. (The alternative category had been established only the year before, an indication of the music industry's awakening interest in underground rock music.) The album's success elevated the band to major rock stars, with successful follow-up albums and tours appearing through much of the 1990s. However, the heavy touring took its toll on the group's members, most notably drummer Bill Berry, who collapsed on stage from a brain aneurysm in 1995 and subsequently retired from the band. The group's later efforts were less successful, and they eventually disbanded in 2011.

Sonic Youth, formed in New York City in 1981, pushed underground rock music in a quite different direction. Influenced by avant-garde experimentalists such as the Velvet Underground, Sonic Youth developed a dark, menacing, feedback-drenched sound, altering the tuning of their guitars by inserting screwdrivers and drumsticks under the strings at random intervals and ignoring the conventional song structures of rock and pop music. On a series of influential (though commercially unsuccessful) recordings released during the mid-1980s on the independent label SST, Sonic Youth began to experiment with more conventional pop song forms while maintaining the discordant sound with which they were so closely identified by fans and other musicians. By the early 1990s Sonic Youth, the former underground phenomenon, had signed with the major label DGC (owned by the media magnate David Geffen) and was being widely hailed as a pioneer of the alternative movement in rock. The magazine *Vanity Fair* went so far as to proclaim Sonic Youth's lead singer, Kim Gordon, the "godmother of alternative rock." The 1994 album *Experimental Jet Set, Trash, and No Star*, their third release on DGC, reached Number 34 on the Top 100 album chart, proof that their national audience, like R.E.M.'s, had expanded beyond all expectations. While this period of commercial success was not long-lived, the band continued to produce both "commercial" albums and more experimental music (on their own label) through 2011, when they went on "hiatus." Band member Kim Gordon published her memoirs, *Girl in a Band*, in 2015.

ROCK'S HARDER EDGE

Around the same time that R.E.M. and Sonic Youth were formulating (and reformulating) their distinctive underground sounds, another influential branch of post-punk music was developing. **Hardcore** was an extreme variation of punk that was pioneered during the late 1970s and early 1980s by bands in London (Crass), San Francisco (the Dead Kennedys), Washington, DC (Bad Brains), and Los Angeles (the Germs, Black Flag, X, and the Circle Jerks). These groups took the frenzied energy of the Ramones and the Sex Pistols and pushed it to the limit, playing simple riff-based songs at impossibly fast tempos and screaming nihilistic lyrics over a chaotic wall of guitar chords. Audiences at hardcore clubs—typically adorned in tattoos, buzz cuts, and combat boots—developed the practice of "slam dancing," or "moshing," in which members of the audience pushed their way up to a mosh pit, an area situated directly in front of the stage, and smashed into one another, sometimes climbing onto the stage and diving off into the crowd. Most hardcore recordings were released by independent labels like SST, Alternative Tentacles, and IRS, and the typical hardcore disc was produced to look and sound as though it had been made in someone's basement. Few of these bands managed to score contracts with major labels, a fact proudly pointed out by fans as proof of their genuine underground status.

By the mid-1980s the hardcore movement had largely played itself out, though aspects of the music's style and attitude were carried on by bands playing thrash, which blended the fast tempos and rebellious attitude of hardcore with the technical virtuosity of heavy metal guitar playing. Thrash was a harder, faster version of the commercially successful speed metal style played by bands such as Metallica, Megadeth, and Anthrax. (The 1991 album *Metallica* was the ultimate confirmation of heavy metal's mass popularity and newfound importance to the music industry: it streaked to Number 1 on the album charts, sold over 5 million copies, and stayed on the charts for an incredible 266 weeks.) Unlike speed metal, thrash didn't produce any superstars—the Los Angeles bands Suicidal Tendencies and Slayer were the most recognizable names to emerge from the genre—but it did exert an influence on alternative rock bands of the 1990s. Although thrash never developed a mass audience, its fans remained devoted, keeping the style alive as an underground club–based phenomenon through the 1990s.

Listening Guide "HOLIDAY IN CAMBODIA"

Written and performed by the Dead Kennedys; recorded 1980

"Holiday in Cambodia" by the Dead Kennedys is a good example of the sensibility of early 1980s hardcore punk rock. The song appeared on the album *Fresh Fruit for Rotting Vegetables*, released in the United Kingdom in 1980 and in the United States on the independent record label Alternative Tentacles the following year. The lyrics—written by the band's lead singer, *Jello Biafra* (Eric Boucher, b. 1958 in Boulder, Colorado)— brim with merciless sarcasm. The song is directed at the spoiled children of suburban yuppies, who Biafra suggests ought to be sent to forced labor camps in Cambodia—then in the grip of Pol Pot's genocidal regime—to gain some perspective on the magnitude of their own problems. The recording opens with a nightmarish display of guitar pyrotechnics, a series of Hendrix-inspired whoops, slides, scratches, and feedback that are evocative of a war zone. The band— guitar, electric bass, and drums—gradually builds to an extremely fast tempo (around 208 beats per minute). Over this chaotic din, Jello Biafra's quavering voice sneers out the caustic lyrics.

The Dead Kennedys' variant of hardcore was lent focus by the band's political stance, which opposed American imperialism overseas, the destruction of human rights and the environment, and what the band saw as a hypocritical and soulless suburban lifestyle. Jello Biafra composed songs with titles like "California über Alles," "Kill the Poor" (a Jonathan Swift–like suggestion for the practical application of neutron bombs), and "Chemical Warfare." As the hardcore scene began to attract right-wing racial supremacists—a problem that the genre shared with 1970s punk rock—Biafra penned a song entitled "Nazi Punks F— Off" (1981) in an attempt to distance the progressive hardcore skinheads from their fascist counterparts. Although the Dead Kennedys did not appear on the American pop music charts during the 1980s, the album *Fresh Fruit for Rotting Vegetables* was eventually certified as a Gold Album in England, a testimony to the enduring loyalty of hardcore punk's fan base. The original band broke up in 1986, following a difficult trial for obscenity inspired by their inclusion of graphic artwork in their 1985 album, *Frankenchrist*.

GRUNGE

While underground bands began to appear on the charts during the late 1980s, the commercial breakthrough for alternative rock—and the occasion of its enshrinement as a privileged category in the pop music marketplace—was achieved in 1992 by Nirvana, a band from the Pacific Northwest (see Box 14.2). Between 1992 and 1994, Nirvana—a trio centered on singer and guitarist *Kurt Cobain* (1967–1994; originally from Aberdeen, Washington) and bassist *Krist Novoselic* (b. 1965 in Compton, California)—released two multiplatinum albums that moved alternative rock's blend of hardcore punk and heavy metal out of the back corners of specialty record stores and into the commercial mainstream. The rise of so-called **grunge** rock—and the tragic demise of Kurt Cobain, who committed suicide in 1994 at the age of twenty-seven—provide some insight into the opportunities and pressures facing alternative rock musicians in the early 1990s.

Cobain and Novoselic met in 1985 in the town of Aberdeen, an economically depressed logging town some hundred miles from Seattle. (Cobain's parents had divorced when he was eight years old, an event that by his own account troubled him deeply and

Kurt Cobain.

left him shy and introspective.) Inspired by the records of underground rock and hardcore bands and the creativity of the Beatles, and frustrated with the limitations of small-town working-class life, the two formed Nirvana in 1987 and began playing gigs at local colleges and clubs. The following year they were signed by the independent label Sub Pop Records, formed in 1987 by the entrepreneurs Bruce Pavitt and Jonathan Poneman. (Sub Pop started out as a mimeographed fanzine for local bands before mutating into a record label.) Nirvana's debut album, *Bleach* (1989), cost slightly over $600 to record—less than the cost of thirty minutes of recording time at a major New York or Los Angeles recording studio—and sold thirty-five thousand copies, an impressive amount for a regional indie rock release. In 1991 the group signed with major label DGC. (By this time, Ohio-born drummer **Dave Grohl** [b. 1969] had become a steady member of the group.) Following a European tour with Sonic Youth, their album *Nevermind* was released in September 1991, quickly selling out its initial shipment of fifty thousand copies and creating a shortage in record stores across America. By the beginning of 1992 *Nevermind* had reached Number 1, displacing Michael Jackson's highly publicized comeback album *Dangerous*. The album stayed on the charts for almost five years, eventually selling more than 10 million copies.

Although alternative bands like R.E.M. and Sonic Youth handled their rise to fame with relative aplomb, success destroyed Nirvana. The group's attitude toward the music industry appears to have crystallized early on, as this 1989 Sub Pop press release indicates:

> NIRVANA sees the underground scene as becoming stagnant and more accessible to big league capitalist pig major record labels. But does NIRVANA feel a moral duty to fight this cancerous evil? NO WAY! We want to cash in and suck up to the big wigs in hopes that we too can GET HIGH AND F—...
> SOON we will need groupie repellant. SOON we will be coming to your town and asking if we can stay over at your house and use the stove. SOON we will do encores of "GLORIA" and "LOUIE LOUIE" at benefit concerts with all our celebrity friends.

The sardonic humor of this public relations document only partially masks the band's intensely ambivalent attitude toward rock celebrity, a kind of "listen to us, don't listen to us" stance. As *Nevermind* rose up the charts, Nirvana began to attract a mass audience that included millions of fans of hard rock and commercial heavy metal music, genres to which their own music was explicitly opposed. This realization impelled the group to ever more outrageous behavior, including baiting their audiences, wearing women's clothing, and kissing one another onstage. Gender theorist Mimi Schippers points to this "alternative" approach to masculinity as a hallmark that unites many disparate styles of indie music that "consciously rejected the masculinist gender order of rock music and asserted an alternative" (2002, 13).

In 1992 Cobain married Courtney Love, leader of the alternative rock band Hole. Rumors concerning the couple's use of heroin began to circulate, and an article in *Vanity Fair* charged Love with using the narcotic while pregnant with the couple's child, leading to a public struggle with the Los Angeles child services bureau over custody of the baby. In the midst of this adverse publicity, Nirvana released the album *In Utero*, a return to the raw sound of the band's early Sub Pop recordings, which shot to Number 1 in 1993 and sold 4 million copies.

In 1994, after the band had interrupted a concert tour of Europe, Kurt Cobain overdosed on champagne and tranquilizers, remaining in a coma for twenty hours. Although the event was initially described as an accident, a suicide note was later discovered. He returned to Seattle and entered a detoxification program, only to check out two days later. On April 8, 1994, Cobain's body was discovered in his home; he had died three days earlier of a self-inflicted shotgun wound. While there is a diversity of opinion concerning the ultimate meaning of Cobain's suicide—he is viewed on the one hand as a martyr of alternative music, and on the other as a self-indulgent rock star—his death has widely come to be viewed as evidence of the pressures faced by alternative musicians who are pulled into the mainstream.

OTHER ALTERNATIVES

Although the term "alternative rock" is most often used to describe bands inspired by the 1970s punk rock movement—like R.E.M., Sonic Youth, Dead Kennedys, and Nirvana—some forms of alternative rock found their inspiration elsewhere. The band *Phish* created a loyal following by extending the approach of the quintessential 1960s concert band, the Grateful Dead. Like the Dead, the members of Phish embraced eclectic tastes and influences. A typical Phish concert would weave together strands of rock, folk, jazz, country, bluegrass, and pop. A band devoted to improvisation, Phish required a live performance environment to be fully appreciated. There are some obvious differences between Phish and the Dead—Phish being a smaller and in some regards a more technically adept band, with a range of stylistic references arguably even broader than that of the Grateful Dead. Be that as it may, bands like Phish, Blues Traveler, and Dave Matthews Band, inspired by the counterculture of the 1960s and the improvisational work of jazz musicians such as Miles Davis and Sun Ra, provide an optimistic, energetic, and open-minded alternative to the nihilism and relentless self-absorption of many alternative rock bands. The fact that Phish has often been dismissed by rock

Listening Guide "SMELLS LIKE TEEN SPIRIT"

Music by Nirvana, lyrics by Kurt Cobain, performed by Nirvana (recorded 1991)

One source of *Nevermind's* success was the platinum single "Smells Like Teen Spirit," a Top 10 hit. One of the most striking aspects of "Teen Spirit" is its combination of heavy metal instrumental textures and pop songwriting techniques, including a number of memorable verbal and melodic hooks. The band's sound, which had been thick and plodding on its Sub Pop recordings, is sleek and well focused (thanks in part to the production of Butch Vig and the mixing of engineer Andy Wallace). The song itself combines a four-chord heavy metal harmonic progression with a somewhat conventional formal structure made up of four-, eight-, and twelve-bar sections. The overall structure of the song includes a verse of eight bars ("Load up on guns . . ."), which we call A, and two repeated sections, or choruses, which we label B (eight bars in length) and C (twelve bars). These sections are marked off by distinctive instrumental textures, which shift from the quiet, reflective, and even somewhat depressed quality of A through the crescendo of B, with its spacey one-word mantra and

continuous carpet of thick guitar chords, into the C section, where Cobain bellows his unfocused feelings of discontent and the group slams out heavy metal–style power chords. This ABC structure is repeated three times in the course of the five-minute recording, with room created between the second and final iterations for a sixteen-bar guitar solo.

Nirvana's "Smells Like Teen Spirit," the first alternative rock single of the 1990s to enter the Top 10, is a carefully crafted pop record. The sleek, glistening studio sound, Cobain's liberal use of melodic and verbal hooks, the trio's careful attention to textural shifts as a means of marking off formal sections of the song, and the fact that Cobain's guitar solo consists of an almost note-for-note restatement of the melodies of the A and B sections, driving these hooks even deeper into the listener's memory—all serve to remind us that the Beatles were as profound an influence on 1990s alternative rock as were bands like the Velvet Underground.

LISTENING GUIDE | "SMELLS LIKE TEEN SPIRIT"

TIME	FORM	LYRIC	DESCRIPTIVE COMMENTS
0:00	Introduction (16 measures)		Bars 1–4: solo guitar plays progression (quiet); bars 5–12: whole band plays progression (loud, intense); bars 13–16: bass plays progression with guitar chimes (soft)
0:34	A (8 measures)	*Load up . . .*	Lead vocal enters; quiet, somewhat depressed tone; gentle instrumental texture
0:50	B (8 measures)	*Hello, hello . . .*	Spacey, one-word vocal, backed with continuous guitar chords; gradual crescendo
1:06	C (12 measures)	*With the lights out . . .*	Vocal angry, growling; heavy metal power chords, loud and distorted
1:31	Interlude (4 measures)		Stop time effect with guitar response
1:39	Introduction (4 measures)		Last four bars of introduction; bass plays progression with guitar chimes (soft)

TIME	FORM	LYRIC	DESCRIPTIVE COMMENTS
1:47	A (8 measures)	*I'm worse . . .*	
2:04	B (8 measures)	*Hello, hello . . .*	Dreamy vocal (like Beatles); continuous bed of distorted guitar chords
2:20	C (12 measures)	*With the lights out . . .*	Vocal angry, growling; heavy metal power chords, loud and distorted
2:45	Interlude (4 measures)		Stop time effect, answered by guitar
2:53	Guitar solo (16 measures)		Guitar plays melody of sections A and B (little, if any, improvisation)
3:25	Introduction (4 measures)		Last four bars of introduction
3:33	A (8 measures)	*And I forget . . .*	
3:50	B (8 measures)	*Hello, hello . . .*	Crescendo; spacey, one-word vocal
4:05	C (20 measures)	*With the lights out . . .*	Vocal angry, growling; heavy metal power chords, loud and distorted

critics—in part because their music doesn't make sense in terms of the rock-as-rebellion scenario that dominates such criticism—didn't impede their success as a live act. Unlike bands such as R.E.M., Nirvana, and Pearl Jam, however, their popularity as a touring act never translated into massive record sales. By the mid-1990s Phish was able to pack stadiums—selling out New York's Madison Square Garden in merely four hours—but none of their albums has sold as many as a million copies.

The twelve-and-a-half-minute track "Stash" from the concert album *Phish: A Live One* (1995) exemplifies the band's loose-jointed, freewheeling approach to collective improvisation. (This is, it must be admitted, a relatively brief selection. For an even better sense of the band's improvisational prowess, we would advise that you listen to one of the longer tracks, perhaps the half-hour-long "Tweezer.") The song—in the sense of a verse-chorus structure with a more or less fixed melody and lyrics—takes up only a small portion of the track, which is an extended collective exploration of the improvisational possibilities of a minor-key chord progression carried along on a rhythmic groove indebted to Latin American music. Certain relatively fixed elements create a sense of structure—for example, the tango-like melody played by guitarist Trey Anastasio at the beginning of the track and periodically throughout. (The audience's familiarity with these structural points is evidenced by the fact that they fill in one part of the melody with collective, and reasonably precise, clapping.) At some points these structural elements seem to melt away completely as the guitar, acoustic piano, electric bass, and drums develop a subtle interplay, taking the performance in unexpected directions. While Anastasio's guitar is generally the dominant instrument in the mix, Phish's approach to improvisation resembles the collective polyphony of early New Orleans jazz (see Chapter 3) more than the hierarchical structure of rock bands, in which the soloist becomes the more or less exclusive center of attention and the rest of the band plays a subservient role.

In a June 1995 interview in *Addicted to Noise* magazine, guitarist Trey Anastasio talked about the fact that Phish has never in over a decade of touring had a hit album or single:

> Lately I've been thinking . . . the worst thing that could happen to a band is to have a hit single. . . . Because you weaken your fan base. People start coming in that aren't interested in the whole thing. And then they're expecting to hear that one song. . . .
>
> Kind of like life. You don't go from being thirteen to being thirty, you gotta go through everything in between. Music is life to a musician. Having a hit single is very similar to going up to someone in eighth grade and saying, "Wow, that thing you did in eighth grade was really great. We're going to skip you to college. Here you go! Good luck!" Take it slow. Life is long.

Life is long, but lives are sometimes short. It is in the end difficult to explain why musicians such as Duke Ellington, Ray Charles, Bill Monroe, Paul Simon, and the Grateful Dead managed to sustain a pattern of creative growth over several decades, while others—for instance, Hank Williams, Jimi Hendrix, Janis Joplin, and Kurt Cobain—burned out almost overnight, consumed by social pressures or personal demons. Anastasio's quote suggests that the key to musical longevity may be the ability to balance the passionate involvement of music-making with a philosophical, and even somewhat distanced, perspective on the business of making a living from music.

BOX 14.2 THE "SEATTLE SOUND"

Regional "sounds" have played an important part in the history of popular music, from the Chicago blues of Muddy Waters to the Memphis rockabilly style of Elvis Presley and the Southern California inflections of gangsta rap. Seattle, where Nirvana honed their sound and built a local fan base, was already home to a thriving alternative rock scene by the late 1980s. (The Pacific Northwest, while somewhat removed from the main centers of the recording industry, had twenty-five years earlier played a role in the development of garage band rock, an important predecessor of punk rock.) The group often singled out as an originator of the "Seattle Sound" was Green River (formed in 1983), whose 1988 album *Rehab Doll*, released on

Sub Pop, helped to popularize grunge rock, blending heavy metal guitar textures with hardcore punk. Green River was also the training ground for members of later, more widely known Northwest bands such as Mudhoney (formed in 1988), which was Sub Pop's biggest act until Nirvana came along; and Pearl Jam (formed in 1990), who went on to become one of the most popular rock bands of the 1990s. One of the first bands signed to the fledgling Sub Pop label was Soundgarden (formed in 1984), a heavy metal band that many insiders expected to be the first group to break the Seattle grunge sound on the national market. However, Soundgarden's first across-the-boards success—the album *Superunknown*, which reached Number 1 on the charts and sold 5 million copies—was not released until 1994.

Today, the push to define a regional style often comes as much from the promotion departments of record companies as from the local artists and fans themselves. The documentary video *Hype!* (1996), a revealing portrait of the role of Sub Pop Records in the Seattle alternative rock scene, suggests that many Seattle-based musicians and fans rejected the grunge label as a commercial gimmick, especially when it was adopted by advertising agencies and upscale fashion designers. This tension between commercialism and authenticity continues to play a central role in the creation and promotion of alternative rock music.

Women's Voices: Alternative Folk, Hip-Hop, Country, and Punk

While the term is most frequently associated with rock music, there are "alternative" artists in almost all genres of popular music. In this section we will look at the work of four artists who established an alternative identity in their respective genres: Ani DiFranco, a folk singer-songwriter, Lauryn Hill, a hip-hop artist, k.d. lang, a country singer, and the riot grrrl band Bikini Kill. In each case, the music industry's application of the term "alternative" to these performers has to do with the fact that women's perspectives—and feminist values—play an important role in their recorded work. While these artists share this commitment, they differ in their relationships to the corporate music business, their performance styles, and the degree of commercial success they have enjoyed.

A folk singer dressed in punk rock clothing, **Ani DiFranco** (b. 1970 in Buffalo, New York) has spent her career resisting the lure of the corporate music business, releasing an album and playing upward of two hundred live dates every year while building up a successful independent record label (Righteous Babe Records) and a substantial grassroots following. By the age of nineteen DiFranco had written over one hundred original songs and relocated from her native Buffalo to New York City to pursue a musical career. In 1989 she recorded a demo album and pressed five hundred copies of an eponymous cassette to sell at shows. The tape—a spare collection of intensely personal songs about failed relationships and gender inequality, accompanied with acoustic guitar—quickly sold out, and in 1990 DiFranco founded Righteous Babe Records to distribute her recordings more effectively.

By the mid-1990s the mainstream media had begun to take notice of DiFranco's homespun, low-tech music. Her 1995 album *Not a Pretty Girl* garnered notice from CNN and the *New York Times*, although it did not appear in the *Billboard* charts. But 1996 brought *Dilate*, an eclectic work recounting a love affair with a man, which debuted in the Top 100 of the *Billboard* charts, an unusual achievement for an independent release. The live album *Living in Clip*, released in 1997, became DiFranco's first gold album. In 1998 DiFranco released the studio effort *Little Plastic Castle*, her highest-charting album yet, which debuted at Number 22 on the Top 200 chart. All of these albums were released on the Righteous Babe label, despite many offers from major record companies.

Ani DiFranco.

"Not a Pretty Girl," from the album *Not a Pretty Girl*, is a typical Ani DiFranco record-ing, with self-revealing lyrics and an austere, minimalist studio sound that focuses on DiFranco's voice and acoustic guitar. The lyrics operate on at least two levels: first, as a response to an individual, a man who has wronged the singer in some way; and second, as a more general indictment of society's treatment of women.

The track opens in a reflective mood, with the solo acoustic guitar playing a four-chord progression. The musical form of "Not a Pretty Girl" is not dissimilar to that of many Anglo-American folk songs, and the song's text, as printed on the CD's liner notes, suggests the format of a traditional folk ballad made up of a series of stanzas. However, DiFranco's performance of the lyrics—which escalates from a sung whisper at the beginning to an assertive growl in the middle before ending with gentle wordless singing—creates an effect entirely different from that of seeing the words laid out on the page. DiFranco lays her lyrics over the structure of the song like ropes, tightening them here, loosening them there, and creating a sense of emotional intensity and musical momentum. She begins the first verse of the song in a whisper, her dislike for the man to whom the song is addressed emerging clearly only on the word "punk," which she spits out derisively. The way the accents in the text are distributed around the strong waltz rhythm of the music—with its *one*-two-three pulsations—creates the sense of a woman who is impatient with the injustices of the world and who insists upon being treated as a person, not a stereotype.

The impact of "Not a Pretty Girl" is closely tied up with its carefully controlled fluctuations in musical texture, verbal density, and emotional color. DiFranco artfully blends the progressive outlook of urban folk music with the rebellious energy of alternative rock. At the same time, her performance—a song-portrait of a woman whose experience of sexism has had profound emotional consequences—implies that matters of the heart cannot simply be reduced to political positions. The cultural impact of Ani DiFranco's music was recognized in 2006 when she received the Woman of Courage Award from the National Organization for Women (NOW).

Lauryn Hill (b. 1975 in South Orange, New Jersey) is a hip-hop artist whose work is a self-conscious alternative to the violence and sexism of rap stars such as Dr. Dre, the Notorious B.I.G., and 2Pac Shakur. Her commitment to female empowerment builds upon the groundbreaking example of Queen Latifah, but Hill raps and sings in her own distinctive voice. She started her recording career with the Fugees, a New Jersey–based hip-hop trio that scored a Number 1 hit in 1996 with their second album, *The Score*. Hill's debut solo album, *The Miseducation of Lauryn Hill* (1998), extended the Fugees' successful blend of rap, reggae, and R&B. The album shot to Number 1 on the charts, selling 7 million copies in a little over a year and spawning the Number 1 hit "Doo Wop (That Thing)."

k.d. lang (b. 1961 in Alberta, Canada) has always occupied a marginal position in the conservative world of country music. Raised in an isolated rural town on the high plains of Canada, lang discovered country music when she played a Patsy Cline–type character in a college play. She began her career in 1982 as a Cline imitator, going so far as to christen her band the Reclines. During the early 1980s she released two albums on the Edmonton-based independent label Bumstead Records, but it was only in 1987, when Sire Records (former label of Patti Smith and the Ramones) released her *Angel with a Lariat*, that lang came to the attention of a broader audience. (The album was played on college radio stations and progressive country stations.) Her subsequent albums—1988's *Shadowland* and 1989's *Absolute Torch and Twang*—moved toward a more traditional honky-tonk sound, producing lang's first appearances on the country Top 40 chart and a Grammy Award for Best Female Country Vocal Performance. Even at that stage, however, lang never sat quite right with the Nashville establishment, which found her campy outfits (rhinestone suits and cat-eye glasses) and somewhat androgynous image off-putting.

A scandal over lang's appearance in a commercial for the "Meat Stinks" campaign of the People for Ethical Treatment of Animals led stations in the cattle-producing areas of

Listening Guide "DOO WOP (THAT THING)"

Written and performed by Lauryn Hill; recorded 1998

"Doo Wop" combines aspects of 1950s R&B—a soulful lead vocal, four-part vocal harmony, and a horn section—with Hill's penetrating observations on gendered behavior. The cut opens with Hill and a few of her friends reminiscing about the good old days. Then the digital drum machine's groove enters, and Hill launches into the first half of her rap, directed to female listeners.

Hill admonishes the women in her audience to be more selective about their sexual relationships and to avoid being hypocritical about their personal conduct. She then turns to the men in her audience, opening up a rapid-fire volley of wordplay that strips the so-called gangstas of their tough-guy trappings, exposing them as mother-dependent, sneaky, woman-beating, sexually immature hypocrites.

"Doo Wop (That Thing)" is essentially a moral parable, delivered in terms that leaven Hill's righteous anger with light-hearted and thoroughly up-to-date hip-hop jargon. She lowers her audience's potential defensiveness by admitting that she has found herself in similar situations and pleads with them to pay attention to the development of an inner life—"How you gon' win when you ain't right within?"—in order to avoid the twin traps of materialism and easy pleasure. The mixture of sweet soul singing and assertive rapping, R&B horns and a digital groove, moral seriousness and playful humor not only announced the arrival of a new and distinctive voice but also made the single "Doo Wop" a unique and important contribution to the hip-hop repertoire.

k.d. lang performing in 1996.

the Midwest to boycott her records and generated an impressive volume of hate mail. In 1992 lang officially announced her homosexuality, a move that rather than hurting her career, led to *New York* magazine christening her an "icon of lesbian chic." During the 1990s lang moved in the direction of adult contemporary pop music, becoming an "alternative" star in that category as well. *Ingénue*, a 1992 album that owed little to country music, sold over a million copies in the United States. A single from *Ingénue*, "Constant Craving," reached the pop Top 40 and won the Grammy Award for Best Female Pop Vocal Performance. Although lang has not been able to repeat this commercial success, she has maintained a dedicated following, and in 2013 was inducted into the Canadian Music Hall of Fame.

The levels of commercial success enjoyed by these three artists, varied as they may be, are different in kind from the "do-it-yourself" (D.I.Y.) aesthetics of the feminist punk collective *Bikini Kill*. Led by singer, writer, and political activist *Kathleen Hanna* (b. 1968 in Portland, Oregon), Bikini Kill was at the forefront of an underground musical and social movement known as "**riot grrrl**." Centered around the Evergreen State College in Olympia, Washington—an established hotbed of progressive political action—the culture of riot grrrl encouraged young women and girls not only to make music, but to create and distribute handmade pamphlets called "zines" that expressed feminist viewpoints and advocated for grassroots community activism. Little distinction was made between "artists" and "fans" in this participatory culture. Riot grrrl bands played mostly all-ages venues and usually eschewed the stage altogether by either joining the crowd on the floor or inviting the crowd onto the stage with them.

Bikini Kill drew on the punk visual aesthetics of women who came before them, both in the UK (Siouxsie Sioux, Poly Styrene) and in the United States (Patti Smith, Joan Jett), complementing this image with a harder and faster punk/hardcore sound. "Rebel Girl," from the band's 1993 LP *Pussy Whipped*, was something of an anthem for the riot grrrl movement. Like most punk music, "Rebel Girl" is in common time and bears a standard verse-chorus structure. Drummer Tobi Celeste Vail (who was responsible for the iconic "grrrl" spelling of the movement) bangs out a march beat with the snare during the verse, then clangs the vociferous crash cymbal over a standard backbeat in the chorus. Throughout both the verses and choruses the guitars and bass play a droning low riff with thick distortion.

This punk simplicity allows the lyrics and vocal delivery of "Rebel Girl" to take center stage. Hanna's expressive singing recalls that of Patti Smith (Chapter 12), incorporating techniques of traditional singing, punk rock screaming, and spoken word. Notable for 1993, the song is an unabashed anthem to same-sex love. A love-struck narrator pines for the "queen of the neighborhood" in the first verse, wanting to take her home and "try on her clothes." The second verse moves from fantasy to reality, with sensual depictions of the rebel girl's hips and her kiss, both of which are said to contain "revolution." Following a brief guitar solo, Hanna's delivery in the third verse becomes agitated as she screams "they say she's a slut" (which the singer gladly affirms). An earlier recording of the song, produced by none other than Joan Jett, replaces "slut" with "dyke." Both pejoratives were reclaimed as badges of honor by the riot grrrl community, exemplifying both third-wave feminism's commitment to sexual empowerment and riot grrrl's alliance

Listening Guide "NOWHERE TO STAND"

Written by k.d. lang, performed by k.d. lang and the Reclines; recorded 1989

"Nowhere to Stand," from the 1989 album *Absolute Torch and Twang* (1989), is a traditional song in musical terms, with a series of four-line verses and a repeated chorus, all in triple meter. In fact, apart from lang's public image, the only thing that marks this as an alternative country song is the content of the lyrics, which are an indictment of the "traditional" practice of child abuse. The song begins quietly with lang's country-tinged alto voice accompanied only by acoustic guitar. The message of the song is not explicit in the first two verses, the second of which is accompanied by a solo fiddle. The song hints at the tradition of abuse in the family by opening with the ominous words "As things start to surface . . ." Although the woman described in the lyric is starting to realize the hurt that she felt at the hands of her abusive father, she is unable to stop herself from repeating this abuse of her own child ("what's taught is what's known" the song's narrator comments).

The intensity of lang's performance builds through the second verse, but only in the chorus—which enters suddenly, a measure early—do we become aware that this is not the typical lovelorn country song and that something hidden, and deadly serious, is being revealed to us. The characterization of child abuse as a "family tradition, the strength of this land"—in which moral values and gender identity are taught with "the back of a hand"—drives lang's message home without resorting to explicit descriptions of violence. The verse that follows sketches the psychological legacy of domestic violence as a deeply buried memory, "like a seed that's been planted and won't be denied," and the recording reaches its emotional peak in the second, final chorus. By juxtaposing traditional Anglo-American song form and country music sensibility with a lyric that in essence questions the sanctity of the family—used by politicians and cultural commentators as the ultimate symbol of traditional values—lang creates a tender but powerful critique of American (and Canadian) culture.

with the LGBTQ+ community. Riot grrrls would in fact often scrawl such words across their bare stomachs at concerts.

The cultural resonance of Bikini Kill and other riot grrrl artists was dampened by their resistance to mainstream trends. Record companies wanted to pitch riot grrrl bands as either mainstream punk (e.g., Green Day, Blink-182) or as "angry women" (e.g., Alanis Morissette, Fiona Apple), both durable musical trends of the early-to-mid 90s. But the artists, fiercely protective of their own D.I.Y. communities, resisted being pigeonholed into these ready-made categories. Ultimately, the legacy of riot grrrl lives on in a new generation of grassroots punk collectives for women and LGBTQ+ folk, the most (in)famous of which is the Russian performance art collective Pussy Riot, three of whom were jailed in 2012 for demonstrating against Vladimir Putin in a Moscow cathedral. Kathleen Hanna now sits on the board of *Girls Rock*, a nonprofit organization dedicated to teaching young women and girls to play instruments and write songs through week-long camps that take place all over the United States.

DiFranco, Hill, lang, and the members of Bikini Kill all achieved the status of alternative artists in their respective genres, and it is worth taking a moment to consider why. The lyrics of DiFranco's "Not a Pretty Girl" do not depart completely from the norms of urban folk music, a genre long identified with social and political criticism.

Kathi Wilcox (left on bass) and Kathleen Hanna (right on vocals) of Bikini Kill performing in 1994.

(DiFranco's respect for the early practitioners of that genre is abundantly clear on her 2012 album *¿Which Side Are You On?*, which features urban folk pioneer Pete Seeger.) What makes this track an alternative folk recording is the introduction of instrumental textures and vocal style from punk rock, and the fact that it was released on a small independent label managed by the artist herself. Hill's "Doo Wop (That Thing)" is classified as an alternative hip-hop recording not because it incorporates aspects of R&B and soul music—many mainstream hip-hop records do this—but rather because the song's lyric challenges aspects of the materialistic and sexist ideology promoted on many of the most commercially successful rap recordings. k.d. lang's "Nowhere to Stand" hews quite closely to the norms of country music in its form, vocal and instrumental style, and emotional tone. Its status as an alternative country song has more to do with the singer's public persona (the only Jewish Canadian vegetarian lesbian in country music) and the subject matter of the song, the secret of child abuse in "traditional" families. Bikini Kill's gender makeup alone sets them apart from mainstream punk rock, a genre populated mostly by straight white men in the early 1990s. But their lyrics are even more outside the norm. Boldly addressing taboo topics such as rape, sexual assault, homophobia, and inclusivity within the trans community, such lyrics wouldn't be heard on Top-40 radio for another twenty years.

While these four songs present an interesting series of contrasts, it is also worth noting the strong parallels among the careers of these artists. All four are innovative singer-songwriters whose "alternative" perspectives are deeply informed by historical knowledge of the particular genres in which they have chosen to work. DiFranco refers to herself as "just a folk singer" and performs at tribute concerts for urban folk pioneers like Pete Seeger, while Hill demonstrates her "old school" credentials by evoking, and verbally citing, the sound of postwar rhythm and blues, and k.d. lang uses the 1960s country style of Patsy Cline to convey her social messages. Bikini Kill drew on accompaniment patterns heard in the rhythm sections of punk rock bands since as early as 1977. All four artists are committed to creating popular music that engages with contemporary social issues, particularly the rights of women and children.

That all four of these artists were shut out from the Lilith Fair Festival—a mainstream festival for adult contemporary music made by women and the highest grossing touring festival of 1997—speaks volumes to their "alternative" status. Despite this shared outsider position, Bikini Kill's antipathy toward fame sets them apart from the three singer-songwriters. In a time when the boundaries of acceptable nonconformity were narrowly drawn, DiFranco, Hill, and lang were all able to achieve a degree of commercial success without compromising their passionate and distinctive voices. By contrast, the political messages put forth by Bikini Kill and other riot grrrl acts were heard only by those who attended their shows, bought or bootlegged their cassette tapes, or read their zines.

Modern Sounds in Country and Western Music: Approaches to Tradition

In the closing decades of the twentieth century and the beginning of the twenty-first, it became undeniable that country and western was one of the most popular genres of American music—some would argue *the* most popular genre of American music. While the pop singles charts might not consistently have reflected this situation, the data on bestselling albums of the 1980s, 1990s, and 2000s attest to a steadily increasing dominance by country artists, and the recent mega-success of Taylor Swift (see the following discussion) indicates the extent to which an artist who starts out with a country identity can not only penetrate, but eventually come to dominate the pop singles charts. We will outline some of the characteristic trends in modern country music by briefly examining the careers of three men who are among the most successful country singers of all time: George Strait, Alan Jackson, and Toby Keith. Then we will look at two very contrasting examples of female country artists who achieved prominence during the first decade of the twenty-first century: Taylor Swift and Gretchen Wilson.

HUNKS IN HATS: GEORGE STRAIT, ALAN JACKSON, AND TOBY KEITH

Striking similarities in the personal backgrounds and music of *George Strait*, *Alan Jackson*, and *Toby Keith* demonstrate the persistence of certain traditions in country music and the culture surrounding it—the culture from which it arises, and which also continues to sustain it. All three were born and bred in the South or the Southwest, the heartlands of country: Strait in Texas (b. 1952), Jackson in Georgia (b. 1958), and Keith in Oklahoma (b. 1961). All three men come from working-class backgrounds—Strait was a rancher, Jackson was a car salesman and construction worker, and Keith worked in the oil fields and as a rodeo hand—and did not fully establish careers as country music performers until they were in their thirties. This trajectory is not atypical of country artists, as country has always tended to be much less of a youth-oriented genre than many other categories of pop music. It is a closely related truth that country audiences often reward their mature, stable, consistent artists with long, steady careers as consistent hit makers, and certainly the music careers of all three men have been characterized by a consistency of style and professionalism—as well as by an attendant downplaying of concern with novelty and current pop trends. Strait came to prominence in the mid-1980s, Jackson in the early 1990s, and Keith in the mid-1990s, but all three continued to rack up Number 1 country hits well into the new millennium.

In surveying the many hit records of these three male superstars, we can observe further significant commonalities. All have recorded songs with lyrics that specifically acknowledge their country backgrounds and country traditions. Strait's "Heartland" (Number 1 country, 1993) starts right out with the singer praising the sounds of fiddles and steel guitar (with appropriate instrumental accompaniment, of course). Jackson's striking, minor-key "Midnight in Montgomery" (Number 3 country, 1992) pays tribute to Alabama's Hank Williams (see Chapter 7) as an enduring presence in his mind, heart, and music. And Keith's very first country hit proclaims his identity with its title, "Should've Been a Cowboy" (Number 1 country, Number 93 pop, 1993). In keeping with long-standing country music practice, the songs of all three artists tend to present straightforward verse-chorus structures, favoring immediate accessibility over formal innovations or intricacies. A characteristic "country sound" also prevails, with the steel guitar acting as a country "marker" in the recordings of all three. Keith, however—the youngest of the trio—does not retain that other country marker, the fiddle, as a significant element of his sound, while this is an approach favored by both Strait and Jackson. All three men sing in a full-voiced manner, clearly articulating the lyrics while neither concealing nor leaning heavily on their regional accents. (It is arguable that those looking for "natural," well-crafted pop singing in a world of rapping, mumbling, belting, and screaming vocal styles are more likely to find it in country music than in many other currently prominent genres—which may help account for the current widespread appreciation of country music, even among those who did not grow up with it.)

Although there is no trace of "hillbilly" yodeling or of the "high lonesome" vocal sound (found frequently in bluegrass) in the output of all three men, in many respects their music suggests a strong continuity with the honky-tonk style of the period immediately following World War II, updated with the addition of a stronger backbeat. The resulting sound is often quite similar to that of the country-flavored pop/rock of the 1970s (see Chapter 11), which illustrates in yet another way the strength and endurance of tradition in country music. To those who might claim that this leaning on tradition results in much music that sounds generic or formulaic, the response could be made that much generic or formulaic music has characterized Tin Pan Alley, blues, early rock 'n' roll, and many other genres of American pop. Furthermore, listeners relatively unfamiliar with or unsympathetic toward contemporary genres like alternative rock and hip-hop—genres that supposedly prize individuality and innovation—might well find that many examples of those genres sound generic or formulaic to them!

None of this is meant to imply that artists like Strait, Jackson, and Keith lack individual musical profiles. Strait, as the oldest, is the most traditional-sounding of the three, but it is worth recalling that a self-consciously traditionalist stance was not the most obvious path for a country singer to embrace in the early 1980s in the wake of the "country pop" and "outlaw" phenomena of the 1970s (see Chapters 11 and 12). Keith leans more typically toward a rock-like sound than do the other two. On a Keith track like "Country Comes to Town" (Number 4 country, Number 54 pop, 2000), this tendency can result in a kind of paradox, as the singer asserts his country roots over music that sounds for all the world like a rock anthem, lacking any obvious country markers. Jackson may be the most versatile of these three singers. His range can embrace an old-fashioned, tear-jerking country waltz (like "[Who Says] You Can't Have It All," Number 4 country, 1994); a knowing satire on those who rushed to embrace suddenly-fashionable country clothing and music in the 1990s ("Gone Country," Number 1 country, 1994); and a gentle and touching response to the terrorist attacks of September 11, 2001 ("Where Were You [When The World Stopped Turning]," Number 1 country for five weeks, Number 28 pop, 2001–2002). Keith released his own more militaristic, flag-waving response to September 11 with "Courtesy of the Red, White, and Blue (The Angry American)" (Number 1 country, Number 25 pop, 2002). He also made a stab at rapping on the clever "I Wanna Talk About Me," an attempt that was evidently successful with listeners, since the song achieved a pop chart presence (Number 28) along with a five-week stay at Number 1 on the country charts in 2001. While Jackson and Keith are songwriters as well as singers, Strait has until very recently relied on professional songwriters for his material—but his astounding quantity of Number 1 country hits attests to his nearly unfailing taste in choosing that material. Strait recordings of songs like "All My Ex's Live in Texas" (Number 1 country, 1987) and "Ace in the Hole" (Number 1 country, 1989) have deservedly become classics.

TAYLOR SWIFT: COUNTRY STAR

When we turn our attention to *Taylor Swift* (b. 1989), we confront a career that seems to contradict every tendency under discussion: a "teen idol" and singer-songwriter pop phenomenon who self-identified as a country artist! But Swift is an exceptional case by any standard. She was still a teenager when her second album, *Fearless* (2008), became the longest-running Number 1 album of the 2000s up to that time, spending eleven weeks at the top spot in 2008–2009 and spawning eleven Hot 100 hit singles. (The remaining two tracks on the album just missed charting on the Hot 100 singles chart.) As of this writing, *Fearless* has sold well over 12 million copies. The "catch" is this: listening to *Fearless*, one might well be excused for asking in what respects it is a "country" album. Neither the lyrics nor the music reflect standard country traditions. The songs center around teenage romance and heartbreak, as is only appropriate, with titles like "Fifteen," "Love Story," "You're Not Sorry," and "The Way I Loved You." (The obvious exception, "Changes," deals in a very general way with triumphing over struggle.) Obvious country markers are inaudible in the music, which has a mainstream pop sheen, and Swift does not project a particularly noticeable Southern (or any regional) accent—in fact, she was born far from the American South, in Reading, Pennsylvania! Nevertheless, *Fearless* won a Grammy Award for Best Album—as well as Best Country Album—in 2008.

Taylor Swift's eponymous first album from 2006, also a multiplatinum seller, helps clarify her status as a country artist. The very first track, "Tim McGraw," is named for a very popular country singer-songwriter, and its opening verse presents images of "Georgia stars," a "Chevy truck," and "back roads," all clearly evoking a "country" ambience. Fiddle, dobro, banjo, and mandolin all figure prominently in the sound world of *Taylor Swift*. The question then became not whether Swift may be identified with country music, but whether *Fearless* represented a conscious attempt on her part to move beyond what might be seen as the limitations of that identity in shaping her career. The extraordinary success of *Fearless* must have had a tremendous impact on Swift, and of course on her enlarging fan base. It seems apparent now that Swift decided to court the largest pop market possible as her career

Taylor Swift on stage.

progressed, and she is now a central figure in the overall pop landscape, standing among the most successful pop artists of the age. (Her career during the 2010s and 2020s will be discussed in the "Twenty-First-Century Divas" section of Chapter 15.) Although Swift has spent her career moving further and further away from the genre that first embraced her music, currently prominent artists such as Mickey Guyton, Kacey Musgraves, and Miranda Lambert have remained firmly in the country camp with a combination of the Nashville Sound (see Chapter 10) and the rock-driven Progressive Country (see Chapter 12), showing that country music is alive and well, even for the millennial generation.

REDNECK WOMAN: GRETCHEN WILSON

Starting out with simply the title of her first hit in 2004, "Redneck Woman" (Number 1 country for five weeks, Number 22 pop), there was no doubting the cultural identity proclaimed by *Gretchen Wilson* (b. 1973 in Illinois). With the huge success of both that song and Wilson's subsequent efforts, including the Number 1 album *All Jacked Up* in 2005, there was also no doubting the marketability of that cultural identity. Wilson presents the most complete contrast imaginable to Taylor Swift. Like many a successful country star, Wilson emerged in her thirties with a fully formed artistic profile, which she has maintained consistently. The subject matter of her songs embraces many standard country subjects, demonstrated by tracks on her 2007 album *One of the Boys*: hard drinking ("There's a Place in the Whiskey"), hard loving ("Come to Bed"), hard losing ("Pain Killer"), and—to be sure—country pride ("There Goes the Neighborhood" and "Good Ole Boy"); her next album (2010), released on the Redneck Records label, was aggressively titled *I Got Your Country Right Here*. Musically, although fiddle and steel guitar players are listed in her album credits, these instruments are usually buried in the mix in favor of a strong, rock-oriented sound. (The featured fiddle parts in the choruses of "Redneck Woman" represent an obvious exception to this general observation.) The style of Wilson's music establishes a certain kinship with that of Toby Keith, while her deliberate "tough woman" image does have something of a precedent in the rockabilly output of Wanda Jackson (see Chapter 8). Whether Wilson's image corresponds directly to her personal lifestyle and ideals or whether it is more of a savvy construct targeted at a very specific audience demographic is the sort of question that typically eludes any definitive answer.

BOX 14.3 MORE COUNTRY ALTERNATIVES: *O BROTHER WHERE ART THOU?* AND THE RESURGENCE OF BLUEGRASS

The unexpected popularity of the Coen brothers' film *O Brother, Where Art Thou?* (2000)—and especially of its bestselling soundtrack album—illustrates once again the power of movies to carry musical styles and artists previously viewed as marginal into the mainstream. The movie deals with the odyssey of three escaped convicts in 1937 as they wander through Mississippi, and the music appropriately emphasizes rural Southern acoustic styles of this period. The soundtrack encompasses several generations of country artists and recordings, extending back to Harry "Mac" McClintock's

1928 version of "Big Rock Candy Mountain" (titled "The Big Rock Candy Mountains" on the original record) and forward to re-creations by twenty-first-century musicians of such "hillbilly" classics as "Keep on the Sunny Side" and "You Are My Sunshine."

From a musical standpoint, the most significant aspect of the *O Brother, Where Art Thou?* "phenomenon" was the way in which it pushed bluegrass music, and the artists associated with it, into the limelight. Bluegrass, a style modeled on that of the early acoustic string bands, was probably the original "alternative country" music, and it continued to flourish steadily as an "alternative" to western swing, honky-tonk, rockabilly, countrypolitan, and any number of other, more "modern," country idioms. The roots of bluegrass may be traced conveniently back to the time period in which *O Brother, Where Art Thou?* itself is set, since it was in 1938 that Bill Monroe formed the Blue Grass Boys (see Chapter 7). Throughout its long history, bluegrass has never lacked an enthusiastic, even passionate, following, but for most of this history that following was not large enough—in terms of actual numbers of fans or numbers of records sold—to move the music out of the margins as far as the big picture of American pop (or even the picture of country music, considered as a whole) was concerned. *O Brother* changed all that.

Among the artists featured on the movie soundtrack is bluegrass veteran **Ralph Stanley** (b. 1927 in Virginia, died 2016); he and his brother Carter (1925–1966) performed as the Stanley Brothers beginning in 1946 and produced a body of outstanding bluegrass recordings. After his brother's death, Ralph Stanley continued his own career as the leader of the Clinch Mountain Boys, another tradition-based ensemble. But Stanley can hold his own simply as a solo vocalist, and his unaccompanied performance of the eerie traditional lament "O Death" on the *O Brother* soundtrack is remarkably powerful. At the other end of the spectrum in almost every respect is **Alison Krauss** (b. 1971 in Illinois), who also sings traditional material on the soundtrack, but whose career before she reached the age of thirty had already ranged much further from strict traditionalism than Ralph Stanley ever desired to go.

A fiddling champion and bluegrass fan by the time she was twelve, Alison Krauss quickly went on to establish her credentials as a bandleader, vocalist, and producer, as well as a valuable collaborator on numerous recordings by other artists; at the time of this writing, she ranks fourth among all-time Grammy Award winners, with twenty-seven to her name. (We might call particular attention to Krauss's collaboration with Robert Plant, the lead singer of Led Zeppelin; this seemingly unlikely pairing resulted in the critically acclaimed, commercially successful, and Grammy Award–winning album *Raising Sand*, released in 2007.) Her fine albums with her band **Union Station** demonstrate both her close connections to traditional bluegrass and her interest in creating a distinctive and original sound that grows out of those connections. While Union Station employs the instruments of a typical bluegrass ensemble (fiddle, guitar, mandolin, dobro, banjo, and acoustic bass), the group also occasionally adds drums and even an upright electric bass to its sound, and their repertoire ranges far and wide—from traditional country material and Woody Guthrie's "Pastures of Plenty" to the 1968 pop hit "Baby, Now That I've Found You" and newly composed material by group member Ron Block and other rising artists in the "alternative country" field (such as Gillian Welch, a talented singer-songwriter who is also heard on the *O Brother* soundtrack). That the term "bluegrass" can be employed to characterize the music of two excellent musicians as different in age, temperament, and musical proclivities—not to mention gender (female bluegrass stars are still unquestionably the exception)!—as Ralph Stanley and Alison Krauss attests to the liveliness and importance of this supposedly "marginal" genre of music. These two artists, as well as the unexpected success of the *O Brother* soundtrack, opened the door for a new wave of bluegrass-tinged indie folk acts—many of whom came from across the pond, including Mumford & Sons (England), First Aid Kit (Sweden), and Of Monsters and Men (Iceland)—to achieve mainstream success in the twenty-first century.

Latinx Superstars of the 1990s

As the worldwide market for Latin music began a rapid expansion during the 1990s, several superstars embodied the ambition of many Latinx musicians to break into the mainstream pop charts while maintaining the loyalty of audiences in their own local communities. These artists shared an ambition to reach the broadest possible audience while remaining true to their musical roots.

Born in Havana, Gloria María Fajardo García, better known to the world as *Gloria Estefan* (b. 1957), fled Cuba with her family when Fidel Castro and the Communists rose to power in the late 1950s. (Her father, a soldier, had worked as a bodyguard for the deposed dictator Fulgencio Batista.) In 1975 she auditioned for the Miami Latin Boys, a local wedding band headed by keyboardist Emilio Estefan. The group soon changed its name to Miami Sound Machine, and four years later Fajardo and Estefan married. Miami Sound Machine's fusion of pop, disco, and salsa earned a devoted local following, and their breakthrough 1985 album *Primitive Love* scored three Top Ten pop hits in the United States. *Primitive Love* included the energetic salsa-meets-disco party song "Conga" (Number 1 dance, Number 10 pop, Number 60 R&B), the first single to crack *Billboard*'s pop, dance, Black, and Latin charts simultaneously.

Miami Sound Machine's next album, *Let It Loose* (1988), sold 6 million copies in the United States and included four more Top 10 hits. Soon thereafter, Gloria Estefan took top billing, and her 1989 album *Cuts Both Ways* yielded her second Number 1 hit, "Don't Wanna Lose You" (Number 1 pop, Number 2 adult contemporary). While touring in support of the album, Estefan's bus was struck by a tractor trailer, and she suffered a broken vertebra that required extensive surgery and kept her off the road for over a year. She resurfaced in 1991 with the album *Into the Light*, again topping the singles charts with "Coming Out of the Dark," a song inspired by her accident. Throughout the 1990s, Estefan stayed in the public eye, recording her first Spanish-language album, the international hit *Mi Tierra [My Homeland]* (1993); appearing at the 1996 Summer Olympics in front of an international audience of 2 billion people; and capitalizing on the late-1990s revival of popular interest in disco music with the dance album *Gloria!* (1998), which included the single "Oye!" (Number 1 dance/club music, Number 1 Latin).

With over 100 million albums sold worldwide throughout the course of her career, Gloria Estefan has in recent years continued her formula of alternating among dance-oriented pop, English-language love songs, and Spanish-language tracks aimed at an international Latin American audience. In 2005 Estefan scored a hit in England with the release of "Dr. Pressure," which reached Number 3 on the UK singles chart and also sold well in continental Europe and Australia. "Dr. Pressure" was a collaboration with the Scottish musician Mylo that combined his EDM hit "Drop the Pressure" (2005) and Miami Sound Machine's 1984 single "Dr. Beat." (This is an example of a **mashup**, a recording that digitally combines two or more pre-existing tracks, usually by overlaying the vocal track of one song over the music track of another.) In 2007 Estefan returned to her roots with *90 Millas*, an album of original Spanish-language songs inspired by her native Cuba that featured a roster of veteran Latinx musicians, including Johnny

Gloria Estefan, c. 1980s.

Pacheco, salsa bandleader and cofounder of Fania Records (see Chapter 12); and rock guitarist Carlos Santana (see Chapter 11). In 2015, her life story was adopted for a Broadway musical, *On Your Feet!*, and she was awarded the Presidential Medal of Freedom.

Selena (1971–1995), known to her fans as "The Queen of Tejano (Texas-Mexican) music," was born Selena Quintanilla-Pérez in Lake Jackson, Texas. Her father was a working musician, and Selena began performing at the age of ten backed by his band, Los Dinos. (Because English was her first language, in her early years Selena had to learn Spanish song lyrics phonetically.) After facing a series of financial challenges, the family relocated to Corpus Christi, Texas, where they made a living performing at fairs, weddings, and *quinceañeras* (a traditional coming-of-age ceremony held on a girl's fifteenth birthday). Their efforts paid off in 1983 when the thirteen-year-old Selena re-corded her first album for Freddie Records, a local independent label.

Selena's reputation as a singer continued to spread in the region, and in 1989 she signed with the Latin division of EMI Records. By the mid-1990s she had released a series of popular albums drawing on the traditional accordion band style of Texas-Mexican music, the romantic *ranchera* song tradition of Mexico, and a pan-Latin dance music style called *cumbia* (a genre that originated in Colombia and eventually became popular throughout Latin America). In 1994 she played a role in the film *Don Juan DeMarco*, starring Johnny Depp, and won her first Grammy with the multi-million-selling album *Amor Prohibido [Forbidden Love]* (Number 1 Latin, Number 29 pop), knocking Gloria Estefan's *Mi Tierra* out of the top position.

In 1995 Selena was recording her first English-language album and preparing for her breakthrough into the pop charts when her life took a tragic turn. Alerted by her family that Yolanda Saldívar, president of Selena's Texas fan club, was embezzling money from the club, she decided to fire her. Soon thereafter, Selena agreed to meet Saldívar at a Corpus Christi motel to retrieve paperwork for tax purposes. After an argu-ment, Saldívar drew a gun from her purse, pointing it at Selena. As the singer turned to run from the room, Saldívar shot her once in the back. Critically wounded, Selena ran toward the lobby to get help and was transported to a local hospital, where she died from a loss of blood.

Selena's death was an event of iconic importance in the lives of her millions of fans, comparable in its emotional impact to the death of Elvis Presley or John Lennon. The funeral of the twenty-three-year-old singer—posthumously characterized by the media as "the Mexican Madonna"—reportedly drew sixty thousand people, and her birthday, April 16, was declared Selena Day in Texas. Selena's album *Thinking of You*, released after her death, was the first ever by a Hispanic artist to debut at Number 1 on the pop album charts in the United States. A film based upon her life, starring the Puerto Rican American pop star Jennifer Lopez, was released in 1997, and in 2005 a concert in her honor, *Selena ¡VIVE!,* became the highest-rated and most-viewed Spanish-language show in American television history. Fittingly, the biggest star to participate in *Selena ¡VIVE!* was Gloria Estefan, who sang Selena's posthumous hit single "I Could Fall in Love." Though they apparently met face-to-face only once, and though their lives took quite different courses—one of them able to sustain a musical career for more than three decades, the other murdered just before her twenty-fourth birthday—the careers of Gloria Estefan and Selena intersected in interesting ways, both on the *Billboard* charts and as important forces in the emergence of a crossover market for Latinx singers.

The success of these women helped make room for Latinx superstars in the late 90s. Although he was the son of internationally renowned Spanish singer Julio Iglesias, **Enrique Iglesias** (b. 1975) was determined to make a name for himself without the aid of his famous last name, marketing his original demo tapes under the nom de plume "Enrique Martinez." Born in Madrid, the young Iglesias was sent to live with his father in Miami after his grandfather was kidnapped by Basque separatists. Because of Julio's rigorous touring schedule, Enrique was largely raised by his nanny, Elvira Olivares. Once a contract was secured with the Mexican label Fonovisa, his self-titled debut album *Enrique Iglesias* (1995, dedicated to Olivares) was released under his real name, and quickly became a hit. Four singles hit Number 1 on *Billboard*'s Hot Latin Tracks chart, and the album won a Grammy for Best Latin Pop Performance.

Breaking into the U.S. market with songs sung entirely in Spanish was, in 1995, a relatively recent phenomenon largely made possible by the success of *Mi Tierra* just two years earlier. Iglesias and Selena continued to jockey for top chart positions through-out the mid-90s. Three singles from Iglesias's sophomore release *Vivir* ("Enamorado Por Primera Vez," "Solo En Tí," and "Miente") set a record in 1997 by collectively hold-ing the Number 1 position on Hot Latin Tracks for twenty-six consecutive weeks. His best-known song in the United States, "Bailamos" (Number 1 Hot 100) was originally released on the soundtrack to the 1999 film *Wild Wild West* (it would later be released on Iglesias's first English-language album *Enrique*). Despite its title, the song is sung mostly in English; only the memorable chorus hook sounds in Spanish. The track's clever blend of traditional Spanish guitar with a dance-friendly Europop beat helped make it a massive crossover hit topping charts world-wide.

"Bailamos" is part of what has been called the "Latin Pop Explosion" of the late 1990s: a high demand for Latinx musicians singing mostly English-language songs with crossover Latin-Europop accompaniment. Puerto Rican pop sensation **Ricky Martin** (b. in San Juan, 1971), whose Spanish-language songs had been internationally successful for years, was a huge player in this explosion. In 1999 his first English-language single, "Livin' La Vida Loca," debuted in the Number 1 position on the *Billboard* Hot 100, and the corresponding album *Ricky Martin* would eventually sell 15 million copies world-wide. Another hugely successful artist who first achieved success in the U.S. in this explosion is the Colombian singer-songwriter *Shakira* (b. in Barranquilla, 1977), whose 1998 record *Dónde Están los Ladrones?* went on to sell more than 4 million copies.

Globalization and the Rise of "World Music"

During the 1980s the boundary between mainstream and marginal music became ever fuzzier, and the twin pressures to expand the global market for American popular music and create new alternative genres and audiences within the American market grew ever stronger. One of the most interesting results of these processes was the emer-gence of a category called **world music**. The term was first systematically used in the late 1980s by independent record label owners and concert promoters, and it entered the popular music marketplace as a replacement for longer-standing categories such as "traditional music," "international music," and "ethnic music." These sorts of records were traditionally positioned in the very back of record stores, in bins containing low-turnover items such as Irish folk song collections, Scottish bagpipe samplers, German polka records, recordings by tourist bands from the Caribbean and Hawaii, and perhaps a few scholarly recordings of so-called "primitive" music from Africa, Native America, or Asia. International records were generally purchased by immigrants hungry for a taste of home, cross-cultural music scholars such as ethnomusicologists, and a handful of aficionados. In general, while transnational entertainment corporations became ever more successful at marketing American pop music around the globe, most of the world's music continued to have little or no direct influence on the American marketplace.

To be fair, we can point to some examples of international influence on the American pop mainstream before the 1980s—Cuban rumba, Hawaiian guitar, and Mexican marimba records of the 1920s and 1930s; Indian classical musician *Ravi Shankar's* album *Live at the Monterey Pop Festival*, which reached Number 43 in 1967, as the counterculture was at its peak; "Grazing in the Grass" (1968), a Number 1 hit by the South African jazz musician Hugh Masekela; or "Soul Makossa" (1973), the Top 40 dance club single by the Cameroonian pop musician Manu Dibango, often cited as a primary influence on disco music. But these cosmopolitan influences were typically filtered through the sensibilities of Western musicians and channeled by the strategies of American and European record companies and publishing firms. A quintessential example of this tendency is the Tokens' rock 'n' roll hit "The Lion Sleeps Tonight" (Number 1 pop, 1961), an adaptation of a hit single by the urban folk group the Weavers entitled "Wimoweh" (Number 14 pop, 1952). "Wimoweh" had in turn been an adaptation of a 1939 South African recording by a vocal group made up of Zulu mine workers called Solomon Linda and the Evening Birds. By the time the Evening Birds' song reached the ears of Americans, it had undergone several bouts of invasive surgery, including the insertion of a pop-friendly melodic hook and English lyrics, and the removal of all royalty rights pertaining to the original performers.

This sort of rip-off—a basic operating procedure for many years in the fields of American rhythm & blues and country music, as well as in the international music market—reflected the global imbalances of power that had initially been created by Western colonialism. Later world fusion or world beat projects—including Paul Simon's pioneering albums *Graceland* (see Chapter 13) and *The Rhythm of the Saints*; the annual World Music and Dance (WOMAD) Festival, initiated in 1982 by Peter Gabriel; and various recordings by David Byrne and *Ry Cooder*—helped to redress this imbalance to some degree. Nonetheless, the unequal economic relationship between "the West" and "the rest" continues to haunt such cross-cultural collaborations up to the present day.

The 1980s also saw musicians from Africa, South Asia, the Near East, Eastern Europe, and Latin America touring the United States with increasing frequency and appearing, even if rarely, on the *Billboard* pop charts. The first indication that musicians from the so-called Third World might gain increased access to the American market was the release in 1982 of the album *Juju Music* by a Nigerian group called the African Beats, led by the guitarist *King Sunny Adé*. Featuring an infectious brand of urban African dance music that blended electric guitars, Christian church hymns, and Afro-Caribbean rhythms with the pulsating sound of the Yoruba "talking drum," *Juju Music* sold over 100,000 copies and rose to Number 111 on *Billboard*'s album chart. The African Beats' next album, *Synchro System*, reached as high as Number 91 on the chart; however, the group was soon thereafter dropped by Island Records and never again appeared on the American pop charts.

In an article published in 1982 in the *Village Voice* by the popular music critic Greg Tate, entitled "Are You Ready for Juju?" the author explicitly identified King Sunny Adé as a potential replacement for Bob Marley, the Jamaican reggae superstar who had very recently died. On one level, this association seems perfectly logical, and it probably reflects the strategic thinking of Island Records, who released the Adé albums. Adé might well have had a shot at equaling Marley's success, but the fact that he sang in Yoruba, a language spoken by precious few American listeners, rather than Marley's richly spiced version of Jamaican English doomed him to failure from the beginning. Twenty-five years later, hits such as "Despacito" by *Luis Fonzi (ft. Daddy Yankee)*, as well as a number of consecutive chart toppers by the Korean boy-band BTS, have made non-Anglophone songs increasingly marketable as the linguistic makeup of the United States continues to diversify. In 2019 the Barcelonian singer-songwriter Rosalía became the first all-Spanish-language artist to be nominated for the Best New Artist Grammy. For his day, Adé did succeed in establishing a market for so-called Afro-pop music, opening the door for African popular musicians such as Youssou N'dour (Senegal), Salif Keita (Mali), Thomas Mapfumo (Zimbabwe), and Ali Farka Touré.

By 1990, when the heading "world music" first appeared above a *Billboard* record chart, it was as a subcategory of the broader heading "adult alternative albums." Interestingly, this latter category also included New Age music, a genre of instrumental music designed to facilitate contemplative and mystical moods that is sometimes loosely linked with the religious and healing practices of Native American, African, and Asian cultures. The larger category "adult alternative albums" suggests an effort on the industry's part to identify forms of alternative music that would appeal to an affluent baby boomer audience, rather than to the younger audience attracted by rock bands such as Nirvana. (Since 1991 the National Academy of Recording Arts and Sciences [NARAS]

Ali Farka Touré.

has limited its Grammy Awards for world music, New Age, folk, Latin, reggae, blues, polka, and various other alternative genres to albums only, presumably on the assumption that such genres are unlikely to generate hit singles.) The world music sections of most record stores usually do not include Latin dance music (salsa) or reggae, genres that sell enough records to justify their own discrete territories.

What, then, is world music? In a strictly musical sense, it is a pseudo-genre, taking into its sweep styles as diverse as African urban pop (juju); Pakistani dance club music (bhangara); Australian aboriginal rock music (the band Yothu Yindi); and even the Bulgarian State Radio and Television Female Vocal Choir, whose evocatively titled 1987 release *Le Mystère des Voix Bulgares* (*The Mystery of the Bulgarian Voices*) reached Number 165 on the *Billboard* album chart in 1988. Bestselling albums on *Billboard*'s world music chart have featured the Celtic group Clannad (whose popularity was boosted in the United States by their appearance in the soundtrack for a Volkswagen advertisement); Spanish flamenco music (played by the Gypsy Kings, a hotel band from France); Tibetan Buddhist chants (presented by Mickey Hart, one of the drummers for the Grateful Dead); and diverse collaborations between American and English rock stars and musicians from Africa, Latin America, and South Asia. The overlap among various types of "adult alternative" music—including New Age, world music, techno, and certain forms of European sacred music—is reflected in the commercial success of albums like *Vision* (1994), a mélange of "twelfth-century chant, world beat rhythms, and electronic soundscapes," as one press release put it. (It's hard to imagine better confirmation of the old adage that "the past is another country.") The attraction of world music for its contemporary American audience is bound up with stereotyped images of the "exotic," whether these be discovered on imaginary pilgrimages to Africa and the Himalayas, or in time travel back to the monastic Christianity of medieval Europe. Nonetheless, not every culture's music proved commercially viable during this world music gold rush. This may explain the almost total absence on the *Billboard* charts of music from East Asia which, prior to the K-pop and J-pop explosions of the 2010s and 2020s (see Chapter 15), had never been successfully marketed to American listeners.

We are all familiar with the assertion that music is a universal language, by which people usually mean to suggest that music can transcend the boundaries separating diverse nations, cultures, and languages. This statement, however comforting, does not stand up to close scrutiny—even within American culture, one person's music may be another person's noise. Nevertheless, the music industry has wasted no time in chaining the rhetoric of musical universalism to the profit motive, as, for example, in this mid-1990s advertisement for the E-mu Proteus/3 World, a digital device programmed with hundreds of samples of world music:

> Enrich Your Music with a Global Texture. As borders dissolve, traditions are shared. And this sharing of cultures is most powerful in the richness of music.... E-mu has gathered these sounds and more—192 in all. Use them to emulate traditional world instruments or as raw material for creating one-of-a-kind synthesized sounds of your own. (Théberge 1997, 201)

Music, with its ability to flow over the boundaries of society and the borders of nations, holds open the possibility that we may glimpse something familiar and sympathetic in people strange to us—that the inequalities of the world in which we live may for a moment be suspended, or even undermined, in the act of making or listening to music. Still, the suggestion that installing a digital device in your home studio in order to emulate the "gathered sounds" of faraway people has anything to do with "sharing cultures" reveals a critically impoverished vision of cross-cultural communication. There is no denying that music has the potential to traverse the boundaries of culture and language and thereby add to our understanding of people very different from us. But the ultimate responsibility for interpreting its meanings, and determining its impact, lies with the listener.

WE HAVE NEARLY completed our journey through the history of American popular music, from the emergence of minstrelsy up through the invention of the phonograph and radio, the Jazz Age, the swing era, and the birth of rock 'n' roll into the age of rock music, rap, digital technology, and global pop. In our concluding chapter, we examine the state of popular music in the twenty-first century focusing on the transformative impact of digital technologies on the production and dissemination of music and the operations of the music business; the emergence of a new generation of rock music and hip-hop artists; and the impact of globalization on American popular music.

Key Terms

alternative music	grunge	raves
electronic dance music (EDM)	hardcore	riot grrrl
	house music	techno
gangsta rap	mashup	world music

Key People

Alan Jackson	Enrique Iglesias	Jello Biafra
Alison Krauss	Eric "Eazy-E" Wright	Johnny Cash
Andre "Dr. Dre" Young	Flavor Flav	Kathleen Hanna
Ani DiFranco	George Strait	k.d. lang
Bikini Kill	Gloria Estefan	King Sunny Adé
Chuck D	Gretchen Wilson	Krist Novoselic
Dave Grohl	Ice-T	Kurt Cobain
DMC	Jam Master Jay	Lauryn Hill

Marshall "Eminem" Mathers	Queen Latifah	Selena
MC Hammer	Ralph Stanley	Snoop Doggy Dogg
Notorious B.I.G.	Ravi Shankar	Sonic Youth
N.W.A	R.E.M.	Taylor Swift
O'Shea "Ice Cube" Jackson	Ricky Martin	Terminator X
Phish	Run	Toby Keith
Professor Griff	Run DMC	Tupac (2Pac) Shakur
Public Enemy	Ry Cooder	Union Station
	Sean "Puffy" Combs	Vanilla Ice

Review Questions

1. Describe the similarities and differences between East Coast and West Coast rap styles. Include significant artists.
2. Does rap reinforce stereotypes, or does it give a realistic depiction of urban life in African American communities?
3. What are the meanings of "alternative" as it pertains to popular music styles?
4. What is the "Seattle Sound"?
5. Name a few of the important styles of world music that emerged in the 1980s.

The Internet Age, 2000–

15

"1,000 songs in your pocket!" This memorable advertising slogan for the Apple Corporation's new iPod music player, launched in 2001, signaled a sea change in the ways that consumers interacted with recorded music. Fast forward to 2007 and the introduction of another product by the same company: the iPhone, whose promotional catch phrase was "This changes everything. Again." Indeed, consumers would now no longer have to devote much effort to collect music; they could just search for any song or video and access it largely for free with the press of a button. Music technology—for both consumers and producers—changed so rapidly over the first twenty years of the new millennium as to strain comparison with any previous era of popular music. The internet became a vast virtual archive, bringing within easy reach music from many historical periods, traditions, and genres.

And yet, amid all of this technological innovation, it is not hard to locate examples of "retro" trends among pop singles of the new millennium. The bestselling single of the 2000s was Mariah Carey's "We Belong Together" (Number 1 for fourteen weeks in 2005), a sentimental song performed by a crooner with cooing background vocalists and a chord progression and lyrics evocative of 1970s soft soul music. "Poker Face" (Number 1 for seven weeks in 2009) featured **Lady Gaga** (Stefani Germanotta, b. 1986), a charismatic singer and fashion icon performing in a high-energy dance music video that was heavily influenced by 1980s synth-pop. The melody, lyrics, strong backbeat, gritty vocal delivery, and rhythmically emphatic backup singing of Adele's "Rolling in the Deep"—the biggest hit of 2011—are an homage to the golden age of 1960s singers like Aretha Franklin.

Perhaps no performer is more emblematic of the retro consciousness of popular music in the new millennium than **Bruno Mars** (Peter Gene Hernandez, b. 1985), a Hawaiian-born musician of Puerto Rican, Jewish, and Filipino descent. Mars's interest in the history of popular music was influenced by the fact that he grew up in a multigenerational family of musicians and from the age of three performed the music of Elvis Presley, the Jackson 5, and the Temptations onstage. His song "Just the Way You Are," the biggest-selling single of 2012, is a pop ballad with an anthemic chorus, sung in a crooning tenor voice to a hip-hop-derived groove. The video of the song opens with images of Mars singing to the object of his affections, who is listening to music on a 1980s Sony Walkman, complete with vintage over-the-ear headphones. Mars unreels magnetic tape from a cassette labeled with his name and manipulates the tape to create a series of animated images of musical instruments, his prospective lover, and himself, all while singing and playing an upright piano. The retro theme established by the cassette tape and Walkman is reinforced at intervals by a barely audible digital imitation of the scratchy surface noise of a vinyl LP record and by Bruno's attire, which includes a fedora hat hearkening back to stars of the past such as Frank Sinatra and Michael Jackson.

Another commercially successful example of Mars's incorporation of earlier musical styles is "Uptown Funk" (the Number 1 digitally downloaded and streamed track of 2015), a collaboration with British producer Mark Ronson. This track evokes the Minneapolis-based funk sound pioneered by Prince (see Chapter 13) and features several members of the Gap Band, a funk outfit from Tulsa, Oklahoma, who had scored a series of gold albums during the early 1980s. In the video of the song (which by 2021, had been viewed 4.1 billion times, making it the seventh most watched YouTube video of all time), Mars's vocal style, clothes, and dance movements reference Prince, James Brown, Michael Jackson, and other pop culture influences from the 1980s and earlier decades.

Of course, genres such as hip-hop, alternative rock, electronic dance music, and Latin pop remain enormously popular, but their recent evolution seems more continuous and gradual than in previous decades, and it is difficult to identify innovative "breakthrough" albums that have redefined the popular musical landscape to the extent of Bob Dylan's *Highway 61 Revisited* (1965), the Beach Boys' *Pet Sounds* (1966), the Beatles' *Sgt. Pepper* (1967), Michael Jackson's *Thriller* (1982), Public Enemy's *It Takes a Nation of Millions to Hold Us Back* (1988), and Nirvana's *Nevermind* (1991). It could be argued that—unlike all the previous decades since the dawn of sound recording—there really is no style of popular music that can be identified specifically as "the sound of the 2000s."

The real story of popular music since the year 2000 has less to do with the rise of a signature or dominant style, or with radical transformations in the sound of music, than with an interlinked set of changes in the technologies used to produce, record, distribute and experience music, and in the structure of the music business. The introduction of digital recording technologies, portable media such as the iPhone, and internet-based promotion, downloading, and streaming of music and video files;

Bruno Mars in performance in 2012.

the decline of physical media such as the compact disc; changes in the relationships between artists, audiences, and entertainment corporations; and the increasing importance of music licensing and concert tours as profit centers for the industry—all have converged since 2000 to produce a musical landscape that is familiar in some ways, yet radically transformed in others.

In every historical period, certain musicians help us make sense of the moment we are living through. The late rock star and actor David Bowie (1947–2016), always ahead of his time, evoked something of the sensibility of the new millennium in the lyrics for his 2002 song "Sunday":

> *Everything has changed*
> *For in truth, it's the beginning of an end*
> *And nothing has changed*
> *And everything has changed*

"Nothing has changed, and everything has changed." In this final chapter of our journey we will assess this most recent phase in the history of American popular music, with an eye toward the past and the future.

The Impact of Digital Recording

Developments in sound recording technology and software have exerted a transformational impact on popular music since the late 1990s. "Digital audio workstation" (DAW) programs such as **Pro Tools**, a virtual sound mixing board designed to run on computers, became the professional standard. Pro Tools (introduced in 1990) was a significant departure from most previous recording systems in two ways. Older recording technology, based on the use of multitrack tape recording, imposed many limitations on the kinds of changes that could be made after the music had been recorded. By contrast, the new, purely digital software-based format allowed virtually unlimited alteration of the music with no loss in sound quality. Furthermore, Pro Tools was based on a visual interface—the sound of the music was represented graphically on the computer screen. This led to new ways of thinking about popular music production, particularly in terms of patterns, repetition, and form. It became a relatively simple matter to cut-and-paste the same chorus of a song each time it came around rather than play it again. This led to a more modular approach to recording, with songs being *assembled* from constituent parts more than *performed* in the recording studio. Ricky Martin's "Livin' la Vida Loca" (1999) was the first Number 1 single to be produced entirely on Pro Tools, rather than in a conventional studio setting.

Today more affordable DAWs permit musicians working on a limited budget to set up a basic home studio at relatively small expense. Programs such as Logic, Ableton, and Fruity Loops are relatively inexpensive and can be run on a laptop computer. Some of these applications are even free (e.g., Reaper), and many, such as Apple's GarageBand, can be run directly on a smartphone. Most of these DAWs contain software synthesizers that can be controlled directly by a MIDI keyboard (or a standard computer keyboard), and thus require no external instruments or microphones.

As with any increase in creative options, the move to digital recording was a double-edged sword. On one hand, it gave musicians an unprecedented amount of control over every aspect of their sound. On the other, it also made possible a new level of musical obsessiveness that could easily destroy the spontaneity that has so often been at the heart of popular music. It is now common practice, for example, for a producer to quickly go through an entire song and erase the sound of the vocalist inhaling before each phrase they sing. Do such gestures serve to improve the sound of a recording or dehumanize it? As the drummer Matt Cameron put it in an interview with the *Philadelphia Inquirer* about Pearl Jam's 2002 album *Riot Act*, recorded "live" in a studio, "This is definitely our anti-Pro Tools record. . . . It's more interesting hearing musicians in a room playing hard, with the tempo fluctuating slightly as the band heats up. Perfection is boring."

One of the most influential, and controversial, aspects of digital technology's potential for altering the sound of the human voice was introduced on Cher's Number 1 hit "Believe" (the bestselling single of 1998). The track featured a highly distinctive, digitally manipulated vocal sound, courtesy of a new audio processor called **Auto-Tune**. Since then, Auto-Tune has been used on recordings by artists across a wide range of popular music genres, not only to correct a singer's pitch, but also to create an effect that can be described as hearing the voice leap from note to note stepwise, like a keyboard synthesizer. (It can also create what has been characterized as a "robotic" or "alien" vocal timbre.) Just as Pro Tools did for DAWs, the original Auto-Tune software (introduced in 1997) spawned an explosion of other pitch correcting options for home engineers. Some of these are competing products (e.g., Melodyne), while others are simply algorithms built into the DAWs themselves. Most DAWs allow the user to change individual pitches manually using a mouse and keyboard, which leads to greater flexibility, including the ability to radically change a vocalist's range rather than simply "correcting" out-of-tune pitches.

Pioneered by the Florida-born rapper T-Pain on singles like "I'm Sprung" (2005) and "Buy U a Drank (Shawty Snappin')" (Number 1 R&B/hip-hop, 2007), the robotic, cool, otherworldly effects of Auto-Tune were soon adopted by established artists such as Snoop Dogg and Kanye West. On West's hit album *808s and Heartbreak* (Number 1 pop and R&B/hip-hop, 2008), it was combined with other digital technology (including the Roland TR-808 drum machine) to create what has been characterized as a minimalist, alienated sound palette. Alongside these more experimental applications, Auto-Tune was soon in wide use by singers in genres ranging from country and western to rock to rhythm & blues, as a means of revising vocal imperfections and saving time and money in the studio.

Some prominent musicians rebelled against the seeming ubiquity of Auto-Tune, which they saw as a technological substitute for musical talent and experience. At the 51st Grammy Awards (2009) the indie rock band Death Cab for Cutie protested against the widespread use of the processing device, framing it as a threat to "the note that's not so perfectly in pitch and just gives the recording some soul and some kind of real character." On the other hand, the Atlanta-born rapper Future (a.k.a. "Future Hendrix") has received critical acclaim for using Auto-Tune as an artistic tool in hip-hop. In an online review of his debut major-label album *Pluto* (2012), *Pitchfork* noted that the rapper "miraculously shows that it's still possible for Auto-Tune to be an interesting artistic tool," asserting that he "finds a multitude of ways for the software to accentuate and color emotion."

Once artists like Future embraced Auto-Tune as a creative tool, other vocal manipulation technologies soon followed suit. Previously treated as a robotic novelty sound (e.g., the droning "Domo Arigato" in Styx's 1983 single "Mr. Roboto"), the **vocoder** has now taken on a different role as a way to enrich vocal tracks. On the track "San Francisco" (2018), Sofia Carson's collaboration with the Swedish EDM producer duo Galantis, several vocoder tracks provide harmonies both above and below Carson's live vocal. Each of these vocoder tracks preserves the intelligibility of Carson's lyrics, but replaces her pitches with those specified by a MIDI keyboard. This makes it possible for a vocalist to "sing" pitches that are not normally within her range. The innovative duo known as 100 Gecs achieves a similar effect through entirely different technological means. By speeding up and manually adjusting the tone of her singing (a vocal sound sometimes referred to as "nightcore"), vocalist Laura Les (b. 1994), who identifies as a woman despite being born male, is able to give her voice an exaggeratedly "feminine" sound. On the 2019 track "xXXi_wud_nvrstøp_ÜXXx" Les starts applying the technique gradually to isolated syllables, creating a melody that gets higher and higher in pitch (eventually reaching a superhuman range), while the tuning manipulation creates a melody that leaps so quickly between distant notes that it would be impossible to sing without the technology.

As we have seen many times, popular music can become a sounding board for larger cultural issues, including the tension between new technologies and notions of authenticity. At one end of the spectrum stand musicians like Death Cab for Cutie and Pearl Jam who have rejected aspects of digital technology and celebrate hands-on, analog, low-fidelity approaches as a basis of their aesthetic. At the other end are artists like Future and 100 Gecs who have avidly incorporated digital synthesis, recording, and mixing techniques into the very heart of their work.

It is also worth noting that the "retro" impulse shown by artists such as Bruno Mars has in some ways been served by the new digital technologies, which have created a deep archive of recordings that allows musicians to explore the past as never before. The techno musician Moby did precisely this in 1999 on his bestselling album *Play*, when he sampled segments of performances by Georgia Sea Islands singer Bessie Jones, Texas blues singer Boy Blue, and the Shining Light Gospel Choir, all of whom had been recorded in the field some forty years earlier by the legendary folk music scholar Alan Lomax. When Moby made all of the tracks on *Play* available for licensing in films and television advertising—an aspect of the music business referred to as "synchronization"—millions of Americans and listeners in other countries were exposed to the sounds of Southern folk music, filtered through digital technology and a distinctly contemporary sensibility.

In a 2015 interview in *Rolling Stone* magazine the singer Adele cited Moby's *Play* as a major influence on her own musical sensibility:

> There's something that I find really holy about that *Play* album . . . the way it makes me feel. Even though there's nothing holy or preachy about it. There's just something about it—maybe the gospel samples. But it makes me feel alive, that album, still. And I remember my mum having that record.[1]

Here we see digital technology and musical memory linked in a kind of symbiotic relationship; and are reminded that what goes around comes around, but never in precisely the same form.

---

1. Brian Hiatt, "17 Things You Learn Hanging Out with Adele," *Rolling Stone*, November 30, 2015.

Moby in Russia in 2011.

Music and the Internet: The Revolution Will Be Streamed

By the beginning of the twenty-first century, digital recording had become the norm, and an unprecedented wave of change was sweeping through every aspect of popular music. The established relationships among technology, commerce, and culture that had sustained the music for most of its life were breaking down, and every aspect of this system was undergoing transformation. Thus far we have focused on the impact of digital technologies on the production of music; now let's turn our attention to parallel changes in the marketing and consumption of popular music.

The digital revolution in music distribution was kicked off in the 1990s by the introduction of MPEG, a digital file compression algorithm that allows files to be squeezed to as little as one-twelfth of their original size. This, in turn, allowed for the first time the wide and rapid dissemination of sound recordings over the internet, a technological precondition for the emergence of a huge market in downloaded music, and for the emergence of personal digital audio players such as the iPod. The introduction of MPEG technology—and its descendants, the **MP3** audio and **MP4** video encoding formats—spurred a series of bitter struggles between entertainment corporations and small-scale entrepreneurs, echoing past conflicts between major and indie record labels, though on an even larger scale.

As with digital sampling, this new way of disseminating musical materials raised a host of thorny legal problems, centered on the issue of copyright. In 1999, an eighteen-year-old college dropout named Shawn Fanning developed **Napster**, an internet-based software program that allowed computer users to share and swap files, specifically music, through a centralized server. Soon thereafter, the **Recording Industry Association of America (RIAA)**—the trade association representing the major labels that controlled the sale and distribution of approximately 90 percent of the offline music in the United States—filed suit against Napster, charging them with "tributary copyright infringement." (This meant that the firm was accused not of violating copyright itself but of contributing to and facilitating other people's violation of the law.) In its countersuit, Napster argued that because the actual files were not permanently stored on its servers but rather transferred from user to user, it was not acting illegally. A federal court injunction finally forced Napster to shut down operations in February 2001, and users exchanged some 2.79 billion files in the closing days of Napster's existence as a free service.

FROM THE IPOD TO ITUNES

The development of new personal listening devices went hand in hand with the rise of file sharing on the internet. As we noted at the beginning of this chapter, in 2001 Apple Computer introduced the first-generation **iPod** player, which could store up to one thousand CD-quality tracks on its internal hard drive. The iPod and other MP3 players soon came to dominate the market for portable listening devices, in part because they provide listeners with the ability to build a unique library of music reflecting their personal tastes. (This trend had been initiated half a century earlier with the introduction of the 45 rpm record changer, which to a more limited degree allowed consumers to play their favorite songs in whatever order they chose; see Chapter 7.) The ability of the iPod to "shuffle" music—that is, to play tracks in a random order, mixing genres, performers, and historical periods—not only exerted an influence on personal listening habits but also provided a metaphor for the contemporary (some would say postmodern) state of consumer culture. (In 2005 Apple introduced the iPod Shuffle, promoted with the catchy slogans "Random Is the New Order" and "Lose Control. Love It.") The iPod has itself faded from popularity, due largely to the massive success of music- and video-capable "smartphones."

In the old days, a music fan who owned a turntable or CD player would go to a record store to purchase new music. The issue naturally arose of how best to sell MP3-based content to a new generation of consumers who owned portable listening devices. In 2001 Steve Jobs, the president of Apple Computers, launched a fee-based music downloading service called **iTunes**, which was designed to supply content for the then-new iPod. The following year Jobs negotiated a deal with the five biggest music corporations—EMI, Universal, Warner, Sony Music Entertainment, and BMG[2]—to make the majority of their recordings available for purchase and download. (At the time, there were a few

---

2. Sony and BMG merged in 2004; EMI was absorbed into Universal in 2012.

major holdouts, including the Beatles, Led Zeppelin, and Radiohead.) In 2003 the iTunes Store was launched, making some 200,000 tracks available for download for 99 cents each; later that year a version compatible with Microsoft Windows was introduced, vastly expanding the potential user base. Within a couple of years, iTunes commanded 70 percent of the online market and by 2008 had become the top music retailer in the United States. The importance of Apple's iTunes service to the commercial success of even the best-known musical acts was underscored in 2010 when the Beatles' Apple Corps (which controls their recordings) finally broke down and agreed to offer the band's music through iTunes. In just two months, the Beatles sold 5 million tracks and a million albums on the service.

STREAMING AUDIO

iTunes's dominance of the download market has been challenged by several competitors. In 2007 Amazon.com launched its own online store offering "open" MP3 files; and in 2008 Google launched Google Play to support its Android operating system, used on many non-Apple smartphones. However, the most fundamental change that took place in the music business during the 2010s was the shift away from downloading—a digital variation on the old model of selling music as a product, through stores—toward **streaming**, in which providers sell users access to music through a subscription model. (These services typically also include a free subscriber tier, which generates revenues through advertisements.)

One of the early pioneers of this format was **Pandora**, a music streaming service that operates like an individualized radio station, offering playlists to listeners based on their own preferences. Using a model that the company calls the "Music Genome," several hundred stylistic "attributes" (and thousands of associated "traits") are assigned to each track; as listeners choose songs to play, their selections are matched with similar tracks that "match" the genomes of these favorites. However, Pandora's listeners cannot select individual tracks and hear them immediately; nor can favorite songs be heard repeatedly. By 2015 the service had over 79 million active listeners around the world, only around 5 percent of whom were paying for the premium, ad-free service. Pandora has relied on copyright clauses that allow it to stream music in more or less the same manner that traditional radio stations broadcast songs on the air. This approach has fueled battles between the company and music corporations over royalty rates, which are higher for downloading services.

Pandora's competitors include on-demand streaming services such as **Spotify**, which launched in Europe in 2008 and in the United States in 2011. Spotify allows listeners to pick and choose the tracks they want to listen to, and, like Pandora, offers both a free and a paid "premium" service. By 2020 Spotify offered access to over 60 million tracks of music and claimed nearly 300 million active subscribers worldwide (around 45 percent of whom were paying subscribers, significantly higher than Pandora's 10 percent subscription rate). It is worth noting that prominent artists such as Radiohead, Coldplay, Adele, and Taylor Swift have at various times withheld their music from Spotify, citing concerns over inadequate royalty payments. Unlike download services like iTunes, which pay a fixed royalty per song or album, Spotify pays artists based on what they call "market share" (the number of streams of a given artist's songs as a proportion of total songs streamed on the service).

In 2015 the hip-hop musician and businessman Jay-Z acquired **Tidal**, a Scandinavian online streaming service that gave listeners access to high-definition, "lossless" files, which (unlike the older MP3 and MP4 formats) preserve all of the information in an original audio and video recording. Tidal attracted positive attention as an artist-owned label (Jay-Z's co-investors have included such A-list stars as Beyoncé, Kanye West, Alicia Keys, Madonna, Chris Martin, Nicki Minaj, and Daft Punk), and generated some market leverage by offering the exclusive release for some bestselling albums. Although Tidal boasted paying a higher percentage of subscriber fees back to artists, reports surfaced in 2017 that Tidal may have been inflating their reported 3 million subscribers, as well as the number of downloads for individual albums. (Tidal no longer discloses such data and has denied any wrongdoing in response to a number of pending suits.) The tension between the evolving revenue models of streaming sites and the demands of artists to be paid fairly for their work promises to remain a hot-button issue in coming years.

The impact of internet streaming on music sales has been unmistakable during the second decade of the 2000s, with revenue from music downloads in decline since hitting a peak of $3.9 billion in 2012. The major online music "stores" responded by introducing their own streaming services, Google's Music Store in 2011 (discontinued in 2020) and Apple's Apple Music in 2015. With over 100 million people in the United States regularly streaming music online, revenues from streaming surpassed all other sources for the first time in 2015. Yet fewer than one in ten of them paid for subscriptions, the majority opting instead for free, ad-supported service. Based upon these figures, *Variety* magazine estimated that the average annual revenue from a paid subscriber was $100 or more, whereas regular users of the ad-supported services were paying only around

Jay-Z.

$4 a year.[3] This means that the number of subscribers to the free music streaming services would have to triple to match the current revenues of the paid services—a target number that exceeds the current adult population of the United States!

Weary of this top-down distribution model, some artists have taken matters into their own hands, distributing their music for free, without the aid of record labels, on incubator websites such as Bandcamp or SoundCloud (e.g., Billie Eilish), while others, such as Lil' Nas X, have taken to the social media site TikTok as a way to generate viral fame. Eilish swept all four of the top Grammy Awards (New Artist, Record of the Year, Song of the Year, and Album of the Year) in 2020, and Lil' Nas X's hip-hop/country single "Old Town Road" (2019) held the Number 1 spot on the Hot 100 for an unprecedented 19 weeks. The success of these and other artists signals that these novel ways of circulating music can be just as lucrative—if not more so—than the old ones. Whether artists decide to release their music through streaming services, incubator sites, social media apps, or some yet-to-be realized internet distribution method, it is clear that the music business, and musicians seeking to make a living from their work, are facing unprecedented challenges and opportunities.

YOUTUBE

Another major outlet for popular music is **YouTube**, an online video website that was launched in 2005. The first big YouTube hit was a quirky video called "A Million Ways" (2005), featuring the Chicago-based rock band OK Go dancing on treadmill machines. The video itself cost the band only $4.99 to make, but it was ultimately downloaded 9 million times, transforming OK Go from locally popular musicians into international superstars. In 2006 Warner Music made a deal with YouTube to make its entire music video catalog available online, and soon thereafter Google bought YouTube for $1.65 billion in stock.

Over the next several years, YouTube became a major medium for the dissemination of popular music, as well as for "breaking" new pop stars. The best-known example of this phenomenon is Justin Bieber, the Canadian teen-pop star who was discovered at the age of fourteen by a music executive who saw a video that Bieber's mother had posted on YouTube. After a brief period of negotiation, Bieber was flown to Atlanta, where he met with the R&B singer Usher and signed a contract with Island Records. With a global fan base—the "Beliebers"—and over 113 million followers on Twitter (and gaining thousands every day), he was named the third most powerful celebrity in the world by *Forbes* in 2012. The singer and pop icon Lady Gaga also used YouTube to build her enormous international fan base. In 2010 Gaga's manager, Troy Carter, explained that her music videos were produced specifically for YouTube, confirming the website's authoritative command over territory formerly controlled by MTV.

Given its global reach, it is not surprising that YouTube has become a launching pad for international pop hits. In 2012 the South Korean K-pop star Psy scored a massive

---

3. Dawson, Jan, "RIAA Stats Mean Music Industry Must Focus on Subscriptions," *Variety*, March 22, 2016.

international hit with his video of "Gangnam Style," named after a trendy area in the capital city of Seoul. (According to Psy, the video humorously parodies Gangnam wannabes, people who claim to be from the neighborhood but dress and dance in a way that betrays their lack of sophistication.) "Gangnam Style," the eighth most watched video in YouTube's history (with over 4 billion views as of June 2021), peaked at Number 2 on the United States pop charts. While hit singles of overseas origin—such as "Grazin' in the Grass" by the South African trumpeter Hugh Masekela (Number 1, 1968) and Los Del Río's "Macarena" (Number 1, 1995)—were rare in the pre-internet days, the success of tracks like "Gangnam Style" and "Despacito" (2017; see Chapter 14) has relied in substantial measure on the global reach of YouTube.

The impact of YouTube has changed the music industry forever. In 2018 music videos became the most popular medium for music consumption in the United States, with 51 percent of all music being accessed on YouTube. The twentieth century saw numerous changes in musical media—the wax cylinder gave way to the shellac gramophone disc, which in turn yielded to the vinyl LP, the LP to the cassette, the cassette to the CD, the CD to MP3 files—but for the first time in music history the pre-eminent medium for disseminating popular music is now audiovisual (MP4). Artists in today's marketplace are just as likely to make as much money, if not more, from paid advertisements and product placements in their music videos on YouTube than from streaming audio royalties. As of 2021 Tidal, Apple Music, and Spotify are now hosting music videos in an effort to capture some of YouTube's market share, yet it remains to be seen how much, if at all, artists will benefit from audiovisual stream revenue with these for-profit subscription services.

Interestingly, the competing performing rights organizations, ASCAP (formed in 1914) and BMI (1940), appear to have reasserted their relevance after a period of readjustment. For many years the bulk of their activities focused on securing payments for the composers and lyricists who comprise their membership from the use of their compositions on radio and television and in films and live performances. The rise of digital streaming caught ASCAP and BMI flat-footed for a few years, but in early 2015 the two agencies announced that during the previous year they had tracked and processed a combined one *trillion* individual performances of songs across all platforms, generating a total of $1.7 billion in royalty payments to members. (This number had risen to $2.4 billion by 2019.) This is a fascinating example of older institutional structures adapting to new circumstances.

"On the Road Again": The New Popular Music Economy

Online downloading and streaming, the emergence of portable technologies for reproducing and listening to music, and the widespread availability of music recording software have posed serious challenges to the popular music industry, which had not changed its essential structures, strategies, and modes of operation since the

BOX 15.1 OLD SCHOOL MEDIA IN THE NEW MILLENNIUM: RADIO AND VINYL

Against the background of these changes in the distribution and consumption of popular music it is worth considering the fate of two long-standing media: commercial radio, introduced in 1920, and the vinyl long-playing disc or LP, which first hit the market in 1948.

In the early years of the twenty-first century, radio broadcasting was dominated by a corporation called Clear Channel Communications. At that time Clear Channel owned over twelve hundred radio stations, thirty-nine television stations, more than 100,000 advertising billboards, and over one hundred live performance venues, ranging from huge amphitheaters to dance clubs—all of which allowed them to present more than 70 percent of all live events nationwide. (This is a strategy referred to as "vertical integration," in which a corporation gains control over all aspects of the production of a commodity and its promotion and delivery to consumers.) Critics asserted that Clear Channel's use of its radio stations and billboards to advertise Clear Channel–booked shows at Clear Channel–owned venues was in essence a monopoly. The corporation also drew criticism for using "voice tracking," a practice in which DJs at the company's headquarters in Texas produced radio shows that were distributed to stations nationwide, but presented as though they were being broadcast locally.

Clear Channel's dominance of the entertainment market declined as outside forces—including the worldwide recession that began in 2008—impinged on its attempt to build a vertically integrated business. From its high point of over 1,200 radio stations, the company shrank to less than 850 outlets, divested itself of its TV and live concert operations, and rebranded its radio services as iHeartMedia. Still, the model of centralizing control in the media landscape continues to trouble some artists and popular music fans. It has been argued that a company's dominance of radio markets makes it harder for local musicians and artists to get their music played on local stations, leading to a homogenization of music broadcasting nationwide. Defenders of companies like Clear Channel argue that they are simply giving consumers what they want. Whatever one's viewpoint on the matter, this controversy is clearly a direct descendant of the introduction of standardized Top 40 playlists and the payola scandals of the 1950s, only on a much larger scale.

What is indisputable is the continuing importance of radio—in both its AM/FM and digital satellite formats—as an avenue for disseminating and promoting popular music. In a 2019 survey of media, Nielsen reported that radio reached 92 percent of adult Americans, more than any other medium, including television, smartphones, and personal computers.[4] Radio was also by a considerable margin the most frequent way that listeners reported discovering new music—at least twice as common as movies, online audio and video streaming sites/applications, or social media sites/applications. Despite the rise of digital downloading, streaming, and music videos, radio keeps chugging away.

Perhaps more surprising has been the recent resurgence of consumer interest in the 33⅓ rpm long-playing (LP) record album, first introduced by Columbia Records after World War II as an alternative to the 78 rpm discs that had dominated the market for several decades. The peak year for vinyl album sales in the United States was 1977, when record companies shipped 344 million of them. In 1988 sales of CDs surpassed LPs for the first time, and by 1993 only 300,000 vinyl albums were sold nationwide. It seemed as though both the record album—not only a vessel of creative possibility that had carried *Pet Sounds*, *Sgt. Pepper*, *Dark Side of the Moon*, and *Thriller* out into the world, but also a canvas for experimentation with the printed word and visual images—was to be relegated to the dustbin of history.

However, the latter half of the 2000s saw a gradual reawakening of interest in the format—a "vinyl revival"—fueled by baby boomer nostalgia for music of the 1960s and 1970s, and by a new generation of millennials interested in analog audio technology and genres of popular music that had

---

4. https://www.nielsen.com/us/en/insights/article/2019/the-steady-reach-of-radio-winning-consumers-attention/

(continued)

BOX 15.1 **OLD SCHOOL MEDIA IN THE NEW MILLENNIUM: RADIO AND VINYL** (*continued*)

originally been released on vinyl discs. While vinyl LPs did not claim a huge share of the overall market in the 2015 Nielsen music industry survey, more than 12 million of them were sold during the course of the year, generating $416 million in revenues, up 32 percent from the previous year, and the most since 1988. This phoenix-like re-emergence of an analog technology now in its seventh decade of existence is all the more extraordinary if you consider that it has taken place at the same time that the market for physical album sales was essentially predicted to disappear.

As might be expected, almost 70 percent of vinyl LP sales in 2015 fell under the heading of rock music, the genre most closely associated with that technology by nostalgic baby boomers and younger fans interested in the history of popular music. (Bestselling vinyl releases for the year 2015 included "classic rock" perennials *Abbey Road* [1969], by the Beatles, and Pink Floyd's *Dark Side of the Moon* [1973], as well as Miles Davis's

groundbreaking jazz album, *Kind of Blue* [1959]). However, it should be noted that several of the Top 10 vinyl albums that year were new releases by contemporary alternative rock artists such as Alabama Shakes, Arctic Monkeys, and Hozier. Even more impressive evidence of this trend can be found in the fact that the two bestselling pop albums of 2015—Adele's *25* and Taylor Swift's *1989*—were released in vinyl versions, driving LP sales in the pop category to rise 163 percent in the space of a year. And though hip-hop became the most popular genre in the United States in 2017 (a position it continues to hold in 2021), in 2018 vinyl sales for R&B (7.9 percent) and hip-hop (6.6 percent) nevertheless still paled in comparison to rock (41.7 percent) and pop (25.6 percent). This genre disparity in vinyl sales appears to be widening. In 2019 seven of the Top 10 spots were occupied by rock and pop bands, with only one of the Top 10 recorded in the new millennium (Billie Eilish's *When We Fall Asleep, Where Do We Go?*).

Shellac record	Vinyl album record	Vinyl single record
10" (25 cm)	12" (30 cm)	7" (18 cm)
78 rpm	33 1/3 rpm	45 rpm
Analog	Analog	Analog

mid-twentieth century. As we have seen, the music business is still adapting, and although it is still early in the process to speculate, two major trends have become apparent.

The first trend, somewhat surprisingly, is a renewed focus on the baby-boom generation as a primary source of revenue. There are clearly several factors involved in that decision. For one thing, it is a generation whose culture and desires are well known to the music industry. There is little risk in releasing a new Eric Clapton or Jimi Hendrix compilation. Moreover, as they age, baby boomers have more income to spend on high-end offerings such as elaborately packaged boxed sets and expensive concert tickets. In the spring of 2011, for example, the Grateful Dead offered a seventy-three-CD boxed set containing recordings of every show from their 1972 European tour. At a retail price of $450, the limited edition set sold out in three days. But perhaps the most significant factor in the baby boomers' appeal to the music industry is their perceived unwillingness (or inability!) to illegally download music files. In other words, they are an important market simply because they're the only ones who are still buying music at all.

A secondary effect of this trend has been the establishment of rock culture of the 1960s and 1970s as the definitive model of rock in general, even for younger listeners. Just to take one rather startling example: If asked to name the top-selling rock group of 2000–2010, few people would guess that it was the Beatles, especially since they hadn't existed as a group since 1970. But that is, in fact, the case. When the Beatles' recordings were finally released for streaming on December 24, 2015, 14 million tracks from their catalog were accessed in the following twenty-four hours, and radio play of Beatles songs increased by 89 percent over a four-day period!

The second trend is a search on the part of record companies for sources of income that do not rely on actually selling records. On the sales end, this often involves placing songs in movies, television shows, commercials, and as cell phone ringtones. On the business end, there is an increased emphasis on making so-called "360-degree deals" with artists. A 360-degree deal is one in which a record company (and their affiliated businesses) handle every aspect of an artist's career, not just the recording aspect. For most of the history of popular music, such things as live performances, T-shirt and poster sales, and even sheet music were handled separately from the artist's recording career; record companies neither wanted to, nor were equipped to, handle these other areas. In the new millennium, however, these different parts of the music business have increasingly been consolidated under large corporate umbrellas, positioning companies much better to address *all* of the artists' business needs. At the same time—by coincidence—income from the sales of recorded music were diminishing, which made these other aspects of the music business more attractive. In short, the music industry is gradually adjusting to an era in which recorded music, measured in "units" such as discs or MP3 files, is no longer the main profit center.

Touring has become an increasingly important component of the total profits generated by the music business, rather than a sideline designed to promote record sales. In 1990 North American revenues from the sale of recorded music totaled $7.5 billion, versus $1.1 billion in concert ticket sales; by the year 2000 this ratio had shifted even more decidedly in favor of recorded music ($14.3 billion versus $1.7 billion), thanks largely to the demand for compact discs. The year-end results for 2014 indicated just how completely the landscape had changed since 2000: live concert ticket revenues had risen to $6.2 billion, as compared with recorded music sales of $6.9 billion, including new platforms such as downloading and streaming. And this does not take into account important ancillary sources of profit associated with the concert economy, including

T-shirts, posters, and refreshments. Digital streaming is usually referred to as the "wave of the future" in the music business, yet in 2015 live concerts generated nearly *six times* as much revenue as streaming!

Another way of looking at the economic importance of live performance is from the perspective of musicians. The *Billboard* list of top "Money Makers" ranks the highest-earning artists and groups across various genres of popular music.[5] In 2015 country-turned-pop singer Taylor Swift led with $73.5 million in earnings over twelve months, of which $61.7 million (about 84 percent) was generated by touring; $7.2 million (less than 10 percent) by the sale of physical and downloaded recordings; $4.1 million by publishing rights connected with various uses of her compositions; and just $564,000 from streaming. That year the next two on the list, country star Kenny Chesney and the venerable Rolling Stones earned 96 and 94 percent (respectively) of their total income from touring. The days of a band going out on the road in order to boost their album sales are long gone. It could be argued that, at least for some artists, one makes new recordings in order to keep fans coming to the arena. And for classic rock and pop artists who rely upon sales of recordings from their back catalog, even that isn't necessary!

Product placements, endorsements, and multimedia have changed artists' financial calculus slightly. In 2019 Taylor Swift once again topped the top-earners list, but this time her income more than doubled ($185 million), due not only to her wildly successful *Reputation* stadium tour, but also through endorsement deals with Apple, AT&T, and Diet Coke. Artists willing to create feature-length films have even more lucrative options. In 2020 the cable network Disney+ paid $75 million for exclusive rights to the film version of Lin-Manuel Miranda's musical *Hamilton*, and Beyoncé secured a $100 million deal with the same network for three films, including 2020's *Black Is King*, an album-length music video much like her 2016 project *Lemonade*, released originally on Tidal.

Of course, making money through extensive touring looks quite different from the perspective of artists who do not have, or want, deals with huge concert promoters like Live Nation, the vertically integrated corporate conglomerate that owns Ticketmaster. And with the average price of a concert ticket hovering around $75, and running into the hundreds and even thousands of dollars on the informal secondary market (including internet-based services like StubHub), the opportunity for millions of Americans to share in the experience of a live tour by the most popular pop, rock, hip-hop, or country artists has become more and more limited.

If the new, mobile, digital technologies are the fundamental drivers of change in the music business, one of the most important outcomes of this process has been a transformation in the relationship between musicians and music corporations. In essence, a new generation of artists has moved to cut out the middleman in an effort to reach their audience directly without the mediation of record companies.

The year 2007 now appears as a kind of historical tipping point in this regard. In July of that year, Prince released his new album, *Planet Earth*, for free with the British

---

5. "Taylor Swift Tops *Billboard*'s Top Money-Makers List of 2015," *Billboard*, May 5, 2016.

newspaper *The Mail on Sunday*, infuriating his UK record label and Britain's music retailers; 2.27 million people received the album, helping to boost sales of tickets for his highly profitable twenty-one-night stand at London's O2 arena. In October 2007 Radiohead made its album *In Rainbows* available on the internet, asking fans to pay whatever they wanted. More than a million copies were downloaded, and the average price paid was $2.26 an album, making the band $2.7 million in direct profits. (An $80 deluxe "discbox" CD version was delivered to stores somewhat later, and in January 2008 *In Rainbows* took over the top spot on the *Billboard* album chart.) However, the idea of selling directly to fans via the internet has not really caught on among major commercial acts.

Madonna continued the trend away from the traditional model of artist–record company relationships, leaving Warner Music after twenty-five years and signing a 360-degree deal with Live Nation, the world's biggest concert promoter. The $120 million deal shared between the artist and the corporation profits from recorded music sales, concert receipts, merchandise, and rights to her celebrity "brand." Artists such as Jay-Z, Nickelback, and Shakira soon followed suit, leaving their record labels to sign with Live Nation's artist management subunit. The major labels responded by seeking to sign their own integrated deals with artists, giving them not only a percentage of the profits made through recordings but also a percentage of revenues from merchandise, concert tours, and other assets.

In his insightful book on the decline of the record business, *Appetite for Self-Destruction*, Steve Knopper (music business contributing editor for *Rolling Stone*) quotes Mark Williams, longtime A&R man for Interscope Records:

> People at the majors for some time have been looking for an answer. The obvious answer is, "There is no answer." . . . It's like, drop a globe and it shatters into a million pieces. It's going to be like in the 50s and 60s, when you had hundreds and hundreds of small labels. It's going to be a lot of trial and error. None of us know whether it'll work right. I laugh when people say, "We're going to try to fix it." They can try, but there's no real answer. (Knopper 2009, 248)

In fact, the picture is more mixed than Williams's description of a shattered globe would suggest. While the old "record business" and its basic modes of operation are gone forever, the *music* business has survived. While it is easier today for emerging or alternative artists to produce their own work and distribute it to local or specialized audiences via the internet and small performance venues, new corporate structures have at the same time arisen to replace the old ones, accommodating and exploiting the shifting balance among sources of profit in the popular mainstream. Radio still plays a critical role in introducing new artists and songs; institutions such as ASCAP and BMI remain relevant; and live performance—the most ancient and fundamental way of making and experiencing music—has taken on an increased importance in the new millennium.

So, while the mix of responses and counter-responses by musicians, audiences, and the people who make money off them has not been neat or predictable, the chaos predicted by many observers does not seem to have occurred. Rather, we are living through profound transformations in the way that music is made, consumed, and experienced, changes that would have been hard to imagine even two decades ago. This convergence of technological and social forces will surely lead to outcomes that cannot be predicted accurately from our present perspective. But it seems inevitable that the role of music in our daily lives will continue to be shaped by new technologies, new business strategies, and the evolving, always complex relationship between musicians and their audiences.

Rock Music in the 2000s

Like all genres in the new millennium, rock music has been profoundly and irrevocably changed by the music industry's shifts in economy, distribution, and media. With the traditional "gatekeepers" out of the way, rock bands in the 2000s were able to experiment with genre in a way that would have been commercially unviable in the age of radio stations and record companies that were focused on specific styles. As we examine rock music in this new era, the question arises: how far can rock music experiment and still be considered "rock"? Is "rock" even a useful category in the new millennium, or has it fused with genres like "pop" and "hip-hop"?

At the onset of the millennium, it seemed as if rock's old-school sensibilities were still commercially viable. One of the first trends to take hold in the early 2000s was known as the **garage rock revival**. Bands linked with this movement adapted the stripped-down rock 'n' roll aesthetics of 1960s rock acts like the Rolling Stones for the modern era. Not coincidentally, many drew attention to this connection through band names that started with "the" (e.g., the Strokes, the White Stripes, the Black Keys, the Hives, the Killers, the Shins). One of the biggest garage rock revival hits of the early millennium was "Maps" by the New York–based three-piece *the Yeah Yeah Yeahs*. In 2004 "Maps" peaked at Number 9 on *Billboard*'s Alternative Songs chart, a wide-ranging category that was created in the late 1980s for lighter "college rock" bands such as R.E.M. but had widened to accept grunge in the early 1990s and even harder nü-metal bands like Korn and Limp Bizkit by the late 1990s.

Born in Busan, South Korea, to Korean and Polish parents, singer-songwriter *Karen O* (Karen Lee Orzolek, b. 1978) began establishing the Yeah Yeah Yeahs when she met jazz drummer Brian Chase while attending Oberlin College in Ohio. After a year at Oberlin, Orzolek transferred to NYU to study film. While living in New York she met guitarist Nick Zinner, and the two began sharing cramped living quarters in Brooklyn's Williamsburg neighborhood with Emily Haines (lead singer of the band Metric). In an interview with BBC, Orzolek revealed that it was these close quarters that led to the spontaneous composition of "Maps": "Nick just had this sample, like kinda playing, you know, in his room, I was walking past the door, heard the sample, came in, I was like 'What is that?' And then, you know, 5 minutes later I was singing basically the lyrics to it."[6]

The sample to which Orzolek refers is the thunderous drum beat that enters "Maps" at 0:13 into the track. Prior to that the only sound is a loop of Zinner rapidly picking a single

---

6. BBC, *The First Time With* . . . "Karen O," September 1, 2019, https://www.bbc.co.uk/programmes/m000837g.

high note on the guitar. While these opening twelve seconds of guitar sound lo-fi and chaotic, once the drum sample enters you can hear that it's actually quite deliberate, with the guitar loop lasting exactly as long as the drum sample. This blend of punk-rock lo-fi aesthetics with the modern technology of looping in DAWs is endemic to the garage rock revival.

Karen O's lyrics are similarly pared down, her delivery earnest and heartfelt. A breakup song about her then-lover Angus Andrews (lead singer of the band Liars, another NYC garage rock band), "Maps" tells the story of a relationship dissolving due to the pressures of two musicians on newly rigorous touring schedules ("pack up/don't stray"). When drummer Brian Chase's live drum track finally enters in the chorus, his jazzy ride cymbal pattern adds levity to Orzolek's plaintiff cry "wait/they don't love you like I love you." Both the quiet verse and emotive chorus build up in volume until a boisterous bridge in which thick multiple tracks of fuzzy guitar churn atop clanging crash cymbals. Because the three-piece band lacks a bass guitar, noisy jams like these, full of fuzz with no bottom end to anchor it, sound as if they were actually being rehearsed in a garage.

A lo-fi instrumental aesthetic also drives "Wolf Like Me" (Number 37 Alternative Songs), another garage-rock revival hit by **TV on the Radio**. (TV on the Radio guitarist David Sitek produced the Yeah Yeah Yeah's 2003 album on which "Maps" appears). The track opens with a variant on the backbeat featuring double hits on the snare that were common in 1960s rock and pop hits (you can hear it in the Beach Boys' "Surfin'

TV on the Radio performing in 2011.

U.S.A."; see Chapter 9). An inordinate level of fuzz is heard on both the guitar and bass, with both getting louder and thicker as the track builds. Multiple vocal tracks also layer into this gradual thickening, beginning in the second chorus with the stereo double-tracking technique heard on a number of 1960s Beatles records. By the end of the third verse the multiple vocal tracks evolve into an overlapping cacophony, in which the lo-fi sound of the track itself (reminiscent of producer Phil Spector's "wall of sound" recordings in the 1960s) threatens to cloud the intelligibility of the lyrics.

Lead vocals in "Wolf Like Me" are provided by Tunde Adebimpe, a Nigerian-American visual-artist-turned-musician who animated the MTV series *Celebrity Deathmatch* and directed the Yeah Yeah Yeah's 2003 video "Pin." His quasi-pitched delivery recalls that of Bob Dylan, with most notes in the verse falling precipitously at the ends of phrases. The choruses in "Wolf Like Me" are unusual, in that they are distinguished from the verse only slightly, with a recurring melody but lyrics that are different each time (choruses are most often identifiable through their recurring lyrics). Though the shared rhyme scheme in these choruses (Chorus 1: "my body's changed/my mind's aflame"; Chorus 2: "I know it's strange/another way") helps to ensure their memorability, the signature lyrical-melodic section of the song occurs only at the ending, with the line "we're howlin' forever" repeated multiple times over the chorus backing track.

THE EVOLUTION OF ALTERNATIVE: RADIOHEAD AND ARCADE FIRE

While the return to simplicity worked for musicians in the garage rock revival, another strategy for rock musicians in the new millennium has been to take a more experimental

Thom Yorke of Radiohead.

Listening Guide "BODYSNATCHERS"

Written by Colin Charles Greenwood, Jonathan Richard Guy Greenwood, Edward John O'Brien, Philip James Selway, and Thomas Edward Yorke; performed by Radiohead; released 2007

It could be argued that the eclecticism of Radiohead's business strategy—and their desire to resist corporate control—have been echoed in the sensibility of their music. The track "Bodysnatchers" (Number 8 rock, 2008) is in a sense a song about the music industry and also serves as an example of Radiohead's creative extension of the basic formula of alternative rock. Like other "alt rock" bands, Radiohead has drawn upon the nihilistic sensibility of hardcore punk rock and the thick, guitar-dominated textures of arena rock and heavy metal. (The band even upped the ante by using three, rather than the usual one or two, electric guitars!) At the same time, they have also brought into play a wide range of musical influences, from progressive rock and electronic dance music to orchestral music, flamenco, jazz, and the singer-songwriter tradition.

Although *In Rainbows* has been described as Radiohead's "gentlest" album in musical terms—with tracks such as "House of Cards," "Nude," "All I Need," and "Jigsaw Falling into Place" featuring acoustic guitar and piano, falsetto singing, and moody electronic textures—"Bodysnatchers" evokes the trademark edginess and sonic power of Radiohead's earlier recordings. The track begins abruptly with a distorted, bone-crunching electric guitar riff, performed with the guitar's lowest string tuned down and left open as a more or less continuous drone. The upper part of the opening guitar riff outlines the song's melody, which is then picked up and developed by lead singer Thom Yorke. The song's lyrics describe the alienation of a person incarcerated within their own body. Like an etherized yet conscious patient, the first-person subject of the song is confined within the limitations of their physical body, unable to connect directly to the world around them.

The musical scale used in the main melody of "Bodysnatchers" is reminiscent of the song "Within You Without You" (from the Beatles' 1967 album *Sgt. Pepper's Lonely Hearts Club Band*), a self-consciously philosophical ode that features instruments and sounds derived from Indian classical music (including the *tanpura*, a drone instrument). The vaguely exotic quality of the instrumental and vocal melodies in "Bodysnatchers" combines eerily with the lyrics'

exploration of a metaphor from 1950s science fiction, rooted in Cold War fears over the loss of free will in society (whether to Communists or extraterrestrials). While the original "pod people" in the 1956 film *Invasion of the Body Snatchers* were interstellar spores that replaced sleeping people with perfect physical duplicates, the alienated narrator of Thom Yorke's song remains fully and ineffectually conscious within their own body. It is not too much of a stretch to connect this sensation of helplessness with the constant demand that musicians harness their creativity to the goal of generating profits. As the *New York Times* reported in 2007:

> After fulfilling its contract in 2003 with its last album for EMI, *Hail to the Thief*, Radiohead turned down multimillion-dollar offers for a new major-label deal, preferring to stay independent. "It was tough to do anything else," Mr. Yorke said during Radiohead's first extensive interviews since the release of [*In Rainbows*]. "The worst-case scenario would have been: Sign another deal, take a load of money, and then have the machinery waiting semi-patiently for you to deliver your product, which they can add to the list of products that make up the myth, la-la-la-la." (Pareles 2007)

This theme—the struggle to retain control over one's creative voice in a profit-driven industry—is emphasized even more explicitly in the second verse of "Bodysnatchers," in which an unidentified "you" is accused of "kill[ing] the sound." A little more than halfway through the track (2:07), the instrumental texture opens up and a solo guitar takes the lead, enhanced by reverb that creates the sense of a great, wide-open space. Thom Yorke then re-enters, a solitary voice in a vast sonic expanse, singing a series of six couplets, beginning with the enigmatic line "Has the light gone out for you?" Another minute into the track (3:09), and the electric guitars take over once again, playing a riff related to, though distinct from, the opening pattern. Yorke sings a wordless, slowly descending line (the "la-la-la-la" referred to in the interview excerpt), doubling it in unison with his guitar. This sequence is repeated, and at 3:32 the guitars move in with a vengeance, tripling the

(continued)

Listening Guide "BODYSNATCHERS" (continued)

riff in unison and creating a massively rocking wall of sound. This three-guitar "rave-up" concludes the track, as we hear the final line, "I seen it coming"—a prophecy in the past tense, too late—shouted four times over the chaotic tumult.

Toward the middle of "Bodysnatchers," Thom Yorke sings, "I have no idea what you are talking about, your mouth moves only with someone's hand up your ass." It's certainly hard to think of a more evocative metaphor than a hollow, soulless ventriloquist's dummy for the frustration and fears of artistic infertility that

appear to have haunted Radiohead's members during the four-year gap between albums that was broken, triumphantly, by the release of In Rainbows. Although the emotional angst of rock superstars and the melodrama of the music business may not seem the most lofty or compelling subject matter, it can be argued that the subtext of "Bodysnatchers"—that is, the role of free will and creativity in a business traditionally dominated by corporate concerns—is both an essential theme in the history of rock music and a key component of the ideology of contemporary alternative rock.

approach to both the sound *and* the economics of rock. Perhaps the best example of this approach is **Radiohead**, who began their career firmly within the boundaries of alternative rock, but subsequently experimented not only with diverse musical influences but also with varied approaches to the marketing and distribution of their music.

Though they had been recording since 1992, Radiohead came to prominence in the United States in 1997, with their third album, *OK Computer*. Over their next two albums, *Kid A* (2000) and *Amnesiac* (2001), they increasingly integrated sampling and other electronic music techniques and approaches. In 2007, Radiohead extended their experimentation to distribution as well, releasing their Number 1 album *In Rainbows* as a digital download and allowing fans to set their own price. Rather than choose between the traditional rock business model and the new culture of downloading, Radiohead chose both.

In the following years, Radiohead's members alternated between issuing solo material while the band went on hiatus and then reuniting for the albums *King of Limbs* (2011; a departure from their previous work, in that it now featured even greater rhythmic complexity, owing to the band having taken on an additional percussionist, Clive Deamer) and *A Moon Shaped Pool* (2016). Both were issued initially via download from the band's website, and then in various streaming and physical formats.

Interestingly, just as the experimental, anticorporate ideology represented by the work of Radiohead has become increasingly mainstream, the very concepts of "mainstream" and "alternative" themselves have begun to lose their meaning. Most alternative music aficionados do not regard the Grammys, awarded each year by the National Academy of Recording Arts and Sciences (NARAS), as a bastion of rebellious individualism and musical authenticity. Nonetheless, there was a good deal of online fist pumping among fans when the Canadian band **Arcade Fire** came from the back of the field to win the 2011 Grammy Award for Best Album of the Year over pop star Lady Gaga and rapper *Eminem*, making them the first alternative rock band to achieve that recognition. The unexpected victory of their album, *The Suburbs*, seemed to some fans to signal the "arrival" of alternative rock at the center of popular music, a kind of culmination of the work of bands such as R.E.M. and Nirvana. (The fact that the band members themselves were not expecting to win the Grammy was revealed by the first words uttered when they came back onstage to accept the award: "What the hell?!?")

Arcade Fire, based in Montreal, Canada, is a seven-piece band centered on the duo of Win Butler, a Texas-raised guitarist and singer, and Régine Chassagne, a Canadian vocalist and keyboardist of Haitian descent. Their third album, *The Suburbs* (Number 1, 2011), evokes the experiences of kids born and raised in the vast stretches of recession-impoverished suburban sprawl that surround most North American cities (including Houston, Texas, where Win Butler grew up). This theme is captured evocatively by the song "Sprawl II (Mountains beyond Mountains)," a meditation on suburban emptiness ("Dead shopping malls rise like mountains . . . and there's no end in sight") carried along on an ironically sprightly, synth-pop rhythm.

The hard-rocking, Ramones-inspired song "The Month of May"—performed by Arcade Fire at the 2011 Grammy concert with bicyclists zooming around and through the band—is even more directly focused on the isolation and desperation of suburban youth. The song's lyric features verbal images of cars driving "around and around and around" a bleak neighborhood decimated by a violent storm (evoked by a roar of digitally generated "white noise") and a teen with "so much pain for someone so young."

A third song, "The Suburbs," takes yet another musical approach to the theme of suburban decline, beginning with a folksy, light-hearted groove with acoustic guitars and piano, reminiscent of some country-rock recordings of the 1970s. The initial charm of the "good ol' days," skip-along-the-sidewalk soundtrack begins to fade, however, as the singer narrates a dream of his childhood, with his friends "still screamin' and runnin' through the yard," and moves on to the subsequent collapse of "all of the houses they built in the seventies," capped with the bleak refrain, "It meant nothin' at all." Trapped in the suburbs and seeking a way out, the singer asks if we can understand

> *Why I want a daughter while I'm still young*
> *I wanna hold her hand and show her some beauty*
> *Before this damage is done*

By the time "The Suburbs" segues into the following track, the texture of the music has gradually become more complex and layered, with Butler singing a falsetto refrain over a continuous bed of strings—"Sometimes I can't believe it, I'm movin' past the feeling . . . in my dreams we're still screaming." Toward the very end we hear a melancholy guitar riff and some virtuoso *Sgt. Pepper*-style melodic runs on the violins, half-buried in the texture, and bathed in studio reverb that gives the impression of a vast, desolated space, a dying community.

The band's success continued with their next album, *Reflektor* (2013), a two-album set that was influenced by Butler and Chassigne's trip to Haiti. Butler noted, "Going to Haiti for the first time with Régine was the beginning of a major change in the way that

I thought about the world. [The trip] I [feel] changed me musically, just really opened me up to this huge, vast amount of culture and influence I hadn't been exposed to before, which was really life-changing."[7] In 2017 they released *Everything Now*, a heavily EDM-influenced departure from their alternative rock roots, produced by Thomas Bangalter of Daft Punk.

Whatever the future of alternative rock—and of the concept of "alternative" within the music industry—Arcade Fire's heady mix of rock concert theatrics and musical versatility, and their drive to explore both the diversity of music and the social and philosophical dilemmas faced by their generation, support the prediction that new voices and perspectives will continue to enrich rock music in the years to come.

EMO GOES MAINSTREAM

Emo (shorthand for "emotional" rock) was a thoroughly underground genre throughout the 1990s. Largely centered in the American Midwest—particularly in college towns like Lawrence, Kansas (the Get Up Kids, the Appleseed Cast), and Champaign-Urbana, Illinois (Braid, American Football)—1990s emo combined the sounds of alternative rock and punk with lyrics that emphasized emotional sensitivity and vulnerability. Emo bands released records on indie labels like Fueled by Ramen and Vagrant, and toured relentlessly to make ends meet. By and large emo was a genre dominated by straight white men whose sorrowful lyrics about the women who wronged them sometimes teetered uncomfortably between self-pity and misogyny.

Most commercially successful genres are not "new" by any stretch of the imagination. Just as garage rock revival bands drew on fashions and conventions from the 1960s, in the mid-2000s a number of artists monetized the cult following of emo by imbuing the same dark lyrical themes with the polished production and designer fashions associated with pop-punk bands like Blink-182. The Fueled by Ramen label pivoted from pedaling underground emo to releasing hugely successful mainstream records by Jimmy Eat World, Fall Out Boy, Panic! At the Disco, and Paramore. Paramore's 2007 hit "Misery Business" (Number 3 Hot Modern Rock, Number 26 Hot 100) was a financial sea change for the label, eventually selling over 3 million units.

Paramore was formed in an outer suburb of Nashville, Tennessee, when vocalist and songwriter *Hayley Williams* (b. 1988)—who had already been signed by Atlantic Records as a solo artist at age fourteen—enlisted a backing band consisting of the brothers Josh and Zac Farro (on guitar and drums, respectively) and bassist Jeremy Davis, who had previously backed Williams in a funk cover band. Their debut record *All We Know Is Falling* (2005), despite having the backing of a major label (Fueled by Ramen, like most successful indie labels, had by this time been acquired by a major, Atlantic Records), reached only a niche emo-punk audience and ultimately enjoyed little market success. Due to its pop-oriented sound and polished production values Paramore's second album,

7. Patrick Doyle, "Win Butler Reveals Secret Influences Behind Arcade Fire's 'Reflektor,'" October 22, 2013, rollingstone.com.

Riot! (2007) quickly went double platinum. One reviewer of the album nicely summed up its crossover commercial appeal:

> There isn't a whole lot of difference between *Riot!* and the better songs from Kelly Clarkson or Avril Lavigne. As punk more extravagantly flirts with pop and pop explores short, sharp rock songs, Paramore finds a comfortable place between the two.[8]

"Misery Business," the lead single from *Riot!*, cannily straddles the line between pop, punk, and emo. First, Williams's highly trained voice—she had taken vocal lessons with Brett Manning, who also coached Taylor Swift, Keith Urban, and Miley Cyrus—soars confidently and articulately over thick instrumental textures in a way that her mumbly (male) emo predecessors rarely could. Her lyrics, which brag about stealing a lover back from a lesser woman, cleverly invert the boy-sad-about-girl emo trope. From a fashion perspective the band's look is nothing more than a shined-up version of punk rock fashion. Williams's hair, razor cut and dyed various shades of yellow, orange, and magenta,

Paramore performing in 2007.

---

8. Jonathan Bradley, *Stylus* Magazine, August 13, 2007.

evokes a punk aesthetic that matches the driving uptempo beat and distorted guitars perfectly. This punk rock look is echoed in the official video, which is organized around the "mean girl" trope common to many popular films about adolescence. The video shows Williams triumphing over her arrogant antagonist, and performing with her backing band—three skinny emo guys with tight black shirts and black bangs carefully swept just over their eyes—in a graffiti-covered room that evokes the album cover.

Of course, the genre-crossing tactics of "Misery Business" inevitably attracted accusations of "selling out." Other indie-label emo bands that morphed into successful mainstream acts did so by trading their punk style for one more oriented toward mainstream rock. In the early 2000s a charismatic lead singer named Chris Carrabba (b. 1975) left his emo band Further Seems Forever to focus on an acoustic solo project called Dashboard Confessional. A heavily inked punk rock singer screaming at the top of his lungs over an acoustic guitar was novel enough to draw a cult following, but his debut record *The Swiss Army Romance* seemed to hold little commercial potential (the original pressing was limited to 1,000 copies). Dashboard's 2001 follow-up *The Places You've Come to Fear the Most* added sparse drum and bass accompaniment and did slightly better (Number 108 *Billboard* 200). In 2003, *A Mark, a Mission, a Brand, a Scar* featured a full electric rock band setup, even re-arranging past album tracks (e.g., the lead single "Hands Down") for this traditional instrumentation. It debuted at Number 2 on the Hot 200, selling over 120,000 copies in the first week alone. By the following year Carrabba had completed his transformation to mainstream hit maker when he recorded the rock anthem "Vindicated" for the Hollywood action film *Spider-Man 2*.

Hip-Hop in the New Millennium

If hip-hop in the 1990s was all about the battles between East and West Coast rappers (some merely boastful and figurative, others deadly and tragic), then hip-hop in the new millennium is about the emergence of new hotbeds located in the South—Atlanta in particular—and transgressing the stylistic norms associated with those East and West Coast scenes. Hip-hop artists in the new millennium developed new vocal techniques (ranging from the heavy metal shouts of Lil' Jon, to the Auto-Tune of T-Pain, to the mumble of Future); new ways of distributing their music (Jay-Z's subscription service Tidal, Beyoncé's Disney multimedia release *Black Is King*, and an entire generation of rappers releasing music for free through the website SoundCloud and various social media outlets); and new ways of earning money, often through entrepreneurship having little or nothing to do with the music itself.

Compared to their near domination of hip-hop in the late 1980s and early 90s, West Coast rappers had a harder time in the mainstream just after the turn of the millennium. Dr. Dre, Snoop Doggy Dogg, and Ice Cube continued to release records that were far less celebrated than their seminal hits of the 1990s. Though the two biggest rookies to come out of the West Coast in the 2000s (Xzibit, the Game) both produced platinum and double platinum albums, respectively, the market share of West Coast hip-hop pales in comparison to that of the East Coast.

Of the two biggest names associated with 2000s East Coast hip-hop only one, *Jay-Z* (Shawn Corey Carter, b. 1969), is a native New Yorker. Jay-Z is candid about his rags-to-riches fame, even admitting to selling crack to make ends meet. Supported by big New York talent—especially Sean "Puffy" Combs and the Notorious B.I.G.—Jay-Z eventually got signed to Def Jam records and from there began to build the biggest financial empire in hip-hop history. Having already started his own record company, Roc-A-Fella (largely as an independent label to release his own CDs), in 2003 Jay-Z branched out to start a clothing line called Rocawear. His most lucrative holdings over the years have included stakes in a professional sports team (the Brooklyn Nets), a champagne brand (Armand de Brignac), and the music streaming service Tidal. In 2019 Forbes crowned Jay-Z the first hip-hop billionaire; as of 2021 he is the richest American musician in history, and third wealthiest worldwide (just behind Paul McCartney and Andrew Lloyd Webber).

In 2003 Jay-Z released his eighth record, *The Black Album*, which debuted at Number 1 on the *Billboard* 200 and has sold over 3 million copies to date. The album is notable for having a different producer on each track, including Rick Rubin for the single "99 Problems." Rubin is known for his signature rap/rock crossover sound, a style he helped to establish in 1986 by producing the Aerosmith/Run-DMC collaboration "Walk This Way," and the Beastie Boys' "(You Gotta) Fight For Your Right (To Party!)." One of Jay-Z's most memorable verses to date is the second verse of "99 Problems," in which he describes his own standoff with a white police officer during a racially motivated traffic stop (in which he was indeed carrying crack-cocaine). His signature line "I ain't passed the bar but I know a little bit/enough that you won't illegally search my shit" helped cast light on racial profiling and was even the subject of a legal analysis published in the *Saint Louis University Law Journal*. After marrying R&B legend Beyoncé in 2008 the two went on to form numerous collaborations. As the Carters, they released a hit video "Apeshit" in 2018, for which they rented out the Louvre museum in Paris as the backdrop for a critique of cultural snobbery and institutionalized racism, and a celebration of their own success. As of 2021 Jay-Z has sold over 50 million albums, and holds a number of musical records, including the most Grammy Awards won by a hip-hop artist (22) and the most Number 1 albums on the *Billboard* 200 by any solo artist (14).

The other big name associated with New York hip-hop in the 2000s is *Kanye West* (b. 1977). Born in Atlanta and raised in Chicago, West is actually an East Coast transplant, having moved to New York in the early 2000s to produce records for Jay-Z's Roc-A-Fella label. As a rapper he first entered the public spotlight in 2004 with a debut album called *The College Dropout*. Kanye's style had previously drawn on New York hip-hop (particularly the music and fashion of Puffy, Nas, and Biggy), but he diverged from the gangsta persona on this album by expressing a great deal of vulnerability. The first single, "Through the Wire" (Number 8 Hot R&B/Hip-Hop Songs), details Kayne's near-fatal car crash, and was actually recorded while his jaw was still wired shut, marking his flow with an inarticulate mumble that contrasts the confident braggadocio associated with gangsta rap. The track also helped establish Kanye's signature "chipmunk" production technique, in which classic vocal samples (such as Chaka Khan's "Through the Fire") are sped up and/or pitch shifted. Vocal manipulation would remain a hallmark of West's sound.

Missy Elliott performing in 2003.

His 2008 record *808s & Heartbreak* used Auto-Tuned singing more than rapping, and continued to explore lyrical themes of emotional distress. In the following decade Kanye West would come to be known as many things in addition to his music: as a fashion designer (both for his *haute couture* line Yeezy, and for a line of children's fashion co-designed with his then-wife Kim Kardashian); as a political rabble-rouser (mostly notably interrupting Taylor Swift's acceptance speech at the 2009 MTV Video Music Awards, and claiming that President George W. Bush doesn't "care about Black people" in the aftermath of Hurricane Katrina); and even as a 2020 U.S. presidential candidate.

Despite the splash made by Jay-Z, Kanye, and others on the coasts in this decade, the 2000s were a transitional period, in which a number of communities in the South—especially Atlanta, Georgia—became the first hip-hop hotbeds not associated with either coast. For fifty-eight of sixty-two consecutive weeks starting in late 2003, a Southern hip-hop artist occupied the Number 1 spot on the *Billboard* Hot 100. Outside of Atlanta, artists like Lil' Wayne, Juvenile (both from New Orleans, Louisiana), and Three 6 Mafia (Memphis, Tennessee) topped the charts.

But the first major commercial success of the 2000s to come out of the South did not come from one of these major cities at all. Four-time Grammy-winning rapper and producer **Missy Elliott** (Melissa Arnette Elliott, b. 1971) was born and raised in Portsmouth, a southern-Virginia Navy town where her father was stationed. Early in life Elliott pursued a career as an R&B singer with her group Sista, whose recordings were produced by her childhood friend **Timbaland** (Timothy Mosely, b. 1972). After eventually getting signed to Elektra records the group moved to New York. Shortly afterward Elliott and Timbaland began working together to produce records for successful artists including Destiny's Child and Aaliyah.

Because Elliott appeared as a guest vocalist on many tracks that she and Timbaland produced, her debut solo record *Supa Dupa Fly* went platinum in 1997, owing in part to her name recognition. Her most successful record, *Under Construction* (2002) went double platinum largely on the back of the first single and music video "Work It" (Number 2 Hot 200). In addition to her work as a rapper and producer, Elliott has come to be known as a director and key innovator in the field of music videos. Co-directing with veterans such as Hype Williams ("The Rain") and Dave Meyers ("Work It"), Elliott's videos usually contain high-tech imagery and cutting-edge CGI graphics that evoke a twenty-first-century version of the Afrofuturism aesthetic promoted a generation earlier by artists such as George Clinton (Chapter 12).

Viewing Guide "WORK IT"

Song written by Melissa Arnette Elliott and Timothy Zachary Mosley; music video directed by David Charles Meyers and Melissa Arnette Elliott; performed by Missy Elliott; released 2002

Co-directed by Missy Elliott and Dave Meyers, Missy Elliott's video for "Work It" won the 2003 MTV Video Music Awards (VMAs) for Video of the Year (in addition to Best Hip-Hop Video), and was nominated for five more (Direction, Special Effects, Art Direction, Editing, and Cinematography). Like most music videos, "Work It" pantomimes many of its lyrics in the visual domain, the most obvious of which (e.g., Elliott raising a glass with her dining companion along with the lyric, "Let's make a toast") are shown in the third column of the Listening Guide chart. Column four of the chart shows how the

video gradually introduces new settings to keep viewers' interest, most of which are timed perfectly with the entrance of a new musical section (e.g., the hair salon arrives right at the onset of Chorus 2). Quickly re-cycling through most if not all previously seen settings in the final chorus is a common music video editing technique; in Chorus 4, we see all of them except the restaurant and the stripper poles.

The video opens with a sample of Rock Master Scott's 1984 dance track "Request Line," which accounts for the "DJ please, pick up the phone" vocal

TIME	SECTION	LYRICS ANIMATED	SETTINGS
0:01	Intro sample	"Pick up the phone"	Timbaland at pay phone
0:11	Beat enters		Missy in abandoned playground
0:31	Chorus 1		Bees; Missy and four dancers
0:49	Verse 1	"Shave my cha-cha" "See my hips big hips" "Glass of water"	Checkerboard dance floor
1:27	Chorus 2		Hair salon
1:46	Verse 2	"Get your hair did" "Let's make a toast" "Halle Berry poster" (Belvedere) "Not a prostitute"	Restaurant; parking garage
2:28	Chorus 3		Playground (child dancers added)
2:47	Verse 3	"Chinese boys" "Girls get that cash" "Prince couldn't get me to change my name" "Kunta Kinte" "Got a Lamborghini" "Why ya act dumb?" "Drummer boy"	"Boys" lined up; "Girls" on stripper poles; Prince look-alike; *Roots* scenery; Lamborghini-in-mouth CGI; Elliott in corner w/dunce cap; Military drummer
3:34	Chorus 4		All except restaurant and stripper poles
3:53	Outro	"To my fellas" "To the ladies"	

(continued)

Viewing Guide "WORK IT" *(continued)*

sample, as well as the snare hits that follow. Timbaland predictably picks up a payphone to animate this lyric. At 0:11 the main beat enters, which features yet another sample; the fast running "blips" in the background are sampled from the intro of Blondie's 1978 synth-pop hit "Heart of Glass." Cleverly, Timbaland reveals his original contribution to the beat by pantomiming the squealing siren-like synth line he has added atop all these samples.

Missy's visual entrance anticipates her vocal entrance. We see her being "dragged" (through trick camera work) through an abandoned playground with lighting and colors reminiscent of a horror movie. "Work It," like many post-millennial pop tracks, begins on a chorus, rather than a verse (as was the norm in verse-chorus forms in the 1990s). Its memorable chorus hook is composed of two stanzas, each of which is punctuated with a backwards speech sample:

> Is it worth it?
> Let me work it
> I put my thing down flip it and reverse it
> [backward speech sample]

> If you got a big [sound of elephant trumpeting]
> Let me search it
> Find out how hard I gotta' work ya'
> [backward speech sample]

The backward speech is actually her line "I put my thing down flip it and reverse it" played in reverse. Achieved with just the click of a mouse in early 2000s DAWs, Elliott has said that it was actually put in reverse by accident, but that she liked the sound and decided to keep it. The video animates the backward speech through its visual analogue, reversed footage. In most of the video's chorus imagery, dancers are shown doing their moves both forward and backward. In the second chorus, the backward speech is animated visually by negative imagery (1:33), in which the brightest lights of the hair salon all appear darkest, and colors are flipped 180 degrees around the color wheel.

Elliott's official video is set to the radio edit of the song. Words throughout the verses that appear in the original, but are changed for the video are as follows:

(0:52)   "put the pussy on ya">> "put a hurtin' on ya'"

(2:03)   "a bitch that's even betta'">>"a chick that's even betta'"

(2:18)   "my ass go">>"my butt go"

(2:25)   "my ass go">>"my tail go"

(3:00)   "shakin' your ass">>"shakin' your [silence]"

Given that Elliott went through the trouble to create a radio edit, it's ironic that the chorus's elephant noise actually appears in the original. As if the sound of the elephant were not clearly understood to represent its trunk—and by extension, her lover's virility—Elliott makes the symbolism clear by grabbing the crotch of her pants when this sound recurs throughout the video.

In Verse 3 the speed with which the video shifts settings accelerates, as does the number of lyrical references directly pantomimed on screen. At this speed of editing, the distinction between settings and individual shots begins to collapse; most settings are introduced only for as long as the lyric they are intended to animate lasts. Beginning with the Lamborghini lyric/scene (3:16), the video version completely replaces four entire lines for less than obvious reasons:

Album version	Video version
Picture Lil' Kim dating a pastor	Got a Lamborghini so I drive faster
Minute Man and Big Red could outlast ya'	Just to make ya' haters even freakin' madder
Who is the best? I don't have to ask ya'	Admit I'm the sh___[silence] ain't no one no badder
When I come out you won't even matter	When I drop this record here you won't even matter

With "Lil' Kim" Elliott name drops one of her rap contemporaries; Minute Man is a reference to Elliott's song "One Minute Man" from her previous album *So Addictive* (2001); and Big Red references a brand of chewing gum who advertised their product with the tag line "say goodbye a little longer." Why didn't these lyrics make it into the video version? With so many of the lyrical references in the verse being depicted literally on screen, it's possible that Elliott didn't want to subject Lil' Kim to the same mockery as she did the grotesque caricature of Prince shown at 3:07 that accompanies the lyrics "Prince couldn't get me to change my name" (a reference to his much publicized name changes; see Chapter 13).

Ultimately, the greatest lasting cultural resonance of this monumental video may be Elliott's popularization of the phonaesthetic expression "ba-donk-a-donk," the meaning of which is spelled out throughout the second verse as Elliott and her dancers repeatedly bounce their derrières to the phonetic rhythm. (Country Musician Trace Adkins released a video called "Honky Tonk Badonkadonk" just three years later, which reimagines the expression as the object of the male gaze in a strip club.) "Work It" also references the fictional character Kunta Kinte from the 1976 novel *Roots*, both lyrically and visually (at 3:11 in the video), an allusion that reappears twelve years later in Kendrick Lamar's song "King Kunta" from *To Pimp a Butterfly* (2015). Whereas in Elliott's video the Kinte-esque character is shown rebelling, slapping the "massa" she references in the lyrics, Lamar's video reminds the viewer that modern-day conditions for Black Americans in places like Compton, California, are not entirely divorced from the history of slavery.

After "Work It" Missy Elliott had only one comparable hit, 2005's "Lose Control" (Number 3 Hot 100), featuring another critically acclaimed music video directed by Dave Meyers that won the 2006 VMAs for Best Dance Video and Best Hip-Hop Video. After this Elliott returned to her work in the studio, producing hits for major artists. She has re-emerged into the spotlight in the past few years, appearing in the 2015 Super Bowl halftime show alongside Lenny Kravitz and Katy Perry, and releasing the 2019 EP *Iconology* (Number 24 *Billboard* 200). As of 2021, Missy Elliott is the bestselling female rapper of all time, with 30 million records sold. Her lifetime of innovation in the field of music video production earned her the Michael Jackson Video Vanguard award at the 2019 VMA Award Ceremony.

More than anyone, the artist who put one particular Southern hip-hop locale on the map—Atlanta, Georgia—early in the 2000s was **OutKast**, an eclectic duo composed of André 3000 (André Lauren Benjamin, b. 1975) and Big Boi (Antwan André Patton, b. 1975). Though they released three hip-hop albums in the late 1990s, it was two genre-bending records in the early 2000s that catapulted them into the limelight. Released in late 2000, the *Stankonia* LP (Number 2 *Billboard* 200) swerved outside of hip-hop norms, especially with André 3000 now augmenting his raps with vulnerable crooning about personal heartache. In the chorus of the second single, "Ms. Jackson" (Number 1 Hot 100), André sings apologies to his "baby mama's mama" (inspired by the dissolution of Benjamin's real-life relationship with hip-hop artist Erykah Badu). Big Boi's fast-paced rapping in the verses adds rhythmic contrast, filling in the nooks and crevices of a rhythmically intricate backing track marked by echo and backward effects.

OutKast doubled down on this experimentation with a double album called *Speakerboxxx/The Love Below* in 2003. The two-part title belies its dual authorship, the first disc featuring songs in Big Boi's Southern hip-hop style, with André 3000 intensifying his efforts as an experimental pop musician—more Prince than P-Diddy—on the second. Both discs spawned Number 1 pop singles. Big Boi's "The Way You Move" features his signature machine-gun delivery over a straightforward beat provided by the Roland 808 drum machine (which he references in Verse 1: "I know y'all wanted that 808"). Because Big Boi and 3000 worked on each half of the album separately at times, sung vocals in Big Boi's chorus are provided not by his bandmate, but by famed Atlanta producer Sleepy Brown, whose vocal style is reminiscent of soul music pioneer Marvin Gaye. (This bridge between hip-hop and 1970s soul music is reinforced by the use of a horn section.)

Compare this with André 3000's hit single "Hey Ya!" from disc two of *Speakerboxxx/ The Love Below*. Inspired by early punk (e.g., the Ramones) and garage-rock revival (e.g., the Hives), André was determined to make as much of the album as he could with traditional instruments, rather than samples; "Hey Ya!" is dominated by strummed acoustic guitar, understated electric bass, and playful keyboard twinkles in the chorus. The track is just as notable for its parody music video, which reimagines the *Ed Sullivan Show* being overrun by young women screaming for a band composed entirely of multiple copies of 3000, rather than the Beatles. Simply put, André 3000's stylistic eclecticism on *The Love Below* transcended the genre norms of hip-hop more than any mainstream hip-hop record of the time.

Catapulted to the top by these two very different singles, *Speakerboxxx/The Love Below* debuted at Number 1 on the *Billboard* 200, where it spent seven weeks, eventually achieving diamond certification by selling over 11 million discs. Riding on the success of these two hit albums by OutKast, a whole new generation of hip-hop artists from Atlanta became household names. Ludacris rose to fame after his single "Act a Fool" was featured prominently in the 2003 film *2 Fast 2 Furious*. CeeLo Green and Danger Mouse, better known as the duo Gnarls Barkley, released the 2006 hit "Crazy" (Number 2 Hot 100) the same year that OutKast released their final studio record. But it was really the next generation of musicians who would realize OutKast's legacy and make Atlanta the undisputed hip-hop capital of the United States. Listing the biggest names to come out of Atlanta in that decade—Childish Gambino, Quavo, Future, 21 Savage, Offset, 2 Chainz, Gucci Mane, Young Thug, and Killer Mike (of Run the Jewels)—looks like a roll call of hip-hop stars in the 2010s.

Hip-Hop Stars of the 2010s

The second decade of the twenty-first century saw the rise of a new generation of hip-hop artists, each of whom navigated the career strategies established by stars of the 2000s—the Hustler-Entrepreneur (Jay-Z), the Star as Artist (Kanye), and the Genre Blender (OutKast). *Drake* (Aubrey Drake Graham, b. 1986), a Canadian artist whose work combines egocentric, abrasive rapping and R&B-influenced singing and features collaborations with British, African, and Caribbean artists, recorded a series of bestselling albums and in 2016 charted the first Number 1 single ("One Dance") to surpass one billion streams on Spotify. *Nicki Minaj* (Onika Tanya Maraj, b. 1982), the Trinidadian-born, New York City–raised rapper and fashion icon creates animated, word-play-filled performances that incorporate a cast of colorful alter egos (including Roman Zolansky, whom she has referred to as her gay Cockney twin brother). Minaj's hit singles range from pop-rap songs like "Super Bass" (Number 2 rap/Number 3 pop, 2012), with its catchy refrain and pink-suffused music video, to 2015's "Anaconda" (Number 1 R&B/ hip-hop and Number 2 pop), which sampled the fundamental theme of Sir Mix-A-Lot's 1992 hit single "Baby Got Back." Minaj's 2018 *Queen*, a sprawling mixtape of solo work and collaborations with rappers like Future and Lil' Wayne, debuted at Number 2 on the *Billboard* 200, just behind the Number 1 slot occupied by Houston rapper **Travis Scott's** (Jacques Bermon Webster II, b. 1991) triple platinum LP *Astroworld*. *Astroworld* (Number 1 *Billboard* 200) won Album of the Year from the BET Hip Hop Awards, and its lead single "Sicko Mode" (Number 1 Hot 100) was nominated for Best Rap Performance and Best Rap Song at the 2019 Grammy Awards. All three of these artists have worked to maximize their earning potential beyond the music business: Drake as ambassador for the Toronto Raptors NBA franchise; Minaj with celebrity endorsements for Adidas and Pepsi and a custom-made Barbie doll; and Scott becoming the first celebrity since Michael Jordan to have a McDonald's meal named after him.

The expressive range of hip-hop in the 2010s is illustrated by **Frank Ocean** (Christopher Edwin Breaux, b. 1987), whose idiosyncratic style straddles hip-hop and contemporary R&B. Raised in New Orleans, Ocean began his career as a "ghostwriter" (anonymous composer) of songs for Beyoncé and Justin Bieber, and in 2010 joined the Los Angeles-based hip-hop collective Odd Future. His first two albums, *Channel Orange* (Number 2 pop, Number 1 R&B/hip-hop, 2012) and *Blonde* (Number 1 pop and R&B/ hip-hop, 2015), incorporate musical influences ranging from the Beatles to David Bowie and Andre 3000, and his contemplative, crooner-like vocal delivery, distinctive melodies, and exploration of issues such as spirituality and sensuality on tracks like "Voodoo" (2012), released on Ocean's Tumblr account, have all contributed to his iconoclastic image. (Back in Chapter 1 we mentioned the personal courage demonstrated by Ocean in "coming out" as the first publicly LGBTQ+ figure in the hip-hop world, a parallel to contemporaneous developments in professional sports.)

The tradition of bestselling white artists in hip-hop was continued by the Seattle-based duo **Macklemore** (Ben Haggerty, b. 1983) **& Ryan Lewis** (b. 1988), who were nominated for seven Grammy awards in 2014, winning Best New Artist, Best Rap Album (*The Heist*), Best Rap Song and Best Rap Performance ("Thrift Shop"). The fact that *The Heist* won the Best Rap Album Grammy caused heated controversy within the hip-hop community, in part because it beat out the debut album by Kendrick Lamar, who, like Macklemore & Ryan Lewis, had received seven nominations, but did not win in any category. In an interview with the hip-hop website thesource.com, Macklemore said, "I am a huge supporter of what Kendrick does. And because of that, I would love to win in a different category. We obviously had massive success on commercial radio . . . but Kendrick has a better rap album."[9] The band's follow-up album, 2016's *The Unruly Mess*

---

9. Osorio, Kim, "Macklemore Graces the Cover of 4th Annual Source Magazine 'Man of the Year' Issue," *The Source*, January 7, 2014.

I've Made, debuted at Number 4 on the *Billboard* Hot 100 and Number 1 on the R&B/hip-hop charts. However, sales dropped over the following weeks and overall the album did not do as well as their debut, leading the duo to go on hiatus in 2017.

Of the hip-hop artists who rose to prominence during the second decade of the twenty-first century, it can be argued that none has made as impressive an artistic or social impact as **Kendrick Lamar** (Kendrick Lamar Duckworth, b. 1987), whose fourth album *DAMN* became in 2018 the first popular music record to be awarded the prestigious Pulitzer Prize for Music. Raised in Compton, California, crucible of the groundbreaking West Coast gangsta rap group N.W.A and its alumni Dr. Dre, Ice Cube, and Eazy-E, Lamar has reaffirmed both the artistic potential of the genre and its community-oriented, consciousness-raising heritage, reaching back to the pioneering work of Public Enemy. Charting his path between "realness" and commercialism—between duty to home, family, and the 'hood and the temptations of fame, fast fortune, and the road—Lamar has created concept albums that are cinematic in scope, drawing in a vast range of musical references, and dealing with topics seldom if ever addressed within the tough-guy framework of rap music, including depression, the fear of failure, and what he has called "survivor's guilt."

Having started his musical career as a teenager under the stage name K Dot, Lamar gathered attention with a series of mixtapes distributed on the internet and an independent studio-produced album, *Section.80* (2011). His first major label album, *good kid, m.A.A.d city* (2012), chronicles, in a nonlinear narrative form, the experiences of the teenaged Lamar growing up in Compton amid the harsh realities of gang-on-gang

Kendrick Lamar on stage in 2015.

Listening Guide   "TO PIMP A BUTTERFLY"

To Pimp a Butterfly, concept album written and performed by Kendrick Lamar; executive producers Anthony "Top Dawg" Tiffith and Dr. Dre; recorded 2015; "i," written and performed by Kendrick Lamar; single recorded 2014, album version recorded 2015

The title of Kendrick Lamar's ambitious sophomore album, *To Pimp a Butterfly* (2015), is a play on the phrase Tu Pimp a Caterpillar (Tu.P.A.C.), an acronym for the 1990s rap artist Tupac Shakur (1971–1996). It is also the title of a poem that appears at the very end of the album. The poem presents the caterpillar as a creature whose "only job is to eat or consume everything around it." This is in contrast to the butterfly that "represents the talent, the thoughtfulness, and the beauty within the caterpillar/But having a harsh outlook on life the caterpillar sees the butterfly as weak and figures out a way to pimp it to his own benefits. . . ."

In his struggle to grow beyond the limitations of his alienation, the caterpillar goes to work on his cocoon, which both traps him and provides a space for creative ideas to emerge, "new concepts" that he can take back to his home community, "this mad city."

> *Finally free, the butterfly sheds light on situations that the caterpillar never considered, ending the internal struggle*
>
> *Although the butterfly and caterpillar are completely different, they are one and the same.*

Over the course of sixteen tracks, featuring a dizzying array of musical influences from soul music to rock to free jazz and contributions by artists such as Snoop Dogg, funkmaster George Clinton, the classic R&B group the Isley Brothers, and jazz musicians Robert Glasper and Kamasi Washington, Lamar explores this theme of struggle, transformation, and reconnection, mapping the creative, generative possibilities of Black masculinity within a community framework. *To Pimp a Butterfly* traces an emotional arc from youthful braggadocio through self-doubt toward an optimistic vision of change based upon self-knowledge and respect for others.

The album opens with "Wesley's Theory" (a reference to the tax evasion conviction of celebrity Wesley Snipes), which deals with the temptations of sudden fame and the exploitative tendencies of the music industry; and the boastful "King Kunta," a hard-edged rap that serves notice to Lamar's critics and competitors,

while at the same time introducing images of the shared oppression of Africans caught up in the slave trade (and of the yam as a traditional symbol of wealth and power).

The role of the rapper as cultural critic and community conscience—a role with deep roots in African American musical traditions—is adopted by Lamar with full seriousness, and he focuses his critical lens fearlessly, in multiple directions: on institutionalized racism, in the music industry and society at large ("For Free?"); on the hip-hop community and many of its stars, driven more by greed than by moral purpose ("Institutionalized"); on hip-hop purists who mourn the passing of socially-conscious rap music, yet don't support contemporary artists who pursue that direction ("Hood Politics"); and, controversially, on the ideological contradiction inherent in lamenting the tragic deaths of Trayvon Martin and other young African American men while celebrating images of masculine toughness that feed internecine violence in urban neighborhoods ("The Blacker the Berry"). But the critical lens of *To Pimp a Butterfly* is always focused most intensively on Lamar himself, in a relentless process of self-questioning about his own position and how he can best make use of his good fortune and celebrity to help the young men and women from Compton who are depicted so vividly in the black and white photographs that adorn the album cover.

One of the album's key pivot points is a shift in tone between the sixth and seventh tracks on the album, "u" and "Alright." In "u," an inebriated Lamar berates his image in a hotel room mirror, questioning his own motivations and character, expressing regret for having let his family and friends down, and admitting to depression and suicidal thoughts, an expression of vulnerability seldom heard in the tough-guy world of rap music. The song's refrain, "Loving you is complicated," addresses a key theme of the album: the struggle to achieve self-love in a world that provides so much negativity. "Alright," the following track, turns the corner toward faith and self-acceptance, recognizing the challenges faced by young African American men, but pushing back with the uplifting refrain, "We gon' be alright." During the summer of 2015 this refrain was adopted by activists protesting the police killings of young Black men, and when Lamar

(continued)

Listening Guide "TO PIMP A BUTTERFLY" *(continued)*

performed the song on the annual BET awards show standing on top of a police car, some political commentators revived the well-worn argument that rap music was a primary cause of social unrest and conflict. In an interview with TMZ, Lamar responded,

> Me being on a cop car, that's a performance piece after these senseless acts . . . Hip-hop is not the problem. Our reality is the problem of the situation. This is our music. This is us expressing ourselves.[10]

Lamar's openness to self-criticism and personal transformation, and his search for the optimism embodied in the metaphor of the butterfly emerging from its cocoon have led some in the hip-hop community to criticize him, implying that he is too "soft." Perhaps the most instructive example of this is the track "i" (counterpart of "u"), which has appeared in two very different recorded versions, first as a single (2014) and, a year later, as the penultimate track on the *To Pimp a Butterfly* album.

The single version (2014), which incorporated a version of the Isley Brothers' classic R&B hit "That Lady" (Number 6 pop, 1973), was widely described as "upbeat" and "uplifting," and won Grammy awards for Best Rap Performance and Best Rap Song. The single's cover depicts members of the Crips and the Bloods making heart signs—rather than antagonistic gang signs—with their hands, and the song's catchy refrain features lines like "I gotta get up, Life is more than suicide . . . I love myself." Some fans of Lamar's previous work felt that "i" was a pop compromise and a repudiation of his origins in the West Coast underground hip-hop scene, despite lyrics that describe urban life in terms evocative of Grandmaster Flash's classic "The Message." In an interview, Lamar's response to such criticism was direct and unambiguous:

> That's great. I would hate to stay stagnant. I would hate for you to say there's no growth. You're supposed to innovate and not only challenge yourself but challenge your listeners.[11]

For fans of the single, the very different version of "i" released on *To Pimp a Butterfly* came as a surprise. To begin with, although it was also produced in a studio, the album version is designed to imitate the experience of a live concert performance. It starts with crowd noise and an MC hyping Lamar as "The Number 1 Rapper in the World." Unlike the relatively subdued opening of the single, the album track launches directly into a high-energy rap, backed by a treble chorus and rock instrumentation. At about three minutes into the recording, we hear a fight break out in the audience, and Lamar stops the band, shouting "Not on my time! We could save that s**t for the streets . . . No, for real, how many ni**as we done lost, bro? This year alone? Exactly!"

After counseling the crowd against violence, Lamar completes the track with a deliberately-paced freestyle rap that returns to the theme of the African slave trade and then moves into an inspired reinterpretation of the N-word, which he translates as *Negus*, the word for "King" in the Semitic languages of Ethiopia. (This was one of the titles applied to Emperor Haile Selassie, whose important symbolic role in Jamaican Rastafarianism and Reggae music we discussed in Chapter 12.) In so doing, he transforms a term of racist derision—the word that Malcolm X and Richard Pryor stopped using when they returned to the United States from trips to Africa—into a signifier of pride and spiritual power. This is a powerful moment in hip-hop history, and a creative transferral of the uplifting sentiment of the single version of "i" into the artistic and social framework of his larger work.

The final track on *To Pimp a Butterfly*, "Mortal Man," pulls together the main themes of the album: struggle, hope, exploration, and the love of self and community. Once again, Lamar triangulates his own journey by reference to Africa, with an invocation of the late South African leader Nelson Mandela (1918–2013). Inspired by a 2014 visit to Robben Island, where Mandela was imprisoned for his resistance to apartheid, Lamar expresses his aspiration to follow in the footsteps of African American icons like Martin Luther King Jr., Malcolm X, Jackie Robinson, and Huey P. Newton, and to embody the spirit of Mandela in reaching out to his young fans. The track starts with a rich sonic texture reminiscent of 1970s soul and R&B recordings, with a loping mid-tempo groove, piano arpeggios, horns, synthesized strings, and voices layered one on top of the other.

10. "Geraldo's Twisting My Message: I'm about Hope, Not Violence." TMZ.com, July 2, 2015, http://www.tmz.com/2015/07/02/kendrick-lamar-responds-alright-geraldo-rivera-bet-awards-controversy-tmz-live/
11. Drew Millard, "Why Do People Hate Kendrick Lamar's 'i' So Much?" Noisey.com, November 5, 2014. https://noisey.vice.com/en_us/article/kendrick-lamar-i-music-video-essay

As the cinematic instrumental music fades to silence, Lamar begins a final recitation of his message, referring to his personal journey, his "survivor's guilt," and focusing on the core value of respect, and the importance of getting beyond the pain that gang warfare has caused Black men of his generation. Then, using segments of a 1994 interview conducted by Swedish music broadcaster Mats Nileskär, Lamar constructs an uncanny posthumous conversation with Tupac Shakur, in which both the points of shared experience and the generational differences between the two men are revealed. At the end, Tupac is heard expressing his view that armed conflict will be the inevitable outcome of America's racist history, and Lamar responds that "music and vibrations" are the only way forward now. As a parting gesture, Lamar reads Tupac his poem, "Tu Pimp a Caterpillar." There is no reply.

Whatever one's taste in popular music or view of the causes of social injustice in the United States today, there is no denying the sheer ambition and creative energy of *To Pimp a Butterfly*. Though their stylistic surfaces and creators' biographies are very different, in many ways, Kendrick Lamar's album could be heard as a descendant of the Beatles' *Sgt. Pepper's Lonely Hearts Club Band* (1967), in terms of its overall conceptual unity, the incorporation of myriad musical influences and cultural references, the flaunting of conventional genre expectations, the creation, in-studio, of elements of a live performance experience, and an air of self-conscious artistry. (Interestingly, Lamar and all four members of the Beatles were between twenty-five and twenty-seven years old when these albums were released.) Perhaps the main distinction is that, while the Beatles' album was a creative response to and catalyst for cultural friction and transformation, *To Pimp a Butterfly* is an artist's refraction of social trauma, at once a dispatch from a war zone, a poetic manifesto, and an inspired sermon on the moral limits of conflict.

violence, endemic drug use, and sometimes brutal law enforcement. Labeled as "a short film by Kendrick Lamar," *good kid, m.A.A.d city* contrasts smooth, atmospheric beats and textures with rough, violent scenarios, creating an overall low-key mood quite different from most contemporaneous rap recordings. In his raps Lamar embodies a series of characters, charting his own personal evolution from a brash, skirt-chasing teen to a more subdued and seasoned young man, struggling to grow beyond, yet stay connected to, the community in which he was raised. The album was widely appreciated within the hip-hop community and praised by critics, scored three Top 40 singles, and debuted at Number 2 on the *Billboard* album chart, signaling the arrival of a significant new voice in popular music.

As we noted earlier, hip-hop and R&B genres finally ended up outselling rock music in 2017, but it is important to note that some of this has to do with the way these genres are defined from a commercial standpoint. *Billboard* still tends to separate music that appears on the hip-hop/R&B charts from music that appears on the rock charts along race lines, just as they did with rhythm & blues and country & western charts in the mid-twentieth century, despite the fact that in most cases many musical characteristics of hit records in these genres were shared. Award nominating committees frequently separate artists along race lines as well. For example, the fact that the single "Blinding Lights" by Black Canadian artist the Weeknd (Abel Makkonen Tesfaye, b. 1990) won a 2020 VMA in the R&B rather than the pop category was clearly motivated more by race than musical characteristics. "Blinding Lights" is a synth-pop banger with more allegiance to the Psychedelic Furs than to Alicia Keys (whom he beat out in the R&B category).

Despite also winning the VMA for Video of the Year, "Blinding Lights" was *not* nominated in the pop category, where all of the nominees were white (Bieber, Halsey, Jonas Brothers, Lady Gaga, Ariana Grande, Taylor Swift).

Another genre polymath, *Lizzo* (Melissa Viviane Jefferson, b. 1988), began her musical career as a member of the rap group Cornrow Clique in Houston, Texas, before studying classical flute at the University of Houston. Her 2016 single "Good as Hell" (Number 44 Hot R&B/Hip-Hop) blended quasi-pitched rap verses with a catchy sung pop hook in the chorus ("I do my hair toss/check my nails"), all over a simple three-chord R&B piano and hip-hop drum machine pattern. Her follow-up 2019 LP *Cuz I Love You* (Number 4 *Billboard* 200) featured three very different singles that reveled in stylistic eclecticism: "Juice" (Number 27 Hot R&B/Hip-Hop) blends 70s soul with 80s synth pop; "Tempo" (Number 5 rap digital songs) is an entirely rapped collaboration with Missy Elliott; and her biggest hit "Truth Hurts" (Number 1 Hot 100) has Lizzo blending rapping with reggae-inflected vocals ("bom-bom bi-dom bi-dum bay-bay") over a downtempo "trap" beat (a signature Southern hip-hop beat type characterized by busy hi-hat patterns). Lizzo received more nominations than any other artist at the 2020 Grammy Awards, ultimately winning three that showcase the album's blend of genres (Urban Contemporary Album, Pop Solo Performance, Traditional R&B Performance).

Lizzo in performance, 2019.

Nowhere is post-2010 hip-hop's stylistic eclecticism more obvious than in the genre known as **emo rap**. Emo rap amplifies the vulnerability heard in lyrics by Kanye West and OutKast by blending rapping with the nasal singing style of punk and emo bands like Blink-182 and Dashboard Confessional. Emo rap crossed race lines more than traditional hip-hop, its biggest stars nearly split between white and Black (e.g., Lil' Peep and Juice WRLD, respectively; that both died in their early 20s from overdosing on pain medication speaks to the real-life impetus for their tortured lyrics). The genre had been popular on SoundCloud for nearly a decade (some in fact call this genre "SoundCloud rap") before it broke into the mainstream in 2017 with Lil' Uzi Vert's "XO TOUR Llif3" (Number 7 Hot 100). *Pitchfork* summed up the impact of the genre in 2017 neatly as "[c]ombining themes of suicide and revenge with trap drums and scraggly guitars" and "reinventing heart-on-sleeve agony for a new generation."[12] By 2018 emo rap was the single fastest growing genre on Spotify.

Defining emo rap as a genre gets tricky because at the same time that these "rappers" were incorporating emo elements into their music, "rock" and "pop" artists were also heading at the same idea from a different direction, replacing their drums and electric guitars with drum machines and synths, while employing sped-up vocal deliveries inherited from hip-hop. One can trace at least part of this evolution back to the highly influential 2003 album *Give Up* by the Postal Service, a side project for the indie-rock/emo musician Benjamin Gibbard (lead singer of Death Cab for Cutie). Named for the peculiar manner in which he collaborated with the album's other contributor, the EDM musician known as Dntel, the duo worked by mailing recordings back and forth, with Gibbard providing emo vocals and Dntel layering the track with synths and drum machines. Would-be indie rockers like Owl City, MGMT, and others continued to adopt and adapt this new "indietronica" style for the top of the pop charts.

By the mid-2010s the sound of mainstream rock had morphed to take on these characteristics: less guitar and drum set, more synths and drum machines. Artists who used to occupy two very different poles of the rock aesthetic—mainstream pop rockers Maroon 5 and emo rockers Panic! at the Disco—now all began to converge on this single, commercially viable strategy. A newer generation of artists seem not to acknowledge the distinction between hip-hop and rock at all. *Machine Gun Kelly* (Richard Colson Baker, b. 1990) released a rap collaboration with Latin pop sensation Camila Cabello that charted at Number 2 on the Hot R&B/Hip-Hop chart, then just three years later released the collaboration with Blink-182 drummer Travis Barker called "Bloody Valentine" that charted on Number 3 on Hot Rock & Alternative Songs. To keep the confusion going, it was white punk drummer Travis Barker who presented the award for Best Hip-Hop Video at the 2020 VMAs, in which four nominated Black male emo rappers (Da Baby, Future, Juice WRLD, Roddy Rich) ultimately lost to Megan Thee Stallion, a decidedly non-emo Houston-based rapper who would go on to "break the internet" the following year with a collaboration with New York–based rapper Cardi B, entitled "WAP."

---

12. https://pitchfork.com/features/rising/10001-tears-of-a-dirtbag-rapper-lil-peep-is-the-future-of-emo/

Machine Gun Kelly and Travis Barker (on drums) performing virtually at the 2020 MTV VMAs.

Watching Travis Barker and Machine Gun Kelly's live performance on the VMAs during that same ceremony, one is confused about whether this is rap crossing over into emo, or emo crossing over into hip-hop; indeed, the distinction would seem beside the point.

With artists from different genres all arriving at the same musical conclusions—quasi-pitched rap-singing over drum machines and synths—a disturbing pattern emerges. By analyzing the amount of vocal pitch present in rap and pop music at the top of the charts (whether with or without Auto-Tune), Robert Komaniecki has recently shown that even when these musical characteristics are quantifiably similar, genre categories remain fixed based on race, with white artists charting in pop/rock, and Black artists in R&B/hip-hop. After winning the 2020 Grammy for Best Rap Album, genre-bending hip-hop pioneer Tyler, The Creator (another member of the Odd Future collective) called the award a "backhanded compliment." He went on to call out the nominating committee's genre-based racism:

> I'm very grateful that what I make can be acknowledged in a world like this, but also it sucks that whenever we—and I mean guys that look like me—do anything that's genre-bending, they always put it in the rap or urban category. . . . I don't like that "urban" word, it's just a politically correct way to say the "n" word to me.[13]

In the wake of emo rap, racist nomination practices, and artists crossing over between rock, hip-hop, or even country in the case of Lil' Nas X's 2019 hit "Old Town Road"

---

13. https://www.independent.co.uk/arts-entertainment/music/news/grammys-2020-tyler-creator-best-rap-album-urban-racism-winners-a9303351.html

(Number 1 Hot 100, Number 19 Hot Country Songs), long-standing arguments over the authenticity of particular hip-hop artists remain, and it has become even more difficult to assess the limits of the category.

Twenty-First-Century Divas: We Never Go Out of Style

At the time of this writing, the twenty-first century is entering its third decade and popular music continues to blur the lines of genre and intended audiences, with artists who continue to reinvent themselves and their music. We will take a close look at three women, each of whom has a unique approach to songwriting, music-making, and celebrity. Despite these differences, each of them maintains an impressive level of commercial and critical success and, in many ways, their recordings are the definitive sounds of the 2010s. Beyoncé, Adele, and Taylor Swift share unprecedented commercial success, with combined album sales of over 69 million and thirty-four Top 10 hits between 2005 and 2016.

BEYONCÉ

Beyoncé Knowles (b. 1981) came to the attention of audiences at the turn of the century as the leader of the group Destiny's Child. As a singer, songwriter, dancer, actress, and celebrity, Beyoncé has become a symbol of feminine empowerment, including personal, sexual, and financial independence. Her music is closely tied to her image as a strong Black woman, and her videos and live performances enhance this image. In many ways, the polished image of Destiny's Child with Beyoncé at the helm was a parallel to that of the Supremes and Diana Ross in the 1960s (see Chapter 9). When Beyoncé embarked on a solo career, she did so conscious of this parallel and has carefully crafted her image to recall the R&B divas of the past; she even starred in the film version of *Dreamgirls* (2006), a fictionalized account of the career of the Supremes, as the "Diana Ross" character. In 2003, she released her first solo album *Dangerously in Love* (Number 1 pop, four times platinum) which spawned four Top 10 hits (including the infectious "Crazy in Love," featuring her future husband, Jay-Z) and garnered five Grammy awards, including Best Contemporary R&B Record.

Beyoncé's music hovers between R&B, hip-hop, dance, and pop, and often includes memorable rhythmic hooks. Her 2008 smash hit "Single Ladies (Put a Ring on It)" (Number 1, pop; Number 1, R&B/hip-hop) from her third solo album *I Am . . . Sasha Fierce* (a reference to her performing alter-ego) perfectly exemplifies Beyoncé's empowered, dance-heavy, pop-friendly music. "Single Ladies" started a world-wide dance craze, and the video has over 824 million hits to date on YouTube.

In 2013, 2016, and 2020 Beyoncé experimented with a new album format: the visual album. The first two included two discs, one purely audio and the second a DVD. The visual album for her self-titled *Beyoncé* (2013) offered a series of music videos which lean toward the short film genre, and *Lemonade* (2016) presented an album-length film in eleven segments directed by an eclectic group of film-makers, including Beyoncé herself. *Black Is King* (2020) was the first not to be released as a stand-alone audio CD (though songs heard in the film appear on her 2019 audio album *The Lion King: The Gift*). The fully integrated multimedia product retells the story of Disney's film *The Lion King* through various styles of African and African American musical genres as a way to express the conditions of the African diaspora. Beyoncé's visual albums acknowledge and revel in the demand for strong visual elements for both the pop star and the music she makes. This format, which relies on multimedia discs or streaming video services, prompts the question: Are we supposed to listen to, or to watch, the music in order to fully experience the album? While the predecessors to Beyoncé's visual albums may be Michael Jackson's *Thriller* and Madonna's *Like a Prayer* (see Chapter 13), the *music* on her multimedia creations depends on the visual elements to a virtually unprecedented degree, behaving almost as an accompaniment to the film. Arguably, the primary experience of this music *is* the film.

By channeling the music and divas of the past, including Diana Ross, Donna Summer, Tina Turner, and Etta James—a 1960s soul singer whom Beyoncé portrayed in the 2008 film *Cadillac Records*, and whose signature song "At Last" she performed at the inaugural ball of President Barack Obama in 2009—Beyoncé is seeking to establish a legacy. With two Super Bowl halftime shows under her belt (2013, 2016), twenty-four Grammy awards as of 2020, and over 100 million albums sold worldwide, it looks as if Beyoncé need not become the "next" anything—she already is the only Beyoncé.

ADELE

Adele Adkins, M.B.E. (born May 5, 1988, London, England), became a pop sensation in 2008 when circumstance placed her in the right place at the right time. On tour in the United States promoting her first album *19* (2008), Adele appeared on the long-running late-night sketch show *Saturday Night Live* on October 18, 2008, performing the singles "Chasing Pavements" and "Cold Shoulder." The episode also featured another guest: Republican vice-presidential candidate Sarah Palin. The episode drew record viewership, and "Chasing Pavements" rose to the top of the iTunes charts. In 2009, she collected two Grammy Awards—Best New Artist and Best Female Pop Vocal for "Chasing Pavements."

In 2011, Adele released her follow-up album *21*, produced in part by Rick Rubin (see Chapter 12), which became the bestselling album of 2011 and 2012, spending a staggering 208 weeks on the *Billboard* 200, and at the time of this writing has sold over 31 million units worldwide, making it the bestselling album of the twenty-first century as of January 2021. The album produced five singles, three of which topped the pop charts and collected individual Grammy Awards in 2011–2012: "Someone Like You" (Best Pop Solo Performance, 2011), "Set Fire to the Rain" (Best Pop Solo Performance, 2012), and "Rolling in the Deep" (Record of the Year, Song of the Year, Best Short Form Music Video, 2011). Additionally, *21* earned Grammys in 2011 for Album of the Year and Best Pop Vocal Album.

"Rolling in the Deep" begins with a driving, somewhat angular acoustic guitar riff over a sparse vocal line. The instrumental arrangement builds, first with a driving bass and bass drum rhythm followed by keyboard, until an explosive instrumental climax arrives, with addition of background vocals at "We could have had it all/Rolling in the deep." The basic structure of the song follows the straightforward verse-chorus form. The vocals also build in intensity through the verse to the chorus. The verse begins with a conversational vocal featuring a fairly static melodic line, then adds melodic interest with a descending vocal line on "The scars of your love remind me of us / they keep me thinking that we almost had it all / the scars of your love, they leave me breathless" before reaching a vocal climax at the chorus, when we finally hear the highest point of Adele's range and an expressive crack in her voice. The stylistic differences between the verse and chorus are notable for how well they work together. "Rolling in the Deep" is a perfectly polished pop song, with slick production, a decidedly vintage style (doo-wop backing vocals), and a subject of heartbreak and survival.

Adele's sudden and accelerated rise into the collective headphones of American audiences was surprising, but was aided by fellow British singer-songwriter Amy Winehouse (1983–2011), whose 2006 album *Back to Black* combined hip-hop with 1960s girl group gloss. Adele's own vocal style is heavily influenced by the 1960s and 1970s soul singers, and by prominent artists of the 2000s, including Lauryn Hill (see Chapter 14) and Alicia Keys. Her albums are full of power ballads and torch songs, with elaborate production and large vocal climaxes reminiscent of Barbra Streisand and Celine Dion. Her public image, like her music, is a throwback to the 1960s, with a Motown-esque performance polish. She remains relatively private about her personal life, opting to present herself in public as a serious musician and performer, an image reinforced by the photos of Adele hard at work in the studio that are included with her albums.

Adele's dedication to making money "the old school way—by moving records" puts her at odds with the growing trend of making money from touring we discussed earlier, with sales of recordings and streaming accounting for a combined 82 percent of her 2015 revenues, and the balance coming from publishing rights to her songs. In addition to her impressive sales, chart success, and Grammy Awards, in 2013 Adele won an Oscar for Best Original Song for "Skyfall," from the James Bond film of the same name. In 2015, she released *25*, the last in her "age" trilogy, which, despite becoming available only during the last six weeks of the year, was the bestselling release of the year, and shattered first week sales records with over 3 million units sold. As of this writing, the album has sold over 11 million units in the United States, making Adele the first artist of the new millennium to reach the elusive "Diamond Certification" for two albums. The lead-off single "Hello," a power ballad which debuted at Number 1 on the pop charts, has sold over 7 million units as of this writing.

TAYLOR SWIFT

Let us now revisit *Taylor Swift*, whose early career was discussed previously in Chapter 14. In 2012, Swift released her fourth album, *RED*, an album still technically classified as "country" (it was nominated for a Grammy for Best Country Album in 2013), but occupying a world away from an early Swift song like "Tim McGraw." Though the lead-off single, and Swift's first Number 1 hit on the Hot 100, "We Are Never Ever Getting Back Together," was purportedly about a high-profile break-up, the song could easily be seen as her "break" from country music, which she had all but abandoned with her previous album *Speak Now*. The acoustic guitar remained, but shrewd marketing helped redefine what the acoustic guitar meant: it was no longer a stylistic marker of country music. Instead Taylor Swift looked toward embracing the great singer-songwriters of the 1960s and 1970s, including Carole King and Joni Mitchell. In case the shift in musical style wasn't obvious enough, a booklet was included with physical and digital albums featuring photos of Swift with long straight hair, blunt bangs, bright red lips, and vintage fashion—a far cry from the innocent, country persona portrayed on her first three albums.

As is the case with Beyoncé and Adele, visual imagery is essential to the way a listener experiences Swift's music, and the space between Swift's public and private persona is negligible. Her Instagram account, which includes heavily curated photos of Swift and her "girl squad," has over 162 million followers at the time of the present writing. Taylor Swift and her music are now about a lifestyle, constantly reinforced in the tabloid press and on social media. Her penchant for tabloid gossip is furthered by the cryptic messages scattered throughout the liner notes of her albums.

Taylor Swift's album *1989*, released in 2015, was the first "official" break from country music. On her website, she made the following statement about this drastic and conscious shift:

> For the last few years, I've woken up every day not wanting, but needing to write a new style of music. I needed to change the way I told my stories and the way they sounded. I listened to a lot of music from the decade in which I was born and I listened to my intuition that it was a good thing to follow this gut feeling. I was also writing a different storyline than I'd ever told you before.

To those listening, the stylistic shift was well in place before *1989*. But that is not to say there isn't a stylistic difference between *1989* and *RED*. While *RED* embraces a 1970s singer-songwriter sound laced with an alternative rock and pop aesthetic, *1989* is an unabashedly synth-pop record which literally sounds like the music from 1989, the year of Swift's birth.

There are consistencies in Swift's songwriting in the past decade, namely her fondness for the "you done me wrong" revenge song. Swift's very public relationships and feuds with other celebrities provide much of the fuel to fire the Swiftian revenge song. A song such as "Bad Blood" from *1989* has striking similarities in subject matter to "Picture to Burn" (*Taylor Swift*); "You're Not Sorry" (*Fearless*); "Better Than Revenge," and "Dear John" (*Speak Now*); and "I Knew You Were Trouble" and "We Are Never Ever Getting Back Together" (*RED*). Although the revenge songs keep Swift's name in the tabloid press, it's often the love songs that provide musical and lyrical high points on Swift's albums. Her most consistent writing may come from a place of joy, as in "Our Song" from *Taylor Swift*; "Mine" from *Speak Now*; and the decidedly more grown-up "Style" from *1989*, an infectious synth-pop track with an unself-conscious fun lyric: "You got that James Dean daydream look in your eye / And I got that red lip classic thing that you like . . . 'Cause we never go out of style/ We never go out of style."

1989 represents a kind of anomaly, a rare recent example of an artist completely and successfully abandoning her home genre at a time of massive success to take a gamble on the pop charts, a place where Swift was previously comfortable visiting, but only with one foot in Nashville's door. The lead-off single "Shake It Off" squelched criticism before it could be uttered with a video showing Swift refusing to conform to different types of dance, featuring the pop-perfect lyrics "I'm dancing on my own / I make the moves up as I go / And that's what they don't know / That's what they don't know / But I keep cruising / Can't stop, won't stop grooving / It's like I got this music in my mind / Saying, 'It's gonna be alright.'" With 10 million digital singles sold and 3 billion YouTube hits for "Shake It Off," a Grammy for Album of the Year for *1989*, 5 million units of *1989* sold in the first eight months of its release, and five Top 10 hits from the album, it's clear that pop audiences needed no pushing to fully embrace Taylor Swift.

Swift has continued to stylistically reinvent herself in subsequent work. Her sixth album *Reputation* (2017) was produced primarily by two Swedish producers, Max Martin and Shellback, who brought to the work their EDM sonic signatures. Her 2019 *Lover*—the bestselling record of 2019—combined the glitzy synth-pop of *1989* with a more personal and confessional lyrical tone. *folklore*, her eighth studio album, swings in quite the opposite musical direction. Full of indie-folk balladry, its "recorded-at-home" aesthetic owes in part to Swift writing and recording a large portion of it during the Covid-19 epidemic in 2020. Having previously won the Grammy for Album of the year twice (for *Fearless* in 2010; for *1989* in 2016), in 2021 *folklore* also won Album of the Year, making Swift the only woman to win this prestigious category three times.

Conclusion: American Popular Music in the Age of Globalization

As we have charted the dynamics of the marketplace for popular music since the year 2000 it has become increasingly difficult to sustain the distinction that we initially drew between the *mainstream* and its *margins*. In part this is because at the outset we were able to conflate two quite different concepts: on the one hand, the idea of a *musical* mainstream and margins, involving cultural and stylistic distinctions that have grown more and more blurry over time; and on the other hand, the idea that the market for popular music has an *economic and institutional* center and periphery.

In the early twentieth century these two dichotomies fit together rather neatly, for the mainstream of popular music—mainly Tin Pan Alley love songs and jazz- and ragtime-tinged dance music—coincided to a great degree with the central institutions of the music business (publishing firms, phonograph companies, and, somewhat later, radio networks). But by the early twenty-first century, the two dichotomies, as well as the correlation between them, had broken down almost completely. Musical genres that started on the margins—rhythm & blues, country and western, urban folk music, soul music, disco, heavy metal, EDM, punk, rap, and emo—came in time to occupy the mainstream, right alongside (and frequently displacing) "adult contemporary" music more directly descended from the Tin Pan Alley tradition. This process was mirrored in turn by the economic evolution of the music business. When BMI was founded in 1941 as an alternative to ASCAP, it represented marginalized genres such as race and hillbilly music. Today both of these performing rights societies license the widest imaginable range of music, from folk to country to hip-hop (and, as we have seen, monitor the use of their member's compositions in digital formats with increasing effectiveness).

While the distinction between "major" and "independent" labels continues in a sense today, the modes of operation of the global music industry have changed radically. In the evolving global marketplace, even the concept of the album is being fundamentally rethought, as streaming opens up new options. While some artists continue to release albums as integrated, unified "works," others are experimenting with more open-ended approaches that incorporate responses from their fans and allow the album to grow over time. Nearly every new album now begins as a "pre-release" on streaming services. Users "add" the album, but only a few tracks appear in their library until months later when the full album is made available. (Sometimes tracks are added gradually, appearing unannounced in the user's library.) These approaches are deeply informed by images of transnational, lateral, collaborative flows, made possible by digital technologies.

Alongside the impact of digital technologies on the structure of the music business and the process of musical creation, the geographical distribution of the music industry has undergone significant change. At the beginning of the twentieth century, New York City was unquestionably the center of the American music industry. A little more than a century later, the spread of digital technology seems to be completing a process of decentralization.

Indeed, the rise of massively popular global pop music stars like Shakira (Colombia), Drake (Canada), Enrique Iglesias (Spain), and Psy (South Korea); the creation of *Billboard* charts such as global dance tracks; and an increase in the number of nation-specific charts—including those devoted to sales in Japan (since 2008), Brazil (2009), and Korea (2011)—all suggest that our center/periphery model of the music industry must now be rethought in truly global terms.

In 2015, for example, half of the ten bestselling global artists—Adele, Ed Sheeran, One Direction, Coldplay, and Sam Smith—were British, joined on that list by The Weeknd (Abel Makkonen Tesfaye), a Canadian alternative R&B artist who is the son of Ethiopian immigrants. The bestselling single worldwide in 2015 was "See You Again" by hip-hop artist Wiz Khalifa (Cameron Jibril Thomaz), an American born in North Dakota and raised in Germany, the UK, and Japan, before settling in Pittsburgh, Pennsylvania, where his music career started. And the bestselling album in the United States was *25* by Adele, born in London, England. It is clear that we have reached a stage where globalization has thoroughly impacted the lives of musicians and listeners everywhere, far beyond the implications of the British Invasion of the 1960s.

Perhaps the best example of the internationalization of the U.S. music business is the reggaeton/Latin trap superstar **Bad Bunny** *(b. Benito Antonio Martínez Ocasio in*

Puerto Rico, 1994), who began releasing his recordings in 2016 on the streaming platform SoundCloud. In 2020, Bad Bunny performed at the Super Bowl LIV halftime show as a guest, alongside Shakira and Jennifer Lopez; released El Último Tour Del Mundo, which became the first all-Spanish-language album to top the US *Billboard* 200 and generated the *Billboard* Global 200 Number 1 single "Dakiti," and became the first non-English language act to be Spotify's most streamed artist of the year.

The United States, which formerly accounted for the lion's share of worldwide sales of recorded music, was neck-and-neck with Japan in 2015 when all sources of revenue were taken into account. The next five largest national markets for recorded music—Germany, the United Kingdom, France, Australia, and Canada—all together generated in total about the same revenues as either the United States or Japan. (The massive music markets in China, India, and Korea are not accurately reflected in such surveys, since reliable statistics are not available, either because of government policies or as a result of the trade in counterfeit recordings.) In 2019 the Big Three multinational music corporations—Universal Music Group, Sony Music Entertainment, and Warner Music International, all headquartered in the United States—were responsible for about 68 percent of recorded music sales worldwide and about 65 percent of sales in the United States, where the share of the market attributed to independent labels has grown markedly since 2015.[14] At the same time, the internet has continued to accelerate the globalization of the music business. Given the challenges facing the European Union market (including the recent departure of its largest music economy, the United Kingdom) and ongoing changes in Asia (including the continued rise of India, China, and Korea as major centers for the production and consumption of popular music), it is hard to predict with any precision the future of the international music business. It does seem likely that the United States will be an important and even indispensable part of the global music system, but it will possibly no longer represent its dominant center.

That's the economic picture. But even if the United States can no longer cling to a mythology of Manifest Destiny in relation to the rapidly growing and diversifying global entertainment industry, there can be no doubt that the sounds and sensibilities of American popular music will continue to exert an enormous impact all over the world. Millions of people worldwide have come to know the United States through its popular culture, as disseminated in movie theaters, on television and radio, on cassettes and discs, and via the internet. This image of America is a song-map: a set of narratives about being "Born in the U.S.A." and "Living in America," and a network of imaginary pathways connecting "Georgia on My Mind" to the "St. Louis Blues," juxtaposing street knowledge "Straight Outta Compton" with the urban delights of "Spanish Harlem," and pitting the seductively mirrored "Hotel California" against the plain white city hall of "Muskogee," Oklahoma. Similarly, the popular narrative of America as a center of novelty, excitement, and mobility has been disseminated by mass-reproduced sonic images

---

14. https://www.statista.com/statistics/947107/recorded-music-market-worldwide-label/; https://www.statista.com/statistics/317632/market-share-record-companies-label-ownership-usa/

BOX 15.2 POPULAR MUSICIANS WHO ENDURED—AND ENDURE!

Throughout its long history, the basic aim of American popular music has always been to capture its own cultural moment and, by doing so, to captivate the audience of its own time. The central goal of popular musicians has been the making of hit songs, not the creation of enduring "art" or the construction of cultural "monuments." And it is therefore not surprising that the story of pop music includes many instances of artists who are "one-hit wonders" (or two- or three-hit wonders), with careers that appear like flashes in the pan of history. Even very successful pop musicians tend to achieve peak success within the span of a relatively few years, facing dwindling influence and audiences after their initial achievements as hit-makers. The most successful pop group of all time, the Beatles, seems to have known when to quit, disbanding while still at a height of popularity in 1970—less than a decade after their initial record-setting conquest of the music scene.

We have, however, encountered striking exceptions to this pattern, in the form of artists with multi-decade careers, who achieved and maintained iconic status in the pop music world for anomalously long periods of time. Most of these are figures who managed successfully to change with, and adapt to, their changing times, such as Louis Armstrong, Frank Sinatra, Aretha Franklin, Dolly Parton, and Paul Simon. With Bob Dylan, we have a songwriting musician who altered his style with great frequency, seeming to follow his own whims while both setting and ignoring trends, all the while managing to bring a large audience along with him. And then there is the exception among the exceptions, Tony Bennett. Bennett's career, spanning seven decades at the time of this writing, is a testament to the integrity of an artist who has remained true to a single aesthetic vision, centered upon a Tin Pan Alley–based repertoire and singing style that were already "old-fashioned" when he made his first appearance on the pop charts in 1951!

Briefly reviewing these figures will offer us a concluding overview of major developments in the history of American popular music.

Louis Armstrong initially distinguished himself as an outstanding ensemble player within the group improvisation style employed by the first prominent African American jazz bands (such as that led by King Oliver). In the later 1920s, his innovative recordings with his Hot Five and Hot Seven expanded the melodic and rhythmic horizons of jazz by virtue of Armstrong's creativity as a solo player, introducing him also as a singer—and as a pioneer of scat singing. In the 1930s, as big dance bands became increasingly popular, Armstrong fronted his own, achieving renown increasingly as a singer of pop songs as well as a jazz trumpet performer. His success in both these realms endured for decades, reinforced by his appearances in popular movies like *A Song Is Born* (1948) and *High Society* (1956), and he even scored a late-career Number 1 hit with "Hello, Dolly!" at the height of Beatlemania in America (1964).

Starting out as a singer with big bands, Frank Sinatra struck out on his own to become one of the most beloved crooners of the 1940s. When his popularity as a hit singles artist appeared to be fading in the early 1950s, Sinatra reinvented himself: first, as a master of the new long-playing record (LP) format, releasing entire albums built on sustained musical moods and specific themes in song lyrics; second, as a non-singing actor in serious films like *From Here to Eternity* (1953, for which he won an Oscar as Best Supporting Actor). Persevering through many changes in the dominant styles of popular music, Sinatra remains to this day one of the bestselling album artists of all time, while he periodically scored major career-reinvigorating individual hits like "Strangers in the Night" and "That's Life" (both 1966), and "Theme from *New York, New York*" (1980). His two trend-setting albums of *Duets* in the 1990s, which paired him with singers decades younger in a repertoire composed chiefly of Tin Pan Alley standards, kept Sinatra in the public ear up to the time of his death in 1998—and beyond.

During the late 1960s and the early 1970s, the great soul singer Aretha Franklin recorded a seemingly unbreakable string of major hits, remaining for years a powerful presence on both the rhythm & blues and pop charts, but her career seemed to sag in the mid-1970s. Her triumphant return to the upper echelons of chart success a full decade later offers a lesson in the ways an "older" artist might regain status as a "contemporary" pop star.

During the brief period 1985–1987, Franklin scored three Top 10 hits: "Freeway of Love," "Who's Zoomin' Who," and "I Knew You Were Waiting (for Me)." All three featured very elaborate arrangements employing synthesizers, giving them an up-to-date sound that was decisively different from that typical of Franklin's earlier soul singles, which had relied on a more basic, stripped-down approach. Synthesized and studio effects are especially noticeable on "Who's Zoomin' Who" and "I Knew You Were Waiting (for Me)," and it didn't hurt that the latter song was a duet sung by Franklin and George Michael (1963–2016); Michael was one of the most popular singers of the 1980s, and his participation surely had a role in pushing the song to Number 1 on the pop charts in 1987. (It won a Grammy in the R & B Vocal Duo category!) "Freeway of Love" and "I Knew You Were Waiting (for Me)" also employed the newly important medium of music video as a means of additional popularization, and Franklin became a well-recognized presence on the era-defining MTV. However, lest long-time fans might have feared that Franklin had left behind her gospel roots, 1987 also brought the release of her highly-regarded album *One Lord, One Faith, One Baptism*, recorded live in church (as was her previous gospel album *Amazing Grace*, in 1972).

Duets are playing an obvious role in this narrative, and become decisively important in recounting the early careers of our next two artists, Dolly Parton and Paul Simon. Dolly Parton was first introduced to a national audience in 1967, via the television show hosted by fellow country singer Porter Wagoner, and she released numerous duets with Wagoner (singles and albums) that made the pair a reliable presence on the country charts for years. During this period, Parton was also honing her considerable skills as a songwriter, and releasing successful solo recordings, both of which prepared her perfectly for her career as a solo artist beginning in 1974. Parton soon set her sights on success beyond the country market, and she began to make her mark on the national Hot 100 charts with pop-oriented material like "Here You Come Again" (Number 3, 1977). She became a movie star in 1980 with her film debut in *9 to 5*, and she wrote and performed the theme song, which became her first Number 1 pop hit. Taking her cue perhaps from Frank Sinatra,

Parton enlarged her audience and demonstrated her acting talent by assuming non-singing (as well as singing) roles in movies, as she did in the very popular *Steel Magnolias* (1989). Entering her fourth decade as an entertainer, Parton both surprised and reassured country fans by releasing *The Grass Is Blue* (1999), which won a Grammy in the Bluegrass Album category, and she followed this with other albums along similar stylistic lines. This "return to roots" echoes Aretha Franklin's gospel "return" cited previously, and suggests another kind of successful career strategy for artists who have the interest, perseverance, and talent to play the "long game."

Following his achievements in the 1960s as the songwriting half of the folk-rock duo Simon and Garfunkel, Paul Simon embarked on a solo career in the 1970s, producing three Top 10 albums and five Top 10 singles during that decade. Simon's music was eclectic in the best sense, ranging stylistically from the reggae-flavored "Mother and Child Reunion" (Number 4, 1972) to the deceptively gentle folk rock of the acid-tinged "50 Ways to Leave Your Lover" (Number 1, 1975). However, his wide-ranging creative embrace of world music in the 1986 album *Graceland*, which continued in *The Rhythm of the Saints* (1990), could not have been readily foreseen. The broad significance of these albums lies in the fact Simon was not following an established marketing strategy for the time in a conscious attempt to reinvigorate his career; rather, by following his own artistic instincts, he ended up playing an innovative role by establishing a newly expanded market for the kind of music that he (and others that followed) wished to make. Simon's efforts to expand his career into movies (*One Trick Pony*, 1980)—and even in writing for Broadway (*The Capeman*, 1997)—proved less successful than comparable efforts by artists like Sinatra and Parton, but Simon continued to release critically and commercially successful albums into the 2010s. Simon announced his retirement from touring in 2018, but assured fans that he would agree to perform on particular occasions to benefit the causes in which he believed (such as preserving the environment).

When it comes to Bob Dylan, a list of the various musical styles that he has embraced would read like the table of contents for a book on American

(continued)

BOX 15.2 POPULAR MUSICIANS WHO ENDURED—AND ENDURE! (*continued*)

popular music over the last century. Such a list might proceed chronologically through the major changes in Dylan's own recording and performing career—from his beginnings as interpreter of classic folk, rural blues, and early country material; to his emergence as an urban folk, acoustic singer-songwriter; to Dylan, the electric rock pioneer; to Dylan, the country crooner; to Dylan, the Christian rock missionary; and on and on. Or the list might proceed chronologically through pop music history itself as recounted in this book—from Tin Pan Alley standards and crooning; to blues and country repertoire; to rock 'n' roll; to urban folk; and so on. The list would serve the same purpose regardless, as an effective chronicle of Bob Dylan's musical interests and achievements. It might seem easier to list a few major stylistic developments in which Dylan was *not* involved, but such an attempt raises some problems of its own. Psychedelic rock? To be sure, Dylan shied away from the elaborate arrangements and studio effects that characterized much psychedelia, but the intensely personal imagery and even surrealism to be found in his song lyrics of the mid-1960s (see "Mr. Tambourine Man," "Desolation Row," and others, for examples) just as surely were a source of inspiration for songwriters identified with the counterculture of the time. His first electric single, "Subterranean Homesick Blues" (1965), with its rapid-fire, half-sung and half-spoken vocal, is often cited as a "proto-rap" record. What about world music? Well, the famous reggae rhythm section of Robbie Shakespeare (bass) and Sly Dunbar (drums) pervades the sound world and provides the backbone of every track on Dylan's 1983 album *Infidels*.

As controversial as many of his career twists and turns may have seemed to many of Dylan's fans at any given time, it should be emphasized that every style this protean artist has attempted—including, it must be stressed, gospel music—represents a major thread in that extraordinary patchwork that constitutes American popular song. From a twenty-first-century standpoint, it wouldn't seem to matter whether Dylan's comprehensive achievements were strategic or simply incremental on his part, the product of a grand design or of a constantly questing spirit. What matters is that Bob Dylan is as essential and defining a figure as any in the history of American music, and that it is his continuing, seemingly unpredictable evolution—his openness to change—that has assured him of this stature.

In complete contrast to Dylan stands Tony Bennett (born Anthony Dominick Benedetto, 1926), who has attained his high status in the pantheon of American performers by determining early in his career exactly the kind of music he wished to sing, and the way in which he wished to sing it, and then remaining true to that vision. In his reverence for the Great American Songbook, and in his commitment to keeping that repertoire alive while remaining open to new material written in an analogous style, Bennett obviously followed in the footsteps of Frank Sinatra, whom he reveres. Bennett arguably has a fuller voice than Sinatra, but he is equally skilled at intimate crooning. And like Sinatra, Bennett has always been flexible enough to wander occasionally outside of Tin Pan Alley and its offshoots. In fact, one of Bennett's earliest hits was an elaborate, mainstream pop-oriented arrangement of country artist Hank Williams's "Cold, Cold Heart" (Number 1 for six weeks in 1951), but this approach ultimately proved atypical. More characteristic of Bennett were recordings of Tin Pan Alley evergreens, interpretations of songs from Broadway shows old and new (his "Stranger in Paradise" from the 1953 show *Kismet* proved very popular), and what we might call neo–Tin Pan Alley songs like "I Wanna Be Around," "Fly Me to the Moon," and, especially, "I Left My Heart in San Francisco," with which Bennett has become indelibly linked.

Written by George Cory and Douglass Cross, and first introduced by Bennett in live performances in 1954, "I Left My Heart in San Francisco" is clearly modeled—in its melody, lyrics, and form—on the sentimental pop songs of the 1920s and 1930s. Bennett did not get around to recording it until 1962, and released as a single that same year, it achieved only the kind of modest chart success (reaching Number 19) that was typical for Bennett in the age of rock 'n' roll. At the time, with the twist craze at its peak, one could have been forgiven for feeling that such a record, with its slow tempo, old-school orchestral arrangement, night-club piano fills, and smooth, lyrical vocal, presenting a song in the seemingly archaic verse-refrain form, was nothing more than a curious anachronism. More than half a century later, with "I Left My Heart in San Francisco" established as an enduring standard and as Tony Bennett's iconic theme song, "timeless" seems a much more appropriate characterization than "anachronism"—for the song, for the recording, and indeed for Bennett himself! Tony Bennett's constant goal, which he has achieved regularly, is delineated in one of his own album titles: *The Art of Excellence*.

Like many of the other artists under consideration here, Tony Bennett's later career was reinvigorated through appearances on visual media. In Bennett's case, in the 1990s, the specific medium was television, in particular his participation in the MTV *Unplugged* series; the recording of this event won 1994 Grammy Awards in both the "Album of the Year" and the "Best Traditional Pop Vocal Performance" categories. Bennett has been receiving Grammys on a regular basis since 1992 (more than ten such awards, and counting, as of this writing). He has frequently collaborated with other prominent musicians, such as jazz greats Count Basie and (pianist) Bill Evans, and recently has joined so many other renowned singers in turning his attention to vocal duets, with partners as diverse as k.d. lang and Lady Gaga. The "Jazz at Lincoln Center" DVD *Tony Bennett & Lady Gaga: Cheek to Cheek Live!*, recorded in 2014, is a special delight. Bennett, just days from his eighty-eighth birthday at the time of this performance, commands the stage in his steady, leisurely, suave, and utterly self-assured way, while Lady Gaga plays his foil in her own characteristic style, dancing around him, gesturing, and changing from one flamboyant costume into another. It all works perfectly, because both artists obviously enjoy and esteem one another, and are united in their love for the Great American Songbook set they chose together to perform: popular music that endures!

of Americans "rollin' on the river" on the "Proud Mary," "Waiting for a Train," "Leavin' on a Jet Plane," driving around in a "Merry Oldsmobile," a "Little Deuce Coupe," or a "Low Rider," and wandering footloose "Like a Rolling Stone." Although music is by no means a universal language, the recurring themes of American popular music—love and sex, home and migration, materialism and morality, optimism and heartbreak—have resonated with millions of listeners worldwide.

Americans are often surprised to discover that country and western music is extremely popular in Africa, has a large following in India, and has even become a kind of second traditional music for Australian aboriginals. The assumption underlying this reaction—that, despite the contributions of African American musicians such as Charlie Pride, Ray Charles, and Mickey Guyton, country music is essentially music by and for white people—is related to the particular racial history of the United States and the impact of slavery, "Jim Crow" laws, and racial segregation on the development and social significance of American popular music, all issues that we have examined in detail in this book. From our perspective, this international appeal suggests that one of the possibilities created by the adoption and creative reinterpretation of American popular music by musicians around the world is the opportunity to hear that music—and, by extension, American identities, values, and histories—through someone else's ears. As the writer G. K. Chesterton once put it, "The whole object of travel is not to set foot on foreign land; it is at last to set foot on one's own country as a foreign land." We began this book with the observation that American popular music has from its very earliest days been the product of multiple influences, brought to our shores by successive waves of immigrants from Europe, Africa, Latin America, and beyond. Today, the global circulation of music continues and extends this centuries-old "conversation" among cultures and provides us with an opportunity to experience America's contributions anew, from a broader perspective.

WE HAVE REACHED the endpoint of our journey, but there is every reason to expect that the energy and creativity, the crassness and commercialism of American popular music—that messy product of almost four centuries of cultural miscegenation—will continue to impress themselves on the world's consciousness, provoking equal measures of admiration and disapproval. Whether one views this process as an extension of cultural imperialism or as proof positive of the unique value of American musical culture, there can be no denying that popular music—forged by the sons and daughters of Africa and Europe, shaped by the diverse musical cultures of the Americas, hustled and hyped by generations of entrepreneurs, molded and remolded by the force fields of identity, technology, and the music industry—constitutes an epochal contribution not only to American culture but also to the wider, incredibly diverse world of music. Rock on!

Key Terms

Auto-Tune	MP4	Spotify
emo	Napster	streaming
emo rap	Pandora	Tidal
garage rock revival	Pro Tools	vocoder
iPod	Recording Industry	YouTube
iTunes	Association of America	
MP3	(RIAA)	

Key People

Adele Adkins, M.B.E.	Jay-Z	Nicki Minaj
Arcade Fire	Kanye West	OutKast
Bad Bunny	Karen O	Paramore
Beyoncé Knowles	Kendrick Lamar	Radiohead
Bruno Mars	Lady Gaga	Taylor Swift
Drake	Lizzo	Timbaland
Eminem	Machine Gun Kelly	Travis Scott
Frank Ocean	Macklemore & Ryan Lewis	TV on the Radio
Hayley Williams	Missy Elliott	the Yeah Yeah Yeahs

Review Questions

1. In what ways have digital technologies impacted the production, distribution, and consumption of popular music since the year 2000?
2. Why has live concert performance become increasingly important in the popular music economy of the twenty-first century?
3. How have changes in the relationships between musicians, their audiences, and the music business affected rock music in the 2000s?
4. What strategies have hip-hop artists adopted to maintain the rebellious spirit of the genre while increasing its mainstream appeal?
5. How has globalization affected American popular music?

Appendix

Understanding Rhythm and Form

Audio tracks corresponding to this appendix are available for download on the book's companion website, www.oup.com/us/starr.

☞ The most basic unit of time in music is a beat or pulse (imagine a ticking clock).

time → | 1 | 2 | 3 | 4 | 5 | 6 | 7 | ...

☞ These beats can be played at different speeds. This is called "tempo."

faster tempo | 1 | 2 | 3 | 4 | 5 | 6 | 7 | 8 | 9 | 10 | 11 | 12 | ...

slower tempo | 1 | 2 | 3 | 4 | ...

☞ Beats can be grouped to form a time signature or meter. Here are a few example meters.

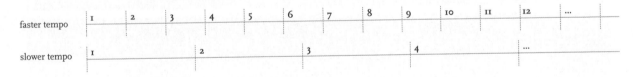

4 beats | 1 | 2 | 3 | 4 | 1 | 2 | 3 | 4 |

3 beats | 1 | 2 | 3 | 1 | 2 | 3 | 1 | ... |

2 beats | 1 | 2 | 1 | 2 | 1 | ... |

6 beats | 1 | 2 | 3 | 4 | 5 | 6 | 1 | 2 | 3 | 4 | 5 | 6 | 1 | 2 | ... |

☞ A meter can be broken up into many different rhythms. A rhythm is defined by a set of notes placed in time with specific accents or intensities. Here are a few example rhythms in a meter of four beats. The larger waves represent accents.

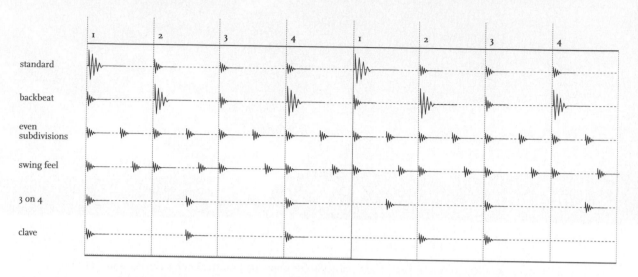

☞ Music can also be grouped on a larger scale to create an overall structure or form. For example, an arrangement can have multiple parts that are played one after the other. Take for example, an AABA form with eight-measure parts in a meter of 4. Here it is with each measure written out. There are 128 beats total.

☞ Here is the above AABA form in a simplified notation.

A - 8 measures	A - 8 measures	B - 8 measures	A - 8 measures

☞ Here is an ABAC form with 8-measure parts.

A - 8 measures	B - 8 measures	A - 8 measures	C - 8 measures

☞ Forms can be much more complex. Here is the form used in "Castle House Rag" (see Chapter 3).

Introduction 4 measures	A - 16 measures	A - 16 measures
	B - 16 measures	B - 16 measures
	A - 16 measures	Transition 4 measures / C - 32 measures
		C - 32 measures
		D - 16 measures
E - 16 measures		E - 16 measures
F - 16 measures		

Glossary

This glossary consists of terms requiring specialized definitions that recur throughout the book. Such terms appear in the text in **boldface** on first use.

a cappella Vocal singing that involves no instrumental accompaniment.

A&R (artists and repertoire) The department of a record company whose responsibility it is to discover and cultivate new musical talent, and to find material for the artists to perform—naturally, with an eye toward commercial potential. As many artists today write and record their own material, the latter function of A&R has atrophied to some extent.

alternative music An early 1980s genre that arose in the wake of punk rock's decline and in opposition to mainstream rock music.

alternative rock An early 1980s genre that arose in the wake of **punk rock**'s decline and in opposition to mainstream rock music. Bands such as Sonic Youth, R.E.M., and the Dead Kennedys were associated with the movement, which emphasized local, anticommerical, guitar-based music blending the abrasive, do-it-yourself sensibility of punk with the thick, heavy sonic textures of heavy metal.

analog recording A system of sound recording in which the energy of sound waves is transformed into physical imprints (as in pre-1925 acoustic recordings) or into electronic waveforms that closely follow (and can be used to reproduce) the shape of the sound waves themselves. *Compare* **digital recording**.

arranger A person who adapts (or arranges) the melody and chords of a song to exploit the capabilities and instrumental resources of a particular musical ensemble. For example, a simple pop tune originally written for voice and piano may be arranged for a jazz "big band" with many horns and a rhythm section.

Auto-Tune Audio processing software capable of altering the pitch of vocal sounds. It has been used on recordings by artists across a wide range of popular music.

backbeat In rock music, the accenting of the second and fourth beat of a four-beat bar.

ballad A type of song consisting usually of verses set to a repeating melody (see **strophic** form) in which a story, often romantic, historic, or tragic, is sung in narrative fashion.

bar (measure) A line drawn vertically through a staff or staves of musical notation, normally indicating division into metrical units (of two, three, four beats, etc.); now also the name for the metrical unit itself, the line being commonly called a "bar line."

big band A popular type of dance music ensemble of the 1930s and 1940s, comprising wind instruments (brass and reeds) and a rhythm section (piano, bass, drums, and sometimes guitar or vibraphone). Big bands thrived during the so-called **swing** era, when jazz was popular on record and radio and often was played to accompany dancing.

bluegrass music A country music style that grew out of traditional fiddle bands and **ballad** traditions. Mandolinist Bill Monroe is generally credited with pioneering the style and establishing its standard instrumentation, including the prominent featuring of the mandolin, five-string banjo (played with metal picks), guitar, fiddle, and bass.

blue notes Expressive notes or scalar inflections found primarily in blues and jazz music. Blue notes derive from African musical practice; although they do not correspond exactly to the Western system of **major** and **minor** scales, it is helpful to imagine them as "flatter" or "lower" versions of the scale degrees to which they are related, and thus one speaks of "blue" thirds, fifths, and sevenths (see Chapter 5).

blues A genre of music originating principally from the field hollers and work songs of rural Blacks in the southern United States during the latter half of the nineteenth century. Themes treated by blues lyrics include the oppressive conditions suffered by African Americans, love gone wrong, alienation, misery, and the supernatural. The lyrics are often obscured by a coded, metaphorical language. The music of the blues is rich in Africanisms and earthy rhythms. Originally an acoustic music, the blues moved to the urban North in the mid-twentieth century, becoming electrified in the process (see Chapters 5 and 7). *See also* **Chicago/electric blues; classic blues; country blues; twelve-bar blues.**

boogie-woogie Popular jazz/**blues** piano style of the 1920s and 1930s featuring strong bass patterns in the left hand and syncopated chords and melodies in the right hand. Key exponents of the style included Pine Top Smith and Meade Lux Lewis.

bridge A passage consisting of new, contrasting material that serves as a link between repeated sections of melodic material. A bridge is sometimes called a **release** (see the discussion of Tin Pan Alley song form in Chapter 4).

Brill Building A New York City office building where several major music publishers and record labels located their operations in the late 1950s and early 1960s. It became associated with producers like Phil Spector and Don Kirshner and songwriters like Carole King and Gerry Goffin, and Barry Mann and Cynthia Weil, and the music that they produced.

broadside A **ballad** that is printed on a single sheet of paper; popular from the seventeenth through the nineteenth centuries. Broadsides were an early form of sheet music.

bugalú **(Latin Soul)** A fusion of rumba and mambo with Black American popular music. "Watermelon Man," a 1963 hit for Ramon "Mongo" Santamaria, is considered a classic example of the genre.

cadence A melodic or harmonic event that signals the end of a musical line or section, or of the piece as a whole.

call-and-response A characteristic feature of much African American music, in which musical forces alternate with one another, usually in quick succession; these forces may be a solo singer with a chorus or backing group, sung lines with guitar or band passages, an instrumental solo with a larger instrumental group, or other groupings. This form of expression has spread to many musical styles and genres but is a characteristically African phenomenon in its origins and so is most associated in America with African American expression.

Chicago electric blues A style of blues employing amplified instruments, that developed in Chicago following World War II and quickly attained widespread popularity, largely through recordings on the Chess record label by artists such as Muddy Waters and Howlin' Wolf. Like the Delta blues before it, this style is characterized by a rough, aggressive approach to vocal delivery and instrumental performance.

chorus A repeating section within a song consisting of a fixed melody and lyric that is repeated exactly each time that it occurs, typically following one or more verses.

classic blues A popularized form of **blues**, often written by professional composers and performed primarily by female vaudeville and recording artists. The style was popularized by performers like Gertrude "Ma" Rainey and Bessie Smith. *See also* **twelve-bar blues.**

composer A person who creates a piece of music. Although the term may be used to describe the creators of popular songs, it is more commonly applied to those who create more extended, formally notated works of music.

concept album A record album conceived as an artistic totality, rather than a collection of individual songs. The Beatles' *Sgt. Pepper's Lonely Hearts Club Band* is generally credited with popularizing the form.

conjunto Spanish term for a musical group or ensemble, used widely in Latin America (e.g., Cuba and Mexico).

counterculture A subculture existing in opposition to and espousing values contrary to those of the dominant culture. The term is most often used to describe the values and lifestyle of young people during the late 1960s and early 1970s (see Chapter 10).

counterpoint The sounding of two independent melodic lines or voices against one another.

country and western (C&W) A term used to describe popular country music from the late 1940s on, replacing the earlier term **hillbilly music**. Popular country and western performers included Eddy Arnold and Patsy Cline.

country blues A style of song and performance developed among rural African Americans in the late nineteenth and early twentieth centuries. Country blues were often performed by a single guitarist who accompanied his own vocals. *See also* **blues; Chicago/electric blues; classic blues.**

countrypolitan A popular style of country music that emerged in Nashville in the mid-1960s and combines elements of traditional country with mainstream pop sounds. Popular performers in the style included Glen Campbell and Kenny Rogers.

cover version The practice of recording a song that has previously been recorded by another artist or group, often involving an adaptation of the original's style and sensibility aimed at cashing in on its success. The most famous examples involve white artists "covering" and reaping disproportionate benefits from recordings by African American artists (e.g., Bill Haley's version of Big Joe Turner's recording of "Shake, Rattle and Roll").

crooning An intimate, gentle style of singing facilitated by the introduction of the microphone and modern recording techniques. Bing Crosby was among the first great crooners.

dialect A regional speech variant; one may allude to regional musical "dialects" to describe stylistic variants of the same basic musical genre, as with Mississippi Delta blues or East Texas blues.

digital audio workstation (DAW) A generic name for any software program that runs on a computer that seamlessly integrates the addition of effects into the **digital recording** process. *See also* **Pro Tools.**

digital recording A system of sound recording that transforms sound waves into a stream of numbers (0s and 1s), which is converted back to an analog wave by a digital-to-analog converter in order to be heard. *See also* **DAW.** *Compare* **analog recording.**

disco Derived from the word "discotheque," first used in Europe in the 1960s to refer to nightclubs devoted to the playing of recorded music for dancing. By the mid-1970s, clubs featuring an uninterrupted stream of dance music were common in the United States, particularly in urban Black and Latino communities. The 1977 film *Saturday Night Fever* launched the music into the mainstream.

Disco is characterized by the heavy use of **synthesizers** and a regular, heavily accented beat.

dissonance A harsh or grating sound. (The perception of dissonance is culturally conditioned. For example, the smaller intervals employed in certain Asian and Middle Eastern music may sound "out of tune" and dissonant to Western ears; within their original context, however, they are regarded as perfectly consonant.)

distortion A buzzing, crunchy, or "fuzzy" tone color originally achieved by overdriving the vacuum tubes of a guitar amplifier. This effect can be simulated today by solid state and digital sound processors. Distortion is often heard in a hard rock or heavy metal context.

DJ (disc jockey, or deejay) One who plays recordings (either on a radio program or in a live performance involving the use of pre-existing recordings, most common in hip-hop and techno music).

doo-wop A style of vocal rock 'n' roll popular in the 1950s and early 1960s and centered on close-harmony singing by groups of four or five members, Originally formed in urban neighborhoods among amateur vocalists inspired by the recordings of 1940s groups such as the Mills Brothers, the doo-wop sound was popularized by groups such as the Orioles and the Moonglows.

double-tracking (multi-tracking) A method used in sound recording that allows for several different parts to be recorded separately and then layered over one another in playback. This technique is also known as **overdubbing.**

drum machine An electronic instrument that can emulate the sound of traditional drums. A drum machine has the additional capability to record specific rhythm patterns and to play them back in various combinations.

electronic dance music (EDM) A broad category of genres, including **house music, techno,** and others, that are created using electronic means including **synthesizers, drum machines, sampling,** and **digital audio workstations,** usually for the purposes of live dancing at a club or **rave.** In the 2010s EDM production techniques became commonplace in **Top 40 radio.**

emo Short for "emotional rock" or "emotional punk," a genre of **alternative rock** music popular in the 1990s and 2000s that usually combined **punk rock** instrumental timbres with sensitive, vulnerable singing styles.

emo rap A **rap** genre popular in the late 2010s and early 2020s that combines hip-hop beats with a blend of rapping and singing in **emo**-like vocal timbres.

feedback Technically, an out-of-control sound oscillation that occurs when the output of a loudspeaker finds its way back into a microphone or electric instrument pickup and is reamplified, creating a sound loop that grows in intensity and continues until deliberately broken. Although feedback can be difficult to manage, it can become a powerful expressive device in the hands of skilled blues and rock musicians, most notably the guitarist Jimi Hendrix. Feedback can be recognized as a "screaming" or "crying" sound.

folk music In the most general sense, music that is orally transmitted and closely bound up with the daily lives and customs of local communities. More specifically, a popular music style of the late 1950s and early 1960s (sometimes called *urban folk music*) featuring guitar-playing singer/songwriters who often addressed topical issues. Bob Dylan began his career as a folk singer.

funk A musical style derived from **R&B** (rhythm and blues) and **soul music** characterized by repeated rhythmic figures and a strong bass line.

gangsta rap *See* **rap**.

garage band A neighborhood group made up of young musicians who play mainly for themselves, their friends, and the occasional high school dance. Their music usually consisted of fairly simple melodies and lyrics accompanied by two or three chords and a simple beat. The rough-and-ready, do-it-yourself attitude of the garage bands paved the way for **punk rock**. *See also* **garage rock revival**.

garage rock revival An **alternative rock** subgenre popular in the early 2000s that drew on the sounds and visual aesthetics of 1960s garage rock and 1970s punk; popular groups include the Yeah Yeah Yeahs, TV on the Radio, and the Strokes.

gospel music Religious-themed popular music performed by both white and African American musicians. White groups such as the Carter Family performed restrained versions of traditional American hymns. Black groups drew their inspiration from the enthusiastic, deeply felt singing of Black church choirs.

groove Term originally employed by jazz, rhythm & blues, and funk musicians to describe the channeled flow of swinging, "funky," or "phat" rhythms.

grunge An **alternative rock** movement of the late 1980s and early 1990s centering in Seattle, Washington, featuring a do-it-yourself, anti-mainstream rock attitude, intense vocals, and loud, unremitting accompaniments. The band Nirvana and particularly its leader singer/songwriter Kurt Cobain exemplified the movement.

hardcore Short for "hardcore punk," a genre that emerged in the late 1970s and early 1980s that distinguished itself from **punk** by faster rhythms and more aggressive timbres. Hardcore's earliest and most successful bands include Bad Brains, Black Flag, and Minor Threat. The influence of hardcore can be heard in later **grunge** and **emo** bands.

hillbilly music A term used from the 1910s through the 1930s for traditional Anglo American folk and dance music styles, and for other music of white rural Southerners stemming from these sources. Artists like Fiddlin' John Carson, the Carter Family, and Jimmie Rodgers are examples of this genre.

hip-hop culture Culture forged by African American, Puerto Rican, and Caribbean American youth in New York City in the late 1970s; includes distinctive styles of visual art (graffiti), dance, dress, and speech. Rap music grew out of the movement, at first spread by pioneering DJs like Afrika Bambaataa and Kool Herc, who spun and mixed different source recordings. DJs formed their own groups featuring dancers and MCs who rapped or rhymed to the musical accompaniment.

honky-tonk A popular style of country music that evolved in the late 1940s and early 1950s around small bars (called honky-tonks) catering to a working-class, white crowd. Hank Williams is considered among the greatest honky-tonk singers and songwriters.

hook A "catchy" or otherwise memorable musical phrase or pattern.

house music *See* **electronic dance music**.

independent record labels ("indies") Smaller, regional record companies, especially those specializing in **rhythm & blues** and **country and western** recordings in the later 1940s through the 1950s and pioneering in the recording of **doo-wop** and early **rock 'n' roll**.

"indie" rock *See* **alternative rock**.

iPod A portable music player created by the Apple corporation capable of playing **MP3** and other downloadable audio files.

iTunes An online hub created in the early 2000s by the Apple corporation for the purpose of circulating digital files, including audio, video, mobile apps, and e-books. Originally created to load files onto an **iPod**, iTunes briefly operated as a **streaming** service before being replaced by Apple Music.

jazz rock A fusion of jazz improvisation with rock instrumentation and rhythms, pioneered by artists like Miles Davis on records like his 1969 *Bitches Brew*.

jukebox A coin-operated record player popular in bars, diners, and honky-tonks.

jump blues An **R&B** style of the late 1940s/early 1950s featuring small combos performing upbeat, danceable songs, often with humorous lyrics. Saxophonist and singer Louis Jordan was a major proponent of the style.

Latin Soulb (*bugalú*) A fusion of rumba and mambo with Black American popular music.

lyricist A person who supplies a poetic text (lyrics) to a piece of vocal music; not necessarily the composer.

magnetic tape recording The process of preserving sound on magnetic tape, which replaced the process of recording directly onto phonograph discs, affording greater fidelity, and the potential for manipulating sounds in the studio.

major A term that refers to one of the two scale systems central to Western music (see **minor**). A major scale is arranged in the following order of whole- and half-step intervals: 1-1-½-1-1-1-½. (This pattern is easy to see if one begins at the pitch C on the piano keyboard and plays the next seven white notes in succession, which yields the C major scale: CDEFGABC.) A song is said to be in a major tonality or key if it uses melodies and chords that are constructed from the major scale. Of course, a song may (and frequently does) "borrow" notes and chords from outside a particular major scale, and it may "modulate" or shift from key to key within the course of the song.

mariachi A Mexican style of music played by ensembles of violins, guitars, and two or more trumpets.

mashup A new musical track created by combining **samples** of at least two pre-existing works. Most often created digitally by superimposing a vocal sample from one song onto the backing track of another. Because of their tenuous legality, mashups are often created anonymously and circulated on the internet. Unlike rap, in which the vocals are added live over a sample, mashups largely exist as recordings only.

measure *See* **bar.**

melisma One syllable of text spread out over many musical tones.

microphone A device that converts sound waves into electrical energy, for purposes of amplification, transmission, and recording. The introduction of the microphone in 1925 revolutionized the music recording industry.

minor A term that refers to one of the two scale systems central to Western music (see **major**); a minor scale is arranged in the following order of whole-and half-step intervals: 1-½-1-1-½-1-1. (This pattern represents the so-called natural minor scale, often found in blues and blues-based popular music; it is easy to see if one begins at the pitch A on the piano keyboard and plays the next seven white notes in succession, which yields the A minor

scale: ABCDEFGA. The two other minor scales in common usage—the melodic minor and harmonic minor scales—have ascending and descending forms that differ somewhat from the natural minor scale.) A song is said to be in a minor tonality or key if it uses melodies and chords that are constructed from the minor scale. Of course, a song may (and frequently does) "borrow" notes and chords from outside a particular minor scale, and it may "modulate" or shift from key to key within the course of the song. In comparison to the major scale, the minor scale is often described as having a "sad" or "melancholy" sound.

minstrel show/blackface minstrelsy A popular form of mid-nineteenth century entertainment featuring white performers performing in black face makeup. The classic minstrel show was organized around a series of more or less independent sketches and songs, featuring characters such as Mr. Interlocutor, a lead performer who sang and provided patter between acts, and Bones and Tambo, who sat at either end of the line of performers.

montuno Spanish term for a formal section within a performance of Afro-Cuban dance music (such as a rumba, mambo, or **salsa**). The montuno, generally the second half of a given piece, alternates a fixed vocal refrain (the *coro*) with a solo vocal improvisation (the ***pregón***), and may also include instrumental solos.

MP3 A variant of the MPEG compression system that allows sound files to be compressed to as little as one-twelfth of their original size.

MP4 A variant of the MPEG compression system used to compress audio or video files, most commonly used for videos that contain audio.

MTV (Music Television) A cable television channel founded in 1981 that featured videos of popular musical performers. It became the major means of promoting new acts during the 1980s and 1990s.

multitracking *See* **double-tracking.**

Napster A pioneering peer-to-peer music sharing system introduced in 1999 which allowed users to share **MP3** and other audio files.

new wave A more self-consciously artistic and experimental side of **punk rock** music, developed by groups like Talking Heads during the mid-1970s.

outlaw country *See* **progressive country.**

overdubbing *See* **double-tracking (multitracking).**

Pandora An internet radio **streaming** service created in the early 2000s that uses algorithms to present individualized playlists to its users.

payola The illegal and historically widespread practice of offering money or other inducements to a radio station or DJ in order to ensure the prominent airplay of a particular recording.

polyrhythm The simultaneous sounding of rhythms in two or more contrasting meters, such as three against two, or five against four. Polyrhythms are found in abundance in African and Asian musics and their derivatives.

pregón Spanish term for "announcement." In Afro-Cuban music *pregón* refers to (1) an improvised vocal solo based on the cries of street vendors, or (2) the improvised solo part in call-and-response singing (as in the **montuno** form).

producer A person engaged either by a recording artist or, more often, a record company, who directs and assists the recording process. The producer's duties may include securing the services of session musicians, deciding on arrangements, making technical decisions, motivating the artist creatively, helping to realize the artistic vision in a commercially viable way, and not unimportantly, ensuring that the project comes in under budget. A good producer often develops a distinctive signature sound, and successful producers are always in great demand. They are often rewarded handsomely for their efforts, garnering a substantial share of a recording's earnings, in addition to a commission.

progressive country A reaction to the country and pop blends of the 1960s, progressive country focused on distinctive singer/songwriters who fused country music with countercultural sensibilities. Musicians like Willie Nelson and Waylon Jennings exemplified the movement in the mid-1970s. Also known as **outlaw country.**

Pro Tools A widespread, industry-standard **digital audio workstation.**

punk rock A mid-to late-1970s movement rebelling against **disco** and the popular rock acts of the day. It was a stripped-down and often purposefully "nonmusical" version of rock music, with lyrics that stressed the ironic or dark dimensions of the human experience. *See also* **hardcore.**

R&B (rhythm & blues) An African American musical genre that emerged after World War II and consists of a loose cluster of styles derived from Black musical traditions, characterized by energetic and hard-swinging rhythms. At first performed exclusively by Black musicians and aimed at Black audiences, R&B came to replace the older category of "race records" (see Chapter 7).

race music A marketing term developed by the record labels of the 1920s to designate records by African American artists aimed at the African American market. Eventually the term was replaced by **rhythm & blues (R&B)** in the late 1940s.

Radio Technology that emerged early in the 1900s that allowed people separated by thousands of miles to hear the same music simultaneously.

ragtime A musical genre of African American origin, later exploited to great advantage by white performers, that emerged in the 1880s and became quite popular at the turn of the century. Ragtime is characterized by melodic accents that fall on "off" or weak beats; it is highly **syncopated.** Scott Joplin is the recognized master of this genre, having composed numerous rags for the piano (see Chapter 2).

raves After-hours dancing venues for **EDM music** often associated with MDMA (otherwise known as "ecstasy") and other drugs. Underground, unlicensed raves gained popularity in the 1990s in cities like Berlin, London, and San Francisco, and have evolved into outdoor EDM festivals that sometime attract ravers in the hundreds of thousands.

Recording Industry Association of America (RIAA) The trade organization representing most record companies and distributors.

refrain In the verse-refrain song, the refrain is the "main part" of the song, usually constructed in AABA or ABAC form (see the discussion of Tin Pan Alley song form in Chapter 4).

reggae A popular form of Jamaican dance music that weds aspects of **R&B** and native musical styles. Bob Marley was the most famous proponent of the style.

release *See* **bridge.**

reverb Short for "reverberation," a prolongation of a sound by virtue of an ambient acoustical space created by hard, reflective surfaces. The sound bounces off these surfaces and recombines with the original sound, slightly delayed (reverb is measured in terms of seconds and fractions of seconds). Reverberation can occur naturally or be simulated either electronically or by digital sound processors.

riff A simple, repeating melodic idea or pattern that generates rhythmic momentum; typically played by the horns or the piano in a jazz ensemble, or by an electric guitar in a rock 'n' roll context.

riot grrrl A music and social justice movement in the early 1990s associated with U.S. Pacific Northwest that empowered women and girls to participate in rock culture primarily through music and "zines." Songs by riot grrrl bands often drew attention to violence and discrimination against women as well as BIPOC and LGBTQ+ community members. Prominent riot grrrl bands in the United States include Bikini Kill (Olympia, WA) and Bratmobile (Eugene, OR).

rockabilly A vigorous form of country and western music informed by the rhythms of Black R&B and electric blues. This genre is exemplified by such artists as Carl Perkins and the young Elvis Presley.

rock 'n' roll A term usually used to describe the popular teen-oriented music of the 1950s to the early 1960s, as opposed to the more consciously artistic "rock" that developed from the mid-1960s on.

rock steady A style of Jamaican popular music that developed from **ska** in the later 1960s, performed in a slower tempo than ska.

salsa A rumba-based musical style pioneered by Cuban and Puerto Rican migrants in New York City. The stars of salsa music include bandleader/percussionist Tito Puente and singer Celia Cruz.

sampling/sampler A digital recording process wherein a sound source is recorded or "sampled" with a microphone, converted into a stream of binary numbers that represent the profile of the sound, quantized, and stored in computer memory. The digitized sound sample may then be retrieved in any number of ways, including "virtual recording studio" programs for the computer, or by activating the sound from an electronic keyboard or drum machine.

scat singing A technique that involves the use of nonsense syllables as a vehicle for wordless vocal improvisation. It is most often found in a jazz context.

sequencer An electronic device that creates automated repeatable sequences of sound. A sequencer can record a section of a pre-existing record for manipulation on playback or a series of MIDI codes or other digital information.

ska The generic title for Jamaican music recorded between 1961 and 1967, ska emerged from Jamaican **R&B**, which itself was largely based on American **R&B**. It emphasized a heavily **syncopated** "jump" beat. Groups like the Ska-Lites helped popularize the style.

slap-back A distinctive short reverberation with few repetitions, often heard in the recordings of rockabilly artists, such as the Sun Records recordings of Elvis Presley.

soft rock A term invented in the early 1970s to describe acoustic folk-rock as well as tuneful, soothing types of popular music that use electric instruments. The work of Carole King in the 1970s is representative. The term is now applied broadly to quieter popular music of all sorts that uses mild rock rhythms and some electric instruments.

soli (plural of solo) Band textures achieved by having a small group of players within the band play certain passages of music together. Soli playing contrasts with tutti sections, in which the entire ensemble plays (see the discussion of swing bands in Chapter 6).

soul music A combination of the intensity of African American **gospel** with popular **R&B** styles, exemplified in the late 1960s recordings of Aretha Franklin and James Brown.

Southern rock A genre of rock music developed in the late 1960s and early 1970s by bands from the American South who emphasized their regional roots via song lyrics and the visual elements in their stage sets and on album covers. Representative groups are the Allman Brothers Band and Lynyrd Skynyrd.

spiritual A type of sacred song created by and for African Americans that originated in oral tradition. Performances by groups like the Fisk Jubilee Singers in the late nineteenth and early twentieth centuries did much to popularize the form, as did later singers like Mahalia Jackson and Paul Robeson.

Spotify A Swedish **streaming** service.

standard A popular song of the 1910s to the 1940s that has been recorded many times, to the point where it has reached iconic status.

streaming The real-time playing of media over the internet without the need for users to download the content first.

strophes Poetic stanzas; often, a pair of stanzas of alternating form that constitute the structure of a poem. These could become the **verse** and **chorus** of a **strophic** song.

strophic A song form that employs the same music for each poetic unit in the lyrics.

swing A style of jazz that gained great popularity from the mid-1930s through the Second World War. Swing music was popularized by the **big bands** of the era, including those led by Benny Goodman and Duke Ellington. The music is characterized by a very danceable beat.

syncopation Rhythmic patterns in which the stresses occur on what are ordinarily weak beats, thus displacing or suspending the sense of metric regularity.

synthesizer An electronic instrument, usually incorporating a keyboard, capable of producing complex sounds through the manipulation of wave shapes.

synth-pop Popular music featuring primarily electronic **synthesizers** as accompaniment rather than traditional instrumentation. The Eurythmics led this movement in the mid-1980s with songs like "Sweet Dreams."

techno Up-tempo, repetitive, electronic dance music that developed in various urban club scenes during the late 1980s and the early 1990s.

territory band A **big band** that was popular in a local area or region but never achieved national prominence.

Tidal A Scandinavian **streaming** service most notable for its focus on high-quality, lossless audio (*Compare* **MP3**). Tidal is or has been owned by a number of high-profile musicians including Jay-Z, Nicki Minaj, and Madonna.

timbre The "tone color" or characteristic sound of an instrument or voice, determined by its frequency and overtone components. Timbre is the aspect of sound that allows us, for example, to differentiate between the sound of a violin and the sound of a flute when both instruments are playing the same pitch.

Tin Pan Alley The center of the commercial songwriting and publishing business in New York from approximately the 1880s through the mid-twentieth century. The term has been applied to the popular songs published there by composers like Irving Berlin, Jerome Kern, and George Gershwin.

tonic Refers to the central or "home" pitch, or chord, of a musical piece—or sometimes of just a section of the piece.

Top 40 radio A style of radio programming based on a set list of selections that are played repeatedly over the course of the broadcast day. It became the prevalent mode of radio programming from the late 1950s to the 1960s.

twelve-bar blues Refers to music based on a particular sequence of chords heard within a rhythmic pattern of twelve four-beat measures. *See* **blues**; **classic blues**; **country blues**; and Chapter 5.

vaudeville A kind of variety show that became the dominant form of popular entertainment in the late nineteenth and early twentieth centuries in America. A typical performance might feature singers, actors, jugglers, animal acts, and other novelties.

verse In general usage, this term refers to a group of lines of poetic text, often rhyming, that usually exhibit regularly recurring metrical patterns. In the verse-refrain song, the verse refers to an introductory section that precedes the main body of the song, the **refrain** (see the discussion of Tin Pan Alley song form in Chapter 4).

vocal harmony group *See* **doo-wop**.

vocoder An instrument that replaces a singer's pitch with pitches specified by the user. Vocoders can either be analog, operated in real time using a **synthesizer** and microphone, or digital, created in a **digital audio workstation**.

waltz A dance in triple time with a strong emphasis on every third beat.

western swing A fusion of country string band music with **swing** style instrumentation and rhythms, popularized in the 1930s and 1940s by bandleaders like Bob Wills.

world music A term developed in the late 1980s to describe non-Western music, usually those that incorporated elements of Western rock or pop music. It can encompass a diverse range of musical traditions.

yodeling A vocalization technique (originally from the Alpine region of Austria) which uses the throat muscles to enable an abrupt change in pitch, usually to a much higher register of the voice.

YouTube An internet video-hosting site, started in 2005 (purchased by Google in 2006), that allows users to upload videos and share them with the world.

Bibliography

This list includes all works cited in the body of this book, along with a small number of others that may be recommended for further reading on individual topics and issues central to the material covered in the preceding pages. No attempt is made to offer a comprehensive bibliography here, or to list books of a general introductory nature in the area of American popular music.

Armstrong, Louis. 1954. *Satchmo: My Life in New Orleans*. New York.

Armstrong, Louis, and Thomas Brothers. 2001. *Louis Armstrong in His Own Words: Selected Writings*. New York.

Austin, William W. 1975. *"Susanna," "Jeanie," and "The Old Folks at Home": The Songs of Stephen C. Foster from His Time to Ours*. New York.

Bashe, Philip. 1985. *Heavy Metal Thunder*. Garden City, New York.

Basie, William, and Albert Murray. 1995. *Good Morning Blues: The Autobiography of Count Basie*. New York.

Baulch, Emma. 2007. *Making Scenes: Reggae, Punk, and Death Metal in 1990s Bali*. Durham, NC, and London.

Baulch, Emma, and Bangkal Kusama. 1994. "The McDonaldisation of Bali." *Inside Indonesia*, December.

Beatles. 2000. *Anthology*. San Francisco.

Bennett, Alan, Barry Shank, and Jason Toynbee. 2005. *The Popular Music Studies Reader*, 3rd ed. New York.

Berlin, Edward A. 1994. *King of Ragtime: Scott Joplin and His Era*. New York.

Berry, Chuck. 1987. *Chuck Berry: The Autobiography*. New York.

Blesh, Rudi and Harriet Jans. 1971. *They All Played Ragtime*, 4th ed. New York.

Brackett, David, ed. 2013. *The Pop, Rock, and Soul Reader: Histories and Debates*, 3rd ed. New York.

Bright, Spencer. 1999. *Peter Gabriel: An Authorized Biography*. London.

Camus, Raoul. 1986. "Bands." In *The New Grove Dictionary of American Music*, vol. 1. New York.

Castle, Irene, Robert Lipscomb Duncan, and Wanda Duncan. 1980. *Castles in the Air: As Told to Bob and Wanda Duncan*. New York.

Castle, Vernon and Irene. 1914. *Modern Dancing*. New York.

Chapple, Steve, and Reebee Garofalo. 1977. *Rock 'n' Roll Is Here to Pay: The History and Politics of the Music Industry*. Chicago.

Charles, Ray, and David Ritz. 1978. *Brother Ray: Ray Charles' Own Story*. New York.

Chilton, John. 1994. *Let the Good Times Roll: The Story of Louis Jordan and His Music*. Ann Arbor, MI.

Clarke, Donald. 1995. *The Rise and Fall of Popular Music*. New York.

Cockrell, Dale. 1997. *Demons of Disorder: Early Blackface Minstrels and Their World*. New York.

Collin, Matthew. 1997. *Altered State: The Story of Ecstasy Culture and Acid House*. London.

Conway, CeCe, and Scott Odell. 1995. *CD liner notes for Black Banjo Songsters of North Carolina and Virginia*. Smithsonian Folkways LC 9628.

Deffaa, Chip. 1996. *Blue Rhythms: Six Lives in Rhythm and Blues*. Urbana, IL.

Dodworth, Allan. 1885. *Dancing and Its Relation to Education and Social Life*. New York.

Ellington, Edward Kennedy. 1976. *Music Is My Mistress*. New York.

Emerson, Ken. 1997. *Doo-dah! Stephen Foster and the Rise of American Popular Culture*. New York.

Escott, Colin, and Martin Hawkins. 1992. *Good Rockin' Tonight: The Sun Records Story*. New York.

Escott, Colin, George Merritt, and William MacEwen. 1995. *Hank Williams: The Biography*, 2nd ed. New York.

Frith, Simon. 1981. *Sound Effects: Youth, Leisure, and the Politics of Rock 'n' Roll*. New York.

Furia, Philip, with Graham Wood. 1998. *Irving Berlin: A Life in Song*. New York.

George, Nelson. 1998. *Hip Hop America*. New York, 1998.

George, Nelson, Sally Banes, Susan Flinker, and Patty Romanowski, eds. 1985. *Fresh: Hip Hop Don't Stop*. New York.

George-Warren, Holly, and Patricia Romanowski, eds. 2001. *The Rolling Stone Encyclopedia of Rock & Roll*, 3rd ed. New York.

Giddins, Gary. 2001. *Satchmo: The Genius of Louis Armstrong*, 2nd ed. New York.

Gillett, Charlie. 1996. *The Sound of the City: The Rise of Rock and Roll*. New York.

Gioia, Ted. 2011. *The History of Jazz*. New York.

Goodwin, Andrew. 1992. *Dancing in the Distraction Factory: Music Television and Popular Culture*. Minneapolis.

Gottlieb, Jack. 2004. *Funny, It Doesn't Sound Jewish: How Yiddish Songs and Synagogue Melodies Influenced Tin Pan Alley, Broadway, and Hollywood*. New York.

Guralnick, Peter. 1999. *Careless Love: The Unmaking of Elvis Presley*. Boston.

Guralnick, Peter. 2005. *Dream Boogie: The Triumph of Sam Cooke*. New York.

Guralnick, Peter. 1994. *Last Train to Memphis: The Rise of Elvis Presley*. Boston.

Guralnick, Peter. 2003. Liner notes for CD *Sam Cooke: Portrait of a Legend, 1951–1964*. ABKCO Records 92642. New York.

Guralnick, Peter. 1986. *Sweet Soul Music: Rhythm and Blues and the Southern Dream of Freedom*. New York.

Hager, Steven. 1984. *Hip Hop: The Illustrated History of Break Dancing, Rap Music, and Graffiti*. New York.

Handy, W. C. 1941. *Father of the Blues: An Autobiography*. New York.

Hasse, John. 1993. *Beyond Category: The Life and Genius of Duke Ellington*. New York.

Heilbut, Anthony. 1997. *The Gospel Sound: Good News and Bad Times*. New York (anniversary edition).

Hines, Earl. 1977. Interview on "Soundsheet" (45 rpm disc) included with boxed LP set *Giants of Jazz: Earl Hines*. Time-Life Records STL-J11.

Holden, Stephen. 1987. "The Pop Life: 25 Years of A&M." *New York Times*, June 10, Section C, p. 24.

Howe, Irving. 1976. *World of Our Fathers: The Journey of the East European Jews to America and the Life They Found and Made*. New York.

Jablonski, Edward, and Lawrence D. Stewart. 1996. *The Gershwin Years: George and Ira*. New York.

Jackson, Mahalia, and E. M. Wylie. 1966. *Movin' on Up*. New York.

Jay-Z. 2011. *Decoded*. New York.

Karlen, Neal. 1985. "Prince Talks." *Rolling Stone*, April.

Keil, Charles. 1966. *Urban Blues*. Chicago.

Keil, Charles, and Steven Feld. 1994. *Music Grooves*. Chicago.

Knopper, Steve. 2009. *Appetite for Self-Destruction: The Spectacular Crash of the Record Industry in the Digital Age*. New York.

Kusek, David, and Gerd Leonhard. 2005. *The Future of Music: Manifesto for the Digital Music Revolution*. Boston.

Laing, Dave. 1985. *One-Chord Wonders*. Philadelphia.

Levine, Lawrence. 2007. *Black Culture and Black Consciousness: Afro-American Folk Thought from Slavery to Freedom*. New York.

Lhamon, W. T., Jr. 1998. *Raising Cain: Blackface Performance from Jim Crow to Hip Hop*. Cambridge, MA.

Lott, Eric. 1995. *Love and Theft: Blackface Minstrelsy and the American Working Class*. New York.

Malnig, Julie. ed. 2008. *Ballroom, Boogie, Shimmy Sham, Shake: A Social and Popular Dance Reader*. Urbana, IL.

Malnig, Julie. 1992. *Dancing till Dawn: A Century of Exhibition Ballroom Dance*. New York.

Malone, Bill C. 1985. *Country Music, U.S.A*. Rev. ed. Austin, TX.

Malone, Bill C., and Jocelyn R. Neal. 2010. *Country Music U.S.A.*, 3rd ed. Austin, TX.

Marcus, Greil. 2008. *Mystery Train: Images of America in Rock 'n' Roll Music*, 5th ed. New York.

Meizel, Katherine L. 2011. *Idolized: Music, Media, and Identity in American Idol*. Bloomington, IN.

Merriam, Alan P. 1964. *The Anthropology of Music*. Evanston, IL.

Morgan, Thomas L., and William Barlow. 1992. *From Cakewalks to Concert Halls: An Illustrated History of African American Popular Music from 1895 to 1930*. Washington, DC.

Morse, Dave. 1971. *Motown and the Arrival of Black Music*. New York.

Neal, Jocelyn R. 2013. *Country Music: A Cultural and Stylistic History*. New York.

Negus, Keith. 1992. *Producing Pop: Culture and Conflict in the Popular Music Industry*. London.

O'Dair, Barbara, ed. 1997. *Trouble Girls: The Rolling Stone Book of Women in Rock*. New York.

Oliver, Paul. 1990. *Blues Fell This Morning: Meaning in the Blues*. Cambridge, England.

Palmer, Robert. 1988. "The Cuban Connection." *Spin* 4, no. 8.

Palmer, Robert. 1981. *Deep Blues*. New York.

Palmer, Robert. 1995. *Rock & Roll: An Unruly History*. New York.

Pareles, Jon. 2007. "Pay What You Want for This Article." *New York Times*, December 9.

Peterson, Richard A. 1997. *Creating Country Music: Fabricating Authenticity*. Chicago.

Peterson, Richard A., and Russell David, Jr. 1975. "The Fertile Crescent of Country Music." *Journal of Country Music* 6: 19–27.

Petkov, Steven, and Leonard Mustazza, eds. 1995. *The Frank Sinatra Reader*. New York.

Pleasants, Henry. 1974. *The Great American Popular Singers*. New York.

Porterfield, Nolan. 1979. *Jimmie Rodgers: The Life and Times of America's Blue Yodeler*. Urbana, IL.

Reid, Shaheem. 2009. "Jay-Z Premieres New Song, 'D.O.A.': 'Death of Auto-Tune.'" *MTV.com News*, June 6.

Reynolds, Simon. 1998. *Generation Ecstasy: Into the World of Techno and Rave Culture*. New York.

Roberts, John Storm. 1998. *The Latin Tinge: The Impact of Latin American Music on the United States*, 2nd ed. New York.

Rose, Tricia. 1994. *Black Noise: Rap Music and Black Culture in Contemporary America*. Middletown, CT.

Schafer, R. Murray. 1977. *The Tuning of the World*. New York.

Schiff, David. 2012. *The Ellington Century*. Berkeley, CA.

Schuller, Gunther. 1968. *Early Jazz: Its Roots and Musical Development*. New York.

Schwartz, H. W. 1975. *Bands of America*. New York.

Sexton, Adam, ed. 1993. *Desperately Seeking Madonna*. New York.

Shaw, Arnold. 1986. *Honkers and Shouters: The Golden Years of Rhythm and Blues*. New York.

Simon, George. 1982. *The Big Bands*, 4th. ed. New York.

Stephenson, Richard M., and Joseph Iaccarino. 1980. *The Complete Book of Ballroom Dancing*. New York.

Stowe, David W. 1994. *Swing Changes: Big-Band Jazz in New Deal America*. Cambridge, MA.

Sublette, Ned. 2004. *Cuba and Its Music: From the First Drums to the Mambo*. Chicago.

Taylor, Timothy D. 1997. *Global Pop: World Music, World Markets*. New York, 1997.

Teachout, Terry. 2011. *Pops: A Life of Louis Armstrong*. New York.

Théberge, Paul. 1997. *Any Sound You Can Imagine: Making Music/Consuming Technology*. Middletown, CT.

Thompson, Robert Farris. 2005. *Tango: The Art History of Love*. New York.

Toop, David. 2000. *The Rap Attack 2: African Rap to Global Hip Hop*. London.

Tucker, Mark, ed. 1993. *The Duke Ellington Reader*. New York.

Wald, Elijah. 2004. *Escaping the Delta: Robert Johnson and the Invention of the Blues*. New York.

Wald, Gayle F. 2007. *Shout, Sister, Shout!: The Untold Story of Rock-and-Roll Trailblazer Sister Rosetta Tharpe*. Boston.

Walser, Robert, ed. 2013. *Keeping Time: Readings in Jazz History*, 2nd ed. New York.

Walser, Robert. 1993. *Runnin' with the Devil: Power, Gender, and Madness in Heavy Metal Music*. Middletown, CT.

West, Cornel. 1993. *Race Matters*. Boston.

Whiteman, Paul, and Mary Margaret McBride. 1974. *Jazz*. New York.

Wiggins, Gene. 1986. *Fiddlin' Georgia Crazy: Fiddlin' John Carson, His Real World, and the World of His Songs*. Urbana and Chicago, IL.

Wolfe, Charles. 1999. *A Good Natured Riot: The Birth of the Grand Ole Opry*. Nashville.

Wolfe, Charles. 1990. "Rural Black String Band Music." *Black Music Research Journal* 10, no. 1: 32–35.

Wynn, Ron. 1985. *Tina: The Tina Turner Story*. New York.

Credits

Front Matter

FM-1 Kristina Kokhanova / Alamy Stock Photo; FM-2 MediaPunch Inc. / Alamy Stock Photo; FM-3 Arterra Picture Library / Alamy Stock Photo.

Chapter 1

TL1.1 Courtesy Library of Congress, Prints & Photographs Division; TL1.2 © James Steidl/ Shutterstock; TL1.3 Courtesy Library of Congress, Prints & Photographs Division; TL1.4 Courtesy Library of Congress, Prints & Photographs Division; TL1.5 Courtesy Library of Congress, Prints & Photographs Division; TL1.6 Used by permission of BenCar Archives; TL1.7 Courtesy Library of Congress, Prints & Photographs Division; TL1.8 Courtesy Library of Congress, Prints & Photographs Division; TL1.9 Bettmann / Contributor / Getty Images; TL1.10 Courtesy Library of Congress, Prints & Photographs Division; TL1.11 Courtesy Library of Congress, Prints & Photographs Division; 1.0 Cavan Images / Alamy Stock Photo; 1.1 Courtesy Library of Congress, Prints & Photographs Division, LC-USZ62-126078; 1.2 Photo by Wisekwai, Creative Commons Attribution-Share Alike 3.0 Unported license; 1.3 Courtesy Library of Congress, Prints & Photographs Division, LC-USCC2-1758; 1.4 Photograph by George Pickow. Courtesy Peter Pickow; 1.5 Used by permission of BenCar Archives; 1.6 Everett Collection Inc / Alamy Stock Photo; 1.7 Pictorial Press Ltd / Alamy Stock Photo

Chapter 2

2.1 Courtesy of Library of Congress, Prints & Photographs Division, LC-USZ62-126131; 2.2 Courtesy of Library of Congress, Prints & Photographs Division, LC-USZC2-1773 and LC-USZ62-24517; 2.3 Courtesy of Library of Congress, Prints & Photographs Division, LC-USZ62-56944; 2.4 Courtesy of Library of Congress, Prints & Photographs Division, LC-USZ62-51599; 2.5 The History Collection / Alamy Stock Photo; 2.6 Courtesy of New York Public Library Digital Collections; 2.7 Courtesy of Library of Congress, Prints & Photographs Division, LC-B2-3982-5; 2.8 Courtesy of Library of Congress, Prints & Photographs Division, LC-USZ62-90925 and LC-USF34-031941-D

Chapter 3

TL2.1 Courtesy of Library of Congress, Prints & Photographs Division; TL2.3 Courtesy of Library of Congress, Prints & Photographs Division; TL2.4 Courtesy of Library of Congress, Prints & Photographs Division; TL2.7 Courtesy of Library of Congress, Prints & Photographs Division TL2.8 Courtesy of Library of Congress, Prints & Photographs Division; TL2.10 Courtesy of Library of Congress, Prints & Photographs Division; 3.1 Courtesy of Library of Congress, Prints & Photographs Division; 3.2 Courtesy of Library of Congress, Prints & Photographs Division, LC-USZ62-54635; 3.3 © Pictorial Press Ltd / Alamy Stock Photo Ltd./Alamy; 3.4 © Pictorial Press Ltd /

Alamy Stock Photo Ltd./Alamy; 3.5 © Pictorial Press Ltd / Alamy Stock Photo Ltd./Alamy; 3.6 © DIZ Muenchen GmbH, Sueddeutsche Zeitung Photo / Alamy; 3.7 Courtesy of Library of Congress, Prints & Photographs Division, LC-USZC4-1396; 3.8 Courtesy New York Public Library Digital Collection

Chapter 4

4.1 Courtesy of Library of Congress, Prints & Photographs Division, LC-USZ62-122087; 4.3 © Pictorial Press Ltd / Alamy Stock Photo; 4.4 Courtesy of Library of Congress, Prints & Photographs Division, LC-USZ62-126268; 4.5 Courtesy of Library of Congress, Prints & Photographs Division, LC-DIG-ppmsca-10443

Chapter 5

5.1 © Pictorial Press Ltd / Alamy Stock Photo; 5.2 Library of Congress, Prints & Photographs Division, LC-USZ62-94954; 5.4 © Pictorial Press Ltd / Alamy Stock Photo; 5.5 Used by permission of BenCar Archives; 5.6 Used by permission of BenCar Archives; 5.7 Used by permission of BenCar Archives; 5.8 Courtesy of Library of Congress, Prints & Photographs Division, LC-USZ62-107998

Chapter 6

6.1 Library of Congress, Prints & Photographs Division, LC-USW3-023097-E; 6.2 Courtesy Library of Congress, Prints & Photographs Division, LC-USZ62-126073; 6.3 Courtesy Library of Congress, Prints & Photographs Division, LC-USW3-023954-C; 6.4 Courtesy Library of Congress, Prints & Photographs Division, LC-USW3-023954-C; 6.5 Photograph by William P. Gottlieb, courtesy of Library of Congress, William P. Gottlieb Collection, LC-GLB13-0421 DLC; 6.6 Used by permission of BenCar Archives; 6.7 © Pictorial Press Ltd / Alamy Stock Photo; 6.8 PF-(bygone1) / Alamy Stock Photo

Chapter 7

TL3.1 Courtesy of Library of Congress. Library of Congress, Prints & Photographs Division; TL3.2 © Murat Baysan/Shutterstock; TL3.4 Courtesy of Library of Congress. Library of Congress, Prints & Photographs Division; TL3.5 Courtesy of Library of Congress. Library of Congress, Prints & Photographs Division; TL3.7 Courtesy of Library of Congress. Library of Congress, Prints & Photographs Division; TL3.8 © tele52/Shutterstock; TL3.9 Courtesy of Library of Congress. Library of Congress, Prints & Photographs Division; TL3.10 Courtesy of Library of Congress. Library of Congress, Prints & Photographs Division; TL3.11 © Liz Van Steenburgh/Dreamstime; TL3.12 ©

Evannovostro/Shutterstock; 7.1 AP Photo/Dan Grossi; 7.2 Photograph by Willliam P. Gottlieb, courtesy of Library of Congress, William P. Gottlieb Collection, LC-GLB13-0779 DLC; 7.3 Photograph by Willliam P. Gottlieb, courtesy of Library of Congress, William P. Gottlieb Collection, LC-GLB13-0161 DLC; 7.4 Courtesy Library of Congress, Prints & Photographs Division, LC-USZ62-120591 and LC-USZ62-124419; 7.5 © Pictorial press Ltd./Alamy Stock; 7.6 Photograph by Willliam P. Gottlieb, courtesy of Library of Congress, William P. Gottlieb Collection, LC-GLB23-0475 DLC; 7.7 Album / Alamy Stock Photo; 7.8 Pictorial Press Ltd / Alamy Stock Photo; 7.9 Used by permission of BenCar Archives; 7.10 Used by permission of BenCar Archives; 7.11 Used by permission of BenCar Archives

Chapter 8

8.1 Photo by Michael Barera, Creative Commons Attribution-Share Alike 4.0 International license; 8.2 Courtesy Library of Congress, Prints & Photograph Division; 8.3 MARKA / Alamy Stock Photo; 8.4 Courtesy of Library of Congress, Prints & Photographs Division, LC-USZ62-126068; 8.5 © Pictorial Press Ltd / Alamy Stock Photo; 8.6 Courtesy of Library of Congress, Prints & Photographs Division, LC-USZ62-126071; 8.7 Pictorial Press Ltd / Alamy Stock Photo; 8.8 Pictorial Press Ltd / Alamy Stock Photo; 8.9 Pictorial Press Ltd / Alamy Stock Photo; 8.10 Pictorial Press Ltd / Alamy Stock Photo; 8.11 Michael Ochs Archives / Stringer; 8.12 Used by permission of BenCar Archives

Chapter 9

9.1 Courtesy Library of Congress, Prints & Photographs Division, LC-USZ62-126069 and LC-USZ62-126067; 9.2 Courtesy Library of Congress, Prints & Photographs Division, LC-USZ62-126065; 9.3 Donaldson Collection / Contributor / Getty Images; 9.4 Pictorial Press Ltd / Alamy Stock Photo; 9.5 Pictorial Press Ltd / Alamy Stock Photo; 9.6 Tracksimages.com/ Alamy Stock Photo; 9.7 © raphael salzedo / Alamy; 9.8 Pictorial Press Ltd / Alamy Stock Photo

Chapter 10

10.1 Pictorial Press Ltd / Alamy Stock Photo; 10.2 Pictorial Press Ltd / Alamy Stock Photo; 10.3 Pictorial Press Ltd / Alamy Stock Photo; 10.4 Philippe Gras / Alamy Stock Photo; 10.5 Pictorial Press Ltd / Alamy Stock Photo; 10.6 Pictorial Press Ltd / Alamy Stock Photo; Alice Ochs/Michael Ochs Archives/Getty Images; 10.7 © The Pictorial Press Ltd / Alamy Stock Photo /Alamy; 10.8 Frank Nowikowski / Alamy Stock Photo; 10.9 Michael Ochs Archives /

Stringer / Getty Images; 10.10 A. F. Archives; 10.11 Pictorial Press Ltd / Alamy Stock Photo

Chapter 11

11.1 ZUMA Press Inc / Alamy Stock Photo; 11.2 Pictorial Press Ltd / Alamy Stock Photo; 11.3 Pictorial Press Ltd / Alamy Stock Photo; 11.4 Pictorial Press Ltd / Alamy Stock Photo; 11.5 Pictorial Press Ltd / Alamy Stock Photo; 11.6 © CBW/Alamy; 11.7 Pictorial Press Ltd / Alamy Stock Photo; 11.8 Pictorial Press Ltd / Alamy Stock Photo; 11.9 © AF archive / Alamy; 11.10 Pictorial Press Ltd / Alamy Stock Photo

Chapter 12

12.1 © Scott Goodno / Alamy; 12.2 Tracksimages.com / Alamy Stock Photo; 12.3 © Zuma Wire Service/ Alamy; 12.4 © Fotomaton/Alamy; 12.5 Pete Still / Contributor / Getty Images; 12.6 Pictorial Press Ltd / Alamy Stock Photo; 12.7 Pictorial Press Ltd / Alamy Stock Photo; 12.8 Pictorial Press Ltd / Alamy Stock Photo; 12.9 REUTERS / Alamy Stock Photo

Chapter 13

TL4.1 Courtesy Library of Congress. Library of Congress, Prints & Photographs Division; TL4.2 ValeStock/Shutterstock.com; TL4.3 © Mark Simms/Shutterstock; TL4.5 catwalker/Shutterstock.com; TL4.7 MarcelClemens/Shutterstock.com; TL4.8 Ken Tannebaum/Shutterstock.com; TL4.10 1000 words/Shutterstock.com; TL4.11 © Pattie Steib/Shutterstock.com; TL4.12 Courtesy of Library of Congress, Prints & Photographs Division; TL4.13 s_bukley/Shutterstock.com; TL4.14 Fiora Watts/ Shutterstock; TL4.15 Chris Pizzello/Invision/ AP/Shutterstock; 13.1 MediaPunch Inc / Alamy Stock Photo; 13.2 Pictorial Press Ltd / Alamy Stock Photo; 13.3 © Peter Jordan/Alamy; 13.4 © Marka/ Alamy; 13.5 Pictorial Press Ltd / Alamy Stock Photo; 13.6 Pictorial Press Ltd / Alamy Stock Photo; 13.7 Pictorial Press Ltd / Alamy Stock Photo; 13.8 AF Archive/Alamy

Chapter 14

14.1 Everett Collection Inc / Alamy Stock Photo; 14.2 ZUMA Press, Inc. / Alamy Stock Photo; 14.3 Golden Richard / Alamy Stock Photo; 14.4 © The Everett Collection/Alamy; 14.5 Pictorial Press Ltd / Alamy Stock Photo; 14.6 Rodolfo Sassano / Alamy Stock Photo; 14.7 The Pictorial Press Ltd./Alamy; 14.8 Ebet Roberts / Contributor / Getty Images; 14.9 Néstor J. Beremblum / Alamy Stock Photo; 14.10 The Pictorial Press Ltd./Alamy; 14.11 © Adrian Arbib/Alamy

Chapter 15

15.1 ZUMA Press, Inc. / Alamy Stock Photo; 15.2 ITAR-TASS News Agency / Alamy Stock Photo; 15.3 Brigette Supernova / Alamy Stock Photo; 15.4 ZUMA Press, Inc. / Alamy Stock Photo; 15.5 © ZUMA Press, Inc. / Alamy; 15.6 Theo Wargo / Staff / Getty Images; 15.7 REUTERS / Alamy Stock Photo; 15.8 ZUMA Press, Inc. / Alamy Stock Photo; 15.9 Paul Froggatt / Alamy Stock Photo; 15.10 © MTV 2020

Lyrics

SON DE LA NEGRA

Words and Music by Silvestre Vargas Vazquez and Ruben Fuentes Gasson

Copyright © 1958 by Promotora Hispano Americana de Musica S.A. Copyright Renewed. Administered by Peer International Corporation. Used by Permission. All Rights Reserved.

NAGÜE

By Luciano Chano Pozo Gonzales

© 1942 (Renewed) Robbins Music Corp.

Rights Assigned to EMI Catalogue Partnership All Rights Controlled and Administered by EMI Robbins Music Corp. (Publishing) and Alfred Music (Print)

All Rights Reserved

Used by Permission of Alfred Music

I WANNA BE SEDATED

Words and Music by Jeffrey Hyman, John Cummings and Douglas Colvin

© 1978 WC Music Corp. and Taco Tunes, Inc.

All Rights Administered by WC Music Corp.

All Rights Reserved

PSYCHO KILLER

Words by David Byrne, Chris Frantz and Tina Weymouth

Music by David Byrne

© 1978 WC Music Corp. and Taco Tunes, Inc.

All Rights Administered by WC Music Corp.

All Rights Reserved

Used by Permission of Alfred Music

WHO AM I (WHAT'S MY NAME)?

Words by Cordozar Broadus, George Clinton, Garry Shider, and David Spradley.

Copyright ©1993 WB Music Corp. (ASCAP), Suge Publishing (ASCAP), Bridgeport Music, Inc. (BMI), and Southfield Music, Inc. (BMI). All rights o/b/o Suge Publishing administered by Entertainment One Group. All rights reserved. Used by permission.

Index

Note: Italicized page references indicate a photo; pages followed by a "*b*" indicate a box.